RIFT
and REVOLT
in HUNGARY

THIS BOOK HAS BEEN PREPARED UNDER THE AUSPICES OF THE CENTER FOR INTERNATIONAL AFFAIRS, HARVARD UNIVERSITY

Created in 1958, the Center fosters advanced study of basic world problems by scholars from various disciplines and senior officers from many countries. The research at the Center, focusing on the processes of change, includes studies of military-political issues, the modernizing processes in developing countries, and the evolving position of Europe. The research programs are supervised by Professors Robert R. Bowie (Director of the Center), Alex Inkeles, Henry A. Kissinger, Edward S. Mason, and Thomas C. Schelling. Book-length studies prepared thus far under the Center's auspices include:

The Soviet Bloc, by Zbigniew K. Brzezinski, 1960 (jointly with Russian Research Center). Harvard University Press.

The Necessity for Choice, by Henry A. Kissinger, 1961. Harper & Brothers.

Strategy and Arms Control, by Thomas C. Schelling and Morton H. Halperin, 1961. Twentieth Century Fund.

Rift and Revolt in Hungary, by Ferenc A. Váli, 1961. Harvard University Press.

RIFT
and REVOLT
in HUNGARY

/\

NATIONALISM VERSUS COMMUNISM

Ferenc A. Váli

HARVARD UNIVERSITY PRESS
CAMBRIDGE · MASSACHUSETTS · 1961

Distributed in Great Britain by Oxford University Press, London •

Library of Congress Catalog Card Number: 61–13745 •

Printed in the United States of America •

To my wife

FOREWORD

This is a notable book. Comprehensive, analytical, and lively, it brings new insights on the turbulent events in Hungary since World War II even to an informed reader who followed those events closely as they took place. Its author is peculiarly qualified to write such a volume: international lawyer and political scientist, professor and public servant, he experienced Communist rule in Hungary from the inside. Arrested by the Hungarian Security Police, interrogated according to the usual methods, condemned for conspiracy and high treason, he spent five years of his life in Budapest prisons.

Ferenc A. Váli has not given us here an account of his personal ordeal, interesting as that would have been. He came to the Harvard Center for International Affairs as a scholar to study exhaustively the complex and many-sided conflicts that resulted when an intensely nationalistic people was drawn into the orbit of the Soviet Union. At times his Hungarian and humanistic feelings shine incandescently in what he has written. Yet the impressiveness of the work flows from his capacity for detached and systematic analysis of the colliding forces in this troubled part of the world.

Professor Váli was born in Budapest in 1905. He received his *Doctor Juris* at the University of Budapest in 1927, and his Ph.D. in political science at the University of London in 1932. In Hungary he engaged in a legal practice of an international character, and from 1935 was on the Law Faculty at the University of Budapest. Besides publishing books in Hungarian and German, he was the author of a standard work in English, *Servitudes of International Law*, first issued at London, and recently reissued in a revised edition at both London and New York. During World War II the Hungarian government sent him to Istanbul on a confidential mission to make contact with the Allied powers. In Turkey from 1943 to 1946 he lectured at the University of Istanbul on various subjects of international law.

Returning to Hungary after the war, he served as international law adviser to the Hungarian Ministry of Finance, and continued teaching at the University of Budapest until he was banned from the faculty and the Ministry by the Communists early in 1949. In 1951, his Western connections led to the arrest of Dr. Váli and his wife. She remained in prison for three years. He was provisionally released on October 18, 1956. Five days later the Revolution broke out, and he was recalled to the university and participated in an effort to reorganize the Hungarian Ministry of Foreign Affairs.

When the Revolution was crushed in November 1956, Dr. Váli and his wife escaped from Hungary into Austria on November 23, 1956. With a fellowship from the Rockefeller Foundation, he did research in London, Paris, and The Hague, and after December 1957, in New York and Washington. From 1958 to 1961, Professor Váli was a Research Associate at the Harvard Center for International Affairs working on the present volume. In September 1961 he joined the government department at the University of Massachusetts.

Rift and Revolt in Hungary falls within one of the major areas of research interest at the Center for International Affairs. In analyzing basic forces of change, the Center has given priority to three main fields of inquiry: development process in the less-developed countries; military policy and arms control; and the evolving role of Europe. An important aspect of the European program is the study of the forces at work in the Soviet-dominated countries of Eastern Europe. The factors for cohesion and conflict in that whole area were analyzed in *The Soviet Bloc,* by Zbigniew K. Brzezinski (Harvard University Press, 1960), which the Center for International Affairs sponsored jointly with the Russian Research Center. In the present work, Dr. Váli, using both published and unpublished sources, makes an intensive study of the clash of nationalism and Communism in one country. But the implications are much wider. His penetrating analysis of the nature, methods, and scope of Soviet domination in Hungary from the late 1940's to the early part of 1961 sheds light on satellitism in general as well as on struggles within the Soviet leadership, and between the Soviet Union and Yugoslavia.

The Center for International Affairs is delighted to have had a part in making this volume possible.

ROBERT R. BOWIE
Director, Center for
International Affairs,
Harvard University

AUTHOR'S PREFACE

THE present work has grown out of a study on the internal rift within the Communist Party of Hungary. This rift, so long hidden from the outside world but closely interwoven with the popular opposition against a Soviet-dominated regime, provided material for a continued study of conflicts in the body politic of Communist Hungary, conflicts which eventually led to the Revolution of 1956. A systematic analysis of the 1956 uprising in all its aspects was undertaken next. Finally, what is believed to be a comprehensive description and evaluation of the postrevolutionary Kádár regime was added.

The Hungarian events cannot be separated from developments outside Hungary; they are, indeed, part and parcel of the current global cleavage. While battles of the Cold War are being fought in many theaters, a mostly inconspicuous but by no means less important silent struggle continues in the East-Central European satellite area. A studious approach to the Hungarian struggles cannot ignore the interaction between the political evolution of the Soviet Union and that of Hungary, nor can it by-pass other foreign factors, such as Titoism and the Suez episode.

The main body of the book is divided into five sections, or "phases." Phase one deals with the Stalinist era in Hungary, characterized by the personal dictatorship of Rákosi. Phase two deals with the "New Course" and the system of diarchy under both Rákosi and Imre Nagy. Phase three undertakes to portray Rákosi's attempt, after Nagy's fall, to stabilize the regime under a restrained dictatorship. Phase four is devoted to an analysis of the events directly leading to the Revolution and of the Revolution itself. In Phase five the aftereffects of the Revolution are examined, as well as the novel features of the Soviet-controlled regime up to the present day. The introductory chapters of the book and the concluding chapter are designed to place the whole study into its proper historic and international perspective.

Source material is more abundant for Hungary than for other members of the Soviet Bloc. But this abundance calls for special caution, especially in the use of the plentiful memoire literature produced by political refugees who left Hungary at the time of the Communist takeover and immediately after the Revolution. I endeavored to draw from such narratives only that which appeared trustworthy, and even when accepting their factual accounts I could not always endorse their opinions or conclusions.

The polemic writings of Imre Nagy, clandestinely brought out of Hungary after the Revolution of 1956, require particular comments. His "dissertation," as he liked to call it, consists of operational papers addressed to Hungarian and Soviet Party leaders. This fact, as well as Nagy's Communist upbringing, determined his style and method of reasoning. Thus the text is often obscure and replete with topical allusions not easily comprehensible without appropriate annotations. But used with discrimination, the former Hungarian Premier's writings provide us with a first-class source of information. I have made use of the English translation of Nagy's memoranda, entitled *On Communism — In Defense of the New Course* (New York, 1957). Permission by Frederick A. Praeger, Inc., to quote from this volume is hereby gratefully acknowledged.

In addition to the extensive published materials, listed in my bibliography, I also relied on sources not generally available to the reading public. I wish to thank Professor Henry L. Roberts, Director of the Columbia University Research Project on Hungary (CURPH), for having allowed the use of reports and interviews obtained from Hungarian refugees of 1956. Other unpublished material was provided by General Béla Király, who studiously answered a lengthy questionnaire on military matters. Free Europe Press opened their research reports, and so did the Kossuth Foundation, Inc. Dr. Kálmán Potoczky allowed me to read and use his manuscript (in Hungarian) on the recent history of Hungary. Mr. William E. Griffith made available his draft manuscript on "The Thaw and Frost in Eastern Europe." Dr. György Heltai, Deputy Foreign Minister during the Revolution in Hungary, gave enlightening information. For all this invaluable help I wish to express my deep gratitude.

I have also drawn much benefit from conversations and interviews with other Hungarians and non-Hungarians. Finally, I have been able to add something through my personal knowledge and experience.

My appointment as Research Associate in the Harvard Center for International Affairs enabled me to devote two full years to the writing of this book. For initiating the project, for perspicacious and helpful suggestions and creative criticism, I am greatly indebted to Professor Robert R. Bowie, Director of the Center. His inspiring guidance accompanied my research throughout. His foreword to this book is also greatly appreciated.

The Center for International Affairs, placed among the manifold libraries and other institutions of Harvard University, proved to be a stimulating workshop. The exchange of ideas with Faculty members, Fellows of the Center, and other scholars, gave unsurpassable assistance. Among my colleagues in the Center special thanks are due to Mr. George A. Kelly, who went through my texts in their early stages and greatly contributed toward their improvement by his useful suggestions.

To Professor Merle Fainsod, who, despite his busy schedule, was kind enough to read the manuscript and to provide valuable advice, I wish to express my sincere thanks. Professor Zbigniew K. Brzezinski, after an exceptionally speedy yet meticulous perusal, offered a galaxy of comments, queries, and friendly objections which I was able to utilize when revising the text. Mr. John C. Campbell, Professor Andrew Gyorgy, and Mr. William E. Griffith were the other experts who gave me the benefit of both their advice and criticism. All their help I gratefully acknowledge.

Mr. Max Hall, Editor of Publications in the Center for International Affairs and Social Science Editor for Harvard University Press, has, in both his capacities, carried out the task of editing this book. In fact, he did much more. By painstakingly reviewing every sentence, by clarifying ambiguities, by weeding out semantic aberrations and incongruities of style and thought, he gave his master's touch to the work. For his travails that must have been a test for both his patience and endurance, I wish sincerely to thank him.

The task of typing and arranging such a lengthy manuscript fell upon the secretarial staff of the Center to whom the author wishes to extend his thanks. Among all these helpers special thanks are due to Mrs. Anne Mayo, who assiduously retyped the manuscript in its final form.

Ferenc A. Váli

Cambridge, Massachusetts
March, 1961

CONTENTS

THE SECOND PHASE
Dual Leadership — Conflicting Policies
1953–1955

THE THIRD PHASE
Single Leadership — Divided Party
1955–1956

Map and Charts

What happened in Hungary demonstrated that the desire for national freedom is stronger even than any ideology and cannot ultimately be suppressed. What happened in Hungary was not essentially a conflict between Communism and anti-Communism. It represented Nationalism striving for freedom from foreign control.

JAWAHARLAL NEHRU

1

Summons to the Kremlin

/\\.\/\\.\/\\.\/\\.\/\\.\/\\.\/\\.\/\\.\/\\.\/\\.\/\\.\/\\.\/\\.\/\\.\/\\.\/\\.\/\\V

He putteth down one and setteth up another.

PSALMS 35:7

Dictators ride to and fro upon tigers which they dare not dismount. And the tigers are getting hungry.

WINSTON CHURCHILL (1938)

STALIN's death exercised greater influence upon Hungary than upon any other satellite country. When the Soviet autocrat died on March 5, 1953, Mátyás Rákosi was his omnipotent lieutenant in Hungary; only Moscow could have dethroned him. And in June of that year, Stalin's successors did so. Though Rákosi was not totally removed from his position of command, his monopolistic rule was brought to an end, a dangerous rival was set up at his side, and he was compelled to undergo a painful humiliation.

This episode marks one of those turning points that sometimes occur in the history of nations. The scene staged in the sanctum sanctorum of the Kremlin on that occasion epitomizes the years of Hungarian agony under Communist rule. It illuminates, as if with a flash bulb, the fact of Soviet control — and the peculiar dual nature of that control, now Great Russian, now Marxist-Leninist, and both simultaneously. This rendezvous in Moscow touched off a conflict of personalities and unlocked forces that led to the Hungarian Revolution of 1956 and may yet lead to events the shape of which is still a matter of conjecture.

Rákosi had been in Moscow in March 1953 to attend his mentor's funeral. That trip had already afforded him opportunity to watch the first sproutings of the new Soviet "collective leadership." We do not know whether he was given any hints that his own version of Stalinism would have to be terminated. His self-confidence seemed unabated; his line of dictatorial policy seemed unshaken. So we must presume that he received no forewarning.

The Hungarian "elections" were scheduled for May 17. Rákosi exposed the program of the Hungarian Workers Party (Communist Party) on May 10 at a mass meeting held in the big square in front of the Parliament building in Budapest. At that time he was both Secretary-General of the Party and Prime Minister of the country. He praised the unprecedented achievements of the last four years, during which Hungary had advanced more than in previous whole decades; in dithyrambic words he extolled the achievements of the Five-Year Plan, over the course of which thirty-five billion forints had been usefully invested and the country covered with flourishing industrial plants. The superiority of agricultural cooperatives over individual farming had become obvious, and the "rapid development of cooperatives was assured." The intellectuals of the nation had been won over to the admiration of the Party and its work. Because of "the progress of building socialism," the class struggle was to become "even more vehement." Rákosi warned his audience to watch ceaselessly for conspiracies, sabotage, and espionage, organized by the United States. The second Five-Year Plan (to start in 1955) would inevitably turn Hungary into a "Socialist society," and its implementation was to insure that "Hungary would surpass most of the advanced capitalist countries in every field of activity." [1]

Other speakers hailed Rákosi, who with Stalin's guidance had been able "to rally the entire Hungarian people into a single camp." They assured the mass audience that all these "great achievements are closely linked with the name of Comrade Rákosi." [2]

On May 17, the approval of 98.2 per cent of the voters elected 298 deputies to the National Assembly on the basis of the single list offered. The monolithic unity of Party and country under the leadership of Rákosi seemed to have been clearly demonstrated.

Less than five weeks later[3] Rákosi was summoned to Moscow. He planned to take with him only his two associates: Ernö Gerö and Mihály Farkas. But then he was told to appear with Imre Nagy and István Dobi. The fifth member of the group was Béla Szalai, acting as Rákosi's secretary. The selection of Nagy must have assailed Rákosi with evil forebodings, for Nagy was already suspected as a rival.[4] Furthermore, Rákosi had already been given the bad news that, in imitation of the separation of the Soviet Party and governmental offices after Stalin's death, the Hungarian Party leadership must be severed from the premiership. There is evidence[5] that Rákosi had been requested to recommend his potential successor in the premiership as early as May, though apparently he still had no fore-warning of the rebuke he was to receive. It seems likely that this consultation took place by telephone. Rákosi was known to have frequent and long telephone conversations with the rulers of the Kremlin; he had a direct line to the Kremlin on his desk.[6] It is certain that he did not recommend Imre Nagy.

Pilgrimages of Communist leaders to Moscow are an important aspect of their duties. Sometimes Party leaders from individual countries are invited; sometimes general or regional conclaves are held. Such visits may be compared to personal reports of provincial governors in the capital of an empire, or — if a somewhat profane comparison be permitted — to visits of Catholic bishops to Rome. During Stalin's lifetime a visit to Moscow was the only opportunity of a Communist leader to be admitted to the sanctum, to the person of the *vozhd,* since the suspicious Georgian — except for his wartime journeys to Tehran and Potsdam — never left Soviet territory.

A new experience now awaited Rákosi: to be formally received by the collective leadership of the Soviet Party Presidium. Members of the Presidium, according to their official ranking, were: G. M. Malenkov (who was Chairman of the Council of Ministers); L. P. Beria (Minister of Internal Affairs, and therefore head of the Security Police services); V. M. Molotov (Minister of Foreign Affairs); K. E. Voroshilov (Chairman of the Presidium of the Supreme Soviet, i.e., the formal head of state); N. S. Khrushchev (acting as highest-ranking Party Secretary); N. A. Bulganin (Minister of Defense); L. M. Kaganovich, A. I. Mikoyan, M. Z. Saburov, and M. G. Pervukhin. It has been well established that a deep cleavage existed at that time among various factions of the Party Presidium. The visit of the Hungarian Party leaders preceded by a very few days the arrest of Beria. It also coincided with the period when a fierce struggle was being fought over the final disposition of the post of first Party Secretary.[7]

Rákosi, a Moscow-trained Communist leader — a "muscovite" — who spoke excellent Russian and had many personal ties with top Soviet leaders, ordinarily possessed an enormous advantage over less-endowed Communist visitors to the Kremlin. Among the members of the Hungarian delegation, Gerö and Farkas were also Moscow-trained, but had been close collaborators of Rákosi and could hardly be thought of as challengers. Dobi spoke no Russian; he was only a latter-day Communist devotee, a dummy in Rákosi's hands, evidently invited only as ceremonial head of the Hungarian State, i.e., Chairman of the Hungarian Presidium of the National Assembly. But, with Imre Nagy, the case was different.

Imre Nagy had spent many years in the Soviet Union, was well acquainted with conditions there, and spoke the language. But his scholarly leanings, his modesty, and his absence from Moscow during a critical period (most of the war), as well as his less significant role in the Party, had offered him far fewer opportunities than Rákosi to rub shoulders with the Kremlin leaders. He then held the title of Deputy Prime Minister, but possessed hardly any authority, and in fact had been in limbo throughout the preceding four years.

When the Hungarian delegation was admitted before the members of the Soviet Presidium, it is recorded that Khrushchev, Malenkov, and Beria gave Rákosi a scolding on what had happened in Hungary during his monopoly of power.[8] Their version of the Hungarian events seems to have borne no resemblance to Rákosi's own account at the mass meeting in Budapest.

The Moscow leadership had been at pains to inform itself of the conditions prevailing in Hungary, and thus knew where to place the responsibility for what had happened. Imre Nagy portrays tersely the broadside of rebuke fired at Rákosi:

The shocking situation was described by the key members of the Soviet Communist Party, who declared that the mistakes and crimes of the four-member Party leadership in Hungary, headed by Rákosi, had driven the country to the verge of a catastrophe, shaking the People's Democratic system to its foundations and that, unless prompt and effective measures had been taken to bring about a change, the people would have turned against them and, to quote Khrushchev, "we would have been booted out summarily." [9]

Khrushchev is also said to have added: "If the situation is not immediately and radically changed, they will chase you with pitchforks." [10] It must be remembered that the date is approximately June 24, 1953, that is, a few days after the Berlin uprising, the Pilsen riots in Czechoslovakia, and strikes and demonstrations in many places in Hungary.

Mikoyan gave an up-to-date description of Hungary's economic status. He reproached Rákosi for having favored an excessive expansion of steel production without regard to a scarcity of iron ore and coke. He told Rákosi that through his responsibility for the tempo of forced collectivization he had brought ruin to Hungary's once famous agriculture. Socialist legality had also been abused.

Thousands of innocents were crowding the jails. The Presidium members rebuked Rákosi for the "cult of personality" which he had introduced to his advantage and for the intemperate rule of his clique. They held him and his associates responsible for the mistakes and crimes committed.

The Soviet leaders did not hesitate to discuss the personal questions as to who should succeed Rákosi as Prime Minister and whether Rákosi was to remain head of the Party. Imre Nagy described this part of the conversation in the following terms:

> Comrade Malenkov pointed out that, in May 1953, they had discussed with Mátyás Rákosi the personal questions also that concerned the separation of Party and state leadership. "We asked, whom do you recommend as your deputy?" He could name no one. He had objections to everyone whose name was mentioned; he had something against everyone. Everyone was suspect except he alone. "This appalled us very much," said Comrade Malenkov. Comrade Molotov declared that Mátyás Rákosi had said that he did want a Premier, "but he wanted a Premier who would have no voice in the making of decisions." Comrade Khrushchev noted: "The matter involved was that the leadership of the Party and the state should not be concentrated in the hands of one man or a few men; this is not desirable." [11]

Evidently Imre Nagy was not considered by Rákosi as a Premier "who would have no voice in the making of decisions." Khrushchev's remarks about the undesirability of having Party and state power concentrated in the hands of one man are noteworthy in view of his subsequent career.

Various sources confirm that the Jewish issue was fully exploited against Rákosi at this encounter. When the "wise father of the Hungarian people" tried to resist Imre Nagy's appointment and eventually suggested a "more reliable" person, it was again Khrushchev who rebuked him with these words: "Do you think that only a Jew can be a leading politician in Hungary?" [12] Beria, who is said to have been the most aggressive, went even further in ridiculing Rákosi: "Listen, Comrade Rákosi, I've heard that Hungary has had Hapsburg emperors, Polish Kings, Turkish sultans as her rulers, but she has never had a Jewish king, and it looks to me as if you were trying to become just one." [13]

These expressions of anti-Semitism, which seem to imply much personal antipathy and hatred, were uttered less than four months after the official demasking of the fictitious Jewish Doctors' Plot — a plot which had probably been directed against Beria's person.[14] Was Beria, in especially stressing this issue, instinctively eager to defend himself against the accusation of philo-Semitism, or was his overbearing attitude due to his anticipated ascendancy over Party and government in the Soviet Union? [15] It should again be recalled that Beria was arrested after the session of the same Presidium which now passed judgment on Rákosi and his clique. The anti-Jewish outburst itself was probably provoked by Rákosi's ultimate recommendation of a certain name as his successor in the premiership: he must have suggested his associate, Ernö Gerö, thus prompting this *argumentum ad hominem* against him and Gerö from some members of the Presidium.

Finally, the Kremlin decided that Rákosi was to hand the premiership over to Imre Nagy but retain the Party secretaryship.* He was enjoined to mend his ways and repair his mistakes. Later Imre Nagy laid great stress on the fact that it was not Rákosi who recommended him for the premiership but the "Soviet comrades." He objected strongly to Rákosi's saying in 1955 that he (Rákosi) felt "heavy responsibility" for the appointment. Nagy cites especially the names of Malenkov, Molotov, and Khrushchev as having been instrumental in his nomination.[16]

Why was Nagy invited to Moscow and selected to become Prime Minister of Hungary? We can only infer the answer. When the masters of the Kremlin first resolved to relieve Rákosi of part of his public duties, they must have sought information through their various agents in Hungary. The information they wanted to obtain might have been formulated thus: the person to be chosen Prime Minister in Rákosi's stead should be a reliable Communist, a muscovite, popular with the people of Hungary, not involved in the excesses of Rákosi, and — an anti-Semite tendency seems to have been paramount — not of Jewish descent. Who filled these qualifications? The Budapest Soviet agent, whoever he was, in trying to find a person who suited Moscow's desiderata, could have chosen no other than Imre Nagy. Besides such a recommendation, Imre Nagy may have had personal ties with one or two of the participants in the collective leadership of the Soviet Union. Most probably he was well known to Malenkov, but possibly to Khrushchev, too.

Before Beria's fate was sealed, the Hungarian delegation was on its way back to Budapest to implement the instructions received from the Soviet oligarchs. Apart from the change of leadership, the Kremlin had given policy directives to the Hungarians. What these directives were is only generally known: the subsequent program

---

* He was soon to give up his title of Secretary-General and adopt the title of First Secretary, following Khrushchev's example of September 1953.

of the Imre Nagy cabinet may be considered as fairly reproducing in its main elements the wishes of Moscow. Imre Nagy is careful to speak of a "recommendation" given by the Soviet comrades, but from his narrative no other conclusion can be drawn than that the Moscow Party leadership had issued direct instructions to the Hungarian leaders concerning the policy to be pursued. On the other hand, we are inclined to think that the new Premier-designate had his own ideas of consequence and that he discussed with one or two members of the Moscow Presidium, or with some of their experts, the main items of a program whose main goal was to repair the material and moral damage caused by Rákosi and his entourage.

Since the Moscow interview took place subsequent to revolts and disturbances in the Soviet satellite area, these events might have had some impact on the directives approved by Moscow. The coincidence of the Berlin events might have served Imre Nagy in obtaining the Kremlin's approval of some points which it would not otherwise have accepted, but in the light of subsequent behavior the historian is justified in assuming that Nagy would have included them even in the absence of such a sequence of events.

In any case, Imre Nagy subsequently laid great stress on the fact that the Soviet comrades approved the June program which he announced on returning to Hungary,[17] and there is no reason to doubt that they did. This program amounted not only to an admission that the country's affairs had been mismanaged for a number of years, a period coinciding exactly with the Stalinist dictatorship exercised by Rákosi and his associates, but it proposed to correct the mistakes committed, securing a policy which in many important respects clashed boldly with the objectives hailed only a few weeks before by Rákosi himself. The June program entailed an industrial reconversion, a complete reversal of agricultural policies, the abandonment of ambitious plans of industrialization, and the endorsement of an urgent necessity for raising the standard of living. It promised the restoration of law and order, the rehabilitation of innocent political prisoners, the abolition of internment camps, and the return of the deported. It was a political outline which in parliamentary democratic countries would have been styled an "opposition program." But in Communist Hungary, under the orders of Moscow, this program was to be carried out with the concurrence and collaboration of those very same persons who had sponsored the opposite policy and had logically to be blamed for its mistakes and failures.

A paradoxical situation was thereby created which inevitably brought into conflict the two heads of the new dual leadership, the Prime Minister and the Party leader. Nothing parallel had happened in other satellite countries nor in the Soviet Union itself. There had been similar changes in Czechoslovakia, in Rumania, and in Bulgaria, involving the separation of Party and state leadership, but nowhere else had two leaders been established in antagonistic equilibrium as in Hungary. The humiliating demotion administered to the pocket dictator Rákosi to the advantage of his suspected and feared opponent would already have been sufficient cause for their subsequent rivalry. A policy substantially disavowing the still-powerful Party leader was bound to create such tensions as had no parallel in magnitude and vehemence in any other satellite country.

If we combine the seething discontent of the country, the incipient split in the Party, the prevailing anti-Russian and anti-Communist sentiment which was bound to hail enthusiastically any such change in policy that manifestly forswore the Stalinist past, an approaching conflict would seem the more unavoidable.

Before entering into the analysis and evaluation of ensuing trends and events during the term of this dual leadership, we must go back to investigate the nature of the Stalinist era in Hungary, a hotbed of divergencies. Indeed, we must begin by going back even further, because there are strands in the history of expansionism and satellitism, and in the heritage of Hungary and Russia, that manifested themselves again in the post–World War II period when nationalism clashed with Communism on Hungarian soil.

2

The Historical Setting:
Expansionism and Satellitism

/\/

Russian Communism was an attempt to reconcile the irresponsible sense of Russian destiny with the ineluctable necessity of cop-
ing with Modern Western technological prowess . . . Lenin and
his successors divined that a policy of fighting the West with a
selection of its own weapons could not hope to succeed if the
weapons were conceived of in purely material terms . . . If Russia's
reaction against the West was to succeed, she must appear as the
champion of a faith that could contend on equal terms with
Liberalism. Armed with this faith Russia must compete with the
West for the spiritual allegiance of all living societies that were
neither Western nor Russian in their native cultural traditions.

ARNOLD J. TOYNBEE

Time after time in the course of history, Hungary and other
East-Central European countries have been subjected to the status
of political satellites by their more powerful neighbors, expanding
either from the east or from the west. After World War II the area
lent itself to Soviet-Communist expansionism. Successively, in the
wake of the Red Army's advance, Bulgaria, Rumania, Poland, Hungary, and East Germany passed under Soviet domination and acquired Communist regimes. Czechoslovakia fell under the Soviet-
Communist system in 1948. Communist Yugoslavia was able to
extricate herself in the same year from Moscow's strangling tutelage,
though her subsatellite, Albania, remained in the Soviet orbit.

THE DUALISM OF SOVIET EXPANSION

Soviet expansionism appears to the peoples of East-Central Europe as a complex system, one which intermingles Communist universalism with nationalistic aspirations.[1] In this satellite area the ambitions of international Communism and the national ambitions of Soviet Russia seem parallel but they act with alternating emphasis. This dualism appears to be, and often is, instinctive, unconscious, and uncontrollable. The Soviet "ego" may be said to be a split personality; one day its expansionism is Dr. Jekyll, the champion of World Communism, and another, Mr. Hyde, the Great Russian warrior.

Tsarist Russian expansionism was split in somewhat the same way. Under the tsars, Russian imperialism went hand in hand with Pan-Slavism and Eastern Orthodoxy. Today, Russian imperialism goes hand in hand with the spread of Communism. Under the tsars, Slav kinship and Slav Messianism were exploited in conjunction with the charismatic authority of the "Third Rome" to further Great Russian ambitions that were purely national. Today the Soviet Union, while professing to be the first "Socialist" state, instead approximates in the eyes of East-Central Europeans its tsarist predecessor, and, according to notable testimony,[2] even surpasses him in nationalistic zeal.

The Soviet Union has not even abandoned the use of Eastern Orthodoxy as an instrument of expansionism. It undertakes to extend the jurisdiction and authority of the Moscow Patriarch over non-Russian Orthodox bishops. With methods never employed by imperial Russia, it forced Uniate (Greek-Catholic) Churches to sever their union with Rome. Not only in territories incorporated into the Soviet Union itself during or after World War II, but also in Rumania, Hungary, and Poland, the Uniate bishops were either imprisoned or forced to give up allegiance to the Pope. Thus the atheism of the Communist regime does not exclude the employment of ecclesiastical affiliations to favor the double objective of Russian nationalism and Communist universalism. And this modern-day phenomenon is far more dangerous to other countries than the tsarist efforts ever were, as its undoubted successes clearly demonstrate.

Soviet Russian nationalism is not as conclusively pro–Great Russian as tsarist expansionism was. Possessing a more composite character, it is more deceptive and opaque, though no less deliberate than its tsarist equivalent. To distinguish whether an action favors international Communism or Russian national interests may often be difficult, if not impossible. Such actions may be spontaneously initiated irrespective of ultimate results, since in the Soviet view the two objectives are indissoluble — at least so far as East-Central Europe is concerned.

The question may thus be put as follows: Is the Marxist-internationalist principle used to further Russian imperialist aims, or is the somewhat artificial Soviet (truly, Russian) nationalism used to serve the cause of international Communism? More tersely, as between ideological cultivation and national expansion, which is the means and which the end? The answer emerging from this book will be that when the proposition was put to a test in Hungary, the objective of Soviet national interests prevailed over the objective of Communism.

In Soviet parlance, ironically enough, "nationalism" is part and parcel of the bourgeois state. To express a legitimate loyalty toward one's "Socialist Fatherland," the term "patriotism" is employed. Until the German attack in 1941, even "patriotism" was considered reactionary in the Soviet Union; thereafter, "Soviet patriotism" grew into an accepted slogan together with "Soviet man," "Soviet culture," and "Soviet science." [3] Again during the war, not only "Russian" as an epithet for patriotism returned to official currency, but even the "Great Russian" notion appeared in the new Soviet anthem. Russian nationalism played an important role in resisting German aggression and invasion, and as such it was exploited by the Soviet rulers. Stalin even toasted it in his victory speech.

There is no doubt that the Soviet Union was satisfying traditional Russian ambitions — closely following in the footsteps of the tsars — when during and following World War II it not only reannexed territories which had been tsarist domains prior to the Revolution of 1917, but also managed to acquire further real estate which had never belonged to Russia, usually by invoking principles of nationality. Thus, Eastern Galicia and Northern Bukovina were annexed, the Czechoslovak ally was deprived of the Carpatho-Ukraine (which formed part of Hungary prior to World War I, and again between 1939 and 1944), and part of East Prussia was incorporated. The Soviet Russian empire obtained a firm foothold below the big semicircle of the Carpathian Mountains, and a harbor in the Western Baltic, advantages never before enjoyed by Russia.

Up to the end of World War II, the adjustment of Russian nationalism with postulates of Marxist-Leninist internationalism remained an internal Soviet problem. In spite of the much-heralded

Leninist principle of nationalities, Russification has been pursued in the numerous nationality groups of the Soviet Union on an increasing scale and with mounting intensity, in the Stalinist era and ever since. Reactions against this Russification are somewhat similar to, but naturally less intensive than, those which we shall meet in the European "captive" area. Sometimes they take the form of a "social-class" character, at other times that of "political-national" attitudes. The essence is resistance, and it makes little difference whether it is labeled and upbraided as "chauvinistic," "revision-istic," "reactionary," or "deviationist."

Nowadays, "Socialism in one state" has been replaced by the "Socialist camp" which includes seven captive satellite countries in Europe. Thus, Soviet Russian nationalism in its interplay with Communist internationalism has outgrown internal Soviet limits; it has become an international problem with which the whole world is concerned, the focal concern of everyday interest, and the hub of sorrows, expectations, and disillusionments in the European satellite area.

The contradiction between Soviet national objectives and Marx-ist-Leninist class-war objectives did not of course originate with the creation of a satellite empire. In the 1920's it led to wrangling between Zinoviev's Comintern, the agency that directed foreign Communist parties, and the *Narkomindyel,* or People's Commis-sariat of Foreign Affairs. When Stalin took a firm hold of the reins of Party and government, he resolved the contradiction by the device of removing the Zinovievists from the Comintern's leadership and making this agency subservient to the *Narkomindyel* and ultimately to his Politburo's strategy and tactics.[4] The people of the Soviet Union were told that in serving the "Socialist Fatherland" they served the cause of international Communism. And to the outer world, as early as 1927, Stalin announced the maxim that an internationalist Communist "is one who is ready to defend the USSR without reservation, without wavering, unconditionally; for the USSR is the base of the world revolutionary movement, and this revolutionary movement cannot be defended and promoted unless the USSR is defended." [5] Though this "uncontested truth" made life rather difficult for the struggling Communist parties all over the world, and forced them slavishly to follow the labyrinthine or zig-zag movement of Soviet foreign policy, from Litvinov's collec-tive security schemes down to the Stalin–Hitler Pact, it relieved Soviet leaders from thinking and scheming in terms other than those of egocentric Soviet Russian power politics. And during World War II the Comintern was ostentatiously abolished.

But when the doctrine of socialism in one state came to an end after 1945 and the Soviet Union resorted to large-scale methods which could only be explained in terms of power politics, the contradiction between the task of spreading Marxism-Leninism and the task of pursuing imperialistic aims became more and more apparent. The Soviet leaders then made a more fruitful use of their Leninist system of dynamic interaction between Party and the state.

PARTY RULES STATE — SOVIET PARTY RULES OTHER PARTIES

The establishment of a number of states "building Socialism" rendered impractical the official maintenance of the axiom concerning the identification of Soviet interests with interests of the Communist revolutionary movement. The official recognition of the independence and sovereignty of the *de facto* Soviet-dominated countries of East-Central Europe made it impossible to enforce discipline, openly and formally, upon the governments of those allegedly sovereign states. Therefore the objectives of Soviet Russian expansionism, parallel with those of international Communism, were to be upheld not so much on the inter-state as on the inter-Party level. As soon as the Communist parties obtained a monopolistic control in the satellites, these countries were to be dominated mainly via the Party channel under the axiom: The Party rules the state, but the Communist Party of the Soviet Union leads all other Communist parties. In other words, Stalin or the Soviet leadership, representing Soviet Russian national interests, was to control other Communist parties, especially those which were running their own countries; thus, Stalin, or whoever ruled the Soviet Party and Soviet Union, was to rule all Communist countries. But such a principle could be more readily observed when the Soviet Union was in a position to maintain a power status enabling it ultimately to enforce a policy which could not be made acceptable by the inter-Party domination alone.

As a further obfuscation of the real state of affairs, the Cominform — successor to the defunct Comintern — was created in October 1947. For some time, Zhdanov seemed to have the ambition of following in Zinoviev's footsteps, creating an organization which, to some extent, might dissociate itself from the Soviet Russian nationalism of Stalin in regard to foreign Communist parties. The seat of the Cominform was originally Belgrade, and evidently Tito was to play an important role in shaping international Communist destinies. But in June 1948 the Cominform conference was convoked not in Belgrade, but in Bucharest, and Tito's Communist party was excluded because it had refused to recognize the "leading role" of the Soviet Communist Party. Evidently, the pro-Russian nationalistic view prevailed over the "internationalists." The supremacy of Soviet Russian national objectives — even at the risk of losing strength and prestige in the Communist parties of the West — was to be strictly upheld, and Soviet Russian domination and grip over the satellite area was to be strengthened.[6]

Centralistic-oligarchic principles in Party organization date from the time of Lenin. It was Lenin who insisted on the essential unity of the Party, and refused to give way to federalist endeavors.[7] Whereas the Soviet Union had been established on a formally federal basis, Party organizations in the member republics became nothing more than lower layers of the Party administration. Similar subordination was required of Communist parties outside the Soviet Union. For example, the organizational statute of the Communist Party of Hungary, adopted in Moscow on November 4, 1918, provided that the Party "submits itself to the resolutions, decisions of the Central Committee of the Russian Communist (Bolshevik) Party."[8]

A restatement of the Soviet Party's leadership is contained in the Moscow declaration of the twelve "ruling" Communist parties of November 22, 1957 (which the Yugoslav Party refused to endorse). In veiled and copious verbiage the declaration promises to safeguard "from enemy encroachments the historic, political and social gains effected in the Soviet Union — the first and mightiest Socialist power — in the Chinese People's Republic and in all the Socialist countries."[9] Again it is maintained that "the vital interests of the working people of all countries call for their support of the Soviet Union," and also of other Socialist countries. This text, while trying to give an expression of the equality of Communist parties, sustains the old claim according to which — using the Orwellian phrase — the Soviet Party is more equal than others. Leaders of eighty-one Communist parties after their meeting in Moscow in November 1960 reaffirmed the Declaration of 1957, unanimously declaring that "the Communist Party of the Soviet Union has been, and remains, the universally recognized vanguard of the world Communist movement, being the most experienced and steeled contingent of the international Communist movement."[10]

With the Kremlin's gradual recognition of Communist China as another leader of the Communist camp, world leadership of Communism appears to have become bipolar, and may even become polycentric. Nevertheless, there is no convincing sign of the Soviet Party's willingness to loosen its grip over the adjoining satellite area of East-Central Europe.

While the main stream of Soviet control is being exercised through Party channels by Party commands emanating from the Kremlin, a great variety of other control and pressure media exist in the satellite countries, such as military occupation or military supervision under the Warsaw Pact, subordination of the Security Police organs to the MVD, and the advisory system in many branches of government (mostly in the ministries of Foreign Affairs and in those of Foreign Trade). In addition, all-out importance must be attributed to the many Soviet-trained Party members who have taken possession of most of the key posts in the Party and in the government of each satellite country.

This Soviet-adopted system of domination through subordination of the local Parties to the Soviet Party, and under the "Party rules the state" principle, is a unique method, unprecedented in the long history of satellitism.

SATELLITISM IN PAST AND PRESENT

Political satellitism* is a method whereby another country may be controlled or made dependent on another state without incorporation or any other legal or official admission of the *de facto* reality of dependency. It is a kind of indirect rule, an autonomy enjoyed by the dependent state which agrees to follow the advice or commands of the dominating power. The subordination may be voluntary or involuntary: it may be in the real interest of the dependent country, or against the best of its interests. We are here concerned with the involuntary type of satellitism.

Imperial Rome had her satellites, her "allies." The Jewish tributary kingdom presents an interesting precedent: Herod the Great, by political and tactical astuteness, was able to balance Roman claims to domination with Jewish nationalism and religious zeal. But under his less skillful successors, and with the increasing pressure of Rome, the inevitable clash between the universalist, polytheist *imperium* and Jewish ethnocentric theocracy could not be

---

* There is a cultural satellitism, too. Its intensity may vary greatly; to some extent the whole Western World is a satellite of Greco-Roman culture. There is nothing wrong with this as long as cultural satellitism is voluntary.

avoided, and the Jewish state collapsed under the weight of Roman legions. It proved to be impossible to adjust the claims of Caesar and those of God.

The victorious French Revolution and Napoleonic imperialism provide ample precedents of unwilling satellitism. The French Republican armies helped to create the Batavian, the Helvetian, the Cisalpine, the Parthenopian and many other Republics. The liberty and democracy promised by the liberators was at first enthusiastically hailed by many patriots; but soon *liberté, égalité, fraternité* proved to be a method of French oppression and economic exploitation. French "stooges," like Schimmelpenninck in Holland or Melzi d'Eril in Italy, had difficulties in explaining to the people that they had been "liberated" by the French. When Napoleon made himself Emperor of the French, members of his family were sent to become "kings" in the various satellite countries from Holland to Naples and from Westphalia to Spain. When the King of Holland ultimately sided with his people against his brother, the French Emperor, he was dismissed and his country incorporated into the empire.*

Russian intolerance and chauvinism have never been very successful in the practice of satellitism. The "Kingdom of Congress-Poland" of Tsar Alexander I ended in a bloody revolution (1830) and outright incorporation. The "Grand Duchy of Finland," fighting Great Russian claims of "one law, one church, one language," was able to survive longer because of its greater accommodation to Russian demands and tactical subtlety; even so, its autonomy was finally suspended (1899), and it had to put up continuous resistance to survive.

When Russia — genuinely — liberated Bulgaria (Russo–Turkish War of 1877–1878), this country, organized and administered by many Russians, became a satellite. But soon tactless interferences by Russian officials and immoderate attempts at Russification turned national sentiment against the liberators. The elections were won by the Liberals, the anti-Russian party, and the rulers of the country were forced for a considerable time to govern against the Assembly or provide for rigged elections in order to maintain the pro-Russian official policy required by the exigencies of survival.[11]

The Soviet Union, in its dealings with the East-Central European

---

* It is interesting to note the psychological parallel between King Louis who conspired in the interest of the Dutch people against the Emperor (according to the French couplet: "Le roi de Hollande fait la contrebande"), and the muscovite Communist Imre Nagy who ultimately turned against Moscow.

satellite peoples, seems to be even less able to maintain satellitism on a voluntary basis than was its tsarist predecessor in Poland, Finland, or Bulgaria. History demonstrates that the basis of successful satellitism must be an essential interest, as conceived by the majority or at least the ruling minority of a country, in maintaining such a dependency, outbalancing the inevitable drawbacks incumbent on a loss of full independence. Otherwise satellitism will degenerate into a mere military or police regime where the military or police elements cannot, furthermore, be entirely indigenous.

The Romans in their supremacy over the Jewish State allied themselves with the Hellenized segment of the population. The French relied on their Jacobin brethren in their satellite republics. Imperial Russia tried to obtain support from the Polish aristocracy and big landowners, and from the Swedish element of the population in Finland. But in all these instances, the satellite status was, or soon became, involuntary, and could be maintained only with the help of forces of occupation.

With the coming of modern communications the imminent potentiality of armed intervention may in itself be a sufficient deterrent to preserve an "unwilling" satellite status. The East-Central European satellite empire fell to the Soviet Union by various direct or indirect methods of pressure, of which the presence or propinquity of the Soviet Army was the decisive influence.[12] Skillful and fortunate Herods — like Gomulka in Poland — are temporarily able to maintain a balance compatible with satellite status but with a minimum of interference by the Soviet Union. In Hungary, the intervention by Soviet troops was needed to preserve a more precarious equilibrium.

THE CASE STUDY OF HUNGARY

Violent outbreaks of anti-Soviet nationalist sentiment in the various satellite countries may be assigned to multiple causes and conditioning circumstances. When one considers such circumstances with reference to the variable countries and peoples, it will appear that Hungary was and is, more than any other satellite country, conditioned for the development of acute anti-Soviet feeling.

The national consciousness of Hungarians — their sense of a historic, ethnic, and linguistic individuality — is highly developed. Through the centuries Hungary has had to fight for her independence. Traditions of liberalism and democracy are also prevalent, and before 1945 the strength of Communist or extreme leftist movements was rather insignificant. Hungarians are not Slavs, and they have entertained a particular national bias against Pan-Slavism and against Russian imperialism. In religious affiliations and general culture, they are definitely Western. Roman Catholicism is the most powerful denomination; Protestantism is also strong. Although Hungary suffered much in the past and in recent times from Pan-Germanism, she does not retain any considerable anti-German sentiment; no territorial anxieties with regard to German expansionism are felt. She has had to suffer probably more than any other satellite country from the excesses of Soviet-Communist rule.

Poland shares with Hungary a strong sense of national consciousness and a strong desire for independence, and nurses an even more violent anti-Russian bias. Roman Catholicism is even stronger and nationally more exclusive than in Hungary. On the other hand, anti-German sentiment strongly competes with the existing anti-Russian phobia, and the fate of Western Poland would be in jeopardy if Germany regained preponderancy.

In Czechoslovakia expressions of national sentiment are less extrovert than in Hungary and Poland, and her struggle for independence has been less violent. Also, she is not quite so homogeneous in mentality; in the Czech parts of the country, democratic sentiment is extremely strong, while in Slovakia religious feeling, especially Roman Catholic, is a powerful factor. Traditions of Pan-Slavism are particularly deep in Czechoslovakia, and the Czechs have always displayed a definite pro-Russian attitude. Fear of Germany has vitally influenced political and national sentiments.

In Rumania the majority, in Bulgaria the whole of the population, belongs to the Eastern Orthodox Church. Their traditions as fully independent nations are more recent, their national sentiment having lain dormant for centuries. Though Rumania is non-Slav, her attitude toward Russia in the past has been dependent on concrete Russian actions (liberation, oppression). The Bulgarians speak a Slav language, and strong pro-Russian traditions have existed always, especially in the cultural field.

In East Germany attitudes toward Soviet Communism are influenced by an extraneous element nonexistent in other satellite areas: the desire to be reunited with the rest of Germany.

The circumstances of any of these satellite areas warrant a case study. The circumstances of Hungary demand one. In Hungary the underlying causes of anti-Soviet and anti-Communist sentiment are unassisted by outside factors. Violent conflicts have arisen even in upper layers of Communist Party leadership. Events have been cataclysmic, leading to a tragic denouement. From an understanding of these Hungarian events conclusions of a more general nature may be deduced. And finally, material for research on Hungarian nationalism in conflict with Soviet nationalism and Soviet-sponsored Communism seems more abundantly available than similar materials in other satellite countries.

The case study begins when the Red Army drives Hitler's troops from Hungarian soil, but in a sense it begins a thousand years ago, for the battles of resistance fought by the Hungarian people against Tartars, Turks, the Holy Roman Empire, the Hapsburgs, and the tsarist Russians are forerunners of the present-day struggle.

SURVIVAL OF A NATION

In 896 A.D., the nomadic Magyars (or, in Western terminology, Hungarians), led by the chieftain Árpád, settled down in the Carpathian Basin and thereby drove a wedge into the Slav world, separating Western Slavs (Czechs, Moravians, Slovaks) from Southern Slavs.[13] In their new surroundings these people from the vicinity of the Ural Mountains were ethnically and linguistically isolated. They have had to fight to defend their national characteristics. They have succeeded in so doing.*

The Hungarians embraced Western Christianity during the eleventh century and thus became amenable to Western cultural and organizational influences. They adopted medieval feudalism as practiced by the western and northern neighbors, Latin became the language for official purposes, and the country was ruled by the kings of the House of Árpád, who were crowned with the Holy Crown of St. Stephen, sent by Pope Sylvester II to the first King of Hungary in the year 1001. This action by the Pope helped the Hungarians to remain outside the Holy Roman Empire despite two centuries of attempts to incorporate them.

The Mongols (popularly called Tartars) fell upon Hungary in 1241 and reduced the population by approximately one half, but did not stay to rule. In those times Mongol-Turkic nomads roved across the steppes of Southern Russia, and under their Khans the rulers of Moscow lived a precarious life of vassalage. Despite the devastating invasion of Hungary, the nation under the House of Árpád maintained itself as a power in that part of Europe. To the south, in the Balkans, the Byzantine political influence receded —

---

* Many other migrating peoples, through no discredit to themselves, have become ethnically assimilated or have changed their language. For example, the Bulgarians, who had settled in the Balkans a century earlier, lost their original language, adopting the tongue and many of the customs of the Slavs whom they conquered.

the Latin Empire was still vegetating in Constantinople. Parochial states were formed, some of them owing allegiance to the King of Hungary.

The Árpád dynasty finally died out, but Hungary was able, under the Anjou kings of French-Italian origin (1308–1382), to maintain her great-power status. Of these kings, Louis the Great ruled over Poland as well. Subsequently, Hungary shared many of her kings with Poland and Bohemia. The last monarch who maintained the independent great-power status of Hungary was King Matthias Corvinus (1458–1490). Since the early fifteenth century the Ottoman Empire had been steadily expanding northward. Hungary stood squarely in the way, and bore the brunt of the fight against this aggressive power. The popes referred to Hungary as the "shield of Christianity."

As a result of the disastrous battle of Mohács (1526) against the Turks, Hungary fell into three parts. The northern and western part, after some initial resistance, recognized the Hapsburg rulers (emperors of the Holy Roman Empire at that time) as kings of Hungary. The eastern end, Transylvania, became a principality owing nominal allegiance to the Sultan. The south and center of Hungary remained under Turkish domination for 150 years.*

Protestantism, like other Western spiritual and cultural currents, penetrated into Hungary in the course of the sixteenth century. The 150 years of Turkish occupation were replete with a struggle for national and religious liberties. Transylvania became the refuge of Hungarian national independence and the cradle of surviving freedom. While Hungarians were participating in the life-and-death warfare against the Turks, there were also in "Royal Hungary" frequent insurrections against Hapsburg misrule. The proportion of Hungarians in the nation declined to the advantage of the other nationalities: Slovaks in the north, Rumanians in the east, and Serbs in the south. After the expulsion of the Turks by the Hapsburg armies at the end of the seventeenth century, these other nationalities, joined by German settlers, entered the devastated empty spaces of the central plain. And now, with the Turks gone, Transylvania joined Hungary proper in recognizing the Hapsburg rulers.

In the early eighteenth century, the constant policy of the Vienna

* After the battle of Mohács the Czech kingdom was also taken over by the Hapsburgs. Poland was a powerful kingdom. The Muscovite Empire, having gotten rid of Mongol bondage a century earlier, was on the way to expansion, at first toward the east and south. The Ottoman Empire was at the height of its power in Europe, Asia, and Africa.

Court in denying Hungarians their constitutional liberties led to the Rákoczi insurrection (1705–1711). Prince Ferenc Rákoczi became an ally of Louis XIV of France. The fate of Hungary, however, as so often before and after, was decided on foreign battlefields. After the French defeats in the War of the Spanish Succession, the insurgents had to surrender, though not without stipulating the maintenance of Hungary's constitution. At that time Peter the Great ruled over Russia, and Poland's power was on the decline. The House of Hapsburg, holding the Imperial Crown, ruled over its Austrian lands, the Czech provinces, and Hungary. The Ottoman Empire was still a formidable power, but had ceased to be a danger to Christendom.

Maria Theresa's reign (1740–1780) was marked by Hungarian economic and cultural development despite her absolutist tendencies. Her successor, Emperor Joseph II, who was never legally king of Hungary, having refused to have himself crowned in order to avoid taking an oath on the Hungarian constitution, undertook to streamline his wide-flung domains by the introduction of identical patterns of government, including the use of German in Hungary as official language in the place of Latin. He failed against the passive resistance of the Hungarians.

REFORM, REVOLUTION, AND COMPROMISE

The French Revolution of 1789 gave an enormous impetus to Hungarian nationalism, as to nationalism elsewhere. The country, though living under its own constitutional feudal regime, was hampered in its development by the suspicious Vienna cabinet, whose will was paramount in military and foreign affairs. Consequently, nationalism together with democratic development came to mean furthering the official use of the Hungarian language (which the people had never stopped using); shaking off the tutelage of the Vienna cabinet; abolishing serfdom; and introducing a Western-type democratic constitutionalism. Writers and poets introduced what is known as the *era of reform*.

The long evolution of the Hungarian dissent suddenly came to a climax when news of the 1848 February revolt in Paris reached Hungary. Repercussions of this event were widespread in Europe, for example, in Italy and Germany, and also in Vienna and Prague,* but nowhere were the tremors so violently felt as in Hungary. A parallelism with the events of 1956 — despite obvious differences

* Warsaw remained quiet; the abortive Polish revolution of 1830 was still in memory.

— offers itself. In 1848, the revolutionary events resulted in a constitutional change approved by the monarch, the adoption of a "responsible cabinet" system on a democratic ballot basis. But the Vienna Court and cabinet, awakened from their initial torpor and confusion, wished to go back on their concessions. They had by now stabilized their position in Prague and in Vienna, and they determined to halt Hungary's manifest trend toward becoming a sovereign, independent state, connected with Austria only by the identity of the sovereign. Emperor-King Ferdinand (who had sanctioned the 1848 laws) was made to resign, and the youthful Francis Joseph was installed as Emperor. The government of Hungary was forced to defend itself when Austrian troops penetrated deep into Hungarian territory. But by the spring of 1849, the military position turned to the favor of the Hungarians. The Austrians were driven back. Pest and Buda were recaptured. At that juncture, Louis Kossuth, the head of the government, resorted to a radical step: the Hungarian Assembly, convened in the city of Debrecen, adopted on April 4, 1849, a declaration dethroning the House of Hapsburg from all sovereignty over Hungary — a document couched in terms similar to the American Declaration of Independence.* At that very moment young Francis Joseph was already beseeching Tsar Nicholas I to send his troops to the rescue of Austria. Russian armies entered the country in the early summer of 1849, and the outnumbered and outflanked Hungarian forces were pushed back, defeated, and finally compelled to surrender on August 13, 1849.

Even today the Soviet leaders are haunted by the evident analogy between the tsarist intervention in 1849 and the Soviet Army's intervention in 1956. During his April 1958 visit in Hungary, Khrushchev undertook to point out the difference between these two interventions, but on another visit in December 1959 he explained, lacking any tact toward his audience's national susceptibilities, that since the Tsar did not quibble about intervening, "how could the Soviet Union have withheld such a help in 1956 . . . ?" [14]

After the 1849 intervention the Russian army withdrew, leaving Hungary at the mercy of the Vienna camarilla. Hungary was made an Austrian province. The political and military leaders who had been captured were executed, including the thirteen generals of

* But, what a difference! The American colonies were separated from the mother country by the full breadth of the Atlantic Ocean, and France was soon to become their ally. Had France not been still in the throes of her own revolution in 1849, the French might possibly have intervened in favor of the Hungarians, anticipating their actions of 1854–1856 and 1859.

the Hungarian army. Hungary fell into a mood of spiritual apathy and passivity. The Austrian oppression, contrary to the Soviet-Communist methods of government, did not require collaboration by Hungarian leaders. Nevertheless, the Russian intervention of 1849 had been characterized by a limited number of "muscovite-guides," as quislings of those days were called.

The internal situation of Hungary greatly weakened Austria. The fear of renewed revolts, together with Austria's military defeats by France in 1859 and by Prussia in 1866, forced Vienna into gradual concessions. The pre-1848 status of Hungary was restored in 1861; but all Hungarian political parties continued to insist on the re-establishment of the 1848 reform acts (though not on the dethronement of 1849). Ferenc Deák was the statesman who, with moderation and steadfastness, succeeded in reaching the settlement of 1867. This arrangement not only restored the acts of 1848, but raised Hungary to the status of equal partner of Austria, thus creating the Dual Monarchy of Austria-Hungary. In addition to the identity of the monarch (who was King of Hungary and Emperor of Austria), foreign affairs and defense were "common affairs" between the two countries.

But Austria-Hungary's days were numbered, and she scarcely survived another half-century. The dissatisfaction of non-Germanic elements in Austria (Czechs, Poles, Italians) and non-Hungarian elements in Hungary (Croats, Rumanians, Slovaks, Serbs), together with the desire of nationalist Hungarian parties to achieve independence, doomed the Monarchy to succumb to the disaster of a defeat in World War I. In 1918 Austria-Hungary's northern and southern territories went into the formation of Czechoslovakia and Yugoslavia. The Rumanians annexed Transylvania and even parts of Hungary proper.

BETWEEN TWO WARS AND AFTER

Hungary declared herself a Republic in November 1918. Under the trauma of having lost two thirds of her territory and more than one half of her population (including nearly three million ethnic Hungarians), she fell prey to a tiny number of Communists, mostly former prisoners of war returned from Soviet Russia, under the leadership of Béla Kun. This early incarnation of the dictatorship of the proletariat lasted only four months (March–July 1919). It was toppled by a stiff show of popular resistance, the advance of Rumanian troops, and the pressure of the anti-Communist armed forces

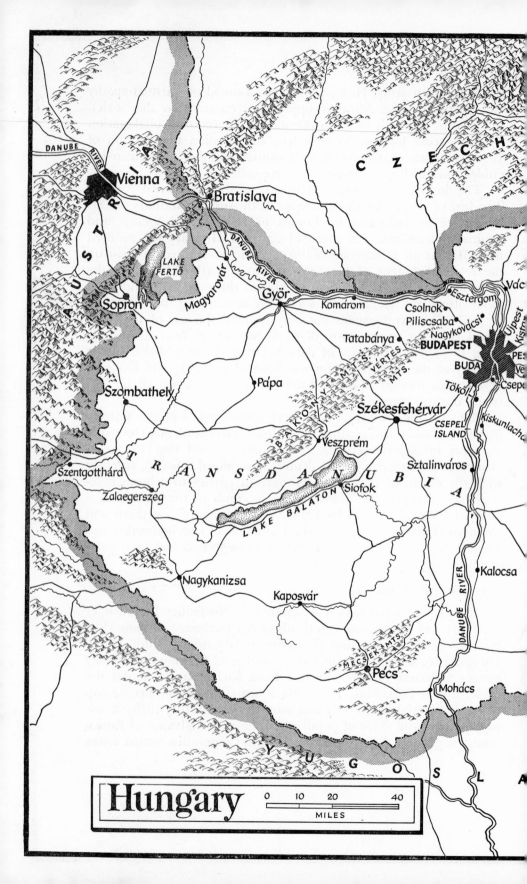

Hungary

| 0 | 10 | 20 | 40 |

MILES

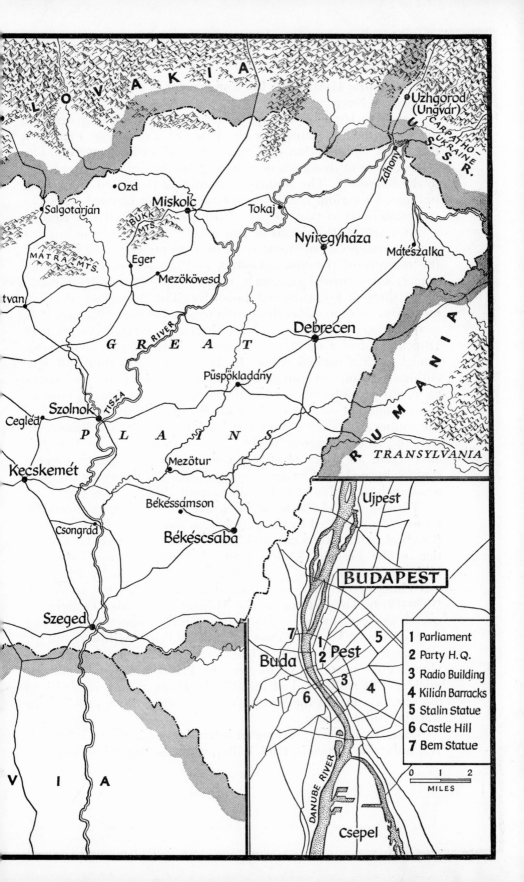

under Admiral Horthy, the last Commander in Chief of the Austro-Hungarian Navy.

For years Hungary writhed under the aftereffects of geographic dismemberment (legalized by the Peace of Trianon in 1920) and the action and reaction of Communist and white terrorism. The influx of tens of thousands of refugees from the lost territories added to the difficulties. The country reconstituted itself into a kingdom, but since for various reasons the throne could not be filled, a regency was established to take its place, with Admiral Horthy as Regent.

Two factors, the results of past events, determined the internal and external policy of Hungary for over twenty years: the desire for the recovery of the lost territories, and the fear of Communism. The country turned extremely nationalistic — partly by instinct, partly through governmental insistence. The democratic development was cut short. The Hungarian regime between 1920 and 1944 was a conservative one with authoritarian leanings. Like pre-1918 Hungary it had a multiparty system (including Social Democrats), though with a limited ballot. In the absence of a thorough agricultural reform, old-fashioned large holdings continued to hamper an all-out development of a healthy farmer class. In fact, the country was a somewhat ossified remnant of Austro-Hungary, with many of the former Monarchy's good and bad qualities. It is inaccurate to style the Horthy regime "fascist," as the Communists do. Whereas, after 1935, all other Central-European countries except Czechoslovakia turned totalitarian or authoritarian, Hungary by comparison remained an island of liberalism until 1944.

The country, because of its irredentist tendencies, lived for twenty years besieged by the isolating pressure of the Little Entente (Czechoslovakia, Rumania, and Yugoslavia) which was the Eastern tier of the French alliance system. When under the impact of Hitlerite Germany and Fascist Italy the Little Entente fell apart and Hungary was able to recover some parts of her lost territories (1938–1940), large strata of the Hungarian population were attracted to Germany and spellbound by German successes in the first years of World War II. Count Teleki, the Prime Minister, and his entourage saw more clearly; when German armies marched through Hungary en route to Yugoslavia, the Prime Minister committed suicide. Half willingly, half unwillingly, Hungary was dragged into the war, first against the Soviet Union, subsequently against Britain and the United States.

Hungary, however, became an increasingly reluctant participant. When the tide turned in 1943, Kállay, who was then Prime Minister, made a tentative secret agreement with the Allies.* Hitler fore-stalled the plan by occupying Hungary on March 19, 1944, and the Regent Horthy was forced to acquiesce in a German-sponsored right-wing cabinet. Now several hundred thousand Jews were de-ported to death camps by the Germans, and the country was made to participate more fully in the war effort. In October 1944, when Soviet troops had penetrated part way into Hungary, Regent Horthy tried to sever Hungary's ties with Germany. The move, however, failed: Horthy was made prisoner by the Germans, and an extreme Hungarian Nazi (Arrow Cross) faction was placed in power by Hitler.

Hungary became a bloody battlefield. Budapest, surrounded by Soviet troops and defended for six weeks by the Germans, was largely destroyed. A Hungarian government was formed in Debrecen on December 23, 1944, under the auspices of the Soviet Army. This government concluded an armistice agreement with the major Allies in Moscow on January 20, 1945.

In April, after the Germans had been expelled from the country, the new government moved to Budapest. It was a coalition cabinet, composed of "democratic" parties which had all been opposition parties during the Horthy regime except the outlawed Communist Party. But the real and direct power — it would be exaggerated to call it administration, because for months the whole country was totally disorganized — was for some time entirely in the hands of the Soviet occupation forces. Thus the Communist Party had a relative advantage over all other parties, in means of communica-tion, occupation of buildings, and the media of propaganda. Most of these initial benefits were, however, counterbalanced by the actions and behavior of their sponsors, the Soviet Army.

* Unconditional surrender, under the Casablanca formula, was offered and ac-cepted by secret agreement in August–September 1943 in Turkey. It was to come into force when Allied forces reached the boundaries of Hungary. C. A. Macartney, *October Fifteen, A History of Modern Hungary, 1920–1943* (Edinburgh, 1957), II, 139–148. When Soviet troops reached Hungary the former agreement was simply ig-nored, and a new armistice agreement was concluded.

3

The Communists Take Over

/\\/\\/\\/\\/\\/\\/\\/\\/\\/\\/\\/\\/\\/\\/\\/\\/

There cannot be true love for one's fatherland if the love is in one way or another opposed to the love of the Soviet Union.

VULKO CHERVENKOV (1948)

No matter how much each of us loves the land of Socialism, the Soviet Union, he can in no case have less love for his own country, which is also developing Socialism.

TITO AND KARDELJ to Stalin and Molotov, April 13, 1948.

CONFLICTS between Hungarian national interests and Soviet control arose as soon as the Soviet Army occupied Hungary. Armies of occupation are scarcely noted for respecting the political, economic, and cultural interests of the lands they conquer. But in this case the brutal behavior of the Soviet soldier and the official attitude of Soviet authorities toward the new Hungarian government contrasted strangely with the Soviet claim of having liberated Hungary from German domination. During the period of the Armistice, and even for some time after the Treaty of Peace came in force in September 1947, the government of Hungary could not be considered as directed entirely by the Communist Party, as it was to become after the "year of transformation" (Communist terminology for the year 1948). This coalition government of 1945–1948 struggled under a steadily increasing Communist pressure, and therefore was bound to be characterized by contradictions and vacillations.[1]

THE RED ARMY AND THE COMMUNIST PARTY

World War II and Soviet occupation reduced Hungary to a state of prostration comparable to that which followed the Mongol destruction suffered in the thirteenth century. Historically minded people asked themselves whether this was to be a Tartar or a Turkish occupation — the first having lasted less than two years, the second a hundred and fifty. The Soviet combat and occupation forces (in contradistinction to the official Communist version) behaved like ruthless conquerors. They looted, committed innumerable brutalities, and appeared to the average Hungarian as primitive, uncouth, but sometimes cunning, barbarians — in contrast to the equally ruthless, but civilized and self-disciplined Germans. Veterans of World War I were ready to compare tsarist and Soviet Russian soldiers: The imperial Russian officer, on the average, had been a Westernized individual, able to check barbarian instincts in the common soldier. In the Red Army practically no difference in standards existed between officers and their troops. It was also noticed that the average Soviet soldier, contrary to expectations, displayed nationalistic rather than class phobias and prejudices.[2]

The behavior and intellectual caliber of Soviet soldiers destroyed a belief, entertained by some, about the superiority of the "Soviet man." In fact it was convincing propaganda against Communism. The originally tiny but aggressive Communist Party which popped up everywhere in the wake of advancing Soviet armies faced difficulties at the outset because of the devastating impressions created by these "Soviet men" all over the country. Hungarian Communists asserted that the Red Army's behavior was in retaliation for Hungary's participation in the war on the side of Nazi Germany, but they often contradicted themselves by maintaining that Hungarian working classes were not to be made responsible — an argument entirely ignored by the Soviet Army.

Many people may have been influenced by a whispering campaign initiated by the Communist Party leadership hinting that the attitude of the Soviet Union vis-à-vis Hungary depended on whether the country was to become truly democratic (meaning Communist). Nevertheless, despite the open support given by the Soviet Army, the Communist Party obtained only 17 per cent of the total votes at the free elections of November 4, 1945, the only free elections ever held behind the Iron Curtain. The Smallholder Party (backed mostly by anti-Communists) obtained 59 per cent, the Social Democratic Party, 17 per cent, and the National Peasant Party, 5 per cent.[3]

Before and after these elections a longing toward the benefits of real democracy was perceptible. Because the Communist movement was represented as democratic the adjective took on an almost pejorative meaning for many, but all but a small minority wished to establish a government elected by majority vote. The election results inspired a wishful optimism, strengthening a belief that after the conclusion of the peace treaty the Soviets would withdraw and refrain from further interference.

Subsequent developments, however, refuted any such optimism. Using tortuous tactics the Communist Party, aided by the Soviet Command, succeeded in undermining, disrupting, and finally eliminating the other parties.[4] In the period of transition the Communist Party found itself compelled to pronounce on vital national questions in which Hungarian interests clashed with policies followed by the Soviet Union.

During this period, owing to the presence of the Red Army, the influence of the Communist Party had outdistanced that of the other parties in the coalition government. Nevertheless, its influence was not entirely controlling. The Party's positions, strictly conforming to the variables of Soviet policy, often came into collision with policies supported by the non-Communist elements of the Hungarian government. Thus Hungary's national interests, even before the all-out Communist takeover, were largely subordinated to the devious line of Soviet policy-making. Furthermore, the Hungarian Communist Party failed to protect the economic interests of its country, interests largely identical with those of the working class whose vanguard it professed to be.

For instance, in the border question between Hungary and Rumania the Communist Party refused to support the revision of the frontier line in favor of Hungary until the Soviet leaders hinted their approval.[5] Even so, eventually, the Soviet Union sided with Rumania on this question.[6] Application of the doctrine of collective responsibility against the German-speaking minority in Hungary, which was to be expelled under the Potsdam Agreement of 1945, was upheld by the Communists of Hungary though running against Hungarian interests.[7] Under the same principle 600,000 Hungarians in Czechoslovakia were also to be removed into Hungary;[8] the Hungarian Communist Party, in fact, temporarily backed this latter ultra-chauvinistic attempt championed by the Czechoslovak Communist Party.[9]

The Hungarian Communist Party, prior to its acquisition of full control, hardly ever intervened for any alleviation of the crushing burden resulting from the various methods of Soviet exploitation, which were: reparation deliveries,[10] acquisition of German "assets,"[11] Soviet — Hungarian Joint Corporations,[12] and occupation costs of the Red Army. Responsibility for acts against Western citizens or their property, committed by Soviet military personnel during the hostilities or after, could never be placed by Hungary on the Soviet Union because of a Communist veto.[13] The Socialist Fatherland was in no mood to take the blame, and eventually Hungary had to assume responsibility and damages.

THE COMMUNIST PARTY'S ROAD TO POWER

From 1945 to the end of 1948 the Communist Party in Hungary fought its way toward a monopolistic control of the country. After the 1945 elections, the idea of obtaining a democratic majority was abandoned and the goal was reached by other means: terrorizing, bribing, or blackmailing leading members of the other political parties. And, as the *ultima ratio,* there always remained the Soviet Army, which, though, would need to be used only once. The Communist Party was able to control the police, and its political branch, the Security Police,* and its grip over the weak Hungarian Army was systematically established through intimidation and infiltration, with the active cooperation of the Soviet Army.[14] Coercive power was thus wielded by agencies subordinate to the Communist Party only.

The majority party, the Smallholders, was weakened by accusations leveled against many of its independent-minded members, who were expelled from the National Assembly as "fascists" or "reactionaries." Also, "conspiracies" were discovered and a further number of deputies were eliminated or arrested, including a cabinet minister. The Assembly, terrorized into servility, removed the parliamentary immunity of the accused members. The turning point was the removal of the immunity of the most powerful anti-Communist leader, Béla Kovács, Secretary-General of the Smallholder Party. In this case the Assembly tried to resist; then the Soviet Command intervened, arresting Kovács on February 25, 1947, on a charge of conspiracy against the occupation forces. Subsequently the Prime Minister, Ferenc Nagy (no relation to the Communist Imre Nagy), while on vacation in Switzerland, was threatened with a similar charge; he could not return for fear of arrest and was forced to tender his letter of resignation in exchange for his child on June 2, 1947. Thereafter all resistance came to a standstill and only persons fully tractable to Communist pressures were allowed to occupy

---

* The Soviet Head of the Armistice Control Commission, Marshal Voroshilov, consented to the holding of the 1945 election only after the political parties agreed to maintain the coalition among them, and to leave the Ministry of the Interior (controlling the police) to the Communist Party.

ministerial positions. Communist infiltration and elimination of resisting elements took place in all political parties. Many leading politicians fled the country.

The elections of August 31, 1947, although fraudulently managed, secured to the Communist no more than 22 per cent of the votes. But their main objective, the destruction of the majority party, was reached, for the Smallholders, now under transparent Communist guidance, obtained only 15 per cent, whereas the two opposition parties (composed mostly of dissident Smallholders) scored nearly 40 per cent. These two parties were the Hungarian Independence Party and the Democratic People's Party.

When the Treaty of Peace took effect on September 15, 1947, the occupation of Hungary by Soviet troops came officially to an end. But Soviet forces did not leave the country. Article 22 provided that they should stay "for the maintenance of the lines of communication of the Soviet Army with the Soviet zone of occupation in Austria."

Within six months after the elections of 1947, the two opposition parties were dissolved, their deputies deprived of their seats and their leaders forced to leave the country. As for the parties that had participated in the government, the Social Democrat Party was forcibly merged into the Communist Party in March 1948 to form the "Hungarian Workers Party," which, for convenience and accuracy, we shall continue to call the Communist Party; and the Smallholders and the National Peasant Party henceforward led only a shadow existence. After February 1949, under the leadership of the Communists, they had to participate in the "Hungarian People's Independence Front" which was to enter the next election with a single list of candidates.

DRAMATIS PERSONAE OF THE COMMUNIST PARTY

In its fight for power the Communist Party leadership wished to avoid conflicts within its ranks. If there were such conflicts — and there is some evidence to this effect — they remained latent or were discreetly thrashed out and settled at the highest level of Party leadership.

The leadership as well as the membership was rather heterogeneous in antecedents. The most important leaders were the so-called muscovites, who had been Hungarian prisoners of war in Russia during World War I and had joined the Bolsheviks there, or who had fled to Russia upon the collapse of the Communist regime in Hungary in 1919 or at some later date.

The uncontested leader of the Communist Party was the muscovite Mátyás Rákosi. Born in Hungary in 1892, conscripted into the Austro-Hungarian Army during World War I, he was taken prisoner by the Russians and came into close contact with the Bolshevik leadership after the Russian Revolution of 1917. Having received a Communist education, he returned to Hungary with Béla Kun in 1918. During the Communist regime of 1919 he was Deputy People's Commissar for Commerce and Transportation, and later Commissar for Production. After the collapse of the regime he fled with Béla Kun's party to Austria, and later to Soviet Russia. In 1924 he was ordered back to Hungary as agent of the Comintern. Promptly arrested and sentenced, he spent sixteen years in Hungarian prisons. The Soviet Union obtained his release in October 1940 when he was exchanged against Hungarian flags captured by the tsarist armies in 1849. Béla Kun and other Hungarian Communists having become, in the meantime, victims of Stalinist purges, Rákosi not only became Hungarian Communist number one but was able to establish a personal contact with Stalin. At the end of 1944, by the grace of the Red Army, the future dictator of Hungary returned triumphant to his country of origin.

In Rákosi's entourage were a number of other outstanding muscovites who were to figure importantly in the coming events. Ernö Gerö, refugee to the Soviet Union after 1919, had been a trustworthy agent of the Comintern, and now was a colonel of the MVD. Jozsef Révai, former secretary of Béla Kun, was about to become chief theoretician of the Party and editor in chief of the Communist Party daily, the *Szabad Nép*. Mihály Farkas was formerly of the Czechoslovak Communist Party and later officer of the Red Army. Gábor Péter had been a Soviet Security Police trainee, a circumstance that predestined him to become, after 1944, head of the Security Police in Hungary.

All those Communist leaders were of Jewish origin. The only conspicuous non-Jewish muscovite in the group that returned to Hungary with the Red Army was Imre Nagy. While Rákosi had the look of a bald-headed paunchy capitalist, Imre Nagy had the appearance of a country schoolteacher, stocky, round-faced, bespectacled, and mustached. Like Rákosi, Imre Nagy was a prisoner of war in Russia during World War I. He joined the Soviet Communist Party in 1917, but returned to Hungary only after the collapse of the Communist regime of 1919. He worked in the clandestine Communist movement until 1930 when he escaped to the Soviet Union. Here he was employed by an Agrarian Institute (Nagy was of peasant stock and his special interest had always been agriculture), and acted also as manager of a Siberian kolkhoz. During World War II he served as Hungarian broadcaster for Radio Moscow. His radio texts were considered to smack of Hungarian nationalism by Rákosi, whose hostility against Nagy may be traced back to that time.[14] This was not the first time that Nagy had come into conflict with an official view of the Party leadership; at the second Congress of the outlawed Hungarian Communist Party in Vienna in January 1930, he stood for a distribution of land to the peasants in Hungary as against the official opinion, which favored the establishment of agricultural collectives. For this he was accused of expressing Bukharinist views, and later made a retraction.[15] In 1944 when the muscovites returned to Hungary, Imre Nagy became Minister of Agriculture in the provisional cabinet of Debrecen.

Only one of the outstanding Communist leaders in 1944 did not happen to be a muscovite, although he was a Communist of long standing and former fighter in Spain. This man was Lászlo Rajk. In contrast to most of the leading muscovites, Rajk was not Jewish, and indeed his family had a peculiar association with the anti-Semitic Hungarian Arrow-Cross movement. In World War II when Rajk was arrested as a Communist conspirator by the pro-Nazi Hungarian movement, his life was saved by his two powerful Arrow-Cross brothers. After the war he repaid this debt by removing the names of his brothers (then in Germany) from the list of war criminals. At the beginning of the Communist Party's recruiting campaign in 1944 a considerable number of former Arrow-Cross rank and file joined up, partly because forgiveness was promised them, partly because the Communist movement, with its slogans and methods of violence and its pretense to uncontrovertible verities, appealed to them. While leading Hungarian Nazis were being tried before the People's Courts, most of these so-called "petty Arrow-Cross" elements turned Communist. Rajk from 1945 to 1947 was more popular with the Communist membership than even Rákosi, his family ties adding to his popularity.

Imre Nagy was popular with the peasant class. Under his tenure of the Ministry of Agriculture, on March 15, 1945, agricultural holdings over a certain size were expropriated and distributed among the peasants who had little or no land. Again ultradoctrinaire Party members had wished to "short-cut" the "inevitable development" and proceed right away with collectivization of the expropriated estates. The dispute was settled when the Soviet Command, under Moscow's orders, decided in favor of distribution.[16]

In November 1945, Imre Nagy exchanged his post of Minister of

Agriculture for the all-important Ministry of the Interior. At that juncture, this Ministry was of greater importance than any other cabinet post: it was the position from which the rest of the coalition parties could be swept off their feet. Nagy, more philosopher than fighter, unsuited for palace intrigue and cloak-and-dagger dealings, did not have the temperament for such a post. In March 1946, Rákosi replaced him with Lászlo Rajk.

During the deplorable economic conditions of the postwar inflation in Hungary, when the value of the dollar reached 4,600,000 quadrillion pengoes, Communist agitators and the Party press incited the working population against "speculators" and "black marketeers." Anti-Semitic excesses, even murders, resulted and the Communist police, under the orders of Rajk, secured impunity for the perpetrators, even though on one occasion a Jewish police officer was killed. There is evidence of some tension between Rajk and the Rákosi-led muscovites, and one may safely presume that considerable tension existed within the Party.[17]

Rákosi, after the 1947 elections, wished to get rid of Rajk, who was no longer needed in the key position of Minister of the Interior. Clashes between Rajk and Gábor Péter, head of the Security Police, were the order of the day. Though Péter's agency was subordinate to Rajk's Ministry, Péter had the support of Rákosi. On August 3, 1948, Rajk was demoted to the far less important position of Minister of Foreign Affairs. His later arrest and execution and the dispute surrounding his posthumous rehabilitation, will be discussed in subsequent parts of this book.

Rajk was the most prominent figure among the "indigenous" nonmuscovite Communists. There was still another group, mostly intellectuals, who had left Hungary in the interwar period and settled in Western Europe. Many of them, as students in the West, had joined local Communist movements and fought in Spain or with the Résistance in France. Outstanding among the "Westerners" was the so-called Swiss Group, whose members were often in contact with Allied intelligence officials during World War II.[18] These "Western" Communists, returning to Hungary after the war, were not attracted by the methods utilized by the muscovites. None of them held key positions, though their influence, especially in the cultural field, was for some time considerable. Their education and Weltanschauung brought them into conflict with Rákosi and his associates during the Stalinist period of terror which was to descend upon Hungary as soon as the Communist Party found itself in the uncontested possession of monopolistic power over the country.

THE FIRST PHASE

Hotbed of Conflicts:
The Stalinist Dictatorship
1 9 4 9 – 1 9 5 3

The essence of the system was the creation of an individual hierarchic ladder of cults . . . In the bloc of Socialist States Stalin stood at the top of this hierarchic ladder. All those who stood on lower rungs of the ladder bowed their heads before him. Those who bowed their heads were not only the other leaders of the CPSU and the leaders of the Soviet Union, but also the leaders of the Communist Workers' Parties of the countries of the Socialist camp. The latter, that is, the First Secretaries of the Central Committees of the Parties of the various countries, who sat on the second rung of the ladder of the cult of the individual, donned in turn the robes of infallibility and wisdom. But their cult radiated only on the territory of their own countries where they stood at the top of the national cult ladder. This national cult could be called only a reflected brilliance, a borrowed light. It shone as the moon does. Nonetheless, it was all powerful in the sphere of its action.

The bearer of the cult of the individual was omniscient, knew how to do everything, solved everything, directed everything and decided everything within the sphere of his activity. He was the most intelligent man, regardless of his personal knowledge, capacity, or other personal qualities.

WLADYSLAW GOMULKA before the Central Committee
of the Polish United Workers Party, October 21, 1956

4

Party and State

/.v...v...v...v...v...v...v...v...v...v...v...v...v...v./

The achievement and maintenance of the dictatorship of the proletariat is impossible without a party which is strong by reason of its solidarity and iron discipline. But iron discipline in the Party is inconceivable without unity of will, without complete and absolute unity of action on the part of all members of the Party . . . from this it follows that the existence of factions is incompatible either with the Party's unity or with its iron discipline . . .

Not a single important political or organizational question is decided by our Soviet and other mass organizations without guiding directions from the Party.

STALIN, *Problems of Leninism*

For the shaping of Hungary into a model Stalinist country it was necessary to employ all the instruments and paraphernalia of power politics, all the economic measures and psychological and physical deterrents that had proved so successful in stabilizing Communist rule in Russia and that had made Stalin's dictatorship the accepted pattern of Soviet government. As Stalin and Stalinism were equivalent with Soviet rule after 1928, so Rákosi and his system of government meant Communism to Hungary in the years between 1949 and 1953. The Five-Year Plan, starting in 1950, the ultimate Sovietization of Hungary's constitution and administration, the systematic growth of Party rule, the overwhelming influence and terror exercised by the Security Police, the purges and show trials against both Party and non-Party elements, the deportations of "reactionaries," the exploitation of the working class and forced agricultural collectivization — all these were part and parcel of Rákosi's system, as they had been of Stalin's in the Soviet Union.

A NEW THEORY OF THE PEOPLE'S DEMOCRACY

By early 1949, the political monopoly of the Communist Party (officially the Hungarian Workers Party) had become an accomplished fact. In January of that year Mátyás Rákosi could dare to proclaim openly that "a People's Democracy is according to its function a dictatorship of the proletariat without the Soviet form." He went on to explain that the Hungarian People's Democracy was in a position to establish such a dictatorship because it could base itself "on the great Soviet Union," and that the dictatorship could be exercised "in comparative peace without a bloody civil war" because of "the presence of the Soviet Army." [1]

The period prior to the "transformation" year 1948 was now considered as a kind of diarchy comparable to the Kerenski era of 1917 in Russia. The "Old Order" of Capitalism and the "New Order" of Socialism had been fighting each other for supremacy; the New Order had won, and the "People's Democracy" (in other words, the dictatorship of the proletariat) had been established with the acknowledged help of the Soviet Union. Up to then, a People's Democracy, in contrast to a "bourgeois" democracy, had been represented as a democratic form of government with greater emphasis on "economic and social equality" than on a mere "voting equality." And now, by one wave of the conjurer's wand, People's Democracy suddenly became a dictatorship of the proletariat in which the intrinsic contradiction between "democracy" and "dictatorship" was exorcised by the allegation that this was a dictatorship not of a minority but of the majority. [2]

In May 1949 new elections were held, for the first time on a single-list basis. Although the list was submitted by the People's Independence Front, in practice all members of the National Assembly to be elected were designated by the Communists. The results were not surprising: 95.6 per cent of the 5,478,515 votes were cast for the single list.

Not for long did the People's Democracy exercise its function of proletarian dictatorship "without the Soviet form." The new National Assembly hurried to adopt a constitution modeled on the Stalinist constitution of the Soviet Union, and paid tribute to the Soviet Union for its "unselfish help" in liberating Hungary and for its guidance in the advance toward Socialism. Becoming effective August 20, 1949, [3] the constitution imposed the council (soviet) system of local government. The first single-list elections of the local councils were held on October 22, 1950. Hungary thus acquired not only the substance but also the form of a Soviet-Communist country. The constitution also changed the national symbol. A new coat of arms of the Hungarian state was made to resemble those of the member republics of the Soviet Union. Despite the servility of the National Assembly, some lobby opposition could be observed against the abandonment of the old Kossuth blazon, a circumstance to which Rákosi referred in his speech introducing the new constitution.*

The Soviet example has demonstrated to the world that a constitution in a Communist-governed country may be largely a face-saving apparatus. Thus, according to the new Hungarian constitution, the National Assembly (and during its recess its Presidential Council) holds supreme legislative power including the right to elect the Council of Ministers. But in fact the National Assembly is convoked only once or twice a year, when it is expected to give rubber-stamp approval to all those decrees having the force of law which have been passed since its last meeting by the Presidential Council.** The Presidential Council acts in complete deference to the Ministry, and ultimately the Ministry (which in the Stalinist era included all the impressive figures of the Party), the National Assembly, and the Presidential Council are all directed and controlled by the Party.[4]

The new constitution formally restated many features of totalitarian regimentation which already had been introduced in the course of 1948 and early in 1949. The leading role of the Communist Party as the vanguard of the working class is defined; the dictatorship of the proletariat is installed for the purpose of eliminating capitalist elements and to enable the country to build Socialism.

Totalitarian legislation, whether Nazi, fascist or Communist, is marked by purposeful vagueness and ambiguity when it attempts to define governmental tasks, obligations of citizens, or certain crimes. Thus, in the new Hungarian constitution certain rights are accorded only to "workers," with the intent of excluding all those who might be arbitrarily classed as "nonworkers" or "exploiters." Likewise the

---

* In the struggle between nationalism and international Communism, national symbols and slogans acquire special significance; the re-instatement of the Kossuth blazon was one of the achievements of the 1956 revolutionaries.

** When in 1950 some Party members questioned the wisdom of the procedure of not having real debates in the National Assembly, they were simply given the answer that "this is the way the Soviet comrades are doing it." CURPH (Columbia University Research Project on Hungary), interview no. 500.

general provisions of a new Criminal Code (Law No. 2 of 1950)
render punishable "every act which violates or endangers the political, social, or economic order of the Hungarian People's Republic
or of its citizens." Under the Cabinet Decree No. 4,353 of 1949, the
State Security Authority was given the right to "take into custody"
anyone suspected of an antistate or antisocial offense without any
limitation as to the duration of such custody. This decree, however,
simply legalized the arbitrary use of detention already practiced
by the Security Police for some years.

STRUCTURE OF THE PARTY

The Party obtained full control over Hungary at a time when
its Soviet counterpart had ruled Russia for over thirty years and
Stalin had enforced his authority for nearly a quarter of a century.
The Hungarian Party's organizational structure was an imitation of
its Soviet parent. There was one main difference. During the 1944–
1948 period the Hungarian Party, in order to compete with other
political groups, especially with the other workers' party, the Social
Democrats, had felt compelled to become a *mass* party. Before merg-
ing with the Social Democrats in May 1948, it reached an alleged
membership of 884,000, and with the adherence of most of the
Socialists it attained a peak of about 1,500,000.[5] After its realization
of monopoly power, the Party could dispense with much of its
membership, and deliberately brought the number down to about
860,000.

Thus the Party had a membership in 1951 which represented
about 9 per cent of the country's population. At the same time the
Soviet Party only numbered about 6,000,000 members, that is, 3 per
cent of the population of the Soviet Union, where the Party had been
in control for nearly thirty-five years. Accordingly, the Hungarian
Party was still a mass party by comparison to Soviet standards, not
the elite or "vanguard" of the working class.

The Hungarian Party had a ready-made plan of organization. As
in the Soviet Union, the highest permanent Party organ was the
Central Committee. Again, reality diverged from avowed principles:
the Central Committee consisting of 78 members was far from being
a parliament of the Party. The majority was a conglomerate of yes
men, who were selected by Rákosi and his associates; relatively few
members had individual ideas. In the course of time, Rákosi was
careful to retain only those who could be relied on to make no
trouble and vote for the resolutions submitted to them by the
Secretary-General of the Party.[6] The Central Committee was thus

made subservient to Rákosi, who framed it to be subservient to the Soviet cause.

From among its members the Central Committee elects the Political Committee (called the Politburo in accordance with the name given to its Soviet counterpart up to 1952), consisting of twelve or thirteen men empowered to make decisions in the intervals between Central Committee sessions. As in the Soviet Union, the Politburo is the highest Party authority and the highest organ of decision-making.

Alongside the Central Committee was its huge, departmentalized secretariat, set up in close imitation of the Soviet Party secretariat as reorganized in 1948.[7] Besides the important sections dealing with cadre, propaganda, and agitation, the Hungarian secretariat had sections corresponding to branches of state administration, such as foreign affairs, planning, finance, heavy industry, light industry, agriculture, and communications. It also had a "special section" devoted to the affairs of the Security Police. The Party secretariat, though subordinate to the Central Committee, was in fact the mechanism through which Rákosi and his clique exercised authority over the whole Party and over governmental and other public organizations. The secretariat headed the entire Party apparatus with its numerous *apparatchiki*.

The various hierarchical layers of the Communist Party also imitated the Soviet model. Primary (basic) Party organizations, also called Party cells, were organized in plants, agricultural cooperatives, offices, villages, and police and army units. Above the primary Party units were local Party organizations in municipal districts, village circuits, and large industrial combines. County and big-city organizations came next. Each of these Party organs possessed a committee and a secretary.

Theoretically the chief Party organ has been its National Congress, assembled in every third year. Though in principle it was free to deliberate, in practice it has been a very obedient assembly. Its delegates are selected carefully by the Party secretaries, and its debates are strictly confined to a program prearranged by the Central Committee. The Congress "elects" the Central Committee, generally by acclamation, on the basis of the lists submitted to it by the secretariat.

The Party took over and controlled the country's mass organizations. Of special importance was the Federation of Working Youth (*Dolgozo Ifjuság Szövetsége,* abbreviated DISZ), which in 1951 was formally incorporated into the Party as its youth organization, the equivalent of the Komsomol in the Soviet Union. After March 1952 the Party confined its own membership to persons 24 or over, and obtained its young recruits from the DISZ. The Communist children's organization in Hungary was the Pioneers; and the Federation of Democratic Women (MNDSZ) was also Party-controlled. After 1948 the National Council of Trade Unions (SZOT) became totally subservient to the Party, and so did the individual unions.

LOCUS OF REAL POWER

Following closely the Soviet example under Stalin, the *de facto* dictatorship was exercised not so much by the Politburo as a corporate organ, but by its leading members, Rákosi, Gerö, Révai, and Farkas.* Other Politburo members, although enjoying immense prestige owing to their exalted position in the Communist hierarchy, wielded considerably less power than Rákosi and his closest associates; many of them were selected only because they proved pliable instruments of the dictator. When they had outlived their usefulness they were quickly discarded.

Rákosi called himself Stalin's "first Hungarian disciple," and among the many Stalinist dictators of Soviet-dominated European countries, he most nearly approached a miniature imitation of the Soviet autocrat. Nowhere else did the cult of personality put down such deep roots. Dimitrov might have reached a similar position in Bulgaria had he lived, but the roles of other Party chiefs such as Bierut, Gottwald, Gheorghiu-Dej, and Ulbricht were extremely modest when compared with that of Rákosi. Perhaps, if we descend to a still more diminutive example, the supremacy of Enver Hoxha in Albania may be likened to that of Rákosi. If we ask why such a personal autocracy existed in Hungary, the answer apparently is that not every personality is apt or willing to become a brutal and cruel tyrant, and that not everywhere did one of the Communist leaders enjoy such a measure of confidence with the Kremlin, or with Stalin. Rákosi's personal dictatorship — subject only to Soviet control — could not have been exercised save with the explicit approval of Stalin himself, and was manifestly part of Stalin's scheme to extend Soviet control over Hungary.

Rákosi seemed peculiarly adapted to the task. He was clever, had a wide knowledge, and was deeply devoted to the Soviet cause.

---

* This list of Rákosi's principal lieutenants during the Stalinist period has been provided by Imre Nagy, *On Communism: In Defense of the New Course* (New York, 1957), p. 15. He scathingly calls them the "foursome."

He was probably one of those top Communist leaders, who, having arrived at a stage of cynicism in matters of ideology, know only one ideology, that of power. Since he could obtain power only by serving his master in the Kremlin, he was easily prepared to do so. In serving Stalin, he served himself. He was an excellent satrap, and an apt imitator of Stalin's methods; he combined a seeming amiability with vengefulness, paternal benevolence with sadism, perplexing frankness with deceitfulness. Physically, he was dwarfish and ugly, but he had the Napoleonic megalomania and an entire lack of scruples as to means and methods.

While Rákosi was doubtless the protagonist in the Stalinist drama of Hungary, its deuteragonist was Ernö Gerö. Rákosi impressed one as an Epicurean, whereas Gerö was a prototype of austerity. Without the affability of Rákosi, he shared the latter's cunning and cruelty. Révai, a Communist-Soviet philosopher, ideologist, and aesthete, was a Hungarian edition of a composite Zhdanov and Suslov. And the least intelligent among the four, Mihály Farkas, was a Soviet *condottiere* with all the recklessness, opportunism, and perversity of a mercenary.

All these four had one thing in common: their only connections with the country they were to rule in the name of the Soviets were their Hungarian birth and their Hungarian mother tongue. They were real Communist "internationalists," that is, champions of Soviet imperialism and agents of the Cominform. Had it not been for their particular aptitude for employment in Hungary, they could have been sent (as Gerö was to Spain, and Farkas to Czechoslovakia) to any country and would have been sure to serve the cause of the Soviet Union with equal fervor. The qualities of these typical Soviet-Communists dominated Hungary's entire Stalinist epoch, and they served as prototypes for those other Russianized Hungarians who were ready to put Soviet interests before the interests of their own country.

But their power was ultimately only secondary; the primary decision-making authority lay with the multiplex Soviet organs of control, with the Moscow Politburo, or rather with Stalin himself. And the mainstay of Soviet domination was the line of Party communications. Frequent personal visits by Rákosi and other top Party leaders to the Soviet Union and personal interviews with Stalin and top Soviet leaders gave a possibility of exchanging views, submitting reports, and obtaining instructions and opinions. These personal contacts were of particular importance, for basic changes in policies and decisions on personal questions were imparted by the Kremlin at such times.

On subjects of secondary importance, the leader of each section of the Party secretariat conferred directly with his Soviet opposite number, who was in fact his superior. Should the Hungarian participant in the discussion disagree with his Soviet counterpart in Moscow — which might have happened occasionally — he was always able to pass the matter to Rákosi or, on economic questions, to Gerö. If, however, Moscow insisted on its own solution, that decision was final.

Soviet control was exercised also by another means — by various "advisers" stationed in Hungary. The influence of the Hungarian Party upon military decisions was smaller than in any other field, since decisions had to come via Soviet military channels — through "advisers" — directly to Hungarian military authorities. Apart from the Army, it was the Hungarian Security Police that was most intensively advised and that possessed the most complete and direct links with its corresponding Soviet agency. An advisory system of lesser significance was extended to the Ministry of Foreign Affairs, and, for a shorter period, to the Ministry of Foreign Trade. The adviser in the Ministry of Foreign Affairs was rather an agency for reporting on this ministry than a channel for giving orders.

The Soviet embassy in Budapest was also an important instrument of communications. Embassy officials regularly visited the Hungarian Ministry of Foreign Affairs. But, since the Minister was not generally an important leader, the Soviet ambassador himself called on the Party secretariat and in matters of importance on Rákosi.

The chief Hungarian economic centers — the Economic Council, as long as it existed, and the Planning Bureau — had direct individual contacts with relevant Party or governmental agencies in the Soviet Union. But matters of principle were dealt with via the Party-to-Party channel.

In general, we can safely conclude that Rákosi's policy was a reflection of what Moscow wanted from Hungary, in some respects, even an exaggerated expression of what Moscow wanted — as is often the case with over-zealous satraps. The Stalinist insistence on uniformity and strict compliance required, and servility of the top personnel guaranteed, no divergence. This explains the cleavage that resulted in the Party in Hungary when not only the rank and file but more important Party members came into conflict with Rákosi's policies and at the same time (since they were deemed to be identical) with those of Moscow.

PARTY AND GOVERNMENT

In view of the supremacy exercised by the Party leadership, the relative importance of persons in charge of ministerial portfolios greatly decreased during and after 1948 unless they also held important Party positions. Except a few very pliable fellow travelers, most of the non-Communist ministers were gradually eliminated, some of them exchanging their ministerial seats for prison cells. From the summer of 1949 onwards a purge of Communists took place, and up to the end of the Stalinist terror many leading Communists (a large proportion of them former Socialists) became victims of Rákosi's clique.

The President of the Republic since 1946, Zoltán Tildy, was forced to resign on July 30, 1948, as a result of the arrest of his son-in-law, Victor Chornoky, the Hungarian Minister to Egypt, on a charge of high treason. Tildy was succeeded by Árpád Szakasits, who had been the pro-Communist leader of the Social Democratic Party of Hungary after 1945. When the new constitution became effective in August 1949, the presidency was abolished and Szakasits stepped down to the lesser dignity of Chairman of the Presidium of the People's Republic, that is, honorary Head of the State under the Stalinist constitutional system.

Szakasits, by being instrumental in aligning his former party with the Communists, had rendered it incapable of maintaining its independence. This overambitious and vain person with narrow horizons believed that his services would earn the gratitude of Rákosi. On April 26, 1950, he was arrested while a dinner guest in Rákosi's house, and, after being pressed into admitting crimes he had never committed, was sentenced to fifteen years' imprisonment.[8] He was succeeded as Chairman of the Presidium by Sándor Ronai, another ex-Socialist, one of the few who strangely escaped liquidation.

As for the premiership, when Ferenc Nagy, the Smallholder leader, had been forced out while vacationing in Switzerland in 1947, his successor had been Lajos Dinnyés. This man was also from the Smallholder Party but was an early fellow traveler of Soviet and Hungarian Communists and an accommodating instrument in Rákosi's hands. He was cashiered on December 8, 1948, when the Minister of Finance, a fellow Smallholder, failed to return from an official mission in the West.

István Dobi, an even more pliable instrument, then became Prime Minister (officially, Chairman of the Council of Ministers).

Of peasant stock, a Socialist who had later joined the Smallholder Party, Dobi soon submitted himself entirely to Communist blandishments. Overwhelmed by an unaccustomed luxury and somewhat a slave to alcohol, he played the role of the model peasant cooperating with the Communists and subsequently entered the Communist Party. Dobi was allowed to hold the office of Prime Minister until August 14, 1952, when this post was taken over by Mátyás Rákosi himself. Rákosi thus joined the office of Secretary-General of the Communist Party with that of Prime Minister, again imitating Stalin. Dobi then became Chairman of the Presidium.

Rákosi had been Deputy Prime Minister before making himself Prime Minister, and in both positions he tended to short-cut the Party channels. Furthermore there were other leading Party functionaries who combined governmental portfolios with their Party offices. Therefore problems concerning the "proper" Marxist-Leninist mode of Party-government relations arose during those years and caused considerable difficulties among Communists. Party intellectuals wished to maintain and apply the principle that the Party "directs and controls the state," but the *de facto* autocratic rule of Rákosi upset the working of the system. Even while Rákosi held only the deputy premiership, it no longer seemed of any consequence to rely exclusively on Party channels for the enforcement of major decisions. And in the premiership Rákosi, still imitating Stalin, issued major orders via his private secretariat directly to government offices.[9] This procedure, depriving the Party organs of even the possibility of consultation, was considered improper by some faithful students of the Leninist doctrine.[10] Of course, after June 1953, when Rákosi retained only the post of First Secretary of the Party and the premiership was passed to Imre Nagy, he wished to reverse the policy he had accepted during his own premiership.

THE PERSONAL DICTATORSHIP AND ITS OPPONENTS

Rákosi and his muscovite colleagues, following in the footsteps of Stalin and his associates, promoted a personal, as contrasted to a proletarian, dictatorship through autocratic and terroristic methods. These methods met with the hatred and fear not only of the people in general, but also of large sections of the Party and even Party leaders.

For a long time the rigged trials conducted against leading Party members led outsiders to suspect the existence of a latent opposition within the Party. Discipline, however, was too strict in the Stalinist era, and fear of political or physical liquidation too great, to allow any overt expression of discontent by upper-stratum Party members. Though the existence of such a concealed opposition is controversial,[11] writings and interviews by former Communists who escaped after the 1956 Revolution, as well as personal contemporaneous impressions of this writer, confirm the existence of anti-Stalinist and anti-Rákosi opposition within the Party before 1953. This opposition, however, became vocal only when the overwhelming risk of expressing contrary views had disappeared. Many former Communists have admitted that their conversion from Communism took place under the impact of Rákosi's regime of terror.[12] Others were converted while in prison.[13] There is sufficient basis for supposing that the fermentation period of the subsequent Revolution dates back to the time of the Stalinist dictatorship.[14]

The excesses of Party and government leadership were largely attributed to Soviet influence and to the personal subservience of Rákosi and his clique to Stalinism. Thus, at least in those years, the Party critics in opposing Stalinist methods were, by the same token, questioning the foundations of Soviet rule. Patriotic feeling clashed with the psychological and physical requirements of being a faithful Party member. As long as Hungarian national feeling was in some way or other slightly compatible with a pro-Soviet Communist attitude, the incipient antagonism could be subdued; but Rákosi's regime too obviously demonstrated the incompatibility of being at the same time a convinced Communist and a Hungarian patriot. As one former Communist expressed it: "The situation was different in 1941, when one could subjectively be both Communist and a Hungarian patriot. In those days I considered myself both a Hungarian patriot and a Communist, but today he who thinks himself a Communist cannot be a patriot. This is objectively true." [15]

Since the events of October–November 1956, the internal cleavage as it existed since 1949 within the Hungarian Communist Party has come more consciously to the knowledge of the world. Much light is cast upon it by Imre Nagy's memoranda written in 1955–1956, which also include information and criticism concerning events and attitudes prior to his first premiership. He complains about the "non-clarification" of the theory which claims that the People's Democracy is a type of proletarian dictatorship that emerged "under the mechanical interpretation of Marxism-Leninism, and the copying of Soviet methods under completely different internal and international situations." He concludes that "the essence of the people's democratic character in all People's Democracies" has been lost, and that "serious contradictions have arisen between the form and the substance of these democracies." [16] If the inference is right, Imre Nagy wished to combine some kind of effective democracy with the "building of Socialism." He seemed to have considered this possible in Hungary under the prevailing conditions though not possible in Russia under the conditions of 1917 and after. Thus, he and his adherents opposed the very essentials of which Rákosi and his clique had built their regime.

The opposing elements within the Party must have felt that only Soviet control and protection had enabled Rákosi to establish and exercise an individual dictatorship based internally upon the terrorism of the AVH (Security Police) and leading to the elimination or even physical extermination of nonsubservient elements within and outside the Party.

A further point of resentment in the eyes of Rákosi's opponents was the overbearing attitude displayed by top Party functionaries toward lower-ranking ones, an attitude apishly followed by many Party functionaries toward the rank and file of the Party membership and non-Party members in general as soon as power seemed to rest safely with the Party. The rudeness and vulgarity manifesting itself in the intercourse between superiors and inferiors in the Party and government was, and was generally considered, an inheritance of the muscovite Party leaders stemming from their Soviet past. The coarseness employed in the Soviet Union by superiors toward inferior officials and the people at large (surpassing the similar tone evident in the Russia of the tsars) was something unknown to the Hungarian character, and sounded alien in a country where, especially within the bureaucracy, polished courtesy and smooth manners had been the rule.

No criticism was allowed in Rákosi's autocracy, even by high-ranking Party dignitaries. It is to be noticed, however, that no muscovite was condemned to execution during the purges initiated in Hungary during the Stalinist era. Nevertheless, the absolute interdiction of disapproval against Rákosi and his entourage extended also to muscovites, like Imre Nagy. Besides the ever-threatening possibility of disgrace, prison and execution, leading and well-deserved Party members were likely to be rebuked in the most provocative manner for criticism of what they considered a minor mistake by Rákosi and his ruling clique.[17] The atmosphere of Ivan the Terrible's court, coupled with toadyism, pervaded the Party headquarters and ministries — to the disgust of many Party members with more backbone.

EDUCATION

The Hungarian Stalinists, while clamping a dictatorship on the nation, also set about to indoctrinate the young. By 1949 the whole educational system had adopted Communist principles of education. Marxism and historical materialism permeated all the curricula, the study of the Russian language became compulsory, the obligatory teaching of religion was banned, and a high degree of isolation from Western ideas and information was attained.

Before 1948 about three fifths of the primary and secondary schools had been denominational in character.[18] Thereafter the Catholic Church was allowed to retain only eight schools, the Calvinists four, and the Lutherans one. Even those schools, however, had to conform strictly to the prescribed curriculum; for example, they were required to teach Marxism-Leninism and dialectical materialism. The teaching of religion in all schools was made "optional" but was restricted by many obstructive rules.*

In all phases of education the imitation of Soviet patterns was apparent. The curriculum, the character and names of the degrees conferred, and even the grading of students were fashioned according to the Soviet model. The number of institutes of higher education was greatly expanded. There was a heavy shift in favor of engineering, applied sciences and Marxist economics, to the detriment of history, humanities, and law. The schools became propaganda grounds for Soviet idolatry, while Hungarian and Western values were degraded and distorted from their true context.

Most students who happened to be of bourgeois origin were excluded from higher education. The class war was carried into the schoolroom, where disfavored pupils, however industrious and qualified, found it more and more difficult to compete with children of working-class origin or children of Party members, even pupils of a very low intellect.[19] From the first, the teaching of Russian offered insurmountable obstacles; there were hardly any qualified teachers. Obligatory Russian — coupled with its political and ideological association — became distasteful to the pupils, and despite enormous efforts by the teaching authorities realized minimum results. There was a widespread longing by students to learn one of the Western

* Parents had to declare in writing before the opening of the academic year that they wished to have religious teaching for their child. Teachers of religion were appointed not by a church, but by the government. Religious teaching could take place only after school classes, and only in the school building. Government approval for religion textbooks and curricula was required.

languages instead of Russian. All these violations of national sentiment affected students to a degree which became perceptible only
when the abolition of compulsory Russian and of academic grading
according to the Soviet system figured among the demands of the
demonstrators of October 1956.

PRESS, RADIO, LITERATURE, AND THE ARTS

With the monopolistic rule of the Communists, the press and
radio became faithful information media of the regime. The newspapers became facsimiles of their Soviet counterparts. By far the most
important morning daily, the *Szabad Nép,* was only a Hungarian
Pravda.[20] After vigorous circulation drives, supported by block
wardens and office chiefs, the Hungarian *Pravda* reached the colossal
circulation of 700,000. *Népszava,* formerly the organ of the Social
Democrat Party, was the paper of the "trade unions." The *Magyar
Nemzet,* also an old newspaper, was allowed to survive in name only,
and was read by intellectuals who would not touch the *Szabad Nép.*
There was one evening paper, a youth daily, just as in Moscow. But
the *Szabad Nép* overshadowed all other Budapest and provincial
papers.

The editorial staff of the *Szabad Nép* was a segment of the Party
officialdom. It was directed from Party headquarters, often personally
by Rákosi or some other top Party leader. Nothing was published
without utmost scrutiny from the Party's point of view, and often
only after consultations with Moscow.[21]

MTI (Hungarian Telegraph Agency) was the Hungarian TASS.
It acted as the monopolistic source of news propagation. Western
news was censored, doctored, and distorted from its context; and
occasionally news already published in the *Pravda* was also submitted
to censorship, and suppressed or manipulated.[22] Julia Kenyeres, the
muscovite editor in chief of the MTI, a former TASS employee
whose husband had deserted both her and Communism, often telephoned directly to Moscow for directions. The MTI, besides providing press and radio with news items, also prepared confidential
news circulars, in which Western press commentaries were digested
and delivered to selected Party and government functionaries. An
even more confidential report, containing mostly Hungarian language broadcasts of the Voice of America, Radio Free Europe, and
the British Broadcasting Corporation, was prepared in twelve copies
and delivered to Politburo members only.[23]

The Hungarian Radio was provided with the same news material
as that published in the *Szabad Nép.* Western radio broadcasts were

assiduously jammed. Nevertheless, those eager to listen to Western newscasts always managed to get them. One wave-length was never jammed, because the monitors of the MTI had to tape-record this news for preparing their confidential reports. But docile Party members who refused to listen to the unlawful sources were deprived of obtaining news of what was going on in Hungary or the rest of the world.

The state of literature and of art degenerated during 1949–1953 into Soviet-modeled anti-Western diatribe. Most writing of the period had little to do with Hungary, except for its language, and even the language became often interlaced with Russian-tinted expressions.[24] Many writers, poets, and artists refused to participate in the debasement, but few had opportunity for open resistance. Some resorted to making translations, or reproductions of art. Still others retired into complete silence. Stalinist totalitarianism seemed to drown out the representatives of what had been the main literary currents of Hungary: the Urbanists and Populists. The Western-oriented and libertarian Urbanists — those not in exile or prison — either embraced Communism or fell silent. The Populists, representing ideals and desires of rural Hungary, were also split under Communist pressure. Some emigrated and some remained inactive. Others collaborated to a greater or lesser degree with the regime, but their indigenous Hungarian outlook differentiated them from the outright Communist writers, even in the Stalinist era.

The majority of active writers were vying with one another in their devotion toward *Zhdanovism* ("Socialist realism"), in a "proletarian hegemony in literature," [25] and in their adoration of Soviet superiority. These pro-Soviet writers (most of them Communist Party members, the others overt or sham collaborationists) had to follow directions issued by Jozsef Révai, the Minister of Culture, and other Communist administrators of art and literature.

Among the Communist writers, those who had lived in the West differed somewhat from the muscovites in their response to the pressures of the regime.[26] Very few details of open resistance are known. György Lukács, the philosopher, who had lived for a long time in Germany, was sharply impugned because of his "deviationism" in literary criticism and Marxist philosophy; he tendered a lukewarm self-criticism on some minor points only, and reserved his opinion on the more important issues.[27] Tibor Déry, who later played an outstanding role in the spiritual preparation of the 1956 Revolution, openly rejected attacks against his writings by Révai as early as 1952, thus revealing a cleavage which existed between the Rákosi clique and at least a section of Communist intellectuals.[28] But, in general, Communist writers and artists had to submit to Party discipline.

At the same time they were favored sons of the regime, enjoying wealth and privileges. The non-Communists were being pressed into conformity by financial and intellectual bribes, by being allowed to enjoy privileges without Party membership, even by being flattered and cajoled by Party and government. A lack of collaboration would have meant for them not only the loss of all these favors, but an imposed silence, the nonpublication of their writings, privations and misery.

For Hungarian writers and artists Party conformism did not mean just the glorification of the Party, "Socialist realism" (whatever that evasive term meant), and adherence to "proletarian" civilization; it also included recognition and belief in the superiority of Soviet culture, adulation of Stalin, of the Red Army, and of everything Soviet. They were also expected to promote hatred and contempt against the Western way of life. The clear aim of Soviet strategy was to isolate Hungary and other satellite countries from the West, and place them in a spiritual bondage to Moscow. Everything Soviet or Russian was privileged, irrespective of its artistic or literary value. While translations of Russian books were printed in tens of thousands of copies, Hungarian books received printings of two to three thousand at the maximum.[29] Every piece of art or literature was compared to something Soviet. There were even cases of direct Soviet intervention, as in the performance of the masterpiece of Hungarian drama, the *Tragedy of Man* (written a century earlier by Imre Madách, and often called the "Hungarian *Faust*"). The play had associations highly displeasing to the regime; for instance one scene demonstrates the drabness of life in a Socialist phalanstery. For some time the drama was still performed (with slight alterations), but when the correspondent of *Pravda* intervened, it was quickly banned. Rákosi declared that it was a "pessimistic and reactionary" work. Incidentally, it contained the line, "I am to be revered and not criticized," which was loudly applauded by the audience; everybody was thinking of Rákosi.[30]

THE MORAL CRISIS

In Lenin's conception the Communist Party was to be like an army, a combat force, the elite of the working class, organized to fight the wars of the working class. The morale of an army is of utmost importance to its operating capability. If the morale of most of the fighters, and especially the officers, reaches a very low ebb, the stamina of the combat troops in question becomes insignificant. In the course of the Stalinist era the morale of the Hungarian Communist Party, a morale which on the average had never been too high, drained away to such an extent that one may feel justified in speaking of an extremely acute crisis of loyalties within the Party.

At the same time a crisis of a somewhat different nature was developing among the entire Hungarian people in their relation to Party and government. Respect for law and authority gradually crumbled. The overwhelming majority of the population had viewed with anxiety the Communists' taking possession of the country. Though they cherished little illusion as to what awaited them, their forebodings were exceeded by the events. But we are not here concerned with attitudes of the average citizen. Under the alleged dictatorship of the proletariat, as exercised in the name of the workers by the Communist Party, the real beneficiaries of the regime as well as the pillars of government were supposed to be the industrial workers, the toiling peasants, and pre-eminently their "elite," the Party members. While registering the discontent and despair which prevailed in all strata of the population, we wish to concentrate on attitudes and sentiments of the Party membership, the industrial workers, and the intellectuals. The reactions of these elements — the only elements which, under the existing autocratic rule, still were able to exert some limited influence on what was happening — were of decisive importance in the course of events which followed upon the end of Stalinist terrorism.

The most portentous result of Rákosi's rule was the complete alienation of most of the formerly convinced Communists. Totalitarian regimes based on closely knit conceptual ideologies aspire to enroll, and indeed have to rely on, zealots — while relying also on their possession of power. When they lose their devotees, they must depend largely on force for the maintenance of rule, and on assistance by opportunists. Since the membership of the Party largely consisted of such "neutrals" — careerists and people who joined in order not to be bothered — the disillusionment and frustration of the relatively small core of dedicated members deprived the Party of its stability, of its capacity to control and govern without resort to crude means of coercion. The disintegration of the Party, we are told and may well believe, did not start with the neutrals, who were never to be relied on, but with those who felt they were cheated.[31]

By 1952, the peak of Stalinist terrorism, when the situation was deemed to be beyond repair,[32] the Party's composition reflected the following shades of mentality: (1) the top Party leaders, Soviet-devoted, cynical, bent on perpetuating their dominant status, "living in their own make-believe world, completely isolated from the suffering masses";[33] (2) the Party functionaries, including the Security Police officers, intent on and anxious for self-preservation, instruments of domination without internal convictions or principles, often frustrated, but, nevertheless, doing their jobs;[34] (3) *hoi polloi* of the disillusioned or characteristically indifferent or hostile members, who performed their Party duties as formal rituals, "practicing Communism but not believing in it." [35]

This cleavage between word and belief, between outward appearance and inner reflection, between truth and falsehood, penetrated into every phase and every expression of Party life, of the government, and of individual or collective action. Make-believe "Potemkin villages" — an old Russian device dating back to Catherine the Great — were manifest all along the line from economic production figures to the liturgical applause given to top Soviet and Hungarian leaders, from citations of "sacred" texts to flag-waving and shouting at public demonstrations.

The discontented, both inside and outside the Party, registered their discontent not only privately, but also by certain kinds of action. Workers and clerical employees, despite the enormous risks involved, acted in self-defense against oppressive exploitation and privation by resorting to thefts and embezzlements, under the widespread belief that defrauding or stealing from the state was no sin, but a merit. From innumerable petty larcenies to big embezzlements, from individual withholding and concealment of agricultural goods to willful collective sabotage of production in cooperatives, the symptoms of the moral crisis spread through Party and population, through town and village. Immorality was spread by the Party itself, which pretended that everything was ethical that served its interests.[36] When reliable Party members started to have doubts and complained about the hard life people had to live, or asked questions about the disappearances of persons, they were rebuked for "petty-bourgeois moralizing." [37]

The Party members who no longer believed in Communism realized that no personal element could be the sole cause of evil; it was the system, the Party, the Marxist-Leninist doctrine, and Soviet imperialism that were to blame.[38] After Stalin's death in 1953, and especially after the revelations at the Soviet Twentieth Party Congress in 1956, the Soviet and other Communist parties worked out an explanatory slogan for something which could no longer be ignored.

Their new doctrine of the cult of the individual undertook to shift all blame on certain carefully selected persons, first of all on Stalin.[39] But long before Khrushchev's revelations the disenchanted element of the Hungarian Party had become convinced that no individual human element alone was to be blamed. It was the Bolshevik system itself.

The Potemkin-village aspect of Hungarian Stalinism was conspicuously demonstrated when Rákosi, after the "elections" of May 17, 1953, which gave a 98.2 per cent majority to the single electoral list, was able to declare that everything was going right, and that everybody was happy and prosperous in Hungary.[40] Later events contradicted his statement. In a different vein, another Communist, Imre Nagy, was to pronounce the following judgment on the Stalin-Rákosi era in Hungary:

The "left-wing" deviationists, primarily Rákosi and Gerö, in the years 1949 to 1953 brought the socialist reorganization of agriculture to a dead end, bankrupted agricultural production, destroyed the worker-peasant alliance, undermined the power of the People's Democracy, trampled upon the rule of law, debased the people's living standards, established a rift between the masses and the Party and government — in other words swept the country toward catastrophe.[41]

5

Security Police: Purges and Terror

/\/

Who is so gross
That cannot see this palpable device?
Yet who so bold but says he sees it not?
Bad is the world: and all will come to naught
When such ill-dealing must be seen in thought.

RICHARD III

AMONG the instruments of coercion at the disposal of the People's Democracy in Hungary during the Stalinist era, special treatment must be reserved for the State Security Police, a necessary concomitant of any Communist or other totalitarian regime, for which terror and purges are essential ingredients.[1]

The Hungarian Security Police had grown out of the political section of the state police. In March 1946 it was detached from the ordinary police and put under the authority of the Minister of the Interior. Its abbreviated name then was AVO (Államvédelmi Osztály, or State Security Section). In December 1949, it was severed from this Ministry and made into a special department, AVH (Állam-védelmi Hivatal, or State Security Authority), subject only to the Council of Ministers.

Ever since the occupation of Hungarian territory the close co-operation between Hungarian and Soviet Security Police had been clearly discernible. At the very outset, Communists who did not fall in with Rákosi's Stalinist line were arrested;[2] and the arrests were made either by the Hungarian political police or by the Soviet MVD. When the occupation status was technically abandoned, the

Hungarian Security Police appeared to act on its own authority, but the cooperation persisted. Of course, this was not a cooperation between equals; it was between higher and lower administrative organs.

AVH — STATE WITHIN THE STATE

From the date of its independent existence the AVH enjoyed a prolific growth. In accordance with the Soviet model, the Frontier Guard was placed under its jurisdiction and special internal security troops were organized under its authority.* At the apogee of its power, from 1950 to 1952, the AVH harbored seventeen clerical divisions in its central office. These offices handled the widespread affairs of the Security Police: the elimination of internal opposition; the conduct of investigations; the arrests and interrogations of prisoners; the surveillance of foreigners; and the supervision of government offices, the Army, religious bodies, and youth social and cultural organizations. Further activities of the AVH included espionage and counterespionage, the keeping of secret files, the maintenance of labor discipline, the continual checking on Party members, and protection of leading Party and government personnel. There also fell into the competence of this mammoth department the administration of political prisons, which were transferred to its domain from the Ministry of Justice, and the administration of internment camps and labor camps and their ancillary economic affairs.[3]

The AVH's activities embraced the life of the whole nation; its personal file system included one million names out of a population of less than ten million.[4] We can infer that an army of voluntary and involuntary informers had provided information as to the acts and pronouncements of all these individuals.

The Hungarian Security Police was at its very beginning permeated with muscovites. Long before the Hungarian Army adopted Soviet methods or organization and training, the security agency had already been streamlined to correspond with its Soviet elder brother. Moscow was especially interested in the results of investigations; therefore "confessions" of persons detained by the AVH

* The development of the AVH followed certain Soviet patterns. In the Soviet Union, in 1943, state security affairs were separated from the NKVD (People's Commissariat of Internal Affairs), and the NKGB (People's Commissariat of State Security) was created. When commissariats were renamed ministries in 1946, the two departments became the MVD and the MGB respectively. In 1949 the MGB was expanded, and frontier guards and troops of internal security came under its authority. This enlarged and centralized MGB apparatus flourished until Stalin's death. See Merle Fainsod, *How Russia Is Ruled* (Cambridge, Mass., 1953), p. 378. The Hungarian counterpart of the MGB was the AVH.

were made out in seven or nine copies, and one copy invariably found its way to the central record office of the Soviet Security Police.[5] The AVH was directly dependent on intercommunications with the Soviet MVD and MGB; channels of communication might by-pass top Party leaders when Moscow wished to contact its Hungarian agency and vice-versa. But decisions of principal importance were, of course, taken in consultation with the Hungarian Party leaders.

The agency was headed by Gábor Péter, who held the title of Lieutenant General of the AVH and participated in the sessions of the Council of Ministers. He grew into the Hungarian version of Yezhov, Yagoda, and Beria, and closely cooperated with Soviet security authorities. We can assume that Péter, in order to strengthen his position vis-à-vis the Hungarian Party leadership, was only too willing to receive orders and instructions from Moscow.

The AVH was working under the control of the Party Politburo, or more accurately, under the personal direction of Rákosi himself, though another member of the Politburo (during the Stalinist era it was General Mihály Farkas) was formally in charge of Security Police operations. The crucial decision of making arrests generally rested with Péter, but important Party leaders could be arrested only with the approval of the Politburo, or, when the leader was a Politburo member himself, the approval of Rákosi personally. But even Rákosi did not always have his own way: the interdependence of the AVH and the Soviet security organs could sometimes thwart Rákosi's orders. Thus when Lieutenant General Sándor Nográdi was to be arrested (he was already under house arrest), he was able to ask for help from the MVD, and was quickly released and reinstated.[6]

The AVH extended its menacing surveillance over all Party organizations, including the Central Committee. The purges administered against leading Communists under Rákosi's personal dictatorship demonstrated that even Politburo members (other than muscovites) were not safe from the Security Police's clutches; the fate of the leading indigenous Communist, László Rajk, remains the most striking example.

RAJK: A VICTIM OF ANTI-TITOISM

László Rajk, the indigenous Hungarian Communist leader, as Minister of the Interior, was instrumental in achieving Communist domination in Hungary. It was a surprise for many when this man was suddenly relieved of his duties and given the less weighty post of Minister of Foreign Affairs on August 3, 1948. The date is significant: five weeks earlier the Cominform excluded Yugoslavia from its ranks, and the anti-Yugoslav campaign by the Soviet Union and its satellites was brewing. Rajk was known to have entertained friendly relations with his Yugoslav comrades, but so had many Communist leaders, and obviously this was not the whole reason for his demotion.

After the death of Zhdanov, head of the Cominform, which occurred about this time, Rákosi's star rose in the Communist camp. The Hungarian dictator became recognized as a leading figure of the Cominform. And he was ready to please his master in Moscow. The idea of sacrificing Rajk as a propaganda scapegoat for the drive against Tito must have been hatched out between Rákosi and Stalin. The personal selection of Rajk must have engendered in Rákosi's head; thereby he could rid himself of a dangerous rival who had already crossed his path. An alternative choice, Imre Nagy, had probably been discarded because he had been a muscovite.[7] It would have been more difficult to assemble fabricated accusations against this modest theoretician than against the resolute Rajk.

Rajk was arrested on June 8, 1949 — while still a Politburo member and Minister — and on September 24 was sentenced to death, together with some "accomplices," after a theatrical trial lasting several days. The military members of the "Rajk conspiracy," headed by General György Pálffy, Inspector General of the Hungarian Army, received their death sentences from a military court.

Rajk admitted in the course of his well-arranged trial that he had been an informer for the Horthyist police against Communists, that he had betrayed his comrades in Spain, that he was an organized spy of the American and French intelligence services, and that he had conspired with Tito to overthrow the Hungarian Communist regime, to murder Rákosi and his associates, and to restore capitalism in Hungary with the help of the "imperialists."

Rajk's confessions were confirmed by an array of witnesses. Dr. Gyula Bokor, a former police officer, testified that Rajk had been an informer for Horthy's police.[8] István Stolte, a former colleague of Rajk, reproached him for having betrayed the existence of a Communist cell in the Eötvös College. (Stolte had been delivered to the prosecutors by the Soviet MVD, which had lured him from Germany to Vienna and kidnapped him there.)[9] Noel Field, an American Unitarian missionary who had been arrested in Poland and brought to Budapest for the trial, testified that Rajk was in the service of American intelligence. Antal Klein, a former member of the National Assembly, gave testimony that Rajk had secretly met Ran-kovič, the Yugoslav Minister of Interior, on his (Klein's) farm where they conspired. Lazar Brankov, Yugoslav embassy secretary in Budapest who had been arrested in disregard of his diplomatic immunity, declared that Rajk was Tito's agent. All the witnesses had been arrested before the trial, and all later were sentenced or disappeared.

The accusations against Rajk — as it was openly admitted at the time of his posthumous rehabilitation in the summer of 1956 — were falsehoods, carefully devised though semitransparent, whose objective was to compromise Tito and the Yugoslav leadership, unmasking them as Western agents before the whole world in order to bring about their downfall. It was the most grandiosely staged trial of Stalin's reign, inside or outside Russia. Whereas the prewar rigged trials in the Soviet Union had served internal Soviet politics, the Rajk trial was intended to bear fruits in the foreign field and have an impact on international events to come.

The Rajk affair was a common Soviet-Hungarian venture with Stalin and Rákosi as chief entrepreneurs. Their managers were General Bielkin, from the Russian side, and General Gábor Péter, from the Hungarian. General Bielkin personally conducted the briefing of witnesses, and General Péter personally directed Rajk's tortures and brainwashing. Rajk, who himself had staged rigged trials in his time, knew what results a confession would have, and in spite of the pressures brought against him, refused to play his role in the trial-show. He was finally persuaded to do so when Rákosi sent János Kádár into his cell. Kádár, an old friend of Rajk's, had succeeded him as Minister of the Interior. Speaking on behalf of Rákosi, he promised Rajk his life, reunion with his family, and a new existence in the Soviet Union under some assumed name. Eventually Rajk consented to play the role Rákosi had planned for him. Despite the promises made, he and his "accomplices" were duly hanged on October 15, 1949.

Rákosi had the Kádár-Rajk conversation taken on a tape recorder without Kádár's knowledge.[10] The discrepancies between Kádár's report and the tape contributed toward Rákosi's enmity against Kádár, and precipitated Kádár's later downfall.

The *Grand-Guignol* story of Rajk's liquidation and its staging by Soviet and Hungarian officials throws striking light on the political morality of the Stalinist era in Hungary and on the methods and goals of the chief protagonists which, if not corroborated by reliable sources, would appear unbelievable for a student of twentieth-century history. Although there had been show trials and mass arrests prior to the Rajk affair, the Hungarian *Yezhovshchina* prefigures its ominous course with this event.

TERROR: INSTRUMENT OF COHESION AND DISRUPTION

The methods and means of terrorism employed by the Hungarian Security Police closely resemble their Soviet patterns of inspiration. A study of Soviet terrorism as a source of power[11] reveals a most striking identity between the Soviet model and its Hungarian counterpart, not only in the techniques of mass arrests, executions, deportations, and forced labor, but also in rationale — or rather irrationality.

In 1945 and 1946 the terroristic methods of the Hungarian Security Police were employed mostly to eliminate real or alleged pro-Nazi elements and war criminals. In 1947–1948 the terrorism was employed to support the Communist Party's struggle for power; it was, together with overt Soviet intervention, the most effective instrument for achieving the required result. The terror and purges were thereafter initiated against remaining forces of resistance: churches, political parties, and foreign (Western) economic interests. The most important spectacles purporting to demonstrate the sinister influences of Western capitalism were the rigged trials against church dignitaries; the "MAORT trial" against the management of the American-owned Hungarian Oil Company; and the "Standard trial" against the directors of the American-owned Standard Electric Company and International Telephone & Telegraph Company, among whom were a United States and a British citizen.

After Rajk's arrest the wholesale and indiscriminate purges and arrests against former Social Democrats, and simultaneously against "reactionary" elements and "foreign agents," ran their full course. Most of the Western and indigenous Communists shared their fate in 1951. Among those arrested were János Kádár (now no longer Minister of the Interior), Gyula Kállai (former Minister of Foreign Affairs), Géza Losonczy, and Ferenc Donáth. All these survived and were able to play a role during subsequent events. Another indigenous Communist, Sándor Zöld, who had succeeded Kádár as Minister of the Interior, preferred death to arrest. At a cabinet meeting on April 21, 1951, he received the impression that he was about to be arrested; so he drove home, killed his wife and children, and then shot himself.

The number of purge victims is not precisely known. About 4,000 former Social Democrat functionaries are estimated to have been arrested by the summer of 1950.[12] Data furnished by prisoners who had been in various prisons, internment camps, or forced labor camps provide a basis for estimating that at the time of Stalin's death the number of political prisoners (including internees, inmates of labor camps, and people uprooted from their homes and confined to some other locality) had reached 150,000, one and one-half per cent of the population.[13] At least 2,000 are believed to have been executed outright.

To explain Rákosi's purges is just as difficult as to provide a satisfactory explanation for the seemingly senseless excesses of the Soviet *Yezhovshchina* of the 1930's.[14] The elimination of real or potential enemies of the regime, and also of persons having connections with the West, may have contributed to the strengthening of Communist rule — directly by removing the forces of opposition, and indirectly by spreading terror in the ranks of relatives, friends, or sympathizers. But the rationale for the proscription of such a number of faithful Party members seems more difficult to establish. Some of these Party members (but only a few) might have been possible rivals to Rákosi's power. Some might have borne the dictator's grudge for present or past opposition to his will. Still others might have been suspected of cherishing independent — possibly anti-Soviet — views. Sadism and cynicism on the part of the main protagonists of the terror, Rákosi, Gerö, and Péter, may also be cited as contributing causes.[15] Nevertheless, the great number of victims can ultimately be explained only by the fact that the terror itself had an independent role to play within the precincts of a totalitarian dictatorship. It was the hallmark of power. Here much weight has to be attributed to the towering presence of the Soviet example. Stalin had displayed his unrestricted power by creating havoc among kulaks, Party members, or army officers through mass purges; and so the petty dictator also had to tamper with the lives, liberties, and human dignity of his subjects. Stalin easily gave his placet to this sort of competition between the Soviet and the Hungarian security agencies. And when the engine of persecution gathered momentum, feeding on its own devices of mass denunciations and accusations fabricated by blackmailed informers or by AVH agents themselves, it became a law unto itself. Otherwise it would be hard to explain the arrest of so many dedicated Communists in the middle and lower Party ranks.[16]

The impact of all this on Party members, intellectuals, workers, and peasants cannot be properly assessed by large numbers of victims alone. For it was multiplied by the fact that these thousands upon thousands, enduring the ordeal of AVH interrogations and torture, exchanged their impressions with one another in their cells or camps. The steadily growing collective experience created a potentially disruptive force which proved to be of decisive importance when eventually Pandora's box was opened.[17] Thus the Stalinist terror brought about more submission and more discipline in the Party and country for the time being only. The treatment inflicted upon so many innocent and influential Party members, intellectuals, and industrial workers was to become a source of fatal weakness. The victims and their families, friends, and compatriots attributed these purges and terror to their real cause: the Soviet domination over Hungary.

RELIGION: A SECURITY POLICE PROBLEM

The atheist Communist regime knows that it cannot extirpate religious feeling overnight; consequently, religion must be made subservient to the state, in order to render it incapable of forming a center of resistance. Furthermore, much care has to be taken to exclude all religious influences from youth groups and Party members, and to separate the churches from all their ties abroad.

Stalin could mold the Russian Orthodox Church into a pliable instrument with relative ease. It had already served as such for the tsars, though to serve an atheist autocrat might seem a less easy task. But the internationalism of the Catholic Church, its ties of allegiance to Rome, and the Western orientation of the Protestant churches in Hungary prevented a simple reiteration of methods utilized in the Soviet Union to subjugate the Church to the needs and requirements of a Communist government.

Rákosi set himself to provide a model for how to deal with the recalcitrant churches of the West.* Jozsef Mindszenty, the Cardinal Primate of the Hungarian Catholic Church, was arrested and, having "confessed" his crimes at a rigged trial, was sentenced to life imprisonment on February 8, 1949.[18] This martyrdom rendered its hero the chief personification of resistance against Soviet Communism; churches became crowded not only with the "religiously" religious, but with "politically" religious people.

The government resorted to mass arrests of priests; it transported most of the members of religious orders to concentration

* He disapproved of Polish methods of relative tolerance. "I told Bierut that they [the Poles] are rightist deviationists. I told them the way they were doing it was wrong, and that they must do it my way: arrest one Church dignitary, and bribe the rest. And that's all there is to it." Quoted in CURPH (Columbia University Research Project on Hungary), interview no. 500.

quarters. In the summer of 1950 the Clerical Peace Movement was founded, ostensibly to support the Stockholm Peace Congress, but in fact, to create a collaborationist faction in the Catholic Church. The bishops disapproved the movement, and few priests joined. Then an Office of Church Affairs was formed (the former Ministry of Religion and Public Education was simply renamed "Ministry of Education"), and it soon openly interfered in diocesan affairs. Mindszenty's see, the archdiocese of Esztergom, was being administered by a vicar capitular. When this man died, the canons elected as his successor the Auxiliary Bishop Meszlényi; he was arrested, and so was another prelate who was elected in his stead. Then a "peace priest" was elected, as suggested by the AVH, but he remained unrecognized by Rome. Instead the Vatican appointed Bishop Endre Hamvas, of the see of Csanád, as Apostolic Administrator of the Esztergom archdiocese; thereupon Bishop Hamvas was put under house arrest.[19]

Up to then the Archbishop of Kalocsa, Jozsef Grösz, had led the Catholic bishops of Hungary in their resistance. He was arrested in May 1951, and after the usual show trial was sentenced to life imprisonment on June 28. A number of bishops were placed under house arrest and the next chairman of the reduced episcopate, Gyula Czapik, Archbishop of Eger, moved the acceptance of the government's terms.

From then on representatives of the Office of Church Affairs assisted the vicars (deputy bishops) who themselves were mostly peace priests. The bishops were reduced to the role of puppets; their mail was opened, their correspondence supervised, and if they refused to sign any paper, it was done by the vicar. The representatives of the government assigned to assist the diocesan vicars (mostly former AVH officers, nicknamed by the people "mustached bishops") were authorized to transfer priests to remote villages, remove popular parish priests, and issue circulars advising pastors what to do and what not to do.

The government announced that it would recognize only those bishops whose appointments it had approved. Since the Hungarian government entertained no relations with the Vatican, and since the Vatican refused to appoint unreliable priests to diocesan posts, the bishoprics gradually became vacant, and were administered by vicars who had received the blessing of the Communist regime.

Though churches were not closed, and Mass and sacraments were not interfered with, those who attended were carefully watched and checked, and sermons were censored. The number of seminaries was reduced, and their inmates carefully screened; the mustached bishops carried out inspections, and frequently expelled seminarists who met with their disapproval. Religious orders were disbanded, except for the Benedictines, Franciscans, and Piarists, which were allowed to function on a restricted scale. The evicted monks and nuns took up jobs in factories and farms; they still considered themselves to be members of the "silent" Church, and their example attracted many workers.

The oppression of Protestant denominations and of the Jewish community was equally drastic; but since their superiors were not appointed from abroad, the task was less complicated. Church leadership was forcibly purged, and the electing bodies were pressed to choose persons approved by the regime. Many hundreds of clergymen, both Catholic and Protestant, were inmates of prisons and internment camps. The atmosphere of religious persecution made many people think of the predicament the early Christians had faced.

TERROR COORDINATED

The Stalinist terror, whether in its Moscow or Budapest version, was all of a piece. Stalin's machine had exterminated most of the leadership of the Communist parties of East-Central Europe during the *Yezhovshchina* or in the course of World War II.[20] Nor were Communist leaders of the Spanish Civil War spared. One may only guess at the rationale of such actions: Stalin wanted to rid himself of local Communist leaders who might not be responsive to his doctrine of Soviet supremacy; in fact, many of the Comintern leaders were among his victims — for example, Béla Kun, the leader of Hungarian Communism in 1919. Without such foresight, he might have faced greater difficulties in establishing the Soviet satellite empire.

The synchronization of the security machinery of the whole Communist camp was clearly demonstrated by the purges and trials following Yugoslavia's expulsion from the Cominform. Stalin embarked upon his campaign to extirpate all anti-Stalinist (e.g., anti–Soviet Russian) Party bosses and their adherents all over the satellite area. At the same time, this was intended to be a propaganda drive against Tito; forceful examples were to be made in order to deter any attempt at independence from the prescribed Soviet line. Although the purges and trials (whether theatrical or secret) were not carried out simultaneously, and individual requirements of each satellite state were respected, the general uniformity of style and arrangement is clearly discernible. Beria and Abakumov, in conjunction with local Security chiefs, shaped the development of events, and General Bielkin, the traveling salesman of terror, acted as stage manager wherever he took up his provisional headquarters.

The earliest genuinely Titoist victim was the Deputy Prime Minister of Albania, Koci Xoxe, who was executed on June 10, 1949. Patrasceanu of Rumania had been arrested earlier (his earlier demotion is attributed to a refusal to consider the "voluntary" incorporation of Rumania into the Soviet Union),[21] but for unknown reasons his physical liquidation was delayed a long time. The Rajk trial (September 1949) was followed by Traicho Kostov's trial in Bulgaria (December 1949). General Markos, leader of the Greek Communist insurgents was also demoted in January 1949, and his liquidation remains shrouded in mystery.[22] Gomulka in Poland was expelled from the Party on November 14, 1949; he admitted having had "Titoist doubts," but he denied other charges and said that his eyes had been opened as a result of the Rajk trial.[23] Although preparations for his trial were made and his parliamentary immunity was lifted, he was spared.[24] The Slansky trial in Czechoslovakia (November 1952) was combined with the eradication of anti-Soviet, national Communist elements; Slansky himself can hardly be counted as anti-Soviet, falling victim instead to the anti-Semitic drive of the senescent Stalin. The delay of the purge in Czechoslovakia is remarkable because Rákosi as early as September 1949 had foretold it.[25] Gottwald was more apt to have become the victim of such a purge than Slansky, but he was nevertheless spared.[26]

The last international Stalinist purge, culminating with the Doctors' Plot in Moscow, was staged with the active participation of Rákosi. The final arrangements, following Slansky's execution, which was to be the prelude, were made in Moscow in December 1952 where Rákosi had gone to explore the situation. Rákosi, himself a Jew, was ready to participate in an anti-Semitic plot. The purge was to be combined with the liquidation of the top "Jewish" leaders of the AVH in Hungary. General Gábor Péter, who entertained special contacts with Beria, had complained against Rákosi, and this was revealed to Rákosi by Abakumov.[27] In January 1953, General Péter and many of the AVH officers were arrested. In full synchronization with the Doctors' Plot, Lajos Stöckler, president of the Hungarian Jewish Community, was also arrested. Stalin's death, however, brought these arrangements down with a crash; and while the subordination of the AVH to the whims of the Soviet

Security Police still persisted, the disappearance of one-man rule in Moscow and the subsequent downfall of Beria did not fail to have their repercussions on the AVH in Hungary and elsewhere in the satellite area.

6

The Army of a Satellite

∧∧∧∧∧∧∧∧∧∧∧∧∧∧∧∧∧∧∧∧∧∧∧∧∧∧∧∧∧∧∧∧

If there is disagreement between the military commander and the political officer and reasons of urgency or other circumstances prevent the opinion of the next higher commander and political officer from being obtained, the decision of the political officer must be accepted. This is particularly so in matters of border violations and incidents requiring the use of arms.

From the regulation concerning political officers in the Hungarian Army

HUNGARIAN ARMY AND SOVIET ADVISERS

THE Soviet Army secured Hungary and other East-Central European satellite countries for Communism and subjected them to the allegiance of Moscow. In order to maintain the *status quo* thus achieved, the satellite armies had to be turned into obedient instruments of Soviet military might, no less than were the Party and Security Police organizations. Under Stalin, who cherished ideas of Korean wars "by proxy," and in view of possible hostilities against recalcitrant Yugoslavia, the satellite armies were strengthened to the point which would render them capable of waging war against the heretic Socialist nation and possibly against the Western Powers as well.

The various stages of politico-military thought in the Soviet mind are reflected by the developments within the Hungarian Army after 1945. Before the end of hostilities, three Hungarian divisions had been trained to participate in the war against Germany. After the German surrender only two of the divisions with some other specialized units were maintained. During the period of the Armistice up to September 1947 (when the Treaty of Peace became effective) it was the allied (Soviet) Control Commission which disposed of the Hungarian armed forces. But even so, in order to strengthen Communist influence over the Army, most of the effective units were transferred to serve as frontier guards, thereby coming under the control of the Army's Communist-led Military Security Section headed by General György Pálffy, who later was hanged as Rajk's accomplice. From September 1947 to September 1948 the Hungarian Army remained extremely weak, and was controlled by the military attachés of the Soviet embassy in Budapest.[1]

In September 1948, Mihály Farkas took over the Ministry of Defense and embarked upon a general reshuffle and Sovietization of the Army. The political officers' corps was introduced (previously there had been orientation officers charged with indoctrination of the troops), and the first group of Soviet military advisers arrived. These military advisers worked in the Ministry of Defense, and were attached to the General Staff and to the individual service commands (infantry, artillery, signal troops, engineer troops, tank troops, and air force). The newcomers, headed by Lieutenant General Prokofiev, were assigned to reorganize the central leadership of the armed forces according to the Soviet pattern. This first group, many of whom had acted as military instructors to the Chinese National Government in World War II, were genuine advisers. They refrained from interfering in the day-to-day activities of the Hungarian command, and emphasized that their role was merely advisory. By the fall of 1949, they had completed their work and were recalled to the Soviet Union.

A much larger advisory staff soon arrived. And now a drastic change was felt. The new advisers were not only more numerous than their predecessors, but their attitude was fundamentally different. They openly indicated that their "advice" was meant to be followed. Step by step, the real command and leadership of the Hungarian Army slipped into the hands of these new "advisers."

Lieutenant General Boykov became the head of the advisory body in November 1949. He also served as Soviet military attaché at the Soviet embassy. His deputy was General Sergei Sergeyevich Sergei, a *politruk* officer, whose uncompromising and brutal behavior determined the conduct of all advisers toward the Hungarian commanders.

The number of Soviet advisers grew; gradually they set up their advisory groups to Hungarian army-corps staffs, then to divisional staffs, and eventually, by the end of 1951, they were even reaching down to regimental staff-commands. Soviet advisory staffs also operated in every military institution, such as officers' military schools, military industrial establishments, and military depots.[2]

The first advisory staff, operating between 1948 and 1949, had been under the command of the Soviet Commander in Chief in Austria, with headquarters in the Burgenland province of that country, and the advisers had commuted there once or twice a month to submit reports and receive instructions. But the second group of Soviet advisers entertained no official contact with the Soviet occupation forces in Austria; their superior contact was the Soviet Military High Command in Moscow.

The Soviet advisers — apart from their official functions of controlling and supervising the Hungarian Army — lived a life apart from the Hungarian community; they and their families kept strictly to themselves in their own living quarters, shopping centers, clubs, and messes. They sedulously avoided all social contacts with Hungarians, just as did the members of the Soviet forces stationed in Hungarian territory.

SOVIETIZATION OF THE ARMY

Under the control of the Soviet advisory staffs the Hungarian Army was thoroughly reorganized. The size of the Army increased steadily until 1952; Soviet arms and ammunition were poured into the country to provide equipment for the new units.[*]

The Treaty of Peace had restricted the size and striking power of the Hungarian armed forces. The land army was not to exceed 65,000, and the air force 5,000. In spite of these treaty restrictions, recruiting started on a large scale. Military service was extended in principle between the ages of twenty and sixty and was made compulsory for three years. The country was divided into four military districts (Budapest, Pécs, Szeged, and Debrecen). The Army reached its peak in 1951–1952 when it probably exceeded 210,000, not counting between 40,000 and 90,000 troops of the Security Police and Frontier Guard. Thus the total armed forces are estimated to have been between 250,000 and 300,000.[3]

The Army was composed of nine infantry divisions, two mecha-

---

[*] The weaponry consisted of World War II Soviet-type arms, a considerable proportion used and worn out. The Hungarian treasury was forced to pay heavily for them, as if they were brand-new. (Information obtained in 1959 from General Béla Király.)

nized divisions forming one mechanized corps, four artillery brigades, nine antiaircraft brigades, four engineer brigades, one paratroop brigade, and ancillary services. Each infantry division — in conformity with the Soviet army structure — consisted of 12,000 men, formed into three regiments, two or three field artillery battalions, and some technical units. The whole Army was grouped into three army corps. The air force consisted of four fighter squadrons and a small force of bombers. The planes, about 550 in number, were old YAK-9 and new MIG-15 types.[4] According to official sources, defense expenditures of the Hungarian budget increased from 1.8 billion forints in 1949 to 7.4 billion forints in 1953 (16.7 per cent of the total expenditures).[5]

The first step taken by the Soviet advisers in 1949 in transforming the Hungarian Army into a Soviet-type organization was the introduction of Soviet service manuals. All old army regulations were gradually replaced by ones modeled on the Soviet example. For example, the Soviet military manual on Internal Discipline, which was translated and put into effect, regulated procedures and behavior, from the military oaths to the training and everyday life of the soldiers. In every military manual of such a kind we find national traditions in digested form. It is to some degree a revealing picture not only of an army but of a nation, since each army's make-up is deeply interwoven with the national character. The morale of a national army is built on the traditions and experience of many decades or centuries, and on the habits and peculiarities of the nation concerned. The Soviet military manuals were still largely based on tsarist Russian traditions; even the uniforms of the Soviet Army resembled those of its tsarist predecessor. The implementation of these alien rules and habits was distasteful to Hungarian officers and soldiers alike; it meant a drastic change in the whole collective life of the army, in its training system, clothing, lodging, and discipline.

A small but not trivial illustration is found in the question of shirttails. Army privates and noncommissioned officers had to wear the *gymnastërka*, the Russian blouse which is worn outside the trousers. They detested this garment, and it brought them the ridicule of civilians: "Wearing shirts outside the pants!" To appreciate the significance of this, one must understand that hanging shirts were part of the national costume of many Balkan peoples, but considered primitive and backward by Hungarians. As far back as the Congress of Berlin (1878), Bismarck reportedly said he trusted only the representatives of regions "who still wear their shirts outside their trousers," meaning that they were the unsophisticated ones. Russian penetration into Hungary has thus again opened the international question of "outside or inside the pants."

But among the many changes the new method of lodging and feeding proved to be most repellent to the average Hungarian soldier. A full company of about 150 to 160 men were quartered in a single big hall, whereas previously soldiers' dormitories in Hungary were built for only 10 to 12 soldiers. According to the Soviet system the sergeant of the company had his bed beside the door in order to watch soldiers going out and coming back at night. Similarly the Soviet feeding system entailed drastic changes in the daily menu as well as in the hour of serving the meals. The Soviet nutrition method was based on semi-Asiatic customs: the principal food was the *kasha* (a kind of grits), and the main hot meal was served in the morning, whereas formerly Hungarian soldiers had received the main hot meal in the evening after their return from the training grounds.

For the full implementation of the new laws and habits, all important orders for the Army (orders for training, organization, maneuvers, parades, and so on) were either drafted by the Soviet advisers and translated into Hungarian, or had to be translated into Russian and submitted to the respective advisers for advance approval.[6] The Hungarian commanders were not entitled to carry out any inspection of the troops without the consent of the advisers. But the advisers were free to go wherever they wished for the purpose of making surprise inspections.

In the Hungarian Army after 1950, the most important positions were held by Soviet citizens of Hungarian descent. We have already mentioned Colonel General Mihály Farkas, the Minister of Defense. His first deputy and head of the Political Officer Section was Lieutenant General, later Colonel General Sándor Nográdi, the man who, as we have seen, was saved from disgrace by the MVD. The head of the Intelligence Section was Géza Révész, whose father had been a World War I prisoner in Russia and, having married a Russian woman, remained there. The Personal Affairs Section was headed by General István Szabo, of Czechoslovak origin. Each of these leading military personalities was either born in the Soviet Union or had spent most of his life there and had married a Russian. The first line of Communist generals who were not muscovites but had helped to introduce Communist power over the Army had all been liquidated.*

In the fall of 1951 more and more Hungarian officers began returning from the Soviet Union where they had been studying military science from one to four years. By 1953 a large number had come back to Hungary. These Soviet-trained (and supposedly loyal) officers were placed in many key positions of the Army. Accordingly, the number of Soviet advisers was somewhat reduced; and in 1953 those assigned to regimental commands were withdrawn.

The members of the armed forces were ceaselessly indoctrinated to respect and admire the Soviet Army. Films and novels idolizing the deeds of the Red Army and the partisan warriors of World War II were typical means of propaganda. The lessons of guerrilla warfare thus depicted certainly were not lost on Hungarian youths; it was this kind of warfare that they practiced against the Soviet armed forces during the Revolution of 1956.

PARTY AND ARMY

The special importance of the Army for maintaining the regime and supporting Soviet influence was fully endorsed by the Communist Party of Hungary. The Party's Central Committee, which possessed agencies of control corresponding to the various ministries of the government, took an extra precaution in the case of the Ministry of Defense, placing its Military Department within the precincts of the Ministry itself. This department coincided with the Chief Political Section (*Politikai Föcsoport Fönökség*) of the Ministry of Defense, as in the Soviet Union.** This Chief Political Section was in the direct charge of Farkas, both as Defense Minister and Politburo member. Its structure (see Chart I) shows that it not only directed propaganda, ideological education, and sports activities within the Army, but also controlled the vital networks of Party secretaries and political officers.

Into the corps commands, and into the divisional, regimental, and battalion commands, a double system of leadership was introduced. In the Soviet Army such a double system had been long

---

* We have seen that General György Pálffy was executed as an accomplice of Rajk. In June 1950, Lieutenant General Solyom (Chief of General Staff), Lieutenant General Illy, the Major Generals Beleznay, Porffy, Révay and Merényi-Scholtz, and many other officers were hanged. Béla Király, "Hungarian Army," *East Europe*, June 1958, p. 4.

** In the Soviet Union the Main Political Administration functions both as a section of the Ministry of Defense and as the Military Department of the Central Committee of the Party. Merle Fainsod, *How Russia Is Ruled* (Cambridge, Mass., 1953), p. 409.

before abolished as a consequence of frictions between the commanding officers and the political commissars (after reinstatement in 1941 had been abolished again in 1942);[7] nevertheless the system was fully adopted in the Hungarian Army. To each commander a

CHART I

STRUCTURE OF THE CHIEF POLITICAL SECTION

of the

MINISTRY OF DEFENSE

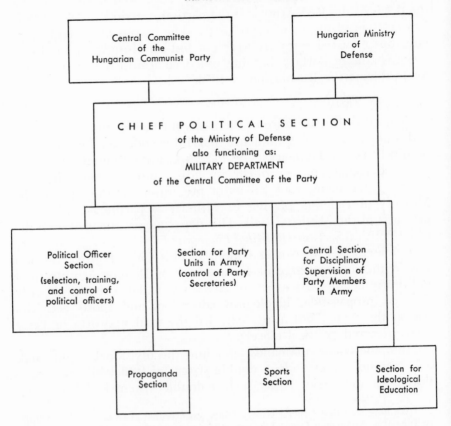

political officer was assigned. Orders issued to the respective military bodies were valid only if signed both by the commanding officer and the political officer. In case of a split between a regimental commander and his political officer, the question had to be referred for decision to the divisional commander and *his* political officer, and so

on up. In the case of an emergency which did not permit seeking
decisions from superiors, the decision of the political officer was to
prevail. On the company level the political hierarchy was represented

CHART II

HIERARCHY OF MILITARY AND POLITICAL OFFICERS

AND OF THE PARTY IN THE ARMY

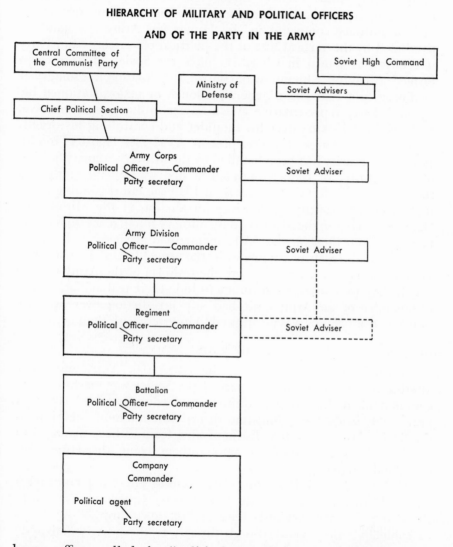

by an officer called the "political agent," but his opinions could
never overrule decisions made by the company commander. Thus,
for all commands above company level, the political officer was
actually a co-commander of the unit.

The political officers, being representatives of the Party, not only participated in the military leadership, but also carried out in their respective units all the responsibilities of the Chief Political Section, including supervision of the Communist Party organizations in the Army units. Each of these organizations was headed by a Party secretary, subordinate to the political officer. Thus the vertical line of military command in the Hungarian Army was (and is) paralleled by the vertical line of the political officer corps and Party secretaries, as shown in Chart II. Since the Soviet advisory corps formed still another hierarchy of control, the situation was somewhat confining to a Hungarian general, colonel, or major, stationed between a Party representative and a Soviet military representative, both of them looking over his shoulder and controlling his orders.

Finally there were the ever-present AVH men. Earlier, intelligence and security had been handled by the Military Security Section of the Ministry of Defense, headed at first by General Pálffy and then by General Révész. But early in 1949 the fast-expanding AVH took over the security (defensive) jurisdiction of the Ministry of Defense, leaving to the Ministry only military intelligence (offensive) matters. From then on the AVH maintained agencies at the headquarters of all levels of command in the armed forces. The Security Police officers and personnel wore the uniform of the Army unit to which they were attached in order to hide their real affiliation. No commander of an Army unit had any jurisdiction over Security Police personnel, nor was he allowed to interfere with their activities.

HUNGARIAN ARMY: UNIT OF THE SOVIET ARMY

In Soviet strategic planning, the Hungarian Army and other satellite armies are treated as part of the Soviet war machine. The common manuals, common training and education, and common armament, made the Hungarian armed forces almost identical to the Soviet Army. Very few distinguishing features have managed to survive, the most important among them being the Hungarian command language.*

Moscow, through its advisers, was able to direct the Hungarian Army as easily as it directed the Soviet Army. Instructions passed to the Hungarian Minister of Defense and on down through the chains of command; they could also go directly to the heavily "advised"

---

* Russian never served as command language in the Hungarian Army. Instructions emanating from Soviet sources had to be translated into Hungarian. The study of the Russian language was, however, compulsory for all officers with a view to facilitating communication with Soviet advisers. Of course, Hungarian officers trained in the Soviet Union were excellent Russian linguists.

Hungarian General Staff (degraded into a group of military counselors), or even to individual commands by simply sending the order to the adviser attached to the unit.

Hungarian units were distributed in accordance with Soviet strategic planning for the eventuality of war. Up to Stalin's death in 1953 the single prospective operational area was Yugoslavia. Consequently, the majority of Hungarian army units were garrisoned between the rivers Danube and Tisza in the southern part of Hungary, and in Southwest Hungary along the Yugoslav frontier.[8] Hungarian units at the outbreak of hostilities were to act as an advance guard for the Soviet Army operating in the Hungarian-Yugoslav area. In 1950, Hungary already had placed in the field an army of sufficient strength to represent a significant item in Soviet war strategy. These troops were to be used exclusively against Yugoslavia.

In the strategic plans of 1950–1951 the main Hungarian thrust was to be carried out between the Danube and Tisza with the task of occupying the Bačka region of Yugoslavia, crossing the Danube and forming a bridgehead in the Fruška Gora range north of Belgrade. The Hungarian planners were told that the bulk of the Soviet Army would follow, attacking out of this bridgehead and moving toward the Yugoslav capital.

In 1952 and 1953, the Soviet-Hungarian strategic plans reflected an even broader scheme, pointing toward participation in a European war. Now the Hungarian Army was to operate in the Western part of Yugoslavia and advance through the Ljubljana gap into the Trieste area. Again the Hungarian units were to serve as an advance guard to establish bridgeheads, through which the Soviet Army was to move on its way to Northern Italy. All these plans were of an offensive character and no defensive plans existed.[9]

The emphasis on building up heavy industry, to be discussed presently, gave Hungary the possibility of producing large amounts of military equipment and arms. These had to conform to the Soviet models, and licenses for the manufacture of Soviet types were given to Hungarian industry. Thus, the T-34 type tanks were made both for the Hungarian Army and for the armies of other Communist states.* Hungarian plants became capable of supplying equipment and ammunition not only to the Hungarian units in case of war but also to less industrialized Communist countries, particularly Bulgaria and Albania.

* While surrendering the manufacturing licenses, the Soviet leadership was always careful to deny the Hungarian industry the license of some important piece, whose absence rendered the tank or ammunition useless. These missing pieces were directly supplied from the Soviet Union.

Since Hungarian territory was to serve as a military base for both the Hungarian and the Soviet armies, it was studded with huge military depots of weapons, ammunition, and other equipment. During the Stalinist period it became a base of logistics with much greater capacity than was needed for the Hungarian Army alone.

Thus, the Army was more totally integrated into the Soviet system than any other Hungarian institution. The reaction of the more nationalist-minded Party leaders to this state of affairs is hardly possible to ascertain, since caution and restraint were even greater in this field than in other matters of Party or state. It may even be doubtful that more than a handful of the leading Party members were fully aware of what was being done in military affairs. Imre Nagy, condemning the Stalinist period in his writings, is far more reserved than usual on this point and restricts himself to a rather cryptic remark concerning Rákosi, "who, as he used to say, had already burned his fingers once by fulfilling excessive demands" in military matters.[10] Excessive demands by whom? It is not difficult to guess.

7

Economics in Stalinist Hungary

∧∧∧∧∧∧∧∧∧∧∧∧∧∧∧∧∧∧∧∧∧∧∧∧∧∧∧

If discussions are to have real meaning, we must be concrete. Thus, so far as the phrase "standard of living of the working class" denotes something real and measurable, it must rise, fall, or remain static. Yet in recent years . . . when we wrote that the standard had risen, it was not, as some of us supposed, the "people's truth" that we proclaimed; alas, we merely lied . . .

MIKLOS GIMES (executed in 1958) in *Béke és Szabadság* (Budapest), October 3, 1956

THE Stalinist economic experiment brought severe hardship on the people of Hungary, and, in so doing, deepened the crack in the top layers of the Communist Party and contributed significantly to the seething popular discontent. The hotbed of conflicts which characterized the Stalinist years from 1949 to 1953 gathered much of its ferment from economic factors. A full analysis of the Hungarian economy does not fall within the task of a book devoted to the struggle between nationalism and Communism in Hungary. For our purposes, it remains only to summarize the economic measures of that period which bore directly upon the later course of history, leading to the explosion of 1956.

THE FIVE-YEAR PLAN

At the end of 1949, Hungary completed a Three-Year Plan which had mainly served purposes of postwar reconstruction, and on January 1, 1950, the first Five-Year Plan was launched. Already in March 1948 all industrial enterprises employing one hundred or more workers had been nationalized (banks and some big steel works even earlier); and in December 1949, in preparation for the Five-Year Plan, all industrial plants employing ten or more employees were also expropriated.

The Five-Year Plan of 1950–1954 set for itself a most ambitious goal: not only to transform Hungary from an "agrarian-industrial" country into an "industrial-agrarian" one, but, what later seemed to be a fantastic project, to turn it into an "iron and steel country." [1] Simultaneously with the collectivization of agriculture, launched in 1949, Hungary was to be forcibly industrialized, and endowed especially with heavy industry. The target figures of the plan were set to achieve this object. The original plan as published in 1949 was drastically revised early in 1951, and production figures were raised by 60 to 80 per cent. According to the original plan, industrial production in general was to increase to 186 per cent of the 1949 figures, but later the target was raised to 310. The output of heavy industry was to increase to 204 per cent, according to the 1949 version, but 380 according to the 1951 version. Plant construction was to increase even more — to 438 per cent.[2]

The plan was, probably from the very outset, an object of controversy between muscovite zealots headed by Ernö Gerö, the Politburo member in charge of Hungary's economy, and the more cautious (also very cautious in their opposition) economic experts.[3] Opposition to the exaggerations of the Five-Year Plan grew with the increase in the target figures and with the devastating effects of the Plan upon the manufacture of consumer goods and upon agriculture. Whatever were the achievements of the plan within the industrial field — and there certainly were notable achievements — complete fulfillment of the plan was impossible, and its impracticable target demands led to a considerable waste of money.[4] The palpable result was a further lowering of the already meagre standard of living of the working class and of the population as a whole.[5] We shall later see that the critics of the plan (Imre Nagy and István Kovács are known to have been among this number) managed to force a downward revision of its targets.

Various features of the mammoth industrialization plan which Rákosi, Gerö, and their associates undertook to force upon the country indicate that it was not only an imitation of Soviet industrialization under Stalin, but was to serve the strategic and economic purposes of the Soviet Union. Many of the goals set by the plan were, both in nature and magnitude, contrary to the genuine interests of Hungary, and even contradicted elementary economic tenets honored by students of Marxist doctrine.

The Communist opponents of exaggerated industrialization seemed to fear that the impoverishment of the population through lack of articles of consumption would eventually be harmful to Communism as such. It is even possible that they had humanitarian motives, considering the hardships people had to endure as a result of the plan. As for agriculture, these opponents were not against collectivization on principle, but considered that collectivization of agriculture undertaken simultaneously with an exaggerated expansion of the industrial base would prove both impracticable and harmful.[6]

Imre Nagy and some of the muscovites probably remembered the events in the Soviet Union at the time of the First Soviet Five-Year Plan which had been enforced simultaneously with wholesale collectivization of agriculture. It had led to a loss of life assessed at from ten to fifteen million people, to famine, deportations, internments, and executions, and to untold misery for tens of millions of others. Very likely Imre Nagy (who must have been an eyewitness to these events) wanted to spare the Hungarian people such a disaster — which a small nation could afford less easily than Russia.

Industrialization and agricultural collectivization in Communist regimes serve both economic and political objectives, and it is sometimes difficult to discern which motive is paramount.* Enforced industrialization in Hungary and elsewhere, aside from serving certain economic and strategic purposes, could absorb a surplus agricultural population (partly engendered by forced collectivization of farmlands) as well as the nation's small artisans, thus making the maximum number of people entirely dependent on the government. Collectivization of agriculture is considered mainly as an instrument for extending full control over the peasantry.[7] Rákosi might have remembered how in 1919 the Hungarian peasant population, by refusing to deliver food to the towns and cities, was instrumental in bringing the first proletarian dictatorship to its knees.

The timid opposition felt, however, that both the Communist movement and the economy of the country would fare better if

---

* In June–July 1951, when great numbers of families (generally former government officials, army officers, aristocrats, and intellectuals) were deported from Budapest and other cities into distant villages, some Party leaders dallied with the idea — in imitation of Stalin's methods — of carrying out full collectivization with the aid of large-scale deportation of kulak families, thus defeating resistance by intimidation and terror (information conveyed to writer by an employee of the Planning Office). Since Hungary had no Siberia to which to deport her kulaks, it was proposed to transplant them from one part of the country to another (peasants from Transdanubia in the West to be deported to the country behind the Tisza River in the East, and vice-versa). The plan was never implemented.

Hungary were to remain under a more liberal economic regime than that imposed by means of the Five-Year Plan and other coercive measures directed from Moscow through Rákosi, Gerö, and their clique. They were confirmed in their thesis when the standard of living (real wages), instead of rising by 35 per cent as predicted by Rákosi, decreased by 15 to 20 per cent.[8] Though extreme destitution was lessened, the average living standard was so lowered that the majority of the population was reduced to a drab existence. In the words of a Hungarian refugee: "The number of people going around in rags decreased, but the number of the shabby ones increased; Hungary was a shabby country." [9]

INDUSTRY AND TRANSPORTATION

Although Western scholars have generally considered the Hungarian Five-Year Plan of 1950–1954 a failure because the production targets were not attained, they have also recognized that considerable progress was made on the road to fuller industrialization.[10] The increase in production in the machine industry and in some areas of light industry had to be acknowledged. Economists of the Western world have criticized the unreasonable growth of investment in heavy industrial construction, but ironically this growth seems to have met with even more severe criticism by Imre Nagy, the heir to Rákosi's economic brinkmanship. We have to assume that the Western analysts based their findings on official Hungarian data, which may or may not be correct, whereas Imre Nagy, during his first premiership in 1953–1955, was better able to acquaint himself with the real results, even for the period prior to his assumption of office.

The index of industrial output at the end of the Five-Year Plan (1954) was announced to have been 258 per cent as against 100 per cent in 1949, and that of heavy industry considered separately, 288 per cent.[11] Though we have no means to contradict the above figures by confronting them with other statistics, Imre Nagy's analysis of the economic picture as he found it when taking over the premiership in July 1953 is not to be ignored. Writing in 1955 for distribution within the Communist leadership, he concluded that at the end of the Five-Year Plan the productive capacity of industry was twice as great as in 1949 (index of 200), hardly consistent with the official figures. He scathingly described the results achieved as an "increase of industrial production for its own sake," which, "combined with the neglect of technical standards, inevitably allowed almost no increase in productivity during the First Five-Year Plan." Although the results, "calculated on the basis of incorrect value indices," show a

significant growth in productivity, "the facts and the existing difficulties plainly contradict such data." [12]

His criticism was directed mainly at what he had earlier called
exaggerated industrialization, an economic policy which "did not
take into account the human being, the society." He specifically
found fault in the overemphasis of the production of capital goods
designed to produce further capital goods.[13] A shortage arose not only
in consumer goods, but also in capital goods designed to produce
consumer goods. He deplored the lack of consideration given to the
specific character of his country, and thus implicitly condemned
imitation of the Soviet pattern. According to Imre Nagy, the Five-
Year Plan "made no basic changes in the technical backwardness of
our industry; while great investments were being made in increasing
production capacity, almost nothing was being done to perfect production and to improve technology. Even a good many of the new
establishments are no exceptions to this." [14] Though he avoided an
open anti-Soviet attack, there can be no doubt that his criticism was
directed against the Soviet machinery, Soviet planning, and Soviet
methods[15] which had been pressed on Hungary: obsolete machinery,
old-fashioned planning, and unsuitable or inferior methods.*

The wastefulness of Soviet supervision in the Hungarian economy is most clearly demonstrated by the history of the large-scale
integrated metallurgical plant at Mohács, a town on the Danube near
the Yugoslav border. This site had the advantage of utilizing the
nearby coal mines of Pécs, and was expected to process Yugoslav ore
brought north on the Danube. After the excommunication of Tito,
this site was abandoned (even though considerable investment had
been made) and another construction started some eighty miles
north, at the village of Dunapentele (thereafter re-christened Sztalinváros, or Stalin-town). The Sztalinváros metallurgical plant, constructed under Soviet advice and expert aid, was considered to be
backward by 20 or 25 years (it is said to have been modeled on an
American plant of 1928–1929 vintage, adopted subsequently by the
Soviet Union), and its construction cost four times what would have
been necessary had proper technical advice been followed.[16]

Hungary's main source of energy is coal. The wartime peak production of 11.5 million metric tons was reattained in 1949. The
target of 27.5 million as set by the revised Five-Year Plan fell short

---

* Soviet machinery and Soviet planning often receives much less credit in the
satellite areas than in the West. Such condemnation results partly from an innate
bias against anything Soviet, partly because the Soviet government often dumps its
obsolete and used machinery in the satellite countries. "Soviet methods" have become
a laughing stock with workers and intelligentsia in the Soviet-dominated countries.

by 5.5 million tons. But the quality of coal extracted considerably deteriorated, its caloric value falling by 12 per cent during the operation of the plan.[17]

Oil production, which during World War II reached a yearly output of 839,000 metric tons, fell back to 490,000 in 1951, owing to improper management and exhaustion of the resources; in 1954, however, owing to the opening of a new oil field in the Great Hungarian Plain (up to then the principal fields had been in southern Transdanubia near the Yugoslav border) the production of oil was raised to 1,190,000 metric tons.[18]

The stellar project of the Five-Year Plan in the field of transportation was the much advertised Budapest Subway. The first line to be constructed was to connect Buda and Pest on either side of the Danube, which there flows from north to south. The most difficult part of this construction consisted in piercing the limestone rock under the river bank and in properly protecting and isolating the tunnel. The planning was done by Soviet experts, and the famous Moscow Subway served as model. A north–south subway line, entirely east of the river, would have been given priority if the commuting interests of Budapest had been determining. But the real reason for the subway construction and the selection of its first line is to be found in Soviet strategic thinking; the line planned would have connected with the Hungarian railway network on both sides of the Danube, and in case of war the railroad connections toward the west bank of the Danube would have been secured even if the railroad bridges had been destroyed (as they were by the Germans in World War II). In spite of the enormous sacrifice of material and manpower, the soil underneath Budapest and the Danube, differing from that in Moscow, resisted Soviet techniques. By 1953, the construction had to be discontinued, in fact, abandoned. The shafts and their outer construction at the sites of the would-be subway stations still disfigure the streets and squares of Budapest.[19]

AGRICULTURE

After the Communist takeover, the Communist Party and government set before themselves the goal of the collectivization of agriculture. Had they proceeded more cautiously in herding farmers into kolkhozes — producers' collectives — and had they helped the socialized sector of agriculture with solid investments (as they did for industry, especially heavy industry), the incentive for peasants to join the kolkhozes might have been much greater. What had been overlooked in economic incentive had to be made up for by other means, such as intolerable compulsory deliveries, low prices for the commodities thus delivered, high taxes, and monetary fines for alleged infringements of a host of administrative regulations relating to all phases of agricultural activity. The more independent farmers, very often irrespective of the size of their holdings, were branded as kulaks, and in order to break their influence over the villages, were subjected to all sorts of pressure, from administrative vexation up to internment, imprisonment, and even execution. Despite this terror, the percentage of arable land cultivated by kolkhozes rose only to 26 per cent by March 1953, with another 13.2 per cent in state-owned farms.[20]

Many leading Party members must have looked with great apprehension at the events in the villages in the years 1950–1953. The alleged federation of workers and peasants looked even more farcical, seen in its true light, than the supposed dictatorship exercised by the proletariat. The measures of collectivization resulted in the abandonment of approximately 10 per cent of all land in cultivation, which thus became waste land.[21]

The kolkhozes and most of the state farms lagged in productivity. It has been pointed out that the production of bread grain was smaller in the period 1950–1954 than it had been in 1911–1915; the yearly average in the earlier period had been 2.79 million tons, and in the later, 2.63 million. In the meantime the population of Hungary had risen by nearly 25 per cent. The resulting decrease in the per capita production of bread grains explains the reduction of real consumption and of agricultural export.[22]

There are many reasons for the decline of agricultural production. In the case of the independent farmer (where the decrease was less conspicuous), the main causes were persecution and the government's failure to amalgamate the widely separated small parcels of land held by individual peasants. In the case of the kolkhozes and state-owned farms, psychological factors were more important.[23] Mismanagement was another adverse factor. The agricultural laborer, as he reflected on his lot in the kolkhozes and state farms, sabotaged and slowed down work as his part in the resistance against a hated regime.*

* For a characteristic picture in one of the state farms, see CURPH (Columbia University Research Project on Hungary), interview no. 402: "Until 1954, the state farm of Puszta-Szabolcs was assigned to the growing of cotton . . . it was found that this was a wrong thing to do — so growing of cotton was abandoned. However, the seed grain ordered from Russia had to be taken over. Due to the fact that it could not be used for anything else, it was used to feed fish." The interviewee knew of a State farm where the slogan of the employees was: "Every day ten forints' worth of damage to the People's Economy."

FOREIGN TRADE

The Five-Year Plan, contrary to the predictions of its planners, completely upset the balance of foreign trade in Hungary. The all too rapid development which had been forced upon the country, especially in heavy industry, required an increasing amount of raw materials that were scarce or nonexistent within Hungary; their importation thus became a necessity for fulfillment of the Plan. In addition, rearmament required large imports of military equipment. In order partly to counterbalance the adverse trend of foreign trade, exportations had to be increased, even if this meant depriving the population of Hungary of some much-needed commodities.[24] In order to sell goods abroad the commodities selected for export were priced considerably below the internal price level, so that the resulting loss had to be supplemented through other sources of income. Imre Nagy wrote that the country was spending 2 billion forints a year to supplement deficits in foreign trade revenue.[25] Soviet-owned corporations were returned to Hungary in 1952, reparation payments to the Soviet Union ended in 1953, and the Joint Soviet–Hungarian Corporations were dissolved in 1954. And with these developments, mutual trade as a source of Soviet economic exploitation of Hungary grew relatively more important. The general pattern of Soviet–satellite trade was to fix prices below the world market for goods imported into the Soviet Union from the satellite countries, and, on the other hand, to fix prices above the world market for goods exported from the Soviet Union to the satellites.[26] Another method was to buy at cheap prices commodities from one satellite state, and to resell them at a much higher price to another satellite — without even importing them to the Soviet Union.[27] All this applied to Hungary.

On January 25, 1949, as an answer to the Marshall Plan, which at the behest of Moscow remained closed to the satellite countries, the Council for Economic Mutual Assistance (CEMA) was established in Moscow. The parties were the Soviet Union, Bulgaria, Hungary, Poland, Rumania, and Czechoslovakia. The objectives were "to realize broader economic cooperation" and to carry out "an exchange of economic experience, the granting of mutual technical aid, the exchange of raw materials, foodstuffs, machines, equipment . . ." among the signatories. Albania was admitted in February 1949, and East Germany in the early fall of 1950.[28] For many years, however, this organization functioned chiefly on paper.[29] Until the death of Stalin, the Soviet Union found it more profitable to insist on trading individually with its satellites.

THE SECOND PHASE

Dual Leadership—
Conflicting Policies
1953–1955

In recent times, we have seen attempts to write history entirely in terms of impersonal forces, with the so-called "great men" dancing like puppets to tunes that the impersonal forces call. But this view, also, is too simple to be convincing. It may be right to play the "great men" down, but it makes nonsense of human affairs if one tries to do away with them altogether. Instead of taking either of these two extreme lines, let us think of history in terms of an interplay between "forces" and "personalities." This approach is really more illuminating.

ARNOLD J. TOYNBEE, "Seventeen 'Great Men' — Or Great Forces?" *New York Times Magazine,* November 8, 1959.

8

The Gladiators Square Off

ΛΛΛΛΛΛΛΛΛΛΛΛΛΛΛΛΛΛΛΛΛΛΛΛΛΛΛΛΛ

There is nothing more difficult to take in hand, more perilous
to conduct, or more uncertain in its success, than to take the lead
in the introduction of a new order of things.

MACHIAVELLI

AT THE memorable Kremlin meeting between the Hungarian
Communist leaders and the members of the Soviet Presidium in
June 1953, it was decided that Rákosi was to be deprived of his monocratic power, and the premiership conferred on Imre Nagy. The
Party leadership was thus separated from the governmental command, as it had been in the Soviet Union since Stalin's death. Malenkov, who had been the first Secretary of the Central Committee under
Stalin as Secretary-General, and had become Chairman of the Council of Ministers on March 6, 1953, gave up his Party secretaryship
to Khrushchev on March 14.[1] Malenkov was still considered the most
powerful man within the collective leadership in June 1953, and
his choosing the premiership and abandoning the traditional leading
post of First Party Secretary (which once had opened the road toward
personal supreme dictatorship for Stalin) could have been interpreted as raising the highest position in the state hierarchy to a
status at least equal to that of Party leader.*

---

* Leadership also became divided in the other satellite countries in accordance with
the Soviet pattern, but in most of these the most powerful leader chose to retain the
Party post: Bierut in Poland, Novotny in Czechoslovakia, Enver Hoxha in Albania,
and Ulbricht in the German Democratic Republic. In Rumania and Bulgaria, however, Gheorghiu-Dej and Chervenkov chose the premiership. Zbigniew K. Brzezinski,
The Soviet Bloc: Unity and Conflict (Cambridge, Mass., 1960), p. 161.

In view of such an initial uncertainty as to the real locus of
power, coupled with the abasement suffered by Rákosi before the
Soviet Presidium and the importance of the task assigned to Imre
Nagy (to repair the damage done by his predecessor), Nagy might
justly have felt his position equal to that of his colleague entrusted
with the leadership of the Party. We may thus feel justified, as Imre
Nagy might have felt, in considering the new era as one of *dual
leadership* for Hungary.

THE CENTRAL COMMITTEE MEETS

Upon the return of Rákosi and his companions from Moscow, the
Central Committee of the Hungarian Party was convoked. It met on
June 27 and 28, 1953, and adopted the famous June Resolutions.
These resolutions of the Central Committee were never published.
According to Imre Nagy, it was Rákosi who prevented their dis-
semination, and we can suppose that they contained a much more
severe condemnation of Rákosi's policies, and possibly of his person,
than did the reserved judgment expressed in Imre Nagy's speech
before the National Assembly on July 4. The real meaning of these
resolutions formed the subject of many disputes during the whole
time of Imre Nagy's first tenure of the premiership. Since only a
short summary of the resolutions had been circulated among local
Party secretaries, the struggle to interpret an esoteric text waged by
the initiated few gave rise to various exaggerated assumptions by the
rank and file of the Party and the population as a whole.

The contents of the June Resolutions may, however, be partially
reconstructed from excerpts quoted by Imre Nagy and others, as well
as from summarized reports. According to Imre Nagy: "The chief
purpose of the Central Committee's June resolution was to stave off
the catastrophe and to counterbalance the effect of the disturbances
in East Germany and Czechoslovakia, to ease the growing tension
manifested in frequent mass demonstrations in the Great Plains, and
in general to bring about a turn of the tide." [2]

The Central Committee's resolutions spelled out in formal
language the rebuke administered by the members of the Soviet
Presidium over the miscarriage of government during Rákosi's autocratic regime. *Inter alia,* they blamed the pre-June leadership of the
Party for having departed from Leninist principles and for having
introduced a "clique leadership." [3] The question of relations between Party and state was extensively dealt with (see next chapter).
Other parts of the resolutions condemned Rákosi's economic policy,

especially the overemphasis on heavy industry, the forcible collectivization, and the excesses committed by the Security Police.*

Imre Nagy, we are told, was already encountering difficulties in drawing up his program — indeed in drawing up the June Resolutions. The essence of the Central Committee's resolutions had been inspired by the Moscow conversations, and most of the texts were drafted by Imre Nagy himself. That he encountered obstacles in verifying some of the data necessary for his program and that the sabotage of his efforts had already started at this initial date may easily be assumed.**

The vote of the Central Committee (unanimous as usual) in condemning the mistakes of the past may rightly be considered as an apology to the man who had been critical of the errors and excesses of Rákosi and his associates, and whose warnings had been neglected and advice discarded. This triumph of Nagy before the highest Party organ was to be a further humiliation for Rákosi which the latter was not likely to forget. The resolve of Rákosi and his group not to give up their hold over Party and country must have been strengthened by the fear that the success of Nagy's program would even more vividly reveal their incompetence and abuses.

A reshuffle in the membership of the Politburo of the Hungarian Party was also approved by the Central Committee. Six members of Politburo were removed: Jozsef Révai and Mihály Farkas, closely associated with Rákosi's personal regime; Lászlo Piros (who had succeeded the imprisoned Gábor Péter as AVH chief); Károly Kiss (who remained, however, chairman of the Committee of Supervision); Árpád Házi (until then a Deputy Prime Minister); and Sándor Ronai (a former Social Democrat).† Two relatively young Central Committee members, Lajos Ács and István Hidas, were now elected to the Politburo. István Bata (a Moscow-trained Army officer) and Béla Szalai (who had been in Moscow with the Hungarian

* According to CURPH (Columbia University Research Project on Hungary), interview no. 500, the June Resolutions also contained the following pronouncement: "The Central Committee deeply condemns the adventurous policy of Mátyás Rákosi, Ernö Gerö, Jozsef Révai and Mihály Farkas, which policy is taking the country on the edge of ruin."

** According to the CURPH report by György Heltai: "The tenets of his program were put together by Imre Nagy himself. The top Party and government functionaries were reluctant to assist in an analysis of the mistakes of the past. Imre Nagy drew up his critical comments on the past partly on the basis of data given to him by the Russians, partly with the help of one or two Hungarian economists, but mostly on the basis of his own notes."

† Other members of the Politburo were: Mátyás Rákosi, Imre Nagy, Ernö Gerö, Antal Apro, István Kristoff, András Hegedüs, and Mihály Zsofinecz.

delegation) became alternate members. The membership of this body was thus reduced to nine in all with two alternate members, a move which also bore the imprint of Soviet reforms in the post-Stalin era.

In this change of membership one can see the reflection of a desire to drop some of the persons responsible for the distasteful aspects of the Stalinist regime, and those who had been most servile in carrying out Rákosi's orders. But the remainder, headed by Rákosi and Gerö themselves, and the newcomers, not one of them a reliable adherent of Nagy, can hardly be considered as favoring the radical changes called for by the Central Committee's resolutions — despite the "unanimous" vote.

THE NATIONAL ASSEMBLY MEETS

On July 4, 1953, the National Assembly met. This was the newly elected Assembly which the country had "delegated" under the slogans and plans presented by Rákosi. Now, this very Assembly was to listen to a program of quite a different sort.

Imre Nagy was elected Chairman of the Council of Ministers on July 4, in accordance with the directives given by Moscow. He then addressed the National Assembly and announced his program of the New Course.[4] The fact that the new policy was first made public before the National Assembly and not before a Party body was novel under a Communist regime and conducive to speculations about the growth of parliamentary rule planned by the new Prime Minister. It must, however, be borne in mind that the new program had already been approved in its essence by the Central Committee of the Party.

The reforms Imre Nagy was able to announce were mainly of an economic nature. The trend of development in the national economy must be modified; excessive industrialization must cease; greater stress must be laid on the development of light industry and food production as against that of heavy industry; increased attention must be directed to agriculture; the accelerated pace of agricultural collectivization was to be abandoned, and individual farming supported. Among noneconomic tasks, the Prime Minister promised greater tolerance in religious questions, the "consolidation of legality," the abolition of internment camps, an amnesty for minor offenses, and revision of sentences against "people who had been wronged." *

* This program somewhat resembles that submitted by Premier Malenkov to the Supreme Soviet about a month later, on August 8. He too promised a better standard of living, support of light industry and of agriculture, and an improvement of the

Imre Nagy's inaugural speech had an unburdening effect upon the Hungarian public. It especially caused great repercussions among the farming sector of the population; they started to abandon and redistribute agricultural collectives in many villages. Many people were even inclined to believe that the end of the Communist totalitarian regime was near, and the relatively small number of Party *apparatchiki* became alarmed for that reason.[5] Neither side sufficiently realized that a dual leadership had been created and that the preponderance of either of the two heads was still a matter which lay in the lap of the gods — the masters of the Kremlin.

SOME OBSERVATIONS ON DUAL LEADERSHIP

It may have been the intention of the Soviet leaders to introduce a *collective* Party leadership in Hungary, rather than the dual leadership they in fact created. The collective leadership of the Soviet Union had come into existence after Stalin's death because, at that juncture, none of his heirs had the necessary influence and power to continue the *yedinonatchaliye* (one-man rule). The character of collective leadership in the Soviet Union, with its hesitations and compromises, the personal predilections or prejudices of its members, and the changing factions within their ranks, may be considered as the true cause for creating a dual leadership in Hungary and also for the struggle which ensued between the two leaders in Hungary.

A one-man dictatorship, when coming to an end with no constitutional successor available, always results in an acute crisis. The crisis is even more serious when the dictatorship has been *de facto* and not constitutionally established. In the early Roman Empire, succession to the emperorship was a revolutionary act. So long as republican forms and traditions survived in the empire, tentative moves were frequently made for the reinstatement of an effective republican system under leadership of the Senate ("collective leadership"). In Rome and elsewhere, coregents have usually come to loggerheads until one of them eliminated the other (like Caracalla and Geta in Rome), or until they agreed to divide their empire. In the Soviet state, as well as in its ruling elite, the Party under the formal constitutional system is far from being monocratic; therefore Stalin's

---

food situation. Moreover the amnesty decreed by the Soviet government on March 27, 1953, is very like that declared in Hungary after Nagy's appointment. But as for the failures and illegalities charged against the pre-June Hungarian administration, no counterpart is to be found in Soviet announcements as early as 1953. A satellite regime more easily lends itself to becoming a scapegoat, under the orders of the overlord, than the administration of the overlord itself.

attainment of undisputed one-man leadership demonstrated a situation of fact contrasting with formal constitutionality.

We can assume that the Soviet collective leadership was in the throes of conflict from the earliest moment. Differences of policy and of the exercise of power must have divided that heterogeneous group, differences they were skillfully able to conceal until such flashing lights as the liquidation of Beria began to dispel the illusion of the monolithic unity of the Presidium.

The stormy reception of Rákosi at the meeting in Moscow gave evidence of the dislike that some members of the Presidium felt for the Hungarian satellite dictator. These were mainly the men who professed to discontinue the dangerous policies of their own dead autocrat. They wished to eliminate the Stalinist dictatorships in all of their dependent countries and to support persons congenial to their way of thinking, persons who seemed likely to follow their lead and their policies. They wanted to install leaders who could cope with the acute problems engendered by the incompetence of the Stalinist regime, and to eliminate the dangers which later so drastically assailed them in Berlin and also in Hungary. On the other hand, former Stalinists still continued to place their trust in the tested and experienced muscovite satrap and were chary of having him replaced by any other person. Whereas we know that Beria, Malenkov, Mikoyan, and Khrushchev were the foremost critics of Rákosi, no words of rebuke from the mouths of Molotov, Kaganovich, or Bulganin have been recorded.

Whether Imre Nagy had earlier been Malenkov's man of confidence or not, he certainly became such as soon as they were able to exchange views in Moscow. It seems immaterial whether Imre Nagy adopted Malenkov's coming economic program or whether their exchange of views had resulted in a common program. The fact that both were primarily interested in raising the standard of living of their peoples and deprecated the overemphasis on heavy industry created a community of interest between them. It is also to be noted that in the early days of the collective leadership Khrushchev wholeheartedly supported Malenkov's endeavors to improve the living standard, to give more and cheaper food to the population, and to eliminate inadequacies in agriculture.[6] When Khrushchev's stature rose, he turned against Malenkov, and also against Malenkov's economic policy — confirming the assumption that in the uppermost strata of the Soviet hierarchy power factors prevail over political or ideological motives. But at that early stage of Moscow's collective leadership, there is no doubt that political solidarity made Khrushchev's position regarding Rákosi and Imre Nagy identical with that of Malenkov.

The reports which reached the Soviet Presidium from Kisselev, the Soviet ambassador in Budapest, and others prompted its members to bring about a change in the Hungarian high command. The principle of collective leadership, no doubt considered advisable for acceptance by other Communist governments (in view of the "law of imitation" always prevailing between paramount governments and their satellites), led the Presidium to dethrone Rákosi from his monopoly of power. By giving a share of this power to an outsider, a person unconnected with past mistakes and not belonging to Rákosi's "foursome," they might have hoped to introduce a facsimile of collective leadership. It was a compromise solution, as often obtains with political bodies in which conflicting views are expressed but where the desire is, nevertheless, to maintain the semblance of unity.

The Presidium therefore did not wish to drop Rákosi but rather to dilute his monopolistic power, to create a more healthy equilibrium between "sectarian" Stalinists and reformists who were nevertheless "reliable." The intense conflict between Nagy and Rákosi resulted from the accidental circumstances of their respective characters: Nagy's inner-directedness versus Rákosi's stubbornness and drive for power. It cannot be presumed that the Moscow Presidium intentionally arranged matters in such a way as to create the struggle; nevertheless the struggle became protracted because of the parallel rivalries within the Soviet leadership and because of the uncertainty of the Hungarian leaders as to what the Soviet Presidium really wanted them to do.

In this respect we have to differentiate among the Hungarians. Though Nagy might have believed that the mission he had received from the Presidium reflected the uniform and settled opinion of its members, Rákosi was probably not deceived by their appearance of unanimity. We shall see that during subsequent developments he was far better equipped to guess Soviet intentions than his idealistic and unsophisticated opponent. Other members of the Hungarian Politburo, including even Gerö, as well as members of the Central Committee, displayed a more or less real "satellite attitude": they were trying to guess whether Rákosi or Nagy was favored by the Soviet leadership, and they gave their allegiances according to the momentary impressions they gained. And the fight going on simultaneously for power positions among the members of the Soviet Presidium often obfuscated not only the vision of these lesser Hungarians but even that of Rákosi and Nagy, who had better opportunities for obtaining first-hand information.

RÁKOSI COUNTERATTACKS

Rákosi, after trying in vain to prevent Imre Nagy from obtaining the premiership, reluctantly acquiesced to the inevitable; but he never gave up in his endeavors to counteract the New Course of his successor nor to achieve in due time the removal of his all too dangerous rival. He was motivated by jealousy (fostered by the popularity of his opponent before the masses), by fear that his abuses might be openly aired, and above all by ambition. He refused to lose everything which he had gained through bitter struggles. With dismay he beheld the tremendous success Imre Nagy was achieving in his parliamentary debut.* He still had the Party apparatus faithfully in hand, and always reminded them that with his fall they would all perish, that only he could protect them. The Party was still ruling the country but the *apparatchiki* became alarmed. Something had to be done to counteract and neutralize the effect that the announcement of the New Course had had over the country. Rákosi could not as yet risk openly opposing Imre Nagy's program; he had to appear to approve it, but nevertheless he had to soften its impact on the country and tranquilize the members of the *apparat*. This conspiracy of Rákosi and his associates of the Party cadres, an alliance based on jointly committed excesses and sealed by the mutual knowledge, started very early. Being a real conspiracy, it often changed tactics and never came out into the open until victory was finally assured.

On July 11, 1953, Rákosi in a speech before the Budapest Party activists[7] warned the public that "those measures which the Party proposes to resort to in achieving their aim, the building of socialism, are unchanged." He stated that it would have been more correct to submit the new program first in the name of the Party, because, as it happened, "many of the comrades were not clear that the proposals presented by Comrade Nagy in the National Assembly were prepared on the basis of the resolutions of the Central Committee of the Party." He particularly warned farmers that they would only be permitted to leave the cooperatives at the end of the production year, that is, in October. And though the "kulak list" was abolished, the "kulaks remain kulaks, with or without a list." He emphasized

* Interviewee, a prominent Party member, met Rákosi on July 4, 1953, in the Parliament after Nagy had delivered his inaugural speech, and told him: "This is just wonderful!" Rákosi retorted ominously: "Oh, yes, you think so? Well, we'll see . . ." CURPH, interview no. 500.

that the Party authorities must maintain their vigilance, and in guarded language he warned the Party not to attribute too much weight or wider interpretation to Nagy's pronouncements. He showed his "teeth" and warned friends and foes that the Socialist Order could not be encroached upon.

In Moscow, just one day earlier, Beria's arrest had been announced, and this may have persuaded Rákosi to fling down the gauntlet at so early a juncture. At the Kremlin encounter in June, Beria seems to have been one of the foremost critics, if not *the* foremost critic, of Rákosi's administration. It can reasonably be assumed that Beria's purge gave Rákosi the much-needed impetus for his first thrust against Nagy. Of course, he may have known earlier of Beria's impending fate, but even if so the announcement itself may have had an encouraging effect.[8] And at any rate it must certainly be said that Beria's downfall somewhat weakened Nagy's position. To understand this fully we have to return to the developments inside the Kremlin.

It was uncertainty which created the collective leadership after Stalin's death, fear of revolution in consequence of the deceased dictator's terrorism, inability to predict both internal and external events, an urge for solidarity in the hours of danger. All rallied to preserve the Soviet regime. Malenkov brought the Party (the leadership of which he had to abandon for the role of Prime Minister). Beria brought the state security organizations. Molotov brought only his past experiences, but Marshal Zhukov, suddenly raised from the limbo where he had been submerged by Stalin after his successful wartime career, added the support of the Red Army. Khrushchev, at that time, was just seen lingering in the background.

Malenkov and Beria had been known as rivals for Stalin's inheritance. Beria himself almost fell victim to Stalinist obsessions during the crisis created by the Doctors' Plot. He was bound to be the most fervent anti-Stalinist after the demise of the autocrat. He violently displayed his anti-Stalinist feelings when meeting Rákosi, the Hungarian Stalin.* At first it seemed that Malenkov and Beria were working hand in hand. Beria's intentions for easing the cold war went even beyond Malenkov's plans to this effect. But Beria was the most hated and most unpopular member of the collective leadership because of his record as Secret Police chief. Aware of this, he

---

* Already the Slansky trial in November 1952 in Czechoslovakia appeared to many as a plot to bring about Beria's downfall. Rákosi was credited with having been instrumental in promoting this anti-Jewish trial, which coincided with his move against Gábor Péter, the Hungarian Security Police chief. If the Slansky trial was indeed directed against Beria, the enmity of the leader toward Rákosi was thus fostered by an additional reason.

wished to climb quickly up the ladder and thus become invulnerable. Whether he really prepared a conspiracy against the Presidium, and if successful, what his policy would have been, are matters of conjecture.[9] From what we know, he warmly supported Malenkov's economic policy, the raising of the standard of living (a slogan which might serve to popularize him with the masses), and the assurances for preventing a new war and establishing peace with the West.[10] We can conjecture, however, that had Beria been successful in attaining the highest post in the Soviet system, Rákosi would have been ousted from even his Party leadership, and possibly Imre Nagy could have achieved some of his objectives.

The downfall of Beria in the summer of 1953 and his subsequent execution, made public in December, provided Rákosi with an appropriate explanation for his demotion from government leadership that could be used in internal Party circles. Beria was his chief opponent in Moscow, and since Beria had proved to be a traitor, he would soon be back in favor again. Rákosi knew that the good Party functionaries would always be watching out for what Moscow had to say.

Rákosi's speech of July 11, closely following Beria's arrest, started the deadly duel* between him and Imre Nagy which lasted for over twenty months, until the fall of Imre Nagy in 1955. The feud remained concealed from the rank and file of the Party almost until Nagy's defeat. Rákosi was able to maintain his control over the Party machinery, and factionalism was thus restricted to the upper echelons of the leadership. The struggle remained largely unnoticed by the masses of the population. Nevertheless, it did not fail to spread uncertainty and disquiet both among the beneficiaries of the regime and those outside the pale.

This internecine combat of two Communist bosses was fought on various grounds: on theoretical questions, principles of economic policy, and principles of Marxism-Leninism. They fought within the Party forums in Hungary and in Moscow, before the plenum of the Presidium, and in the presence of individual members. Basically it was a fight for power, but this was probably less apparent to Imre

---

* Wrote Nagy later: "Owing principally to Rákosi's obstructive attitude, the Political Committee began and continued its struggle to combat the deterioration of Party life amid great political vacillation. One manifestation of this, which I have already mentioned, was Rákosi's July 11 speech to the Party activists of Budapest. This speech left the Party inclined to feel that there was no need for great changes in Party life, leadership, and policy; that actually the old policy could be continued. Even the Political Committee was unable to keep Rákosi from this endeavor." Imre Nagy, *On Communism: In Defense of the New Course* (New York, 1957), p. 283.

Nagy, who fought for power that would enable him to implement his political ideas. For Rákosi it was rather a fight for power for power's sake. But in any case — and this is a fact always to be remembered — it was not a fight for the leadership of an independent state. The struggle had to be carried out under the watchful eyes of the Kremlin masters and both men must have known that it was the Kremlin which would ultimately act as arbiter between them and would mete out its judgment. Thus the battle differed essentially from similar internecine battles fought within the walls of the Kremlin. When Stalin struggled to rid himself of real or potential rivals, or when later Khrushchev discarded one by one his adversaries within the collective leadership, both men had only to be concerned with the moves and countermoves of their opponents. The fight within the Hungarian Party was a "satellite duel," a fight for the power to rule the satrapy of Hungary. And Imre Nagy, like the others, seemed to acquiesce in the role of arbitrators which the Soviet comrades would inevitably play.* At least he did at that time.

* Imre Nagy in these years is assessed thus by a non-Communist observer: "he should be looked upon as one of Moscow's chessmen for the purposes of carrying out alternate policies. I could not tell whether Nagy is playing consciously his part, or whether he does not know that he is being used for a dummy." CURPH, interview no. 118.

9

Rivalry of Party and State

/\.\/

Confucius when guest in the Kingdom of Wei, was asked what he would do first if called to head the government. He replied: "Evidently, I would see to it that things are called by their right names."

W ITH Imre Nagy the head of the government and Rákosi the Party leader, the struggle between the two rivals often assumed the character of a conflict between the state administration and Party organization couched in terms which could be verbalized under the Marxist-Leninist doctrine. Since one of the chiefs of the antagonistic forces was the Prime Minister and the other the First Secretary of the Party, the question of correct relationship between government and Party easily disguised the power aspects of the struggle. At the same time one must emphasize that, owing to the peculiar nature of the Party-government relationship in a Communist state, this problem in fact offered a subject for genuine ideological discussion. Thus the period of dual leadership was characterized by disguised or concealed antagonisms appearing in forms of doctrinal or ideological disputes, and there was not always a readily observable line between admitted subjects of dispute and the disguised substance of the conflict.

The issues were still further befogged by the intermingling of Party organization and government administration. High Party functionaries often held high state offices, and former Party functionaries now participated in the administration of state operations and often maintained their allegiance toward their former chief and benefactor, Rákosi. The situation in the all-important State Security and Army branches of the government was peculiarly characteristic: only reliable Party members could hold posts in these organizations, and in most cases their Party affiliations proved to be a stronger tie than the administrative relationship. Besides, the Communist system of infiltrating state and municipal administrative staffs with Party and Security Police watchdogs, stooges, and spies made a clear-cut differentiation between Party and government even more unrealistic.

THE EXTRACONSTITUTIONAL POWER PATTERN

The question of the proper relationship between Party and state had been extensively dealt with in the June Resolutions, and Rákosi must in large measure have suffered demotion for his earlier disregard of the "principles" concerning such a relationship. As the full text of the June Resolutions is not available, we are compelled to try to reconstruct the nature of the criticism leveled against Rákosi from the pertinent parts of a report which had been submitted to the Central Committee prior to the June plenum meeting. The text of this report, largely embodied in the resolutions themselves, was probably drafted by Imre Nagy and inspired by the conversations he had in Moscow.

It is important to examine some parts of this Report as reproduced by Imre Nagy:

The unprincipled and un-Partylike leadership of the Party has brought with it a violation of the fundamental principles of the People's Democracy, as regards the relation of Party and state and of state and the masses . . . The fault is that the Party has excessively dominated the state and economic leadership of the country; the Party not only has made the rules and the decisions but to a large extent it has also executed the measures prescribed. The Party is not suited, either in its organizational structure, its operation, its make-up or its social character, for attending to state functions, nor is this its job. Nevertheless, it has interfered excessively in the execution of state tasks, thereby violating the independence of state organs, paralyzing their operations, and discrediting their reputations . . . Added to this is the fact that Comrade Rákosi combined in his own person *all the power in the country* — he was First Secretary of the Party and Chairman of the Council of Ministers [Premier], and he took the State Security Authority [AVH] under his immediate direction. He has committed serious errors, both in his leadership of the Party and of the state and in the work of the AVH, errors that contain within themselves great dangers . . . We can assert that the government was in reality a *shadow government*, which approved Party resolutions that had already been passed, and that the authority and responsibility of the ministries was also greatly curtailed . . . Such governmental organs and methods are *not suitable* for absolutely guaranteeing legality in all aspects of state and economic life. Here are the most serious evils of our state life, the roots of the violation of socialist legality, which, in the last analysis, derive from a separation from the masses . . . It must be stated frankly that, owing to the errors of the leaders of the Party, we have deviated from the principles of Lenin as far as our popular democratic state is concerned.[1]

During the Moscow meeting in June 1953, an agreement must have been reached by the Soviet leaders, whereby the overwhelming power of Rákosi, as Party leader, would be restricted in favor of both the collective Politburo, and the government administration as represented by its head, the new Prime Minister. One can assume that Nagy was unwilling to accept the role of a puppet and wished, as Premier, to have a voice in decision-making. The grievance against the supreme position of Rákosi and Nagy's desire to share in the wielding of power may have been the chief reasons why the question of Party-state relationship came into the foreground in Moscow in June 1953, and after. Up to June, Hungary had had only one ruler, who, with the help of a few associates, presided over Party and government; after June, there were to be two.

In the Soviet Union and in Soviet-dominated lands the significant role played by the Communist Party in shaping the destinies of the countries concerned engenders a political problem of extreme importance when the heads of Party and government are divided, and both of them wish to exert real power. Stalin, as Secretary of the Party, was able to destroy his opposition and control Party and state many years before adding the office of Chairman of the Council of Ministers to his supreme Party post.[2] The struggle between Malenkov, the head of the government, and Khrushchev, the First Secretary of the Party, ended with the victory of the latter.

Situations where the true sphere of power is not correlated with the constitutional organs of the state, that is, governments by proxy, have been known to various countries in the course of history. In Rome the imperator and *princeps senatus* wielded supreme power while the republican constitution remained unchanged. Under the last Merovingian kings in France the *maire du palais* was the real depository of power until Pepin the Short assumed the title of king. In Japan the relations between the *tenno* (emperor) and the *shogun* offer similar analogies. Even approximate analogies may be found in certain phases of the French Revolution, when real political power rested with the "clubs" (first Girondist, then exclusively Jacobin) or with the Municipal Council of Paris, and the government merely fulfilled functionary tasks. Analogies may be instructive but often also misleading. In many respects the present-day Communist extra-constitutional Party regime lacks precedent. It seems appropriate, however, to compare the bicephalous Hungarian state of 1953 and 1954 with realities of power in other Communist satellite countries.

In Poland, Boleslaw Bierut was President of the Republic and Secretary-General of the Party until 1952. Under the new Polish Constitution, which abolished the presidency, Bierut assumed the role of Prime Minister while simultaneously reserving that of Party Secretary. Under the influence of Soviet developments, he relinquished the premiership in 1954, but as First Secretary of the Party remained the leading personality of his country.*

In Czechoslovakia, Klement Gottwald, President of the Republic, took over the duties of Party leadership in September 1951 when disgrace fell upon Rudolf Slansky, the Secretary-General. When Gottwald died after his return from Stalin's funeral in March 1953, Prime Minister Zapotocky was raised to the office of President of the Republic; Antonin Novotny succeeded as First Secretary of the Party, and Vilem Siroky as Prime Minister, thus creating a more balanced distribution of power.

In Rumania, Gheorghe Gheorghiu-Dej, the Party chief, after having gotten rid of his two colleagues in a triumvirate of power (Vasile Luca and Ana Pauker), assumed also the post of Premier in June 1952. (The former Prime Minister, Petru Groza, had been a puppet in the hands of the Party leadership, as István Dobi had been in Hungary before Rákosi became Premier.) Thus all power was concentrated in the hands of Gheorghiu-Dej, and he was still the strongest leader after Gheorghe Apostol became First Secretary of the Party in April 1954. In Bulgaria, beginning in 1951, Vulke Chervenkov joined the Party secretaryship with the office of Prime Minister until he yielded the Party post to Todor Zhivkov in March 1954. It is interesting to note that in both Rumania and Bulgaria the most powerful man retained the premiership, and gave up the formal Party leadership, just as Malenkov had done in the Soviet Union. This might have suggested to Imre Nagy that in a satellite country a Prime Minister may wield the most influential authority.

In Albania, Enver Hoxha ruled supreme over Party and government alike, even after Stalin's death. In East Germany, the office of the Prime Minister had never been joined to that of the Party

---

* Josef Cyrankiewicz, a former Socialist, became Chairman of the Council of Ministers, a post which he retained after Gomulka's advent to the Party leadership in October 1956.

chief, but Prime Minister Otto Grotewohl, a former Social Democrat, was always a person of lesser stature than Walter Ulbricht,
the Secretary-General of the Party.

Nowhere else in the satellite area was such a bipolarized leadership established as in Hungary with the juxtaposition of Rákosi
and Imre Nagy.

THE EXTRA-PARTY POWER PATTERN

The above examination of the distribution of power centers
in the People's Democracies does not provide a uniform picture.
During Stalin's lifetime, the tendency shifted toward a monopoly
of control concentrated in the hands of the Party chief, who, in most
cases, subsequently assumed the government leadership as well.
The supreme leader either surrounded himself with a number of
lesser colleagues (establishing a sort of triumvirate, as in Rumania,
or in Poland where Jakob Berman and Hilary Minc were nearly
coequals to Bierut), or strictly retained the totality of power himself, though assigning important tasks to a restricted number of
associates, as Rákosi did in Hungary.

The personal character and antecedents of the holder of supreme
power were influential in determining whether and why he wished
to surround himself with the halo of a demiurge (imitating on a
more modest scale the example of Stalin), as did Rákosi, or con-
tented himself with lesser attributes, like Bierut. But no matter
who, uniquely or collectively, occupied the top leadership position
in the Party, the pretension of the Party's controlling role within
the state was studiously maintained.

In Leninist doctrine and practice the Party is the propelling
force, not the propeller itself. The Party is the spirit, the source of
political action, rather than the "secular" arm that turns policy
into practice. The Leninist political doctrine envisages the Party
as the elite, the storm troops of the working class, a group of the
enlightened and advance guard of the Communist creed, who should
not be identified with officers of administration. The role of the
Party is to be that of leading, decision-making, policy-giving, supervision, and exhortation, not execution.

However, Iosif Vissarianovich Stalin revised the Leninist doctrine
according to his own image. No longer, especially after World War
II, did the supreme Party organ or its leader, as such, control the
body politic; Stalin created the form of extra-Party rule whereby
all power was concentrated in his person — combining centralized
Party leadership, governmental control, and army command to a

degree unprecedented in history. He directed, controlled and super-vised state and Party affairs through his personal secretariat; nobody could say with certainty whether this secretariat was a Party or governmental organ. Its head, Stalin's Grey Eminence, was Lieu-tenant General Poskrebyshev,[3] who mysteriously disappeared after Stalin's death. In Stalin's last years his secretariat directed the Party (mainly through Malenkov), the government (through Molotov), and the army (perhaps through Bulganin), while the all-embracing MVD and MGB were kept busy sometimes over the head of Beria, their official leader.[4] In these years the Soviet Central Committee was never convened in plenary sessions, and the Politburo, which later became the Party Presidium, was reduced in importance by being split into various subcommittees, as we are informed by Khrushchev's secret speech at the Twentieth Party Congress.[5]

The situation in Hungary under the monocratic rule of Rákosi developed into a small-scale imitation of this procedure: all the power which was not withheld from the satrap by his foreign masters became concentrated into Rákosi's private secretariat (which being located in the central Party building could still be considered as a Party bureau). It was a matter of rather willful choice or momentary expediency as to whether instructions were sent through Party or governmental channels. By and large it may be said, how-ever, that Rákosi preferred to use the Party machinery for carrying out his orders and policies even after he had become Prime Minister, thus relegating the governmental machinery to an inferior position. The advantage gained by an overemphasized and unjustified em-ployment of the Party hierarchy to influence implementation of policy greatly widened Rákosi's capability to thwart Nagy in the execution of his New Course program.

IMPLEMENTATION OF NAGY'S PROGRAM FAILS

Imre Nagy, under the duumvirate imposed on Hungary by the Kremlin, had no means to avail himself directly of the services of the Party apparatus. He was a member of the Politburo where he was generally outnumbered by Rákosi's followers. He had no post in the Party secretariat. In the Central Committee he had to fight hard to find a majority for his projects, unless he could directly take advantage of support from Moscow. The servile group were only amenable to his proposals when they were certain that he was backed up by the Soviet leaders.

The June Resolutions had been unanimously endorsed by the Central Committee; nevertheless such a resolution was bound to remain a dead letter unless the means for its implementation were also safely secured. And they were not. To carry into effect the details of the new program, the concurrent support of both the Party apparatus and the government administration would have been necessary. The personnel changes made in the Party leadership and in government posts — at the time of Nagy's advent to the premiership — fell far short of installing a cadre ready to serve the New Course. Two top Party men, members of the "foursome," had been removed from the Politburo; but no genuine adherent of Nagy had replaced them. Nor had he any friend among the Party secretaries. Though Gerö had been made Minister of the Interior (thus able to intercede in Security Police matters), he still maintained his hold over economic affairs. The Economic Subcommittee of the Politburo (without whose consent no important economic measure could be taken) was headed by Rákosi and Gerö; the Rehabilitation Committee pertaining to treatment of political prisoners was also headed by Rákosi. The Chairman of the Planning Office after June 1953 was Béla Szalai, also one of Rákosi's creatures.

Imre Nagy, in his endeavors to implement his policies, had to rely on the governmental machinery. This apparently stood at his disposal. Even so, he was in most cases powerless to prevail against the intentional interferences of the Party machinery, a machinery which during the Stalinist era had so abundantly penetrated the governmental hierarchy. Clashes between government orders and contradictory Party instructions, clashes between government supporters of Nagy's program and Party representatives upholding the principle of Party primacy became the order of the day. These daily squabbles, penetrating to the highest strata of Party and government leadership, up to the peaks represented by Rákosi and Imre Nagy respectively, opened the way for the theoretical dispute as to the proper Party and state jurisdictions.

Rákosi quickly seized the opportunity of accusing Nagy of an anti–Marxist-Leninist offense, that of wishing to push the Party into the background, thereby reducing its role to mere servitude to the government.* The issue is recorded by Nagy:

We prescribed the relations of the Party and state on the basis of the principles worked out at the Moscow conference and laid down by the June resolution of the Central Committee. This was not very easy

* It should be remembered that similar accusations were made against Tito by the Cominform resolution of June 28, 1948, which expelled the Yugoslav Communist Party from its ranks. *Documents on International Affairs, 1947–1948* (London, 1952), pp. 390–397.

— in several respects it did not work at all — and the results achieved were soon defeated because of the resistance on the part of Mátyás Rákosi within the top leadership of the Party. It was he who from the outset saw that by regulating the Party-state relationship in the spirit of the advice given in the June resolutions and at the Moscow conference, the Party would be forced into the background and would be made subordinate to the organs of state. This is the source of the often repeated but baseless charge against me that I allegedly undervalue the leading role of the Party, and that I raise the state organs above the Party. Mátyás Rákosi considered the actions taken in the spirit of the June resolution of the Central Committee concerning the relation of Party and state to be an undervaluation of the leading role of the Party, and he could not conceive of solving the problem except in the pre-June fashion.[6]

It seems well established that Imre Nagy, in order to be able to implement a policy which had been agreed upon and which he was eager to pursue, had to undertake at least a relative emancipation of the state administration from the shackles imposed upon it by the Rákosi system of government. Nor did Nagy shrink from struggling for his thesis on an ideological basis; he was a theoretician too well trained in Marxist-Leninist dogmatism to abstain from this type of defense. When this question came up later before the Hungarian Third Party Congress in May 1954, Imre Nagy was able to hold his ground.[7]

Nagy subsequently formulated his view in the following terms:

The Party exercises direction and control over the state organs. But expropriation of the functions of state organs is incorrect and harmful, as was clearly shown by the practice prior to June, 1953. In that period, the activities and role of the Party in the area of state functions represented a swing toward degeneration of the dictatorship of the proletariat.[8]

The "degeneration of the dictatorship of the proletariat" meant, in Nagy's mind, an unnecessary acuteness of class struggle whereby the "oppressive functions" of the state were too much in the foreground, in other words, a situation where state organs, instead of remaining within the sphere and limits of their jurisdiction as prescribed by law, participated in the class struggle by means of illegal oppression.

Nagy was also able to point out that Rákosi had not always held the view which he championed at present; when he had been Prime Minister "he did not think that placing the state in the foreground was rightist deviation and an undervaluation of the role of the Party." [9]

NAGY APPLIES TO MOSCOW

The opposition of Rákosi to the program originally pronounced in Moscow, and existing differences between Nagy and Rákosi were brought before the Soviet Presidium each time that any or both of these Hungarian leaders made a pilgrimage to Moscow. In January 1954, after half a year of indecisive battle, Nagy submitted his complaints to Malenkov, the Soviet Prime Minister, who still held the position of pre-eminence in the Kremlin and professed to be his protector. He also addressed his complaints to Khrushchev, then a slowly emerging potentate in the collective leadership, and to others. He describes this episode in the following terms:

By the end of 1953 and at the beginning of 1954, it had already become evident to the Soviet comrades, too, that there was opposition to the June resolution, and for this they blamed primarily Mátyás Rákosi. Comrade Malenkov said, "The faults we noted in June are being remedied very slowly. Rákosi has not taken the lead in remedying the faults." Comrade Khrushchev also noted, "Gerö has no words of self-criticism or feeling or responsibility for the serious mistakes of the economic policy; at best he admits, 'It is possible that Comrade Nagy is right in feeling that I am held back by the old economic policy.' " [10]

It seems that as a result of his January 1954 visit to Moscow, Nagy's complaints were at least partly successful, though not to the extent of having Rákosi ousted (which must have been his main concern, although no evidence exists that such an attempt was ever made). Rákosi was evidently ordered by the Kremlin to give up his opposition to the implementation of the June Resolutions. By January 1954, Khrushchev must have been well on his way to consolidating his position as Party chief, but his opposition against Malenkov had not yet come into the open. We can therefore presume that, apart from the disappearance of Beria from the scene (which must be assessed as a negative gain for Rákosi, who thus lost his most violent critic), the attitude within the Soviet Presidium toward the Hungarian situation remained unchanged. The die-hard Stalinists must have supported Rákosi's Party leadership, whereas the others, continuing to argue that faults of the past must be eliminated, placed their confidence in the person of Imre Nagy.

Rákosi now resorted to novel tactics. He no longer openly opposed Imre Nagy, but tried instead to place devious and concealed obstacles along his way (what Nagy later called "double-dealing").[11] Since the downfall of Beria, though helpful to Rákosi, had not wrecked Imre Nagy's position, Rákosi may have resolved to follow a strategy that promised long-range results.

An excellent example of Rákosi's diminished, and of Nagy's increased, prestige within the Politburo is offered by a rare insight into that innermost sanctuary by Tamás Aczél and Tibor Méray.[12] A memorandum on the situation and tasks of Hungarian literature was twice discussed before the Politburo. At the first session Imre Nagy was absent, and the memorandum for consideration was rejected for containing elements of deviationism against the Party's supremacy in the literary field. On the second occasion, when the same memorandum with slight amendments was again discussed, Imre Nagy was present. Referring to the "new political line" of the Party and the "new program" of the government, he moved the acceptance of the memorandum. Rákosi did not dare to oppose him.[13] This happened in February 1954, shortly after Rákosi must have received the warning from Moscow.

MOSCOW RESCUES NAGY

The lull was soon broken; an all-out attack was undertaken by Rákosi against Imre Nagy prior to the Hungarian Third Party Congress which was originally scheduled for April 18, 1954. One of Rákosi's adherents, István Kovács, Party Secretary for Budapest, addressed a letter to the Central Committee for clarification of the question of unity in Party leadership. Most probably this letter was prompted by Rákosi himself. But István Kovács, a person of acute flair, did not wish to antagonize Imre Nagy (he later, though temporarily, professed to be his follower), and accordingly his letter was drafted in a noncommittal form, revealing a genuine anxiety as to the disorganization and disorder caused by the dissent of governmental and Party leadership. In the absence of Nagy, who was detained by a prolonged illness, Rákosi first had the letter discussed in the Politburo, then caused the Central Committee to pass a resolution which was detrimental to the stand taken by Nagy in this matter. This resolution must have placed the blame for disorganization on Nagy; it commented ambiguously on the role of the Party and of the government in the implementation of the principles of the New Course. This resolution could also be interpreted as a condemnation of Nagy and of his program.

Rákosi, after having successfully rallied the Central Committee, wished to visit Moscow without the company of the Prime Minister. He must have rated it a bad omen when he was refused reception without Nagy. Since Nagy was ill, the visit had to wait until his recovery in May, and the Third Party Congress in Budapest was in due course postponed to May 24.[14]

The visit to Moscow in May 1954 proved again to be a complete defeat for Rákosi. The resolution of the Central Committee, if upheld, would have sufficiently discredited Nagy as to compel his loss of the premiership. But it failed because it was not seconded by the Soviet Presidium. Rákosi's action proved to have been premature. He failed to appreciate properly the prevailing situation within the Presidium, where Malenkov's influence was not yet broken. His proceeding against the Prime Minister without prior endorsement by Moscow was the result of the cleavage prevailing within the Soviet Presidium, which thwarted its unity of vision and action and prompted faulty anticipations on the part of its provincial satraps.

We have to rely largely on Nagy's version of what happened in Moscow. But there is no reason to doubt the veracity of his narrative. Of course, we must be constantly reminded when using this source that it was constructed to refute Rákosi's contentions, to compromise his stand with the Hungarian Party leadership, and also to convince the Soviet potentates of the justice of Nagy's cause. For this last reason, Nagy rigorously refrains from any remark which might be viewed askance through Russian eyes. He also refuses to give any impression to the reader of possible dissension within the Soviet Presidium with regard to the struggle of the leadership in Hungary and its consequences. We may even take it as possible that such was the impression he received in the Kremlin; the members of the Soviet collective leadership might have thrashed out their differences prior to the arrival of the Hungarians, and having come to a decision, preferred to present a harmonious unanimity to their guests. Such was the effect of Party discipline over the members of the supreme body of world Communism.

According to Nagy's story, the Moscow Presidium blamed Rákosi for the delay in putting the affairs of Hungary in order, for the unhealthy conditions in the Party. They further exhorted the Hungarian leaders to practice intra-Party democracy and criticism, and they explained to them how to put collective leadership into practice.

Khrushchev is reputed to have said about Rákosi: "He has lost the self-confidence required to correct mistakes, and it can happen that proper leadership will come into being over his head, which is a catastrophe for a leader." Malenkov, too, according to Nagy, found "that we were slow in correcting our mistakes in Party leadership and that Rákosi, as Party First Secretary, was not doing the job well." [15] Other members of the Soviet Presidium (Nagy refrains from giving their names) commented thus on the Hungarian situation: "Comrade Rákosi must take the lead in the fight to correct previous mistakes and to implement the resolutions of the Central Committee. He must put a final end to the mistakes of the past, bravely, manfully, and like a Bolshevik. He does not have to put the blame on Beria, the international situation, or anything else. Rákosi must promote Party unity by fighting consistently against the mistakes." [16]

Members of the Soviet Presidium were ready to admonish their Hungarian partners in terms which they might have equally addressed to themselves:

Franker and more theoretical debates, Party-type criticism, and intra-Party democracy must be ensured. Lack of experience of training must not be looked down upon. Divergent opinions and possibly mistaken points of view must not be capitalized on politically to the detriment of those who hold them. There is no highest and lowest man in the Political Committee. Much more care must be devoted to the complete clarification of the principles involved in the questions. This is the only quick way to dispel the duality existing on certain points within the leadership.[17]

And they went on to point out to the Hungarian leaders:

The policy of airing grievances must be terminated, and the remnants of Führerism, of disdainful, insulting, and offensive conduct must be eliminated. The Party leadership needs Comrade Rákosi, but he must know and realize that he will have to merge into the collective leadership because that is the only way in which he can do his work.[18]

It is characteristic of the measure of Soviet penetration into the affairs of a satellite country that even such a relatively minor event as the Kovács letter did not remain unnoticed by the "Soviet comrades," who condescended to give their opinions in this matter as well. The comrades, Nagy recalled, emphasized "that Rákosi's report had side-stepped and failed to clarify the question of the unity of Party leadership." They said the debate on the Kovács letter "lacked Bolshevik frankness and got off on the wrong track, ending up as it did with a compromise of principle." They accused the Hungarian Politburo of having been "afraid to face the duality in leadership and its true cause." [19]

It was at this meeting in Moscow that Rákosi submitted before the Russian masters the argument (propounded previously in Hun-

gary) according to which he himself had been Beria's victim, and
that his partial removal from office and the rebuke he had earned
were due to false accusations fabricated by the traitorous chief of
the Secret Police. However, he had less success before his Moscow
audience than before his admirers in Budapest. Khrushchev (according to Imre Nagy) told him:

> In June, 1953, we correctly passed judgment on the Hungarian
> Party's leadership, and that judgment is still entirely correct today. They
> can't hide behind Beria as Rákosi is trying to do. We were there, too,
> when these errors were ascertained, every one of us! We were right, and
> what we decided then is also right today. This should have been acted
> upon already! [20]

Thus Rákosi's coup to have Imre Nagy defeated by the vote of
the Central Committee failed because Moscow refused to agree in
it. Ironically, Imre Nagy, the "nationalist" (as he was already considered), had to appeal to the Soviet leadership for a reversal of a
decision by a Hungarian Party organ brought about by his "internationalist" opponent. Under Moscow's pressure Rákosi had to admit that he had been regarding all issues wrongly, and had to move
the adoption of contrary resolutions by the Politburo and the
Central Committee.[21]

ON DUALISM IN HUNGARY AND IN THE SOVIET UNION

The Nagy reports relative to the meeting of May 1954 in Moscow
convey the impression that during these conversations the leading
figures on the Soviet side were Malenkov and Khrushchev. Such an
observation coincides with impressions gained by other visitors who
met Soviet leaders in the summer of 1954.[22] But a useful parallel
could hardly be drawn between the Malenkov-Khrushchev duumvirate, as it took shape after Beria's liquidation, and the dual leadership imposed upon Hungary in June 1953, which curtailed Rákosi's
monopoly of power. True, in both cases one of the leaders in the
diarchy controlled the Party bureaucracy and the other was head
of the state administration. But in Russia, the government head,
Malenkov, had been the Party chief and preserved for some time an
influence over Party personnel even while Khrushchev was bringing
the Party under his control; in Hungary the government head, Nagy,
had never controlled the Party. A parallel, however, between the
two countries with respect to the allocation of functions among
Party and government organs may be appropriate: rivalries between
competing authorities and contradictory instructions arriving either

via governmental or Party channels are presumed to have existed then in the Soviet Union, and to have extended as far as the administration of East Germany.[23]

It may be asked, why Moscow refrained from dropping Rákosi altogether in May 1954, when such an acute antagonism was felt against him by at least some members of the Presidium, and when he was judged incapable of restoring order to the affairs of Hungary. Inferences drawn from a general pattern of Soviet attitudes may be useful in answering the question.

The Soviet leadership is inclined to follow certain patterns in organizing its political structures, in planning its policies, and in its behavior. These patterns are extended to dependent countries in identical terms, irrespective of objective local characteristics or the subjective desiderata of the governed. In international politics, however, the Soviet government has often displayed versatility and a capability of divesting itself even of those natural responses imperatively prescribed by ideology (even to the extent of allying itself with Nazi Germany). Likewise, in countries where Communist parties were striving for power, the Soviet rulers (whether under the name of Comintern or Cominform) often showed aptitude for adaptability to local conditions. But all these feats of versatility and adaptability seem to have been dictated by necessity only; an accommodation to another's way of thinking never has been a strong side of the Soviet rulers. Soviet experts who studied forms of adjustment relevant in a transition period were discarded as soon as domination over a country seemed safely secured. Why strain one's knowledge and the tenets of Marxist-Leninist doctrine, why waste such energy, when it was so much easier either to have one's own system adopted or methods of general application conceived for the use of dependent countries? Standardization also served to advertise Soviet methods and Soviet thinking, and in the ethnocentric mental world of Soviet leaders, poorly informed about the non-Communist orbit as a result of the Iron Curtain, the spread of the gains of Soviet experience seemed to benefit both the receiving country and the cause of international Communism as well.

In 1954, strict Stalinist uniformity was giving way to the more general principles of conduct required of People's Democracies. These principles were demonstrated by the conduct of the heirs to Stalin's autocracy, and the law of imitation was again expected to apply. The main components were: the principle of collective leadership, the separation of governmental and Party leadership, a decompression in the use of Security Police terrorism, a softening of the foreign policy, and the lessening of emphasis laid on development of heavy industry. These lines of conduct were gradually pushed through in the satellite regimes, especially the separation of top governmental and Party offices (except where monopoly of power had never fallen into one hand). It is to be remarked, however, that no essential changes in the top personnel were required; in all satellite countries (apart from Hungary) the old Stalinist leadership continued to operate. After all, even in the Soviet Union the Stalinist old guard, except one Beria, was still on the job.

In Hungary, where monopolistic rule had sprung up in the Stalinist era and where terrorism and economic incompetence rose to heights exceeded by no other satellite regime, the masters of the Kremlin required special remedies for forestalling disaster: Rákosi was to be deprived of his omnipotence, and another person, uncompromised by Stalinist excesses and suitable as an antidote to Rákosi's megalomania, would be given the reins of government. That was how the collective leadership was supposed to operate as prescribed for Hungary. Rákosi continued to be the trusted man of confidence of most of the members of the Presidium. The excesses and mistakes he had committed were not anti-Soviet — an unpardonable sin — but only anti-Hungarian. He was a person not to be dispensed with. The fact of his frequent verbal chastisement was not necessarily a sign of nonconfidence; in the atmosphere of the Kremlin even physical "persuasion" administered to trusted comrades was not out of the question. As long as scolding and humiliation were imparted discreetly, without publicity, confidence still persisted; the comrade thus reminded of his duties was expected to correct his mistakes, abide by the instructions received, and otherwise continue "business as usual." When somebody was to be liquidated (either physically or politically), the rulers of the Soviet Union did not waste their energies in chiding and fault finding. On the other hand, a Party member could never hand in his resignation (unless required to do so). He had to obey and continue to serve, whether a member of the Soviet Party or of any other Party which recognized the supremacy of Moscow.

Rákosi must have had personal supporters in the Soviet Presidium. Imre Nagy never mentions by name Molotov or Kaganovich among those members who were foremost in denouncing Rákosi's mistakes, whereas Malenkov and Khrushchev (after Beria's disappearance) are often quoted as such. And, as we have seen, Imre Nagy also must have had his own personal supporters. A deadlock within the Soviet Presidium therefore favored the maintenance of the dualistic system whether or not it was to the eventual benefit of Hungary or conducive to an implementation of Nagy's program. The members of the Soviet Presidium might have thought that abuse poured over the head of Rákosi might still have the effect of reducing the tension between the rivals, and be helpful to Nagy in his task of carrying out the program which they themselves had proposed for Hungary.

The kaleidoscopic picture of the Soviet Presidium, as it appeared at interview after interview, must have been disconcerting to the two Hungarian rivals. Rákosi, no longer certain of his influence in Moscow, a victim of misleading information or an erroneous assessment of the Soviet Presidium's internal balance, grossly miscalculated his chances in April and May 1954. Imre Nagy, even less familiar with the ways of Moscow potentates, and inexperienced in palace intrigue, must have been confident that his arguments had finally convinced the Soviet leaders. Still, he must have been disappointed by their failure to silence Rákosi's resistance once and for all. In retrospect his outlook might seem naïve, but the encouragement which he gained by his renewed diplomatic victory over his adversary may have strengthened his belief in the righteousness of his cause and his hope in ultimate victory over the powers of evil, as represented by Rákosi and his minions. He must have felt that Rákosi had been decisively defeated and would have to give up the battle.

Rákosi, despite his premature attempt at a coup and his gross error in assessing his chances, refused to consider himself beaten. He still had a better insight into the silent struggle going on within the Soviet Presidium. He must have foreseen that eventually the balance would shift against Malenkov (the member whose policy, after Beria's fall, seems to have coincided most closely with Nagy's program). He may even have concluded that Khrushchev's actions were not ideologically founded, but were simply moves to improve his own power position. Other members of the Presidium still trusted Rákosi, and mistrusted Imre Nagy.* But, for the time being, Nagy had won the day: he had won a battle, but not the war.

---

* Eugenio Reale, the Italian Communist leader, who broke with his Party as a result of the Hungarian Revolution, gave a description of how Rákosi wished to prevent him from meeting Prime Minister Nagy in 1953 and 1954. Rákosi told Reale: "He is not a comrade in whom we have complete confidence." *The New Leader*, Sept. 1, 1958, pp. 13–15. It can hardly be assumed that Rákosi dared to make such disparaging statements before a leading foreign Communist unless assured that his view was shared by at least some of the influential Soviet leaders.

10

The Third Party Congress and
the People's Patriotic Front

/\/

"I always voted at my party's call,
And I never thought of thinking for
myself at all."
W. S. GILBERT, *H.M.S. Pinafore*

THE conversations the Hungarian leaders had in Moscow and, no doubt, the instructions received from the Soviet Presidium determined the program and the main tendencies of the Hungarian Third Party Congress at Budapest in May 1954. Despite Nagy's success in Moscow, Rákosi was by no means defeated, a fact demonstrated to his followers by the outstanding role he played during the Congress. But how could it have been otherwise? He still was the First Secretary, the head of the Party. He had only to obey Moscow's instructions, to adapt himself and his associates to the policies thus prescribed. But, he had to take pains to behave so as not to increase the prestige of the Prime Minister, his rival. As the Hungarian saying has it — the wind must be taken out of the sails. That purpose was fully achieved by Rákosi and his adherents when they delivered their speeches before the Congress.

HARMONY SEEMINGLY RE-ESTABLISHED

The main address to the Congress was given by the First Secretary and lasted five hours. This speech, while fully endorsing the principles of the New Course, enlarged especially on the "harmful effects" of some measures initiated since June 1953, such as increased "kulak influence" over individual peasants, the laxity in agricultural deliveries and also in industrial production, where the permissiveness of factory management encouraged slackness of discipline, lowering of productivity, and often resulted in the overpayment of wages. Rákosi admitted that the New Course had been made necessary by past mistakes which he enumerated without, however, mentioning personal responsibility in this regard.[1]

Rákosi's harangue was followed by the speech of Marshal K. E. Voroshilov, head of the Soviet delegation, in his capacity as member of the Soviet Presidium.* He, most significantly, praised the collective leadership as practiced in Hungary, approved its endeavors to implement the New Course, and especially pointed out the role which the private farmers were to play in the fulfillment of this policy. Supporting Rákosi's theses were Ernö Gerö, Mihály Farkas, and Márton Horváth. Violations of socialist legality and abuses committed by the security authorities were criticized by Károly Kiss, Chairman of the Central Supervisory Committee, who in the same breath inveighed against liberalism and laxity in the period after June 1953.

The participation in the debate by the Prime Minister, although attracting the greatest interest, resulted in an anti-climax: he dealt mainly with the problems of administration raised by the New Course, and he submitted to the Congress a plan of decentralization which somewhat resembled what had been done in Yugoslavia and what was to be done in the Soviet Union under the orders of Khrushchev in 1957.[2] Rákosi and other speakers had previously pointed out the low Party morale and the lack of rapport between the Party and the masses. In response to such complaints Imre Nagy hinted in his speech that a new People's Front was to be created in order to establish a close link between Party and non-Party elements, and to give the People's Democracy greater reality.

An analyst of the data submitted in various reports and speeches to the Third Congress might have found many signs of a weakening of the Party's impact on the "toiling masses," data which may explain many later significant events. The most remarkable facts were the decline in the membership of the DISZ (Federation of Working

* The importance attributed by the Soviet leaders to Party events in the People's Democracies is reflected by the choice of heads of Soviet delegations: in Voroshilov's case, the fact that he was also the Chairman of the Presidium of the Supreme Soviet (titular head of the USSR), cannot be overlooked. Prior to the Hungarian Party Congress, Mikoyan was sent to the East German Congress while Khrushchev represented the Soviet Party in Poland and Pospelov in Bulgaria.

Youth, the Hungarian *Komsomol*), and the decrease of the membership of the MNDSZ (Hungarian Women's Democratic Federation) from one million in 1952 to 560,000 in May 1954. Though the official figure on Party membership rose from 700,000 in 1951 to 810,000 in 1954, the number of candidates to the membership declined from 163,000 to 54,000 in the same period, illuminating the difficulties of recruitment and the resistance of young people to joining the Party.[3]

The Congress adopted important changes in the composition of supervisory Party organs. Though 26 of the 71 members of the Central Committee were replaced by new members, no observer could have discovered any increase in Nagy adherents in the ranks of this body. Membership of the Politburo also underwent change. Three members, István Kristoff, Rudolf Földvári, and Mihály Zsofinyecz, were dropped, and only the name of Béla Szalai, Chairman of the National Planning Office, was added. The number of the Politburo members was thus reduced from eleven to nine, the latter being identical with the Soviet Presidium membership. No improvement of the ratio of pro-Nagy members in the Politburo may be discerned as a result of this change; in fact he had no genuine adherent in this all-important body.[*]

THE LONELY MAN AT THE HELM

No attempt is known to have been made by Imre Nagy to have any of his closer associates included either into the Party secretariat, or as members of the Central Committee, not to speak of the Politburo. It is an interesting phenomenon, partly a proof of his straightforwardness, partly a measure of his political shortsightedness,[4] that the Prime Minister failed to introduce any of his collaborators into the channels of Party hierarchy. Or did he try, and was he successfully resisted by Rákosi? The evidence supports the view that Imre Nagy, during the time of his first tenure of the premiership, was rather a lonely man. Of course, many of his later friends and advisers had just left prison and were — physically and morally — in no shape to be useful. (These were: Géza Losonczy, Sándor Haraszti, Ferenc Donáth, György Heltai, György Páloczi-Horváth, and Szilárd

---

[*] The three Politburo members dropped may rightly be characterized as Rákosites, but there is no evidence that they were eliminated because they were followers of "Stalin's best Hungarian pupil." And Béla Szalai may equally well be described as Rákosite, while no adherent of Nagy was added. Thus there is no evidence that these three members were left out under the orders from Moscow, as has been proposed by Paul Kecskemeti, "Limits and Problems of Decompression: The Case of Hungary," in *The Annals*, May 1958, p. 101.

Ujhelyi.) Others, like Miklos Vásárhelyi, or former members of Populist Colleges,[5] had little opportunity except to give advice, and none of them was able to climb up the Party ladder. Nor is there any evidence that Nagy, in those days, was ready to listen to political advice offered by some of his adherents; even after his fall he estranged some of his followers by refusing to heed their lines of argument.

There were, however, a limited number of leading Party members who, temporarily at least, supported his policies. Exceptional among them, Zoltán Szántó refused to desert him later as the others did when his fall became imminent.* Szántó, an old muscovite, was Hungarian ambassador in Paris when Imre Nagy selected him to become head of the Information Office, a bureau which provided information to foreign journalists and to Hungarian missions abroad. But this office exercised no influence upon the Hungarian Press or Radio, which remained subjected to the control of Party Headquarters or the Ministry of Culture.

Mihály Farkas, formerly head of the Hungarian Army, member of Rákosi's "foursome" in the Stalinist era, had been dropped from the Politburo upon Nagy's rise to power. A muscovite, however, could not be so easily discarded. He sought help from the Soviet side, and such help was afforded him by the Soviet ambassador, Fedor Danilovich Kisselev. The ambassador pleaded with Imre Nagy to support Farkas' return to a leading post and to the Politburo; he personally wished to guarantee that Farkas not only would be willing to endorse Nagy's program, but also would become a man on whom Nagy could rely, who would represent Nagy's point of view. The Prime Minister — realizing his isolation — gave his consent, and in August 1953 Mihály Farkas was readmitted to the Politburo and made one of the secretaries of the Central Committee under the leadership of Rákosi.[6] At the Third Party Congress, Farkas advanced to the position of second Secretary under Rákosi; he was no longer in charge of military and security police matters, but rather the Politburo member who exercised control over art and literature. Thus, formally, Farkas was supposed to be a help to Nagy; subsequent events would belie this supposition.

It seems somewhat difficult to understand how, under such circumstances, without genuine support within the leading Party organs, Imre Nagy had even hoped to be able to thwart Rákosi's influence, to defeat his deadly opponent — unless it was with the

* Sándor Nográdi, Antal Apro, Árpád Kiss, Kálmán Pongrácz, and Ferenc Nezvál may be named as others who temporarily supported Nagy's policies.

help which he obtained and hoped to obtain from Moscow. He certainly failed to rally his followers, to push their elections into high Party bodies, in short, to create a faction which would be ready to sustain his policies. He discouraged those of his followers who were writers and journalists from any organized opposition against the leadership of the Party. At first he took too seriously Lenin's admonition not to form factions undermining the Party's prestige.[7] And when he might have realized the necessity for such action, it was too late: "He did not start organizing an opposition to Rákosi until he was out of power."[8]

Imre Nagy ignored the well-known political axiom that one cannot carry out an opposition policy, calculated to repair past mistakes and crimes, with the very same personnel who committed the abuses and crimes in question. Nobody can humanly be expected to implement a policy whose effect is bound to be his own exposure and condemnation. Self-criticism is one thing, but bringing about by concerted action one's own condemnation is another. Rákosi and his associates, together with the majority of *apparatchiki*, well knew that anything beyond paying lip service to the correction of past mistakes would result in the airing of so many criminal deeds that it would only end in a complete political, perhaps also physical, liquidation of those responsible. And almost everybody who had occupied a leading post had been involved. So Imre Nagy had mostly to rely for the implementation of his program on persons guided by the wire-pulling of Rákosi.[9]

Apart from sabotaging the New Course, Rákosi, together with Gerö and others, studiously endeavored to destroy the popularity of Nagy. They not only undertook to destroy his influence with the masses; his prestige within the Party leadership and in Moscow also had to be systematically undermined. Rákosi is said to have spent hours every day on the telephone talking to his adherents, mostly Party functionaries, and thus trying to strengthen their morale. He also attended Party meetings down to lower echelons (which he had carefully avoided previously) in order to secure the loyalty of the Party bureaucracy and the rank and file of the Party.[10] It is an old Communist habit to collect "charges" against others, including one's own collaborators. Charges against Imre Nagy were collected and forwarded via various channels to Moscow, or in some cases merely collected to wait for the propitious moment when they might be presented to the omnipotent leaders of the Kremlin.

It is also likely that the Prime Minister felt so intensely the lack of support within the Party that he started to seek help from other

Hungarians. As hinted by several speakers at the Third Party Congress, something was to be done to have the popular masses brought closer to the body politic, to obtain support in circles of the public wider than the Party itself. Was this the way Imre Nagy wished to disengage himself from the inimical and monopolistic influence of Party domination? Unquestionably, in initiating the People's Patriotic Front Imre Nagy intended not simply to create a propaganda machine for the Party. On the contrary, it can be established that his genuine intention was to widen the circle of people taking an active part in the affairs of state, to democratize his government, if not to liberalize it — a term not permissible in Communist parlance because it would have the connotation of wishing to introduce a multiparty system of government. But in this respect, as in others, he proved unable to carry his plans into effect.

PEOPLE'S PATRIOTIC FRONT: RIVAL OR SERVANT OF THE PARTY?

In Communist practice the attempt is frequently made to rally people, including eminently qualified and influential persons not admitted to or unwilling to join the Party, into some organization generally called a "front," whose mission is to strive for an objective vaguely described as supporting the regime for the "building of Socialism" or the "struggle for peace," or "to fight imperialism." Inert remains of former political parties are sometimes attached to the ruling Party under the scaffolding of such a front.[11]

The Hungarian Independent People's Front had been created in 1949, to include the remnants of existing political parties, under the aegis of the Hungarian Workers' (Communist) Party. This front ceased operations in 1951, thereby extinguishing even the skeleton party organizations which had aimlessly vegetated with it up to that time, though the front was briefly resuscitated for the purposes of electioneering in 1953.

Prior to the Third Party Congress, the Prime Minister submitted a plan to the Hungarian Politburo for the rejuvenation of the dormant Independent People's Front under the name of "People's Patriotic Front." The Politburo adopted the idea, but held a prolonged debate around the significant question whether the new front should grow into a mass *movement,* embracing other existing mass organizations, but not having individual membership of its own, or whether it should be shaped into a mass *organization* with both collective and individual membership. Nagy wanted it the latter way, and referred to the weighty precedent of the Bulgarian Otechestven Front. The Politburo, however, decided in a contrary manner. Its proceedings were duly reported to the Soviet Presidium and evidently obtained the Presidium's blessing.[12]

The question of the establishment of the People's Patriotic Front was to be fully discussed and resolved at the Third Party Congress. But again the Prime Minister's plans were upset. Though the idea of rejuvenating the People's Front was mentioned by Rákosi and other speakers, the question itself had not been included as an independent item on the agenda of the Congress; accordingly no individual resolution was passed which dealt *in extenso* with the formation of this organization. We must assume that this item of the agenda had been discarded so as to prevent a renewed discussion of the problem of individual membership, lest the Congress overrule the Politburo on this point.

The dispute over the character of the People's Patriotic Front appears as a typical example of how what had degenerated into a power struggle was nevertheless clothed in an ideological garment. Despite the Bulgarian precedent, Rákosi and his adherents obstinately refused to accept individual membership for the new Front, which otherwise had unanimously been approved by the Politburo. Later, on March 4, 1955, the Hungarian Central Committee charged against Nagy that "the establishment of the People's Patriotic Front initiated by our Party, was followed by rightist endeavors to suppress the significance and leading role of the Party, to turn the People's Patriotic Front into a power to supervise state- and council-organs." [13]

If individual membership had been admitted, the new front might (though not necessarily) have become an organization competing with the Party's political activity, and possibly overshadowing the Party. Whether such a scheme had been in Imre Nagy's mind, we do not know. Still, one has to presume that the conspicuous position of the front in Yugoslavia might have exercised a great attraction on him. Quite obviously, the Yugoslav precedent must have been in the mind of Rákosi and his associates as well. Despite Stalin's death and the ebbing of the anti-Yugoslav campaign by 1954, they might have remembered that part of the Cominform resolution of 1948 excommunicating the Yugoslav Party had run as follows:

The fact that in Yugoslavia it is only the People's Front which figures in the political arena, while the Party and its organizations do not appear openly before the people in its own name, not only belittles the role of the Party in political life of the country, but also undermines the Party as an independent political force, which has the task of winning the growing confidence of the people and of influencing ever broader masses of the working people . . . The leaders of the Yugoslav Communist Party are repeating the mistakes of the Russian Mensheviks regarding the dissolution of the Marxist party into a non-party, mass organization.[14]

After his downfall Imre Nagy emphatically denied having harbored any intentions such as those imputed to him by the March 4, 1955, resolution of the Central Committee. He declared that he had been ready to submit to the Politburo a resolution discarding individual membership in the People's Patriotic Front. He stressed, however, that even so his New Course was enriched by the new front, "supported by the masses."

As to the nature of membership, only a small concession was made to Imre Nagy's wishes by the Politburo in 1954. Persons of individual merit and prestige could become members of the People's Patriotic Front, *if so invited.*

The People's Patriotic Front was to be drawn into close relationship with local councils; thus the problem of decentralization raised by Imre Nagy at the Third Congress was to some extent linked up with the creation of the front. In his speech at the Congress the Prime Minister also dealt with the new front to be created. His ideas on this subject can best be interpreted on the basis of those pronouncements, which do not smack of polemic as his subsequent remarks do. He told the Congress: "It is one of the biggest tasks facing our Party to increase the power of the People's Democratic State . . . and its mass influence and respect in every direction . . . This role can only be played by the People's Front, or a movement in the nature of the People's Front." [15]

The need for the introduction of practically all elements or strata of the population into active participation in the nation's affairs (a postulate glaringly contradicting the class-war principle) was thus expressed by Nagy: "Intellectual, petty bourgeois and non-proletarian strata have a part in the building of Socialism and are active participants. Thus Socialism cannot be built without their cooperation." He said too that "even the slightest possibilities must be utilized in order that we can win over a mass of allies, no matter whether they are provisional, undecided, uncertain, or unreliable." [16]

He explained why it was necessary to establish a new front in the place of the decrepit Independent People's Front:

The mere formal existence of the Independent People's Front with its activities limited to occasional action did not at all correspond to the important mission which it would have had if it had been included into our People's Democratic system by creating the broadest popular unity and expanding the democratic basis of the proletarian dictatorship . . .

. . . a new People's Front must be established . . . and in shaping its form, a broad field must be left for the mass initiative and in reviving traditional forms, farmers' circles, readers' circles, etc. The new People's Front must be broader and more democratic than it has ever been in the past . . . a mass movement comprehending the broadest layers of the workers and popular committees in which there is a place for the trade unions, the DISZ, the MNDSZ, social organizations working in the field of science, culture, and sociology, the National Peace Council and its committees, leading personalities of the government, church, and social life, representatives from the intelligentsia, and so forth.[17]

If we take these May 1954 pronouncements *ad verbum* — and there is every reason for doing so — the following conclusions may be drawn:

(1) Imre Nagy did not wish simply to create another mouthpiece for the Communist Party by constructing the new People's Front. Although the objective of this organization was directed toward building Socialism, he maintained that Socialism cannot be built relying only on the Party (a most heretical view, indeed), and in his view the active participation of practically the whole people is indispensable for such an endeavor.

(2) In speaking of the nature and goal of the new People's Front, the Prime Minister had not stressed or even mentioned the "leading role" of the Party, as is usually done in Communist parlance under such circumstances. He had not defined what formal relationship was to exist between the Party and the People's Patriotic Front, and we have to assume that the question was left open on purpose. Of course, whatever formal relation he intended, it was the factual relation that mattered. And, again, there is no clue which can clearly enlighten us on this question.

(3) The new mass movement was to include people who were not unconditional adherents of the regime: waverers and even unreliable elements, from the regime's point of view. Is such a step not tantamount to the admission of the "enemy" into the ranks of "the builders of Socialism"?

(4) The new People's Front was planned by Imre Nagy to undertake continuous activity (like the Party) and not be restricted to occasional performances, such as elections or special campaigns (e.g., "peace campaigns").

(5) Imre Nagy also mentioned the revival of "traditional forms" of organization, like farmers' circles and readers' circles — long-

established rural groupings which had been discontinued under the Communist regime.

There is no clear-cut evidence that Imre Nagy wished to dominate the Party through this new People's Front — as he was accused of planning to do — nor can it be ascertained that his initiative ultimately aimed at the re-establishment of a multiparty system.[18] On the other hand, there is no doubt that he wished to construct outside the Party a broadly popular and democratic political organization which was to reflect the popular will. It was intended to replace the oppressive and one-sided Party dictatorship by channeling all strata of the population into a movement expressive of popular trends. How, in fact, he wished to implement his idea and how it would have operated had Imre Nagy achieved his aim, remain matter for conjecture.

Such a system of obtaining popular consensus, though neither democratic nor liberal in the Western meaning of these terms, nevertheless must have seemed intolerable to a Communist autocracy which really did not care whether it enjoyed popularity or not. The Moscow Presidium, approving a watered-down version of Nagy's original proposal, probably relied on the watchfulness of Rákosi and on his ability to keep the new People's Front under the Party's thumb. As subsequent events demonstrated, there had been hardly any risk involved in the creation of this organization as progressively shaped by Rákosi and his clique. The fact, however, that Imre Nagy was later charged with having endeavored to jeopardize the leading role of the Party sheds light on the potential danger inherent in the movement originally envisaged by the Prime Minister. It appears almost axiomatic that any opposition to a totalitarian system — failing the possibility of revolt — may be expressed only within a still permissible framework, that is, by voicing disagreement in a language adjusted to the limits of acceptance so that the real reasons of discontent and opposition remain concealed. The People's Patriotic Front, as it eventually evolved, proved inadequate for an expression of disguised opposition. It will be seen that other approved bodies subsequently served as mouthpieces for the expression of concealed antagonisms.

After the Third Party Congress a conference was convoked on August 12, 1954, in the Parliament building in Budapest. Rákosi and Imre Nagy were present. Most of the participants were influential persons outside the Party. There were many fellow travelers and peace priests, but there were also bishops of various confessions, academicians, literary people, artists, and so on. The conference entrusted a committee of nine (including Rákosi) with the drafting of the statutes of the People's Patriotic Front. The front itself was formally inaugurated on October 24.

Whatever Nagy's intention might have been in creating the People's Patriotic Front, it was turned by his successors into a propaganda machine of the Communist Party — which Nagy at all pains wished to avoid — and no one was misled by it. The People's Front was to play a limited role during the Revolution of 1956, but was being used again as an electioneering gimmick by the Kádár regime at the elections of 1959.

11

Economic Problems of the New Course

/\/

Vincere scis, Hannibal, victoria uti nescis.
You know, Hannibal, how to gain a victory, but not how to use it.

PLUTARCH

THE clandestine struggle between Rákosi and Imre Nagy continued unabated after the Third Party Congress; another clash was likely to occur at the October 1954 meeting of the Central Committee. During that summer the rivalry seemed to have shifted to the economic field of battle.

At the June 1953 meeting in Moscow, Rákosi had been blamed for his mismanagement of the Hungarian economy. He practiced self-criticism there, and admitted that corrections would have to be made. Up to that date Rákosi and the chief economic minister, Gerö, had been rather critical of the economic achievements of the past; they wished to enforce a faster tempo of industrialization and demanded even greater sacrifices from the toilers. When their economic management was violently criticized by the masters of the Kremlin, their attitude changed. Having admitted their mistakes, they started to praise previous achievements of the Hungarian economy so as to provide themselves with an *ex post facto* justification for their actions.[1] Furthermore they wished to demonstrate by all means that the new Prime Minister could not be more successful than they in manipulating the nation's economy.

AGRICULTURE — NAGY'S "OPPORTUNISM" JUSTIFIED

Agriculture was an especially touchy field in the altercations between Imre Nagy and the First Secretary of the Party. We have previously seen how precarious the condition of agriculture was when Nagy took over the governmental leadership. The June Resolutions of the Party's Central Committee in 1953 gave pointed satisfaction to him with regard to the stand he had taken on the question of forced collectivization. The pertinent part of the resolution ran as follows: "The exaggerated tempo of socialization in agriculture was an error aggravated by the fact that within the Party Comrade Imre Nagy opposed this policy, but instead of adopting these views the Party leadership improperly called them 'opportunist' and subjected Comrade Nagy to Party discipline." [2]

We have mentioned that in his inaugural speech of July 4, 1953, Nagy gave special assurances to the peasants that they would not be forced into collectives any longer and could even abandon existing cooperatives. He also promised a reduction of taxes and of delivery quota obligations. All this was necessitated by the catastrophic situation of agriculture in both Socialist and private sectors. The new Prime Minister's announcements relied on the Central Committee's June Resolutions which had carried out the "advice" of Moscow. Nagy wrote later:

> The conclusions of the Central Committee's June resolution dealing with farm cooperatives and the advice of the Soviet comrades proved correct and were direct consequences of the brutal and widespread violation of the principle of free choice for the sake of exaggerated collectivization by intimidation and financial pressure (taxes, crop requisitions, etc.), and by the application of punishments and other lawless procedures, in the course of which dissatisfaction in the villages flared high, and hundreds upon hundreds of unviable farm cooperatives came into existence wherein the forcibly recruited members simply did not work.[3]

As a result of the Prime Minister's speech, about half of the farm cooperatives, not waiting until the end of the harvest, dissolved at once, and the peasants redistributed the land among themselves.

It was mainly against the voluntary disbandment of these kolkhozes that Rákosi inveighed in his speech (July 11, 1953), which had the effect of a wet blanket on the enthusiasm created by Nagy's announcements. The adherents of Rákosi blamed Nagy for the loss of prestige which the Party was suffering in the villages. Nagy was able to point out that "the above directive with reference to the cooperatives [i.e., their disbanding] did not get into the Central Committee's resolution by accident but was proposed by the Soviet comrades." [4] He also informs us that the Hungarians explicitly obeyed Soviet orders when they allowed farmers to leave the kolkhozes:

the fact is that when we expressed some anxiety concerning the question of the farm cooperatives at the June, 1953, Moscow conference, Comrade Molotov (and not Beria) reassured us as follows: "The farm cooperatives must not be disbanded by fiat, but, should they choose to disband voluntarily they shouldn't be hindered. No harm will come of it." Thus, and for this reason, did the June resolution provide for the free disbandment of cooperatives.[5]

A decree providing for a more orderly procedure in the withdrawal from cooperatives was issued in October 1953. All in all 250,000 members withdrew. During 1954 and even more in 1955, new attempts were made to induce peasants to rejoin the kolkhozes, but with meagre results. Toward the end of 1954, the living standard of members of cooperatives was, on the whole, lower than that of independent peasants.[6] Of course, the members had to work less — an attraction for those lacking ambition.

IMPLEMENTATION OF THE ECONOMIC PROGRAM

At the end of October 1953, three months after the initiation of the New Course, the Central Committee met to review the economic program. Rákosi gave a report on economic developments. He stated that the chief aim of the new economic policy was to effect a real improvement in the people's standard of living, while socialist construction still remained the Party's basic objective. Accordingly, the pace of industrialization had to be slowed down, and the principal problem for the coming years was the development of agriculture. Rákosi thus gave a fair interpretation of the policy, though he stressed that the measures discussed did not imply the beginning of a program similar to the Soviet NEP (New Economic Policy), but only the correction of errors committed previously. The country had moved "into a new phase of socialist construction" and nobody should be misled into thinking that this was "a policy of renunciation or of deviation from the true line of protecting Socialism." [7]

Nevertheless, the Central Committee, acting "in the spirit of the June resolution," proceeded to summarize the major tasks of the new economic policy in the following words:

In the future, the primary goal of our economic policy will be to raise constantly and considerably the standard of living of the people, especially that of the working class; to improve the social and cultural situation of the workers; and to continue at a slower pace the socialist policy of industrialization, which will remain the main line of our Party. In accordance with this, the pace of industrialization must be retarded, especially the pace in the development of heavy industry, and plans for economic development as well as relevant investments must be reviewed. On the other hand, investments in agriculture must be raised, and agricultural production and yield must be increased, including that of the independent peasants. The numerical increase of the producer co-operatives must be slowed down.[8]

Nagy's difficulties in implementing his economic program were by no means smaller than those of carrying his general political aims into effect. The chief directing agency for the Hungarian national economy remained the Economic Policy Committee of the Party. This Committee worked out the main directives of the economic policy and passed them on to the various sections of the Party secretariat which in turn ultimately conveyed them to the corresponding economic ministries for implementation. Ernö Gerö, despite his assumption of the portfolio of the Interior, remained First Deputy Prime Minister and Chairman of the Economic Policy Committee of the Party. In this latter post he was assisted by István Friss, the chief economic expert of the Party. Both Gerö and Friss were Rákosi's collaborators.

Accordingly, implementation of the Prime Minister's economic policy depended on Rákosi's two aides (that is, on Rákosi himself), and Rákosi and his associates were able to thwart or sidetrack measures aimed at carrying out the program of the New Course. Thus, in his main field of endeavor — the economic front — the Prime Minister was least successful, because operations were directed not by himself but, through circuitous Party channels, by Rákosi and Gerö. In preventing the New Course from attaining its principal aim, the raising of the standard of living, they pursued a double goal: they wished to demonstrate the accuracy of their prior economic policy (or rather to demonstrate the absence of any basic mistake of miscalculation) and they endeavored to destroy the dangerous popularity Imre Nagy enjoyed with the masses of the population.

Nagy's efforts were concentrated on introducing "proper ratios between production, consumption, and accumulation," ratios utterly upset in the Stalinist era. On January 23, 1954, before the National Assembly he made the following statement:

Economic planning, in its broader aspects, has to determine the outline and details of the government's economic policy activities for 1954. The mistakes of the past have to be eliminated; plans have to be made on a more secure basis and more realistically, because we cannot afford to repeat the mistakes of the past. With scientific foresight that will prevent any upsets in the national economy, we must plan those far-reaching changes that are necessary to correct the mistakes of the past.[9]

Though during 1954 the New Course succeeded in raising the average standard of living of industrial workers by 15 per cent, Nagy was immediately blamed for having departed from sound economic policy by giving "advance payments" to workers, payments which had not been earned by increased production. Within the Party a cry was raised by the Rákosi clique against the Prime Minister for extravagance in expenditure and promoting slackness in industry. Imre Nagy, in reply, pointed out that the increase of salaries (which resulted in the raising of the standard of living) was long overdue, and was to be considered as a "debt" incurred before his taking office in 1953. In his view, the "left-wingers," as he pleased to style Rákosi and associates, had promised a much greater rise in the living standard for 1950–51, a promise never implemented.[10]

For 1954, the industrial targets of the Five-Year Plan (this was the last year of the plan) had been somewhat reduced, especially those of heavy industry. Even the reduced goals were not attained — either in production or productivity.[11] The general industrial production, which was to reach 310 per cent (the 1949 level being equal to 100) at the end of the plan according to the increased 1951 version, was reduced to 265 under the New Course, and officially reached 258 per cent. The target for heavy industry, which was reduced from 380 per cent to 315 per cent under Imre Nagy's administration, was announced to have attained 288 per cent.[12] Thus ended the Five-Year Plan. For 1955 only a One-Year Plan was adopted, with notable emphasis on an increase in consumer goods. After Nagy's fall, in April 1955, this plan, already in operation, was revised and targets for heavy industry were again increased. All these oscillations took their toll in waste of wealth and human labor.

BUDGET CUTS AS A LEVER AGAINST NAGY

Imre Nagy must have known how industrial workers had been harassed by unattainable production norms, labor competitions, "voluntary" campaigns involving longer working hours, "voluntary" peace loans, and other means of exploitation during the Stalinist period. As a natural reaction, after the inauguration of the New Course, productivity decreased in proportion with the reduction of pressures against the working population.

The campaign of the Rákosi group against dangers of inflation, the decrease in productivity and output, and the extravagant mode of living of the workers — as the very modest increase in the standard of living was described — was not restricted to critical outbursts. During the summer of 1954 the Economic Policy Committee under Gerö adopted (and even undertook to implement) a number of resolutions which attempted to remedy the economic situation by introducing cuts, totaling about 2 billion forints for the year 1955, in economic, social, and cultural expenditure. These measures, according to Nagy, included reductions in social insurance, factory canteens, sports programs, day homes, and nurseries. The Committee also proposed tax increases, mainly on individual peasants, and higher tax allotments on municipalities to the benefit of the state.[13] In order to re-establish discipline and increased productivity in industry, Rákosi suggested a "humanitarian" remedy: that "artificial unemployment" be created to spread awe among the employed, leading them to increase their efforts so as not to be turned out of work.*

In fact, these measures were old-fashioned capitalistic methods for solving inflationary evils and for re-establishing budgetary equilibrium. If implemented, they would have largely upset Nagy's endeavors to raise the standard of living and would have brought the Prime Minister and his ideas into disrepute before the people. The pressure against the workers envisaged by the Rákosi clique would have been tantamount to a return of the Stalinist methods. It is to be doubted whether these measures would have been appropriate for increasing production, and even if they had solved the toughest problems of national economy, one must ask: at what price?

The Prime Minister had left early in that summer (1954) for a long vacation in the Soviet Union. He stayed mostly in the Crimea, but also went for an "unofficial" visit to Moscow. During his prolonged absence Rákosi and his camp prepared their new onslaught. Economic difficulties (exaggerated both by Rákosi's followers and surreptitiously by the enemies of the Communist regime), together with rumors of restrictive measures, discouraged adherents of the New Course and simultaneously emboldened Stalinists throughout the Party network. The impression was created that most of the

---

* There was widespread unemployment already, under the New Course, as a natural consequence of industrial reorganizations, technological change, and decentralization in industry. The government had to allocate unemployment benefits — a thing unheard of in a Socialist country — and the man in the street was heard asking: "What sort of Socialism is it where dismissals can occur?" See *Free Europe Press*, Research Report 19, p. 1.

promises made under the June 1953 program were to be repudiated.[14]

Before Nagy's return in September, the Politburo had approved a report endorsing the harsh deflationary economic measures that had been proposed by the Economic Policy Committee. This report had a general anti–New Course tendency. That was the state of affairs when the Prime Minister returned from his vacation, once more reassured and armed with the solid conviction that he possessed the full confidence of the Moscow Presidium.

NAGY'S PYRRHIC VICTORY

The Prime Minister, as soon as he was informed of the economic improvement plan submitted by Gerö and approved by the Politburo, stubbornly opposed it. He also fought against any "administrative" methods to increase labor productivity. He wrote about these happenings in the following terms:

Charges must be brought against those — and the extent of their responsibility must be established — who are trying to increase labor productivity even today, not through technical improvement but primarily by administrative methods. Such a course is unpardonable under the conditions of socialist building, and it only introduces capitalist methods in labor productivity and production cost cuts. Leading Party circles are familiar with Mátyás Rákosi's views, which he has repeatedly expressed since June, 1953, and has tried to incorporate in our economic policy, according to which an artificial unemployment had to be created in our industry, which he claimed was the most effective method to improve labor discipline and to increase productivity.[15]

The battle was fought in the plenum of the Central Committee in its session from October 1 to 3, 1954. A reversal of the anti-Nagy trend, a reversal clearly inspired by the conviction that Nagy had obtained renewed approval in Moscow, was perceptible in the press from the middle of September on. Full emphasis was again laid on the implementation of the New Course. Another convincing sign of Moscow's approval of Nagy's stand was Gerö's hurried departure for a vacation.[16]

Imre Nagy's speech before the Central Committee plenum was an outstanding success. This time, his presentation overshadowed Rákosi's lukewarm and hesitant report. Only István Friss, the co-author of the repressive economic plan, stood up for Rákosi's ideas. Under the impact of Nagy's speech the Politburo report was quietly dropped. The Prime Minister spoke up against the opponents of the New Course, against "leftism" and "sectarianism." Since evidently Nagy had Moscow's backing, the members of the Central Committee acclaimed him and pledged their support for the implementation of the objectives of the New Course.[17] The Central Committee's resolution contained a scathing rebuke of those Party elements who opposed the New Course, that is, Rákosi and his group, without, however, calling them by name. These were the "elements clinging to old false ideas," "left-wingers" with a "narrow-minded and sectarian" attitude.[18] The *Szabad Nép* reported that the Central Committee had taken a determined stand against those Party elements who believed that "the Party and Government have advanced too rapidly in the direction of raising the standard of living." [19] The resolution stated that "all opposition against the policy of the New Course not only hinders a solution of our transitory difficulties, but therein lies the main source of the difficulties themselves. Our Party has to conduct a most energetic struggle against any expression of opposition, because these deeply hurt the interests of the working class and of the people as a whole." [20]

Nagy's success before the Central Committee marked the apogee of his first tenure of the premiership. His firm stand and victory rallied a number of important Party leaders to his camp. Rákosites such as Andor Berei, Márton Horváth (the *Szabad Nép* editor), István Kovács (the Budapest Party Secretary), and even Zoltán Vas (a former fellow prisoner of Rákosi) were ready, for the time being at least, to follow his lead. Most of the influential journalists, on the staff of the *Szabad Nép* and elsewhere, and the majority of Communist writers and artists stood up for him against the Politburo report, and even assisted Nagy in drafting the Central Committee's resolution. In the editorial office of the *Szabad Nép* the dissent with Rákosi's line of policy was marked by what can aptly be styled a revolt of the staff. They refused to submit to the Party censorship which compelled them to refrain from writing the unpolluted truth and from taking sides against leading Party members who had been guilty of crimes and mistakes. They wished to assist Imre Nagy in his struggle against Rákosi and associates, a struggle which slowly became known to even wider circles of Party membership.[21]

In that month of October 1954, the split within the Party between adherents of Nagy and those of Rákosi was more conspicuous than ever before. The Party leadership was mostly opposed to the Prime Minister, but the lower echelons and the rank and file of the Party sided with him. At that moment he still seemed to possess the confidence of Moscow, and the Rákosi group had been severely mauled by the condemnatory resolution of the Central Committee. It may be asked why Imre Nagy did not pursue his victory in trying to unsaddle if not Rákosi himself, at least some of his fiercest opponents. Surely he might have rid himself of Ernö Gerö, the chief author of the repressive Politburo resolution and chief lieutenant of Rákosi. Gerö and other Party leaders were violently attacked in Party meetings of the journalists and writers. But the only change was that Béla Szalai was removed from the chairmanship of the Planning Office, and replaced by Andor Berei.

The reasons why Imre Nagy refused or was unable to exploit his victory are manifold. He was unconscious of the role which he played in the eyes of not only his followers, but also of practically the whole country. Through modesty he refused to admit that he was regarded by his Party adherents as the anti-Stalinist leader par excellence, the man who could achieve Socialism without violence and by combining it with real democracy. He was even less aware that the large masses of Hungarians were ready to ascribe intentions and characteristics to him which he was far from possessing. He had felt neither a dedication nor a vocation to redeem his country from the Soviet-Communist yoke; he was only ready to fight for his ideals, Communist-Socialist ideals interwoven with streaks of humanitarianism and a sense of democracy. He was ready to attribute similar intentions to the successors of Stalin, and thus he readily cooperated with them, followed their lead — even obeyed them, because he still trusted them.

He had become a leader, a national leader, not because he strove for such a role or had felt a vocation for it. He had become a leader by necessity, by the force of circumstances, because he was considered the embodiment of ideas which could be ascribed to him alone. But he was not aware of his exalted status, of his own incarnation as a depository of hopes and ideas. That is why he appeared passive in the eyes of his followers when they wanted him to be active. He was not the hero-leader that many who knew him and even more who never met him imagined him to be. He was no plotter — and only in conspiring, as his opponents did, could he have attained an ascendancy within the Party over his enemies. He had neither the inclination nor the aptitude to organize his camp, to surround himself with disciples, recruit others, and intimidate the foe. He was rather a teacher than a statesman, an apostle of his ideas, and not a revolutionary conspirator.

It is not suggested here that Nagy would have been successful if he possessed the faculties which would have enabled him to become a real leader, a man of action with conspiratorial zeal. The Party leadership, or even all his genuine admirers, probably would not have agreed to the only measures that could have assured him victory. The removal of Rákosi and his clique would have seemed to most of them at that time an unacceptably radical step. The Hungarian Central Committee members, the *apparatchiki,* and the heads of the armed forces, kept a perpetual eye on Moscow. Their reactions, their approval of Nagy or their disapproval, hinged mostly on the impression these servile souls gained when crystal-gazing into the Kremlin's real or anticipated line of action. A complete victory for Nagy would have presupposed the complete approval of the Soviet leadership for the measures assuring and perpetuating his triumph. There was no such approval available at any time, neither before October nor after.

Thus Imre Nagy's success proved to be a Pyrrhic victory. He was not in the position, either subjectively or under prevailing objective circumstances, to fully exploit his success. Rákosi was still the outstanding leader of the Party despite the discomfiture he had to undergo. He was still a formidable opponent.

Furthermore there was another economic field in which Nagy utterly failed — the field of foreign trade. Here the Prime Minister's responsibility was rather remote; yet in this very field is to be found one of the immediate reasons for his coming eclipse.

FOREIGN TRADE FIASCO

An exaggerated industrialization, uneconomic management of investments, massive importation of military equipment, and the disadvantageous trade agreements with the Soviet Union — these and other methods of Soviet exploitation had left Hungary heavily indebted at the outset of the New Course. Thus, the Imre Nagy administration also inherited a heavy liability in this field. By 1954, the effects of such past mismanagement not only did not disappear, but even were aggravated by the interplay of various factors: the tentative reconversion from heavy industry into a greater production of consumer goods, unsuccessful endeavors to rid the country of unequal trade agreements, and lastly, the resistance of Rákosi and his group against the implementation of the new government economic policy. A considerable part of the indebtedness was due to importation of military equipment, that is, deliveries of an unproductive character. Using guarded language (Soviet trade policy being involved), Nagy later described the situation he had to face in the following terms:

The serious consequences of an erroneous and harmful economic policy that has been pursued for years cannot be eliminated in eighteen months, especially when the government's new corrective economic policy is resisted to a great extent. Not only internal, but much more powerful external forces and factors exerted a harmful influence, especially in the field of foreign trade agreements; this made it all but impossible to overcome the difficulties. Since it is a state secret, I will give no figures and be brief, but it must be pointed out that a considerable part of our foreign debt derives from expenditures and investments for security and defense, which place a heavy load on our foreign trade balance. The June, 1953, resolution pointed out that there were excesses in this field also.[22]

It is not difficult to guess what the "more powerful external forces and factors" were that exerted a harmful influence on the country's foreign trade balance. Unfortunately, that portion of the June Resolutions which dealt with the "excesses" aggravating Hungary's indebtedness is unknown to us; but as for the resistance placed on the road of the new corrective economic policy of the government, the circumstances may fairly well be reconstructed.

The Prime Minister's ability to exercise even less influence over foreign trade than over other economic affairs was due partly to the close Party control of this field and partly to the fact that foreign trade, being closely allied to Soviet interests, was surrounded with great mystery, impenetrable to the uninitiated. (In Soviet practice foreign trade is one of the *arcana imperii,* subject to particular secrecy.) The lamentable position in which the Prime Minister of a Communist country, devoid of decision and implementation in the vital field of foreign trade, found himself is thus presented to us in a pathetically candid manner by Imre Nagy:

our economic policy, including our foreign trade, was directed by the Party, and every new foreign credit action had to be carried out on the basis of Party resolutions. And finally, I cannot be held accountable because, within the Council of Ministers, foreign trade was not under my direction but under the supervision and direction of Ernö Gerö, First Deputy Premier. As far as actual responsibility is concerned, it must be asserted that all important foreign trade resolutions — such as those concerning trade and pay agreements, credits, export-import-plans, foreign exchange management, and long-term contracts and their terms — were made on the basis of the decision of, and in entire agreement with, the Political Committee. After the questions had been debated, the decisions were pronounced by First Party Secretary Mátyás Rákosi, who presided over the meetings of the Political Committee. In not a single instance did the Political Committee's decision concerning any question related to foreign trade run counter to, or fail to agree with, the opinion of Mátyás Rákosi. So, if certain persons want to blame any one person, they can and must blame Mátyás Rákosi, who as Party First Secretary and leader of the Party directed economic policy as he directed all aspects of the implementation of the Party's leading role. Furthermore, since Rákosi considered foreign trade his special field, he kept it under his immediate direction.[23]

A transformation from heavy industrialization to the greater production of consumer goods, as envisaged by the New Course, would have necessitated new investments and the importation of new machinery. For such reconversion, new capital and new credits for financing importations were badly needed. They proved to be unobtainable equally from the East and from the West.

The imbalance in foreign trade presented particularly acute problems in the period between November 1954 and January 1955. It became difficult to obtain necessary materials on a credit basis and consequently to continue the realignment of production. Badly needed imports had to be reduced for lack of foreign currency and credits. A huge credit transaction could have materially eased the situation by rendering a large-scale reconversion of industry possible while permitting a simultaneous and regular inflow of foreign commodities and raw materials. The Western market was chary of participating in such an operation; the export of some basic metallurgical materials to Hungary from the West was prohibited under the cooperative trade controls of Western governments, even if foreign exchange had been available for such purposes.

As for the East, an unexpected blow was struck against the economic policy of the New Course by the Soviet Union, when it suddenly revealed that its deliveries of essential raw products in 1955 would be only half those in 1954. Similar retrenchment was being exercised by other countries of the Soviet bloc in their foreign trade relations with Hungary.[24] It may be asked whether this was a deliberate policy directed against Imre Nagy's person; but nothing indicates that the Soviet government had to resort to such measures if it wished to bring pressure on Hungary. Instead it is likely that the Russians' decision to restrict credits was due to the uncertainty of their economic and foreign trade planning. They had come to the end of their most recent Five-Year Plan in 1955, and their new plan was under discussion; also the forthcoming changes in Soviet leadership augured a cautious trade policy. And the satellite governments simply echoed the Soviet example. Thus the blow which Imre Nagy received from the Communist governments as he tried to remedy an adverse trade position happened to be just a coincidence; nevertheless, it was a coincidence which greatly worsened the predicament in which he found himself.

Under the impact of the refusal by Soviet and other Communist countries to extend credits, the Prime Minister decided to renew a bid for credits from Western countries. Whether these overtures ever reached the Western governments is not known. But in any case, according to Nagy, the attempt met the open hostility of Rákosi and his colleagues, and we may assume that Soviet leadership was swiftly informed about the Prime Minister's intention to improve the foreign trade situation by asking help from capitalist countries.[25] It would be excessive to attribute Nagy's fall to this intended action. Yet, considering the touchiness of the Soviet leadership ever since their refusal to participate in the Marshall Plan and their interdiction of such participation by the satellite governments, such a step undertaken without their prior approval must have added to his guilt in the eyes of some members of the Soviet Presidium.

Unable to find room for maneuver in approaching the West, the initiator of the New Course turned again toward the Soviet Union and to other satellite countries for support in January 1955. However, the Soviet Union was still unwilling to guarantee more than 50 per cent of the 1954 volume of materials. All this happened after the Hungarian government had included in its foreign trade estimate an increase of Soviet importations and of credits. Poland and Rumania likewise wished to reduce their raw material exports to Hungary, and insisted that Hungary supply certain goods obtainable only from the West (e.g., ball bearings, silicates), in exchange for certain valuable materials solicited from them.

At the end of 1954 and the beginning of 1955, much confusion appeared to have existed in the trade relations among the countries of the Soviet bloc. Despite extensive planning, no coordination was apparent; the CEMA vegetated and indeed existed only on paper. How could it otherwise occur that the Hungarian Politburo directed its government to increase foreign trade with the Socialist camp, and released for this purpose an additional billion forints? At the same time, as we have seen, the Soviet Union, and at least two other People's Democracies, the most important suppliers of raw materials to Hungary, "planned" to reduce considerably the volume of their trade with their fellow planner.

When Imre Nagy was ousted from his post of Prime Minister, the foreign trade situation was as bad as when he had first advanced his ambitious program. Later he admitted to a "share in the collective responsibility that falls upon the Party and the leading government organs for having been unable to overcome the serious consequences of the harmful economic policy practiced by the Party and the government under the direction of Mátyás Rákosi during the First Five-Year Plan." [26] Clearly the main reason for this failure was that Rákosi had never lost his grip on the reins.

Nothing is more illustrative of Rákosi's preponderance in power than the fact that in spite of his recurrent defeats before the Soviet Presidium and in the Hungarian Central Committee, he still was able to prevent the Prime Minister from putting into effect an all-important item of his program, the solution of the problem of political prisoners. This question of crucial significance — for it subsequently proved to be one — was fraught with ominous implications for the Communist Party of Hungary and for the history of the country itself.

12

Political Prisoners— Liability and Peril

∧∧∧∧∧∧∧∧∧∧∧∧∧∧∧∧∧∧∧∧∧∧∧∧

Will all great Neptune's ocean wash this blood
Clean from my hand? No, this my hand will rather
The multitudinous seas incarnadine,
Making the green one red.

MACBETH

In the spring of 1953, when Stalin died and Rákosi was still at the height of his power, prisons and internment camps were crowded with tens of thousands of political prisoners. These captives had undergone months of torture in the cellars of the AVH and had been either delivered to humiliating mock trials or sent by administrative orders straight to one of the many internment or labor camps, to rot there without any time limit or possibility of appeal. The prisoners who escaped the death sentence considered themselves lucky, for many did not. Those who did found themselves in a prison where — as in the internment and labor camps — they had to live under a regime of harsh treatment, renewed beatings, and often inedible food, and where few could expect to survive for a protracted period.

In the Stalinist era Mátyás Rákosi and the Lieutenant General of the AVH, Gábor Péter, violated not only justice but also the elementary principles of political prudence when ordering the arrest, torture, and execution or imprisonment of tens of thousands of people, irrespective of their objective or subjective guilt, their responsibility for acts ascribed to them, or even the existence of the crime allegedly committed. A doctrine of guilt by assumption had even been worked out by Vilmos Olti, the principal Judge Jeffreys of the Hungarian bloody assizes, as a means of incriminating persons without factual evidence.

All strata of the population and all political creeds were involved in these purges. In the prisons and internment camps former government officials, officers, ex-Nazis, and war criminals were crowded together with genuine Communists, Social Democrats (whether or not they had joined the Communist Party), leaders of former political parties, industrial workers, former big landholders, kulaks, priests, students, members of intellectual professions, all types of Yugoslavs (anti-Tito or pro-Tito), foreign citizens (Communists or not), males and females, and even adolescents. Their numbers did not reflect the general character of the total population, for the more intelligent, influential, and talented people — workers, students, farmers, and professional people — comprised the bulk of inmates.

ATTEMPT TO RESTORE LEGALITY

When Imre Nagy took over the reins of government, he gave an assurance that arbitrary arrests would be stopped, internment camps dissolved, "law and order restored," and unjustly sentenced persons rehabilitated.[1] However, the question of political prisoners proved to be a much tougher problem for the new Prime Minister than he had originally believed. Going into the matter more thoroughly, he found to what extent Rákosi and his accomplices had abused their unlimited powers in dealing with the liberty, life, and human dignity of such a great number of people, including many faithful Party members. These facts were generally known by the public, but ignored by the higher echelons of the Party.[2]

The problem of political prisoners had a much wider and deeper significance in Hungary than in any other Communist country, even including the Soviet Union. In the years since World War II the ruthlessness and cruelty of treatment, the number of persons and families involved relative to the population as a whole, the irrationality[3] of such conduct (e.g., imprisonment or execution of enthusiastic Party members) were nowhere so conspicuous as in Hungary. The impact of these events on subsequent political developments was so outstanding that it would be difficult to overemphasize their significance. Even if we assume that the mass imprisonments, labor camps, and deportations in the Soviet Union affected a proportionately equal or greater number of individuals and families, the difference in personal outlook and traditions of civilization has also to be taken into account. It is not suggested here that the monstrous feats of Stalinist dictatorship were acceptable or tolerable to the average Soviet citizen; but the greater impact on Hungarians and members of traditionally Western civilizations is to be underscored.[4]

In the ministerial shuffle after the Central Committee session of June 1953, the Rákosi group, the official policy of the Party notwithstanding, maintained their control over the fate of the political prisoners. Whether the appointment of Gerö, Rákosi's first deputy, as Minister of the Interior was accomplished under instructions by Moscow is not known. But it had probably been a condition set by Rákosi that the key post of the Interior, including jurisdiction over police and Security Police matters, be bestowed upon his reliable adjutant.

By the end of August 1953, the internment and the labor camps were indeed closed, though not without the pressing of many hundreds of their inmates into confessions so as to make possible their speedy condemnation by special People's Courts sitting within the precincts of the camps — a fact not reported by any of the commentators on the dissolution of internment camps under Imre Nagy. These victims were added to the already overcrowded prison population.

The Prime Minister was also successful in alleviating the treatment of political convicts. After July, the hitherto neglected prison regulations were slowly put into application again in the political prisons, and many abuses, such as the use of iron shackles or systematic beatings, were brought to an end. In November 1953, political prisoners were allowed to write to their relatives, and short visits to the prisoners were also permitted.[5] But the retrial or reconsideration of cases, as heralded by the Prime Minister, failed to take place.

Imre Nagy's endeavors to restore legality, including the release of innocent purge victims, give every appearance of sincerity; therefore, it seems somewhat difficult to understand why the Prime Minister could not carry out his objectives in this respect, objectives included in the program approved by the Party and the National Assembly, and also by Moscow. Again one has to recall the extreme delicacy and hazard involved. The fate of so many thousands of persons, sentenced on concocted charges or in flagrant violation of procedural rules, became a threatening liability to the Party and to the whole Communist system in Hungary. The misdeeds of Rákosi and his accomplices would have necessarily been unmasked by released prisoners (many of them former Party members, influential workers and intellectuals), and the retrials, even when held *in camera,* would have revealed the depravity prevailing within the Security Police (supported and condoned by Rákosi and his friends). An avalanche of accusations and impeachments against the Party leadership, the Security Police personnel, and the judiciary would have been inevitable. Such a course would have been a revolutionary act, and revolutions are never initiated and carried out by those against whom they are to be directed.

Of course, the Party might have avoided some scandal by releasing political prisoners without retrials, under a general amnesty. But such a measure would have had the effect of indiscriminately opening the gates of prisons, and its impact would have been equally disastrous. The amnesty decreed on July 26, 1953, commuted only short sentences, and hardly touched the hard core of thousands of political convicts.

THE REHABILITATION COMMITTEE AT WORK

The importance of the problem of political prisoners was acknowledged by the Party itself when it created a special Rehabilitation Committee to study the question and evidently also to select prisoners to be "rehabilitated." It is known that Prime Minister Nagy, and also Rákosi and Gerö, had been members of this Party Committee; Erik Molnár, the Minister of Justice, also participated in its work. The Committee was to decide whether group retrials or only individual revisions of cases should take place. It was also to recommend procedures to be followed when the selected prisoners were to be released, and how the prosecutors and judges were to operate.

Rákosi and his associates were able to prevent rehabilitations, even of faithful Party members, for over a whole year. Representatives of the Security Police must also have fought hard against Imre Nagy's endeavors to proceed in this matter. Although a vital issue was involved, the Prime Minister proved totally helpless. Was it because in this field he could not rely on the wholehearted support of the Soviet leaders? The close collaboration existing between the Soviet Security authorities and the Hungarian AVH has been described in an earlier chapter. It would seem well founded to attribute greatest responsibility for the delay to the interference or influence of the Soviet leadership, an influence welcomed by Rákosi and the Hungarian Security authorities.

But this neglect and delay on a subject requiring such urgency had further disastrous effects on public sentiment and greatly increased the pressures between various fractions of the Party. Imre Nagy, very outspoken in this respect, bequeaths us the opinion that it would have been far better to attend to the problems in the autumn of 1953 instead of continually deferring them, "as this caused serious uncertainty and tension among Party members and the broad masses of the workers. We long since could have worked out these touchy Party problems. Numerous circumstances, *pointed out more than once by the Soviet comrades,* hindered solving the problem with reference to the *long-range interests of the Party"* (italics added).[6]

The policy of Rákosi, advocated by the Security Police and supported by the Soviet advisers, seemed to have aimed at gaining time. Prisoners after a lapse of time might become forgetful of what had happened to them after their arrest. Some of them might die (as some did). Relatives and friends might be less outraged when meeting liberated prisoners again after a more prolonged time. Nevertheless, hard fighting and bickering went on within the Party headquarters over the "bodies" of their imprisoned comrades. The bitterness of the struggle within the Politburo and within the Rehabilitation Committee is reflected by the fact that eventually the Prime Minister resigned from the Committee, having been unable to make his view prevail.[7] The AVH, though formally incorporated into the Ministry of the Interior, was still a state within the state, and it preferred to listen to the Soviet "advice" and follow Rákosi's directives rather than those of the Prime Minister.

THE PROBLEM REACHES THE SOVIET PRESIDIUM

Rákosi presented the question of the release of political prisoners before the Hungarian Politburo and also before the Rehabilitation Committee as one which, if implemented, was likely to have a devastating effect on the authority of him and the Party with which he identified himself. He used a similar argument when submitting reports on this subject to Moscow. On the other hand, Nagy was able to point out that the real Party interests would suffer if the prisoners were not rehabilitated. He later wrote: "It was . . . and still is my opinion that it is not a matter of how the question is posed, but rather that the commission of the crimes in question was and is detrimental to the Party and to leadership authority." [8]

It is remarkable that in this context "commission of crimes" meant the unjustified imprisonment of Communist Party members; there seemed no further doubt about the authenticity of the crimes committed. And when speaking of "leadership authority," Nagy was thinking of his own and his group's leadership, whereas Rákosi, in fearing the rehabilitation of prisoners and consequent shattering of the Party's prestige, was thinking of *his* personal "leadership" and "authority." Naturally, Nagy and his friends were disinclined to take into account the fact that reviews of condemnations of faithful Party members would reveal crimes committed by Rákosi and his associates, and that such revelations were bound to have disastrous effects on the standing of those responsible. For those who might have been affected by the stigma of these crimes it was not only a question of Party or governmental posts. It might easily be a question of life and death.

The problem of the release of innocent Party members was several times brought up before the members of the Soviet Presidium during the talks which Imre Nagy and Rákosi had with them. Nagy records the following conversation on this subject held with Khrushchev on January 1, 1954:

Comrade Khrushchev . . . urged the rehabilitations, saying, "The detainees are being released slowly. This is Rákosi's fault, because he hasn't taken the matter in hand. Rákosi alludes to the fact that his nerves are bad. Nerves don't count. He has lost self-confidence in the correction of errors." [9]

Khrushchev's reproach to Rákosi is no refutation of the fact that the Soviet comrades advised against their release. It is a device frequently employed by imperial masters to reproach their satraps for things which they have been summoned to do by other representatives of the imperial power. Was not Rákosi reproached for having done what he was enjoined to do during the Stalinist era? And would Imre Nagy not be accused for a program which had received the hallmark of approval by the same Soviet comrades? Evidently, when faced with the question of releasing innocent Party members, Khrushchev could not have acted any differently, even if contrary directives had been passed on to Rákosi, directives which Rákosi was only too glad to follow.

Though Rákosi's apologetic allusions to the state of his nerves seem to have made little impression on Khrushchev, the utilitarian argument based on the jeopardy of Rákosi's authority must have touched the heart of the Moscow potentate. Nagy reports concerning the Moscow talks of May 1954:

Comrade Khrushchev likewise said the following: "Rákosi is responsible for the arrests. Therefore he does not want to release these people. He knows that he is guilty and will compromise himself. It is not permissible to denounce men and to throw suspicion on them." Comrade Khrushchev advised that "the rehabilitations should be carried out so as not to destroy Rákosi's authority." But, so that his words would not be misinterpreted, he added, "We will protect Rákosi's authority only in so far as it is not prejudicial to Party authority." [10]

At that juncture Moscow was anxious to preserve Rákosi's authority, which it was necessary to identify with the prestige of the Hungarian Communist Party, and — it must be added — with the prestige of Soviet authority as well. At the same time, it was felt that something should be done in favor of the detainees. Again we must remember that all these discussions centered around the review of sentences pronounced against reliable Party members.[11]

At the May 1954 meeting, Khrushchev's final instructions were as follows:

It may happen that on the pretext of protecting Rákosi's authority, the old policy will be reinstated and the freeing of the prisoners will not proceed. Of course, it is difficult for Rákosi to free the prisoners . . . because he ordered the arrests. Despite that, what happened must be told. Neither silence nor glossing over will increase the authority of the Party; rather it will take frank discussion.[12]

This pronounced hesitancy on Khrushchev's part again confirms the view that Soviet "advice" had a considerable part to play in the detention of imprisoned Communists.

RELEASE OF FAITHFUL PARTY MEMBERS

At last, in the months from August to October 1954, after prolonged "frank discussion," the Prime Minister succeeded in having most of the Communist prisoners released. Their number was relatively small in proportion to that of all political prisoners, and they did not include former Social Democrats, most of whom had become Communist Party members after the merger of the two parties in 1948.* This writer estimates the number of the released in 1954 to have been over a hundred but less than two hundred. The fact that the overwhelming majority of political prisoners were not released at this time should be emphasized because many of the commentators on this subject have created the impression that during Imre Nagy's premiership the political prisoners were released.[13]

The liberation of the Communist prisoners was first mentioned publicly by István Kovács, the Budapest Party Secretary, who on October 14, 1954, announced the release of those "unjustly con-

---

* Among the non-Communist former Social Democrats, only Anna Kéthly had been released as early as November 21, 1954. The British Labour Party had often intervened on behalf of her and other Socialists.

victed." Imre Nagy himself wrote in the *Szabad Nép* of October 20, 1954, that "the Party resolutions were implemented by the rehabilitations, by the liberation of unjustly sentenced comrades." Nagy was then attacked by Rákosi's adherents because of this article. He was accused of having weakened unity and authority of Communist leadership. In his later testimony, however, Imre Nagy retorted that it was not his article but the illegal imprisonments that were detrimental to the Party and to the leadership authority.[14]

As mentioned earlier, General Gábor Péter and many staff officers of the AVH had been arrested in December 1952. On March 13, 1954, it was announced that a military court had sentenced Péter to life imprisonment and his two associates, Gyula Décsi and István Timár, to nine and eleven years, respectively, for "criminal activities against the State and the people." These condemnations seem lenient if one bears in mind that the accused could have been charged with murder and the torturing of prisoners in plenty of cases. However, those charges were not brought against them (they could have been leveled against Rákosi as well), and their lives were spared, perhaps through Soviet intervention or because Rákosi wished to reserve them for ulterior procedures. He also believed that by eliminating the Head of the AVH and some of his collaborators he had done his share to acquit the conscience of the Party and the public for the crimes committed. His error in miscalculating the strength of subsequent waves of indignation proved to be fateful to him and the Party.

So, in Hungary's period of dual leadership from 1953 to 1955, large masses of prisoners were not released. The Prime Minister was powerless in this respect. In March 1955, shortly before his dismissal, in a report addressed to the Central Committee, he again raised the question of political prisoners.[15] His last appeal, as was to be expected, was of no avail either. And around October 1955, no longer in power, he was still writing that "Rákosi does not want to settle these matters — i.e., the great trials, principally the Rajk trial — frankly and thoroughly, but rather in a way to gloss over former mistakes and to hide crimes and criminals. Mátyás Rákosi's attempt to induce various comrades to help him to hush up this affair regardless of the truth or of the facts is proof of that." [16] But did not Nagy know that by admitting the truth Rákosi would have had to stamp himself a wilful murderer? Or was Nagy equally unaware of the Soviet complicity in these matters? In so writing did Imre Nagy reveal his naïveté, or was it deliberate astuteness to prescribe Rákosi a formula which would certainly destroy him — without directly impeaching him as responsible for these crimes? An interesting and characteristic example of Communist internecine warfare.

Thus the problem of political prisoners remained a deadly cancer in the Communist body politic, and, in its time, it did not fail to have its decaying and disintegrating effect upon both the unity of the Party and the stability of the Communist regime. Imre Nagy gives the impression of a successful prophet when writing in the same memorandum in the fall of 1955:

The denial of human honor, of Communist morality, and of socialist legality, however, brings grim retribution. Whoever acts contrary to this has only himself to blame and should not charge me with damaging the authority of the Party.[17]

13

About-face in Moscow: Nagy's Fall

∧∧∧∧∧∧∧∧∧∧∧∧∧∧∧∧∧∧∧∧∧∧∧∧∧∧∧∧∧

The arts of power and its minions are the same in all countries and in all ages. It marks its victim; denounces it; and excites the public odium and the public hatred, to conceal its own abuses and encroachments.

HENRY CLAY

Victrix causa diis placuit, sed victa Catoni.
The cause of the victor pleased the gods, but that of the vanquished pleased Cato.

LUCAN

AFTER the October 1954 session of the Central Committee, the Rákosi clique appeared to accept defeat, and Prime Minister Nagy's position was considered more secure than ever before. Rákosi himself ostensibly withdrew from maintaining the dual leadership with Nagy.[1] Gerö suddenly discovered his enthusiasm for the Prime Minister and after returning from the Soviet Union sang eulogies in favor of the Nagy program.[2] Nevertheless, the Prime Minister still had reasons for complaint; the opposition against his ideas still persisted on all essential questions; the tactics alone changed.[3] Only if his opponents had been totally crushed — expelled from the Party or arrested — could Nagy have reached his objectives; but he had neither the despotic abilities for such procedures nor the Security Police at his disposal, nor the support of the Soviet Presidium: this paramount body had never forsaken Rákosi, considering Imre Nagy more expendable.

BEFORE THE STORM

The pro-Nagy section in the Party, which had now acquired somewhat greater strength through the influx of a number of opportunists, became more vocal. While the Rákosi group objected to the Prime Minister's article of October 20, 1954, in the *Szabad Nép*, Tibor Déry, the veteran Communist writer, in an open letter published in the *Irodalmi Ujság*, congratulated Imre Nagy for his initiative.[4]

At the inaugural congress of the People's Patriotic Front held on October 24, three weeks after the triumphal Central Committee session, Imre Nagy again was the principal speaker. At the end of his address he asked the members to support his policy with their votes, a gesture which earned him much approval. This democratic method, unusual with Communists, and his snub to the Party on that occasion gave the impression that the new front might become a political force equivalent to the Party itself. Such a belief, while essentially erroneous, was not immediately disavowed, and the thought for some time persisted that now the door had been widened for the voice of non-Communists to be heard. It was hoped that at least one step toward real democracy had been taken. Such a view was repeated in veiled language by fellow travelers of the regime, especially by the editor of *Magyar Nemzet,* the official daily paper of the People's Patriotic Front.[5]

The Rákosite whispering propaganda, of which Imre Nagy had so often complained, tried to discredit the People's Patriotic Front by alleging that it had slipped into the hands of the enemy. The *apparatchiki* were alarmed by rumors that a "hostile right-wing wave was sweeping the country." [6] Economic and political crises were envisaged. Simultaneously, the international situation was proclaimed to be extremely tense, and even the danger of war was threatened. While the Party functionaries were frightened by such alarming forebodings, the general public, favorable toward the Prime Minister and his policy, was disillusioned by rumors according to which Imre Nagy was just the chessman of the Kremlin for carrying out a "soft" policy, that when he was dropped the old policy would be resumed. It can be stated with fair accuracy that the Prime Minister never considered his June 1953 policy a tactical move nor a diversion to gain breathing space; he seemed honestly to believe in it, and also to believe that such a policy had once and for all been approved by the Kremlin.

At the end of October 1954, Rákosi set out for a prolonged journey to the Soviet Union. He was in need of a rest. It has been reported that he made use of his recuperation in Russia to visit top Soviet Party men and hold long conferences with the Stalinist Kaganovich.[7] Later Rákosi represented Hungary at the European Security Conference convoked by the Soviet government in Moscow and attended only by members of the Soviet bloc. While participating from November 29 to December 2 in this "family reunion" which foreshadowed the signing of the Warsaw Pact,[8] the First Secretary of the Hungarian Party had ample opportunity to acquaint himself with the changes of alignment within the Soviet Presidium and the creation of the front that eventually brought about Malenkov's fall. Rákosi seems to have been very well briefed by his Soviet friends concerning the coming trend of events in Moscow. Once back in Budapest he launched a series of broadside attacks against the Prime Minister, an action in strange contrast with the normal consequences of a defeat he had suffered two months before.

Now Nagy was more openly attacked as a rightist deviator[9] and the People's Patriotic Front depicted as a counterrevolutionary organization. Another item of accusation against Nagy was based on his alleged intention to have the DISZ (Federation of Working Youth) joined to the People's Front and thereby separated from the Party. Evidently, people were indeed attempting to dissolve the DISZ and hand over responsibility for organizing the youth movement to the People's Front. This attempt if successful would have had the far-reaching effect of extricating the youth movement from Communist Party ideological control. Imre Nagy disclaims having had anything to do with this plan, which remained a plan only. In a speech on November 18, 1954, at the occasion of the forthcoming local council elections of November 28, he stressed that the People's Front be given opportunity to assist the DISZ, but that the latter should not be merged with the former and so lose its identity.[10] These council elections were the first where the single-list candidacies had been sponsored by the new People's Front. Although this time one third of the selected candidates did not belong to the Party, the procedure demonstrated that the People's Patriotic Front did not establish even the semblance of democracy and hardly broadened the political base of the regime.

On December 22, 1954, the Tenth Anniversary of the convocation of the Provisional National Assembly and the formation of the Provisional Government was celebrated in the East Hungarian city of Debrecen, the original scene of these events.* According to eyewitnesses, the Rákosi-Nagy feud was visibly entering an acute phase at this time. Rákosi, the principal speaker, delivered a programmatic speech about building Socialism, devoid of any reference to past mistakes. Imre Nagy's address was colorless and unpolemic.[11] After the celebrations Party and governmental leaders withdrew to the restaurant of the *Arany Bika* (Golden Bull) Hotel. The Prime Minister sat with his friends, mostly writers and journalists, at one table, and Rákosi and his group at another, the two groups eyeing each other across the tables. Imre Nagy then told his friends that Mihály Farkas had just confronted him with the following provocative words: "There is no New Course . . . it is rightist to pursue it . . . the old road must be pursued, only some mistakes to be corrected." But we are told that the Prime Minister said he would refrain from fighting back so as not to jeopardize Party unity.[12]

Evidently, the cynical Farkas must have had some knowledge of what was in the air. Having sided with Imre Nagy after being "converted" to the New Course, he found it of vital importance to demonstrate his loyalty to Rákosi as soon as the latter's star was definitely in ascendancy. Yet Farkas' enthusiasm in rejoining the side of Stalin's first Hungarian disciple did not ultimately save him, as will appear later.

By the end of 1954 not only Farkas but other intimate observers must have realized that it was the Prime Minister's position which was in jeopardy. For many who did not know the circumstances underlying the situation, however, the outward appearances must have been unconvincing, especially to believers in Imre Nagy's mission.

MALENKOV VERSUS NAGY

The parallel between Malenkov's demotion from the Soviet premiership and the ouster of Imre Nagy from the same post in Hungary has struck many observers and given rise to many speculations. Besides the principal argument for the belief that Malenkov had been Nagy's chief supporter, it was also an illustrative example of Moscow's overwhelming control over its satellite. But we must be careful not to rely solely on an inference of *post hoc, ergo propter hoc*.

---

* Ironically, Professor Béla Zsedényi, original President of the Provisional Assembly in 1944, and a leading member of the Smallholder Party, died in prison about the time of the celebration.

It has been observed that Georgi Malenkov's downgrading can be traced back as from the spring of 1954.[13] But evidently his strength was not broken for some time. On December 21, 1954, the continuing struggle between the Soviet Premier and his opponents on the Presidium was demonstrated by a strange and glaring inconsistency between *Izvestiya*, the government daily, which insisted on an increase of consumer goods production, and *Pravda*, organ of the Party, which directed the Soviet people's main attention to the increase of heavy industry targets.[14] Subsequent pronouncements provided the necessary evidence that the issue of consumer goods versus heavy industry was the rallying ground for the forces mustered for and against Malenkov.[15]

Some have suggested that the anti-Malenkov rallying originated during the trip of Khrushchev, Bulganin, and Mikoyan to Peiping in October 1954.[16] But clearly these three members of the Soviet Presidium would have had opportunity of conferring without having to journey together to and from China, and it seems that Mao Tse-tung's ability to intervene in Soviet domestic politics was comparatively restricted in those days.[17] At any rate, the active cooperation with the Stalinists (Molotov, Kaganovich, and others), and with Marshal Zhukov of the Army, one of the beneficiaries of the forthcoming change, would seem to have had greater consequence than the approval by the Chinese leader, and these Stalinists were not represented in the party which traveled to China.

The chief instigator of the anti-Malenkov coup must have been its chief beneficiary, Nikita Sergeyevich Khrushchev. The anti-Malenkov coalition, whenever it was originally formed, must have gathered momentum after the contrasting articles appeared in the leading Soviet press. It was this event which probably brought the struggle to its climax. Heralding the supremacy of the new coalition, Mikoyan abruptly abandoned his earlier support of Malenkov. The final outcome appeared already determined when Khrushchev made his devastatingly violent utterance before the Soviet Central Committee on January 25, 1955, upbraiding adherents of pseudo-theoretical views on the priority to be given to light industry against the neglect of development in the field of heavy industry, and comparing them to such heretics as Rykov and Bukharin.[18] Though he did not name the targets of his accusations, Khrushchev unquestionably intended Malenkov and his group.

Prior to the meeting of the Soviet Central Committee, a Hungarian delegation had appeared before the Soviet Presidium in Moscow. The date of this confrontation is in doubt, but appears to have been in the first half of January 1955.[19] Malenkov's star was already in decline; for this reason, he now showed much accommodation toward the views of his colleagues, and was willing to pose as spokesman, on behalf of the Presidium, in denouncing the Hungarian Prime Minister. Malenkov had also been accused of endangering, by his economic and foreign policy, the orderly development of the People's Democracies. In attacking Nagy, he had the opportunity to correct his mistakes.[20]

This meeting has been given less notoriety than any prior collective audience of the Hungarian leaders. Imre Nagy does not explicitly disclose anything of value about it in the writings he left us. But he told the story to some of his close friends, and it is possible to reconstruct a fairly accurate version of the scene and also the nature of accusations raised — this time not against Rákosi, but against Imre Nagy.[21]

Nagy was reproached first of all for the economic failures of the New Course: the setback in industrial production,* the collapse of most of the agricultural collectives, chaos in foreign trade, and hopeless indebtedness. All these were fields where the Prime Minister had very little control; the accusations were addressed to the wrong person. There were accusations of a different kind, more general in nature: unrest in the country, formation of factions and cliques in the Party, open activity of the "enemy," too many liberties permitted to anti-Party and counterrevolutionary elements.

The most detailed charges directed against Nagy's person were delivered by his former patron, Malenkov, who in the course of his philippics frequently resorted to quotations of speeches made and articles written by Nagy. Thus Malenkov accused Nagy of having hinted in one of his articles that the economic policy prior to his premiership had taken account "neither of man nor of society." [22] This Malenkov considered a slander against the Party. Nagy had also written that "Party members should have an important role not only in carrying out the tasks ordered by the leadership, but also in the *formation* of the policy of the Party." This — said Malenkov — is contrary to the well-known Leninist principle of democratic centralism.[23]

In addition Imre Nagy had dared to describe the People's Patriotic Front as "the living conscience of the country." He was told

---

* The Hungarian Office of Statistics reported this same month that in 1954, compared to 1953, industrial production generally increased by 3.1 per cent, the production of consumer goods increasing by 13 per cent and the output of heavy industry *decreasing* by 3.1 per cent. *Szabad Nép*, Jan. 30, 1955.

by Malenkov that the living conscience of a Communist country is the Party and only the Party, and there can be no other conscience. In the same speech Imre Nagy had also said that "the hearts of nine and one-half million Hungarians are set on the same goal." Does the Prime Minister deny the existence of a class struggle? [24] Even a quotation of a line from a poem by Sándor Petöfi, the famous Hungarian poet who was killed in a battle against the Russians in 1849, was to smack of chauvinism and demagogy in Malenkov's eyes.* Finally, an anti-Soviet demonstration during a water polo match in Budapest was laid to the account of the Prime Minister. [25]

Thus Imre Nagy was receiving a treatment similar to Rákosi's some eighteen months before — but a treatment which this time seemed undeserved and the injustice of which must have been keenly felt by the Prime Minister. We are told that he was unable to explain his points, was being constantly shouted down — which must have been the usual way of brainwashing satellite leaders in the Kremlin. So Imre Nagy had to endure a scolding like a schoolboy; he was told that he had not done what was expected of him. It is related that he answered back to his tormentors in a way forbidden by the code of Communist ethics, laying before them their own failures in forming agrarian cooperatives. [26]

After all this, one might expect to find Nagy deprived of his office. But he was not. He was simply told to admit and correct his errors, to revert to an expansion of heavy industry, and to help in restoring discipline within the Party and in the country. Shortly, he was being given instructions to accept Rákosi's lead. We can assume that this time the dossier of accusations was prepared by Rákosi rather than by Soviet advisers or the Soviet embassy in Budapest.

THE CHANGE OF FRONT: A PARALLELISM

What was the underlying reason for such a volte-face of the Presidium in its attitude toward Imre Nagy? An obvious reply to such a query would be that, parallel with Malenkov's decline, the policy inaugurated at the beginning of his incumbency declined also, and in the satellites, as elsewhere, adjustments had to be made. But this is not the full explanation. One must also consider Hungary's unique position in the extension of Malenkov's New Course

* Imre Nagy, after his eclipse, referred to this accusation in the following terms: "It is stupid ill will . . . to quote against me a line by Petöfi — 'If the earth were God's hat, then our homeland is the bouquet upon it' — as if this were a manifestation of nationalism. I believe that our Party accepts the 'nationalism' of Petöfi, together with the quoted line." Imre Nagy, On Communism (New York, 1957), p. 238.

into the Soviet satellite area. Not only had Stalinist terror and irrational purges been more violent in Hungary than elsewhere,[27] but the impact of the changes initiated by Stalin's successors was sharper in Hungary than elsewhere. When examining policies pursued by European vassals of the Soviet Union in the post-Stalin period we find, it is true, that relaxation of police terror and irrational purges took place, the violence of the anti-Tito campaign was reduced, and shifts from heavy industry toward more consumer goods were carried out. But nowhere else was there such a momentous turnabout both in top personnel and in fundamental policy as in Hungary. And Hungary's distinction was due partly to the fact that the Stalinist era had not bequeathed a need for such thorough-going changes in other People's Democracies, and partly to Nagy himself — for no Nagy showed up in the other satellites.

The New Course, as implemented within the Soviet bloc, had accordingly taken account of local conditions and requirements in contradistinction to the uniformity required, if not always realized, within the Soviet empire during Stalin's monocratic rule.[28] No doubt, by this token, Hungary had received a very individual treatment under the New Course. Now, when the chapter of the New Course was closed for the Soviet Union, when a return to an economic Stalinization was on the way, and when Soviet statesmanship had taken a step away from collective rule, Hungary again was to receive an individual impact. And again this was because the pendulum had swung wider in Hungary; de-Stalinization had traveled too far away from its expected course. Besides, there was again the personality of the Prime Minister to deal with, and also the feud within the Hungarian leadership.

The dual leadership in Hungary, the Moscow-tolerated conflict between the two Hungarian leaders, the support of Nagy, the reprimand of Rákosi without his liquidation, had all been results of the simultaneous internecine rivalry existing within the Soviet Presidium. When Rákosi was demoted from his monopoly of power in June 1953, this was done out of fear of internal troubles in Hungary, and also to divest this most Stalinist of countries from intolerable tyrannic shackles. When things came to a crisis in Hungary — owing to Rákosi's autocratic temperament and Nagy's tenacity in his convictions — the existing equilibrium within the Soviet Presidium determined the consequences for Hungary: Rákosi was blamed, but never dropped; Imre Nagy praised and encouraged, but never given the means of enforcing his program. When, after December 1954, the equilibrium of forces within the Soviet leadership underwent a change, when the Khrushchev-Bulganin-Mikoyan clique, deserting Malenkov, rallied against him together with die-hard Stalinists, the new balance of power quickly found a reflection in the Presidium's assessment of the Hungarian scene. Accusations were leveled now against Imre Nagy and his policy, and he was ordered to correct his views and bring them closer to those of Rákosi, who gained correspondingly in prestige and influence. Of course, the influence of Rákosi in Moscow and his intrigues against Nagy also had much to do with this result.

Since the balance of power had shifted against Georgi Malenkov, since he found himself not only in the minority but with hardly any support in the Soviet Presidium, he was compelled to give way and make concessions. The outward unity of the Presidium had to be maintained; so things were discussed and decided before the Hungarians were admitted to the sanctum sanctorum. As usual with Soviet practice, Malenkov, the scapegoat, was commissioned to act as the "executioner" of Imre Nagy.

That the rebuke was violent and unjust was not unusual; this was the way satellite statesmen were handled in the Kremlin. Rákosi himself had earlier been treated in a similar manner and he had accepted such treatment compliantly, as a satrap was used to receiving reprimands from the mouth of a Great King, or as the Bonapartes, whom Napoleon had installed on Europe's thrones, accepted scoldings from Paris; after all, they owed gratitude to the person who had enthroned them. The privilege and power accorded to the leadership of World Communism, the Moscow Presidium, was to be respected. A faithful servant of the "Party," a Party which promotes "Socialism," must bow and scrape before the paramount leaders and accept their rebukes with all humility.

But Imre Nagy, strangely for a Moscow-trained Communist, did no such thing. He resented his treatment. He refused to accept an undeserved humiliation, and would not obey the recantation order. This played into the hands of Rákosi, especially when Malenkov fell from his premiership.

THE SECOND LANDSLIDE IN MOSCOW

On February 8, 1955, that is, about three weeks after he played the role of a principal spokesman in the rebuke administered to the Hungarian Prime Minister, Georgi Malenkov "requested" to be relieved from the post of Soviet Prime Minister. In his letter of resignation he referred to his lack of experience in governmental work, and admitted his guilt and responsibility "for the unsatisfac-

tory state of affairs in agriculture." Nevertheless, he assured the
Supreme Soviet (to which his resignation was directed) that he
would carry out the duties to be entrusted to him in a most con-
scientious manner "under the leadership of the monolithic and
unified Central Committee of the Communist Party of the Soviet
Union." [29] The fallen angel was spared, and Malenkov remained,
for the time being, a member of the Party Presidium and was given
the posts of Deputy Prime Minister and Minister of Power Stations. He was replaced as Premier by Bulganin, and the latter's post
of Minister of Defense was given to Marshal Zhukov. There was no
change, thereafter, in the Party leadership itself until July 1955, and
the personnel of the Presidium remained likewise unchanged.

Imre Nagy and his companions had returned from Moscow, and
for a few days Nagy continued his work as if nothing had happened.[30]
But now he was urged by Rákosi and his associates to practice self-
criticism as Moscow had demanded. It seems unlikely that Nagy
consented to recant; if he did agree there is no way of explaining
why he failed to carry out the agreement. According to one version,
he merely consented to admit difficulties of an economic nature, and
this only on the condition that at the same time he would again
expose the mistakes of Rákosi's management which had led to these
economic difficulties, as well as the sabotage initiated by the Rákosi
clique to prevent the implementation of his economic program.[31]
If this version of the story is accurate (and there is a likelihood that
it is), one can easily perceive why such a form of self-criticism was
unacceptable to Rákosi.

Nearly three months passed between the return of the Hungarian delegation from Moscow in January and Imre Nagy's final
removal from the premiership. This delay signifies that much
bickering and haggling had to take place before Rákosi was able
fully to achieve his objective: the total, as he believed, political
liquidation of Imre Nagy.

The fall of Malenkov must have been interpreted by Rákosi
as a green light for his actions against Nagy. He was greatly helped
in his endeavors by the temporary physical incapacity of the Prime
Minister. Beginning early in February, probably as a consequence
of the emotional strain caused by his disillusionment in Moscow,
Imre Nagy suffered from a heart disorder. He may have suffered a
light heart attack followed by palpitations. His doctor was Professor
István Rusznyák, President of the Hungarian Academy of Sciences
and chief Party physician. Rákosi, who exerted control over Rusznyák, saw to it that both the treatment of Imre Nagy and the

medical reports of his condition were handled in the best interests of the maneuver he was undertaking.[32] For over one month Imre Nagy was confined to bed, and physically cut off from the exercise of the powers of his office. No member of the cabinet nor any leading Party member visited him during his illness. When he wrote letters to Rákosi and other leaders, he had no reply.[33]

The scenario of the Moscow meeting in January was arranged while Malenkov was still in his Prime Minister's post. Undoubtedly, as with other decisions reached according to formulas of compromise, the Hungarian Premier was to be rebuked, enjoined to mend his ways, but not removed from his office. Now, however, after the fall of Malenkov, was this compromise decision still in force? Evidently it was for Rákosi to sound out what Moscow thought in this matter after Malenkov's humiliating removal had been achieved. We may assume that by March he had received word from the Kremlin, or perhaps only hints, that Nagy's removal would be tolerated and even approved. Now he knew how far he could proceed, and he acted accordingly.

IMRE NAGY'S CENSURE AND OUSTER

A session of the Hungarian Central Committee was convoked for early in March. When Imre Nagy heard of this and the fact that his case would be on the agenda, he wrote a letter of protest to the Central Committee. He wished to be present when his case was to be dealt with, and he was still unable to appear in person. His letter contained the following passage: "There are those who wish to silence me, to influence the members of the Central Committee with only one side of the story. I regard this as an arbitrary attitude, contrary to the spirit of the Party and inadmissible." [34]

The Central Committee sat from March 2 to 4. Its members were well briefed by Rákosi and his associates; they were told what had happened in Moscow, perhaps even told things that did not happen. At any rate, they were assured that Imre Nagy was politically dead, since that was the decision of Moscow, and that therefore Rákosi was again their sole master. The events in Moscow, the parallel of Malenkov's fall, must have impressed even those members of the Central Committee who had willingly voted just a few months before for Imre Nagy and against Rákosi.

The Central Committee unanimously adopted a resolution calling attention to the dangers, this time, of rightist deviationism. It contained such passages:

The principal task of the Party consists in the ideological crushing of rightist views . . . Especially great damage has been done by those rightist views alien to Marxism-Leninism which appeared in the important question of our Party's policy concerning the peasants.

The strengthened rightist opportunist deviation also expressed itself in undervaluating the leading role of the Party. Some persons denied this leading role within the People's Patriotic Front. The creation of the People's Patriotic Front — initiated by our Party — had been accompanied by such rightist endeavors which were aiming at the suppression of the significance and leading role of the Party in order to endow the People's Patriotic Front with the power of supervising even the state and council organs. To enable the Front to fulfill this "supervisory and controlling" role some persons wished to turn it into the all-embracing mass organization of the People's Democracy; thus they wished to give the Front a greater role than assigned to the local councils which — as it is well-known — are the widest mass organizations and at the same time the local organs of state power . . . These rightist views, in their essence, wished to revise the Marxist-Leninist doctrine of the dictatorship of the proletariat.[35]

Furthermore, the resolution was not chary of naming the chief deviationist, the chief propagandist of these heretical tenets:

It has been possible for rightist conceptions to become so dangerous in our Party because Comrade Imre Nagy has supported such anti-Marxist views in his writings and speeches, and has even been the first advocate of them.

The resolution was quickly circulated among the Party functionaries and a few days later published in the newspapers, whereas all the previous resolutions censoring Rákosi had been withheld even from the Party membership. Soon the whole country resounded with the deprecations against rightist deviationism, and the press and radio expressed horror of the Prime Minister's many misdeeds.

Rákosi wanted to force Nagy to tender his resignation; he even wished to press him to full recantation of his errors and into self-criticism. But the Prime Minister refused to recant, and even refused to tender his resignation. He preferred to be discharged from his office.[36] Rákosi's insistence on Nagy's self-abasement was prompted by the desire to see his popularity destroyed; it always vexed the vanity of Rákosi that Imre Nagy was able to muster such enormous popular support in spite of his lack of political success.

After the results of the March plenum became public on March 9, 1955, everybody expected some swift action: the removal of Nagy from the premiership or his resignation, possibly also his arrest, even a new show trial à la Rajk. But nothing of the sort happened. The nation waited.

April 4 was Liberation Day, the tenth anniversary of the expulsion of German troops from Hungary. The Soviet Party was represented at the celebration by Mikhail Andreyevich Suslov. The marching troops and workers saw only a gesticulating, exuberant Rákosi in the center of the tribune; the Prime Minister was not to be seen.

After these festivities, the Central Committee was convoked once again. By this time, Rákosi had clearly obtained a full fiat for his actions against Nagy. Suslov attended this meeting, and it is said that he himself drafted the points of accusations against Nagy.[37] Prior to the meeting, Suslov undertook to persuade Nagy to retreat from the premiership in a Malenkov manner. But the strong-headed idealist refused; he wished to submit his defense in person before the Central Committee, and declared that he would resign only when defeated after a thorough examination of his case. That, of course, Rákosi could not afford to risk.

This time the accusations were more specific. Imre Nagy, the Central Committee was told, was guilty of the following offenses:

Attempting to form an opposition group within the Party. This accusation was based on a casual remark which Nagy is supposed to have made to István Dobi.[38]

Trying to put himself above the Party by becoming President of the People's Patriotic Front. He was the Vice-President of this organization, the Hungarian Politburo having turned down his request for the presidency.

Clericalism. His daughter had married Ferenc Jánosi, a Calvinist pastor, in 1945. The marriage, in view of her husband's status, had to be concluded according to ecclesiastical forms, and the father of the bride attended it. Also, István Bata, the Defense Minister, stated that he had difficulties in obtaining access to the Prime Minister but "it was quite otherwise when it came to bishops." [39]

Nepotism. His son-in-law, Jánosi, was made Secretary-General of the People's Patriotic Front. Jánosi was one of the so-called peace priests, and at one time had been Deputy Minister of Education in Rákosi's cabinet.

And this time the Central Committee was ready to administer more than a rebuke. On April 14, it unanimously excluded Imre Nagy (who was still Prime Minister) from his Central Committee membership, and consequently from the Politburo and all his other

Party functions.[40] He was to remain — for the present — a simple Party member. On April 18, 1955, the National Assembly met. Nagy still refused to tender his resignation as Prime Minister. Therefore, István Dobi, Chairman of the Presidium of the National Assembly, moved that the Assembly discharge Nagy from the premiership "for having failed properly to carry out his duties." This resolution was unanimously adopted by the Assembly with great enthusiasm. Shortly afterwards, Imre Nagy was also deprived of his dignity as a Vice-President of the People's Patriotic Front and expelled from the National Assembly. He was even banned from his university chair and from the Academy of Sciences. His formal exclusion from the Party had to wait for some more months. But no prosecution or arrest had been instituted against him. Evidently, the Soviet comrades did not wish to repeat these Stalinist methods. Even so, Rákosi evidently hoped that he had finally rid himself of his dangerous rival.

SIGNIFICANCE OF NAGY'S PREMIERSHIP

Both the rise of Imre Nagy to the premiership and his fall from that position are primarily attributable to oscillations in the internal balance of the Soviet Presidium, oscillations which were based on real or manipulated policy and on ideological issues molded by factional power rivalries and resulting in frequent shifts of balance within the paramount Party body. The Presidium must have felt that matters were getting out of hand, that the ferment engendered by Nagy's personality, by his program and idealism, might have perilous results.[41] A man of independent judgment was not the kind of person the Soviet leaders like to deal with.

On the other hand, Rákosi had been running Hungary safely for the Soviets for a number of years; he was a trusted servant in spite of all his shortcomings. He was no danger. The mistakes and crimes he had committed were not shocking events for the members of the Soviet Presidium, who had had their own share in similar excesses during Stalin's reign, excesses, perhaps, on an even larger and more brutal scale than those in Hungary. The damage had to be repaired by a stern hand, which Nagy did not possess. The Soviet leaders were not concerned with the hopes which the people of Hungary had placed in the program of Imre Nagy. Their concern was focused on the maintenance and preservation of their own power system.

It may also have been that Moscow got tired of Nagy's continual complaints against Rákosi, the man who still essentially enjoyed their confidence. Nagy was considered expendable whereas Rákosi was not. Perhaps some of Nagy's daring ideas, which he subsequently entrusted to paper, had become known to the masters of the Kremlin, and they (under special pressure by the Stalinist faction) made use of Malenkov's elimination to have the Hungarian Prime Minister simultaneously degraded.

The second landslide in the Soviet leadership — Malenkov's reproof and removal from the premiership — together with Nagy's reluctance to recant and Rákosi's continued nagging brought about the complete removal of the Hungarian Prime Minister. The final word was probably said by Suslov after he vainly tried to obtain Nagy's self-criticism or resignation. Moscow must have believed — and for some time Rákosi, too — that Nagy had been rendered harmless by being politically neutralized. Since he was politically dead he might as well physically live; no more unnecessary bloodshed, nor more imprisonment of powerless former Party leaders. One can imagine Suslov saying, "Just leave him alone, Comrade Rákosi; no harm will come of it."

Evidently, the Soviet leaders as well as Rákosi were completely unaware of what impact Imre Nagy's unsuccessful premiership had on the Hungarian psyche. The agonizing years of the Stalinist era had ended when the New Course, so intimately linked with the Prime Minister's person, had for a moment given rise to hopes for a better future. The new program, professing to operate within a Marxist-Leninist ideological frame, had opened a much wider horizon than the former Stalinist system. The ambiguity of Nagy's concepts led the non-Communist masses to believe that an evolution toward abandonment of Soviet-Communist Party rule was in the offing.

The general public, apart from the small stratum of convinced Communists, had, from the very outset, attributed a different significance to Imre Nagy's administration and program from that intended by the Prime Minister himself. His admirers had quickly exalted his qualities in their imagination; he was assigned a gift of astuteness by which he would be able to extricate Hungary from Soviet and Communistic thralldom. At first only a few dissented from this judgment and classed Imre Nagy as "a Communist and muscovite like the others." [42] Later, however, when the Prime Minister seemed to have failed, the number of skeptics increased and these hopes slowly faded away.

The more immediate circle around Imre Nagy, those initiated

in Party affairs, who watched the clandestine fight between Rákosi and the Prime Minister with eager eyes, reacted differently from the general public. Many of them became fervent adherents of Imre Nagy's concepts. Their evolution from Stalinist dogmatism to the vague democratic Communism of Nagy, and even further into the realm of liberal democracy, paralleled the frustrating struggle of the "old man." These never lost faith in him, although he soon lagged behind his followers in their endeavor to escape the strait jacket of Marxism-Leninism. This group, forming the shock battalion of Party opposition in the subsequent phase, remained Communist only by the fact of their membership cards. They used Marxist-Leninist phraseology to oppose official Party and governmental views, and becoming concealed enemies of the regime, cloaked in an ideological garment of heresy, they fought an anti-Soviet and anti-Communist battle.

When Imre Nagy was removed from office he regained the sympathy of the masses. Had he submitted to recantation or self-criticism, the larger public, already skeptical, would have lost interest in him. But, because of his inflexibility, he grew from a redeemer into a martyr, revered even by some of his former foes, and became even more a symbol of frustrated desires than when he had taken over the reins of the government.

Frustration and resentment, accumulated under the Stalinist terror, had not abated during the relative relaxation of the "thaw." The disappointment felt in the frustration of Nagy's endeavors and in his eclipse greatly added to existing resentment and strengthened aggressiveness. Thus the Nagy experiment, instead of releasing some of the pressure, increased tensions and created an atmosphere more propitious for an ultimate explosion than did the continuous, consistently harsh Stalinist regime in countries like Czechoslovakia or Eastern Germany.

The Imre Nagy premiership also revealed more than any previous experience that Moscow was well able to exercise an intense despotism even when the government leader was not an outright puppet. It demonstrated that Hungarian questions (political, economic, and personal) were being submitted to Moscow by the Hungarian Party for decision, that dicta of the Kremlin prescribed the political attitudes and the economic and cultural policies of a supposedly independent country. It showed that those who held important government or Party posts had been selected by the Soviet Presidium. This august body passed judgment upon the

Hungarian Party and government leaders, and arbitrated their differences, acting in every respect like a central authority controlling and directing a provincial or colonial government. If anybody had doubts as to how far, in what manner and respect, Moscow ruled its satellite empire, Nagy's drama dispelled any misunderstanding. All this happened not in Stalin's lifetime, but under the more enlightened regime of his successors.

It has been emphasized that during Rákosi's Stalinist dictatorship, his regime could be entirely identified with that of his muscovite masters and, in principle, there could be no conflict of interest, at least not on a higher governmental or Party level. During Nagy's first premiership, however, we have to presume (as substantiated by subsequent events and also by his subsequent writings) that he and some of his collaborators, Communists though they were, at least tried to represent genuine Hungarian interests as against those of Russia, as far as it was possible for them within the narrow limits of their jurisdiction. Rákosi's "double-dealing" and the fact of rigorous Soviet control prevented either a real defense of Hungarian interests or even a candid expression of them by Nagy and his followers. Nagy's whole tenure of office was absorbed by an incessant struggle with the open or concealed endeavors of Rákosi to prevent a more independent exercise of power by the initiator of the New Course in Hungary. For that period it is difficult to identify genuine Soviet interests in everyday political matters. Was Malenkov (who until his eclipse, seemed to favor Imre Nagy), or Khrushchev (who seemed to steer a somewhat middle course), or the Stalinist group in the Presidium the real representative of Soviet interests with regard to Hungary? However, it is certain that the treatment of Hungary (and any other satellite country) as a satrapy of Moscow was certainly against her real and lasting interests, whether the paramount ruler was Malenkov, Khrushchev, or the Stalinist diehards.

In view of this situation, Imre Nagy during his first premiership was able to represent Hungarian interests only to the extent of his opposition to the subservience of his country to the whims of the Kremlin. The Prime Minister, fully engaged in a life-and-death struggle with Rákosi and his adherents, could hardly have been expected, in his precarious position, even if he had wished to, to utter the slightest complaint concerning the subordinate situation of the Hungarian Party and government vis-à-vis Moscow. His only hope was to obtain final victory over Rákosi, especially with the help of the "Soviet comrades," and then to bide his time; but even in this he failed. In 1956, when Premier again, he was faced with a choice, a difficult one. But in the course of his first tenure his only practical choice — even if it was not his heart's choice — was to hearken to the imperious demands of Moscow.

THE THIRD PHASE

Single Leadership —
Divided Party
1 9 5 5 – 1 9 5 6

It is impossible for a man to mount two horses and stretch two bows, and it is impossible for a slave to serve two masters. Either he will honor the one and despise the other, or he will hate the one and love the other.

Apocryphal Gospel of Thomas

14

Rákosi Sole Master—but with Strings Attached

⋀⋀⋀⋀⋀⋀⋀⋀⋀⋀⋀⋀⋀⋀⋀⋀⋀⋀⋀⋀⋀⋀

Is not the sound of his master's feet behind him?

2 KINGS 6:32

THE same session of the National Assembly that demoted Imre Nagy from the premiership in April 1955 elected his successor.[1] Rákosi, evidently following instructions from the Kremlin, did not again assume the premiership, but installed his cat's paw, András Hegedüs (a rather insignificant Politburo member), in that post. Rákosi now had a Premier who had "no voice in the making of decisions." [2]

Hegedüs belonged to the younger generation of Hungarian Communist leaders who had joined the Party in and after 1945. He came from a peasant family. After his organizing talents were discovered, he was sent to Moscow to study at the High Party Academy, where his preparation predestined him for higher posts in the Hungarian Party hierarchy. For some time he worked as Gerö's secretary and belonged to Rákosi's intimate circle. On March 1, 1951, he became a member of the Central Committee and junior member of the Politburo. In Imre Nagy's cabinet he served as Deputy Prime Minister. He thus could claim to be a junior muscovite, enjoying confidence both of Moscow and of Rákosi. In fact, however, he was simply a mouthpiece of Rákosi.

THE RESTRAINED DICTATOR

Rákosi thus returned as supreme master of Hungary by the grace of Moscow; but this time, he was considerably shorn of his claws. We may imagine he was told by the collective leadership of the Kremlin: "No more bloodletting of Party comrades, no more staged trials and no undiluted terror — you must get along without this as we do, Comrade Rákosi — our advisers and representatives in Hungary will report to us whether or not you and your Security Police adapt to these instructions!"

Although a recrudescence of Security Police activity was noticeable, no return to the indiscriminate terror of the Stalinist era occurred. "Enemies" of the regime were rigorously prosecuted and, in many instances, executed,* but the Security Police still continued to act with restraint — compared to the Stalinist, not Western, standards — almost as it had under the administration of Imre Nagy. However, the release of political prisoners came to a standstill and was only resumed later at a very slow pace and with evident reluctance.

An interesting by-product of Imre Nagy's removal was the purge of Mihály Farkas, a Politburo member and Party Secretary. It is to be recalled that Farkas had been dropped from the Politburo in June 1953, probably at the behest of Imre Nagy; previously he had been considered one of the "foursome" of Rákosi, and he was responsible for many illegalities of the AVH as the Politburo member in charge of security affairs. His son by his Russian wife, Vladimir Farkas, colonel of the AVH, acted as chief torturer of Party members and former Social-Democrats. When subsequently rehabilitated again at the request of Nagy and readmitted to the Politburo and the Party secretaryship, Mihály Farkas professed to pose as an adherent of the New Course and a supporter of the Prime Minister; nevertheless, in December 1954, he was one of the first who openly turned against him. In spite of this he was unable to regain the confidence of Rákosi, and the same Central Committee resolution which ousted Imre Nagy from his Party posts in April 1955 removed Mihály Farkas from the Politburo as well as from the secretariat of the Central Committee.[3]

* A widespread conspiracy was "discovered" early in 1955 which was headed by a former detective inspector, Jozsef Fiala. Many hurdreds of arrests were made, especially in East Hungary; in some cases the Security Police picked up and transported in buses to neighboring towns a considerable number of male inhabitants of some villages. Fiala and five of his accused companions were sentenced to death on April 13, 1955, and later executed; a hundred or more were given prison sentences.

There is no evidence — apart from the Farkas case — that Rákosi took revenge on Nagy's collaborators at that juncture. The former Premier's genuine collaborators were not to be found in any of the higher Party or state positions, perhaps with the notable exception of Zoltán Szántó. This man suffered a minor setback. He had been head of Imre Nagy's Information Bureau (an organization whose research enabled the Prime Minister to gather information independently from the Party organs) and before that had been ambassador to France. In June 1955, Szántó was sent as Hungarian ambassador to Poland.

Under the new regime the former economic line (emphasis on heavy industry) was restored. This emphasis was considerably softer now. But nothing was heard of an increase in the standard of living. The collectivization of agriculture continued to be soft-pedaled, and there still was a marked restraint in the exploitation of workers when compared with the situation prior to June 1953.

Imre Nagy's program had particularly affected the countryside. He was considered the man who had saved the farmers from further enforced collectivization, from the pressure to join the feared and hated kolkhozes. It was only natural that the first significant reaction against Nagy's removal came spontaneously from the villages. Food deliveries fell short and there was, particularly, a shortage of meat.[4]

One important weakness of the new regime soon became apparent: the international situation moved in a direction tending to compromise Rákosi's position. The cold war, instead of increasing in tension — as presaged by Rákosi[5] — softened considerably as a result of the Austrian State Treaty and subsequent evacuation of Austria. The atmosphere of the Geneva Summit meeting of 1955 notably reduced the vehemence of psychological warfare on both sides of the Iron Curtain. The reconciliation between the Soviet Union and Yugoslavia sharply undermined Rákosi's prestige, even in the eyes of his followers.

The opposition within the Party, slowly but increasingly rallying around the now even more popular personality of Imre Nagy, became more and more outspoken, as will appear presently. The surreptitious feud between the members of the Soviet Party Presidium rendered Rákosi's stand the more insecure, thwarting his will and capacity to act and perplexing his attempts to guess the real intention and policy of Moscow. Similarly his followers were confounded when international developments failed to justify the acts of the First Secretary of the Party. In vain did Rákosi try to dispel doubts concerning infallibility by describing Soviet political actions as mere "tactical moves." [6]

People both outside and inside the Party viewed with dismay the likelihood of a return to the Stalinist days of terror. As for those within the higher echelons of the Party who had been sincere admirers of Imre Nagy and his policies, they preferred to remain silent, for at least a few months. As time went on, they gained some encouragement, partly from developments on the international and Soviet scenes, partly from the daring attitude displayed by native writers and journalists. For it was the writers who first launched a systematic campaign against the Rákosi clique in the post–New Course period.

Rákosi could pretend that complete uniformity of opinion had been achieved within the Party,[7] and for the time being the outward picture seemed to confirm such a view. But uniformity even within the leading Party circles proved soon to be lacking. As for the rank and file of the Party, their attitudes did not basically differ from those of the rest of the population, that is, opposition to the regime.[8] The situation could be described as one in which the Party membership had split into two major parts: an insignificant minority which, nevertheless, ruled the Party and the country, and the overwhelming majority which opposed the existing Party and state regime.[9]

CANOSSA AT BELGRADE

Among the international events that did not correspond with the continuation of Stalinist rule in Hungary, the most jarring was Khrushchev's Canossa visit to Belgrade, reminiscent of a medieval emperor's self-humiliation before the Pope at Canossa. The Soviet-Yugoslav reconciliation, which widened the already existing dissension within the Soviet Party Presidium, also was bound to jeopardize Rákosi's position all over again in the eyes of this paramount political body. Within the Soviet Presidium the main adversary of concessions in favor of Tito had been Molotov, who, from this point of view, found himself in a position somewhat similar to that of Rákosi. Both of them had been in Stalin's advance guard in his onslaught against Yugoslavia; both of them had attacked Tito as being a capitalist agent, the "chained dog" of the West. Rákosi — under the direction of Stalin, Molotov, and Beria — had staged the Rajk trial in order to demonstrate Tito's complicity with the Western "imperialists." He had persecuted members of the Yugoslav community in Hungary and had ordered many leading

Yugoslavs imprisoned. There could be no genuine reconciliation between Hungary and Tito's Yugoslavia as long as Rákosi was head of the Hungarian Party, and no essentially improved relationship between the Soviet Union and Yugoslavia as long as Molotov was conducting the foreign affairs of his country.

Molotov, before and after the Khrushchev-Bulganin pilgrimage to Belgrade in the last days of May 1955, opposed apologies, concessions, or even sympathetic gestures to Tito,[10] though he did not oppose state-to-state *rapprochement* with Yugoslavia. Rákosi, as far as his voice had weight in the Communist camp, also advised against yielding to Tito.[11] But Molotov was voted down by the Soviet Presidium before the pilgrimage to Belgrade, and also at the July 1955 session of the Soviet Central Committee when the Tito issue was discussed at considerable length.[12] Molotov's discomfiture not only undermined his position in the Presidium, but added to Khrushchev's stature. In fact, the Yugoslav question was the one that Nikita Sergeyevich used as a lever to unseat Molotov, just as he had employed the heavy-industry issue against Malenkov.

The July 1955 plenary session of the Soviet Central Committee was also the occasion for a full-scale discussion of the relation between the Soviet Union and the People's Democracies. Molotov insisted that the demands of this relation had dictated the need for a strong attitude toward Yugoslavia (even though he was ready to deplore the violence of the rupture). He asserted that many of the People's Democracies (or rather their Communist parties) had wavered on account of Tito's heresies. Gomulka's attitude in Poland was cited as an example. On the other hand, Khrushchev took the view that the Communist parties in the People's Democracies might be drawn toward Yugoslavia as long as that country was so harshly treated.[13] During the Central Committee debates, which lasted seven days, M. A. Suslov sided with Khrushchev against Molotov and was eventually rewarded with a seat in the Party Presidium. So was A. I. Kirichenko, a fervent Khrushchev adherent. The Central Committee also listened to a speech by Mikoyan, who branded as undesirable the Soviet exploitation of the People's Democracies through the means of the "Joint Companies" (in Hungary these had been dissolved in November 1954), and who also denounced the arrogant and patronizing behavior of Soviet experts and advisers in those countries.

Molotov experienced further humiliation when forced to publish a letter of abject apology in the *Kommunist* of September 1955 recanting his statement made on February 8, 1955, at the session of the Supreme Soviet, wherein he had dared to pronounce the heretical view that the Soviet Union had only so far established "the foundations of a Socialist society," and not Socialism itself, as the correct ideological view ought to have been.[14] Kaganovich, another staunch Stalinist, found himself also on the decline. Simultaneously with Malenkov's eclipse his assignment as chief industrial minister was changed to that of a Deputy Prime Minister without any particular duties.

The Belgrade visit by Khrushchev and Bulganin resulted in the famous melodramatic apology to Tito at the airfield, where Khrushchev again made an attempt to shift responsibility for past mistakes on the shoulders of the liquidated Beria.* It also resulted in the declaration of June 2, 1955, which pledged the two governments to observe "mutual respect and non-interference in one another's internal affairs for whatever reason — whether of an economic, political, or ideological nature — in as much as questions of internal organization, difference of social systems, and difference in the concrete forms of socialist development are exclusively the concern of the peoples of the respective countries." [15]

The Belgrade pilgrimage of Soviet leaders was intended to be an initial approach. The agreement reached was one between the two governments only, with the two Parties still remaining officially dissociated. Nevertheless, almost ten months passed before anything positive contributed to a further improvement of Soviet-Yugoslav relations. We can assume that among Tito's demands were the dissolution of the Cominform and the removal of objectionable characters like Molotov and Rákosi from their respective responsible posts. The ideological questions involved in the inter-Party relations were equally thorny. Tito himself stated that "this was a little difficult to settle." [16]

The Belgrade reconciliation had at first very little impact on Hungarian-Yugoslav relations. The Hungarian government, while paying some lip service to improved relations,[17] proceeded an inch at a time with the obvious task of releasing Yugoslav prisoners. These Yugoslav officials, refugees, kidnapped persons, and members of the Yugoslav minority in Hungary were transferred to other prisons, presumably in preparation for their release. But not until after they

---

* From the Soviet side it was proposed, prior to the visit, to share responsibility for the rupture: the Soviets would blame Beria, and Yugoslavia would blame Milovan Djilas (who had at that time been expelled from the Party). Tito, however, refused this deal and insisted on full Soviet apology. See Richard Lowenthal, "Tito's Affair with Khrushchev," *The New Leader*, Oct. 6, 1958, p. 11.

had staged a number of hunger strikes, revolts, and acts of sabotage, were they finally released during the winter of 1955–56.

No doubt, Tito was particularly vexed because of Rákosi's continuing survival as dictator of Hungary. While the big Soviet Union was prepared to offer humble apologies, the leader of a small neighboring state had shown no repentance. On July 28, 1955, Tito railed bitterly against Rákosi and associates:

There are still people who do not like the normalization of relations. They dare not speak out, but are acting under cover. They will not recognize what the Soviet leaders have said. They raise objections against Yugoslavia whenever they can, and continue to arrest men who happen to be in favor of friendship with Yugoslavia. They say that what has happened is only a manoeuvre, and that the Soviet Union is conducting a cunning policy with a knowledge of how to deceive others. There are such people, especially in Hungary . . . These men have their hands soaked in blood, have staged trials, given false information, sentenced innocent men to death. They have had Yugoslavia mixed up in all these trials, as in the case of the Rajk trial, and they now find it difficult to admit before their own people their mistakes.[18]

Ever since 1949 the economic relations between the two countries had been practically at a standstill. On September 5, 1955, a Hungarian financial and trade delegation journeyed to Belgrade. But after three weeks the negotiations were broken off, the Hungarian party alleging that exaggerated pecuniary claims had been made by the Yugoslavs.[19]

For Rákosi the Tito issue was not just a matter of Magyar-Yugoslav relations; it was a most personal matter. Even if Rákosi had made his apologies to Tito and Tito had accepted them (a hardly realistic conjecture), the matter could not have ended there. Because Rákosi had accused Tito of being a fascist, a Western spy, and a murderer, recognition now that Tito had been slandered would have implied that László Rajk and those implicated with him had been innocently executed, that the whole Rajk affair had been concocted and managed by Rákosi and his clique, as in fact it had been. The needless slaughter of innocent persons would possibly have made little impression on the Party leadership — but in this case the victims of this judicial murder had been faithful Party members. Even in the corrupt atmosphere of the Communist Party the liquidation of innocent Party members was considered — using the cynical Talleyrandian expression — worse than a crime, a fault. And a fault which could not be forgiven or redeemed by simple self-criticism. The skeleton in the cupboard was the skeleton of Rajk, and any apology to Tito would leave the cupboard door wide open.

It was not only the executed Rajk that haunted Rákosi and his collaborators; living persons bothered them too, for many of their victims who had been tortured in prison had been released. Rákosi avoided the sight of them as far as he could.[20] One of them was Mrs. Rajk herself. She had shared the Communist convictions of her husband and had been a prominent Party member. When Lászlo Rajk was arrested a special "treatment" had been reserved for Julia Rajk by Rákosi. From her cell she could see the execution of her husband and of the others; her baby had been taken away from her to an unknown destination. But in July 1955, six weeks after the Belgrade accolade, she was released. Still Rajk's name remained anathema; she was allowed to work as an assistant librarian, but only under an assumed name. She had to put up a hard fight to have her child returned to her. Only after the Twentieth Soviet Congress in February 1956 was she permitted to use her own name again, and at the same time she was readmitted to the Party.[21] This woman of energetic character, seething with a desire to avenge her husband though still subjected to humiliations by petty Party officials and others acting under Rákosi's orders, grew into a symbol of vengeance, and, like the Erinyes of Greco-Roman mythology, haunted those Party functionaries with bad conscience. And there were many such.

Rákosi was placing his hopes on the opposition which a full reconciliation with Tito would receive in the Soviet Presidium. To be sure, Moscow made the financial sacrifice to meet Yugoslavia's claim for damages,[22] but the ideological and personal conditions for the re-establishment of friendly cooperation, not only between the two governments but also between the respective Party organizations, were still unacceptable to the Stalinist members of the Presidium. And the Stalinist members remained the majority of this body. Thus Rákosi's hopes were not entirely unfounded. He repeatedly tried to bolster the courage of his adherents with the assurance that the treatment Tito was receiving from Moscow was just another tactical move, the gloved hand instead of the big stick, and that Yugoslavia would eventually have to renounce her heresy and return to the fold or be annihilated. The slowing down of the *rapprochement* during the period after Khrushchev's Belgrade visit seemed to substantiate the soundness of this view; had Rákosi not been right in predicting the abrupt end of the Nagy episode? But the time was coming — and it was no further off than February 1956 — when Khrushchev's Twentieth Party Congress would suddenly break the deadlock in Moscow-Belgrade relations, with unfortunate results for Mátyás Rákosi.

HUNGARY AND THE "SPIRIT OF GENEVA"

Meantime, in 1955, the Khrushchev-Bulganin visit to Belgrade was not the only international event that limited Rákosi and affected Hungary's future. The Soviet government, by signing the *Staatsvertrag* recognizing the sovereignty of Austria in May, and by participating in the Geneva Summit meeting of the heads of government in July, seemed to aim at one objective: the improvement of its foreign relations, which had soured during Stalin's reign. This had been Malenkov's goal too, but he had been unable to implement it against the opposition both of the Stalinists and of the rising star, Khrushchev. Now, with Malenkov reduced to a more modest position, Khrushchev was able with the help of his followers (and possibly with the reluctant consent of Malenkov himself) and against the resistance of Molotov, to create a few holes in the Iron Curtain.

The victory of the Khrushchev-Bulganin group was limited in scope: full reconciliation with Tito was still unattained, and, as subsequent events would prove, the Geneva meeting resulted in no real thaw in the cold war. The evanescent "spirit of Geneva" totally faded out when the Geneva conference on German reunification from October 27 to November 16 became deadlocked. Though Molotov had played only a secondary role at the Summit conference (and no role whatsoever in Belgrade), he led the Soviet delegation to the conference on Germany, which by its failure reasserted the pattern of the cold war.

As for the Austrian treaty, the departure of Soviet troops from Austria had been an event long hoped for by the people of two satellite countries in particular: Hungary and Rumania. Their inhabitants had cherished a well-founded belief that the evacuation of Austria by Soviet armed forces would bring about the departure of Soviet troops from their territories as well. It was common knowledge by the man in the street both in Budapest and Bucharest that their respective 1947 treaties of peace permitted the Soviet Union to keep armed forces on their soil only to the extent that it might need them there "for the maintenance of the lines of communication of the Soviet Army with the Soviet zone of occupation in Austria." [23] In these two countries the presence of Soviet troops appeared to be connected with the continued existence of Communist rule.

The *Staatsvertrag* and the ensuing departure of Soviet troops from Austria in October 1955 was preceded by a diplomatic-military move of the Soviet Union designed to counteract the adverse effects of these steps. In weighing the pros and cons of the Austrian settlement, the Soviet Presidium, after defeating Molotov's opposition,[24] resolved to transform the defense system of the Soviet Union — up to then based on a series of bilateral agreements with the People's Democracies — into a formal collective defense organization which became known at the Warsaw Treaty system.

Heretofore the Soviet Union had not been anxious to create a collective treaty system paralleled with NATO. Whereas the establishment of the Marshall Plan organizations had soon been followed by the creation — at least on paper — of the CEMA (Council of Economic Mutual Assistance), no similar step in the military field was taken when the NATO conventions were signed in 1949. The bilateral instruments with the satellite states, the uniformity of Party command, the military advisory system, and the stationing of military forces in Austria, East Germany, Poland, Hungary, and Rumania were considered sufficient means for the maintenance of the military and political *status quo* in East-Central Europe.

But when the evacuation of Austria was in sight, the Kremlin judged the existing ties insufficient for maintaining Soviet military power in the satellite area. A framework had to be created which could formally empower the Soviet to maintain occupation forces in Hungary and Rumania, and which might, in case of necessity, furnish the pretext for stationing such troops in other satellite territories as well. We also have to assume that Party leaders in Hungary and Rumania had been imploring Moscow not to withdraw its forces from these areas.

Already, in late 1954, Soviet and satellite representatives had discussed the possibility of a collective defense system. On May 11, 1955, four days before the signing of the agreement on Austria, representatives of the Soviet Union, Poland, the German Democratic Republic, Czechoslovakia, Hungary, Rumania, Bulgaria, and Albania assembled in Warsaw where, in the presence of Bulganin and Molotov, the Treaty of Friendship, Cooperation and Mutual Assistance was signed on May 14.[25] The Treaty does not explicitly provide for the right of the Soviet Union to station its armed forces on the territory of any signatory state; there is, however, a provision for a Joint Command of their armed forces. The Soviet Army Command, already existing for the East-Central European theater under the command of Marshal Konev, was skillfully turned into a "joint command" without essentially changing either its commander or its character.[26] No official explanation for the continued presence of Soviet troops was given in Hungary, though in Rumania, Premier Gheorghiu-Dej told a Western journalist that his government had invited the Soviet troops to stay. In Hungary, however, the Party leadership quickly circulated to the Party apparatus the tranquilizing item of news so important to the security of the regime.

While thus allaying high-level disquiet in Budapest, the Soviet leadership enjoined Rákosi to undertake something on his part for an improvement of the international atmosphere prior to the Geneva Summit meeting of July. The Soviet government wished to bring about an agreement with the Western Powers concerning the admission of Hungary, Rumania, and Bulgaria into the United Nations. The reluctance of the West to agree to their membership, and the ensuing Soviet veto blocking all other admissions to the United Nations, had created a deadlock which all concerned wished to overcome. The admission of the three People's Democracies had been opposed mainly because of their violations of human rights guaranteed by the Paris Peace treaties. The arrest, mock trial, and condemnation of Jozsef Cardinal Mindszenty, Roman Catholic Primate of Hungary, was considered the foremost example of violation of human rights and of fundamental freedoms. To allay Western susceptibilities, Rákosi was ready to make a demonstrative move. On July 17 it was announced that Cardinal Mindszenty's sentence had been suspended, though he would still be confined in a dwelling put at his disposal by the Catholic bishops.[27] We shall not try to ascertain here whether the non-Communist world was sufficiently impressed by this gesture. In Hungary it was interpreted as an expression of the regime's ardent desire for entry into the United Nations. For Cardinal Mindszenty the gesture meant only a change of his prison. He was transferred from a prison where he already enjoyed privileged treatment to a provincial mansion where he was kept under close and continuous surveillance, and he remained separated from the outside world.

Communist Hungary having thus made her contribution to the easing of world tension, the Geneva Summit conference resolved to open the way for an admission of Hungary, Rumania, and Bulgaria, together with other states, into the United Nations. Prior to Hungary's formal admission her government made a further concession: Archbishop Jozsef Grösz, the second ranking Catholic prelate in Hungary, was released outright, together with a few other Catholic priests connected with his case.[28] The entry of Hungary to the world organization was received with mixed feelings in Hungary. Some people felt that the admission was wrong because it was contrary to the clear provisions of the Charter concerning qualifications for membership. Others hoped that Hungary's membership might influence her government to pursue a more liberal policy. Officially the admission was greeted as a great triumph, and expressions of profuse gratefulness were addressed to the Soviet Union.

Another international event of 1955, though far away, had considerable impact on Hungarian Communist and non-Communist circles. This was the Afro-Asian Conference held in Bandung, Indonesia, from April 18 to 24, where Sir John Kotelawala, Prime Minister of Ceylon, for the first time in an international conference introduced the term "Soviet colonialism" in connection with the East-Central European satellites. The so-called "Five Principles of Peaceful Coexistence" agreed on by all participants did not fail to have an impact on a country as distant as Hungary.[29] The Soviet adoption of these principles in the joint statement of Nehru and Bulganin of June 22, 1955, in Moscow[30] gave rise to hope that a new era of Soviet-satellite relations was approaching.

A lonely man, the former Prime Minister of Hungary, isolated in his Budapest residence, followed with great interest the developments at Bandung, Belgrade, and Geneva. He was ready to apply all these events to the case of Hungary.

15

Imre Nagy: "Withdrawal" and "Return"

The withdrawal makes it possible for the personality to realize powers within himself which might have remained dormant if he had not been released for the time being from his social toils and trammels. Such a withdrawal may be a voluntary action on his part or it may be forced upon him by circumstances beyond his control; in either case the withdrawal is an opportunity, and perhaps a necessary condition, for the anchorite's transfiguration; "anchorite," in the original Greek, means literally "one who goes apart"; but a transfiguration in solitude can have no purpose, and perhaps no meaning, except as a prelude to the return of the transfigured personality into the social milieu out of which the human social animal cannot permanently estrange himself without repudiating his humanity and becoming, in Aristotle's phrase, "either a beast or a god." The return is the essence of the whole movement as well as its final cause.

ARNOLD J. TOYNBEE

IMRE NAGY, demoted from his Party and governmental posts, ostracized by the Party to which he had belonged for over thirty-five years, had refused to admit his guilt or to practice self-criticism. He had not even abandoned fighting for what he considered right, nor opposing the person who, in his view, had wronged him. This refusal to resort to the Communist ritual of recantation in the face not only of the Central Committee's resolution but also of Suslov's demand personally delivered from Moscow, already showed him to be a Communist of a different breed. His behavior was not the kind expected of an "old Bolshevik."

He might have been ready to admit mistakes, if the Central Committee had conducted a trial-like procedure, cross-examined both him and Rákosi, and found him guilty. He never gave up his belief that the June 1953 program had been the proper way to correct past errors, the proper way to advance toward what he considered Socialism to be, and he rightly suspected that the March and April 1955 resolutions of the Central Committee — while paying lip service to the June Resolutions — not only had censured him but had in effect reverted to the pre-1953 policies.

He does not seem to have been fearful for his own person. He rather was alarmed that, because of an exaggerated suspicion of a "rightist deviation," Party members might believe that his June 1953 policy had been an error. He admitted, though, that "the Party must be prepared to fight against . . . rightist mistakes and view-points, but in such a manner as not to disable the Party from dealing with the mistakes and dangers of the left, which probably have deeper roots in our Party than elsewhere." [1]

Nagy's ideological approach to his problem reflects his adherence to Soviet-Leninist thinking. He must have been aware of the fact that his dismissal was not due primarily to a mistaken ideological view adopted by the Central Committee, but to Rákosi's lust for power, supported by the will of Moscow. Still he insisted on clothing his arguments in an ideological garb. He still professed to believe in Party democracy and in his right to discuss the issue before the "parliament" of the Party. Was this an ill-advised idealism on his part or simple naïveté? Did he sincerely believe that the cogency of his arguments would persuade the Central Committee, this group of "absolute non-entities," [2] as he himself had called them, and convert them to his viewpoint?

Nagy's seeming lack of sophistication and his legalistic approach may be explained by reference to other heretics in history who simi-larly placed their trust in institutions rather than in the leaders of these institutions, in observance of strict legality, irrespective of the nature of the men who might decide their fate. Savonarola wished his case to be brought before the Council of the Church instead of Pope Alexander. Sir Thomas More invoked the jurisdiction of a "higher court" than that of his king. Martin Luther in the early day of his "deviation" wished to appeal from the ill-informed to a better-informed Pope. And all these deviationists displayed a similar insistence on procedural accuracy or on a change of venue, from which they hoped to obtain essential justice. Imre Nagy considered his exclusion from office and Party post not only unjust, harmful, and inexpedient, but also illegal, that is, determined in violation of the Party statutes and governing principles. Because of his persistence in observing legal rules, Nagy reminded some people of the image of the Hungarian county judges of old times as described by the novelist Jokai, judges who by their steadfastness, incorruptibility, and meticulous adherence to constitutional principles and rules helped to uphold Hungarian independence against encroachments by the Vienna Court.

SECLUSION AND APOLOGIA

Imre Nagy, had he been able to plead his case personally before the Central Committee, might have realized that he was to be betrayed not only by men but also by institutions (which are created by men) — but he was certainly not mistaken in the eyes of average people. These supported him. Clear knowledge of this he did not have, but his sense of mission never deserted him.

This sense of mission led Nagy — like other persons imbued with missionary zeal — to write what he called his "dissertation" as soon as he recovered from his illness in the summer of 1955. It was intended to be an apologia, a written defense in refutation of the charges brought against him; but it developed into a credo. His memoranda are not, like Milovan Djilas' *The New Class*,[3] an attempt to disprove the Communist doctrine; on the contrary, they are intended to show what Communist doctrine and practice really ought to be — following Marx and Lenin, according to Nagy's interpretation. We shall refrain for the moment from discussing the question of whether Nagy recognized that the idealized Communism he was proposing might, in the long run, fail to be Communism at all. What he wrote was originally intended for submission to the Central Committee so they might be convinced that the accusations against him and their resolutions condemning him had been erroneous both for factual and ideological reasons.

Imre Nagy finished the main body of his writings by September 1955, expecting them to be considered by the Central Committee that fall. In November he was expelled from the Party — to him a dumfounding event. "I was expelled from the Party," he reported, "without having had my views clarified within the framework of the ideological battle or by legal Party procedure."[4] In December 1955 and January 1956 he inserted two more chapters into his dissertation. Later he wrote an introduction. In 1957 a copy of the whole

book-length document was smuggled out of the country and published in New York and Paris. That same year the document was
printed clandestinely in Hungary by some of Nagy's friends.[5]

The Imre Nagy dissertation is an unsystematic and often in-
congruous document. It reflects not only an advance beyond the
June Resolutions, but also a strong evolution in the course of
writing the different chapters.[6] Internal inconsistencies and unsystematic and arbitrary treatment are characteristics of missionary
scriptures. Statements prompted by particular situations are often
employed as generalizations. Mohammed's Koran — if the parallel
is permissible — also abounds in seeming inconsistencies, explained
by the fact that the various suras were written under the impact of
varying motives and events. Similarly Nagy's changing circumstances
affected his pronouncements.

Though he saw things with changing eyes as he turned out his
various chapters, Nagy hardly ever, from beginning to end, mentions
the dictatorship of the proletariat.[7] He thus eliminates one of the
fundamental conceptual additions by Lenin to the Marxist doctrine.
There has been lengthy discussion as to whether, and if so when,
Imre Nagy ceased to be a true Communist.[8] The reply to such a
query presupposes the exact definition of what is meant by the
word "Communist." Whether Nagy ever ceased to be even a
"national" Communist, or whether he just ceased to be a Leninist
while still remaining a Marxist, will be discussed as our study
proceeds. Meanwhile it is important to examine some of Nagy's
theses, the impact of his forced retirement on the public, and the
hortatory value of his papers for his contemporaries.

Imre Nagy in his dissertation unblushingly describes the encroachments of the Soviet Union on the alleged independence and
sovereign statehood of Hungary: appointments to Hungarian ministerial or Party posts are made in Moscow; directives are given and
accepted concerning political lines of conduct to be followed in
Hungarian matters; accusations and complaints against Hungarian
Party and political leaders are brought before the Soviet Presidium
and their decisions accepted as final. Such procedures he must have
accepted as inevitable; he himself practiced them in his fight against
Rákosi. But he also included in his later chapters a strong indictment
against these violations and neglect of Hungarian independence.
True, he did so in veiled language, and this is understandable since
he submitted his memoranda also to the Soviet embassy, directed
to Khrushchev. His condemnation of such practices is nevertheless

severe. The impetus for such a mental process must have come partly from his own experiences, but partly also from the international developments of 1955, especially those at Belgrade and Bandung.

Nagy's withdrawal unto himself gave him the necessary leisure to contemplate the lessons of his premiership and draw the moral from it. The Soviet interference that brought about his downfall, though perhaps failing to weaken his belief in the tenets of Marxism-Leninism (as he interpreted them), must have had a shattering effect on his views regarding the existing status of Soviet satellite relations. He now became more aware of the real character of Soviet supremacy and its impact both on the development of the Communist camp and the world outside.

Though it would be foolhardy to pretend that a complete volte-face, a conversion in the Pauline sense, had taken place within Imre Nagy, or that henceforward he was prepared with King Clovis to "adore what he destroyed and to destroy what he adored," certainly a subtle metamorphosis had occurred within his ego. Once the change of mind had taken place, it was deep and irreversible. His dissertation, mainly polemical in nature, and committed in self-defense, already contained many views heretical to the accepted tenets of Soviet Communism. But the really revolutionary papers are those which he wrote after his expulsion from the Party. The months of withdrawal leading up to his forcible ejection may be regarded as a period of fermentation. When this blow fell on him, he suddenly visualized the underlying greatest evil — the fact of Soviet domination.

IMRE NAGY'S YUGOSLAV ORIENTATION

During the summer of 1955, while drafting his testimonial, Nagy had been much impressed by the Soviet-Yugoslav reconciliation. He hails it in his chapter entitled: "The Peaceful Coexistence of the Two Systems," meaning the Soviet and Yugoslav systems of "building socialism." In his view, lessons of "great historical significance" can be learned from the declarations made during Khrushchev's visit to Belgrade in May–June 1955: "To apply Marxism-Leninism to other countries by upholding its principles without modification can cause only the distortion or stagnation of Marxism," and "to copy or mechanically ape the application of scientific socialism" is both improper and unscientific.[9] And, Nagy continued, "In this sense, 'Hungarian socialism,' which was meant to be a disparaging label for the independent application of scientific socialism, is in effect nothing else but . . . the application of Marxism-Leninism to specific Hungarian situations." [10]

Imre Nagy in the summer of 1955, already under the impact of the events in Belgrade, is ready to pose as an advocate of "Hungarian socialism," just as he recognizes Titoism as the legitimate political principle of Yugoslavia. He inveighs against the policy of the Cominform as stemming from a "rigid, mechanical interpretation of Marxism that disregards the necessity for exchange of views and debates within the Party." Finding many words of praise for the Yugoslav methods and their endeavors "to build socialism," he characterizes the break between the Cominform and the Yugoslav Communist Party as a schism within the Communist Camp, as a civil war in which the Hungarian Party, under the leadership of Rákosi, played an unfortunately outstanding role.

In Nagy's opinion the Yugoslav-Hungarian friendship "on a brotherly basis" should quickly be re-established in view of the "political and economic interdependence of the two countries." Nagy's advocacy of a definite orientation toward Yugoslavia, a closer link than with other Communist countries, may be inferred from the following:

> The construction of the national economy of the two countries, the direction of their development, the supply of raw materials, the geographic location, the transportation lines, the pathway to the sea, moreover the political and internal security angles and other mutual points of interest, make it imperatively necessary that the Hungarian Party should work out the questions, forms, and methods of political, economic, cultural, and other types of cooperation between the two countries.[11]

Nagy greets the Soviet-Yugoslav reconciliation as a new era in the connections among Communist parties. Accordingly, the Hungarian leadership, which played such an "overly compromising" role in the anti-Titoism campaign, and which has done nothing substantial so far to remove the sources of conflict, is out of step with the action initiated by the Soviet Communist Party. He cites Tito's speech made at Karlovać on July 27, 1955, that the Hungarian Party and its leaders prevent the restoration of good relations and still continue their "old detrimental policies." [12] He ridicules the allusions in Rákosi's speeches to "Gábor Péter and his band," intended to shift responsibility onto them for the Yugoslav conflict, and simply labels as a lie the allegation that Gábor Péter and his gang "misled" the Party leadership. Rákosi and his clique must accept responsibility for the break and its consequences — which, as we know, were the Rajk trial and the executions of innocents.

Nagy's goal of political orientation toward Yugoslavia was a policy which he could never implement, but one which underlay some of his actions during the revolutionary period of 1956. Here we already find the source of a political concept which he shared with Tito, that was nipped by the Soviet intervention: a close cooperation between Hungary and Yugoslavia, in friendship with the Soviet Union but also with the West, a policy of neutrality with such overtones as "democratic socialism" and collaboration between Danubian countries.

IMRE NAGY, THE "BOURGEOIS MORALIST"

The impact of Imre Nagy's expulsion from the Party in November 1955 is clearly perceptible in the chapter written in December under the significant title, "Ethics and Morals in Hungarian Public Life." It is directed against the Hungarian Party leadership, and characteristically starts with the following sentence:

The party of the working people that stands at the head of the nation and leads it towards socialist society must be the embodiment of social ethics and morals, and must encompass within itself all the moral virtues and values that our people developed in the course of their history.[13]

If we were not aware of Imre Nagy's individuality this statement would seem satiric. The Communist regime of Hungary — in true imitation of that of Stalinist Russia — had introduced a low standard of political morality, or rather a high standard of immorality which, except for Nazi brutality, reached levels of terrorism and violence familiar only to students of Caligula and Nero.

Communists never professed to adhere to that common morality which they scoffingly despised as "bourgeois morality"; they referred, however, to Socialist or Communist morality which, in its essence, is no morality at all but a rule of expediency for the attainment of the Party's goals. To orthodox Communists it must have sounded heretical when Imre Nagy thus defined his own concept of political morality (italics ours):

The *eternal moral precepts* and laws of progressive mankind are adopted on the same basis by our society, which is developing toward socialism. The new and higher morals and ethics of socialist society unite within themselves the moral ideals and ethical principles *common to mankind as a whole* and peculiar to the Hungarian nation; they develop and perfect these ideals and principles while preserving their characteristic features.[14]

Imre Nagy had, evidently, an ideal Communism in mind, imbued with social ethics and morals "that must prevail in all aspects of public life and individual activity." He seemed to believe in the possibility of elevating a "socialist country" to a "higher plane of humanity," not only materially but also "by our superior moral point of view and pure ethical principles." It appears that his belief was rooted in the Socratic ethical doctrine.

From this idealistic approach, he bewails the absence of morals and ethics in Hungarian public life. He speaks of the intensification of crisis in social and Party life. Considering, in a true Marxist-Leninist sense, ethics and morals as a "reflection of the substructure," he states that "the moral crisis indicated that we got off on the wrong road in laying the basis of social economy and the social system." [15]

The reader must wonder whether Nagy is so enveloped in his idealistic thinking as to be oblivious of the degree and magnitude of depravity into which the Party, the administration, and the whole country had sunk as a consequence of Stalinist misrule, lies, and brutality. Or did he have a clear conception of what had happened — as one is rather inclined to believe — and, being fearful of expressing himself too frankly in his memorandum, did he venture opinions which might still be palatable to those Communist leaders — including Khrushchev — for whom his writings were intended? Only in trying to particularize causes and persons responsible for the absence of morality and ethics do Nagy's views become more realistic and his denunciations more violent. After deploring the abandonment of the "June way" which would have rejuvenated the Party, and condemning the return to a "stupid policy" which cannot tolerate any criticism, he attacks the Party dictatorship "which does not rely on Party membership" but whose power is permeated by "a Bonapartist spirit of minority dictatorship." He says political guidance and persuasion have been replaced "by the use of force and the devices of power, all of which raised the AVH above society and Party." [16] He accuses Rákosi of having subjugated the Party to his will and, with the aid of the AVH, of having forced the Party to execute his wishes. Bonapartism, he says, did not become predominant automatically, and if it had not been for the policy of Stalin in aiding the liquidation of anti-Bonapartist forces, "Rákosi would have been unable to achieve individual dictatorship." To bring about the triumph of Bonapartism, "the allies of social democracy had to be destroyed" and "the Party's leading cadres had to be exterminated." And this, he grimly adds, "is all historical fact." [17]

How far Nagy's eyes had been opened since his "withdrawal" is shown by his somewhat exaggerated assessment of repressive events after March 1955. He wrote that the "abuse of power and the use of illegal devices reached alarming proportions in 1955 and exceeded even the malpractices of the period from 1950 to 1952." [18] Actually the illegalities and abuses, though present in 1955, were less exorbitant than those of the Stalinist era. For Imre Nagy, who started to see more clearly after his involuntary retirement and especially after his expulsion from the Party, the malpractices of the present appeared worse than those which he had perceived as a participant in power.

Nagy's emergence as what might be termed a "bourgeois moralist" is well demonstrated by his attitude toward keeping in office those persons accountable to past crimes:

It is not compatible with public morality to have in positions of leadership the directors and organizers of mass lawsuits, or those responsible for the torturing and killing of innocent people, or organizers of international provocations,* or economic saboteurs, or squanderers of public property who, through the abuse of power, either have committed serious crimes against the people or are forcing others to commit these crimes. The public, the Party, and the state organs must be cleansed of these elements.[19]

One should bear in mind that these words were written before the Twentieth Party Congress of the Soviet Union, before the denunciation of Stalin's crimes by Khrushchev. Khrushchev simply wished the condemnation and eradication of the "cult of the individual," whereas Nagy had a different remedy and a different "socialist" society in mind. Nagy wished to abolish all degeneration and corruption of public life, such as "falsehood and careerism," "self-abasement, cowardice, hypocrisy, lack of principle, and lies." In their place he wished to see "courage, resolution, sincerity and frankness, consistency of principle, and strength." [20] Could we imagine the implementation of such standards as compatible with a Soviet-Communist system at all?

Imre Nagy, naturally, did not wish to omit the Rajk affair. At the date when he wrote the chapter on ethics and morals, Lászlo Rajk could no longer with any seriousness be considered an imperialist or Titoist spy. Rákosi and his clique, in private conversations, now were reproaching the executed leader for cowardice, because he had admitted to fake charges. Nagy is righteously indignant:

* Imre Nagy's transliteration of the Russian word "provokatsiya" is used similarly to that word in Western languages. In Communist jargon this word means "plot" or "conspiracy" achieved usually by the methods of the *agent provocateur*.

Why do they outrage the memory of the deceased Rajk, and why do they protect and conceal the real criminals who are well known by name, i.e. the members of the clique, the so-called "foursome," Rákosi, Farkas, Gerö, and Révai? Is this considered compatible with Communist morality, with human honor and dignity? They do it in the interest of Party unity — as they keep saying — but they forget that *the Party is not a den of criminals, whose unity must be preserved by hiding their crimes* [italics added]. What kind of unity is it that is held together by knowledge of and participation in crime? Their answer is that "we do not moralize," and that this is a political question and not a moral one. They do not perceive that they have thereby condemned their policies and have admitted the loss of all moral ground.[21]

Nagy goes on to assert that this sort of view seeks to identify Party interests with the interests of "a clique of criminals," and while ostensibly trying to guard Party unity is actually protecting the true criminals from exposure. He claims that "real Party unity can be established only through the exposure of crimes . . . Neither suppression, glossing over, nor lies can undo the commission of the crimes." [22] Nevertheless, Nagy tries to draw a distinction between the *Party* and the *ruling clique,* between the Communist system and the present leaders — as many disillusioned Communists have tried to do. One wonders whether Nagy, like many of his friends, had finally come to the conclusion that not only persons who had behaved immorally were guilty, but that the whole system was immoral, that the Party as such lacked political morality and decency. In any case, for Nagy in December 1955, it was already a great leap forward to express himself in such an outspoken manner.

Imre Nagy's attitude during the Revolution in 1956 becomes more understandable in the light of some paragraphs of his chapter on ethics and morals. He considered that the Communist Party had fallen into moral decay and that the necessary condition for its survival was a "moral and political regeneration." In Nagy's view, the Stalinists and, in the case of Hungary the Rákosi clique, guilty of crimes and mismanagement, had caused the Communist Party to degenerate. A complete process of regeneration, of purification, was needed; such a process could be carried out only by those elements that were unstained by the faults and crimes of the past. Nagy claimed that there were still such Communists, and said they must undertake the struggle "to restore the reputation of the Party and of Communists, to reacquire, guard, and increase the faith and confidence of the people." [23]

Imre Nagy's evolution, as evidenced by his writings, was not an evolution restricted to himself; it was one through which many thousands of Party members had passed during the years of 1953–1956, if in less articulate fashion. No less did the results of his "transfiguration" affect himself alone; his scriptures, though never officially considered by the Central Committee, were circulated among his friends, including leading Party members, and among wide circles of intellectuals and even workers. Therein lies the political significance of his literary work. It expressed what many others felt, and his ideas found resonance in those who had been unable to give proper expression to their sentiments.

THE FIVE BASIC PRINCIPLES OF INTERNATIONAL RELATIONS

By January 1956, Imre Nagy was mentally prepared to embark upon writing yet one more chapter, in which he would explain the main source of national evil: the lack of independence. Even then he could not afford to be entirely candid on these fundamental issues. Hoping that his memorandum would reach Khrushchev and Bulganin — to whom it was evidently addressed — he used an obvious stratagem. When raising the question of national sovereignty of Hungary, her desire for equality among other nations (especially the Soviet Union), and the general problem of equality among the members of the Communist camp, he paraphrased the concept of *Panch Sheel,* or Five Principles, for his purpose. The following five points had been accepted as guides for conduct in a 1954 declaration by India and the People's Republic of China: (1) mutual respect for each other's territorial integrity and sovereignty; (2) mutual nonaggression; (3) mutual noninterference in each other's internal affairs; (4) equality and mutual benefit; (5) peaceful coexistence.[24] They also formed the basis of the 1955 agreement reached at the Bandung Conference of Afro-Asian Powers. Nagy entitled this chapter "The Five Basic Principles of International Relations and the Question of Our Foreign Policy." He called the Five Principles a new and extraordinary event of world politics, and said that not a single declaration had been made that opposed or even questioned their justice and correctness. "From these facts we must arrive at conclusions of utmost importance: that these will have a decisive influence on the great changes that are taking place in the field of international relations." [25]

Of course, it was well known to Imre Nagy that Khrushchev and Bulganin, when visiting India and other Asiatic countries in November 1955, had pledged themselves on various occasions to observe these principles. Nagy now shoots the arrow home by arguing for an application the Soviet leaders hardly had in mind. (The italics in the following quotations are ours.)

The "facts indicate," he says, "that the five basic principles cannot be limited to the capitalistic system or the battle between the two systems, *but must extend to the relations between the countries within the democratic and socialist camp.* The five basic principles do not spring from differences between the two systems — capitalism and socialism — they do not express this difference, but they are factors independent of social and political relationships in the international field." He proceeds to point out emphatically why this is so. He attacks existing "erroneous views" to the effect that clinging to the Five Principles in the relationships between the Communist countries is "contrary to proletarian internationalism and nationalism, and indicative of a deviation toward chauvinism, and thus weakening the democratic and socialist camps." On the contrary, he says, "they strengthen them, because the socialist camp can become *the rallying point of independent sovereign countries possessing equal rights, respecting the principle of noninterference in each other's affairs.* Moreover close cooperation within the socialist camp in the economic, political, and cultural fields can insure a healthy relationship if the five basic principles are mutually respected." [26]

While exculpating himself and all other adherents to the Five Principles from the accusation of chauvinism, Nagy asks himself: "Can the ideals of socialism, proletarian internationalism, and national independence be reconciled?" His reply is that this question "must without doubt be answered by an unqualified Yes." [27]

Almost openly addressing himself to the masters of the Kremlin with words which might appeal to their ears, Imre Nagy continues:

It cannot be doubted that it is more difficult to enforce these five principles against the imperialist great powers than between countries of a democratic and socialist type. But from this it does not in the least follow that among the latter these guiding principles have become "superfluous," or that they should be interpreted differently. On the contrary, there they are more easily realized and offer wider possibilities for application. The decisive question is: who does respect these basic principles, and who does not? [28]

Imre Nagy warns his readers that negligence in respecting the Five Principles within the Socialist camp may produce serious consequences, and that those who refuse to follow them are, in effect, professing Stalinism. "These situations arise from improper anti-

Marxist views which declare that socialism supersedes nationalism, denying the national characteristics of socialism, falsifying international proletarianism — in reality this means a cosmopolitan distortion of Marxism. The working class, if it wants to fulfill its historical role and accept, as it must, the burden of solving national problems, must above all insure its independence and sovereignty." Nagy wishes these Stalinist ideas completely discarded and replaced by "the Marxist-Leninist theory of locally characteristic socialism." [29] What is this, if not a sublimated Titoism?

The following passage, in which Nagy wishes to apply his principles particularly to Hungary, reveals more than any other his impatience with those who argued for a "voluntary" relinquishment of these ideals:

> The noble traditions of these five basic principles have roots in our country also, which were formed during our historical development. There were periods in history when the light of these principles and ideals of ours shone brightly in all of Europe. The noble traditions of battles for independence are still alive today, and have their effect, nurturing these principles as our greatest national virtue. Attaining national independence and sovereignty where it is nonexistent, or preserving it, has always been the greatest national problem in past periods, as it is today and will be in the future, even under the socialist system's development. While nations and national states exist . . . the five basic principles will remain the motivating power of the development of the socialist system. *That is why the nation clings to its independence, sovereignty, and freedom. That is why it cannot and does not yield to force or "voluntary" relinquishing of these ideals.* There were and are difficult times in the life of a nation, when *those in power alluding to the best interests of the people and the nation, accept dependence, subordination, humiliating slavery — betraying the cause of national independence.* There are many instances in history that show that the former ruling classes accepted slavery for the nation, instead of independence, sovereignty, liberty and equality, to ensure their own specially privileged status. However, according to the lessons of history, *these betrayals of the nation do not end with the destruction of the nation but with that of the traitors,* following which the ideals of freedom and independence burn with a stronger and brighter flame in the hearts of the masses.[30]

Nobody who has closely read the latter part of this excerpt will fail to understand that Nagy was alluding to his opponents who wished to preserve the nation's "humiliating slavery" to ensure their own privileged status.

Nagy summed up this momentous chapter by pointing out the

reasons for the explosive situation in Hungary: "The inner tension of Hungary, which is chiefly political, is caused by the fact that the leadership is opposing the ideals of national independence, sovereignty, and equality, as well as Hungarian national feeling and progressive traditions." [31]

IMRE NAGY'S HUNGARIAN PATRIOTISM

What is most characteristic about Imre Nagy is that he managed to combine his faith in his conception of "Socialism" with genuine Hungarian patriotism. However futile such a combination must appear to an outsider and however tragic the eventual disillusionment, his conviction in this regard, even during his first term of office, can hardly be questioned. In order to dispel any doubt as to his Hungarian feelings and to dissociate himself from Communists who "are foreign to the Hungarian people and to their ambitions," he inserted in his dissertation the following pathetic apologia, written during the summer of 1955:

At the same time, in order to avoid all misunderstanding, I want to emphasize that as a son of the Hungarian people and as a member of the Hungarian nation I am proud of my Hungarian past. I do not deny my Hungarian nationality and ardently love my Hungarian homeland and my Hungarian people. True patriotism, together with a love and respect for other peoples and nations, is the basis and essence of proletarian internationalism. This distinguishes and separates me, even today, from the cosmopolites and the "leftist" extremists who are foreign to the Hungarian people and to their ambitions — which are fused with the ideal and grand design of socialism — and who are also incapable of true patriotism. They are the ones who, in the past as well as in the present, have turned against the national feelings of the Hungarian people. It is they who sow the nationalistic and chauvinistic seeds of dissension, wittingly or unwittingly.[32]

These words sound strange in the mouth of a Moscow-trained Communist. They were written before his expulsion from the Party, and we must surmise that these ideas were never alien to his thoughts, not even after his return from the Soviet Union in 1945, nor during his term of office and after. As he and his friends clearly saw, Rákosi, Gerö, Farkas, Révai, and many other muscovites were in fact Soviet Comintern or Cominform agents. It simply happened that they were of Hungarian mother tongue, and had therefore been primarily assigned to work in Hungary. In a different context they would have been able and ready to work in any other country, as so many of them had worked in Spain, Paris, Brussels, Berlin, or in other centers for the Communist cause. Nagy, despite his Moscow training, remained essentially Hungarian.

In his writings, Imre Nagy gave voice to complaints long felt by members of groups in opposition to the Rákosi regime. Complaints concerning the dependent status of Hungary had become more and more acute since the demotion of the Prime Minister, which was rightly evaluated as stemming chiefly from foreign intervention. The crux of all national problems was considered to depend on the unequal relationship existing between Hungary and the Soviet Union. The genuine interests of Hungary could never be safeguarded as long as Party and government were unable to act as free agents in both international and internal affairs. Here lay the source of the evil. As Nagy wrote concerning the Party leadership, "We never examined the international situation thoroughly in the light of our own country's interests." [33] Independent economic and foreign trade policy, national cultural development, education, and national political objectives could be achieved only when there was no more subservience to the orders and whims of Moscow. And Imre Nagy was far from being alone in thinking so.

16

The Eager Flock of an
Unsuspecting Shepherd

ΛΛ.ΛΛ.ΛΛ.ΛΛ.ΛΛ.ΛΛ.ΛΛ.ΛΛ.ΛΛ.ΛΛ.ΛΛ.ΛΛ.ΛΛ/

The star that bids the shepherd fold

JOHN MILTON

THOSE who formed the most dangerous opposition to the existing regime and brought influence and pressure even upon leading Party members were heterogeneous groups, mostly intellectuals, and most of them members of the Party. They included writers, journalists, educators, and students; released prisoners (themselves either Party members, such as most of the Rajkists, or else former Social Democrats); and also some lower Party functionaries. These circles never truly rallied to a common cause; lacking common ideas they nonetheless shared a thorough disappointment and resentment for the failures and crimes of the regime. They felt cheated for having followed the Party line. Now they were all disabused of their former attachment to the Party, and they wished to have revenge on those who had swindled them. Their hopes had been raised during the Imre Nagy interlude; this frustrated expectation turned into passionate hatred and exasperation after Nagy's initiative failed and he had become a victim of Rákosi's intrigues and of Soviet interference. Furthermore, their aggressiveness was no doubt increased by their subconscious feelings of guilt.

A common political endeavor to achieve active results needs a visible head. Nagy's reputation, his personality as contrasted with that of other Communist leaders, his recognized patriotism, and primarily his suppression by Rákosi predestined him to play this role in the eyes of all resistance groups whether Communist or not. The split in the Party, the struggle between Nagy and Rákosi — not widely known prior to the Premier's downfall — had now become a matter of common knowledge. His refusal to resort to the Communist gimmick of self-criticism and self-abasement rendered him a martyr, and, even more than before his ostracism, people looked upon him as the providential statesman of Hungary.

Imre Nagy himself had no inkling of his "leadership" over discontented thousands of intellectuals, Party members or not. He also must have been unaware, at least until the outbreak of the Revolution, of the extent of his popularity with the masses. They eagerly desired his return as the leader of Hungary, not because they had shared the majority of his views (of which very little was known) nor because they were sympathetic toward any portion of Communist doctrine, but because it gave them joy and satisfaction to support a brave "nationalist"–Communist against the followers of Rákosi. Their provisional acceptance of this type of "Communist" was cherished as a feat of realistic politics.[1] Meanwhile the unannounced symbolic "leader" of all these contradictory elements that focused their hopes on his return sat in his house, unaware of his prophethood, and wrote the "dissertation" in which he vindicated his right to return to the Party leadership as well as the right of his country to be free, independent, and prosperous. In the fall of 1955, when his writings began reaching his friends and many leading Party members, his prestige further increased in their eyes.[2] In 1956, after the Soviet Twentieth Party Congress, he gradually gave up his secluded life and enjoyed great social popularity.[3]

JOURNALISTS AND WRITERS

We have seen how, during Imre Nagy's premiership, the politically important class of journalists almost unanimously sided with him and supported the implementation of his program. After Nagy's fall the majority of his followers fell silent, depressed by the turn of events. Soon, however, there were developments to raise their spirits. The most prominent one was the visit of the Soviet statesmen to Belgrade.

Following Nagy's dismissal from the premiership in April 1955, a number of the journalists who favored his position were also demoted. The staff of the *Szabad Nép,* the Party daily, was cleansed of opposition elements. The editor in chief of the *Irodalmi Ujság* (Literary Gazette) was removed.[4] All these persons were either transferred to less important journalistic posts, assigned to Party schools, or sent abroad as correspondents. No arrests were made, however. Deviationists ran a smaller risk now than in Stalinist times.

After the Soviet reconciliation with Tito, the rehabilitation of the name of Rajk and his followers was urged in journalistic circles. Miklos Gimes and a few other journalists were expelled from the Party because they asked unpleasant questions concerning the executed leader. The Rajk affair was not the only subject of discontent. The September 1955 issue of the *Irodalmi Ujság* was confiscated because it published a veiled attack against the Minister of Culture; half the issue, however, had already been sold in the streets.[5] Within each of the editorial offices there was a concerted effort to oppose or sabotage the regime — yet always without openly attacking Communism. Writers and journalists pursued their assaults through allusions well understood by the readers.* And criticism was also delivered at meetings of Party cells and editorial committees. However, no centrally planned or coordinated actions were carried out prior to November 1955, except the campaign for the rehabilitation of Rajkists and other political prisoners.[6]

The journalist critics of Rákosi and the regime were mostly those who had lost all illusions about Communism and cherished no hopes for the improvement of Soviet attitudes. If they seemed to endorse the actual line of Soviet policies, it was only to contrast them to the Stalinist line pursued by Rákosi and his clique. When the ruling Party leaders could themselves be accused of being "anti-Soviet" they felt hurt as if touched by a spear of Ithuriel.[7]

Harassment against the ruling clique gathered momentum in the fall of 1955. The confiscation of the *Irodalmi Ujság* furnished an excellent excuse for retaliation. The Writers' Association asked for official explanations, for reparations, and the punishment of those responsible for suppressing a "Communist" paper. Seeing all satisfaction refused, the Communist members of the Presidium of the Writers' Association resigned from that body, a step unprecedented in the history of the Hungarian Communist Party; "resignation" traditionally took place only at the behest of the Party leadership. Since the whole cultural and press policy and the question of "freedom of expression" was at stake, the Party could not give way. Neither, however, did the rebellious writers.

---

* For example, Péter Kuczka in his review of the Soviet film "The Rumyantsev Affair" in *Szabad Nép*, March 25, 1956, under the disguise of praise for the Soviet film, criticized arbitrary arrests and cowardly behavior of the arrested persons' friends. The article ends with the words: "a Communist does not tolerate injustice, does not tolerate cowardly submission."

As a next move in this literary combat, fifty-nine writers, poets, journalists, actors, and artists, the cream of Hungarian intellectuals, submitted a memorandum to the Central Committee, passing in review their grievances, protesting against the activities of those Party functionaries who "are distorting the cultural policy of the Party" and who "are applying anti-democratic methods which cripple cultural life." [8] This "Writers' Memorandum" was to date the most daring action of the inchoate opposition. It emanated from a group of Party members who had been the favorites of the regime, who lived in relative luxury and had been endowed with the highest honors — such as the Kossuth Prize — which a People's Democracy can bestow upon the faithful.

Many of the writers had been ardent sycophants of Stalin and Rákosi. Now, feeling disabused, they turned against their erstwhile idols, and with the zeal of converts set themselves to the task of destroying, from within, the regime they had helped to build.[9] It is by no means an exaggeration to attribute the volte-face of many to the shock treatment they received when listening to the narratives of ex-convicts who were their former colleagues.* Some of the Communist writers had believed in the guilt of these prisoners and even inveighed against them in writings and poems; now they felt shame and remorse, and this feeling equipped them with the audacity and ferocity to turn openly against Rákosi and his clique.

The writers — as well as the University students — had a traditional claim for the task which they wished to assume. There had been periods, in Hungary and elsewhere, when writers, poets, journalists, and students had been able to play an outstanding role in the shaping of political events. Under genuine democratic conditions such a role could not entirely devolve upon literary societies or students' associations; but in autocratic systems where no

---

* A vivid description of the anti-Communist "brainwashing" administered by former prisoners to their colleagues merits quotation: "Many of the former political prisoners were left-wing intellectuals, writers and journalists who had always moved in the Budapest literary set and now made it a point to tell all to their erstwhile cronies. Nights were spent going through what had happened — a story of unspeakable, gruesome tortures, revealing the Communist state apparatus as a monster of depravity. The recipients of these confidences wished they were dead, for as Communist writers they had provided a richly orchestrated literary accompaniment to the purges. They had exhausted the remarkable resources of the Hungarian language to vilify the victims and render thanks to their torturers for saving humanity and Socialism from harm. Now they felt that they had no excuse whatever and began to hate themselves and Communism, the cause of their utter moral degradation. This was one of the decisive impulses behind the revolt two years later." Paul Kecskemeti, "Limits and Problems of Decompression: The Case of Hungary," *The Annals*, May 1958, p. 102. See also Tamás Aczél, "The Honest Sinners," *The Review*, June 1959, pp. 70–86.

popular representation exists, writers and students, or their associations, can acquire great political significance. In the absence of other means of expression they become the mouthpiece of the masses. One needs only to recall the role which writers played in the age of enlightenment in France, and in the German cause of unification in the eighteenth and nineteenth centuries, and in the political convulsions of Russia in the nineteenth and twentieth. Abdul Hamid II, the last autocratic Ottoman sultan, was forced to forbid all literary publications in 1901 because, despite strict censorship, writers were able to criticize his administration in a disguised form.

In Hungary, the way toward national emancipation and freedom had been paved by poets and writers and journalists, whose experience was to influence the imagination of the revolutionaries of October–November 1956. A sense of mission, similar to that felt by their nineteenth-century predecessors, was felt by Hungary's writers and poets in 1955 and 1956 (except for a handful of muscovites and their imitators). And they were in the fortunate position of being able to express their feelings without excessive risks. Under the relaxation that followed the Stalinist terror they only risked expulsion from the Party (which now meant nothing to them sentimentally), or a loss in revenue, or the loss of their jobs. Many of them were ready to risk all these things.

The Leninist structure of government is based on the presumption that not only the state administration but also all other organizations or movements are strictly controlled or run by the Party. Rákosi and his staff, after initial hesitations and attempts at compromise, properly assessed the significance of the revolt within the Writers' Association, an important organization in the Communist system. Since most of the rebels had been members of the Party, the discipline had to be administered by the Party in some appropriate form.

RÁKOSI RESISTS REBELLION

The first reprisal against the Writers' Memorandum was aimed at Imre Nagy although he had been involved neither in the drafting nor in the adoption of it.[10] Either Rákosi presumed that Nagy stood behind this sedition or else he wanted to discourage all opposition by selecting such a prominent victim, the "unintentional" leader of the resistance. Thus the Writers' Memorandum was the pretext for an event which, as already mentioned, shocked Nagy and affected the course of his writing — his expulsion from the Party.

The memorandum had been presented in the early days of

November 1955. A week later Nagy was summoned by the Central Control Commission of the Party. Its chairman, Károly Kiss, read out the accusations: Nagy's refusal to recant, his activity to form an anti-Party group which had made him a "rallying point of the enemies of Socialism." [11] After a short examination of the accused by the members of the Commission, the decision was announced to Nagy: he had been expelled from the Party for "rightist deviationism," for "incompatibility with the Party-spirit," and for diversive activities.

For a man who for over forty years had served the Communist movement, expulsion must have been a jolting experience. According to witnesses he again suffered a slight heart attack.[12] But it did not prevent him from adding the two vigorous chapters on morals and foreign policy to his political testimony in December and January and thereby setting foot on the road to Damascus.

The Party summoned the rebellious writers to attend a mass meeting of Party functionaries on December 6, 1955, where the attitude of the writers, their memorandum, and their debates were severely taken to task by carefully selected Party members. A few days later the Central Committee published a resolution, adopted prior to the mass meeting, which condemned "the rightist tendencies" in the literary field, stating that "rightist opportunism presents itself in the most dangerous, overt and organized form within the field of literary life." [13] Thereupon, most of the sponsors of the Writers' Memorandum revoked their signatures. Those who did not were either expelled from the Party (like Sándor Haraszti and Miklos Vásárhelyi) or severely reprimanded. Though none was arrested at that time, they suffered financial sanctions as a result of the return of unpublished manuscripts, the withholding of royalties, and other discriminations against their works.

The failure of the writers revealed that Rákosi and his associates were still firmly in the saddle. Exchanges of views during the writers' revolt also revealed that many influential Party leaders sympathized silently with their resistance but still dared not oppose Rákosi openly. The rebellion had been muted, but only a new signal, a new sign of weakness, was needed to open the sluices for a new revolt. As it happened, this signal was to be the Twentieth Party Congress in Moscow.

HIDDEN CLEAVAGE IN HIGH PLACES

The cleavage within the Party leadership remained latent prior to the Twentieth Congress, with no clear-cut factions visible. The weakness as well as the strength of the unorganized opposition was its multiform nature. Most of the Party functionaries had served under Rákosi; many of them had turned against him now, but were ready to act openly only when this could be done without incurring risks.[14] In leading Party circles only close friends knew each other's genuine sentiments. Often fear, caution, or mere opportunism determined the stand of one or another Party official. According to all reliable testimony, the Party structure had been greatly undermined from 1955 on. The Imre Nagy experiment, the recognition of crimes committed during and after the Stalinist era, fear of subsequent reprisals, the internal contradictions and lies of the regime, and the triumph of Titoism contributed to the agony of the system.[15]

Despite the absence of definite factions in the leading echelons of the Party, certain tendencies may be discerned. Former prisoners of the Stalinist era, now rehabilitated and given Party or other official assignments, together with their numerous friends and sympathizers, had special reasons for disliking the ruling clique. These disgruntled Party members, however, were far from being uniform in their impulses. János Kádár and his circle of friends (Gyula Kállai, György Marosán, Béla Biszku, Béla Kelen, and others),* though anti-Rákosi in their views, were "conformist," adaptable, and agreeable to any solution which would decrease Rákosi's power but increase their own. Their attitude toward Imre Nagy and his friends was rather hostile, suspicious, and guided by jealousy; Nagy's adherents were intellectually superior, and Kádár felt that he could never himself rival the popularity and intellect of Nagy should the latter be again given a leading role. On the other hand, Géza Losonczy, Ferenc Donáth, and their friends (who included most of the intellectual elite of the Party) ** were not only fervent adherents of Imre Nagy, but had mentally turned away from the Marxist-Leninist kind of Communism. Operating within the Party framework to promote the "rejuvenation" or reform of the Communist-Socialist movement, they had been much influenced by Nagy's ideas and had likewise brought certain of their views to bear on the former Premier.[16] Even some men in important

* All these held important posts in the Hungarian Party and government as late as the spring of 1961, Kállai being at that time the First Deputy Prime Minister, Marosán a Party Secretary (formerly Minister of State), Biszku the Minister of the Interior, and Kelen the Party Secretary of Budapest.

** Losonczy and Donáth had both been imprisoned from 1951 to 1954. After their rehabilitation both rejoined the Party. Losonczy became deputy editor of the *Magyar Nemzet* (daily paper of the People's Patriotic Front), and Donáth, after a prolonged journey in the Soviet Union, was made head of the Economic Institute.

Party positions sympathized, at times, with this faction.[17] The split of the last days of the Revolution and its aftermath, between "anti-Stalinists" like Kádár and those of the Losonczy-Donáth type, who favored and even outdistanced Imre Nagy, was already slightly discernible by the middle of the year 1955.

Years later — June 17, 1958 — a Hungarian regime was to charge that "Imre Nagy and his most intimate accomplices, Géza Losonczy, Ferenc Donáth, Miklos Gimes and Jozsef Szilágyi, established in December, 1955, a secret anti-state organization with the aim of seizing power by force and overthrowing the Hungarian People's Republic." [18]

There is no trace of any such "organization" as mentioned in this indictment. Private conversations on political subjects and exchanges of political ideas should be called neither organization nor conspiracy. There is no evidence that Nagy ever contemplated conspiracy. If Losonczy or Donáth "conspired," they did it without collective assent and organization, and this is not "conspiracy" in the legal sense of the term. What Losonczy, Donáth, and others were doing was to exploit hatred, jealousy, and personal antipathy between leading Party members, persuade local Party leaders to arrange debates on delicate questions, promote "reliable" persons to key posts, and form pressure groups. Similar activities, such as lobbying for oneself and friends, had always taken place within the Party. In early 1956 all these acts in combination acquired a significance larger than mere discontent with the ruling clique. Stalinists were opposed by those who wanted personal and political change. Kádár and his coterie employed similar methods, with the exception that they sought only changes in personnel (removal of Rákosi and his clique) rather than in policy. Kádár had the advantage of being promoted in the fall of 1955 to the secretariat of the Central Committee, a key position where he was joined by his friend Kállai. Whatever the motives, the anti-Rákosi activity in leading Party circles remained clandestine until the Soviet Twentieth Congress — and meanwhile clandestine opposition was mounting throughout the populace.

DISGUISED OR CONCEALED OPPOSITION PATTERNS

History teaches us that whenever an autocratic or totalitarian system of government prohibits the expression of overt opposition, antagonism against the regime is likely to find expression through other channels and in forms approved or at least tolerated by the rulers. In the autocratic Byzantine Empire national sentiment found hidden expression in theological controversies.* Chariot-racing factions at the circus in Constantinople revealed themselves as political parties.[19] In tsarist Russia the self-governing local councils created in 1864, the *zemstva*, soon became centers of opposition to the autocratic government.[20] Between contending Communist leaders, in the Soviet Union and elsewhere, struggles for power have often been concealed beneath the garment of ideological dissent.

The fight against the Hungarian regime — not only against Rákosi or the Stalinist elements of Party leadership — was carried on in the disguise of Marxist-Leninist slogans. These tactics have been widely employed all over the satellite area. It was nowhere prudent to attack the basic features of Communism: the Party rule, the dictatorship of the proletariat, or Soviet Russian domination. Nationalistic or democratic opposition remained anathema, tantamount to counterrevolutionary activity, and was severely prosecuted. On the other hand, after Stalinist terrorism had passed away, "deviationism" was no more a capital offense; no one in a satellite country could finally decide what constituted such a heresy if Moscow had not clearly expressed itself on the subject. In the post-Stalin era, Leninism could be opposed to Stalinism, inter-Party democracy to the cult of the individual, Socialist legality to excesses and illegalities. Furthermore, it was possible in the satellite area to invoke Moscow's dicta against the local Communist leadership, thereby confusing the Party chiefs and promoting their fall. And it was hard for the regime to distinguish between genuine "deviationists" and those who resorted to ideological arguments only on tactical grounds and were, in fact, aiming at the system itself.[21]

To defend itself against accusations of "Stalinism," the Party leadership had to invoke arguments of orthodoxy; it would declare its opponents rightists (or leftists, as the case might be), deviationists, or anti-Party groups. But by 1955 heretics were no longer burned. They were expelled from the Party, removed from their jobs, or transferred to lesser posts. But, as we have seen in the case of the writers, Rákosi, less staunchly supported by Moscow, weakened by the Yugoslav issues, and no longer sure of the unconditional support of his own adherents, resorted with reluctance to even such relatively anodyne sanctions.

---

* Monophysitism in Syria and Egypt masked nationalistic anti-Greek feelings in the fifth and sixth centuries A.D. The clash between image-worshippers and iconoclasts in the tenth century was the cloak covering the struggle between the Greek element of the Empire and racial elements of Asia Minor, represented by an army of recruits from Isauria, Phrygia, and Armenia.

This form of fighting the Party "from within" had its dis-advantages. It might be misunderstood by those who were prepared to fight the regime openly should the opportunity present itself. In Hungary, as in the other satellite countries, Communist ideology had developed for the average citizen into an empty ritual or even an object of contempt or ridicule. The more the workers, employees, or farmers were subjected to indoctrination, compelled to listen to a phraseology and dogmatism whose inaccuracy and mendacity re-vealed itself in their everyday life, the more apathetic and disdainful they became in the face of ideological jargon. It was not easy to convey to out-and-out opponents of the system the expediency of resorting to the devious tactics of concealed opposition cloaked in Communist ideological terms. Unsophisticated elements — outright enemies of the Communist system — were often reluctant to join writers and students who, compelled to fight on ideological ground, were outwardly professing loyalty to the regime itself.[22]

Disguised antagonism against the regime and the Soviet Union could also be expressed through sports enthusiasm which might be either genuine or a façade for political feeling. During the summer of 1954, the unsportsmanlike behavior of the Soviet water polo team had given rise to anti-Soviet demonstrations in Buda-pest.[23] In the summer of 1955, when the much advertised Hungarian soccer team, after a number of outstanding victories, finally lost the world championship, "soccer enthusiasts" demonstrated in the streets of Budapest, breaking the windows of the sports journal, shouting with indignation against the team captain until police broke up the riot. It must have been evident that thousands of demonstrators were not impelled by the fury at losing a sporting event. This was popular indignation in disguise.[24]

The concealed anti-regime campaign reached and permeated many institutions and Party organizations. Youth organizations were especially affected by it. We shall later discuss the Petöfi Circle, a debating society organized under the auspices of the DISZ (Federa-tion of the Communist Youth). Party cells, Party branch organiza-tions, and local groups of the People's Patriotic Front also provided cloaks for disguised resistance. In most of these cases systematic ideological sabotage of the regime took place under the initiative of individual members; yet one may also recall the example of an official Communist organization that devoted its full energy to anti-regime activity: the local DISZ group of the village of Békés-sámson in the Great Plains.

From its very outset the Békéssámson group was a cover organization to fight the regime. Its members had been selected among "reliable" young men, mostly sons of farmers, and entry was never permitted to any outsider who would not be ready to participate in the activity of this disguised resistance group. Its members circulated pamphlets against collectivization and compulsory deliveries, and terrorized Party secretaries and Party members, while outwardly maintaining the appearance of a successful and active Communist Youth organization. For over a year they assured a non-Communist life for their village; and their anti-regime activity reached out into the whole neighborhood. When finally discovered, early in 1956, the members of this conspiracy were brought to trial, and the prosecutor accused them of having damaged the reputation of the kolkhozes and caused a sharp decrease in food deliveries all over that part of the country.[25]

Disguised opposition — using a false pretext to conceal real intention — is practiced not only in satellite areas but also within the precincts of the Soviet Union; it is the special resort of national minorities in that country. The most conspicuous incident of this character occurred in the Georgian Soviet Republic in March 1956, when bloody rioting broke out in Tiflis. Ostensibly the demonstrators were protesting against Moscow's refusal to permit them to honor Stalin on the anniversary of his death. Of course the genuine intention of the ringleaders was to oppose the Communist regime as such, and to use as a pretext Khrushchev's condemnation of the "great son of Georgia." [26]

Thus, many of the events within the Soviet satellite area, and also some occurring within the Soviet Union itself, can be correctly assessed only when taking into account the existence of opposition either ideologically disguised or appearing in tolerated forms, and professing limited aims within recognized Party or state institutions. The leaders of the Party, on the other hand, have just as frequently disguised their simple power motives by resorting to ideological or political excuses — a device employed by Nikita Sergeyevich Khrushchev when he took the rostrum at the Twentieth Party Congress.

17

Effect Beyond Intent—Impact of the Twentieth Party Congress

/\

For greatest scandal waits on greatest State.

SHAKESPEARE, *The Rape of Lucrece*

AFTER Khrushchev and Bulganin re-established tolerable but limited relations with Tito and created the "spirit of Geneva," Molotov and his group nevertheless managed to prevent a strengthening of ties with Tito's Communist Party. Molotov himself undid most of what had been achieved at the Summit by his stand at the Foreign Ministers' Conference of October–November 1955, thus reasserting his authority at least within the field of foreign affairs. There were even signs that Stalinist prestige was again in the ascendant. On Stalin's birthday, December 21, 1955, celebrations greater than those of the preceding year were devoted to his person and his military achievements. Renewed attacks against Malenkov indicated that even his star was still dimly shining, and we may assume that by then the old Stalinist faction had allied itself to that of Malenkov in trying to prevent Khrushchev from attaining supremacy in the Party and government.[1] In view of the temporary deadlock in the Soviet Presidium, Rákosi was able to preserve his status in Hungary.

KHRUSHCHEV BREAKS THE DEADLOCK

The Twentieth Party Congress opened in Moscow on February 14, 1956. Khrushchev, as First Secretary of the Party, submitted

his political report on that day. It contained some courtesies toward
Yugoslavia, but the standard of "brotherly relations" was accorded
only to allied People's Democracies. Khrushchev, quoting Lenin,
admitted the possibility and historic necessity of various forms of
transition to Socialism. He referred to the People's Democracies as
a form of transition different from that of the Soviet Union. He
also spoke of China's way toward Socialism, and devoted some words
to the manner of building a Socialist order peculiar to Yugoslavia.[2]

But Khrushchev's main blast was yet to come. Allied with
Mikoyan, he wished to impose a kind of shock treatment on the
Congress which he believed might tilt the balance in his favor both
in the Central Committee and within the Presidium. The plan was
kept top secret. Prior to the Congress nobody outside Khrushchev's
inner circle seems to have had an inkling of what was to happen.
In Hungary, influential Party members guessed that the Tito question might be in the foreground of discussion, but they did not
assume that Stalin and Stalinism would be so vigorously attacked
as it was.[3] Mikoyan started it in his foreign trade report, and then
Khrushchev took up the assault at much length and with great
violence in a secret speech before a select audience on the night of
February 24–25.[4]

This bombshell was aimed at destroying the "Stalin myth," and
at the same time evicting from leading positions those former aides
of Stalin who could be described as Stalinists. Khrushchev — somewhat clumsily — tried to demonstrate how he avoided taking part
in Stalin's atrocities, but he was careful to hint at the part Malenkov,
Molotov, and Kaganovich had played during the heyday of Stalinist
terrorism.[5] Khrushchev was also careful enough not to mention
a word about the East European satellite peoples' treatment under
Stalin; he restricted himself to denouncing the deportation or
liquidation of some minority national groups in the Soviet Union
during Stalinist rule.[6] He provoked much hilarity in his audience
by mentioning that the Ukrainians avoided meeting such a fate
only because they were too numerous and there was no place to
deport them. Khrushchev himself is known to have carried out
purges in the Ukraine, especially after the liberation of that country by the Germans, and he must have had personal knowledge of
Stalin's plans for the Ukraine.

Considerable space was devoted to the Yugoslav Affair in
Khrushchev's secret speech. He recalled Stalin's "shameful role"
in artificially inflaming Soviet-Yugoslav relations. According to
Khrushchev, Stalin "had completely lost consciousness of reality; he

demonstrated his suspicion and haughtiness not only in relation to individuals in the USSR, but in relation to whole parties and nations." Khrushchev fully described Stalin's behavior toward the Yugoslav Party and nation. But we also know of Stalin's physical liquidation of whole Party leaderships, such as that of the Polish Communist Party, and also of his ruthlessness toward nations other than Yugoslavia.

Though Khrushchev gave full details of the paranoiac misdeeds of his former master against loyal Party members after World War II (omitting those committed during the Great Purges of 1934–1938), he made no accusations against Stalin for terroristic mass arrests, tortures, and executions in Hungary, Czechoslovakia, Bulgaria, Rumania, Poland, and Albania, ordered or at least approved by the Soviet leader. Neither did he say anything with regard to the rigged trials (Rajk, Kostov, Slansky, and others) organized by General Bielkin under the orders of Beria and, naturally, the orders of Stalin himself. This silence is most significant. Stalin's crimes in the international field, such as the Katyn affair and the actions in the Baltic states, Finland, and the East European satellite area, were not to be mentioned, for the sake of Soviet international prestige and for reasons of foreign policy. It was left to the individual Communist bosses in the satellite countries to cope as best they could with the analogies drawn from Stalinist excesses. The Soviet Union and the Soviet Party were not to be blamed for whatever sins had been committed at the behest of Stalin and his lieutenants.[7] This concept of irresponsibility for acts committed outside the Soviet Union, acts for which Stalin might have been blamed, eventually led Khrushchev to a contradictory position: anti-Stalinism within the Soviet Union, and neo-Stalinism in most of the satellite countries. The neo-Stalinism was to become particularly manifest after the events in Hungary in the fall of 1956.*

Khrushchev's revelations of Stalin's crimes were euphemistically called an attack on the cult of personality. They were evidently intended for internal consumption only. Delegates of non-Soviet Communist parties were not permitted to be present when Khrushchev made his portentous pronouncements, though some outstanding foreign leaders had been given a forewarning just before

* See Khrushchev's speech in Moscow on January 17, 1957, before a Chinese delegation. He said: "When the cause of the revolution was at stake . . . Stalin courageously and relentlessly defended the cause of Marxism-Leninism . . . On these cardinal and main issues, God grant, as they say, that every Communist may fight as Stalin did." *Izvestiya*, Jan. 19, 1957, as quoted by David J. Dallin, *Soviet Foreign Policy after Stalin* (Philadelphia, 1961), p. 441.

he spoke, or were subsequently briefed about what went on at the secret session. In this way they learned of the official admission that Stalin's dictatorship had led to mass murders and tortures unknown to Europeans outside the Soviet orbit since the excesses of certain sadistic Roman emperors. Even the extermination of the Knights Templar by the French king Philip II appeared a relatively mild affair in comparison with the maniac despot's terrorism carried out not only against his own Party comrades but also against entire national groups during the twenty years of his undisputed reign.

UNINTENTIONAL EFFECTS OF A SPEECH

Care was taken to prevent the knowledge of Khrushchev's revelatory speech on Stalin's crimes from spreading beyond controlled limits. At the same time, official Soviet and foreign Communist commentators tried to insure that the Twentieth Congress would have no impact other than the intended one. And this was to condemn the "cult of the individual," the neglect of "intra-Party democracy," the "degeneration" of security organs, the lack of self-criticism, the violations of Leninist norms, and other mistakes.[8] Party leaders in the People's Democracies tried to mitigate the effect of the Khrushchev revelations, and to save at least their own prestige by retaining part of the Stalin myth. *Hoi polloi* of the Party, however, and people all over the Soviet-dominated areas quickly grasped the real significance of this event. Now even the ostrich policy of shutting one's eyes to the obvious had to come to an end. There is no doubt that as soon as the essence of Khrushchev's secret speech became available to the peoples of the satellite countries, every Communist and non-Communist was induced to seek analogies between Stalin's behavior and the actions of their own Communist leaders. Naturally, they did not stop at the condemnation of a person or set of persons, but proceeded to blame the whole Soviet-Communist system.[9]

Foreign Communist leaders could not fail to foresee the disastrous consequences of Khrushchev's gruesome revelations on Communist parties abroad and on the general public. When warned by Thorez and Togliatti, Khrushchev is said to have replied that the Soviet Union needed such a "shock" in order to embark on a "new course," and that such a step had been decided in spite of the temporary damage that would be suffered by other Communist parties and the Communist cause itself.[10] The temerity of Khrushchev's procedure is certainly remarkable; no doubt, he must have been blamed subsequently when the Polish and Hungarian events occurred ten months later. That he is still being blamed for his "rash" action is suggested by the fact that he often feels the urge to defend himself in the matter. Later, on December 1, 1959, in a speech before the Hungarian Party Congress, he said:

> And it was right, even though some people have said that certain complications in the public life of the Socialist countries stem from the Twentieth Congress of our Party . . . No, Comrades, it had to be done. It was necessary to get cleansed and to throw off all the accumulated extraneous matter.[11]

Khrushchev's line of conduct in 1956 was prompted by parochial Soviet considerations, or rather by power considerations. He acted in order to eliminate from his path those elements which so far had withstood his onslaught, and to move away from the deadlock which for a year had blocked his advance toward supreme leadership of the Soviet bloc. As often in the past, the disadvantages accruing from his strategies vis-à-vis other Communist parties, including the Parties in the satellite area, were to be ignored when questions of Soviet power or Soviet leadership were at stake.

An article published in the Yugoslav *Borba* of March 20, 1956, provided the first extensive summary of Khrushchev's speech available to the satellite countries and to the world outside the Iron Curtain. When the U. S. State Department published the full text of the speech in English on June 4, the unabridged version reached many leading persons in the Soviet-dominated countries, where both accurate and apocryphal texts were already in circulation.[12] In Hungary, to forestall the effects of the speech, Rákosi circulated doctored excerpts of it within the Party.[13] The full text has never been published in Hungary.

The Congress had been attended by a Hungarian delegation led by Mátyás Rákosi, with István Kovács and Béla Szalai as members. Rákosi himself addressed the Congress on February 17 — a week before Khrushchev's revelations — and announced that by 1960 Hungary would have laid down "the solid economic foundation of Socialism." [14] He avoided the name of Stalin in his speech, but relied much on quotations and principles stemming from Lenin.* Thus Stalin's foremost Hungarian disciple had also become un-

---

* Rákosi, after Stalin's demise, had already tried to connect his own person with Lenin rather than with the deceased dictator. At his behest, Béla Illés, a muscovite Hungarian writer, composed an essay published in the Hungarian press under the title "The Young Eagle Learns How to Fly," which describes an entirely invented story of Rákosi's meeting with Lenin (CURPH, Miklos Molnár, "History of the *Irodalmi Ujság*"). This is the Communist version of a parvenu autocrat's desire to provide himself with a respectable and respected ancestry.

faithful to his erstwhile master. This fact did not remain unnoticed.

Rákosi's position as Hungarian Communist number one received a blow when Mikoyan in his speech at the Congress implicitly rehabilitated Béla Kun, the leader of the Hungarian
Communist regime of 1919 who, after the collapse of the Budapest
Commune, had fled to the Soviet Union, only to be subsequently
purged and executed during the *Yezhovshchina* in about 1937.
Rákosi, partly to accommodate his policies to Stalin's actions, partly
to emphasize or fraudulently glorify his own insignificant role in
1919, had taken pains to have Béla Kun and his politics in 1919
vilified. During the Congress, Evgeniy Varga, the Hungarian-born
Soviet economist, wrote an article in the *Pravda* praising Béla Kun
significantly on the seventieth anniversary of his birth. The *Szabad
Nép*, much to Rákosi's discomfiture, reproduced this article (which,
however, did not mention the time and circumstances of the death
of the eulogized hero).[15]

IMPACT ON HUNGARY

Rákosi, having returned from Moscow, submitted his report on
the Soviet Congress to the Hungarian Central Committee on March
12 and 13, 1956. He displayed no inhibition in declaring that the
"cult of personality is alien to Marxism" and that "the principle of
collective leadership is an elementary affair for a proletarian Party"
— thus quoting Mikoyan. The Central Committee, approving the
report, called on the Party to fight for the implementation of collective leadership and intra-Party democracy and for a strengthening
of Socialist legality. The People's Patriotic Front was to be supplied
with "political content," whatever that meant.[16]

The Central Committee, in its resolution, undertook to transplant some or most of the Twentieth Congress' theses to Hungarian
soil. It dealt with problems of collective leadership, with internal
Party democracy, with suppression of illegalities and control over
the Security Police, with the rehabilitation of innocent victims of
Stalinism, with the introduction of sounder economic planning and
more liberal cultural policy. But all these efforts carried over from
the Soviet political atmosphere into the Hungarian environment
produced results essentially differing from those achieved in the
Soviet Union. The difference was simply this: the Soviet Stalin had
died, whereas the Hungarian Stalin still directed the country.

For Rákosi and his ruling clique, despite their evident endeavors, the implementation of the principles obvious or implicit in the Twentieth Congress offered considerably greater difficulties than for the Soviet authors. It was easy for Rákosi to say that "collective leadership" existed in Hungary, but it was harder to find people to believe it — at least so long as the Hungarian dictator ruled supreme over Party and government in Hungary. Nor could Rákosi convince anyone that internal Party democracy had been firmly established, or that illegalities had ceased, or that "control" over the Security Police had been firmly secured. The average man would ask: control by whom? Nobody doubted that Rákosi and his aids had control over the Security Police at the time when illegalities now even admitted by Rákosi had taken place. Even those who had participated "physically" in all these excesses had still not been eliminated, with the exception of a handful of scapegoats. The Hungarian saying that "the goat should not be entrusted to watch over the cabbage" was widely quoted when Rákosi presented himself as the promoter of collective leadership and intra-Party democracy, and as the redeemer from the excesses of the Security Police. The very existence of Rákosi and his clique at the top of the Party, and consequently the government of the country, violently contradicted the very principles and aims adopted by the Twentieth Congress.

All that people had to do was replace the name of Stalin with that of Rákosi in that sketch of a sadistic paranoiac despot so ably provided by Khrushchev. Analogies could so easily be drawn between, on the one hand, the execution of "Comrade Eikhe," the honored veteran Communist, or the NKVD instructions given to "Comrade Rozenblum" prescribing his "confessions," and, on the other hand, the liquidation of the many Hungarian Communist victims, headed by László Rajk, whose "confessions" had been extorted by the AVH. It was not the last instance in which the logical consequences of de-Stalinization proved more vexing outside than inside the Soviet Union. Already the era was announced when anti-Stalinism would strengthen the Soviet regime internally but would threaten the disintegration of the Soviet satellite empire.

In spite of this contrasting picture, the stubborn Rákosi proceeded in his attempt to implement the principles adopted by the Twentieth Congress. On March 28, 1956, before the Party activists of the county of Heves in the town of Eger, he delivered a speech in which he reviewed those measures which had been adopted in accordance with the spirit and letter of the resolutions accepted at the Moscow sessions. On the delicate problem of László Rajk's rehabilitation (which so far he had strenuously refused to consider) and on the question of the release of political prisoners, he made the following electrifying statements:

After the unmasking of Beria, the imperialist agent, and in Hungary that of Gábor Péter's gang, the Rajk case has, on the initiative of our Party, been reviewed. It has been established that the case was based on provocation.* Therefore, in accordance with the Central Committee's June resolution, the Supreme Court has rehabilitated Comrade Lászlo Rajk and other comrades. Other cases have similarly been reviewed: the innocently condemned have been rehabilitated; others have obtained pardon. Successively cases of former Social Democrats have likewise been re-examined. Most of them have already been released; the last of them are being released these days. Those who were not guilty have been or will be rehabilitated. Who had been guilty of an offense against the People's Democratic order, has received pardon . . . Since June 1953 we have introduced many measures to secure the strict observance of Socialist legality everywhere.[17]

Rákosi, very tactfully, refused in his speech to distinguish clearly between those who had only been rehabilitated posthumously, like Rajk and many others, and those who had been or were being released. Nor did he make any clear pronouncements with regard to the innocently condemned who were neither "comrades" nor former Social Democrats. The great majority of political prisoners belonged to this class, and they were still in prison and remained there for some time after his speech. The curtness of his language — so much in contrast with his usual Soviet volubility — reveals the understandable embarrassment that he must have felt in making his admissions. He did not explain why most of the "innocently condemned" who had really been freed had to wait two or three years after Stalin's death before their rehabilitation had taken place.

The Rajk case and the associated condemnations of "comrades" presented a Sisyphean task for even a Rákosi. When, prior to Stalin's death, AVH General Gábor Péter and some of his associates had been arrested and sentenced, there was as yet no need to provide for Rajk's rehabilitation; Péter had been imprisoned for other undisclosed charges. Subsequently, Rákosi tried to connect the condemnation of the "Hungarian Beria" with the abuses committed in connection with the Rajk trial. After the Belgrade visit of Soviet statesmen, Rákosi, aware of public resentment in the Rajk affair prepared to arrange another theatrical show trial, this time a pro-

---

* As pointed out earlier, *provocation* in Soviet jargon means a plot carried out mainly through the agency of an *agent provocateur.*

Tito and pro-Rajk case in which General Péter, the principal accused, would admit his guilt in the anti-Titoist campaign and the judicial abuses committed in this respect.

In the summer of 1955, Péter was transferred to the Security Police prison in the Fö-utca in Budapest (Chief Investigation Section). There he was mistreated and urged to play his part in a courtroom performance. Other prisoners were able to overhear shouts and screams uttered by him: "Rákosi is lying!" "I shall never admit it!" "They want to execute Gábor Péter!" "What are the Soviet leaders to say when they will hear of what was done to Gábor Péter!" [18]

But the former chief torturer knew very well where confessions of such a nature would lead (to the grave). He could not be persuaded, either by promises or physical measures. Eventually Rákosi had to give up his master plan of making Gábor Péter, by the latter's own admissions, his chief scapegoat for the purpose of reconciling Tito and Hungarian public opinion. The Security Police had by then become reluctant to torture prisoners (including Gábor Péter) into theatrical confessions, and probably the Soviet leaders had refused to consent to such a deeply compromised Stalinist solution. An open failure, or a flaw in the stage management of the case, or Péter's overt revocation of his confession would have had unforeseeable consequences. And so, under the impact of the Twentieth Congress, Rákosi at last had to admit Rajk's innocence, without the possibility of shifting the blame to Péter, except by oblique reference.

To demonstrate his attachment to the principle of intra-Party democracy, Rákosi submitted the Second Hungarian Five-Year Plan to the Party and country for public discussion.[19] The First Five-Year Plan had ended in 1954; there was to be a one-year intermission to prepare for the second. But, as in the Soviet Union (where a new Plan projected for 1956 had to be abandoned), no new Five-Year Plan was ready in 1956, and the one under preparation was scheduled to begin in 1957. In the meantime, the country's economy had been run on a day-to-day basis. Though heavy industrial development had increased slightly, the policy of the Nagy premiership was pursued with few changes. The foreign trade debt had not further increased; during 1955 even a small surplus had been achieved, and thus the indebtedness was somewhat reduced.[20] But old Western credits were not going to be indefinitely extended. The Soviet Union, in the summer of 1956, was prepared to relieve Hungary, and on October 4, 1956, ten million dollars in convertible currency and a further sixty million rubles were granted on a long-term credit basis.[21] But the economy of Hungary had been managed for many years in a cloud of mystery, and the failures and excesses of the First Five-Year Plan had not been forgotten. When an opportunity arose to discuss the new Plan openly, expert economists subjected Rákosi's and Gerö's Second Five-Year Plan to a devastating array of criticism. Economists took pains to explain how their past advice had been set aside, causing the nation vast damage.[22] The internal Party democracy in the field of economics thus backfired, exposing the Rákosi-Gerö clique to sharp recriminatory attacks.

Under the impact of the Twentieth Congress the Party in Hungary, ostensibly to advance cultural liberalization, approved on March 17, 1956, a plan to form a debating club within the framework of the DISZ (Federation of Working Youth). This was the Petöfi Circle, named for the nineteenth-century poet. Its creation was an event of historic importance. The primacy of influence upon developments in Hungary passed from the Writers' Association to this new organization, where students, writers, scientists, and influential Party members found a platform for engaging in vehement battles against crimes, blunders, and deficiencies of the regime. It was here, for example, that the economists attacked the Second Five-Year Plan. The intellectual prelude of the Revolution took place within the debates of the Petöfi Circle, and their impact on the whole country was out of all proportion to the original objectives set for this discussion club by its rightist promoters. Rákosi's real purpose evidently was to create an escape valve for dangerous pressure. The steam released by the Petöfi Circle largely contributed to his eclipse.

18

Rákosi's Fall

/\\.\/\.\.\/\.\.\/\.\.\/\.\.\/\.\.\/\.\.\/\.\.\/\.\.\/\.\.\/\.\.\/\.\.\/\.\.\/\.\.\/\.\.\/\.\.\/\/

Intravit ut vulpes — Regnavit ut leo — Obiit ut canis
He came in like a fox — he ruled like a lion — he went out like a
dog.

Medieval epigram on Tarquinius Superbus

The Twentieth Congress did even more to increase Yugoslavia's stature among the "Socialist" countries than had the pilgrimage of the Soviet Party leaders to Belgrade. Whereas the
pilgrimage had been intended as an expiation for the past, the
Soviet pronouncement and principles of February 1956 legitimized
the "Yugoslav road" toward Socialism, equalizing it with other ways
to Socialism and finding comparable merit in it. Furthermore, in
the secret session where Stalin's crimes were exposed, the anti-
Yugoslav campaign was stigmatized as a "crime" — not only an
error but an evidence of Stalin's "shameful" and "uncomradely"
policy.

The emancipated Socialist system of Tito had thus grown into
an article triumphantly offered by Tito for export to other Communist countries and coveted by many of his admirers in the People's Democracies. The possibility of abandoning the Soviet way for
the Yugoslav way seemed to become even more practical when
Moscow on April 17, 1956, dissolved the Cominform on the ground
that it "had outlived its positive role." If it was evident that in the
Stalin-Tito dispute Tito had been right and Stalin wrong, it was
easy to jump to the conclusion that the Yugoslav system of Socialism
might in fact be better than the Soviet one. Yugoslav ambitions

did not restrict themselves to the export of their ideological approach; they had a vision of extending their "neutrality," their bloc-free system, to neighboring areas, and creating a Yugoslav-led group of uncommitted nations. To this end they set their eyes mainly on Hungary (also Austria), and regarded with sympathy the activities of the Hungarian "revisionists" and their unsuspecting spiritual leader, Imre Nagy.[1]

The mere existence of Rákosi at the head of the Hungarian Party, even aside from Tito's personal antipathies, seemed to clash with the aspirations cherished by the Yugoslavs after February 1956. This line of Yugoslav policy — apparently then not regarded with antagonism by Khrushchev, who seemed intent on strengthening the Yugoslav tie — ran parallel with the Hungarian internal opposition against Rákosi and his clique, an opposition which gained significant momentum from the Twentieth Congress. But Rákosi, despite the Yugoslav pressure and the forceful harassment by his Hungarian adversaries, was able to maintain his power position for another five months. His only support was Moscow, but this time Moscow let him fall. These last months of Rákosi's rule and his eventual eclipse manifest glaringly how the Soviet overlordship could maintain a person in power against the desire of the overwhelming majority of his own Party, and also how the Hungarian Central Committee was totally dependent on the will and whim of the Kremlin.

TITO VERSUS RÁKOSI

Rákosi, sensing the danger which threatened him from Tito's direction but assured by Moscow that Soviet-Yugoslav relations would not weigh on the internal affairs of Hungary, tried vainly to win back Tito's confidence. In numerous addresses, on March 12 before the Central Committee, on March 29 in the town of Eger, and on May 18 in Budapest, he wooed Yugoslav friendship and expressed hopes for a further improvement of relations. On April 20 a new Hungarian financial and trade delegation, headed by the Minister of Finance, was dispatched to Belgrade to resume the economic talks that had been suspended in September 1955. After protracted negotiations, a financial and economic agreement was concluded in Belgrade on May 29. Hungary had to agree to the payment of 85 million dollars in goods within five years as final settlement of Yugoslav war claims and damages for nonexecution of contracts. But none of these gestures appeased Tito: he remained adamant concerning Rákosi's removal.

Meanwhile, other Communist countries were offering Tito the required human sacrifice. In Bulgaria, Vulko Chervenkov, the local Stalin, who had been one of the chief vilifiers of Tito, resigned from his post as First Secretary of the Party on April 17, 1956, an event preceded by the posthumous rehabilitation of the executed Traicho Kostov.[2] As mentioned above, the Cominform had been dissolved in Moscow on the same day. At the same time, A. Čepička, the foremost Stalinist member of the Czechoslovak Politburo, was dropped. On May 30, Tito set out by rail on a circuitous trip to Moscow, a trip that had been long expected. On June 1, immediately before Tito's arrival, the arch-Stalinist Foreign Minister, Vyacheslav Molotov, tendered his resignation (while preserving his seat on the Soviet Party Presidium).

To the Soviet leaders it was a surprise that Tito did not travel via Hungary but chose the railroad across Rumania. In Moscow, Tito explained that he would not have gone through Hungary "even if it would have meant making the journey three times shorter." [3] His visit to the Soviet Union lasted over three weeks. He undertook to persuade the Kremlin to have Rákosi and his associates removed from the Hungarian leadership; but the Soviet Presidium steadfastly refused. The Soviet leaders, or at least most of them, were still hopeful that Rákosi would surmount his internal difficulties; they told Tito that "they know of no one else whom they could rely upon in that country." [4] The Soviet Presidium member, Suslov, visited Budapest (officially on a vacation) and talked to many members of the Central Committee, apparently reassuring them that Rákosi was not to be removed.[5]

The Rákosi issue had certainly been one on which the Yugoslav and Soviet leaders could not agree. The net result of the Moscow visit — a joint declaration on June 20 — stressed the necessity and usefulness of cooperation between the two Communist Parties. The essential third paragraph of the declaration seemed to pertain to all inter-Communist relationships when it announced:

Believing that the path of socialist development differs in various countries and conditions, that the multiplicity of forms of socialist development tends to strengthen socialism, and proceeding from the fact that any tendency of imposing one's opinion on the ways and forms of socialist development is alien to both — the two parties have agreed that their cooperation shall be based on complete voluntariness and equality.[6]

During these months that followed the Twentieth Congress, the sympathy between Khrushchev and Tito — and there was such a sympathy — was centered around de-Stalinization; but the difference between the two leaders consisted in their varying interpretations of de-Stalinization and the geographical range of this concept. Khrushchev wished to get rid of the Soviet Stalinists in order to attain supreme power, as well as to improve Soviet-Yugoslav relations to the extent of bringing the "prodigal son" back into the fold. According to Tito's interpretation the declaration of Belgrade (and also the declaration of Moscow of June 20) was to apply not only in mutual Soviet-Yugoslav relations but also "in relations among all socialist countries." We now know that one of the major impediments to further improvement in relations between the Soviet Union and Yugoslavia, and between the Soviet and Yugoslav Parties, was Tito's desire to declare outright the "equality" of all Communist states and Parties and their right to choose their own way to build Socialism. It seems that the Yugoslavs preferred a collective declaration to this effect with the participation of all People's Democracies. Khrushchev's statements in his public report at the Twentieth Congress had apparently persuaded Tito that equality of status and independent choice of Socialist methods are "intended for a wider circle than Yugoslavia and the Soviet Union." [7]

It is significant that Imre Nagy in his writings had expressed a similar interpretation of the 1955 Soviet-Yugoslav declaration at Belgrade. On the other hand, according to the Soviet interpretation, both the Belgrade and Moscow declarations "do not concern the others because the situation there is . . . different." [8] We may safely add that the difference, as seen by the Soviet leaders, consisted in the fact that their control was firmly entrenched in those other People's Democracies whereas they no longer imposed their domination in "stubborn" Yugoslavia. This divergency between Khrushchev and Tito — not only one of interpretation but one of fundamental policy — was never patched up between the two partners. But despite this impediment, Tito still pursued his aim of having one or two of the satellite countries relieved of their Soviet allegiance — in peaceful agreement and with the consent of the Soviet Union itself.

OPPOSITION CAMPAIGN

The Twentieth Congress had exercised a galvanizing effect upon the rank and file of the Hungarian Party, its intellectual elite, and in fact on all strata of thinking people in the country. As one of the most vociferous writers said: "After the Twentieth Congress, everything went like lightning." [9] Prior to the Congress much anxiety was felt by writers and journalists when Péter Erdös, a young journalist, was arrested. There was a general belief that a new wave of terror was coming on. Readers of Nagy's memoranda hastened to burn their copies of them.* But with the news of developments at the Congress, fear and reticence dissipated. A spontaneous anti-Stalinist campaign led by intellectuals of every description was launched, in the Writers' Association, in Party organizations and Party cells, in factories, in government offices, and principally through the activity of the new Petöfi Circle. Since journalists formed the vanguard of the campaign, the press soon began to reflect signs of breaking away from the line prescribed by the Party leadership. In the Party daily, the *Szabad Nép,* editorials (drafted in Party headquarters) differed in style and tendency from the rest of the paper. Periodicals which dared to publish especially critical articles, such as the *Irodalmi Ujság* (Literary Gazette) and the *Béke és Szabadság* (Peace and Freedom) gained enormous circulation all over the country.[10] The opposition campaign was couched in the convenient terms of "anti-Stalinization," "implementation of the principles of the Twentieth Congress," and "the Hungarian road toward Socialism." Paradoxically, it was now the stalwart Stalinists in Party bureaus who insisted that "Soviet methods and resolutions would not be mechanically copied." [11]

After Rákosi's admission of the "fabricated charges" against Rajk, personal attacks against the First Secretary of the Party became more violent. On March 29, 1956, in a session of the Party organization of the Writers' Association, Sándor Lukácsy, a literary critic, denounced Rákosi as a Judas.[12] Before the Party activists of the Thirteenth District of Budapest, György Litván, a young writer, told Rákosi that he had lost the confidence of the Hungarian people. At the Party membership meeting in a government enterprise, "Ferenc Kiss slandered the whole Socialist system." In the Party meeting of the Twelfth District of Budapest, one Mrs. Jozsef Szilágyi "spoke with hatred of the Party." All these events were reported in the Party press; it is easy to imagine how many other more violent expressions of antagonism against the Party and its leaders occurred elsewhere, unreported.[13] Open criticism and hostility grew in magnitude and fervor when people became aware that none of Rákosi's assailants had been imprisoned, but had only received serious warnings from Party headquarters.

* Imre Nagy when told that his papers had been destroyed, angrily retorted: "That manuscript should have been defended, not burned!" Tamás Aczél and Tibor Méray, *The Revolt of the Mind* (New York, 1959), p. 384.

The immediate objectives of the anti-Stalinist campaign —
spontaneously conceived by vocal intellectuals and spread by word
of mouth into wider strata of the population — were the removal of
Rákosi and his clique and the return of Imre Nagy. No broader goal
seems to have been set by the promoters of the campaign. The idea
was to impress the members of the Central Committee by the
impulsiveness of attacks against the person of Rákosi and by the
immense popularity of Imre Nagy that was sweeping over the
country. Simultaneously, friends of the reluctant leader of this unorganized opposition tried to persuade him to take an open stand.
For him, an expelled Communist, however, any political action
performed outside the framework of the Party was abhorrent. He
hardly ever attended public meetings, even after the Twentieth
Congress, though he gave up his hermit-like mode of life and
frequently appeared on the street and in public places. The results
of the Twentieth Congress strengthened his belief in the correctness
of his theses and ideas, a belief which he referred to in the introduction which he now wrote for the dissertation he had earlier composed.[14]

After the Soviet Congress, the circle around Imre Nagy greatly
increased. Many who had avoided visiting him (for reasons of safety
or opportunism) now turned their faces toward his rising star. His
closer associates and friends, Haraszti, Losonczy, Donáth, Bibo,
Ujhelyi, Szilágyi, and many writers, including Aczél, Méray, Zelk,
Benjamin and others, spent long evenings with him, discussing
every detail of his ideas and exchanging thoughts. This was no
conspiracy; it was a private debating society. Some of his friends
were more radical in their anti-regime views than others; some had
lost hope that Marxist-Leninists would ever voluntarily consent to
give up their oppressive domination over Party and country; others
hoped that the Soviet leaders would abstain from interfering in the
life of People's Democracies, as they had promised Tito. Then it
would be possible to rejuvenate the Party and introduce genuine
democracy. The developments of the Twentieth Congress seemed to
vindicate the "moderates," to which Imre Nagy had always belonged.
His inherent faith in institutions and his innate sense of obligation
toward the Soviet Union[15] seemed to reaffirm themselves. He refused
to listen to those who had wished him to become the overt leader of
an "anti-Party" opposition.[16]

The anti-Rákosi wave reached even the innermost sphere of
Party leadership. Many of the most overt Stalinists — turning against
their former idol — contrived a plan of eliminating Rákosi and,

having thrown the ballast overboard, saving themselves. They sought a *rapprochement* with the "left-wing" anti-Stalinists led by János Kádár; and through such alliances Kádár's importance came to outweigh his personal mediocrity. He and his former prison friends (e.g., Kállai, Marosán, Péter Mod) were ready to cooperate with the Stalinists and only retained a grudge against those personally blameworthy for their imprisonment and torture, whereas other anti-Stalinists rehabilitated into the Party, such as Losonczy, Donáth, Haraszti, and Ujhelyi, refused to have commerce with Stalinist elements of any description. Even Ernö Gerö, Rákosi's first lieutenant (the only remaining associate of Rákosi from the former ill-famed "foursome") was prepared to betray his leading colleague. He proposed an alliance to Kádár for the purpose of overthrowing Rákosi, whom he described as discredited, senile, and deficient in Marxism-Leninism. But Kádár, uncertain about Rákosi's favor with the "council of gods" in the Kremlin and himself vulnerable in the Rajk affair, declined at that juncture to accept the offer. In June 1956 the magnetic tape of Kádár's 1949 conversation with Rajk in the latter's cell, when Kádár as Minister of the Interior persuaded his "friend" to confess on charges which they both knew were untrue, was played before the Central Committee plenum on the orders of Rákosi. This gimmick, aimed at frightening Kádár into submission, backfired somewhat against Rákosi when the tape was replayed at the request of the committee, this time without omitting the opening words of Kádár: "I come to you on behalf of Comrade Rákosi." [17]

While Rákosi was plotting and devising schemes to save his position, Imre Nagy's sixtieth birthday on June 19 became an occasion for celebration for all his friends and would-be friends. All reports confirm that in the course of the afternoon and evening many hundreds of intellectual leaders and important Party members came to his house to manifest demonstratively their sympathy with the person they considered the providential statesman of Hungary. Rákosi, in his helpless wrath, telephoned warnings to many of those who attended.[18] But the most devastating onslaught against him, and indirectly against the regime, was being displayed at the sessions of the Petöfi Circle.

BROADSIDES IN THE PETÖFI CIRCLE

When the Politburo acceded to the request of university students and other intellectuals in forming the Petöfi Circle and arranging debates on topical questions, it hardly conceived the magnitude and violence of criticism which would come from this platform. Similarly,

Mao Tse-tung had been oblivious of the prevailing resentment when he had said: "Let a hundred flowers bloom, let a hundred schools of thought contend!" But there were no "hundred schools" to contend in Hungary; the debates in the Petöfi Circle assumed the role of an unofficial parliament in an autocratic society. In this parliament there was an overwhelming opposition, just faintly resisted by a few representatives of the ruling Party clique.

The topics selected for discussion and the way these discussions proceeded are highly indicative of the partly overt, partly concealed, tactics of the opposition. The majority of the participants were Party members, and they spoke as Party members, making use of Marxist-Leninist vocabulary and arguments. When — as it often happened — an official Party representative protested against the insults heaped upon the Party, the audience almost unanimously burst out into the cry: "*We* are the Party, *we* are the masses, not you!" The purpose of the exercise was to embarrass, confuse, and perhaps also convince members of the governing Party faction. Yet it did much more. It encouraged large sections of the population who followed the debates with utmost interest, gave heart to the "underdogs" who had lived for years in bondage, and created a revolutionary spirit all over the country.

The first debate concerned the creation of a separate organization for college and university students. Their federation had been forcibly merged into the DISZ, and now seemed the time to ask for its autonomous re-establishment. Next on the program was the historical problem of György Dozsa, the cruelly executed leader of the Hungarian peasant revolution of 1514; this gave an opportunity for discussing the situation of the peasants. There followed a professional debate on the economic situation of Hungary; this permitted a discussion of the past and future Five-Year Plans, past errors and future follies. Then came the turn of the historians. Communist historical writing had been tantamount to official falsification, as acknowledged by the Soviet Twentieth Congress when it resolved to have the Party history rewritten. This gave an excellent opportunity to attack the Party leadership.[19]

The Petöfi Circle debates were generally presided over by high-ranking Party officials. These chairmen and also the leading Party members who took up the defense of past policies put on a very poor show. Soviet and Soviet-indoctrinated leaders are not generally good orators. When they make a speech they usually have their text (approved by the Politburo) ready; they are not trained to extemporize, nor are they prepared to retort to interruptions or refute

arguments spontaneously.* At the historians' debate it was Erzsébet
Andics, the chief historian of the Party, who presided; her stammer-
ing and lack of presence gave ample evidence of her confusion of
mind.

The next session was devoted to questions of pedagogy. Under
this heading the dissolution of the People's College Movement was
deplored. This movement, which dated back to the 1930's, had aided
many hundreds of working-class and peasant students to complete
high school and university studies. Hegedüs, the Prime Minister,
and many other Communist leaders had benefited from this organization; but, since its protagonists were the "populist" writers and
since it did not originate from Soviet Communist sources, the People's Colleges had been closed since 1949. This debate was followed
by an address given by Professor György Lukács on "Contemporary
Questions of Philosophy" and by an agitated discussion on that
subject.

Professor Lukács, a world-renowned scholar of Marxist philosophy and aesthetics, had always been a controversial figure in the
ranks of pro-Soviet Communists. He had been People's Commissar
of Public Education during the 1919 Hungarian Communist regime,
and had lived thereafter in Germany and later in the Soviet Union.
His best known writings were published in Germany during World
War I and in the interwar period. In 1945 he returned to Hungary
and obtained a chair at the University of Budapest. Lukács was one
of the few Marxist-Leninist philosophers, if not the only one, whose
writings have not consisted of a series of quotations from the
"sacred" texts. This quality elevated his theories to the level of
Western philosophical writing, but brought suspicion concerning his
orthodoxy from the Communist side. Already accused in the 1920's
of "rightist deviationism," he made a partial recantation. In 1949, he
was again compelled to practice self-criticism. Afterward he restricted
himself to teaching and only re-emerged from semiobscurity after
the end of the Stalinist era.[20]

Now Lukács had his revenge on those who had persecuted him
during all those years. His slashing criticism of Stalinist cultural
policy was directed both against the Party and the Ministry of

* Khrushchev is an exception, because he often resorts to extemporizations or
off-the-cuff harangues. Such impromptu addresses, however witty at times, are full of
indiscretions, contradictions, incoherent and tactless remarks, and when published in
the Soviet press bear little resemblance to the original versions. See, for instance, an
illustrative juxtaposition of Khrushchev's speech made in Moscow on his return from
Hungary on April 10, 1958, as in fact delivered, and as printed in *Pravda* of April
11, 1958, in *East Europe*, June 1958, p. 19.

Culture. He borrowed his expression from the irony of the Middle Ages when characterizing the work of these "uncultured and stupid" elements as "glossing the glosses of the glosses" (*glossant glossarum glossas*). He exhorted his audience to abide by "independent thinking," and warned them against collecting a *citologia* (as he called it) of Lenin as they had previously done with citations from Stalin. He expressed hope that the Soviet Twentieth Congress would not produce such a disappointment as had been experienced after the Seventh Congress in the 1930's. Not only Marx but Plato, Hegel, and Schopenhauer had to be studied; he condemned any monopoly of Marxism-Leninism in the teaching of philosophy. He indicated in his concluding words that Marxist-Leninist philosophic ideas had not conquered the mind of the Hungarian youth.[21]

This address by Lukács was delivered on June 14, 1956. Some of his critics apologized and practiced self-criticism on the platform of the Petöfi Circle.* Anxiety was voiced in Party headquarters because of the damaging influence of these debates. Nevertheless, the next meeting was transferred to one of the theaters to allow the attendance of an increasing number of people.

The problem of the judiciary was next debated. Károly Kiss, the Chairman of the Party Control Commission, presided. The meaning of "Socialist legality" was submitted to close scrutiny. The speakers, well-versed in Marxist-Leninist ratiocination, pointed out that Stalinism had collided with Leninism in wishing to exploit "law" for influencing the natural development of economic forces. State and law, according to Marxist-Leninist doctrine, were supposed to be of the nature of a "superstructure" only, depending on developments of the fundamental infrastructure (means and forces of production); but Stalin had reversed this "natural" trend of development by introducing "law" (i.e., purges, terrorism, and the like) for the purpose of shaping economic and social developments. Accordingly, Stalin had been anti-Marxist and anti-Leninist, an instrument of the enemy both in the Soviet Union and Hungary, and so were all the Stalinists. No doubt, this line of reasoning must have confused and left speechless those former admirers of Stalin who suddenly found themselves pictured as hostile to the Marxist-Leninist creed.

The peak of the debate on "Socialist legality" was reached when the widow of László Rajk obtained the floor. She described her

---

* Jozsef Szigeti, a former student of Lukács, was one of the chief apologists. After the Revolution, Szigeti became Deputy Minister of Culture, and one of the most violent critics of his former teacher.

tribulations in the prisons of the AVH. Julia Rajk demanded not only full rehabilitation for her late husband, but also the punishment of his "murderers." In a shrill voice she pierced a deadly silence: "The Communist word can never be pure in Hungary while murderers of my husband sit in ministerial seats!" [22]

The last of the series of Petőfi Circle debates took place on June 27, 1956; this time it was devoted to the role of the press. To accommodate some thousands of participants, the Officers' Hall of the People's Army (formerly, the Officers' Casino) had been hired. Some thousands more who could not squeeze into the hall were listening outside in the street to a loudspeaker relay. Writers and journalists inveighed against the fetters laid on journalism and literature; they trespassed into the field of politics in exploring whether anything structurally wrong, above and beyond personal defects, had caused the crimes and mistakes committed in the past. Official Party orators had little success, whereas popular writers, such as Tibor Déry, Tibor Tardos, and others, were greeted with ovations. Géza Losonczy, the last orator, reproached the Party leadership for procrastination on Imre Nagy's readmission to the Party. The hall and the adjoining streets (it was nearly 4 A.M.) resounded with applause for the former Prime Minister.

Two days after this memorable demonstration, news of the Poznan riots arrived in Hungary. Rákosi and his clique considered the occasion ripe for arranging the first counterstroke directed against the organizers of the Petőfi Circle debates. Even so, the best he could do was a resolution by the Central Committee, temporarily suspending but not dissolving this chief center of opposition against the regime:

Anti-Party elements, encouraged by the patience of the Party and the Communists, have launched attacks, growing in strength, against the policy and leadership of the Party and against our People's Democratic system.

The center of these attacks has been the Petőfi Circle of the DISZ . . .

At the last debate of the Petőfi Circle some speakers (Déry, Tardos) went so far as to deny the leading role of the Party and of the workers' class and expressed bourgeois, counter-revolutionary views . . .

These onslaughts against the Party and the People's Democracy are chiefly organized by a certain group which formed around the person of Imre Nagy . . .

The press has not taken a stand against the anti-Party views; some newspapers and periodicals have published misleading, unprincipled praising reports on these debates . . . confusion has been created within the Party membership by the erroneous article of June 24 in the *Szabad Nép** which refrained from opposing these hostile, demagogue attitudes.[23]

Forces within the Party leadership had successfully prevented an all-out prohibition of the Petöfi Circle. The Poznan riots, because of the leniency with which the Polish demonstrators were treated, did not prove sufficient excuse for the immediate crushing of the opposition. Expulsion from the Party had been the most severe punishment that Rákosi was able to mete out to his enemies, and this was mild punishment against a Déry who, as publicized by the Party press, had even propounded the thesis that "our liberation has yet to come."

RÁKOSI'S LAST STAND AND OUSTER

One may ask why Rákosi and his clique behaved in such a lenient manner, one unusual for a dictator, during the campaign aimed at their downfall. The fact is that their leniency was not a sign of strength, but of weakness. Rákosi's hands were bound: he must have been told, repeatedly, by the Kremlin to refrain from violent repression; no longer were the Hungarian Politburo and the Central Committee obedient tools in his hands. These agencies were tools but tools of Moscow, not of Rákosi, and developments during and after the Twentieth Congress made them cautious. We do not pretend that Rákosi harbored a genuine feeling of guilt. But many of his collaborators did, and they did not wish to participate again in actions which later might be considered criminal acts, or even "anti-Party" ones. Even the Security Police were not entirely trustworthy. They had their direct channels to Moscow, and unless so commanded from this distant capital, they would give only lukewarm assistance to Rákosi, as happened when the arrest of one or two of the recalcitrant writers was ordered.

Procrastination was the only strategy Rákosi could usefully employ to maintain himself. He must have felt that he was closely watched by the Kremlin and by his secret and open enemies in the Party and country. Tito, his deadly foe, did everything he could to have him ousted. The Hungarian dictator could not risk making any more mistakes. Slow, cautious moves might efface memories of

---

* The article referred to bears the title: "The Sunlight of the Spirit," and contains a glowing appraisal of the Petöfi Circle debates. It ends with the following ambiguous reference: "These days a Western radio station . . . expressed pleasure with regard to the debates in Budapest. To avoid misunderstandings: *we* have reason to be pleased in listening to these debates and not *they*." The author of this article evidently wished to protect organizers and participants of the debates from accusations of complicity with the West.

past crimes and excesses. He had to accept the presence of rehabilitated Party members who openly defied him and whom he tried to avoid meeting. Furthermore, he was compelled to add to their number by the gradual release of political prisoners. All these elements, directed by the dictatorial character of the regime into Party channels and organizations, created an ever greater pressure against Rákosi. His leadership was being openly challenged in Party meetings of workers, where he was actually referred to as the "bald murderer." Still the collective leadership of Moscow permitted no executions, no large-scale imprisonments of Party members, not even preventive purges. A dictator without punitive sanctions is a very poor spectacle; a satrap whose hands are bound by his overlord is a rather helpless creature.

Rákosi contrived to adjust himself to the requirements of the situation as demanded by the Kremlin, or at least tried to guess the intentions of the elastic majority in the Soviet Presidium. He had to provide a picture of a peaceful, prosperous Hungary with a satisfied population. Partly to demonstrate this state of affairs, partly to meet continual Austrian objections, the Hungarian Council of Ministers instructed the Minister of the Interior on May 9, 1956, to dismantle the "technical border obstruction" (barbed wire fence and minefields) on the Western frontier.[24]

To appease public opinion and to assure the country that no renewal of terrorism was to be expected from him, Rákosi reiterated his abject self-criticism in his Budapest speech of May 18. He again condemned the cult of the individual, and admitted that he, too, had "tolerated, even supported" it. He confessed before his audience that he had been "guilty of the fact that grave illegalities could have been committed in the country." He expressed deep sorrow for having tolerated violations of Socialist legality. There had been no proper system established by the Party and the state for supervising the activities of the AVH. He accepted part of the guilt for this omission, which he said rendered possible "the excesses of Beria's agents, and those of Gábor Péter's gang."[25]

Subsequent events have shown that Rákosi miscalculated the strength of animosity and hatred accumulated against him and against what he represented. His self-criticism was viewed with contempt and ridicule; hardly anybody outside the narrow ruling clique felt the slightest doubt that Rákosi and his associates were responsible for the crimes committed, and no unperverted soul could be satisfied with empty expressions of regret. They asked for punishment. Such a glaring anomaly could only be solved by drastic surgery; either Rákosi had to disappear, or he had to be given means for destroying his opposition.

For Rákosi the Central Committee's condemnation of the Petöfi Circle and the accompanying censure of Nagy and his group in early July was to be an initial step. He saw he could still induce the Central Committee to pass repressive though mild resolutions against his enemies. He dared hope for something stronger. After careful preparations and collection of incriminatory material he would be able to persuade the Politburo and the Central Committee — in strict obedience to the principle of collective leadership — to have the whole array of his opponents arrested. It is not known whether he tried to obtain the prior consent of Moscow for an implementation of his master plan; he may have been told to rely on collective leadership or been given a Delphic answer (as overlords, uncertain themselves, are wont to give their subordinates). And he may have thought of obtaining an ex post facto approval which would have relieved the Kremlin of responsibility in the matter. In any case, he misjudged the prevailing sentiment in Moscow; the impact of the Poznan riots was not as sharp as he had expected; the pressure by Tito was incessant; and it may well be that the Soviet Presidium was already waiting for a well-suited opportunity to rid themselves of Rákosi.

After about two weeks of careful preparatory work, Rákosi submitted his plan to the Hungarian Politburo. Orders of arrest against four hundred persons were to be issued, the Petöfi Circle and the Writers' Association were to be dissolved, and publication of the *Irodalmi Ujság* suspended. The list of people to be arrested was headed by Imre Nagy, and it included names of writers, poets, journalists, student leaders, and Army officers, all of them present or former Party members. The members of this "Imre Nagy anti-Party plot" were to be subsequently brought to trial.

On July 16, the Politburo was unconvinced concerning Rákosi's project; the discussion was postponed to the following day. Ernö Gerö now renewed his intrigues against Rákosi, and others were ready to turn against the First Secretary of the Party. Politburo members, presumably including István Kovács, reported Rákosi's scheme to Yuri V. Andropov, the Soviet ambassador in Budapest, and asked for Soviet intervention. On July 17, the Soviet Presidium member Anastas Mikoyan arrived by plane and joined the Politburo session. After listening to the debate, he conveyed to the Hungarian comrades the Soviet Presidium's "advice" to relieve Mátyás Rákosi from his duties and to appoint Ernö Gerö as First Secretary of the

Party. Rákosi first questioned Mikoyan's authority to speak on behalf of the Soviet Presidium; he telephoned to Khrushchev in Moscow and received a confirmation of the decision. Thereupon he, too, acquiesced in the inevitable. On July 18 he tendered his resignation to the Central Committee plenum and made his last speech before that body.[26]

Rákosi in his speech, after expatiating on the precarious state of his health, referred to his previous admissions of error and added that "after the Twentieth Congress of the Communist Party of the Soviet Union and Comrade Khrushchev's speech, it became clear to me that the weight and effect of these mistakes had been greater than I had thought and that the harm done to our Party through these mistakes had been more serious than I had previously believed." Rákosi also admitted that these mistakes had hindered the development of Party life, the establishment of collective leadership, and democracy in Party and state life, and had offered opportunity for attack to the enemy. He confessed to having neglected to repair these mistakes sufficiently and to not having resolutely combatted "sectarian and dogmatic" views. This time there was no reference to "rightist deviationism" in his speech.

The Central Committee duly accepted Rákosi's resignation and elected Ernö Gerö as First Secretary in his stead. The nonentity András Hegedüs remained Prime Minister. The Committee added four new members to the Politburo. Two of them, János Kádár and György Marosán, were "anti-Stalinist" victims of Rákosi, but the other two, Károly Kiss and Jozsef Révai, were members of the old guard who, however, had not lately been conspicuously pro-Rákosi. To appease public opinion, the Central Committee decreed the abolition of the much hated "peace loans" (technically voluntary, but in fact compulsory contributions). Rákosi himself was swiftly dispatched to the Soviet Union; fallen dictators are never safe in their own country.

Gerö, the new First Secretary of the Party, declared in his inaugural address that now the past was to be regarded as closed, and a clean leaf in the history of the Party was to be opened; unity in the Party must henceforward be the main objective of every faithful member.[27]

Mikoyan proceeded from Budapest to Yugoslavia, where he was able to present Rákosi's head to Tito. On his return journey he stopped in Budapest on July 21 (when he had a short interview with Imre Nagy). On that day the Central Committee met again and deprived Mihály Farkas of his Party functions, also setting in motion the withdrawal of his military rank for "violations of Socialist legality." [28] This fourth member of the Stalinist "foursome" had been victimized by Rákosi at the same time as Imre Nagy (he had then been sent to a military school in Moscow), and now he had to suffer again with Rákosi. In the eyes of the public neither of these censures was adequate punishment for the monstrosities he had committed. Nevertheless, he played the convenient role of whipping boy, while, for the time being, others escaped reprobation.

RÁKOSI'S FALL AND GERÖ'S ADVENT: AN APPRAISAL

The view is held by some that Rákosi's downfall was prompted less by his unpopularity and total loss of prestige in Hungary than by Tito's pressure upon Moscow.[29] But the timing of Rákosi's ouster seems to point out rather that, although Tito's pressure persisted throughout, Rákosi's fall was ultimately caused by the open demonstrations against him and by his impotence to cope with his difficulties by means other than wholesale arrests of Party members. Tito himself attributed Rákosi's ouster to the "increasingly strong dissatisfaction" within the ranks of Hungarian Communists," and he would not have done so if this event had been due solely to his intervention.[30] The Stalinist faction within the Soviet Party had been greatly reduced in authority since Tito's visit to Moscow; its main representative, Molotov, once the main patron of Rákosi, was no longer able to protect somebody who had shared so abundantly in Stalin's crimes.

Whatever the wider or narrower motives of the Soviets in ousting Rákosi, no one can pretend that either the Hungarian Politburo or the Central Committee initiated by its own volition the removal of its First Secretary. Thus, Rákosi's ouster cannot be compared with the changes in Party leadership that occurred in Poland in October 1956, when the Polish Central Committee took the initiative in exchanging its First Secretary, without the prior consent and indeed against the will of the Soviet Party leadership. Rákosi was expelled from office by the Soviet Presidium — as a provincial governor is relieved from his authority by the central government; his resignation and its endorsement by the Central Committee were empty formalities implementing a decision taken in the Kremlin. This was a fact known to all the actors of the play, the members of the Politburo and of the Central Committee, and also to Tito, who was not loath to admit it. It was only the official communiqués which, as always, tried to portray a façade of independent Hungarian Party and government resolutions.

Equally the appointment of Gerö to succeed Rákosi was the choice, and we may add, the choice alone of Moscow. The intrigues of Gerö intended to open up the road to First Secretary were inconclusive; they merely served to strengthen his claim of succession, to convince the Soviet leaders of his ability to cope with the situation. Gerö may have been approached earlier by Soviet agents concerning his chances of succeeding Rákosi. He had his own lines of communication to the precincts of ultimate power and may even have been encouraged to sound out his possibilities as heir to Rákosi's vacant throne. As always in the past, the decision of Moscow on Hungary reflected a sense of compromise: Rákosi was to go, but Gerö was to succeed him. This meant no radical step: the exchange of the satrap for the deputy satrap. The idea was expressed by Tito in the following words: "They [the Soviet leaders] made it a condition that Rákosi would go only if Gerö remained." [31]

This was not a condition approved by Tito; he had not been consulted regarding the change. We may surmise that this was the condition which one faction of the Soviet Presidium accepted in return for the removal of Rákosi, which was required by the other faction. Tito himself was to say publicly a few months later that the Soviet leaders "committed a mistake by not allowing the removal of Gerö and other Rákosi followers, who had compromised themselves in the eyes of the people . . . And this was a mistake, because Gerö differed in no way from Rákosi. He pursued the same kind of policy and was to blame just as much as Rákosi was." [32]

The appointment of Gerö as Rákosi's successor proved to be a significant and fatal step. Any crime attributed to Rákosi could equally have been that of Gerö, his closest collaborator. Since 1948, he had been top administrator of Hungary's economy, responsible for the failures of the Five-Year Plan, for the exploitation of the workers, and for forced peace loans. He bore a special share of responsibility in the forcible transfer of people from one locality to another, and in the frustration of Imre Nagy's program. He was generally open to attack for the whole Stalinist policy and all the fateful decisions taken by the Politburo since 1948. Lastly, he was a muscovite, an international Soviet agent, a colonel of the Soviet Army. Why did Moscow resort to such an unhappy choice?

The only alternative would have been Imre Nagy. Evidently the Kremlin was not prepared to accept this unfrocked Party member as the leader of Hungary. We may, however, presume that Imre Nagy was the preferred choice of Tito; it is known that no one had been watched by Belgrade with greater interest. Kádár was an inconspicuous figure, and not pictured as a possible heir to Rákosi. Imre Nagy's assumption of power would have augured a pro-Yugoslav policy and greater elbowroom for Hungary vis-à-vis the Soviet Union. This reason alone sufficed to make Nagy *persona non grata* to Moscow. Talks between the Soviet Union and Yugoslavia, as well as contacts between Soviet and other Communist leaders with regard to their reciprocal relations, were the order of the day during the summer of 1956. A *Pravda* editorial of July 16 (the day when the decision on Rákosi's ouster was taken in Moscow) reveals the acute anxiety felt in the Kremlin concerning the possible disruption of the "Socialist camp." The article accuses the United States of false solicitude for the independence of the People's Democracies. The readers are warned (italics ours):

> It should not be forgotten that in some places there are still opportunist elements on which the enemies of the working people undoubtedly rely. It should also be remembered that among people who are not politically mature and who are extremely gullible there may be some who will rise to the bait of the bombastic words about "national Communism," about the fact that the *international bonds among Communist Parties* have become "superfluous," etc.[33]

Imre Nagy, on the evidence of his writing, was certainly one of those "gullible" persons who believed that "international bonds between Communist Parties" as interpreted by Soviet leaders, that is, in terms of Soviet supremacy, were a matter of the past. The same *Pravda* article further points out:

> Marxism-Leninism teaches that the national interests of the working people, correctly understood, cannot contradict their international socialist interests. In his well-known article "National Pride of the Great Russians," V. I. Lenin emphasized with very great force that the interest of the Great Russians' national pride, *correctly understood,* coincides with the socialist interest of the Great Russians and of *all other proletarians.*[34]

This was certainly not an interpretation of Marxism-Leninism to which Imre Nagy would have subscribed; his interpretation — as witness his writings — boldly conflicts with that of the official Soviet Party daily.

The Soviet Presidium must have known that the majority of the Hungarian Party membership, in fact the whole country, wished to see Nagy at the helm, but this scarcely appealed to their hearts. He did not enjoy their confidence, not even to the extent that he had before his expulsion from the premiership in 1955 — when his activity had been counterbalanced by Rákosi's presence. At any rate, Nagy must have been considered unmanageable. The choice of Gerö clearly indicates that the Kremlin was intent on retaining full control over Hungarian affairs. The choice of Nagy, in view of his oral and written views, would have meant a repudiation of Soviet control, an insistence on safeguarding Hungarian interests, termination of all forms of economic exploitation, and even a Titoist independent foreign policy. The choice between Gerö and Nagy was ultimately one between the maintenance of Hungary as a Soviet satrapy and its transformation into a Communist state which might or might not collaborate. It was essentially a decision between vital Soviet power interests and vital interests of Hungarian independence.

It is not easy to surmise what would have happened if the Hungarian Central Committee had insisted on electing Imre Nagy its First Secretary, as the Polish Party did three months later with Gomulka. It may be that Moscow would have then swallowed Nagy, as it did Gomulka, but it also may be that Soviet military intervention would have imposed Moscow's choice. However, the Hungarian Central Committee was far from displaying such a patriotic spirit of independence as its Polish counterpart did three months later; its servility toward Moscow prevented any such action.

Mikoyan, representing the Soviet Presidium, probably surmised the drawbacks of Gerö's selection; for one thing, Tito must have warned him against this decision at their encounter on July 19–20. To counterbalance the disappointment generally felt because of Gerö's appointment as Party First Secretary, the Soviet leaders ordered Gerö to continue a soft line. Moscow hoped that public opinion might thus be placated.

During the following months it became the consistent policy of the Kremlin to have Gerö made "acceptable" to Tito. It was believed that a complete reconciliation between the Yugoslav and the Hungarian Party would solve the internal problems of Hungary and neutralize Yugoslav efforts to promote "anti-Stalinism" in Hungary through the promotion of anti-Soviet elements. But Tito refused to be reconciled to Gerö's succession, considering him unstable. He desired to see somebody at the top of the Hungarian Party totally untainted with "Stalinism," and foresaw that the Imre Nagy question was far from being settled. The former Hungarian Premier — apparently still unaware of his "leadership" of the opposition — was similarly an "unknowing" ally of Tito. But Tito had placed his bet on the ascendancy of Nagy and was anxiously watching and secretly promoting his return to active Hungarian politics. Even so, the real initiative for things to come rested this time with the people of Hungary.

THE FOURTH PHASE

The Revolution
1 9 5 6

The justified revolt and uprising against a clique turned into an uprising of the whole [Hungarian] nation against Socialism and against the Soviet Union.

TITO at Pula on November 11, 1956

19

Rajk's Body and
Imre Nagy's Return

/\.\/.\.\/.\/.\/\.\/.\/.\/\.\/.\/.\/\.\/.\/.\/\.\/.\/.\/\.\/.\/.\/\.\/.\/.\/\/

John Brown's body lies amoulding in his grave,
But his truth goes marching on.

THOMAS BRIGHAM BISHOP

The people have always some champion whom they set over them
and nurse into greatness.

PLATO

THE new First Secretary, Ernö Gerö, initiated his policy of the
"clean leaf" under apparently auspicious circumstances. The impetus
of the opposition, focused on the removal of Rákosi, had lost its
momentum after the ouster of Stalin's foremost Hungarian disciple.
Though hardly any thoughtful person was deceived by the exchange
of one Stalinist for another, it is human to repose after a noteworthy
triumph, and the heat of the summer months favored relaxation.
Lack of organization among the small opposition groups both
inside and outside the Party also added to the abatement of tension.
Gerö and his Stalinist clique may have been misled by the rejoicing
and subsequent calm following Rákosi's disappearance. Gerö must
also have been assured not only of Moscow's backing but of Khrushchev's willingness to intercede for him with Tito. He knew that he
had to conduct a rear-guard action until the time had come to stop
his opponents; and since attacks momentarily abated, he believed in
making no concession that went beyond mere lip service. But as

soon as the summer was over and the opposition (the overwhelming majority of the country) began to feel deceived, the pressure and attacks again mounted. The opposition now concentrated on two vulnerable points of the regime: the final and total rehabilitation of Rajk, and the readmission of Imre Nagy to the Party and the leadership of the country.

GERÖ'S "CLEAN LEAF"

The inaugural speech of Gerö and the Central Committee's resolution of July 18, 1956, already foreshadowed the policy which the new First Secretary of the Party was intent on pursuing. The difference between Rákosi's line and the new line may best be analyzed on the basis of two editorial articles (composed in Party headquarters) in the Party theoretical magazine, the *Társadalmi Szemle*. The first, published in the June–July issue, still reflects Rákosi's approach; in fact, he may have drafted it. The second article, appearing in the August issue, mainly reflects the resolution of the Central Committee.

The first of these two editorials inveighs against the "Imre Nagy group," against attempts to oppose Socialist industrialization and collectivization of agriculture, and against those who wished to replace the Party by the People's Patriotic Front, and is essentially critical and polemic in nature. But the second no longer mentions Imre Nagy, and in warning of dangers it cautions against leftist and rightist deviations alike. The later editorial bears the ambitious title: "With the Unity of the Party for a Socialist Democracy." It traces the mistakes of the past to the failure to implement measures against abuses such as the cult of the individual and violations of Socialist legality, or measures for the rehabilitation of innocent comrades. The Central Committee — says the article — had correctly blamed the Politburo for its lack of energy in implementing those measures;[1] thus we learn that not only Rákosi but the entire Politburo had been responsible for the situation that had arisen. The editorial (following the text of the Central Committee's resolution) is not content with abiding by "declarations of principle," but wishes instead to enumerate "concrete measures" for the correction of mistakes. But when we examine these concrete measures we only find the repetitive injunction against the cult of the individual and for the re-establishment of collective leadership. In implementing collective leadership, Party organs were instructed to arrange "wide and democratic debates" before taking decisions. A further admonition was to "create such an atmosphere that in Party meetings the Party members should be able to submit their observations about the policy of the Party and the work of the respective local organs." [2]

Gerö thus wished to convey the impression of steering a middle course, of deploring equally "right-wing" and "left-wing" deviations. In refraining from attacking Imre Nagy openly he wished to contribute to the "unity of the Party," a need which had constantly been emphasized during the summer of 1956. Central Committee member Márton Horváth, asking for unity, was compelled to admit publicly: "From one point of view the situation has become worse than in 1948; it has never occurred in the history of the Hungarian [Communist] movement that one part of the intelligentsia within the Party came to oppose so violently the leadership of the Party." [3]

On September 1, the Politburo resolved to abolish the remnants of the cult of the individual. The resolution forbade the naming of institutions after living Hungarian citizens.[4] Consequently, plants, schools, and streets named after Rákosi had to be rechristened. A further concession of the Party was to discontinue Party punishments against the writers Aczél, Háy, Karinthy, Kuczka, Méray, and Zelk.[5] And the September leading article of the *Társadalmi Szemle* — with a bravado so characteristic of the system — triumphantly declared that "due to the resolution of the Central Committee, the unity of the Party had been strengthened." But despite such an assurance, anxiety concerning deep-seated divergencies was perceptible between the lines. The article also sought to refute such erroneous views that the policy of the clean leaf and the July resolution had meant to persecute such Party functionaries "who might have committed some mistakes or employed incorrect methods" but always were ready to carry out the policy of the Party. Nobody was encouraged to believe that Party life was to be promoted by some kind of "changing of the guard." [6]

A possible changing of the guard, the replacement of all Party leaders and functionaries responsible for past illegalities and crimes, had been the nightmare of all those who now clung together around Gerö. Among these were Kádár and his group, who now occupied important posts within the Party. János Kádár was selected leader of the Hungarian Party delegation which left on September 9 to attend the Chinese Eighth Party Congress in Peiping. Kádár was accompanied by Politburo member István Hidas, and also by Imre Nagy's former staunch supporter, Zoltán Szántó, who had now been recalled from his ambassadorship in Warsaw and made Chairman of the Institute of Cultural Relations.[7] Another concession to opposition demands appeared in a Politburo resolution decreeing the re-establishment of the Popular College Movement and of its associated colleges.[8] We should not forget that many of the Communist leaders — Stalinists (like Prime Minister Hegedüs) and anti-Stalinists alike — had profited by being educated in one of these popular colleges. Rajk himself had been a protector of these institutions; so also had Jozsef Révai, reinstated as a Politburo member on July 18.

These were the "concrete" measures which the government was ready to make between July and September 1956. Of course, there were other less concrete ones: the press had not been so outspoken since 1947, and life had become easier. Laudatory articles on Yugoslavia and the Yugoslav way of life (couched purposely in euphemistic terms) and also reports from the West (no longer pejorative) gave a happy-go-lucky atmosphere of relief but simultaneously brought new criticism on the regime and its foremost representatives. The oppositionists within the Party preferred to have matters settled within the precincts of the Party itself; they urged the leadership to make adjustments to forestall actions and interference of groups on the outside.

REBURIAL OF RAJK

Julia Rajk had been invited several times to Party headquarters; there she had been treated by turns haughtily and courteously, and more than once cajoled by flattery and promises of indemnity. She had remained unimpressed by threats, and refused to accept promises.[9] Kádár, the former friend of her husband, refrained from being helpful; he personally had much to fear from a complete investigation into the Rajk affair. His role from the beginning of his reinstatement to the Party hierarchy had been duplicitous; he had encouraged the opposition but incited Rákosi against them. Now, entrenched in his Politburo seat, he became the chief flagbearer of the slogans: "unity of the Party" and "the Party first." Observers seem to agree, however, that his motives were always primarily egocentric.[10]

Despite the obstacles in her way, Julia Rajk and the friends of her husband insisted on formal reparations. A demonstrative Party funeral was to be given the executed Rajk. They were supported in their claim by Party members and nonmembers all over the country. Rajk, Pálffy, and others had originally been despicable figures in public opinion, for they had served Soviet-Communist domination with all the ruthless means at their disposal. But, having fallen victims to the Rákosian terrorism, they were transformed in the eyes of many into real patriots and martyrs. Many others favored their rehabilitation for *disguised* motives, in order to strike the regime in its vulnerable spot.[11]

Toward the end of September or beginning of October, Gerö managed to meet Tito in the Crimea — an event to be described fully in the next chapter. This gave Gerö hope of becoming acceptable to Tito; and now the Politburo decided to act swiftly and to arrange the reburial of the victims of the anti-Titoist campaign in Hungary. But first the bodies had to be found. They had been buried by the AVH in a deserted forest clearing near the town of Gödöllő. A party, guided by a former major of the AVH (who had selected the original burial ground) and including members of the victims' families, proceeded there. Rajk's dentist was able to identify his skeleton; similarly other corpses were recognized in this Hungarian Katyn.[12] Under pressure of opposition groups the Party headquarters consented to a public funeral on October 6, the anniversary of the execution of the thirteen generals of the Hungarian Army after the downfall of the War of Independence in 1849. This grandiose reburial of the "martyrs" in the Central Cemetery of Budapest provided the gruesome scene for an unprecedented mass demonstration — silent but the more impressive — against the regime, a dress rehearsal of the forthcoming revolution. Ferenc Münnich, then Hungarian ambassador to Belgrade, and Antal Apro, a Politburo member, made speeches on behalf of the Party. Neither Gerö nor Kádár was present; both were in Moscow (Gerö traveled there from the Crimea and Kádár joined him on his way back from China), where they had talks with Mikoyan and Suslov, the two Presidium members who had been particularly assigned to deal with the affairs of Hungary.[13]

Münnich announced in his speech that "we are fighting for such guarantees which will vouchsafe that only guilt supported by objective evidence should be punishable." Münnich's announcement sounded ludicrously anachronistic — this principle had been guiding the English Common Law for centuries, had been adopted in the legislation of other civilized countries since the work of Beccaria and Filangieri in eighteenth-century Italy, and had been part and parcel of Hungarian criminal law for nearly a hundred years. Apro's assurances were little more convincing when he asked: "What is the guarantee that similar violations of the law will not recur? . . . The guarantee is the Party. We are the guarantee, because we are determined, and we can learn from the errors of the past." [14] The audience remained convinced that the roots of these crimes emanated from the system, from the Party itself.

The following days witnessed a number of such reburials. The most outstanding, an event of October 13, was that of the "innocently" hanged army and police officers, Lieutenant Generals Solyom and Illy, Major Generals Porffy, Beleznay, and Révay, and the police leaders Korodi, and Horváth-Höniger.[15] This scene, in front of thousands of officers, including the Minister of Defense and other loyal leaders of the Army (who were considered responsible for the misdeeds by all), was scarcely conducive to strengthening the morale of the armed forces nor their determination to fight for the Party and the Soviet cause.

The series of reburials of "innocent" victims inevitably raised the question of responsibility. The saying had it: "so many crimes and no criminals." Inside and outside the Party, people wished for the incrimination of those who had been responsible for the acts committed. There was no more a quest for *political* responsibility, since such a notion is alien to Bolshevik thinking. The Party, irrespective of mistakes committed by its leaders, could not abandon its hold upon the country, and theory and practice supported the thesis that the Party can do no wrong. When its leaders made mistakes, it would be guided by expediency: perhaps they would have to practice self-criticism only, or perhaps they would be removed, even physically liquidated. Everything depended on whether or not the cause (i.e., the Party) profited by it; if the cause profited, even innocent victims might be sacrificed. The "murder" of Rajk and associates had been deplored not because it was morally or criminally wrong, but because it was a political error, an inexpedient and dangerous act. The question arose whether it was still expedient to victimize leaders of the Party for these errors, however grave. Of course, Gerö and his entourage, steeped in the Communist mentality, believed that it would be unwise and inexpedient (as well as personally uncomfortable) to become victims themselves. It would jeopardize the future and present of the Party. And "the Party first" was their battle cry.

Such a perverse way of thinking was still alien to the rank and file of the Party and the people at large, in spite of indoctrination. They still clung to the time-honored principles of morality and elementary justice; they wished to call a spade a spade, and a murder a murder. Since the Communist system ignored the idea of political responsibility, this principle could not be usefully invoked, even if there had been an opportunity of doing so. But since the "mistakes" committed were criminal acts under existing law, it seemed easier and more satisfactory to ask for criminal responsibility. Even under this heading most of the Party leaders could be included in the vast array of culprits, since practically all were vulnerable for having instigated, abetted, or themselves committed the crimes in question.

The pressure was so enormous and inescapable that the Politburo could not avoid taking certain very limited steps toward inculpating those responsible for the "judicial murders." It resorted to the old device of making a few suffer for something that others were equally guilty of — in this case the Farkases (father and son). On October 11, the arrest of young Vladimir Farkas (and also that of three Security officers) was announced. Two days later the former General Mihály Farkas was taken into custody.[16] However, these arrests failed to produce the expected soothing result. The Petöfi Circle (now reactivated), the Writers' Association, and many other Party organizations asked for an open trial. Such a trial would have compromised the entire Party leadership, since Mihály Farkas was known to have threatened to expose all the Stalinist Party leaders and also "the Russians" if anything happened to him.[17]

IMRE NAGY AND THE PARTY

The resolution of the Imre Nagy problem had led the Party leadership to some no less agonizing decisions. It was evident to everybody that the return of Nagy into the Party — especially if he were to get the fair hearing he wanted — would automatically make him a leading figure, not only outside but within the Party itself. He would rally around him all the opposition elements, those still wavering and those who out of fear and opportunism had refrained from siding with him. The conditions which would accompany his return might become of decisive importance for the leadership of the Party.

We can safely assume that the readmission of Imre Nagy to the Party had formed a topic of discussion not only within the Hungarian Politburo, but also between Gerö and Kádár, on the one hand, and members of the Soviet Presidium, on the other. After Rákosi's downfall, Nagy began paying visits to Soviet Ambassador Andropov,[18] and he had met Mikoyan in July. The Soviet leaders, though distrusting Nagy, guessed his immense popularity and hoped to utilize him, once again, for their purposes, if only he would give up his embarrassing righteousness and stubbornness. The Yugoslav leaders were also interested; copies of his writings had been handed to the Yugoslav embassy,[19] and had no doubt reached the ruling circles in Belgrade. His "Yugoslav orientation" both in international and internal politics, must have been known to them. He was the man they wished to see at Hungary's helm, though the desire was cherished secretly so as not to raise Soviet suspicions. The questions of his reinstatement with the Party, however, might possibly have been a subject of discussion between Tito and the Soviet leaders, and certainly had been one between Tito and Gerö.

The semiofficial expression of the Party leadership's view on Nagy's readmission was voiced in the *Szabad Nép* on September 23. The article, signed by Colonel General Sándor Nográdi, dealt with the general session of the Writers' Association, where many speakers had raised the question of Nagy's readmission and future role. The article called upon Nagy to admit his mistakes in order to assure his reinstatement in the Party. A similar view was taken the next day in an article by Marosán entirely devoted to the "Imre Nagy problem." Since Rákosi's fall Nagy had several times been invited to Party headquarters to discuss his problem. There he had alternately received a friendly welcome or a haughty rebuke.[20] Significantly, it was Gerö who offered him an "alliance," whereas Kádár expanded upon his guest's "rightist deviationism"; evidently Kádár sensed a dangerous rival to his career. The Party's offer to Nagy included a plan to cast all responsibility for the "exaggerated" measure of his expulsion upon Rákosi; but, simultaneously, the Party leaders insisted on some mild form of self-criticism from Nagy himself.

But Imre Nagy felt that he had been expelled unjustly in violation of Party rules, and he wished the Central Committee to withdraw its censure and apologize to his face. He still harped upon the June (1953) Resolutions which had not been implemented by Rákosi nor insisted upon by the Central Committee. Rightly or wrongly, he believed that these resolutions, approved by Moscow at the same time as his rise to power, had been collaborated in by the Soviet leadership, and he wished to argue for their readoption both against the Hungarian Party leadership and against the Soviet Presidium.[21] Nagy wanted to be reinstated; he now had a full program, spelled out in his dissertation. This program went beyond the policies of the New Course, and he hoped to be able to carry it out through the Party. This planned "regeneration" of the Party would have been tantamount to a destruction of the "operating principles of Leninism," [22] but he seemed to ignore that his concepts were irreconcilable with basic Leninist doctrine.

We have seen that Nagy's friends and close adherents had suggested to him the formation of an opposition outside the Party, a path which he tenaciously refused to follow. During the summer of 1956 an opportunity was offered to him to sidetrack the authority of the Party. Attila Szigeti, Chairman of the Györ County Council, a non-Party member of the National Assembly, offered to raise the "Nagy problem" and other fundamental political questions during the forthcoming session of the National Assembly. Since parliamentary interpellations had to obtain prior approval, he proposed to submit an innocuous topic and under this pretext embark upon his principal issue. If he were interrupted, a scandal would ensue; if not, he would have created an opportunity for a debate. This procedure, a matter of routine under genuine parliamentary systems, was a revolutionary action under a Communist regime.[23] Characteristically, the former Premier absolutely refused to approve of this method or any other not directed through recognized Party channels. His actions seemed to imply — although he was unaware of it — the destruction of the Party, as a Leninist Communist Party, by its own initiative.

It appears that eventually Imre Nagy consented, not to repent, but only to "ask" for his readmission to the Party; he would then be given opportunity to defend his thesis before the Central Committee. He wrote his letter on October 4, which happened to be two days before the reburial of Rajk. According to reports this letter, as printed in the October 14 issue of the *Szabad Nép*, was not the verbatim replica of what Nagy had written, and there are different versions in circulation.[24] But, essentially, all versions express the same idea: Nagy wished to return to the ranks of the Party in order to preserve its unity and in the interest of a "firm and homogeneous policy." He was ready to cooperate in a manner "compatible with [his] convictions and with [his] Marxist-Leninist principles," but he demanded a "re-examination" of his case by the Central Committee. He did not practice self-criticism; he did not recant anything.

The Politburo replied to Nagy's letter in a resolution of October 13. The delay was partly due to the absence of Gerö and Kádár from Hungary; nevertheless, Nagy's adherents resented the nine-day lapse. The text of the resolution also caused disappointment, because it was not entirely free from censure of Nagy. Though the resolution annulled the former decision to exclude Nagy from the Party, and though it conceded that the expulsion had been unjustified, it also stated that he had been "guilty of political errors." The blame for the excess of the expulsion was thrown upon Rákosi, who had "exercised personal control over the Party." The Politburo further resolved to submit to the Central Committee the unsettled questions of Imre Nagy's alleged errors. This body would have to detail those errors and "to clarify the ideological questions involved in the matter." [25]

Imre Nagy seemed to acquiesce in this procedure, and was immediately reproached by his adherents for a weakness in having consented to return to the Party without prior clarification of his status, and before the Central Committee had consented to make the necessary amends.[26] The impression one gains is that Nagy wished to forestall any extra-Party move by his followers and wished to impress the Central Committee by a personal appearance. Still trusting in his Socratic approach, he hoped to convince the Committee of the propriety of his cause. He may also have been persuaded to follow this course by the conversations he had with the Soviet ambassador and perhaps with other representatives of the Soviet Party. But he might also have foreseen the danger of further delay and perceived the symptoms of the coming upheaval that he sought to prevent. Now that he had been promised a full discussion of his case in the Central Committee, he considered that he was giving way on procedure only, and not on substance.

FIRST REVOLUTIONARY ACT: RESHUFFLE IN THE WRITERS' ASSOCIATION

The originality of Lenin's Bolshevik system consisted in the fact that the Party exercised control of a universal and total character over all governmental bodies and nongovernmental organizations while preserving at the same time the *formal* democratic framework and autonomy of many of these institutions. Despite their outward autonomy and democratic form, all these organizations and institutions were reduced to sham institutions, controlled by the Party. Elections affecting them are only sham elections; nominees are selected by the Party and no opposition candidates are tolerated.[27] Tho totality of Party control is the mainstay of Communist rule, and any miscarriage of arrangements, especially with regard to purported "free" elections, may produce unhappy results for the regime. The first of these Party-directed sham institutions that emancipated itself from Party tutelage was the Writers' Association.

After Rákosi's ouster a fresh breeze of intellectual freedom began to penetrate Hungarian literature, journalism, and the arts. The writers and journalists who had "revolted" in vain less than a year earlier found themselves in the position of victors over the bureaucrats who had tried to prevent the development of their artistic and literary talents. This atmosphere of relative liberty entered the editorial offices of newspapers and periodicals, the state editorial

bureaus, film studios, and theaters. After many years of restriction
or of self-imposed silence, writers produced a wealth of poetry, novels,
and plays, and also journalism of the best type. Symbolic and veiled
writing on delicate political subjects alternated with more outspoken
criticism and attacks of a political character. The craving for "truth,"
so long suppressed, turned into an obsession: writers and journalists
were constantly making vows always to abide by "truth" and to
repudiate the venomous concept of "double truth," one "Socialist,"
the other "bourgeois." [28] Thoughtful persons realized the paradox
of the situation. There was still a dictatorship; the police power of
the state was still intact and Soviet control unabated.[29] Was the
Party to give up its hold over the country? Was the Soviet Union
ready to abandon its prey? The touchiness of Hungarian-Soviet
relations was keenly felt by almost everybody: no direct reproach
or even veiled attack was made by the reawakened literature or
poetry against the paramount power, though writings railing at
autocracy and oppression could have been applied to the Socialist
Fatherland as well as to Hungary.

In this buoyant atmosphere it is not surprising that the first
structural break of Party control occurred in the Writers' Association, long the hotbed of the discontented. On September 17, 1956,
the Association held its annual General Meeting and proceeded to
the election of its Executive Committee and its secretaries. The
Party candidates, all of them former Party watchdogs and stooges,
including Jozsef Darvas, the Minister of Culture, were defeated in a
secret ballot. In their stead, leaders of the struggle against Stalinism
and "Socialist realism," some of them non-Party writers, were
elected. Among the non-Communists was Pál Ignotus, a former Social
Democrat, who had spent six years in prison.[30] The Writers' Association, as a result of this election, became a free, autonomous body,
relieved of Party control. In the Communist system this action was
something more than a prodrome of a revolution; it was a real
revolutionary act. The Party leadership expressed its bad temper by
making no mention of the results of these elections in the Party daily.

Other expressions of intellectual freedom were becoming quite
abundant in September and October. In the same issue of the
Szabad Nép that announced Imre Nagy's return to Party membership, Professor Lukács expressed views more daring than ever before:
no administrative interference with artistic or literary work should
be permissible; in more general terms, no views should be suppressed
by administrative means; an interrelation between Socialist and
national categories must be found to forestall disaster. He sorrow-

fully admitted that the prestige of Marxism had considerably decreased in Hungary and elsewhere.[31] Also the Petöfi Circle re-opened its meetings; in September a session was held to discuss some aspects of Hungarian agriculture. Ferenc Donáth was in the chair, and Zoltán Vas lamely defended the government's policy. Compulsory deliveries, collectivization, and the financial burdens of individual farmers underwent scathing criticism. Zoltán Tildy, the former President of the Republic, who in May had been released from the house arrest imposed since 1948, also attended this meeting to face the public once again after eight years. Tildy, who had in the past shown all too great servility toward the Communists and had therefore mostly lost the sympathies of the former members of his party, the Smallholders, profusely vowed his approval of the government's agricultural policy (his special field of interest). At that meeting of the Petöfi Circle he possibly became aware of the short-sightedness of his slavish loyalism, having had a glimpse of popular sentiment and the new possibilities for free expression and contact. Thereafter he tried to re-establish some of his former Smallholder contacts, with the help of István Dobi, a renegade Smallholder, now a Communist Party member and Chairman of the Presidential Council of the People's Republic, who, in view of the brewing storm, was trying to mend fences with his former political friends.

Tildy and Dobi attended a farmers' meeting in the town of Kaposvár on October 20, 1956. It was one of the stormy meetings of this period when Party leaders, overawed by the immense outburst of spontaneous hatred, sat silently in their seats, wishing they were elsewhere. This meeting almost turned into open revolt, and it was Tildy who, with his timely intervention, saved it from becoming so. He reminded the audience that there were "Soviet occupation troops" in the country (the debate had taken an open anti-Soviet turn), and that only such policies might be reasonably pursued which were not in conflict with the political conceptions of the paramount power.[32] Tildy's activities on this occasion, and at other times, foreshadowed the role which he was to play in the subsequent course of the Revolution.

GERÖ'S MASTER PLAN

Ernö Gerö, a revolutionary of the old school, after some months in the post of First Secretary came to realize that the revolutionary temper of the nation and the opposition against the ruling Party clique could not be ended unless a dramatic event should enable him to display force and crush the enemy. Thus Moscow might be persuaded that the use of violent measures had been inevitable; then he could restore his and the Party's authority, and be able to rule over the country as his fellow Party secretaries did in countries like Czechoslovakia, the German Democratic Republic, or even in Rumania and Bulgaria. Why should he be unable to control the country assigned as his bailiwick by Moscow? He knew well that because of Rákosi the Kremlin had been under constant pressure from Tito, and that the same pressure continued against him. Evidently no violent method could be resorted to: Moscow would never give its permission for such an action as long as the present Party leadership and Gerö himself were *personae non gratae* in Belgrade.

There is evidence that the Stalinist faction (even its pro-Rákosi group) did not remain entirely inactive during the summer months and the early fall. In September 1956, Gerö had to prevent the publication of an editorial in the *Szabad Nép* which was to bear the title: "We welcome the return of Comrade Rákosi." [33]

Imre Nagy was first warned in August that Gerö's clique was preparing a provocation to save itself from being replaced by Moscow.[34] At that time Gerö was still uncertain whether Khrushchev would be willing to intervene on his behalf with Tito, and whether the Yugoslav pressure would not bring about his fall, like that of Rákosi. But after his personal meeting with Tito, he could more seriously consider the idea of forming a "master plan" to crush his enemies. We should also recall that Rákosi, in exile in Moscow or some other place in the Soviet Union, did not remain inactive: he was sending memorandum after memorandum to the members of the Soviet Presidium, no doubt warning them against adopting a "kid glove" treatment for a "Fascist people" and advocating stern measures.[35] The Gerö clique, with the help of the Security Police and with the active concurrence of Kádár and his group, were yet unable to use brute force, but they tried to cow the opposition by various means. The writers were discouraged by being told that Rákosi's fall was not due to their propaganda campaign. The Security Police permitted the return to Hungary of Antal Páger, a well-known actor with pro-Nazi leanings who had fled to Germany in 1944; and they even sponsored his appearance on the stage, probably to frighten the (mostly Jewish) leaders of the intellectual opposition.[36]

It was a necessity for Gerö, through some planned provocation, to come to grips with the ubiquitous opposition that confronted him inside and outside the Party. He was somewhat hampered by the ostensibly loyal attitude of the opposition. This opposition, especially its Party faction, advocated "purification" and not liquidation of the regime.[37] Gerö knew, and so did many of the members of the Party opposition, that this position was only tactical, but it was difficult to persuade Moscow that he was facing not genuine anti-Stalinists of the Khrushchev type, nor even rightist deviationists, but, *horrible dictu,* clear-cut counterrevolutionaries. He wished to be able to label them as such, in a way that would leave no trace of doubt with the members of the Central Committee, many of whom were now wavering between the Gerö-Kádár faction and the opposition led by Losonczy and Donáth.* To do this, and also to convince the membership of the Party in general — and even more importantly the masters of the Kremlin — he needed his little "Berlin" or "Poznan." Of course, he would not be as weak as the Polish leaders had been in regard to the Poznan revolt; his "Poznan" would crush all leaders of the opposition who could be regarded as dangerous. Imre Nagy, in Gerö's eyes, was not so great a peril as he had been in Rákosi's; his passivity, idealism, and theoretical proclivity were not of the nature to trouble Gerö, who, proud of being a man of action, despised Nagy and his popularity. Consequently, Nagy might be spared, though he would have to be deprived of his following. Then he might even be usefully employed perhaps as Prime Minister, a puppet in the hands of an all-powerful, versatile, and indefatigable Gerö; a figurehead to mitigate the effects of his repression.

Ruthless regimes and the autocrats who dominate them often stage revolts, thus gaining the opportunity to reveal and smash dangerous enemies. From the times of the ill-famed Roman emperors to the reign of Stalin, such "provoked" rebellions or plots have been employed. Only the methods varied: sometimes the use of *agents-provocateurs,* provided by the secret police, sufficed; in other cases the opposition was thrown into despair by extremely harsh measures which gave them no other alternative than to revolt; or perhaps some small event, even an individual act, was inflated into a great *affaire*

* The situation is thus depicted by Khrushchev himself: "I was told by Comrade Kádár and by other friends of the difficult position in which the working people of Hungary found themselves when the revisionists raised their heads with impunity. The First Secretary of the Central Committee, Gerö, would say one thing: Losonczy . . . would say another. Both were speaking on behalf of the Party. Who should be believed, who should be followed — this was the question not only for non-Party workers and peasants but also for members of the Party. This is only one instance which describes the atmosphere utilized by the counter-revolutionaries to raise insurrection against the people's regime. The former Hungarian leadership which committed gross mistakes of Socialist legality and repressions against honest workers, looked the other way while enemies of Socialism were organizing their conspiracy against the people." Speech after his return from Hungary on April 10, 1958, in Moscow; *Pravda,* April 11, 1958; *East Europe,* June 1958, p. 19.

and repression hit those who had nothing to do with the original event. Of course, not infrequently, such staged or provoked revolts overstepped the limits set for them by their planners. Autocratic regimes generally do not realize the extent of their unpopularity, nor are they always accurately informed as to the reliability of their army and police. In such cases, the staged revolt is not as easily suppressed as was thought. It may also happen that the regime is brought down altogether, or at any rate is overthrown more swiftly than if the revolt had not been provoked. If the temper of the people is ripe for an insurrection, that is, if psychological, social, and political conditions favor the possibility of a revolt,[38] then the artificial provocation of the masses is like oil poured on fire. It becomes a very perilous experiment indeed when the forces of the planned repression prove to be unreliable. When Charles X of France, emboldened by the capture of Algiers, issued his harsh ordinances in 1830, he believed that the ensuing resistance would easily be taken care of by the army. He was mistaken, and was ousted by the revolution called forth by his provocative measures.

When Gerö was contemplating his staged revolt, he did not realize the extent of dissatisfaction throughout the country. He certainly did not foresee the anti-regime sentiment of the working class and the students, or the rapid disintegration of the Party. He was equally ill-informed concerning the reliability of the police and the armed forces. He was counting on a reconciliation with Tito to restore him to an honorable place among anti-Stalinist leaders, but he overestimated the impact of his Yugoslav overture on the Hungarian masses. Most of all, he failed to calculate the electrifying influence on the Hungarian nation of the portentous events which took place in Poland just at a time when he and Kádár were undertaking to seal their friendship with Tito.

20

Yugoslavia Complies — Poland Rises — Hungary Revolts

VVVVVVVVVVVVVVVVVVVVVVVVVVVVVVV

And when the war broke out its real horrors, its real dangers, its menace of real death were a blessing compared with the inhuman reign of the lie, and they brought relief because they broke the spell of the dead letter.

BORIS PASTERNAK, *Doctor Zhivago*

THE replacement of Rákosi by Gerö, as we have seen, had not satisfied Tito, who considered that Gerö had "pursued the same kind of policy and was to blame just as much as Rákosi was," and consequently from Yugoslavia's point of view that "things were not going as they should." [1] Nevertheless, Khrushchev had not given up the idea (which had the backing of the Soviet Presidium) of having Gerö made acceptable to Tito. Since Rákosi had been "sacrificed" for friendship's sake, why should Tito not make a step on his part toward restoring the amicable relations with Yugoslavia's northern Communist neighbor? Since Tito's visit to Moscow, Khrushchev must have been in frequent contact with his Yugoslav colleague. They probably had exchanges of views on all topics which interested their two countries, and on all ideological Party problems of the Communist orbit. Titoism had helped Khrushchev to strengthen his stature as a Soviet leader, though he was not yet the single autocrat of the Soviet Union, as he was to become a year later. His agreements with Tito, although ambiguous and incomplete, impressed the Communist bloc and its peoples. It was desirable that Hungary's Gerö should not remain an apple of discord between these two Communist leaders who, in agreement, could ensure the solidarity and success of the Socialist camp.

TITO "ACCIDENTALLY" MEETS GERÖ

Tito's ambition to participate in the leadership of world Communism had been frustrated by Stalin's veto and the Yugoslav Party's excommunication from the Cominform. When, thanks to Khrushchev's help, Yugoslavia seemed about to return to the Socialist camp, not like the prodigal son to his father's house, but with flying colors, it was only natural for Tito to revert to his *idée fixe:* his "Macedonia" was too small. It may be that he had even received some initial encouragement from Khrushchev, who was intent on re-establishing the unity of the Communist community and thereby increasing his prestige and power within the Soviet Union. It has even been suggested that Khrushchev solicited Tito's support for Gerö and stabilization in Hungary on the ground that Stalinists might otherwise regain power in the Soviet leadership and endanger his (Khrushchev's) position.[2] Under such circumstances, Tito's reflex must have been not to disappoint his "friend." Tito's ambitious projects were not altogether favored by more Western-minded members of his entourage. Kardelj and Bebler had never ceased to be suspicious of Soviet designs, and still hoped for *rapprochement* with a Hungary which had shaken off the shackles of monopolistic Soviet control, a relationship which they valued more highly than Tito's other leading project: a federation of Communist Balkan states. These more "progressive" Yugoslav leaders had been well informed about the split in the Hungarian Party, Imre Nagy's writings and his popularity, and the instability of Gerö's position. They advised Tito against befriending the still Stalinist-tainted Hungarian leadership.

Tito, torn between his desire to please Khrushchev and his prejudice against Gerö — a prejudice magnified by the advice of his assistants — had not made up his mind on the point when he met Khrushchev in Yugoslavia and accompanied the Soviet leader back to the Crimea. At this time the Soviet host staged an "accidental" meeting between his Yugoslav guest and Gerö, who just "happened to be there." [3] The date was at the end of September or the beginning of October, in 1956. Tito and Ranković consented to talk to Gerö, who apologized for having slandered the Yugoslav leaders and, promising to correct all past mistakes, begged Tito for his friendship. We can assume that Khrushchev acted as mediator and conciliator throughout these discussions.

Finally the Yugoslav leaders invited a Hungarian Party delegation to Yugoslavia; Tito became convinced either of the sincerity of Gerö's abjuration of Stalinism or of the usefulness of strengthening his ties with the Hungarian Party leaders (he must have had Kádár in mind, but also Imre Nagy, for he urged the readmittance of the latter to the Party). He must have been aware, though, that his reconciliation with Gerö would strengthen Gerö's position; evidently this was the motive of both Khrushchev and Gerö and, in this respect, the Yugoslav leaders thoroughly miscalculated the situation, as Tito was compelled to admit subsequent to the Revolution in these words: "We wanted to establish relations with the Hungarian Workers Party because we hoped that by not isolating the Hungarian Party we could more easily influence that country's proper internal development . . . However, matters had already gone pretty far, a fact which we did not know, so that Gerö's coming to Yugoslavia and our joint declaration could no longer help." [4]

Gerö had already diplomatically undertaken to prepare his journey to Belgrade. Ferenc Münnich, a muscovite who had suffered degradation under Rákosi's rule, had been sent as minister to Yugoslavia on August 7, 1956.[5] The government displayed a conciliatory attitude toward writers. The release of many political prisoners (other than Communist or Socialist) had taken place in the course of the summer and also during September and October. The readmission of Imre Nagy to the Party was timed to take effect on the eve of the Hungarian delegation's departure for Belgrade. We can assume that this readmission was a precondition of the visit. The Hungarians set out for Belgrade, after a delay of several days, on October 14. The members of the delegation were: Gerö, the First Secretary; Kádár, Party Secretary; Politburo member Apro; and Hegedüs, the Prime Minister.[6] The delegation spent one week in Yugoslavia, having lengthy conversations with their hosts. It is to be noted that Tito and his counselors had ample opportunity to discuss matters not only with Gerö but also with Kádár. Tito may have been favorably impressed by Kádár, especially since Kádár had been a victim of Rákosi, a circumstance which could be favorably interpreted as punishment for incipient Titoist sympathies.[7] The representatives of the two Parties signed a declaration of friendship and cooperation, a document which could not be published in Hungary after the return of Gerö because of intervening events.

When, on the night of October 22 and 23, the Hungarian Party journeyed back from Belgrade to Budapest, Gerö must have been satisfied with his achievements. He, with Khrushchev's help, had been able to break the Yugoslav ice; he had been received with all honors by Tito, and had re-established friendly inter-Party relations; he had obtained not only Tito's recognition of his role as First Secretary, but also a promise of friendly assistance and support of his policy. Gerö as well as Kádár no doubt had explained their intra-Party difficulties to the Yugoslav leaders, and had complained of the stubbornness of Nagy and his followers — the deplorable Augean stable bequeathed by Rákosi. Gerö and Kádár seem to have belittled the importance and extent of their Party opposition in the picture they gave Tito; nevertheless, we can presume that Gerö suggested to the Yugoslav leaders the necessity of using harsher measures for discouraging reactionaries hiding behind the cloak of Party opposition. It is not known whether Gerö communicated elements of his master plan to crush the opposition, but his attitude after returning showed that he felt very much at ease in resorting to violent measures of suppression. Gerö must have felt that Tito's backing was a step toward the stabilization of the Communist camp, whereas Tito must have considered the gesture as one that enhanced his own stature in the world Communist movement.

THE POLISH OCTOBER AND HUNGARY: ANALOGIES AND DIFFERENCES

The "triumphant" visit of Gerö and his delegation to Yugoslavia failed to make the expected impression on the Hungarian public. Gerö miscalculated the intensity of the people's aversion for him. Then, too, an unexpected development in Poland had diverted practically all attention from his journey and focused Hungarian interest and enthusiasm on what was considered a magnificent victory of Polish nationalism over Soviet Russian domination. The incomplete accounts appearing in the Hungarian and other Communist presses on the dramatic encounter of the Soviet and Polish leaders, on the refusal of Gomulka to submit to Soviet threats, and on the final acquiescence of the Kremlin — seasoned by foreign broadcasts and circulated in exaggerated versions by word of mouth throughout the country — did not fail to create an atmosphere of satisfaction and aggressive confidence among the enemies of the regime; and these enemies were almost identical with the nation as a whole.

The epidemic spreading of revolutionary movements is a well-known historic phenomenon. The Hungarian Revolution of 1848 broke out under the impact of the February Revolution in France, and so did many other revolutions in the same year. Friendship toward Poland has always been a deeply anchored sentiment in

Hungary, and frequent political commerce between these two nations had taken place, especially in the course of the nineteenth century. Both countries had experienced threats of annihilation from the East and the West, and both had fought hard for ten centuries to preserve their independence. They had been neighbors for almost the same period (and had even had, on occasion, common rulers). They were the only two contiguous nations in Europe that could boast they had never waged war against each other. The Polish events recalled historical precedents, such as the help received from Polish officers and volunteers in 1848–1849. The already existing anti-Russian sentiment was further stimulated.

Wishful thinking and obscured vision failed to reveal the differences prevailing between the political developments of the two countries; existing analogies reflected only the common anti-Soviet and anti-Russian sentiment and sense of frustration, and the similarities in the Communist state structure. The fact is that attitudes and the evolution in the Polish and Hungarian Communist Parties differed utterly; so did the two personalities in whom national confidence had been placed.

In Hungary, as we have seen, the evolution of Communist thinking through which intellectuals and many other Party members had gone since the Stalinist dictatorship had little affected the leading Party bureaucracy and the members of the Central Committee. While intellectuals and the rank and file of the Party (if they were ever convinced Communists) had become "rightists," or professed Communism only to disguise their real sentiment, the Central Committee and Party functionaries remained opportunists and struggled for the maintenance of their position only. For them the safest method for survival was to listen to the voice of Moscow, to guess or anticipate the real wishes of the Kremlin. Thus they had managed to navigate the stormy waters of the Rákosi-Imre Nagy rivalry. Now they felt safe aboard the Gerö-Kádár bandwagon, which they saw as being supported by the Soviet leaders, and they were unwilling to give up their security for the risks of bringing Imre Nagy back to power.

The Polish Party was also split like the Hungarian, but in the case of the Poles the cleavage had reached the upper echelons, notably the Central Committee membership and the Politburo.[8] After Bierut's death, and particularly under the impact of the Poznan riots, the Polish leadership gradually grew sympathetic toward Gomulka's restoration to power; this evolution in sentiment was recognized by Ochab, the First Secretary, who, by October 1956, seemed to be in favor of handing over his post to Gomulka.[9] He and other "evolutionists" in the Polish Politburo and Central Committee now had to face the resistance of a minority group which wished to avail itself of the support of the Soviet Union in order to prevent its exclusion from positions of power. The majority of the Polish leadership, backed by the Army and also the Internal Security Corps, thereupon acted, bringing Gomulka and his friends into the Politburo and designating Gomulka as First Secretary on October 19. All this without the prior approval (perhaps with the explicit objection) of the Soviet leaders. Neither the threat of Soviet military intervention nor the unscheduled visit of an impressive Soviet delegation including Khrushchev, Molotov, Mikoyan, and Kaganovich (two anti-Stalinists and two Stalinists) could deter the Poles from their decision; and the Soviet Presidium, finally persuaded to chart a conciliatory course and convinced of Gomulka's loyalty toward the Soviet Union, acquiesced in the change on October 21.

The revolutionary character of the Polish event consisted in its deviation from accepted norms of Soviet supremacy; it was a revolutionary act carried out by the Central Committee of the Polish Party, thereby violating rules of Communist conduct set by Moscow. It was a revolt within the Communist orbit carried out against the paramount Soviet leadership by the local Communist Party organ, like a vassal state acting against the accepted customs of vassalage. In Poland it was not the people that imposed their will upon the government by revolutionary action (although we know that the overwhelming majority of the Polish people approved of the change). The local Communist Party itself rose against the bondage imposed by Soviet Party authority. The anti-Soviet demonstrations accompanying and following the Party coup brought about the eventual removal of Marshal Rokossovsky as a head of the Polish Army, but otherwise had no significance in the shaping of Polish internal or external affairs. The Polish change, albeit supported by the masses, was not a people's revolution in the sense that the Hungarian Revolution was. It was a coup by the Polish Communist Party which succeeded partly in loosening the shackles imposed by the domineering Soviet Party. Herein lies the historic significance.

No such move could have been expected from the Hungarian Party leadership. Never had Gerö been willing voluntarily to cede his post to anyone, especially Nagy, nor had he or the Politburo or the Central Committee acquired the pluck to make any essential changes in the Party leadership without the prior approval of their

Soviet masters. Though Ochab had been installed by Khrushchev (against the candidacy of Zambrowski) as First Secretary of the Polish Party, he dared to nominate his successor without Soviet consent; no such initiative was forthcoming from Gerö or the organs he controlled. In July 1956, some members of the Central Committee had complained to Moscow against Rákosi, but they refused to take action at any time before the Soviet Presidium intervened. Then they sheepishly accepted the new First Secretary legitimized by the Kremlin. The servility of the Hungarian leadership toward its Soviet comrades made any independent, much less revolutionary, action unthinkable. Consequently, the Hungarian Revolution was not a revolt of the Hungarian Party against the supreme Soviet Party leadership, as in Poland, but a revolt of the Hungarian masses *both* against their Hungarian Party-government leadership and against Soviet domination. No comparison between the two events seems possible in view of the differences of method, personnel, and objective between the two revolutionary actions, although a mutual influence clearly existed between events in Poland and those of Hungary.*

The submissiveness of the Hungarian Central Committee to Moscow, so much in contrast to its Polish counterpart, was not due solely to the fact that its members had been chosen by Rákosi. Except for the muscovites, the leading Hungarian Communists, like other individual Hungarians, had very little personal contact with Russians. Unlike Poland, of which a considerable part had been a Russian province for well over a century, no part of Hungary had ever been under direct Russian rule. In Poland the knowledge of Russian was and is widespread, and the affinity of the two languages was also helpful toward mutual intercourse; but in Hungary the incidence of Russian speakers remained low, despite compulsory instruction, and the great majority of leading Hungarian Communists could only converse with Soviet comrades with the help of interpreters. Although Hungarians now share with the majority of the Poles a dislike and even contempt of anything Russian, the Poles have had far more experience in understanding the Russian mind and dealing with Soviet individuals. Their approach toward things Soviet is more intelligent and sensible than that of the Hungarian. The average Hungarian contemplates the

---

* Polish manifestations of sympathy for the Hungarian cause increased popular revolutionary fervor in Poland, but the collapse of the Hungarian Revolution was utilized by Gomulka as an excuse for restraining his compatriots. See Zbigniew K. Brzezinski, *The Soviet Bloc* (Cambridge, Mass., 1960), p. 259.

Russian — this strange being — with considerable awe, yet despises him. The indoctrinated Party member feels this same awe, but combines it with an admiration not felt by the average citizen. The majority of the Central Committee members, being half-educated and being indoctrinated by Marxist-Leninist literature, would thus be ready to bow and scrape before the "superior" Soviet being, whereas their Polish counterparts would consider him accessible, persuasible, and even gullible. The lack of comprehension and the toadyism of the leading Hungarian Communists prevented the majority of them from cultivating a psychology toward the Russians that would have favored any judiciously independent action.

DEMONSTRATION AND ARMED REVOLT: THE QUESTION OF "SPONTANEITY"

Since the Hungarian Revolution was the work of the masses in the streets, there was no principal or central assembly or other body which might have been considered the agent of revolutionary will. The English Revolution of 1642–1648 centered around the struggle between Parliament and the King. The French Revolution of 1789 arose from the rebellion of the representatives of the Third Estate, constituting themselves as the National Assembly. In the American Revolution it was the Continental Congress which became the spokesman for revolutionary forces. Even the Russian March Revolution of 1917 possessed the Committee of the Duma, which appeared as the representative of national revolution. In all these revolutions, significant or even overwhelming roles were played by demonstrators, street fighters, and popular masses; but whatever their share in revolutionary victory had been, they served only as an accompaniment to the "official" revolutionary body. The almost unique characteristic of the Hungarian Revolution of 1956 may be considered its complete lack of a revolutionary body which, at the time of the outbreak, might have been the formal embodiment of the revolting masses. All the revolutionary institutions which assumed importance were formed only after the uprising was well under way.

Agitated by the Polish events, various student groups acting under the mantle of DISZ organizations (including the Petőfi Circle) held meetings to arrange demonstrations, to draft petitions, and to formulate demands. An analysis of the manifold "points" of these demands reveals that the first set of them was conceived within the framework of the Communist state. Its implementation would not have involved a change of system but only a change of personnel and an emancipation from Soviet predominance, in the Polish style.

The first of the meetings took place in the city of Szeged on October 20. The purpose was to elect the new leadership of the DISZ; but the meeting devoted most of its time to discussing the formation of an organization of university and high school students that would become independent of the DISZ. This assembly drew up a demand of twelve points for submission to the government. Meetings in all other university towns now followed quickly. The most important was a meeting in the Technological University for the Building Industries in Budapest where the students were joined by engineers and workers from many factories. On the evening of October 22, while Gerö's special train was en route from Belgrade, this assembly adopted a demand consisting of sixteen points.[10] The petition was spread by handbills all over the city. The sixteen points were: (1) withdrawal of Soviet troops from Hungary according to the peace treaty; (2) new elections in the Communist Party by secret ballot; (3) Imre Nagy to be made Prime Minister, and Stalin-Rákosi adherents to be discarded; (4) public trial in the case of Mihály Farkas and accomplices; (5) general elections with the participation of several parties; (6) re-examination of Hungary's relations with the Soviet Union under the principle of equality; (7) reorganization of economic life as recommended by experts; (8) publication of foreign trade agreements; (9) revision of working norms in industry; (10) readjustment of the agricultural delivery system; (11) release of political prisoners; (12) freedom of opinion and of the press; (13) removal of the Stalin statue; (14) readoption of the Kossuth coat of arms; (15) expression of solidarity with Poland; and (16) convocation of a Youth Parliament. The sixteenth point also set the stage for an event that was to become explosive; this point called for the laying of a wreath before the statue of General Bem in Budapest. General Bem was a hero of both the Polish Revolution of 1830 and the Hungarian Revolution of 1848. The demonstration was scheduled for the afternoon of Tuesday, October 23.

Even wider circulation was given to ten demands submitted by the Petöfi Circle and published on the morning of October 23 in the last prerevolutionary issue of the *Szabad Nép*. The Circle demanded, among other things, the convocation of the Central Committee plenum, open disclosure of the state of the economy, institution of democratic Socialism, formation of a popular front to ensure the workers' democracy, participation of Imre Nagy and of "other comrades" in the government, exclusion of the Rákosites from the Party, open trial for Mihály Farkas, and publication of foreign trade agreements. Most of these demands were vague, revealing the "reformist" spirit for a rejuvenation of the Communist system. The Petöfi Circle laid particular stress on trade questions and asked for "equality" in the relationship with the Soviets.

The scheduled demonstration at the statue of General Bem was planned to be an expression of sympathy toward the Polish freedom movement. Of course, it was to be also a demonstration for the sixteen points adopted at the Technological University, and furthermore a demonstration against Stalinism and everything meant by that term; but it seems evident from the nature of the debates held, the resolutions adopted, and their approval by such responsible persons as the Rector of the Technological University that only a peaceful demonstration was planned. The *Szabad Nép* of October 23 registered the great number of meetings which had taken place in the high schools and universities, and, while expressing solidarity with their resolutions, at the same time warned the students that the "struggle is being fought for Socialist democracy, and that counter-revolutionary voices and bourgeois provocations will favor sectarianism only."

At 12:53 P.M. on October 23 the radio announced that the Minister of the Interior had forbidden the demonstration planned for that afternoon. At 2:23 P.M. the radio proclaimed that the prohibition had been withdrawn, and that Ernö Gerö, the First Secretary of the Party, would make a speech over the radio at 8 P.M. During the next hours these announcements were five times repeated.[11] The procession to the statue of Bem, owing to the great number of participants, turned into mass demonstrations at various points in the city of Budapest. The crowd, at first consisting mainly of students, snowballed as it was joined by passers-by, workers, and even soldiers. Tempers rose from minute to minute, and soon anti-Soviet slogans were mixed with hurrahs for Imre Nagy and for Poland. After the ceremony the square before the Parliament building, across the Danube from the Bem statue, became the main rallying ground. Here the crowd demanded to hear Nagy. At last the Party functionaries approved Nagy's appearance. Persuaded by friends to address the crowd, he walked uneasily onto the balcony, having no official assignment to speak and still waiting for the Central Committee to vindicate his claims. Imre Nagy gave a maladroit talk which by no means quieted the masses as the Party intended it to do. For example, he addressed the crowd: "Comrades!" Many shouted back: "We are not comrades!" This shout was probably the first open repudiation of the Party, inasmuch as many of these early demonstrators were Party members.

Not merely one crowd but several crowds had gathered in the streets by nightfall. The vicinity of the radio building became one of the centers of excitement. On the outskirts of the city another group took it on themselves to bring down the big metal statue of Stalin. They worked at it a long time without success, until finally some ironworkers severed the legs just above the boots. The statue toppled at about 9:30, and the throng dragged it to a prominent place nearer the center of Budapest.

By that time, the whole city was in an uproar. Perhaps two hundred thousand people were in the surging crowds. The greatest single incitement to bloodshed is generally regarded to have been Gerö's 8 o'clock radio speech, which was heard by many in their homes or over street loudspeakers and was swiftly reported to larger numbers by word of mouth. Tito later declared that "the hundreds of thousands of demonstrators," at that stage, were still "only demonstrators," but that the "blind" Gerö "insulted nearly the whole nation." Said Tito, "In such a critical moment, when all was in turmoil and when the whole nation was dissatisfied, he dared to fling the term 'mob' at people among whom a large number, perhaps even the majority, consisted of Communists and youth." [12] Tito's statement that Gerö had upbraided his audience as a "mob," and other reports according to which he had referred to them as "fascist rabble," are not confirmed by the published text of his speech nor by the recollections of some who heard it.[13] But unquestionably there were contemptuous passages which, in view of the prevailing atmosphere and temper of the crowds, can be interpreted as violently provocative. Furthermore, he exasperated the populace by the abundant use of outworn Communist phraseology, by frequent repetitions of assertions that nearly everyone knew to be brazenly false, and finally by his own personality and his sharp and offensive voice.

Gerö spoke of the threat that menaced "the achievements of our People's Democracy." He said enemies were trying "to undermine the power of the working class" and "to loosen the relations which link our Party to the glorious Communist Party of the Soviet Union." These enemies "heap slanders on the Soviet Union" and pretend that "we are trading with the Soviet Union on an unequal footing, that our relations with the Soviet Union allegedly are not of equality, and that our independence must be defended not

against the imperialists but against the Soviet Union." All this —
so Gerö said — was impudent untruth, hostile propaganda which
did not contain a grain of truth. He proclaimed that good Communists were patriots, but stated that "we are not nationalists. We
are waging a consistent fight against chauvinism . . . therefore
condemn those who strive to spread the poison of chauvinism among
our youth and who have taken advantage of the democratic freedom
insured by our state to working people to carry out a demonstration
of a nationalistic character." Concerning the events in Poland, Gerö
— most awkwardly — announced that "we . . . do not want to
interfere in the internal affairs of Poland . . . but this cannot in
any way mean that we should not follow our own road" — a statement which was taken as a repudiation of the Polish reforms so
much admired and celebrated by the demonstrators.

Gerö promised that within a few days the plenum of the Central
Committee would be convoked in order "to discuss the political
situation and the tasks of the Party, as well as organizational problems." This was not a promise likely to appease impatient and
emotional masses, nor was the open question that Gerö flung out at
his audience: "One has to state frankly that the question now is
whether we want a socialist democracy or a bourgeois democracy."
In the mind of the masses there was no doubt that they ardently
desired a change, and since they were supposed to have lived under
"socialist democracy" (which all of them identified with Bolshevik
Communism) they unhesitatingly sided with the "bourgeois" kind,
whatever meaning they attributed to this term.

After Gerö went off the air the crowd at the radio building and
in the surrounding streets became more and more noisy. This
crowd was demanding the broadcast of the sixteen points that had
been formulated at the Technological University. The building was
protected by a Security Police unit. The first shots were fired here —
by the Security Police on the still unarmed crowd — and thus it
was here that the unarmed demonstration turned into an armed
conflict. Later the United Nations Special Committee on the Problem of Hungary painstakingly examined the problem of the "first
shots." It concluded: "Shortly after 9 P.M. tear gas bombs were
thrown from the upper windows [of the radio building] and, one or
two minutes later AVH men opened fire on the crowd, killing a
number of people and wounding others." [14]

It has puzzled many observers how unarmed demonstrators were
able to obtain weapons so quickly and how they were able to handle
them so successfully, and these facts were used to support the thesis

that the revolution had been organized well in advance and with outside help.[15] On the other hand, there is ample evidence to prove that the demonstrators did not obtain firearms until during the events which occurred in the vicinity of the radio building, and the sources of these arms have been well substantiated.[16] One source was soldiers who either joined the insurgents or simply handed over their arms to them. Another was army and police depots that were opened to the revolutionaries. Still another was the workmen of arms factories, who provided weapons for the fight. The United Lamp Factory (a cover name for an arms plant in Budapest) in the beginning provided most of the arms and ammunition for the rebels; more than one thousand rifles came into their possession there. Also truckloads of arms were transported from various barracks by workers to the scene of battle with the connivance of the military authorities. In view of compulsory military service, premilitary training within the DISZ, and target practice by the workers' militia, the experience in the use of these arms can easily be explained, whereas there is no evidence that suggests a concerted and planned action.

The question of spontaneity or of preparation in a revolution has often occupied historians.[17] It seems appropriate to distinguish here between the two extremes — between a planned armed revolution (military coup, *Putsch*) and a revolution that originates in unarmed demonstration by civilians. The armed revolt is premeditated and organized, and clearly intends to overthrow the existing government by force; the unarmed demonstration only acquires the nature of a revolution *en passant*. There is no human mass activity without some direction or resolve; the question really depends on what the immediate objectives of the pressure groups or other forces have been in directing their members to demonstrate. If the intention was a street procession or demonstration pure and simple, no immediate revolutionary scheming can be attributed to such political action; the revolutionary intent, the *animus insurgendi*, will be adopted by the crowd only in the course of the peaceful demonstration when, in view of the defection of the armed forces, they come to realize their capability of overthrowing the government. Lenin's coup in November 1917 and Franco's military revolt in 1936 were planned armed revolutions. On the other hand, the Russian Revolution of March 1917 started with street demonstrations and only turned into a rebellion for overthrowing the tsarist regime when troops refused to shoot at the demonstrators. Thus, scheming to demonstrate for political reasons is not tantamount to the planning of a revolution. History records a great many demonstrations (and there have been many others not important enough to record) which never ended in a revolution because the necessary requisites — such as incitement to overthrow the regime, intensity of frustration, and defection of armed forces — were absent.

The Hungarian Revolution was never planned or organized; there was no central directive organ or organization in existence to plan, nor did the various student bodies that resolved to demonstrate on October 23 have any idea, much less any intention, of proceeding toward a revolution. The revolutionary inspiration came to them as a consequence of subsequent provocations which, according to the principles of mass psychology, increased their sense of resentment and favored aggressiveness. Thus, the scene around the radio building, the shots of the Security Police, the sight of the wounded and dead, gave them the impetus to storm the building, though they were armed only at first with bricks and cobblestones. Later, the defection of the armed forces other than the Security Police (even the latter wavered and gave way in many instances), the acquisition of arms, and the ensuing successes turned the unarmed peaceful demonstrators into armed revolutionaries intent on putting an end to the Communist regime. The demonstrations at their outset were closely akin to the meetings in the Petőfi Circle or within various student organizations, except that the activity had been transferred to the streets. The slogans adhered to the various "points" previously adopted, and were more "revisionist" or "reformist" than anti-Communist. In the night hours after Gerö's speech, anti-regime slogans became heard. The fight at the radio building was directed against the Security Police. During the early morning hours of October 24, the first Soviet intervention began. And, with that, the Revolution acquired a pronounced nationalist character — a fight for liberation from alien rule, a fight for self-determination and effective democracy.

Had the Revolution been deliberately planned, the objectives of the ensuing armed struggle would have been more clearly defined. The administrative center of the regime was located in the Party headquarters and in the Parliament building (seat of the Prime Ministry); yet no attack was made by the insurgents against either one of these centers of power during the days of the revolt, even though tens of thousands of persons thronged in the Parliament square and adjacent streets on October 23, and even though they did so again on October 25 when about a hundred unarmed demonstrators were killed by salvos from the Security Police. The crowds did penetrate into the radio building about midnight of October 23, and also into the editorial offices of the *Szabad Nép* at approximately the same time; but those assaults were prompted by specific reasons: the radio had not broadcast the "sixteen points" that had been circulated by handbills; the people demanded their broadcast. Nor had the Party daily printed them; the people demanded their printing. In both places, shots fired by the Security Police changed the demonstrators into armed besiegers. There had been no governing scheme or plan directing the movements of what people overnight began calling the Freedom Fighters; and when the first intervention by Soviet troops occurred, the insurgents were easily put on the defensive and were not able to pursue their attacks.[18]

As in Paris in July 1789, the several crowds were joined by people in the various quarters of the city where they happened to operate. Besides the storming of the radio and *Szabad Nép* buildings, the various groups during the night occupied Party locals, police stations, and also some plants. There was at no time any concerted action among the fighting groups, which were headed by self-appointed leaders. What they did have was a sense of community of purpose hardly ever surpassed by previous spontaneous revolutionary movements. The acute feeling of resentment and consequent aggressiveness, and the common goal for action impressed on them by the Soviet intervention, largely replaced the original lack of planning and gave outsiders the impression of a large-scale organization and direction which were, in fact, totally absent.

THE CRUCIAL MOMENT: GERÖ'S MASTER PLAN FAILS

Historians of revolutions often devote careful examination to the question of who shot first. This is indeed an important clue in elucidating the immediate causes of the revolt; but, on the other hand, chroniclers know of many riots where shots were fired and no revolution followed. Evidently the crucial condition for the success of a revolt is not so much whether the demonstrators or the armed forces summoned to repress them fired the first shot, but whether one party was able to defeat the other. In many revolts of the past, even though the armed forces were fully loyal, the government out of weakness refused to use them against the insurgents; but wherever a government possessed both loyal troops and the full determination to use them, the revolutionary movement collapsed unless it could muster capable and reliable fighters of its own. In most of the successful revolutions of the nineteenth and twentieth centuries, the rebels were not adequately equipped to fight the armed forces but success was, nevertheless, achieved by subverting the army and police in favor of the aims of the revolution. In France both the July Revolution of 1830 and the February Revolution of 1848 succeeded because of the defection of the army. The course of the Russian Revolution of March 1917 was similarly determined by the unwillingness of the army to fight the demonstrators of Petrograd. Louis XVI, on the other hand, was reluctant to use his reliable mercenaries against the besiegers of the Bastille, whereas General Bonaparte had no scruples about turning his guns against the rebels of Vendémiaire in 1795.

The siege of the "Bastille" of Budapest, that is, the struggle for the radio building, was the crucial event of the Hungarian uprising.[19] Not only were the first shots fired here, but it was here that the unwillingness of the Hungarian armed forces to fight the rebellion first manifested itself. Had the army and the police been reliable instruments of the government, there is no doubt that the Revolution could have been clipped off in the incipient stage. But, as it turned out, not only did these coercive forces of the regime prove to be wholly reluctant to enter into action, but even some of the Security Police regiments refused to fight their fellow countrymen.* The almost complete passivity of the armed forces in the face of the open rebellion must have been a deadly shock to the ruling Party clique, and particularly to Gerö himself. As we have seen, he had cherished the idea of provoking a riot or insurrection which could enable him to liquidate the "anti-Party" elements. But the indispensable requisite for such a plan was the reliability of those armed forces which were to be called on to smash the uprising.

Gerö must have planned to make his provocation some time after his return from Yugoslavia; his *rapprochement* with Tito would by then have disarmed the less aggressive members of the Party opposition. Against the rest of them he would have to use violent measures after they had tried openly to rebel against the regime. But the Polish events and the speedy developments which followed in Hungary had somewhat outdistanced his plans; arriving back in Budapest on the morning of October 23, he was not able to make sufficient use of his Yugoslav triumph to be ready for his "little rebellion." The demonstration at the statue of General Bem

* These regiments were recruited (not professional) members of the Security Police force: but AVH professionals also turned over their arms to the revolutionaries. One of the co-defendants in the conspiracy case of the journalist Obersovszky after the Revolution was a Security Police officer (Ferenc Kovács) who was sentenced to death and executed (*Népszabadság*, July 5, 1957); see also CURPH (Columbia University Research Project on Hungary), interview no. 616.

had been forbidden by the Minister of the Interior; but Gerö, back in his office, listening to threats that the ceremony would take place despite the interdiction, collecting information from the Security Police and from various Party offices, conferring with the Soviet ambassador and perhaps speaking on the telephone with Moscow, came to the conclusion that the intended showdown might as well take place without the cooperation of his body of *agents provocateurs*. He then decided that the demonstration should be allowed, and if it happened to result in open insubordination, the resistance was to be smashed by force and repression. Orders were then issued to permit the demonstration, and simultaneously Gerö's speech was announced, and both announcements were repeated insistently during the afternoon. Ambiguous invitations to the crowd to participate were mixed with alerts to the Budapest garrison and the Security Police units. Those and other units were then concentrated at various points of the city. Gerö's speech, when it came, was provocative and stern. The combination of these circumstances can only indicate that Gerö wished to induce the demonstrators to commit irretrievable actions so that he could turn his full force against them. Gerö's resolve to fight the crowd by all means became manifest when a group of writers visited him on behalf of the Writers' Association and begged him to abstain from making his speech and have the sixteen points broadcast instead. Gerö made it sufficiently clear to the delegation that he was ready to give orders to shoot at the unarmed crowd.[20]

The events up to a certain moment developed as Gerö had wished. His speech excited the crowd; the stubborn refusal to read the sixteen points over the radio (after they had become common knowledge through handbills distributed in the streets and after the demands of the Petöfi Circle had appeared in the *Szabad Nép* in the morning) added fuel to the fire. It is a fair assumption that if the sixteen points had been broadcast and if Gerö's speech had shown some understanding and been conceived in a more conciliatory spirit the demonstrations would have remained, as was intended, a peaceful manifestation of sympathy toward Poland and of the desire for reforms modeled on that pattern. His intransigence and provocations, and the shots fired by the Security Police, not in self-defense but with the intent to frighten and disperse the demonstrators before the radio building, brought the demonstrations to a degree of emotion that produced a willingness to die rather than withdraw from the demands. The Security Police in the radio building were insufficient to cope with the situation. The regular police had disappeared from the streets. Therefore the Politburo sent army units to the fighting area. The crucial moment approached.

Apart from the Security Police, already in action, three kinds of military personnel happened to be in the radio building area between 10 and 11 P.M. There were individual soldiers and officers who had already joined the demonstrating crowd; there was a detachment from a mechanized army division which had been ordered to the scene from its headquarters in Piliscsaba, west of Budapest; finally, there was a company of the Frontier Guard Command, a unit considered most reliable and under the control of the Security Police. The soldiers and officers who had already joined the rebels, together with individual members of the crowd, enjoined the hesitating officers and men of the armed formations not to shoot at the crowd. Details of the events as told by eyewitnesses vary, but all have concluded that eventually the mechanized detachment refused to fight, and the Frontier Guard company even handed over their weapons to the rebels.[21] Major General Hegyi, chief of the training section of the Ministry of Defense, tried in vain to take over command of the armed forces. Threatened by the crowd and left undefended by his own men, he was finally glad to escape from the scene.[22] He must have been the first high-ranking officer to report the defection of the armed forces.

The fate of autocrats had thus befallen the Hungarian Communist regime: for years they had strengthened their armed might, partly in obedience to the Soviet order to prepare for war against the imperialists, but partly to protect the "People's Democracy" against internal uprisings. They had the People's Army, the police, the Security Police, and the workers' militia. Now within a few hours all they had built seemed to crumble away in their hands: the army refused to fight and turned over its weapons to the rebels, the police disobeyed and disappeared from the streets, the workers' militia joined the rebellion, and the Security Police changed from hunter into hunted. Nothing remained for them but the Soviet Army. Had the Soviet Army not been called upon to help, the entire Communist regime would have collapsed within twenty-four hours. In the absence of the Russians, if the revolutionaries had marched against the supreme Party headquarters and Parliament building, they would have no doubt taken possession of them. We cannot assume that the armed forces concentrated around these key centers would have been willing or able to put up an effective and successful resistance. The immediate collapse of the regime, however, was averted by the intervention of the Soviet forces stationed in Hungary.

THE FIRST SOVIET MILITARY INTERVENTION

The Politburo, in session during those turbulent hours, debated whether to call on Soviet forces for help.[23] Whether the Politburo formally decided to ask for this help is not known, and the person who did make such a request (if it was made at all) is likely to remain unidentified; the choice is among Gerö, the First Secretary; Hegedüs, the Prime Minister; and Marosán, a Politburo member who boasted later that he had called for Soviet military help.[24] Sometime in the middle of that fateful night Imre Nagy found himself catapulted back into the premiership and we now know that Gerö, on October 24, tried to have Nagy sign an antedated document which was to be presented as a note asking for military help from the Soviets.[25] The signature was never obtained.* In the United Nations General Assembly, on November 19, 1956, Soviet Foreign Minister Shepilov quoted a telegram which he had received from the Hungarian Prime Minister on October 24 asking the Soviet Union to send its troops to Budapest in order to put an end to the disturbances; he omitted, however, to state which Prime Minister had signed this telegram. One rightly inquires: how could Soviet tanks arrive in Budapest at 2 A.M. on October 24, in response to a request received in Moscow on the same day? [26]

The contradictions and uncertainties relative to the alleged invitation extended to Soviet troops to intervene on October 24 have led the United Nations Special Committee to doubt whether any formal invitation was made at all.[27] It is no surprise for a student of Soviet-satellite relations that questions of such importance cannot be clarified in the light of conventional international dealings; the relationship in question is, in essence, not an international but an inter-Party one where the principle prevails that the "Soviet Party rules the satellite Party." The problem of intervention by Soviet forces, like any other important question, was discussed between

---

* The Hungarian White Book on the Nagy "trial" provides us with the revealing testimony of a witness according to which Imre Nagy had declared on October 27 before a workers' delegation that "it was not he who had called in the Russians, only that they wanted subsequently to obtain his signature to this effect." *Nagy Imre És Büntársai Elenforradalmi Összeesküvése* (Budapest, 1958), p. 71. On October 29, Imre Nagy declared before other witnesses that it would have been impossible for him to have called in the Soviet troops, since they arrived in Budapest about or even before the time that he was appointed Prime Minister; *U. N. Report*, p. 37.

the Hungarian Party headquarters and the Kremlin. Possibly Soviet Ambassador Andropov, or the Soviet adviser in the Hungarian Party headquarters, or the chief Soviet military adviser, also intervened in the matter. Soviet reinforcements had been on the move into Hungary since the events of Poland, and the Soviet troops in both Rumania and Hungary had been alerted between October 20 and 23.[28] The movement of Soviet forces on Hungarian soil did not require any consent by Budapest, and they could have intervened even without an explicit invitation by the Hungarian Party or government. Gerö and the Budapest Party headquarters were always in telephonic communication with Moscow, and many conversations were carried on daily between the seat of central power and the "provincial" authorities. During these hurried conversations, eventually augmented by those between Andropov and the Soviet advisers in Hungary, it was decided that Soviet forces should intervene for the restoration of order. Subsequently, the need for documentation appeared, and Gerö, after having in vain tried to obtain Nagy's signature, simply sent a telegram to Moscow (with or without Nagy's name on it) in the name of the "Council of Ministers of the Hungarian People's Republic." To justify such a procedure in the customary framework of international relations might be perplexing for a judicial investigating body or for scholars of international law.[29]

During the next four days after the intervention of Soviet military forces began, Soviet tank units engaged in intermittent fighting with Freedom Fighter groups established in various parts of Budapest and with industrial worker groups entrenched in factories. Guerrilla fighters harassed the Soviet contingents, occupied some public buildings and Party offices, and freed political prisoners. The first Soviet military action officially ended with the announcement on October 28 that Russian forces were to be withdrawn from Budapest. This armed intervention proved to be a fiasco both from the military and the political point of view. Militarily the intervention was abortive; it did not restore order or annihilate the armed revolutionary forces. Politically, it greatly strengthened the resistance, turned it into a genuine national revolution, added numbers to the insurgents, and even further alienated "faithful" Party members. This first Soviet military action did not even prevent the collapse of Communist dictatorship in Hungary; it only postponed the collapse for a few days. When the military action slowly lost its momentum and had to be canceled, the maintenance of a Communist one-Party dictatorship became impossible.

At the time of the outbreak of the uprising, two mechanized Soviet divisions were stationed in Hungary, the Second and the Seventeenth, together with some additional army and air force units. The Soviet Thirty-second and Thirty-fourth Mechanized Divisions stationed in Rumania entered Hungarian territory on October 24. Most of these forces were employed to fight the insurgents in Budapest and its suburbs; the rest took up positions in various provincial towns of Hungary. The stories of how the poorly equipped Freedom Fighters, many of them not yet out of childhood, successfully fought Soviet tanks and mechanized units has been related by many eye-witnesses and commentators.[30] The failure of the Soviet armed forces was due not only to the heroic resistance they encountered, but also to the lack of infantry and artillery support; the inadequacy of tanks for combat in narrow streets; poor logistics; and the low morale of the troops assigned to a distasteful task. The Soviet forces had been given the task of fighting and suppressing the rebellion, and probably had been told to spare civilian lives and refrain from devastating houses. Though many noncombatant civilians did lose their lives and many houses were destroyed — even during this first Soviet intervention — a reluctance on the part of the Soviet forces to carry out a ruthless operation was perceptible. This may be attributed to their low morale when forced to combat students and workers. Some Soviet units appeared to sympathize openly with the Hungarian population; others abstained from fighting and assumed somewhat neutralist attitudes.* Regular armed forces seem to require an ideal, a meaningful objective, when engaged in a life-and-death struggle. Though the Soviet soldiers were told that they were fighting a "fascist counterrevolution," those who had been stationed in Hungary for a considerable time could hardly convince themselves that their student and worker adversaries had anything to do with "fascism." ** In some provincial towns the Soviet commanders on the spot entered into implicit or overt agreements of

---

* This writer was able to observe fraternization between Soviet tank crews, hoisting the Hungarian flag, and Hungarian civilians. He also saw mechanized units stationed passively for a whole day in one of the squares in the city while a few blocks away some other units were engaged in a desultory struggle with Freedom Fighters.

** The story told by a Soviet officer seems characteristic from this point of view. He had been ordered from the town of Kecskemét to Budapest on October 23, and told there was a "counterrevolution"; he was sent back to his original post on October 29 on being advised that it was merely a "revolution"; on November 4 the same officer was ordered back again to Budapest with the reiterated claim of a "counterrevolution." CURPH, interview no. 500.

"noninterference" with the local revolutionary authorities, and both sides refrained from fighting.[31]

Were the Hungarian Freedom Fighters the victors against the first Soviet onslaught? Or were they merely saved by the reluctance of the Soviet command to impart the *coup de grâce*?[32] To assess whether a military action has been successful, the objectives must be taken into account. Would the available Soviet forces have been capable of suppressing all resistance, had they continued their fight after October 29? By that date the Soviet forces in Budapest had in fact ceased all offensive fighting, and had restricted themselves to self-defense whenever attacked in their positions. The Freedom Fighters, on the other hand, refrained from attacking idle Soviet units in order to save their scarce ammunition. When the cease fire was announced on October 28 by the Hungarian government, it was a cease fire agreement between the government forces and the Freedom Fighters, to assure the Freedom Fighters that they would no longer be attacked. (Actually no fighting had been going on between the insurgents and the Hungarian Army units, only sporadic fighting between the insurgents and the Security Police.) No such cease fire agreement was ever concluded between the Soviet armed forces and their adversaries; the fighting ceased *de facto*.

There is no doubt that if the Soviet Army in late October had obtained reinforcements such as those which resumed the fighting on November 4, it could have defeated the Freedom Fighters at that time. However, no such reinforcements were yet available, and furthermore the Soviet Union seemed to have decided to discontinue the fight. The officers of the Zrinyi Academy, in the outskirts of the city, were able to observe from their windows that the Soviets towed away 200 damaged or destroyed tanks, that is, half of the armor they had originally thrown into combat.[33] If they had continued the fight, they might have lost their remaining armor. It is thus not unfounded to maintain that the Soviet forces broke off the engagement because of inability to sustain pressure on the insurgents.

The Freedom Fighters had won a battle, but not the war. Nobody could have reasonably pretended that the Soviet forces were altogether defeated. Nevertheless, the impact on the population from having at least partially repulsed the "invincible" Soviet Army was one of utmost exhilaration and satisfaction.

21

Party and Government during the Revolution

/\.\/\V

You have sat too long here for any good you have been doing.
Depart, I say, and let us have done with you!

Cromwell to the Long Parliament (1653)

He whose honor depends on the opinion of the masses must day
by day strive with the greatest anxiety, act and scheme in order
to retain his reputation.

SPINOZA

THE Communist dictatorship had gradually been built up in
Hungary, as in other People's Democracies, by the support of Soviet
occupation forces and the terrorism of a militant Communist Party.
Now, under the pressure of the Hungarian revolutionaries, backed
by the overwhelming majority of public opinion, the carpet had to
be rolled back. The monopolistic rule of the Party disappeared, and
revolutionary institutions came into being which competed, not
with the disintegrated Communist Party, but with the newly emancipated governmental power. Soon other political parties, resuscitated from their slumbers, began to organize a more militant
membership than the compromised remains of Communism. Finally,
the Communist Party reconstituted itself in an attempt to regain
a modicum of prestige. This reversal of the course took place in
ten days — an enormous speed when one considers that Communist
Party dictatorship had required years to construct. The reversal
took place amidst revolutionary struggles and birth pains, and al-

most six of the ten days were spent in armed conflict with an interfering foreign army.

During the night of October 23 to 24, 1956, Gerö's provocative action having failed, the whole coercive power of the Communist regime seemed to be nearing collapse. Resort had to be made to Soviet military support, but on that very same night this gesture of the "hard stick" was accompanied by a "soft hand" measure. A reshuffle took place within the Politburo, new members were called to the Central Committee, and Imre Nagy, who had only ten days earlier been readmitted to the Party and whose "deviation" case was still pending, was again installed in the seat of Chairman of the Council of Ministers. The readmission of Nagy to the ruling circles of the Party and country was by demand of both the intra-Party and non-Party opposition. Now Gerö, no doubt in consultation with Moscow, resolved to use Imre Nagy's popularity to disarm the resistance and counteract the shocking impression created by the Soviet intervention.

DE-STALINIZATION: TOO LATE AND TOO LITTLE

The full Central Committee had been scheduled to assemble on October 31. Gerö, in his radio speech of October 23, said vaguely that the meeting would take place within the next few days. But shortly thereafter, at 10:22 P.M., the radio declared that the plenum would be convoked immediately.[1] Around midnight the Central Committee met in utter confusion; Stalinists and moderates clashed on such issues as how to deal with the revolt and what changes to make in the leadership of the Party and government. The resignation of Gerö as First Secretary and the appointment of Imre Nagy as Prime Minister were demanded by many. Gerö surprised the conclave with the news that Soviet troops had been asked to intervene in the battle; simultaneously he moved the co-optation of the members of the opposition into the Central Committee and the election of a new Politburo. He also asked the Central Committee to recommend the promotion of Imre Nagy to the premiership. The Central Committee complied, and then proceeded to vote a state of martial law.[2]

The next morning, in the absence of newspapers, the radio announced the news: Nagy was back in the premiership. Premier Hegedüs was demoted to First Deputy Premier. New members of the Central Committee were Imre Nagy, Ferenc Donáth, Géza Losonczy, György Lukács, and Ferenc Münnich. Six Stalinists had been dropped from the Politburo; in their place were five new members: Imre Nagy and three of his friends, Sándor Gáspár, Jozsef Köböl, and Zoltán Szánto, and Gyula Kállai (a friend of Kádár). Losonczy became an alternate member of the Politburo. On the other hand, Gerö remained First Secretary of the Party, and only Donáth had been added to the secretariat.[3]

During that riotous night and the following days, Party and state competencies became befogged. It was never announced when and whether the Presidium of the National Assembly had acted upon the "recommendation" of the Central Committee to appoint Imre Nagy as Prime Minister. Evidently this mere "formality" had still been overlooked when Nagy, as Prime Minister, made a broadcast to the nation at 11:10 A.M. on October 24, soon after the announcement of his being "recommended." Martial law was announced as having been decreed by the Council of Ministers, but it was only stated that "governmental organs" had asked for Soviet military help.[4]

The "de-Stalinization" undertaken by the Central Committee *in articulo mortis* of the Communist regime in Hungary was typical of autocratic governments threatened by massive popular uprisings: belated concessions amounting only to half-measures. Gerö was still able to persuade the Kremlin that his position was indispensable for maintaining Soviet control and Communist rule. He must have harped on Nagy's reputation of unreliability and caused the Soviet Presidium to believe that if he used Nagy as a shield, while keeping him under his thumb, he would be able to master the wave of dissatisfaction — at the same time restoring order with the help of Soviet forces. The evidence of the early part of Nagy's premiership makes it manifest that Gerö intended him as nothing more than a dummy to be employed in appeasing the crowds. After Nagy's unsuccessful oratorical exercise on the balcony of the Parliament building on October 23 he was taken to Party headquarters and kept incommunicado from the outside world for almost three days. It is not known that he in any way participated in the discussions of the Central Committee during the critical night, and nothing indicates that he was consulted on the crucial decisions of summoning the Soviet forces, reorganizing the Party leadership, and decreeing martial law. As to his own appointment as Prime Minister, he was confronted with a *fait accompli*. As Prime Minister, he was placed in a room inside Party headquarters instead of in the Prime Minister's office located in the Parliament building. His status must have been that of a recluse if not a prisoner.[5]

The psychological effect that the unexpected explosion had on all leading Party members — including even Imre Nagy — must be taken into account if we are to evaluate the attitudes displayed by individual members of the Communist leadership during the first three days of the revolt. Communist leaders, more than those of other autocracies, live in a self-created world where personally inspired illusions vie with realistic assessments of facts. Their estimates of threats from the non-Communist realm may be exaggerated and therefore inaccurate, but paradoxically their decisions to rely on force against dangers from both within and without are generally the results of realistic calculation. Thus the Hungarian leaders, in selecting their objects of trust and distrust, became victims of their own ideology and propaganda. The illusion of a dictatorship of the proletariat which had been propagated for so many years grew into "reality" in their vision. In their distorted view, the "People's" Army had become a force ready to defend the "achievements of Socialism." They had too much faith in the efficacy of indoctrination, and therefore believed others to be as successfully indoctrinated as they themselves. Though they must have sensed the discontent of the people, they were prepared to minimize both its numerical and qualitative significance. Furthermore, they could never have believed that the most favored elements, the workers and students, would, as one body, turn against their alleged benefactor, the Party. They could not have imagined that indoctrination would prove utterly useless also in the case of the armed forces or that the whole population, including its most "democratic" elements, could ever defy the "glorious" Soviet Army.

Imre Nagy himself, who had warned the Party of the catastrophe into which the country was inevitably being swept as a result of the "rift between the masses and the Party and government," [6] had been stunned by the developments. Wishing to halt the bloodshed through the powers of persuasion, and motivated by a sense of mission, he agreed to put his name, popularity, and ability at the disposal — not of Gerö and his clique — but of the nation. His sense of duty coupled with his idealism and optimism (which might also be called naïveté) persuaded him to accept the post of Prime Minister, even though it meant serving with Gerö and the other Stalinists who still occupied all the other key positions. He apparently fancied that in the course of time, after he had aided in re-establishing peace and order, he would be able to get rid of the tainted elements of the Party. His compromising attitude had not been shared by the "rightist" members of his circle of friends. Donáth and Losonczy refused to accept their Party posts, which had been assigned to them without their prior consent (though to a Communist every assignment is theoretically a duty), and until October 26 they did not occupy these positions.

The contrast between Imre Nagy's radio address of October 24 and the radio announcements and speeches made that day by others is quite striking. While the others threatened the insurgents with reprisals, called them counterrevolutionaries, and wanted to apply martial law (involving the death sentence), Nagy implored the Freedom Fighters to lay down their arms and promised them not only full amnesty but also "systematic democratization of our country in every field, Party, state and economic life." [7] In fact, the martial law was never applied against any of the captured Freedom Fighters, owing to Nagy's intervention. When subsequently arraigned on charges of having prevented the use of this sanction, he is said to have replied that the measure was to apply only to common criminals and not those who fought the regime.[8]

During the afternoon of October 24, Mikoyan and Suslov, the same members of the Soviet Presidium who had acted as troubleshooters in Hungary on earlier occasions, arrived in Budapest and called on Party headquarters. Here they encountered the pandemonium of despair and bickering which reigned among the leading Party members. Since the previous night, reproaches and counterreproaches had been exchanged among the Stalinists and the adherents of Kádár and the Imre Nagy group. The panic had increased when the leaders saw that despite their claims of defeating the rebels, and their repeated invitations to surrender, the number of revolutionaries increased and the resistance hardened. Mikoyan and Suslov, representing the two opposing factions within the Soviet Presidium, spent many hours in discussion with the Hungarians and postponed their decision until the next morning. They wished Gerö replaced as First Secretary by János Kádár, but Gerö — like Rákosi before him — delayed the decision by trying to contact Moscow and by other subterfuges. The bloodbath before the Parliament building on October 25 was the last straw, and shortly afterward Gerö's demotion was announced, together with Kádár's succession to the first Party post.[9] For another twenty-four hours the indefatigable Gerö tried to thwart Nagy's and Kádár's independent course of action, still hoping for a reversal of the verdict by Moscow, until he was finally spirited away to the Soviet Union.

Mikoyan and Suslov, in agreement with the Soviet Presidium, which had been continuously consulted, agreed to certain policy changes which soon were reflected by the speeches made after Gerö's fall. On October 25, Kádár, the new First Secretary, first accused "anti-democratic and counterrevolutionary elements" of causing the peaceful demonstrations to "degenerate" into an armed attack. Then he promised that "after order had been restored, the government would conduct talks with the Soviet government in the spirit of complete equality . . . for the equitable and just settlement of questions pending between the two Socialist countries." [10] Imre Nagy was even more explicit in his address of the same day when he promised an "all embracing program of reform" and talks with the Soviet Union "concerning the withdrawal of the Soviet forces stationed in Hungary," [11] a public demand which overshadowed everything else at the moment. Prior to these speeches, the radio had invited the public to hoist the national tricolor on all houses, a gesture which seems to have indicated that the Party leadership at last understood that it was facing a full-scale national revolution.* The new tone of the radio messages thus contrasted sharply with the earlier announcements, such as the bloodthirsty and vengeful address which István Bata, the Minister of Defense, made before Gerö's removal from office.

Mikoyan and Suslov, after Gerö's demotion, held long conferences with Nagy and other leaders, resulting in agreement on what should be done to stabilize the situation. Evidently, Mikoyan and Suslov had some solution in mind running parallel to the Polish model — that is, wider internal autonomy for the Hungarian Party, measures of liberalization, "domesticism" taking account of Hungarian peculiarities, discarding of compromised Stalinists, revision of trade agreements with the Soviets, and also the later withdrawal of Soviet troops. They thus hoped to arrive at a compromise which would help to maintain the essence of Party rule and Soviet control, but would do away with ostensible shortcomings and satisfy the sensitivities of national feelings. On Friday, October 26, while street combat was still going on between Soviet forces and the Freedom Fighters, Mikoyan and Suslov rode to the airport in a tank escorted by other tanks and armored cars, and left Budapest, to report to the Soviet Presidium.

Imre Nagy, with Gerö out of the picture, recovered a capacity for action and freedom of movement that enabled him to gain information about the real state of affairs in the country. The most

* According to Lenin's advice Communist parties deprecate "khvostism" (following behind popular trends like a "tail"). Whenever possible they want to set themselves at the head of and direct, or, if possible, channel, popular movements. The Hungarian Party had sadly fallen behind the events.

significant and remarkable change, which he must have seen with unbelieving eyes, was the almost complete disintegration of the Communist Party of Hungary.

DISINTEGRATION OF THE COMMUNIST PARTY

Gerö's departure induced some of Imre Nagy's friends, who so far had disapproved the Prime Minister's readiness to cooperate with Stalinists, to join him and assist him with their counsel. Donáth and Losonczy now were willing to fill their Party posts. Gimes and Vásárhelyi acted as liaison between Nagy and the press, and between the Prime Minister's office and the various revolutionary organizations which now sought contact with the Party and government. Many other friends and sympathizers of Nagy were soon to join them in forming the official and unofficial entourage of the Premier. Imre Nagy, released on October 26 from the informational and administrative embargo imposed on him by Gerö, transferred his activities to the Prime Minister's office in the Parliament building. This may almost be taken as a symbolic step, because the controlling authority of the Party over the country's affairs had ceased, and within the Prime Ministry a new central authority was emerging to control and amalgamate under its direction not only the remains of the old administration but also the most efficient part of the new revolutionary institutions.

The Party leaders had lived through a stupefying spectacle: the almost complete disappearance of the Communist Party — the disbanding of its membership, the collapse of its administrative network, and the decay of its local organizations. According to Leninist tenets the Party was to be omnipresent and omnipotent in all matters of state; nothing was to happen which was not controlled, promoted, or suggested by the Party, and this was all that mattered. Since the outbreak of the armed Revolution everything had been done without and against the Party. Its grip over the state administration, the local organizations, and every activity in the country had gone limp and lifeless. To the Party leaders, who had been spiritual outsiders in respect to their rank and file and the people at large, and who had not realized that their structure was a house of cards, the collapse must have been shocking.

We have described in previous chapters how even fervent adherents to the Marxist-Leninist doctrine and faithful Party members had lost their belief in Communism and in the Party. The terrorism and exploitation of the Stalinist era, the unblushing facts of Soviet domination, and the disappointments of the New Course had turned frustrated Party members — like the rest of the population — into vehement anti-Party, anti-Soviet, and generally anti-Communist persons. However paradoxical it may seem, the great majority of Hungarian Party members were "anti-Communist Communists." [12] Only the *apparatchiki*, not by conviction but by self-interest and self-preservation, kept the Party machine running during the years that the system suffered internal agonies. When open and armed resistance against the regime appeared, the middle and lower Party functionaries proved reluctant to fight and possibly die for a cause to which they owed no conviction or affection. Those who had wronged others feared vengeance and tried to climb aboard a new bandwagon; those who had never harmed anybody did the same lest they suffer for having merely served the Party. When the news of the revolt spread throughout the country, the Party machinery became paralyzed as if by a stroke. Party functionaries and others with bad consciences embarked upon a skin-saving campaign in towns and villages alike. The Party was practically reduced to its Budapest headquarters in the *Akadémia-utca*.[13]

That present motives and prior actions, rather than political credentials, were uppermost in the public mind was apparent in the attitude of the masses toward Party members who engaged in anti-Soviet and anti-Party activity, whether as Freedom Fighters or in other revolutionary organizations. The dividing line between "reliables" and "unreliables" (a crucial test in any revolutionary movement) was not the fact of Party membership; the sole test was the record of each person's former actions. Many Party or non-Party people emerged as if awakened from a bad dream. Persons who had taken refuge in a stubborn taciturnity suddenly returned to their former affability and talked freely as they had before. This is why a keen observer could have said that "the Hungarian nation again found itself." [14] In industrial areas the liberated spirit of the oppressed workers was exhibited in the mass destruction of their Party membership cards, thousands of which were seen strewn along the streets of the suburbs, Csepel and Ujpest. The Party, formally composed of over 800,000 members, many thousands of whom had been considered "activists" or "militants," lost in practice its whole body. The brain — the central headquarters — continued to live, but even it was rendered helpless by antagonistic ideas and trends.

Outside the supreme Party headquarters, district and local Party offices were abandoned by the members of the *apparat*. In a few places, where the Security Police offered resistance, the buildings were stormed.[15] The deserted Party offices were occupied by revolutionary organizations or became bureaus of newly constituted political parties. In the villages, the Party secretaries abandoned their posts, and those who had ruled harshly escaped to places where they were less known. Simultaneously, the exodus of deeply compromised Stalinist leaders began; muscovites were easily able to secure transportation by Soviet military aircraft, and the Soviet embassy soon made arrangements for the departure to the Soviet Union of other Communist leaders who might become "dangerous" if they fell into the hands of the revolutionaries. Not only Gerö but also Hegedüs disappeared. So did Minister of the Interior Piros and Minister of Defense Bata. And so did such persons as Olti, who had been the judge of the Mindszenty, Rajk, and many other rigged trials; Erzsébet Andics, the Stalinist historian and literary dictator; and her husband, Andor Berei, Chairman of the Planning Bureau. Their departure was accompanied by the evacuation of Soviet advisers and their families.

The effect of the Mikoyan-Suslov-Nagy conversations appeared in a declaration of the Central Committee on October 26.[16] This declaration admitted the existence of a "fratricidal battle" raging in the nation's capital (no more reference to fascists and counter-revolutionaries). It announced a proposal to the Presidium of the People's Patriotic Front "to put a recommendation before the Presidential Council of the People's Republic for the election of a new national Government." Heretofore the Politburo and the Central Committee of the Party had nominated the Chairman and members of the Council of Ministers; now it was to be left to the People's Front to make such formal recommendations. The Central Committee declaration further stated that "this Government shall have the mission of making good without fail the mistakes and crimes of the past." This was the first time that this supreme Party organ had admitted the existence of any past *crimes*. The declaration said that the new government was to rely "on the whole nation," a very unorthodox admission of the termination of class struggle. The aim of the new government was to "create a free country of prosperity, independence and socialist democracy." The October 26 declaration promised negotiations with the Soviet Union "on the basis of independence, complete equality, and non-interference in one another's internal affairs." It also approved the formation of workers' councils in factories; here again the Party was lagging behind events, for the first workers' councils had already been formed the day before.[17] Furthermore it forecast wage increases, and invited the insurgents to lay down their arms not later than 10 P.M., in which case they would be granted amnesty.

The fear that the survival of Communist rule was at stake is clearly revealed by the Central Committee pronouncement: it stated that it wished "to leave no room for doubt" of being resolved "to defend the achievements of our People's Democracy and would not budge an inch on the issue of socialism." Evidently the Central Committee, as a result of the talks with the Soviet Presidium representatives, wished to emphasize that its concessions were a "last stand."

In the declaration the Central Committee stated that it was being led by "Comrade" Imre Nagy. Nagy was thus elevated to the highest pedestal of the Party, while no mention was made of János Kádár, the First Secretary. The "heretic" who only two weeks before had not even held Party membership was certainly enjoying a Gomulka-like career. That the new Polish-Soviet relations served as a pattern for the Soviet and Hungarian leaders in regard to internal development in Hungary and external relations with the Soviet Union may clearly be inferred from a direct reference of the Central Committee manifesto, according to which Hungarian-Soviet friendship was to be rebuilt on a basis by which "relations between Poland and the Soviet Union are now being shaped anew."

This declaration of the Central Committee, largely free of the usual Marxist-Communist jargon, is a sober document if compared to previous announcements by that body. The Central Committee now seemed to understand the abhorrence felt by the masses toward Communist idiomatic phraseology and Marxist-Leninist ideology, and must have realized that any such verbal legerdemain would be repudiated by the population *ab initio*.

Nevertheless, the Central Committee's invitation to the rebels to give up their arms failed to have any effect, just as previous attempts to stop the fighting had failed. Day by day, hour by hour, the Party prolonged its offer of a "last chance" to surrender within the terms of the promised amnesty. The continually advancing deadline glaringly reflected the impotence of Party and government vis-à-vis the open resistance, and exposed the continued mendacity of current radio announcements. Those announcements were continually celebrating victories of the armed forces, even though no Hungarian armed forces, apart from the Security Police, fought effectively against the insurgents. The official reports claimed that order had been re-established in certain districts, and even that the rebels had surrendered. On October 27, after another "last appeal" had unsuccessfully been made, only "continued fighting" was reported.

On that day Nagy formed a new government, which he called the People's Patriotic Government. Its personnel contradicted the assurances of a "national government" given by the Central Committee the day before, and it evoked little enthusiasm from the revolutionary institutions which by now had taken over exclusive control in the provinces. The new government under Nagy's chairmanship was intended to be somewhat like a "popular front" cabinet, but it differed very little from the usual Communist-dominated governments that Hungary had experienced in the past eight years. The Deputy Prime Ministers were Antal Apro (Stalinist), Jozsef Bognár (renegade Smallholder), and Ferenc Erdei (renegade of the former Peasant Party).

The really new features of the cabinet were the inclusion of Zoltán Tildy, the former President of the Republic, as Minister of State, and of Béla Kovács as Minister of Agriculture. But Tildy had the record of a fellow traveler (despite his detention for six years), and there was general disbelief concerning Kovács' willingness to participate in the government. Kovács was the former Secretary-General of the Smallholder Party, and his capture by Soviet Security agents in 1947 had weakened the resistance of his party against the advances of Communism. He had then spent nearly eight years in Soviet captivity and had been returned to Hungary broken in body and spirit. The radio comment on his nomination fraudulently stated that he had been imprisoned by Rákosi,[18] though his real fate had been common knowledge. Béla Kovács, who on October 27 was still at his home in southern Hungary, never gave his consent to this appointment.[19] Thus the prominently Communist character of the new government could not be disguised. Apart from Tildy (himself tainted) and Kovács (absent), only Communists occupied ministerial posts. It is true that some interesting and distinguished names added a limited prestige to the ensemble. Thus, Professor Lukács, the philosopher, accepted the portfolio of People's Culture, and Antal Gyenes, a former administrator of the Populist Colleges and one-time assistant to Imre Nagy, became Minister of Crop Collection.

Various provincial radio stations had by now become completely independent of central control. Hardly had the personnel of the new cabinet been announced when these free radio stations heaped continuous attacks on some of the members, especially Münnich (Minister of the Interior) and Lajos Bebrits (Minister of Communications), both of whom were muscovites, and Apro, Kossa, and Csergö, well known to be Stalinists. The attacks occurred before Imre Nagy belatedly announced the program of the new government. This program, broadcast by Nagy himself on Sunday, October 28, undertook mainly to reiterate parts of the Central Committee's declaration of October 26. Its novelty consisted in an express condemnation of the viewpoint that the "present formidable movement" was a counterrevolution, and also in a series of promises: to dissolve the "organs of State Security," to restore the Kossuth coat of arms, and to re-establish the national holiday of March 15, anniversary of the Revolution of 1848.[20]

The most important announcements of October 28 concerned the actual fighting. A few hours before Nagy's address the radio had reported the cease fire order issued jointly by the ministers of Defense and of the Interior to all Hungarian armed forces, which were summoned to return to their respective quarters and await further instructions.[21] The Prime Minister's address contained a passage according to which the Hungarian government had come to an agreement with the Soviet government "that the Soviet forces shall immediately begin their withdrawal from Budapest and simultaneously with the formation of our new armed forces evacuate the city's area." [22] These declarations signified that the revolutionary armed forces had not been defeated and that they were no longer being attacked. The reference to new armed forces already forecast their adoption and incorporation into the official armed forces of the country. The withdrawal of Soviet forces, proclaimed by the government, was fervently greeted as the beginning of the abandonment of the Soviet grip over Hungary.

The disintegration of the Communist Party was also marked by a meaningful resolution of its Central Committee on that same Sunday, October 28: "In view of the exceptional situation which has emerged, the Central Committee transfers its mandate to lead the Party, which it received from the Third Congress, to a six-member Party Presidium whose chairman is Comrade János Kádár and whose membership includes Antal Apro, Károly Kiss, Ferenc Münnich, Imre Nagy and Zoltán Szánto." [23]

The composition of this Presidium still failed to reflect the development of the country's sentiments and the wishes of the deserting membership of a decayed Party; it still upheld compromised muscovites and Stalinists, and refused to admit the more popular "rightists," the friends of Nagy, such as Losonczy and Donáth. On the same day as this Presidium began to direct the bankrupt Party, its voice, the *Szabad Nép,* broke away from the control of Party headquarters and engaged in a sharp polemic with *Pravda* on the meaning of the Hungarian Revolution.[24]

The disintegration of the Communist Party and the resulting *de facto* secession of the provinces from the sway of the central government in Budapest, accompanied by the setting up of revolutionary organs of administration, exercised a profound influence on the Prime Minister and some members of his entourage. They were also affected by the pronounced anti-Communist and anti-government attitudes freely expressed in provincial newspapers and over the provincial radio stations, and by the workers' delegations arriving in Budapest from the country voicing shrill anti-Communist principles. At last the government seemed to comprehend that the whole country had risen against Soviet Communism and all that it stood for.

SECESSION IN THE PROVINCES

While the desultory fighting proceeded in and near Budapest between the Freedom Fighters and Soviet forces, the provincial centers did not remain inactive. Where there were institutions of higher education, demonstrations had taken place, similar to those in Budapest. These did not usually degenerate into armed conflict. In some places, like the towns of Magyaróvár and Miskolc, the Security Police tried to maintain their authority by shooting at unarmed demonstrators; they killed over 80 persons in Magyaróvár alone, and 16 in Miskolc.[25] Eventually in all these provincial cities the regular police and army sided with the revolutionaries, and the Security Police were either neutralized or disappeared from the scene. Sporadic fighting with Soviet units took place in some of these towns, Nyiregyháza and Mezökövesd in particular, but nowhere did the Russians try to safeguard Communist rule. In some places, as stated earlier, the local Soviet commanders made it clear they would not interfere with the new authority, especially in Györ, Pécs, and other cities where the Security Police and local Communist organs happened to sympathize with the Revolution.

In the villages, as in the larger places, the transformation from a Communist-led administration and society to popular rule was generally carried out without major violence. The Party secretaries and Communist members of the local councils gave up their posts; the Security Police guards gave up their arms or fled. Uncompromised members of the councils or other local revolutionary bodies took over the duties of administration. Here, as well as in larger centers, the bitterness and resentment of eight years occasionally exploded in the form of personal vengeance. Since no Soviet military interference could be exercised in the many hundreds of villages and smaller towns, no fighting took place there, and the village populations were not directly involved in the revolutionary events. This did not mean, however, that they remained entirely passive; the countryside, especially around the capital, abundantly provided the urban and industrial areas with foodstuffs, which were often transported by the farmers themselves and distributed gratis among the needy. The loosening of Party control also expressed itself in the disbanding of agricultural cooperatives; the area under cultivation by kolkhozes shrank by 63 per cent during the Revolution.[26] On October 30 the government abolished the compulsory delivery system of agricultural products and hides, and also canceled the delivery of arrears.[27]

The provincial towns, many of them important industrial and mining centers, and all the rural areas had thus been freed from Party influence, governmental control, and Soviet interference within a few days after the outbreak of the revolt. The Hungarian provinces, as in most other countries, had always been more conservative, more religious, and more nationalistic than the capital, and Communist or Marxist indoctrination had been even less effective there. In Budapest the workers simply stopped their work (except essential services) because of the fighting and because of the curfew imposed by the government; but in the industrial and mining towns of the provinces, strikes were explicitly declared and carried out. Here, the various strike committees refused to return to work until the fighting had ceased in Budapest and the Soviet troops had returned to their quarters.[28] After the formation of the new cabinet on October 27, the provincial radio stations began their personal attacks on individual Communist ministers, as we have seen. While professing trust and faith in the person of the Prime Minister, the provinces refused to acknowledge the legitimacy of a government still harboring Stalinists.[29] The first workers' councils were formed not in Budapest but in the industrial district of Miskolc. The first delegation of workers that reached Imre Nagy (on October 26), submitting demands including an invitation to Soviet troops to leave Hungary before the end of the year, was also from this important mining and industrial center.[30]

Parallel with the developments in Budapest but with greater

speed and always in advance of the pressure upon the government and Party in the capital, the provinces set their demands. Soon they began formulating them in terms of ultimatums: the strikes would continue until Hungary had a national government (and by "national" they meant overwhelmingly non-Communist) and until the evacuation of Soviet troops had been agreed upon. The provincial towns and their revolutionary administrations drifted more and more away from the political attitude still observed in Budapest. Soon they would no longer speak of the Hungarian government but of the "government of Budapest" — a term reminiscent of June 1919, when Georges Clemenceau, the French Minister and Chairman of the Paris Peace Conference, had addressed the Communist government of Béla Kun as the "gouvernement de Budapest." On October 30, even the formation of a "countergovernment" opposing that of Budapest was considered in Győr, the seat of the National Council for Transdanubia, which was formed that same day. Two days later this new Council discussed a similar proposal from a representative of Jozsef Dudás, the leader of a Freedom Fighter group, but turned it down.[31]

Transdanubia, the part of Hungary west and south of the Danube, though deciding against a countergovernment, was first to organize itself into something resembling an autonomous provincial government. The lead had been taken by the revolutionary organizations in Győr, and the radio station of this city was able to attract a large and attentive audience not only in Transdanubia but also in the industrial districts of the Northeast. It was this radio station which first broadcast news of a strike which was to last until "the last Russian division had left Hungary."[32] "National councils," so named in order to contrast with councils of the Communist regime, had been formed in many cities and counties of the nation. The national councils of Transdanubia met in Győr on October 30 and agreed to form the National Council for Transdanubia. Attila Szigeti, the non-Party deputy who had approached Imre Nagy earlier in the year with a daring plan to raise the "Nagy problem" in the National Assembly, was elected chairman. Each of the seven counties was represented by four members, and each town by two.

The Transdanubian counties and towns also undertook to contact other provincial revolutionary organizations (national councils and workers' councils), and the National Council for Transdanubia at its outset was able to announce the adherence of the national council of Borsod County in Northeast Hungary and that of Bács-Kiskun County south of Budapest on the east bank of the Danube, also the adherence of the Workers' Council of Csepel, an industrial suburb of Budapest. It then presented the following demand to Imre Nagy: after the withdrawal of Soviet troops from Hungary, but not later than January 1957, free elections were to be held; the composition of the government was to be changed by including Freedom Fighter leaders in its ranks, the government was to announce to the United Nations the neutrality of Hungary. The National Council for Transdanubia threatened to withdraw its recognition of the central government in the event its demands were not fulfilled. Significantly the announcement also referred to the fact that the Hungarian Army units stationed in Györ, Pápa, Tata, and Zalaegerszeg had pledged assistance to the council.[33] On November 1, the radio station of Eger announced the formation of an East Hungarian National Council with the seat in the City of Miskolc; and on that same day the National Council of Debrecen sent its representatives to Györ. The provinces were thus preparing to oppose the central government should it be unwilling or unable to accede to their wishes for ending monopolistic Communist control.

RESTORATION OF THE MULTIPARTY SYSTEM

When Imre Nagy and his entourage resumed their work in the office of the Prime Minister and started to take stock of the situation, they must have blinked like Rip Van Winkle waking up to a world transformed. The shots fired in the streets of Budapest, the efficient resistance against Soviet aggression, the collapse of the entire Communist Party system, the paralysis of the government, had changed within a few days the whole psychological and political face of the country. The fictitious image of a Soviet-Communist–modeled "worker-peasant" country had been replaced by a free and outspoken — though still convulsive — society. The "leading role of the Party," "dictatorship of the proletariat," and other Marxist-Leninist slogans seemed outworn and unreal when juxtaposed to such jolting facts as: the people fighting the regime "of the people"; the armed forces of the Soviet Union ("eternal friend and glorious liberator of the Hungarian nation") fighting and killing workers and students; the Party members leaving the sinking ship; and the Security Police, "the fist of the working class," hunted down by the workers. And the Party leaders and government, deprived of any means for enforcing their will, stood condemned to the role of helpless spectators. Nor could they expect Soviet representatives to refloat the wreck of a Communist state during those last days of October. As we have already seen, the Soviet government decided to withdraw its combatants from Budapest.*

The Party leaders and the government, including Imre Nagy, were faced with the dilemma of either being swept away or gradually giving in to an irresistible pressure. The difference between Stalinist rigorists, on the one hand, and the Prime Minister and the "rightists," on the other, lay in the means each group chose to approach the inevitable. The first did so out of necessity; the second did so with evident willingness, influenced by a realistic assessment of the situation and persuaded that a common denominator between real democracy and Communistic objectives might be established.

During the last week of October enormous pressure had been exerted on the Prime Minister by delegations of workers, by representatives of workers' councils and revolutionary committees, by the national councils, and by friends and advisers. They all demonstrated the futility and impossibility of maintaining the fiction of one-party rule. Finally on Tuesday, October 30, one week after the first shots were fired, Zoltán Tildy, the only "bourgeois" politician in the cabinet (Béla Kovács being still absent), was instrumental in persuading the cabinet ministers of the urgent necessity for restoring the multiparty system in order to prevent the total annihilation of the Communist Party and the destruction of all "socialist" achievements. He demonstrated before the twenty Communist ministers the reality of the collapse of their system and its profound unpopularity. According to his view, only a democratic plural party system, similar to that which ruled the country in 1945–46, could guarantee the survival of the Communist Party, now a target of hatred and contempt, and save the country from a swing toward the reactionary right.[34]

This session of the Council of Ministers was followed the same day by a meeting of the six-member Communist Party Presidium in Budapest. After deliberations, the Party Presidium unanimously approved the plan to restore the multiparty system, thus dethroning themselves of supreme authority in the country. Before the day was out, János Kádár, the First Secretary of the Party, made an address containing this statement: "I declare that every member of the Presidium of the Hungarian Workers Party is in agreement with the decisions reached by the Council of Ministers today."[35]

---

* The whole question of the Soviet actions during the revolution will be analyzed in Chapter 24. Soviet declarations toward the end of October strengthened the belief that the Soviets wished to refrain from renewed interference in Hungarian affairs.

This decision was also influenced by the renewed attacks against some Communist members of the cabinet by many workers' councils of the provinces and even those of Budapest. On October 29, one of the targets of these accusations, Lajos Bebrits, the muscovite Minister of Communications, had "resigned," [36] and on the morning of October 30, István Kovács, the Stalinist Party Secretary for Budapest, had handed over his office to Jozsef Köböl, an Imre Nagy adherent.[37] The Party slowly came to understand that it had completely lost the support of its alleged mainstay, the industrial working class.

Pursuant to the decision by the Communist Party Presidium, the Council of Ministers reassembled and approved the motion to restore the multiparty system of government. And in the early afternoon of the 30th the Prime Minister announced by radio (italics ours):

The national Government, acting in complete agreement with the Presidium of the Hungarian Workers Party, has arrived at a decision, vital for the nation's life . . . In the interest of the further democratization of the country's life, the Cabinet *abolishes the one-party system* and places the country's Government on the basis of democratic co-operation between the coalition parties, reborn in 1945. In accordance with this it sets up an *inner Cabinet* within the national Government. The members of this Cabinet are Imre Nagy, Zoltán Tildy, Béla Kovács, Ferenc Erdei, János Kádár, Géza Losonczy, and a person to be nominated by the Social Democrat Party. The Government will submit a proposal to the Presidential Council of the People's Republic to elect János Kádár and Géza Losonczy as Ministers of State.[38]

Immediately thereafter, Zoltán Tildy went on the air and declared that "the people of the country must decide the future of the nation freely and without interference," and he drew the following momentous inference: "consequently we have to prepare for free elections." [39] He also invited his own former party, the Smallholders, as well as the Social Democrats and the National Peasant Party, which had participated in the government in 1945, to reorganize their ranks.

Those three political parties promptly re-established themselves. They had to face many difficulties, not least among them personal issues. During the years 1945 to 1949 many of their leading members had fallen prey to Communist pressures and political ambition. They had become collaborators or outright fellow travelers of the Soviet-Communist regime, or later even joined the Communist Party. Many of these persons now wished to rejoin their former party. Some of them presently occupied important positions in the state hierarchy. Many leaders and members of the reorganized parties had spent years in prison for their intransigence. They generally refused to readmit any of the Party renegades and wished to eliminate them from public life; but for expediency's sake, coupled with reasons of national interest, certain provisional exceptions were made.

The first group to reconstitute itself was the Smallholder Party. A nine-member Executive Committee was formed, and Béla Kovács was elected Secretary-General.[40] Neither Tildy nor István Dobi (who now tried to find his way back into his former party) was included in the party leadership; the party's constituent assembly decided provisionally to allow their presence in the government and in the Presidential Council of the Republic. Otherwise the assembly refused readmission to such Communist collaborators as Lajos Dinnyés (former Prime Minister) and the Smallholder members of his cabinet, and also to ministers who had joined the Communist Party, such as Jozsef Bognár.

The Social Democratic Party announced its re-establishment on November 1. Anna Kéthly was elected Chairman; Gyula Kelemen, Secretary-General; and András Révész, Deputy Secretary-General. Each of them had served six or seven years in prison.[41] Renegades and Communist fellow travelers were most rigorously excluded from their ranks; thus Árpád Szakasits (former President of the Republic), Zoltán Horváth, and Sándor Ronai — all accused of having contributed to the merger of the Social Democratic Party with the Communist Party — were refused readmission. The Social Democrats were at first reluctant to join the government, and agreed only when the Socialist International, meeting in Vienna at just that time, gave its formal consent.

In proportion to its size the National Peasant Party could muster the greatest number of renegades and Communist Party stooges among its ranks. Consequently it adopted a new name: the *Petöfi Party*. It elected Ferenc Farkas as Secretary-General and an eleven-member Executive Committee, which included Professor István Bibo and Attila Szigeti, the Chairman of the National Council for Transdanubia.[42] One of the foremost "traitors" of this party, Ferenc Erdei, was still at that time a Minister of State in the government; the leadership of the party voted his removal from the post.

In addition to these so-called "coalition parties," which began participating in the government, a number of new political parties were created during the days of political freedom from October 30 to November 3. The Catholic People's Party, the Christian Democratic Party, and the Democratic People's Party announced their formation. If the free system of government had survived, these parties bearing the hallmark of "Christian" or "Catholic" could have been expected to emerge as powerful mass organizations, dangerous rivals to the formerly strong Smallholders, particularly in the rural areas.[43]

The three coalition parties wished at once to attain a status of equal representation in the government with the Communist Party which, by virtue of its previous monopoly of power, still held the majority of portfolios, and whose membership outweighed other parties even in the inner cabinet. Attacks against the composition of the government still continued. A demonstration before the Parliament building demanded the immediate resignation of Ferenc Münnich, the muscovite Minister of the Interior.[44] Provincial national councils objected to the maintenance of twenty-one ministers.[45] The participation of the Social Democratic Party had brought forth a number of objections and was still in abeyance.[46] Béla Kovács, the Smallholder leader, though he at last arrived in Budapest on November 1, was still reluctant to join actively in governmental work.[47]

Under all these pressures and difficulties the coalition government was again reformed in order "to be adjusted and strengthened." On November 3 the radio announced the resignation of all the cabinet ministers and the formation of a new cabinet. This time all the muscovites and Stalinists were left out — also Professor Lukács, who, however, continued to support Imre Nagy. The Prime Minister assumed besides his premiership the management of foreign affairs. The new government gave a representation of three to the Communist Party (Nagy, Kádár, Losonczy); three to the Smallholders (Tildy, Béla Kovács, István B. Szabo); three to the Social Democrats (Kéthly, Kelemen, and Jozsef Fischer); and two to the Petöfi Party (Ferenc Farkas and Bibo). General Pál Maléter (nonparty) also joined the cabinet. Each of these except the Prime Minister was titled Minister of State, and the vacant portfolios were to be distributed among them.[48] It was an emergency cabinet, intended to be a true representation of the four coalition parties, and including the powerful leaders of all of them. Throughout these metamorphoses of the Imre Nagy government, legality was sedulously observed (in contrast to the confusion of October 23–24); the Presidential Council of the Republic made the appointments, and its Chairman, István Dobi, administered the oath of office.

The new government had no time to submit a program to the

nation before its overthrow by the second Soviet intervention, nor were the three non-Communist parties partaking in the coalition able to draft formal party programs. The leaders of these parties — so far as their official policy pronouncements are known — all professed to stand on the basis of "freedom, independence and democracy." [49] The Social Democratic Party stressed that Hungary must become a "socialist" country. Both the Smallholders and the Petöfi Party emphasized the right of the peasantry to decide freely whether to own their property or to remain in kolkhozes. There was general agreement among all three parties that Hungary should not participate in any "military bloc," but should remain "neutral." [50] As for the Communist Party that participated in the coalition government, it looked strangely different from its old self, having formally proclaimed the birth of a "new" Communist Party.

THE "NEW" COMMUNIST PARTY

The complete bankruptcy of the "old" Communist Party and its impotency to continue the destinies of the country had led to its abandonment of one-party rule, which also meant the forsaking of the alleged dictatorship of the proletariat. Kádár, the First Secretary, in his speech of October 30 following the re-establishment of the multiparty system, had admitted that "the ranks of the Party will break" and that "the bad leadership of the past years has left a legacy of great and serious burdens" for the Party.[51] The Communist Party had not given up its monopoly without serious internal struggles and convulsions; the common catastrophe was far from uniting the leading stratum. The ruling clique had been forced to embrace members of opposition groups as far to the "right" as Donáth and Losonczy, and it had to acknowledge not only the formal but the effective leadership of Imre Nagy, whose ideological and political concepts were familiar because of his circulated memoranda of 1955 and early 1956. We find no allusion in these memoranda to the necessity of restoring multiparty rule, though he had urged democratization and the elimination of the excesses and abuses of the Stalinist regime. A multiparty system was apparently foreign to his views, and we are told that he struggled at length against the principle before adopting it.[52]

One should not forget that in the heyday of the revolutionary activity after the revolutionary institutions and Freedom Fighter groups had become more solidly entrenched, accusations were lodged not only against the Soviet system of government but also against the Prime Minister, whose popularity had waned because of his

gradualism. During the Communist Party's fight for its survival under the impact of the revolutionary earthquake, even Imre Nagy's
position was not entirely secure. The invitation to Soviet troops to
intervene and also the declaration of martial law had somewhat undermined his prestige. After his awareness of events had become
clarified, the Prime Minister sensed this danger and through his
secretariat undertook to dispel these rumors and deny these accusations. On October 30 it was officially announced that the Prime
Minister had known neither of the invitation to the Soviet troops
to fight the revolutionaries, nor of the extension of martial law.[53]
Nagy had certainly been innocent of summoning the Soviet troops,
but his secretaries seemed a trifle overzealous in denying his knowledge of the declaration of martial law. Still it is clear that he never
wished to apply these rigorous measures against the revolutionaries,
and during his tenure of office he never did so. He still remained
an idol in the eyes of the masses, only now the people, freed of
former reticence, firmly wished their idol to conform to the image
which they had conceived for him. Ever since the first days of the
New Course in 1953, a trend of opinion had stubbornly maintained
that Imre Nagy was only nominally a Communist; he had merely
been compelled to act as he did, and, only disguised as a Communist,
he was actually a genuine patriotic Hungarian. The hesitancy and
gradualness of his concessions toward abolition of the monopolistic
Communist Party rule caused much bitterness among his anti-Communist admirers. But each step by which he separated himself from
the policies of the previous regime rendered his position less vulnerable and further increased his popularity. In acting thus, he now
increasingly relied on those of his friends and advisers who professed Communism in name only and who had, in fact, crossed the
Rubicon, leaving even "national Communism" on the far shore.

The collapse of Communist Party rule and the desertion of the
Party's rank and file had sharpened the already existing split between
various factions of Party leadership. In the last days of October 1956
four such factions could be discerned: (1) the hard-core Stalinists,
most of whom had been deeply involved in Rákosi's and Gerö's
crimes and excesses, and many of whom had already left for the
Soviet Union; (2) a "centrist" group formed around János Kádár
and his friends, which only reluctantly consented to the abandonment of one-party rule and still set its hopes on Soviet support; (3)
a group of "revisionists" or "national Communist" Party members,
such as Professor Lukács and some of Imre Nagy's original adherents,
who, while stressing the "Hungarian" road toward Socialism, and

independence vis-à-vis the Soviets, still clung to *their* interpretation of Marxism-Leninism; and (4) the "rightists" or "reformists" who wished to establish a democratic Communist Party, competing along parliamentary lines with other political parties, renouncing any formal adherence to Marxist-Leninist tenets and any form of dictatorship or autocratic rule. In this fourth group were Losonczy, Donáth, and most of the writers, all adherents of Nagy. These four factions became even more pronounced when such issues as multiparty rule, and later issues during the second Soviet intervention, had to be decided. These crucial questions promoted the further division of the factions, divisions which were to have significant consequences in the postrevolutionary period.

The stalwart Stalinists had no voice in the decisions taken after October 29. The three other groups in the Party regarded them as the culprits who, in having compromised the Party, were responsible for its collapse. The question may be asked: what persuaded the centrists, Kádár and his group, to accept the multiparty system with free elections — a decision which was tantamount to the suicide of the Communist Party? This group (which included the anti-Rákosi muscovite, Ferenc Münnich) never ceased to harken to the advice of Moscow. We have to assume that even after Gerö's departure the telephonic contact between the Hungarian Party secretariat and its counterpart in Moscow was continuously in service. Kádár also could have contacted Andropov, the Soviet ambassador.* Before agreeing to the restoration of the multiparty system, Kádár had certainly consulted the Kremlin. Mikoyan and Suslov again descended on Budapest on October 30, and Kádár had long conversations with them during the following two days. All witnesses agree that the Soviet leaders had seconded the Hungarian decisions, and Tildy, who had also been asked to discuss matters with Mikoyan, has reported that the multiparty system, the withdrawal of Soviet troops from Hungary, and noninterference in Hungarian affairs had received express Soviet consent.[54] The two Soviet Presidium members must have advised Kádár and his group that the best course for the preservation of "social gains" (as well as for the calming down of anti-Soviet sentiment) was the restoration of the 1945 status. The Hungarian Party was to fight for its life as best it could.

* One of the Soviet ambassador's telephones was connected to the Budapest "K" (közvetlen-direct) circuit, which served the telephone exchange of top Party leaders and ministers and could not be tapped in any of the telephone exchanges. Thus the ambassador, from the point of view of telephones, shared the same system with Hungarian leaders. No other embassy possessed such a telephonic device.

Under such circumstances Kádár and his group had no alternative but to approve the self-degradation of the Party; the other two groups also agreed, the revisionists more by necessity, the rightists more by conviction. The concept, expressed by Nagy in his dissertation, of a "rejuvenated," "regenerated" Communist Party was now to be given expression. A declaration introducing the "new" Communist Party to the public was read over the radio by Kádár on November 1.[55] It bears the impact of Nagy's ideas and criticisms of the past; it is also based on the concept that the revolution was fought by Communists, that it had been a revolt against the "despotism" of the Rákosi regime. Consequently the "new" Party did not wish to assume responsibility for past crimes and errors. It was to be new in name and in spirit. Kádár declared that "in a glorious uprising, our people have shaken off the Rákosi regime" and have "achieved freedom for the people and independence for the country." Kádár prided himself in stating that: "We can safely say that the ideological and organizational leaders who prepared this uprising were recruited from among your ranks" — meaning, of course, the ranks of Communists.

Some of the motives which inspired the adoption of the multiparty system may be gleaned from this declaration. Kádár said flatly: "The Hungarian democratic parties will either have enough strength to stabilize our achievements or we must face an open counter-revolution." This fear of reactionary rule — which did not seem justified by the demands of the revolutionaries — seems to be a reiteration of anxieties allegedly expressed by Mikoyan.[56] Kádár continued:

Either the uprising secured for our people the basic achievements of democracy — the right of assembly and of organization, personal freedom and safety, the rule of law, freedom of the press, and humaneness* — or we sink back into the slavery of the old gentry world and with it into foreign slavery.

He also expressed fear of "foreign armed intervention" (meaning intervention by the West) which might impose on Hungary "the tragic fate of Korea." He said that elimination of the "nests of counterrevolution and reaction" and the restoration of peace, calm, and order might prevent such a "grave danger." Kádár made a point of announcing that the *new* Party "will break away from the crimes of the past once and for all." The main political program of this new Communist Party was stated thus:

---

* Kádár's definition of the "basic achievements of democracy" might well be compared with his subsequent pronouncements and attitudes.

On the basis of national independence, does it [the Party] desire friendly relations with every country, far and near, and in the first place with the neighboring socialist countries. It defends and will defend the achievements of the Hungarian Republic [sic!] — the land reform, the nationalization of factories, mines, and banks, and the indisputable social and cultural gains of our people.

This is a program to which many social-democratic or labor parties of the West might subscribe; but Kádár also added that for the implementation of these goals (expedient though they were) the new Party wished to rely on the peculiar characteristics of Hungary, and also on the "teachings of Marxism-Leninism, on scientific socialism free of Stalinism and any kind of dogmatism." The name of the new Party was to be the "Hungarian Socialist Workers Party" and its Party daily was to be published under the title of *Népszabadság*. Kádár announced the formation of a preparatory committee to direct and organize the new Party, composed of himself, Imre Nagy, Ferenc Donáth, Sándor Kopácsi, Géza Losonczy, György Lukács, and Zoltán Szántó.

This directorate omitted all the Stalinists and retained but one muscovite, Szántó, who did not share the unpopularity of Münnich. Kádár was the only member belonging to the centrist group, whereas Lukács and Szántó definitely may be considered revisionists. Donáth, Losonczy (and probably Kopácsi) were rightists, and Imre Nagy may be classified as oscillating between the revisionists and the rightists. After the second Soviet intervention he must definitely be ranked among the rightists.

In its November 1 declaration the new Communist Party refrained from any direct indication that it wished to establish or maintain the rule of the "working class"; we seek in vain any remark concerning the dictatorship of the proletariat — either the proletariat alone or allied with the peasants. This goal is of course explicit in Marxism-Leninism, on which the Party wished to rely. In general, the declaration is devoid of the usual Soviet-Communist slogans and phraseology. It gives the impression of a desperate effort to retain or win back a reliable membership, to appeal to common sense and reason in place of faith in an abused ideology, and to reacquire some modicum of sympathy among the masses. By playing on the fear of Western intervention the declaration wished to counterbalance the prevailing anti-Soviet hatred (just as Gomulka has frequently used the national suspicion of West Germany). One of the last sentences of the declaration clearly reveals this attitude: "We do not want our country to become a battlefield."

Kádár's announcement of the new Party was only one of the events of Thursday, November 1. During the preceding night, the Soviet overseers, Mikoyan and Suslov, once more left for Moscow by air. At 7 P.M. on November 1, Prime Minister Nagy made a dramatic announcement which we shall discuss in detail in a later chapter: Hungary's withdrawal from the Warsaw Pact. And two hours after that, Kádár declared the formation of the new Communist Party. The Warsaw Pact decision, we are told, had been taken with the consent of the Communist Party leadership,[57] but Kádár made no reference to this decisive step. Perhaps, with Mikoyan and Suslov gone, he had been unable to sound out the reactions of the Kremlin — or had deliberately been kept in the dark. Shortly thereafter, he strangely dropped out of sight. When Nagy reorganized the coalition government on November 3, Kádár therefore was only nominally a participant, not being there in person. Soon the fears he had voiced on November 1 would prove well-founded: Hungary would become a battlefield. But the military intervention would not come from the West.

22

Hungarian Armed Forces during the Revolution

/\/

In the early hours of last Wednesday [October 24] I received an order from the then Minister of Defense to set out with five tanks against the insurgents in the Eighth and Ninth city districts and to relieve the Kilián Barracks. When arrived at the spot I became convinced that the Freedom Fighters were no bandits but loyal sons of the Hungarian people. So I informed the Minister that I would go over to the insurgents.

From an interview on November 1, 1956,
with General Pál Maléter

THE Hungarian armed forces, consisting of the police, the Security Police, and the army, proved ineffective in the fighting; yet their attitudes toward the Revolution significantly affected the course of events. The Gerö regime had been ready to suppress the rebellion at all costs. Its failure to accomplish this by means of the Hungarian armed forces was not due to its unwillingness to use them, but rather to the unwillingness and unfitness of the forces themselves.[1] This fiasco necessitated the Soviet military intervention, without which the revolutionaries would have been fully victorious within a short time. According to the usual pattern of revolutions, the military units sympathizing with the revolutionaries ought to have joined them, thus speedily overthrowing the regime. But the Soviet support for the regime frustrated the otherwise "natural" development, and the regular military commands underwent soul-searching fluctuations of opinion.

THE POLICE

The Budapest Police, and also those in the provincial towns, refrained from any action against the demonstrators on October 23 or the following days; still less did they participate in any way in the repression of the revolt. On the contrary, as already mentioned, the police contributed arms and ammunition to the insurgents. Their motives and those of Sándor Kopácsi, the Chief of Budapest Police, have been considered enigmatic by students of the Revolution.[2] The explanation may be found in the nationalist and anti-Soviet attitudes of most of the members of the ordinary police, and also of its chief.

The ordinary police had not lived an isolated life like the Security Police. They participated in the daily tribulations of the masses, and shared their joys and sorrows. Since the police was not called to arrest or detain political suspects, a task which fell uniquely to the Security Police, their indoctrination and discipline were less stringent and their recruitment less selective. The regular police force lived under constant supervision by the Security Police force, which displayed a haughty, condescending, or violently critical attitude toward its stepbrother. This treatment was greatly resented by the regular police officers. No additional explanation seems necessary to establish the motives of the policemen and their sentiment toward the national and anti–Soviet-Communist upheaval.

Chief Sándor Kopácsi was one of the frustrated Communists who had first turned for salvation to the Prime Minister of the New Course. He soon became first a secret, later an open, admirer of the national leader; later he joined the group which, if not physically, at least spiritually surrounded Imre Nagy. He sympathized with the rebellious writers, with the proceedings of the Petöfi Circle. In a short time, he had become a leading member of the opposition. He knew better than anyone that the demonstrators of October 23 were no "bourgeois reactionaries" or "fascists." Consequently, both because of his political views and his desire to avert bloodshed, he evidently gave orders to his subordinates not to interfere in any way with the demonstrations. On October 24 he gave orders, after initial hesitations, to provide the insurrection with weapons; before this order was issued some local police stations had already handed over rifles and pistols to students and workmen. Subsequently, it has been related, Kopácsi also sent weapons to some groups of Freedom Fighters. He was also instrumental in securing free movement and activity for the Prime Minister, thereby "rescuing" Imre Nagy from the restrictions imposed on him by the Security Police during the first three days of his second premiership.[3]

The Budapest Police, followed by the police all over the country, thus practically joined the insurrection, even if it refrained from participating in the fight against the Russians. This fact must have been known to the Party leadership as early as October 24. The general confusion and uncertainty presumably prevented Gerö from taking any stern measures against Kopácsi; and even if such a step had been taken, it would have proved ineffective and only provoked the ordinary police to engage openly in the fighting against the regime. The Chief of the Budapest Police had his well-guarded headquarters which remained free of interference by the harassed Security Police, and when Imre Nagy regained his liberty of action, Kopácsi must have felt secure against dismissal or physical threat. During the first days of the Revolution he successfully disposed of his Soviet adviser, who had been seen on the night of October 23–24 sitting frightened at his desk repeatedly muttering, "grazhdanskaya voyna" (civil war); later he disappeared.[4] Soon the Police headquarters were to become the center of the "legitimized" revolutionary armed forces.

On October 28, the Minister of the Interior (Münnich) and the Minister of Defense (General Janza) of the government which had been formed the preceding day, in a joint order, exhorted commanders and members of the police and of the army "to obey instructions, orders and commands" of the new national government.[5] This constituted an admission of the independent attitude displayed by the police and also by units of the army during the first four days of the Revolution. The order also abolished the heretofore compulsory form of address, "Comrade," and exchanged the national emblem for the red star on police and military caps. As far as the police were concerned this instruction was merely a recognition of the situation already obtaining.

The order evidently had little effect in bringing the police back under the authority of a government that was still Communist-dominated. The Minister of the Interior found it necessary to issue a second order on October 29 foreshadowing the formation of a "unified democratic police force." This meant the abolition of the Security Police's separate status, an important gesture designed to placate the ordinary police. The police were again enjoined to prevent illegal excesses and other infringements of the law. The Minister, in an attempt to prevent revolutionary usurpation, insisted that "the reorganization of the police on a national scale is the exclusive task of the Ministry of the Interior." [6]

Münnich's endeavors to enforce his authority remained fruitless, and on October 30 the government placed the police, together with the army, under the supreme authority of a revolutionary body, as will appear presently. The same day the police force of Hungary formed its own revolutionary council. This council announced with pride that the police force had not abandoned the people in its fight for freedom, that rather it had helped the Freedom Fighters. The police — it stated — had started to disarm the Security Police and taken the criminal elements of that agency into custody to await trial. In this and other respects the police was strictly co-operating with the Freedom Fighters and other revolutionary bodies.[7]

The faithful cooperation between the police and the revolutionaries and the increased prestige of the police as a reliable patriotic and anti-Soviet body had helped Kopácsi's reputation even more than his friendship with the Prime Minister. Consequently, his stature within the Party rose with that of the other Nagy adherents, whether they belonged to the revisionist or the reformist group. On November 1, Kopácsi became a member of the seven-man directory which was to organize and control the "new" Communist Party. He was the only member who in any way represented the armed forces within that body, and his later role might have been even of greater significance had the second Soviet intervention not brought the Hungarian Revolution to an abrupt end.

THE SECURITY POLICE

The previous role of the Security Police in the maintenance of Soviet-Communist domination, its methods of purge and terror, and the hatred which it provoked have been outlined earlier. The AVH had been formally reincorporated into the Ministry of the Interior in the fall of 1953, resuming its former name of AVO, but had maintained its independent and important status. However, even after Imre Nagy's demotion in 1955, it practiced some self-restraint; leading Party members in particular were relatively secure from its clutches. Otherwise the Security Police kept its whole apparatus of spy networks, economic privileges, and special ties with the Soviet Security organs. The AVO personnel consisted of professionals (officers, noncommissioned officers, detectives, clerks) and of recruited personnel organized into military units (internal security services). These recruits generally served three years and then were demobilized if they did not re-enlist as professionals. Reliability and devotion toward the regime varied greatly as between the professionals and the recruited personnel. Only the professionals proved to be reliable tools of the regime — though not without exceptions. Few were fanatic devotees; the majority fought for reasons of self-preservation and for fear of punishment for past abuses.

Had the full military strength of the Security Police been a trustworthy force for suppressing the rebellion, they could probably have defeated the revolutionaries. However, the AVO, in general, proved to be poor fighters. The recruited element wavered and in many cases deserted unless forced at gun point by the officers. And the officers themselves, frightened by the magnitude and force of popular wrath, quickly panicked.[8] Soon, all over the country, the AVO was forced to the defensive although this did not prevent them from provocative actions stimulated by orders from their headquarters — actions that increased the fury of the masses. We have previously indicated how the Security Police's first shots ignited the flame of rebellion, and how the massacre two days later on Parliament square drove the masses into a frenzy. In the provinces it was also the AVO which by its panicky action brought death to many innocent persons. By such behavior the Security Police rushed to its own ruin.

The Security Police also attempted to infiltrate the ranks of the Freedom Fighters. Civilian AVO agents posed as insurgents, but chiefly preferred the role of snipers, shooting unarmed civilians in order to compromise the Revolution. Most of these agents when attempting to join revolutionary units were discovered, because their speech and behavior revealed their occupation.

During the first phase of the Revolution (October 23 to about October 28), the AVO's cooperation and collaboration with the intervening Soviet forces was slipshod. Suspected by the Russians, who fought under unfamiliar circumstances and could not distinguish foe from friend, the Security Police were more an encumbrance than an aid to the Soviet tank units roaming the streets of Budapest.

After the Soviet attacks diminished and the cease fire was declared on October 28, the Freedom Fighters, assisted by the ordinary police, continued their mopping up operations against the remnants of the Security Police. The members of the AVO fled, tried to hide, or gave themselves up voluntarily. On October 29, the government declared the dissolution of the agency,[9] thus acceding to one of the principal demands presented by workers' councils and other revolutionary institutions. The Security Police had been such a target of indignation and hatred that its alignment to the revolutionary movement had been out of the question. The recruited members of the AVO were generally released after they reported to the police or to revolutionary organizations, but most officers were detained. The Kádár regime subsequently stated that over 3,000 in all had been imprisoned.[10]

During the fighting, and subsequently until about November 1, sporadic lynchings of Security Police officers and agents occurred. The victims of these popular outbursts were mostly snipers or defenders of public buildings who were either caught *flagrante delicto* or gave themselves up after prolonged fighting. A number of the AVO, of course, were killed in action. The Kádár regime later declared that there were altogether 234 victims of the "white terror." [11] This is a remarkably low number, considering that at least a hundred AVO men must have died in regular action. The number of those who fell victim to popular revenge was infinitesimal when compared with the over two thousand executed victims of the Rákosi era, or the number killed in the Revolution (estimated by Prime Minister Nehru at 25,000 Hungarians and 7,000 Russians).[12]

The Security Police, as a fighting force, had been annihilated by the first days of November; their most daring and most deeply compromised elements, however, went into hiding. After the second Soviet intervention, when the imprisoned AVO officers were liberated, the others reappeared and offered their services to the Soviet forces and to the new government. In the Soviet operations against the guerrilla Freedom Fighters, officers and agents of the AVO proved more successful than before.

THE ARMY

The status and composition of the Hungarian Army, as we saw it under the Stalinist system, had not much changed up to the outbreak of the Revolution, although its manpower had been somewhat reduced since the easing of tensions toward Yugoslavia and the West. On paper, the Hungarian Army, like the armies of other signatories of the Warsaw Treaty of 1955, was to be directed by the central Joint Military Headquarters of the alliance; but this headquarters, under the "chairmanship" of Marshal of the Soviet Union Ivan Stepanovich Konev, had been a purely Soviet organization. Marshal Konev was the commander in chief of the Soviet land forces in Europe and actually in control of the satellite armies as well. No Hungarian officer was known to have participated in the Joint Military Headquarters, nor had any Polish, Rumanian, Czechoslo-

vak, Bulgarian or other non-Soviet officer been permanently attached
to Marshal Konev's staff.

At the time of the outbreak of the Revolution the Soviet military
advisory system reached down to divisional level in Hungary's
Army. Upon the news of the events in Budapest, the Soviet advisers
quickly issued instructions to disperse the units of the Hungarian
Army so as to prevent its employment on short notice. This order
for dispersion must have been the automatic reaction of the Russians,
who sensed the unreliability of the Hungarian forces. Thus divisions
were fragmented by the transfer of their component units to different
localities.* With that action, the participation of the Soviet advisers
in Hungarian military affairs came to an end — for the time being.
Their prestige crumbled as the Soviet war machine suffered set-
backs in the streets of Budapest; their role was rendered insignificant
by the open denunciations of Soviet domination. It is not known
whether any bilateral agreement was reached concerning the withdrawal of the advisers. Presumably their loss of control had made
them expendable, and their exposed situation amidst Hungarian
units or in Hungarian offices made them vulnerable to attack and
capture. No bilateral state agreement had ever been published
establishing their status in the first place; probably there had never
been any written agreement at all. Since their position was rather
de facto than de jure, the Soviet military headquarters simply decided
their speedy withdrawal. On October 28–29, 1956, all Soviet advisers
relinquished their posts, and during the following three or four
days they departed from Hungary with their families. Thus the
Hungarian Army was bereft of its "advisers" but remained inter-
spersed with other Soviet "agents," officers of Soviet affiliation, and
others who had been trained in the Soviet Union.

The Army's attitude toward the Revolution, as already mentioned, was a true reflection of general popular sentiment in Hungary. The rank and file of an army recruited under compulsory
military service are much more susceptible to the reactions prevailing in the population than are their permanent officers' corps
or professional troops. Consequently, Hungary's army could not
remain immune from the violent anti-Communist and anti-Soviet
feeling that dominated the masses. Whether stemming from proletarian, peasant, or intellectual families, the soldiers had known what

---

* For instance, the infantry regiment of the division stationed in the town of
Kaposvár was transferred to Budapest and the motorized unit to another place, while
the artillery unit was left in Kaposvár. See Béla Király, "Hungary's Army under the
Soviets," *East Europe*, March 1958, p. 14.

Stalinist and post-Stalinist dictatorship meant to those categories of society; they were witnesses to the vexations of the "working norms," the cruelties of agricultural collectivization, and the psychological torments of fear and insecurity. Even those more receptive to Communist indoctrination could never be taught that it was permissible to shoot at students and workers. It was "imperialists," "capitalists," and the "bourgeois" that they had been taught to fight; on October 23 and thereafter they were not facing this kind of enemy.

The majority of officers, including even the political officers, had themselves not remained aloof from the general sentiment of the country. Many officers were engaged in the military instruction of university students, the most revolutionary segment of the population, and had come under their spiritual influence. Others, having attended military academies, shared the views of the cadets.[13] The example of a political officer who sided with the revolutionaries in front of the radio building at the crucial hour and influenced many of his soldiers and other persons to join him can be cited as evidence of the fact that even professional indoctrinators refused to fight against what they considered a genuine popular uprising.[14] Among the staff officers and the graduates of Soviet military academies the impact of anti-regime hostility was less pronounced and less effective. These men had lived lives similar to those of leading Party members, secluded from the rest of the people by the artificial barrier of political devotion. Fear, opportunism, and a limited intellectual outlook also blurred their clarity of judgment.

Many officers and soldiers participated voluntarily in the fighting in Budapest, as they had previously participated in the debates of the Petöfi Circle, or the students' debates in the Technological University. Not to appear as deserters they divested themselves of their uniforms and added their expert knowledge to the heroism of the other Freedom Fighters. Thus the attitude of the army was not entirely passive. While swelling the number of insurgents, it also contributed to the cause by its unwillingness to fight the revolutionaries. Even after the failure of October 23, the Army Command made several attempts to induce its units to participate in the fighting on the side of the Soviet forces. An official announcement on the morning of October 25 proclaimed that during the preceding night the counterrevolutionary coup has successfully been "liquidated." Two hours later the Minister of Defense ordered the army to join with Soviet troops and liquidate the remainder of hostile forces by noon. He further instructed those members of the army who had been "separated" from their units to report to their commanding officers. On October 27, the Army Command reported that since many of the insurgents had shown no understanding of the clemency proclamation of the government, the fighting was still continuing. Five hours later Lieutenant General Károly Janza, the newly appointed Minister of Defense, issued orders to the army to continue the struggle relentlessly until final liquidation of the rebels. All these orders amounted to nothing but shadowboxing, for as we have seen, no Hungarian Army unit participated in the fight against the insurgents. If they were called out for concrete tasks, they either malingered or joined the revolutionaries. In some barracks, officers and soldiers deserted to avoid executing unpleasant orders. Most revelatory in this respect is the next announcement of the Minister of Defense (issued on October 28) calling for surrender and assuring those members of the army who fought with the insurgents that they would be allowed to return unmolested to their respective units. Six hours later the Prime Minister announced the cease fire order; Hungarian armed forces were enjoined to shoot only if attacked.[15]

We may add that although the Hungarian Army did not participate in the attempted suppression of the rebellion, neither did it fight openly in organized units against the Soviet forces. In addition to individual participation of individual soldiers in the anti-Soviet struggle, an example of organized — though well camouflaged — military action against Soviet forces can be recorded.

On October 23, the members of the Military Academy for Communications and Engineering at Szentendre (a town north of Budapest) were ordered to defend the Party headquarters in Budapest. These students, all of them of "proletarian origin," had been considered a very reliable military unit. Proceeding to Budapest they occupied quarters in a block near the Party headquarters. From October 24 on, the cadets were assigned to make sorties, especially at night, into the districts controlled by the Freedom Fighters. These military actions were duly carried out. Each time the unit returned, they brought back their wounded with triumphant reports of having annihilated groups of "fascists." The optimistic announcements of the government might have been based on such reports. But the boys of this military academy never fought the revolutionaries; instead they attacked Soviet units, destroyed many tanks, and spread consternation among the Soviet soldiers who saw themselves suddenly assaulted by well-trained and well-equipped opponents.[16]

Other military academies also proved to be a source of disappointment for the Party and the regime; their student bodies sympathized with the revolt, and individual members often joined the rebels.

The sentiments of the cadets is especially noteworthy since all these students had been selected from the point of view of reliability toward the Party and Communist ideology in general. But cadets and rank and file soldiers were not the only military men who approved of the Revolution. Among the higher-ranking Hungarian officers who sympathized with the revolutionaries, the outstanding figure is that for Pál Maléter, who joined them at a propitious moment.

Maléter had been a lieutenant in the Hungarian Army during World War II and together with other officers had been taken prisoner by the Russians. After the war ended he joined the new Hungarian Army and the Party; during the Stalinist purges he was spared because of the unimportance of his rank, and by 1956 had become a colonel. On October 24, Freedom Fighters of the Ninth Budapest District joined members of a labor unit who were quartered in the Kilián barracks. Colonel Maléter, commanding a tank force, was assigned by the Minister of Defense in the early hours of October 25 to take possession of this barracks and restore discipline. When he appeared before the building, a parley ensued between the insurgents and Maléter. At first hesitant, he became persuaded that the rebels were neither "fascists" nor "mercenaries in foreign pay," and promptly joined their movement. Maléter soon became the leader of this important group of Freedom Fighters, and under his command the Kilián barracks successfully withstood several violent onslaughts of Soviet tank forces during the following days.[17] After the government recognized the revolutionary forces, Maléter, enjoying immense popularity, was made Deputy Minister of Defense and appointed major general. In the coalition cabinet formed on November 3 he became no less than Minister of Defense. In June 1958 he was executed.

In the provinces, where over ninety per cent of Hungary's army was stationed, most units kept aloof from events. However, they expressed their sympathies with the revolutionary movement, and many of their individual members joined the fighting insurgents, especially during the second Soviet intervention. In Transdanubia, the Hungarian army units offered their services to local revolutionary councils; in the town of Magyaróvár they even helped to defeat the terrorist Security Police command. In Northeast Hungary, officers and soldiers dispersed and returned to their towns and villages. Among the four army corps commands — Budapest, Székesfehérvár in Transdanubia, Debrecen in Eastern Hungary, and Kecskemét in the South — only Kecskemét was able to maintain a limited form of discipline, because of the pro-Soviet attitude of the corps commander and some of his subordinates. Even so, one of his divisions, stationed in Békéscsaba, sided with the Revolution and established a revolutionary council.[18]

Other army sympathizers with the Revolution dramatically liberated Jozsef Cardinal Mindszenty from his internment in Felsöpetény, north of Budapest. On October 3 a group of officers, acting on their own authority, disarmed the Security Police guard, and the following day gave the Cardinal a tank escort to his Budapest residence in a procession which had all the earmarks of a political demonstration. Thereupon the Nagy government decreed that he had been unjustly imprisoned, and ratified his release.[19]

THE ATTEMPTED DE-SOVIETIZING AND REORGANIZATION

The Communist Party and its pro-Soviet government had lost control over the country because they could not govern the armed forces in the face of the open resistance of the population in general and the revolutionaries in particular. To the new government, relieved of the monopolistic influence of the Communist Party and of Soviet domination, the recovery of authority over all the armed forces, including the Freedom Fighters, was a question of life and death. The presence of Soviet forces in Hungary and the possibility of renewed intervention under the pretext of restoring order necessitated an integration of command and the revamping of the entire defense system of the country. The Ministry of Defense was considered an unsuitable agency for such purpose; it still remained staffed with unreliable pro-Soviet "cadres," and the Freedom Fighters would never have submitted to its authority in its state of existence at that time. The centralization of all armed forces and the de-Sovietization of the Defense Ministry and of the army had to be undertaken by a body outside the ministry itself. The same was true of the Ministry of the Interior, which officially controlled both the police and the Frontier Guard, an important military force.

Therefore on October 30, 1956, the same day the multiparty system was restored, the government announced the creation of a Revolutionary Committee of Armed Forces. This remarkable body included representatives of the army, the police, and the *National Guard*. The National Guard was none other than the Freedom Fighters, who had adopted the new name. The committee was given power to organize and control "the new armed forces composed of units which participated in the revolutionary fighting, of the army, of the police, of workers and youth units." The powers of this joint revolutionary-governmental body were to extend "until the entry into office of the new government to be formed as a result of general free elections." [20]

In this way the Freedom Fighters found themselves legitimized. The swiftness of events is again illustrated by the changing announcements of Minister of Defense Janza. On October 29, in announcing that Soviet troops had evacuated the Eighth Budapest District (where the fiercest fighting had taken place), he declared that Hungarian Army units were going to take over the district and he ordered the insurgents to surrender their arms to them.[21] The next day, October 30, while the Revolutionary Council of the Hungarian Army was being formed under the orders of the Prime Minister, Janza issued another command which placed the maintenance of order in Budapest in the care of the army, the police, and the National Guard.[22] Thus the Freedom Fighters were treated as a legitimate armed force coequal with the army and the police. And this fact added even more urgency to the complete reorganization of the whole military establishment, especially the army, which, after the disbanding of the Security Police, remained the most pro-Soviet of all branches in its higher echelons.

The key figure of the Revolutionary Committee of Armed Forces was Major General Béla Király. In 1951 he had been sentenced to death. He was later reprieved, and was released in September 1956. A few days after the outbreak of the Revolution he had been asked by the Freedom Fighter groups to take over their supreme command. Together with Colonel Maléter he became joint head of the Revolutionary Committee of Armed Forces, and was reinstated in his former rank.[23] On October 31, Király was appointed commander in chief of the armed forces in Budapest. The Committee also elected him supreme commander of the National Guard, with Sándor Kopácsi, the police chief, as his deputy.[24]

The Revolutionary Committee of Armed Forces set out to remove the pro-Soviet elements from the Defense Ministry and from the army. In this work it was helped by another revolutionary body, the Revolutionary Council of the People's Army. Four "Stalinist" generals were abruptly removed on October 30,[25] and General István Kovács was appointed Chief of Staff. General Janza, the Minister of Defense until November 3, was untrustworthy, and until his formal removal the reorganization of the army and its amalgamation with the National Guard and police units could not be effective.[26] Furthermore, it was not an easy task to distinguish between "reliables" and "unreliables." As proved subsequently, those who had been openly pro-Soviet in the past were not the only "unreliables"; others, less conspicuous for this attitude, behaved opportunistically, and, sensing the seriousness of the new Soviet menace, refused to take the ultimate step of opposing the army of the "Socialist Fatherland." [27] Little time was left for the effective reshuffle of the armed forces, the purge of unreliables, and the establishment of a uniform chain of command. In fact everything was still in flux when the second Soviet intervention brought a quick end to the process.

Besides, the Soviets were able, during the few days available for reorganization, to achieve a further infiltration into the wavering higher ranks of the army. During the successful days of revolutionary fighting, a group of Hungarian officers studying in one of the Soviet military academies had cabled its sympathies toward the revolutionary aims and asked to be recalled. These officers had not been returned home; but on November 1, a very different group of Hungarians arrived from Moscow. They came directly from the highest military institution, the Voroshilov Academy. Among them were Major Generals Ilku, Uszta, Borbás, and Székely, and Colonel Fehér. This group was anxious to occupy key positions, and since no accusations could be made against them they succeeded remarkably with the help of other Moscow-trained staff officers. For instance, General Uszta, who spoke fluent Russian, was made liaison officer between the Hungarian Ministry of Defense and the Soviet headquarters in Hungary. In this capacity he often participated in the sessions of the inner cabinet and made frequent visits to the Soviet embassy and Soviet headquarters. (It is assumed that he betrayed the confidence placed in him; after the Revolution he was made Deputy Defense Minister.)[28]

The regular armed forces of Hungary were not in any way prepared to resist a new Soviet attack. When, at last, orders were issued to put up resistance, the widely scattered units of the regular army participated only sporadically in the renewing battle, because effective centralized leadership was lacking (orders had generally not reached the troops) and because pro-Soviet officers sabotaged the efforts and others hesitated. The police were also unfitted to take part in open or street battles. Only the National Guard, some workers' units, some cadets, and a few small military units stood at the disposal of the revolutionary command when the combat opened on November 4.

23

Revolutionaries and Revolutionary Institutions

/\

We are opening a new chapter in the history of the Hungarian radio at this hour. For long years past, the radio was an instrument of lies; it merely carried out orders; it lied during the night and in the daytime; it lied on all wavelengths. Not even in the hour of our country's rebirth did it cease its campaign of lies. But the struggle which succeeded in securing the nation's freedom, and independence in the streets, has spread to the radio, as well . . . In future you will hear new voices on the old wavelengths. As the old saying has it, we shall tell "the truth, the whole truth, and nothing but the truth."

Broadcast by the Revolutionary Committee
of Radio Budapest on October 30, 1956

IN A revolutionary struggle, power is the decisive factor. To a large extent it replaces moral authority, law, and other political, social, or psychic factors which ordinarily contribute to the construction of the political and social order. Students of revolutions have observed that in the course of successful revolutionary explosions, at least during a certain period, the legitimate governmental machinery operates side by side with a more powerful revolutionary organization until the time comes when the latter is ready and able to incorporate or set aside the former. This dual power or dual sovereignty system,[1] particularly conspicuous in Russia between the initial March Revolution and the Bolshevik November Revolution of 1917, and described as *dvoevlastie* by

Soviet scholars, was apparent also in revolutionary Hungary, though differing in many respects from ordinary revolutionary patterns.

In a Leninist-Communist state a dual sovereignty always exists: a real one, exercised by the Communist Party, and a formal, sham sovereignty purportedly invested in the government. Furthermore, in a satellite country like Hungary, ultimate power and authority is of course vested with the Soviet Union. After October 24, the revolutionary movement proved strong enough to resist both Hungarian and Soviet pressures, and the Communist Party disintegrated as the controlling power. And when those things happened, the newly formed revolutionary institutions, holding *de facto* power, and the government, largely deprived of coercive means, faced each other. Both had been able to extricate themselves from the traditional Soviet chain of command.

In the Hungary of 1956 the formation of revolutionary organizations had not been prompted by revolutionary fervor alone; it was an act of necessity as well. The collapse of the Communist Party apparatus left behind a vacuum which had to be filled. The council (soviet) system of public administration relied on the permanent control and direction by the Party. But eclipse of the Party rendered its role in the state administration impossible. Without the Party's assistance its agents could not function properly, and those who desired to function were curtailed by the uncertainty surrounding their orders. Totalitarian regimes produce a boomerang effect in cases where their system is tottering under hostile pressures: the administrative shares in the guilt attributed to the regime and has to give way. In Hungary, revolutionary and national councils were created in lieu of local organs of administration; revolutionary councils were also formed in ministries and other governmental agencies; and workers' councils took over factories and plants.

The government itself underwent successive transformations from October 23 to November 4, as already related. From a Communist administration, subservient to the Party, it became successively a pseudo "national" government, an inner cabinet of mixed allegiances, and finally a balanced, representative coalition government. To allay difficulties and counteract aftereffects of monopolistic Communist rule, it had to resort to extraconstitutional revolutionary measures, such as the creation of the Revolutionary Committee of Armed Forces. The central government, under revolutionary pressures and in view of its own de-Sovietization and democratization, had to acknowledge the existence of the *de facto* revolutionary groups and institutions. These acts of "legitimization" started on October

26 with the Party's recognition of workers' councils and the encouragement of their formation; continued with the opening of governmental negotiations with the Freedom Fighters on October 28;[2] and reached a climax in a declaration by the Prime Minister on October 30 which (with italics added) ran as follows: "I announce, on behalf of the national government, that it recognizes the democratic organs of local autonomy which have been brought into existence *by the revolution,* that it *relies on them* and asks for their support." [3] Thus, the revolutionary organizations in Budapest and in the provinces had, with one stroke, been declared legal and, so to speak, incorporated into the administrative system of the country. The problems of their amalgamation with bodies that now found themselves in functional or jurisdictional competition, and finally their logical termination after the transformation of the state had been carried out, would have taken considerable time had the second Soviet intervention not restored the former Communist Party-state regime.

THE FREEDOM FIGHTERS

The original core of the Freedom Fighters, the armed groups which successfully defied the Security Police and Soviet interventionists, had emerged from among the demonstrators of October 23. They were students (mostly university students but also many from secondary schools), young workers, deserters from the army, and passers-by who had joined the demonstrators. The procession to the statue of General Bem, the mass assembly before the Parliament building, the destruction of Stalin's statue, and lastly the demonstration before the radio building had attracted crowds which were estimated to number 200,000.[4] Considering the state of excitement, and the magnitude of resentment and corresponding aggressiveness of the demonstrators, we may safely infer that at least ten per cent of them were ready to engage in armed action and to risk their lives for their objectives. The number of actual fighters was limited only by the lack of firearms.

Many of the Freedom Fighters were former political prisoners. The revolutionaries opened the political prisons of the country, whereupon many of the younger inmates joined the battle. A large number of the Freedom Fighters consisted of former or still active Party members and members of various Communist youth organizations. These converts from Communism excelled in deeds of bravery, driven by the proselyte's zeal and by a desire to redeem themselves by sacrifice.

During the night of October 23, and on the following day, the

Freedom Fighters occupied certain buildings — district police stations and district Party headquarters. They retained some of these as their own headquarters, usually selecting "bases" that were difficult of access and could be defended against tanks. Thus, in certain parts of Budapest and its suburbs, the Freedom Fighters began to form groups having a definite topographic area to control or to defend. These groups were often reinforced by volunteers living in the neighborhood, making it possible to organize shifts, thereby allowing those on continuous active duty to be relieved at regular intervals. Gradually leaders emerged who had been tacitly or expressly accepted by the rank and file. The selection of leaders and deputy leaders was determined by superior intelligence and leadership talent, knowledge of weaponry, or individual prowess.

Certain major groups of Freedom Fighters played particularly important roles. One was the group established in the vicinity of the Corvin block (Eighth Budapest District); these fighters, by acclamation elected Gergely Pongrácz to be their leader on October 26.[5] We have mentioned the forces entrenched in the Kilián barracks (Ninth Budapest District); Colonel Malêter, owing to his rank and experience, *ipso facto* became their leader. Another group ranged in Buda around the important intersection of Széna square (leader: "Uncle" Szabo). A group, or rather groups, operated in the industrial suburb of Csepel (Twenty-second Budapest District). Still other forces under the leadership of Jozsef Dudás made their headquarters in the building of the *Szabad Nép*. Finally, a group operating under the auspices of the National Committee of the Second Budapest District included Buda Castle Hill within its field of action and drew support from a military academy unit stationed on this hill. In addition, several military barracks served as potential arms and personnel reserves; some of their inmates collaborated with the Freedom Fighters, occasionally joining them or providing them with ammunition and arms, and giving them expert advice.

In the second phase of the struggle, after the second Soviet intervention, the Command of the National Guard (Freedom Fighters) moved from the Budapest Police headquarters to the Buda Hills. Its first base was in the Frontier Guard barracks on the slopes of the Szabadsághegy, surrounded by two defense rings. On November 10, the location of National Guard headquarters had to be removed farther away from Budapest to the village of Nagykovácsi. At the same time units of industrial workmen continued the fighting in the outskirts of the capital (especially in the Csepel suburb); in the town of Sztalinváros; in the mining areas of Tata and Csolnok, and also near Piliscsaba. The National Guard Command was able to maintain limited communications with these groups; but after November 11, the Command had to be dissolved, and orders were issued for a retreat across the Austrian border.[6]

There were some other Freedom Fighter groups that fought in November without maintaining contact with the National Guard Command. Some of these operated on the Mecsek Hill, north of the city of Pécs; most of the men had been recruited from among miners of the district. Other groups retreated into the Bakony Mountains. Still others took up temporary positions along the Austrian border until they were forced by Soviet units to make the crossing. Smaller military units of the Hungarian Army and many individual soldiers took part in the second phase of the combat; and these, too, were mostly able to find refuge on neutral territory.

REVOLUTIONARY COUNCILS WITH TERRITORIAL JURISDICTION

Shortly after the first news of the armed revolt in Budapest spread over the country, the "revolutionary" or "national" councils, or committees, which we have mentioned from time to time, assumed the direction of administrative functions in lieu of the despised and compromised local soviets. As we have seen, the creation of these revolutionary bodies and their assumption of control was generally achieved without bloodshed in the provinces. Where resistance was offered by the Security police, it was quickly overcome by massive popular effort.

These councils were not set up according to a uniform pattern; their mode of establishment, composition, and activities varied from place to place. In industrial areas (the city of Szeged, for example), the workers' councils, as we shall see, often also assumed the role of local administration.[7] In university cities, students participated in the election of the revolutionary councils and also accepted membership therein.[8] Occasionally representatives of the army took an active part in the establishment of a revolutionary body, and were represented in it. Sometimes it even happened that a local Communist Party branch initiated the creation of such a council.[9] The character and composition of a council was often determined by the way in which it had been set up and by the opposition its establishment had met. Where the local Communist Party offered no resistance or even cooperated, the great majority of the members of the revolutionary council were selected from former or present Communist Party members; in other places Communists were on principle excluded. The selection of the membership was carried out sometimes by professional organizations, sometimes by secret ballot or acclamation at a general assembly. Occasionally councils were set up by self-instituted leaders without election and then recognized by the population.[10] The popular and representative character of these councils was confirmed by the *Szabad Nép* when it said on October 28:

> News comes all the time from all parts of the country about the creation of municipal and county councils, workers' councils, national councils or revolutionary Socialist committees — using various names. All are alike, however, in being spontaneous, popular bodies which came into existence through the upsurge of a new democracy in this country. We do not know who the members of these councils are; we do know, however, that they are representatives of the workers and that they have been elected in a democratic way . . . Among them are those Communists who are respected and loved by the people.

By October 30 these councils had taken over the administration of the territorial areas under their control, establishing local units of the National Guard from among volunteers (mostly students and workers) and dealing with all sorts of local problems, but without neglecting the national political issues. The demands they put forward with great insistence exerted overwhelming influence on developments in Budapest and within the central government.* These demands, during the final week of October, generally included calls for an immediate cease fire, the withdrawal of Soviet forces from Hungary, and free elections. There were also additional demands stressed by one or another of the councils, such as withdrawal from the Warsaw Treaty, proclamation of neutrality for Hungary, the liberation of Cardinal Mindszenty and other political prisoners, the abolition of the AVO, guaranteed freedom of speech, press, religion, and association, and the abolition of compulsory deliveries of agrarian produce. Many of the councils made their recognition of the government conditional of the acceptance of their demands.

The most powerful of all these provincial councils was the National Council for Transdanubia, whose birth was recounted above. While the first meeting was in session at Györ on October 30, news came from Budapest concerning the restoration of the multiparty system, the creation of the inner cabinet including Béla Kovács

---

* The provincial revolutionary councils controlled the radio stations in the provinces, of which those of Györ, Miskolc, Szolnok, Debrecen, and Szombathely were the most important; here they functioned on both medium and short waves, and in other places on short waves only.

and Zoltán Tildy, and the agreement with Soviet troops for their withdrawal from Budapest. The favorable impression created on the four hundred delegates by this news persuaded the conference to abstain from any idea of a countergovernment, but the prevailing suspicion of the Budapest government was given expression by a resolution which empowered the leaders of the National Council for Transdanubia to open negotiations with the Prime Minister with regard to the following points: (1) reliable guarantee to be given by the government regarding the implementation of all promises, first of all those concerning the withdrawal of Soviet forces from Hungary; (2) general elections under secret ballot with the participation of several parties to be held after the departure of Soviet forces, but not later than January 1957; (3) local organs of administration to be set up with the approval of the competent revolutionary councils; (4) a central council for the whole nation to be set up by representatives of the revolutionary councils, and all senior appointments to be approved by this council; (5) the government to be made more representative and to include representation of the Freedom Fighters; (6) the neutrality of Hungary to be proclaimed and announced to the United Nations; (7) freedom of speech, religion, press, and assembly to be guaranteed. The resolution also included a threat: should these demands not be fulfilled, the Transdanubian council would withdraw its recognition of the government and would open negotiations with other revolutionary or national councils for the formation of a new government.[11]

In pursuance of the council's resolution its chairman, Attila Szigeti, led a delegation to Budapest and met the Prime Minister on October 31. Imre Nagy was able to impress the delegation with his sincerity, and his assurances that the council's demands would gradually be met were considered satisfactory. The delegation, upon its return to Györ, reported to the council. The council approved the report, but decided not to cancel the strike that had been proclaimed in the provinces until a formal agreement for the withdrawal of Soviet forces from Hungary had been reached. It was at this point that the idea of forming a countergovernment was rejected for the second time.

The grass roots foundation of these revolutionary councils is noteworthy. Such organizations were not, however, restricted to the Hungarian provinces alone; they were to be found in the capital city as well. Provisional revolutionary councils had been quickly set up in different districts of Budapest. The local Freedom Fighter groups helped to establish them, and it was not surprising that the first ones were formed in those districts most thoroughly controlled by armed revolutionaries: in Buda's Second District; in the Seventh, Eighth, and Ninth Districts on the Pest side; in South Budapest; and in the industrial suburb of Csepel. These district councils cooperated with the Freedom Fighters, undertook to organize their supplies, and fulfilled all sorts of emergency tasks contributing to public welfare — for example, supplying food to the public, repairing buildings, and clearing rubble from the streets. Some of these district revolutionary councils were formed by popular vote, but not all local elections had been organized when the Soviet forces again intervened on November 4.

A central revolutionary authority to administer Budapest was created only after the rebirth of the political parties and the official recognition of revolutionary organs. On October 30 representatives of the "coalition" parties assembled and established a Revolutionary Council for Budapest, which assumed the political administration of the capital. On November 2, the council elected the new Mayor: Jozsef Kővágo, a former Mayor, a leader of the Smallholder Party. At the same time Péter Bechtler, a member of the Social Democratic Party, was elected Vice-Mayor.[12]

With the establishment all over the country of a provisional revolutionary administration ("until the free elections"), Hungary had within a few days ceased to be a country organized and administered according to the Soviet-Communist pattern. The new administrative system, which never pretended to be permanent, was still in a rudimentary and inchoate state; but it was generally able to fulfill the tasks laid before it. It achieved the transition away from a Communist regime, the preparation of stable and orderly conditions in which free elections could be held, and the choice of a new leadership to replace the compromised and often criminal Communist elements. The development in this direction was sharply interrupted by the events of November 4.

REVOLUTIONARY COUNCILS WITH FUNCTIONAL JURISDICTION

Besides the revolutionary institutions created in order to reorganize the armed forces and bring the Freedom Fighters under the same tent with the army and police, similar though often less significant revolutionary organs were set up by manifold professional groups, youth organizations, government departments, teaching bodies, and simple pressure groups. The aims pursued by these organs depended on the type of functions they were supposed to serve; some were called on to replace a Communist or compromised leadership, and some to voice certain political demands or exert pressure on the government. Occasionally, their task was to operate in lieu of an existing government department or institution which was distrusted or otherwise incapable of fulfilling its role under the changed circumstances.

The role which writers, poets, artists, journalists, and students played in the intellectual preparation of the Revolution predestined that they would be active and important during the Revolution itself, and even after its downfall. On October 28, at the University of Budapest, a committee was set up representing students, writers, journalists, artists, and musicians, and also representing universities, the People's Colleges, and the Petöfi Circle. Subsequently the national council formed in the Hungarian Academy of Sciences also sent its representatives. The new body called itself the Revolutionary Committee of Hungarian Intellectuals (later "Committee" was changed to "Council"). Throughout the rest of the revolutionary period the pressure it was able to exert on the government was considerable. The Committee also addressed itself to intellectuals abroad, and undertook to gain sympathy for the Revolution both behind the Iron Curtain and in Western countries.[13]

The students, whose demonstrations had led to the armed conflict, were also the first who tried to shape their masses into an organized form. Shortly after the outbreak of the revolt, the Student's Revolutionary Council had been set up; its initial task was the provisional coordination of Freedom Fighter groups, particularly their student elements. Later this Council participated in organizing the Freedom Fighters as the "National Guard," whose representatives negotiated with Imre Nagy and with the commanders of the armed forces. The Free Hungarian National Revolutionary Youth Council, of which the National Guard was a constituent member, sought to replace the DISZ, the all-embracing Communist youth organization. The Fighting Organization of Young Workers was established to recruit workers and peasant youth groups which were to be added to the National Guard.[14]

There were various attempts to coordinate and unite the activities of all the revolutionary committees and councils, but none proved successful before the Soviets struck on November 4. Probably no such objective could have been achieved without the active participation of the most important revolutionary institutions and the approval of the government. None of the revolutionary bodies had

sufficient authority and prestige to assume this task, though the
National Council for Transdanubia had come closest to taking such
a role. The People's Patriotic Front, much compromised as a crypto-
Communist organization, had played a relatively small part in the
revolutionary events. Only one or two cases are recorded where
the local organization of the front took over administrative duties
in villages;[15] and the front's attempt on October 28 to set up a
central national council failed to bear fruit.

One of the most dramatic attempts to establish an all-embracing
Hungarian National Revolutionary Committee was made by Jozsef
Dudás, the most remarkable *condottiere* of the Revolution. Dudás
had been an anti-Moscow Communist. Arrested in 1947, released
in 1954, he worked as an engineer. When the uprising started he
formed his group of guerrillas, mostly industrial workers, and fought
successfully. After the official recognition of the Freedom Fighters,
Dudás displayed an independent and defiant attitude toward the
government. Indeed, Dudás persistently sought to set up a sort of
rival government. He asked all revolutionary bodies to send their
delegates to a National Congress on November 2. This was to be
a provisional parliamentary body which would elect a countergovernment. No delegates gathered, however, and on the appointed
day, Dudás, instead of presiding over a historic assembly, was
arrested on the orders of Imre Nagy, and the idea was dropped.[16]
Dudás was soon released; his men temporarily demoted him from
their leadership, but after November 4 he again led a group of
fighters. Kádár, toward the end of November, under the pretext of
a parley, lured him to the Prime Ministry, where he was arrested.
Dudás was executed on January 19, 1957.

Among the revolutionary committees set up mainly for functional purposes, those established in most governmental departments and other public agencies were the most important. All the
ministries, the courts of law, the Chief Prosecutor's Office, the
National Bank, the Budapest Radio, and the Administration of
Hungarian Railways had organized such committees, which in
many cases had taken over control of the respective department or
agency. When the Prime Minister, in announcing the new cabinet
on November 3, stated that the ministers in charge of special portfolios had been relieved of their duties, most of the Communist
ministers had already been removed from their offices by the revolutionary committees which had been set up gradually since October
30. In many of the Hungarian foreign missions abroad, *ad hoc*
revolutionary committees established themselves.[17] The Ministry of

the Interior (seat of the Security Police) is not known to have had a "revolutionary committee"; we have to assume that this department had practically ceased to function as soon as the Revolution appeared to be successful.

The case of the Ministry of Foreign Affairs, a department heavily staffed with muscovites, former AVH officers, and disguised Soviet citizens, offered a special problem. Like other ministries, the Ministry of Foreign Affairs had set up a revolutionary committee. On October 30 and November 1 this committee issued declarations condemning those leaders of the ministry and of the foreign missions who were "alien" to the people, approving the "eternal neutrality" of Hungary, and inviting the government to ask for financial help from the great powers.[18] At that time the Foreign Minister was the Stalinist Imre Horváth and his deputy was the muscovite Endre Sik. The most violently attacked representative of Hungary abroad was Péter Kos, the Permanent Representative to the United Nations. Péter Kos had appeared before the United Nations Security Council on October 28 and opposed the consideration of the Hungarian Question. Subsequently it came out that he was a Soviet citizen and his real name was Leo Konduktorov. On October 29, Imre Nagy's government recalled "Péter Kos" and appointed another representative.[19]

Despite the formation of the new committee, Imre Nagy placed little confidence in the Foreign Ministry, for on November 1, three days before the general dismissal of the Communist ministers, he personally assumed the direction of foreign affairs.[20] During the following days, until November 4, the main line of his foreign policy was directed from the Prime Ministry so as to exclude the interference of Ministry of Foreign Affairs personnel. Nagy appointed György Heltai to the post of Deputy Foreign Minister. This man had been head of the Political Division in the Hungarian Foreign Ministry from 1945 to 1948; he was arrested in 1949 and sentenced to fifteen years, but was released and amnestied in 1954 under Imre Nagy's first premiership. Heltai acted as Nagy's foreign affairs adviser during the rest of the revolutionary period.[21] In this way the Prime Minister himself resorted to extraordinary revolutionary institutions for implementing his policy through his own staff, thus by-passing the unreliable Foreign Ministry. In fact a careful plan was developed on November 3 to reinstate many former employees dismissed since 1947. The ministry was to be taken over on November 5 by the new personnel, but events prevented this.[22]

The establishment of workers' councils — aptly called the "anti-Soviet soviets" [23] — shortly after the revolt had broken out, was due to various factors and was to serve, in the eyes of its founders, differing objectives. The trade unions, which throughout the "reactionary" Horthyist regime had maintained their autonomy and in a cautious way had served the interest of the workers, had turned into a helpless tool of the Party after the Communists' assumption of power. Like all other pseudo-autonomous institutions in the country, they obeyed the commands of the Party leadership, their functionaries were appointed by the Party, and the election of the members of the shop committee in the plants became the usual farce of unanimous acclamation of the Party's candidates. Since the trade unions did nothing to prevent the utter exploitation of the workers, the general discontent with their unrepresentative character had been one of the main incentives to the creation of councils that would truly act in the interest of the toilers, who would thus regain their primary weapon: the right to strike.

Neighboring Yugoslavia was known to the average Hungarian as having developed a system of workers' councils which had been managing the plants and factories of that country and had successfully raised the social and economic status of the workers to a level which surpassed that of the Soviet-bloc Communist countries. The importance and autonomy of the Yugoslav workers' councils had probably been overestimated by their Hungarian admirers; nevertheless, the fact of their existence and their impact on the management of factories presented a picture which could only be envied by the workers of Hungary. The nature and operation of workers' councils in Yugoslavia had been studied by Hungarian economists and trade union leaders; these questions had been debated in the Petöfi Circle, and also at meetings of students and factory workers. Among the "points" presented prior to the outbreak of the revolt, reference had frequently been made to the necessity for winning autonomy for factories and their workers. Plants were to be run "by workers and specialists," and the trade unions were to be changed into agencies truly representing the interests of the workers.[24]

The establishment of the first workers' councils after October 24 has been previously described. Somewhat *ex post facto*, the Central Committee of the Communist Party approved the election of the councils in its manifesto of October 26, and on the following day the National Council of Trade Unions announced that "the wish of the working class has been realized: enterprises will be managed by the Workers' Councils." [25] By this time workers' councils had been established in all the major factories, mines, hospitals and state farms. The councils had been elected by the workers in democratic elections; in some places where time and circumstances had prevented regular elections, provisional *de facto* councils had constituted themselves. On the whole, the election of Communist Party members had been avoided, and the representatives of the discredited trade unions were also ignored.[26]

The workers' councils, upon being constituted, immediately took over the management of their plants; but, in view of the current revolutionary events, their activities were more of a political than an economic character. While fighting was going on in Budapest, the councils organized and supported Freedom Fighter groups. Furthermore, they directed the strikes which were declared or spontaneously observed all over Hungary. They dismissed members of the management who had not proved worthy of confidence; they took over the control of funds, paid out salaries, and provided help to families of their combatant members. Factory guards were also set up to protect the plants.

After the fighting in Budapest had come to an end in late October, the principal endeavor of the workers' councils consisted in getting ready for the resumption of work — the repair of buildings and machinery. In the meantime, they never ceased to discuss questions of political significance, and other revolutionary institutions, as well as the government, often asked for their advice, support, and cooperation. Workers' councils or their coordinating committees had put forward political demands throughout the revolutionary period. On November 1, the government appealed to them to bring about an end of the work stoppages. Negotiations dragged on for two days, and on November 2 the workers' councils of Greater Budapest declared their readiness to resume work because, in their view, the government had fulfilled the demands of the Hungarian people. Thereupon, general agreement was reached between representatives of the workers' councils and the government to the effect that work was to be resumed in all Hungarian plants and mines on Monday, November 5.[27]

Meanwhile the workers' councils, feeling the necessity of creating superior organizations, in some areas had set up central bodies, such as the Central Workers' Council of Csepel. But the organization of all workers' councils of Greater Budapest would only be established after the second Soviet armed intervention, when it would be called on to play a major role.

The spontaneous establishment of workers' councils, the popular and democratic voting which generally determined their leadership, and the fact that they participated in the formation of revolutionary councils and sometimes even took over the administration of industrial areas — all these circumstances were proof that they were genuinely representative instruments for the expression of the will and opinions of the working class. As all evidence demonstrates, the workers' councils included only a small minority of Communists,[28] and those were uncompromised Party members who had themselves turned against Communism. The pronouncements and manifestos of the councils do not indicate an adherence to Marxism or any other definable economic and social doctrine; they contain views and demands of a strictly matter-of-fact and pragmatic character. On the other hand, all appeared to agree that plants and factories should remain national property and be managed by the workers themselves.

The discredited trade union movement also underwent a transformation in the course of the Revolution. On October 30, the National Council of Trade Unions assumed the name of National Council of *Free* Trade Unions, dismissed the former Communist leadership, and set up a provisional revolutionary committee selected from among former trade union functionaries, most of whom had been imprisoned for a number of years. The new leadership announced the withdrawal of the Hungarian trade unions from the Communist-dominated World Federation of Trade Unions, and expressed willingness to join other international trade union organizations.[29] The reorganization of unions in the individual trades and professions had also begun but had not been completed before November 4.

"IDEOLOGY" OF THE REVOLUTIONARIES*

The Hungarian Revolution, a combination of national upheaval against foreign domination and revolt against a tyrannical regime, was characterized by its being fought both in the name of national independence and democratic freedom. From beginning to end

---

* "Ideology" is to be used here in its widest sense, including the absence of, or opposition to, a doctrinal ideology. For a differentiation between doctrinal ideology, such as the Marxist-Leninist creed, and ideology in a wider sense (philosophy of life or *Weltanschauung*) see our final chapter.

these spiritual values predominated over economic and social aspects of the uprising.

The aim of any revolution is the overthrow of the existing regime or government; that of a *national* revolution is directed also against domination by a foreign country. Popular forces may be united for action in achieving these ends, but these same forces may differ on the question: what kind of a regime is to replace the old one? Though revolutionaries mostly agree on the initial objective — the removal of an oppressive regime or liberation from foreign domination — they may and often do disagree, after the victory has been won, on how to supersede the former governmental system. The clash between moderates and extremists after an initial revolutionary success may be described as inevitable even though this conflict can often be solved without resort to violent measures.[30]

The primary aims of the Revolution in Hungary had been achieved by the removal of the Communist one-party dictatorship and by the emancipation of the government from Soviet control. All parties seem to have agreed that free democratic elections should be held; thus the people were to have the verdict as to what type of government should be formed and what policy pursued. It is difficult to conjecture in retrospect what the results of these free elections might have been, but some sort of judgment can nevertheless be ventured. Thus, for instance, no prophet is needed to forecast that a Communist Party, even with Imre Nagy's name at the head of the ballot, would have obtained an insignificant number of votes.[31] We can furthermore assume that defeated political parties, unless supported from abroad, would have abided by the decision of the free secret ballot.

As for the political, economic, and social system which the majority of Hungary's people would have chosen, had it been allowed to express its free will, we have to rely on those demands, pronouncements, or programs which were announced in the period between October 23 and November 4 by the various revolutionary committees and councils, the workers' councils, political parties or other pressure groups, and also by outstanding leaders such as Cardinal Mindszenty and Prime Minister Nagy himself.[32] Inquiries based on interviews with Hungarian refugees concerning political and social attitudes may also be usefully consulted for such purposes.[33]

The most significant impression one gains when studying the demands presented to the government by the revolutionary bodies is the complete lack of Marxist-Leninist habituation in describing political, economic, and social problems. As if the ten years of Soviet-Communist indoctrination had simply by-passed both the mature and younger elements of the population, the formulation of these demands was matter-of-fact. Neither Marxist-Leninist doctrines nor their cumbersome terminology were adopted; simple direct language superseded the familiar circuitous phraseology. This pragmatic method of expression showed, if nothing else, that the people of Hungary had not been influenced by the Communist way of thinking and that their "ideology" was not identical with that professed by the slender Communist leading element.

The spiritual values prominently stressed by revolutionary bodies and promoters of the Revolution were based on no abstract doctrinaire theories, Communist or otherwise. Though they demanded freedom and independence, no parallel exists with the philosophic justifications of those concepts, as expressed, for instance, in Kossuth's declaration of independence of 1849, which was modeled on similar pronouncements of the American and French revolutions. The Revolutionary Committee of Hungarian Intellectuals, when submitting ten demands on October 28,[34] called upon the government "to settle our relationships with the Soviet Union on a basis of equality"; "to cancel all disadvantageous foreign trade agreements"; and "to arrange for a general secret ballot where the people might freely set up its candidates." Factories and mines "should effectively belong to the workers"; "factories and land should not be given back to capitalists and big landowners"; and "the exploiting industrial norm system should be abolished." And "complete freedom of speech, of press and of assembly" must be guaranteed. The Workers' Council of the Iron and Metallic Works of Csepel submitted demands to the Prime Minister on November 1, asking *inter alia* for "the immediate release of political prisoners and Freedom Fighters"; "the withdrawal of Soviet troops from Hungary"; "free elections with the participation of several parties"; "complete political, economic and military independence"; "independent free trade unions and the guarantee of the right to strike"; the "supervision of our foreign trade, publication of trade agreements, and the utilization of our uranium ore deposits for our national interests"; "an agricultural system conforming to the Hungarian way of life"; and the placing of "the education of youth on a religious moral basis." [35] These were demands put forward by genuine representatives of the working class of "red Csepel."

The prevalence of the spiritual, rather than materialistic, approach was also evident in the articulation of economic demands.

Human dignity requirements prevailed over material welfare. In the demands for the abolition of detrimental trade agreements, the national equality principle served as an argument rather than anticipated material losses. The demand for a national — instead of Soviet — exploitation of the Hungarian uranium mines is to be found in most of the manifestos;* the wording of these uranium demands implies that Hungarian management was demanded for reasons of national honor and prestige rather than for any material benefit to be gained thereby.[36] The system of agricultural collectives was assailed not because of its theoretical advantages or disadvantages, but because many of the collectives had been formed under compulsion. Voluntary agrarian collectives were not therefore objectionable.[37]

The synthesis of all these demands and views appears to support the thesis that the overwhelming popular consensus favored some form of democratic parliamentarianism based on popular free and secret elections under a multiparty system; the maintenance of large nationalized industry with participation of the workers in its management; a free agricultural system with maximum limits to land holdings; national independence and neutrality; guaranteed freedoms and religious liberty. No expression of "reactionary" policies, no demand for the restoration of royalty or for "Horthyism" had been voiced; remarkable was also the absence of any expression of anti-Semitic or irredentist sentiment.[38] We should, however, point out that the numerically strong peasantry contributed relatively little to these conclusions. Their voice could have been heard only with the implementation of the promised free elections. It is believed that their contribution toward the formation of a new Hungarian political-economic philosophy would have consisted mainly in a greater emphasis on the "Christian-Social" content of democracy and political freedom. Cardinal Mindszenty's address may be considered illustrative from this point of view.

The Cardinal, having been freed from his imprisonment and escorted in triumph to Budapest, spoke on the radio on November 3. Apart from obvious distortions of his remarks, his address has been criticized on the grounds that he adopted a less conciliatory and constructive attitude toward Imre Nagy than Cardinal Wyszynski had taken toward Gomulka in Poland.[39] Critics fail to appreciate the

* In the revolutionary days the Hungarian public learned that Hungary possessed uranium. The Politburo had been able to keep this a secret, as well as the fact that Hungarian uranium deposits were being exploited by and for the benefit of the Soviet Union (see United Nations, *Report of the Special Committee on the Problem of Hungary*, New York, 1957, p. 71).

fundamental difference of the two positions. The Polish Cardinal had to deal with the First Secretary of the Party, who had been confirmed in his position by Moscow and who controlled the essential affairs of Poland. Waging war against Gomulka with all the strength the Catholic Church possessed in that country would have jeopardized Gomulka's newly won leadership, which he promised to exercise in moderation and with respect for Catholic institutions, and would have brought about a Soviet intervention which would have devastated Poland and re-established the former Stalinist regime. Mindszenty, on the other hand, faced a Prime Minister who was not in sole command of the government and who was caught between Soviet power and domestic uncertainty. Imre Nagy, while threatened by Moscow from one side, was still very unlikely to survive as head of the government after free elections. The Hungarian Cardinal had to be careful not to commit himself to any candidate in those elections — least of all a Communist. In any case, a warm endorsement of Nagy by the Cardinal on behalf of himself and the Church would scarcely have been expected to elevate Nagy in the eyes of the Kremlin. Within these imperative limitations Mindszenty's address was a moderate, realistic, and conciliatory one.[40] Pronounced on the eve of the second Soviet intervention in a tense atmosphere, it can only be described as statesmanlike. In parts, it could have been less ambiguous, and framed so as to give rise to less contradictory interpretations. Whatever its tenor was, the address had no impact whatsoever on the fatal developments in whose approaching shadow it had been made. The speaker must have been aware that his declaration would achieve few practical effects but be weighed in the scales of history.

The Cardinal left no doubt of his support of the Revolution, though he referred to it rather as a *struggle for freedom*. He evidently wished to underline the character of the fight as one for national independence against foreign oppression, rather than simply for the overthrow of a government. The Cardinal expressed a desire that his country be allowed to live in peace with all other countries, first of all with the "Russian Empire." He asked whether the leaders of this empire would not consider that "we would cherish a much greater esteem toward the Russian people if it would not subjugate us?" He advocated new elections without abuses with all the political parties participating and under international supervision. He warned against interparty strife and discord, and against individual vengeance. He recognized the classless character of the present Hungarian society, and hoped for "a system of private property but limited by social interest and justice." As Primate of the Catholic Church of Hungary, he declared that he did not wish to oppose the "justified line of historic development," which was even to be promoted. He called, however, for an end to Communist oppression of the Church, and for the elimination of the peculiarities of the bankrupt system which the Party had introduced into the ecclesiastical precincts.[41]

Despite some obscurities in his address, Mindszenty's words reflected the caution and restraint that were shared by a significant element of the country. They also reflected the general feeling that the people should freely vote and decide under what system they wished to live, that nothing should be done to thwart such a development, and that events of an international character might finally resolve whether Hungary was to quit her satellite status and re-enter the world arena as an independent country. Mindszenty, like most of his thinking countrymen, turned frightened eyes toward the colossus of the East where the solution essentially lay. Moscow's appreciation of the significance of Hungarian events counted for more at that moment than any other opinion or assessment.

REVOLUTION OR COUNTERREVOLUTION

When János Kádár announced the formation of a new Communist Party on November 1, 1956, he recognized the justification of the uprising but warned against the dangers of a "counterrevolution" should the Hungarian democratic parties not have enough strength to stabilize the situation. According to this statement — to which the new Party directorate and evidently Imre Nagy himself had given their consent — the criterion of whether the Hungarian liberation movement was to be assessed as revolution or counterrevolution depended on its ability to maintain the "basic achievements of democracy — the right of assembly and of organization, personal freedom and safety, the rule of law, freedom of press and humaneness." Otherwise Hungary would "sink back into the slavery of the old gentry world and with it into foreign slavery." [42]

When the fateful November 4 arrived, nothing had happened to indicate a victory for "reactionary forces" in changing the "revolution" into "counterrevolution." Nevertheless, Kádár's new Party by December 5 was defining the past events as "a Horthyite-Fascist-Hungarian capitalist-feudal counter-revolution." [43] A more detailed appraisal was accorded to this question by Kádár on January 5, 1957,[44] when he stated that his government's aim was the furtherance of the proletarian dictatorship which was exercised through the vanguard of the working class, the Party. The leading role of the Party in all matters should secure the building of Socialism, and the attempt — which had been made with the help of Imre Nagy's treachery — to restore bourgeois democracy, was to be considered as counterrevolutionary in its essence and therefore reactionary and retrograde.

Thus the test of "counterrevolutionary" had been changed from anti-democratic to anti-Communist. We may as well add that since Kádár's change of opinion coincided with the Soviet decision to suppress the Hungarian attempt at democratization, the "counter-revolutionary" stigma of any revolutionary movement was determined also by its anti-Soviet character.[45]

According to the latest interpretation of a counterrevolution in Soviet-Communist terminology, a genuinely democratic and popular movement would be classified as belonging to the nefarious category when directed toward the downfall of the dictatorship of the proletariat as propagated by and enforced by the Soviet Union. Such an interpretation, of course, would not satisfy all Party members in Hungary when the accurate "ideological assessment" of the Hungarian Revolution became a major political issue in the postrevolutionary period.

The new, regenerated Communist Party of November 1 stemmed directly from the Revolution, and in those early November days may correctly be considered a revolutionary institution. It was not intended to oppose vital requirements of Hungarian national life; its purpose was to disclaim Soviet assistance and its own superiority above other political parties. In fact, its *raison d'être* was to denounce the past ten years. The ideology of the "new" Party may best be gleaned from the leading article of the last issue of *Népszabadság* before the second Soviet intervention, an article which has missed the attention of most commentators.[46] This article of November 3 was entitled "Purified." The Communist Party — so the article announced — wished to return to the "traditions of the revolutionary Hungarian workers' movement." The Party could not again be organized from above; its organization had to start from below, spontaneously, in the plants, villages, offices, and universities. "We shall not be a Party of one million, we shall have to operate within more modest frames and more modest possibilities than before." The new leadership wished to discard "a false superiority supported by bayonets." Fewer in numbers but "purified" they stood before the nation. The Party desired everything that gave its program a closer resemblance to that of the other coalition parties.

Recognizing that public opinion "gravely and irresistibly condemns" the criminal policies of former Communist leaders, it wished to dissociate itself finally and absolutely from the discredited former Communist Party.

Kádár, the First Secretary, had by now disappeared, and this Party manifesto was probably composed by Losonczy or Donáth, with the consent of Imre Nagy. The article evidently envisaged the formation of a "Socialist" Party that would deviate from all aspects of the program and practice which had turned its predecessor into a target for national hatred and an instrument of foreign domination. No proletarian dictatorship, no one-party system or autocracy, no curtailment of political liberties and of human rights would be endorsed — only the maintenance of "socialist achievements accruing to public benefit and welfare." It was no doubt a modest program, but the only possible program for a Communist Party that wished to undergo the scrutiny of a free electorate. Only through honesty, in glaring contrast with past mendacity, could a "disgraced" [47] Communist movement face the nation again.

At a press conference on the evening of November 3, Géza Losonczy, who that morning had been appointed a Minister of State, declared that his Party and the government wished to preserve all the achievements of the Revolution, especially independence of the country. At the same time, they did not wish to restore the estates and factories to their former owners, nor infringe on any real social advances of the previous years. "The land belongs to the peasants, the factories to the workers!" He expressed the view that Hungary should maintain equal friendship with the countries of both East and West; this must be emphasized, he said, because there are appearances that in some countries building Socialism the character and policies of the Hungarian government are misunderstood and erroneously interpreted.[48] He no doubt had in mind that the new Party's ideas would be stigmatized as counterrevolutionary by Moscow.

Losonczy's pronouncements reflected anxieties which, on that date, were shared by the Hungarian nation. The Revolution had taken the initiative into its own hands; it preserved this initiative, despite Soviet intervention, for many days until it was able to convert the government to its own creed, have its ideas accepted, and thus obtain full victory. No indigenous Hungarian force could have, at this juncture, turned the wheel of history back to the point where it stood on the eve of October 23. But the towering menace of Soviet armor seemed likely to embark on an action which would deprive the country of its hard won independence and freedom. International events of consequence — the Suez expedition and the ensuing cleavage in the West, and Yugoslavia's hesitating attitude — came as factors which boded ill for the country which wished nothing more than to be left alone in order to heal its wounds, clear away the rubble of revolutionary fighting, and start work on Monday, November 5.

24

Foreign Factors: The Soviet Union, Yugoslavia, and Suez

Nobody who has not actually watched statesmen dealing with each other can have any real idea of the immense part played in human affairs by such unavowable and often unrecognizable causes as lassitude, affability, personal affection or dislike, misunderstanding, deafness or incomplete command of a foreign language, vanity, social engagements, interruptions and momentary states of health. Nobody who has not watched "policy" expressing itself in day to day action can realize how seldom is the course of events determined by deliberately planned purpose or how often what in retrospect appears to have been a fully conscious intention was at the time governed and directed by that most potent of all factors, — "the chain of circumstances."

HAROLD NICOLSON

Foreign interventions have played their part in most of the revolutions in ancient and modern times. Even if these revolutions were not directed primarily against a foreign nation whose domination they intended to throw off, foreign powers often found themselves compelled to intervene—either for dynastic purposes, or for expression of a solidarity with the ruling stratum threatened by the revolution, or simply for fear lest the successful revolution would find imitators in their own land. In ancient Greece, aristocratic city-states intervened against the democrats for their political friends dispossessed in other cities, and vice-versa. Similar interaction existed between the Guelphs and Ghibellines in medieval Italy. Outside interference, if not speedily successful, generally added to the revolutionary fervor by increasing its national aggressiveness. Thus the abortive foreign intervention by the armies of Austria and Prussia contributed to the downfall of the French monarchy in 1790–1792, and the operations of the "interventionists" during the Russian Revolution in 1918–1920 increased the chances of Bolshevik success. We have also observed that the first Soviet intervention in the fighting of Budapest on October 24 significantly aroused the momentum of national resentment and ordained that the demand for a withdrawal of Soviet forces would become the foremost battle cry of the revolutionary movement.

The multiplex character of the revolution in a country allegedly independent but essentially under foreign domination, a revolution directed both at the overthrow of a totalitarian regime and against a vassalage to a foreign power, makes it difficult to fit the Hungarian uprising into one of the known revolutionary patterns. The situation is rendered even more complicated by the metamorphosis of the Hungarian government within ten days from one imploring Soviet intervention into one which assiduously invited the same power to withdraw its forces from the country. Though the first Soviet intervention was aimed at preserving the existing Communist regime of Hungary against insurrectionist forces, the second was designed to overthrow the government, which had adopted and was implementing the principles of the Revolution, and to re-establish the *ancien régime* of the Communist Party together with the political tutelage exercised by the Soviets. This second intervention especially bears characteristics analogous to actions under the Holy Alliance system aiming at the maintenance of reactionary regimes in Spain and Naples after the end of the Napoleonic Wars in Europe. The Warsaw Treaty is cited by the Soviet Union as the instrument justifying intervention, just as the Holy Alliance served to preserve a *status quo* created in 1815 against the democratic and national pressure throughout continental Europe. Just as the principles of this alliance system were not enthusiastically supported by all the powers favoring restoration, the "un-Holy Alliance" headed by the Soviet Union and seconded by Communist China was viewed with suspicion by Yugoslavia. This country, while desiring the preservation of "Socialism," objected to the Soviet overlordship over other Communist states and parties, and undertook to sell its own brand of "national" Communism. The fears of Yugoslavia with respect to the Hungarian events and her endeavors to bring about a solution consonant with her political objectives formed an important influence on the decisions to be reached.

The Bismarckian phobia of a two-front war is not restricted to military operations. A double front of a different sort — simultaneity in political and military action — is the nightmare of both the statesman and the military man. It may not only make demands surpassing available strength but also necessitate a difficult and painful choice of priority. In any case, it may cause an awkward and dangerous division of forces and attention. Often either political or military action has had to suffer temporary or indefinite postponement because it would have conflicted with other actions of greater urgency. Frequently, states have availed themselves of some urgent preoccupation of their opponents to carry out an operation which otherwise they would be chary of doing. Thus Napoleon III, making use of the United States' weakness while engaged in the Civil War, sent a military expedition to Mexico and installed an emperor on its throne. The Soviet Union, safely covered by the state of war existing between the Western Allies and Nazi Germany, annexed, with Hitler's consent, the Baltic states and tried to annex Finland.

The tremors in the Soviet empire of 1956, the convulsions of Poland and the cataclysm in Hungary, must have been events of first-class importance for the Western powers engaged in a "cold war" with the Communist camp since the end of World War II. Irrespective of the attitude — inactivity or interference — they wished to pursue, these events had carefully to be watched and assessed in their real significance. When Hungary's government managed to regain an independent status and divest itself from its erstwhile Communist character in the last days of October, the maintenance of this independence, in view of its far-reaching impact on the Soviet bloc, must have appeared as an event of world-wide significance, bearing upon the outcome of the East-West Manichaean conflict. Still the attention of statesmen in the West was diverted by the occurrence of another conflict, the Suez affair, which simply by its simultaneity exercised a fatal influence on the developments in Hungary, and thus on the future of the global cleavage as well.

MOSCOW CONCILIATORY

The two Presidium emissaries, Mikoyan and Suslov, made their first return from Budapest to Moscow on October 26. In reporting to the Presidium they must have pointed out (1) the violent anti-Soviet feeling of the population, (2) the blunder of Soviet interven-

RIFT AND REVOLT IN HUNGARY

tion which, far from easing, aggravated the Hungarian government's position, (3) the necessity of a complete elimination of Stalinists from the Hungarian leadership, and (4) the need for the "democratization" of the Hungarian regime by including leading non-Communists in the government. They may have expressed the hope that the withdrawal of Soviet forces from Budapest and their restraint from further action, the expulsion of Gerö and other Stalinists from leading positions, the conciliatory leadership of Imre Nagy and Kádár, the proclamation of amnesty for the rebels, and the inclusion of Zoltán Tildy and Béla Kovács in the government would be sufficient to calm down the workers and students, end the armed uprising, and save the Communist Party's monopoly of power in Hungary, which would continue to cooperate as a member of the Soviet bloc. These views are clearly reflected in a *Pravda* editorial of October 28,[1] and are consonant with Imre Nagy's programmatic declaration, and the decisions adopted by the Hungarian Central Committee on the same day.

The question of durable relations with the satellite countries of the Soviet Union, discussed with Tito and presumably hotly debated within the Soviet Presidium, assumed an urgent importance with the coming of the Polish and Hungarian events. The split of opinion — admitted by Khrushchev in regard to the second armed intervention[2] — must have prevailed throughout the various phases of development. Adherents of a more speedy "de-Stalinization" may have reproached the others for having nominated Gerö to succeed Rákosi, and the ill-considered first Soviet army intervention may also have been a bone of contention between Presidium members. They all must have agreed, however, that the situation in the satellite countries, and particularly in Hungary, had been largely mishandled. On receiving the firsthand reports by Mikoyan and Suslov, the Presidium, on or around October 28, certainly agreed to undertake to mollify the satellite areas by consenting to the maximum "democratization" compatible with the maintenance of Communist Party rule and the allegiance toward the Soviet Union as represented by the Warsaw Treaty system. They were thinking in terms of the arrangements made with Gomulka, and they believed that a similar modus vivendi could apply to their relationship with Hungary.

Consequently, orders were issued to Soviet forces in Budapest to stop fighting the rebels and successively to evacuate Budapest; instructions were also on the way for the withdrawal of some of the Soviet forces which had entered on October 24 and 25 from Rumania and the Carpatho-Ukraine.[3] Nagy and Kádár were encouraged to come to a peaceful understanding with the insurgents, to stop the bloodshed, to agree to some demands (such as the dissolution of the AVO and readoption of March 15 as a national holiday), even to recognize the legitimacy of the revolt, and to proceed to "the broad democratization" of the government. Well knowing that the crux of the problem lay with the Soviet-satellite relations, the Soviet Presidium resolved to go one step further and make a clear statement concerning the nature of these relations, which they hoped would have a placating effect on Hungary and at the same time neutralize Tito's aspirations of converting Hungary and other satellites to "national Communism."

The declaration of the Soviet Government dated October 30, 1956,[4] must be interpreted in the light of this attitude; it represents a tentative effort to place, at least theoretically, the relationship between the Soviet Union and other signatories of the Warsaw Treaty on an equal footing, and to repair past mistakes committed in this respect. It must also be viewed as a last-resort offer for Hungary, setting the permissible limits of deviation for a "Socialist" country.

This declaration of October 30 emphasizes the "complete equality," mutual "respect for territorial integrity, state independence and sovereignty, and noninterference in one another's internal affairs" which are to govern the relations of the Socialist countries (called for the first time the "great commonwealth of Socialist nations"). It admits the occurrence of "violations and errors which demeaned the principle of equality among Socialist states." Referring to the decisions of the Twentieth Party Congress and to "recent events," the Soviet government declares its readiness to review the economic and military ties binding it with other Socialist countries, and, in particular, to recall its advisers, military or other, from the respective states. The Soviet government states that Soviet units are stationed in Hungary and Rumania "in accord with the Warsaw Treaty and governmental agreements," without specifying the date and nature of these agreements. It declares its readiness to review, together with the other members of the Warsaw Treaty, the question of Soviet troops stationed on the territory of these countries, but with the proviso that

In so doing the Soviet Government proceeds from the general principle that stationing the troops of one or another state which is a member of the Warsaw Treaty on the territory of another state which is a member

of the treaty is done by agreement among all its members and not only
with the consent of the state on the territory of which and at the request
of which these troops are stationed.

This condition set by Moscow regarding a possible withdrawal of
its force from satellite countries presupposes the existence of a *collective* agreement between Warsaw Treaty members concerning the
stationing of Soviet troops in certain specified areas or countries.
No reports of such a multilateral agreement reached the world before, or after, the above Soviet declaration; consequently, we have
to assume that the stationing of Soviet forces in Hungary rested on
a bilateral governmental (or probably intra-Party) arrangement and
had never been approved by the collectivity of the Warsaw Treaty
signatories. In view of this, the Moscow proviso for the withdrawal
of troops seems only a lame excuse to avoid the necessity of with-
drawing its forces upon the mere request of one of the affected countries, namely Hungary.

A special statement concerning Hungary in the Soviet declaration
reiterates the accusations according to which the "legitimate and
progressive movement of the working people" has been adulterated
by the joining of "forces of black reaction and counter-revolution."
It expresses deep regret because "the developments of events in
Hungary had led to bloodshed." While Soviet troops had entered
Budapest at Hungary's request "to bring order to the city," the Soviet
government, "having in mind that the further presence of Soviet
military units in Hungary *could serve as an excuse for further aggra-
vation of the situation,* . . . has given its military command instructions to withdraw the Soviet military units from the city of Budapest
as soon as this is considered necessary by the Hungarian Government" (italics added). Moscow also declared its readiness "to enter
into the appropriate negotiations" with Hungary and other members
of the Warsaw Treaty on the question of the presence of Soviet
forces on the territory of Hungary.

With regard to political developments in Hungary, the Soviet
declaration warns that country that *"to guard the Socialist achievements of people's democratic Hungary* is the chief and sacred duty
of the workers, peasants, intelligentsia, of all the Hungarian working
people *at the present moment"* (italics added). In the conclusive
paragraph of its declaration Moscow "expresses confidence that the
peoples of the Socialist countries will not permit foreign and domestic reactionary forces to shake the foundations of the peoples democratic system," that is, they will not abandon the system of Communist
Party rule or the hegemony of the Soviet Union in that area. How-

ever, on the same day when the Kremlin adopted the above declaration, intended to become the Magna Charta of satellite rights and duties, the government of Imre Nagy, in Hungary, was already overstepping the permissible limits of a "Socialist country" as set forth by the same document. It had reintroduced the genuine multiparty system, thereby divesting the Communist Party of its monopoly of power and, consequently, denying the Soviet Union its supremacy over Hungary.

MOSCOW IRRESOLUTE

Mikoyan and Suslov, again dispatched to Budapest on October 30, were to be the harbingers of the new Soviet concept of a "Socialist commonwealth" and of the other theses laid down in their government's declaration. But they found a different picture from that which they might have expected: a rebirth of political democracy with several parties, the almost complete disintegration of the Communist Party, the end of the dictatorship of the proletariat, and a Prime Minister intent on forming a coalition government which would take no more instructions from Moscow. When Mikoyan and Suslov met the Hungarian statesmen Imre Nagy and Zoltán Tildy, they were asked when negotiations could be started for the complete withdrawal of Soviet troops from Hungary. It was also suggested to them that Hungary, owing to popular pressure, would have to relinquish her membership in the Warsaw Treaty and replace it with a bilateral convention of friendship and neutrality on the Finnish and Austrian model.[5] The Soviet emissaries were unable to give clear and conclusive answers to these questions. Mikoyan gave reassuring replies, especially in matters of withdrawal of Soviet troops; he suggested that the Prime Minister take the initiative in inviting the Soviet government to open negotiations to this effect. Mikoyan evidently could not make any declaration which went beyond the Soviet statement of October 30. The representatives of the Soviet Presidium could give no reassuring promises to the Stalinists and the Kádár group when they visited in the Party headquarters. No doubt, many of them begged for Soviet help; but Mikoyan and Suslov were only able to convey to them the impact of past Presidium resolutions. Stalinists were advised to abstain from activities; the more important ones were told to take refuge in the Soviet Union; and as for the rest, the Soviet leaders refused any promise of intervention and exhorted their comrades to find their way out of the chaos as best they could.[6] Thereupon, Kádár, on November 1, made his notable pronouncement of the formation of the new Communist

Party, implicitly recognizing the loss of the Party's leading role and promising to cooperate with other democratic parties. When Mikoyan and Suslov again left Budapest there seemed no chance that a Soviet intervention would reverse the inevitable course of destruction to which the Communist Party was doomed.[7] The reason for Kádár's conformism up to his disappearance during the night of November 1–2 may be found in the lack of any encouragement from the Soviets.

During the absence of its two emissaries in Hungary, the Soviet Presidium must have been split on the issue of Hungary. When the report confirmed the disquieting impressions the Presidium must have gained from its other sources, the necessity for a clear-cut decision imposed itself. We do not know the stand individual Presidium members may have taken on the question of a new armed intervention, whether the Stalinists opposed the anti-Stalinists, as they had on the Tito issue, or whether the split occurred along the lines of a temporary alliance between Malenkov and the die-hard Stalinists against the moderates. We must assume that Mikoyan, who appeared always to support the most conciliatory position, and also Voroshilov, who had spent some time in Hungary in 1945 and personally liked Imre Nagy, warned against a violent solution, whereas the die-hard Stalinists must have favored drastic military measures. Khrushchev and his close associates probably hesitated over the action to take; the First Party Secretary's prestige must have reached a low ebb since he was held responsible, through his inadvertency, for endangering Soviet supremacy and Communism in the satellite area.[8] Still, according to his own statement, it was Khrushchev who finally decided to cut the Gordian knot by persuading reluctant Presidium members of the correctness of the course of intervention.[9]

In taking its decision the Presidium of course had to consider many other important questions, connected or unconnected with the Hungarian issue. Since October 30 the Suez dispute had come to the fore; messages and reports were pouring in from the People's Democracies imploring the Soviet masters to prevent the secession of Hungary, an event which might have fatal consequences for their own status. Czechoslovakia and Rumania, which include large Hungarian minority groups, appeared to be alarmed by the mere possibility of a resurrection of a nationalist Hungary.[10] Since October 26, the situation in Poland had again become explosive. Reports of disturbances in Slovakia and Rumania, provoked by university youths, had been arriving, and also news of demonstrations in favor of Hungary in the universities of the Soviet Union.[11] The Soviet Army command had already taken some preventive measures, ostensibly to forestall Western penetrations which already threatened Egypt and which might be expected elsewhere. Since the night of November 1 new Soviet units had been entering Rumania (where they were depriving the Rumanian Army of its heavy equipment) and also entering Hungary itself. The ambiguous position of Yugoslavia toward the Hungarian developments had also to be weighed before the final decision could be reached, and the advice of China had to be assessed.[12] Finally, the United Nations Security Council had been "seized" with the Hungarian Question at the request of the United States, Britain, and France. At an emergency meeting on October 28, the Hungarian representative Péter Kos, alias Leo Konduktorov (soon to be recalled), submitted that the Hungarian government had requested the intervention by Soviet forces and that, therefore, the question fell within the exclusive domestic jurisdiction of Hungary, and the council possessed no legitimate right to discuss the matter. Thereupon the meeting was adjourned, but the topic remained pending on the council's agenda, and the Soviet Presidium had reason to consider United Nations reactions in case of renewed armed action in Hungary.

Before analyzing the determining reasons which convinced the Soviet Presidium to make the irrevocable decision to administer a military coup in Hungary and install a "new" Communist regime, we must examine the Yugoslav attitude and the impact of the Suez episode.

BELGRADE ALARMED

When Tito, upon Khrushchev's entreaties, had consented to forgive and receive Gerö, he did not know that "matters had already gone pretty far" in Hungary.[13] Thus Yugoslavia was taken by surprise with the revolt in Hungary, just as the Soviet leaders had been astonished by the events. Early developments seemed to justify previous Yugoslav contentions: the people had risen against the Stalinists and against foreign domination. Gerö's expulsion, the final disgrace of other Stalinist leaders, Imre Nagy's new premiership and Kádár's Party leadership appeared to coincide with Yugoslav aspirations and plans.

Imre Nagy's Yugoslav orientation as expressed in his writings was known to Tito and the Yugoslav leaders. During the visit of the Hungarian Party delegation in October 1956, Tito's long talks with Kádár entitled him to believe that the accession of Nagy and

Kádár would eventually result in a Yugoslav-like Communist system in Hungary and the loosening of ties with the Soviet Union. An uncommitted Communist bloc — under the spiritual leadership of Tito — would have been compensation for the loss of a potentially high position in the world Communist movement. On October 28 the Yugoslav leader sent a letter to the Hungarian Party leaders to express his sympathies and approval of developments, but also to warn against further bloodshed and exploitation of the revolution by reactionaries. He told them that "the significance of these events extends far beyond the frontiers of Hungary, for they also directly affect the interests of international socialist development generally." Tito further expressed a hope that the "justified bitterness" of the Hungarian working people would not "undermine the faith . . . in socialism and the inevitable development of socialist democracy." He hailed the new political platform of Hungarian political leadership, the introduction of workers' self-management in particular and of democratic self-government in general, the initiative for negotiations on the withdrawal of Soviet troops, the settlement of relations "between Socialist countries" on the basis of equality and respect for sovereignty. In Tito's opinion the Hungarian government had now made a realistic appraisal of the nature of past events, and its declared policy proved that "the present state and political leadership and the genuine socialist aspirations of the Hungarian working people *have merged*." [14]

Tito's reliance on the Hungarian political status and program of October 28 showed itself to be wishful thinking when two days later the bankrupt Communist Party had to give up its monopoly of power, with the promise of a multiparty system and free elections. He tried in vain by epistolary intervention to save the Party rule and also to influence Hungary on the road towards "neutrality." The Yugoslav leadership became alarmed: they now would have to face the possibility of either having a non-Communist (and presumably anti-Communist) Hungary along their northern borders or the return of a neo-Stalinist regime with the help of Soviet bayonets and the collapse of their dreams for a reformed Soviet-satellite relationship. [15] Yugoslavia, like Czechoslovakia and Rumania, has a Hungarian minority. The Yugoslav government had entertained excellent relations throughout the revolutionary period with the government of Imre Nagy; the Yugoslavs had been informed of every move made, but they had not been consulted ahead of time. Nagy's counselors and friends maintained a constant line of contact with the Yugoslav embassy. There was, nevertheless, disappointment in the Hungarian line of development, even though many of the Yugoslav leaders, secretly harboring ideas similar to those of Djilas, or Losonczy in Hungary, hoped for a parallel development in their own country.[16]

More adventurous and sanguinary elements of the Yugoslav leadership even considered the eventuality of a military intervention, partly to save "Socialism," partly to forestall a Russian move. The threatening world situation as a result of the Suez incident, their desire to prevent Hungary (and their own country) from becoming a field of battle, and the lack of any encouragement from either the Soviets or the Hungarians persuaded them of the peril and futility of such an action.[17] They only hoped that the Soviet government would refrain from any *unilateral* military engagement, and, in case of necessity, might prefer a concerted action of "Socialist countries" to stabilize the Hungarian situation in accordance with their own vision.

In observance of "democratic principles in the field of international cooperation," the Yugoslav leadership noted with satisfaction the Soviet declaration of October 30 on the relations of Socialist countries.[18] They particularly approved of the Soviet determination to regulate economic relations with other Socialist countries to their mutual advantage and equality and to discuss with other signatories of the Warsaw Treaty the stationing of Soviet troops on their territories. These two decisions were characterized by the Yugoslavs as "concrete steps in the direction of settling relationships among the Socialist countries on the basis of correct principles." The easing of the Hungarian situation was accordingly expected on account of the additional remark that "the problem of relations between the USSR and Hungary is especially acute." The Yugoslav Party also lavished daily praise on the Soviet attitude expressed in the declaration of October 30 when contrasted with the aggression which simultaneously occurred near the Suez Canal.

Tito enjoyed excellent opportunities for being informed of internal developments in Hungary. Still he viewed the Hungarian situation solely in his cherished image of a Communist system which is not subordinate to the Soviet Union. Even in the last days of the Nagy government he had not given up hope of having "national Communism" triumph in Hungary or his belief that Imre Nagy might be the instrument of such a conception. The Yugoslav government, through its ambassador in Budapest, suggested to Imre Nagy and to members of his government as early as November 1 that the Yugoslav embassy building be used as a refuge should the need arise; in the early morning hours of November 4, before the opening of the Soviet attack, the invitation was reiterated.[19] Yugoslavia not only wished to secure the person of Nagy at that moment but also wished to be able to exercise influence on him. On the other hand the Soviet Union wished Hungary to be both Communist-ruled and subservient to Soviet leadership, while the Hungarian people desired to be neither Communist-ruled nor Soviet-dominated. Since only the Soviet Union possessed both the necessary physical power and — as we shall see — the unscrupulous determination to impose its will, neither the people of Hungary nor Tito were able to attain their objectives.

The Soviet coup and the ruthlessness of Soviet military actions, nevertheless, surprised Yugoslavian leaders and shocked Yugoslav public opinion. After Tito's frequent intercourse with Khrushchev and other Soviet leaders, the Yugoslavs had entertained illusions about the effects of "de-Stalinization" and change of Soviet attitudes toward small nations. The diplomatic defeat which Yugoslavia experienced by the unilateral Soviet action of November 4 and by the flagrant disregard of points of agreement reached between Khrushchev and Tito in regard to the treatment of "Socialist" countries was not mitigated by rumors spread at that time that Yugoslavia had been previously consulted concerning the Soviet action in Hungary and that her consent had been given.[20] Though the premonition of impending action may have been given to Yugoslavia — just to allay her suspicions — it seems improbable that express Yugoslav assent had been obtained by Moscow. Tito denied such an agreement.[21] Though he accepted the second Soviet intervention, the reservations he attached to his justification of this event seemed to indicate his annoyance at having been left out. This drastic Russian action, borne with restraint by the West, dissipated Tito's dreams of a "national" Communist Hungary, possibly led by the Hungarian Premier who had, in his writings, shown a signal appreciation of the Yugoslav road "toward Socialism."

We can merely conjecture how Tito might have behaved had the West assumed a more energetic and threatening attitude against Soviet aggression in Hungary; certainly Tito, together with other uncommitted nations, would have had an opportunity to act as a bridge between the East and West. Yugoslavia showed a complacency with regard to Soviet imperialism in Hungary which she was not to show with regard to Israeli and Franco-British actions against Egypt. But, of course, none of these was a "Socialist" country, nor were these events happening at her own doorstep.

THE SUEZ EPISODE: "WRONG WAR, WRONG PLACE,
WRONG TIME AND WRONG ENEMY" *

It is not the task of this study to discuss the political and legal merits of the Suez military action of 1956 as an isolated Franco-British and Egyptian conflict or as a phase of the Israeli-Arab quarrel. The pertinent fact here is that the Suez affair exercised a significant, if not decisive, influence over the happenings in the satellite empire of the Soviets. This influence took various forms. The division of the West at the fatal hour no doubt encouraged Soviet action; it also rendered a convincing politico-military front against Soviet aggression in Hungary impossible. Britain and France politically, militarily, and psychologically made themselves incapable of standing at the side of the United States. At the same time the United States government let its attention be thoroughly diverted from the events whose priority in global significance ought to have been obvious. Furthermore, the action to be taken by the United Nations — whatever its practical value might have been — was delayed because of mutual recriminations by the Western powers and the scattering of attention caused by Suez. In any case, concerning the Hungarian events the Western powers showed a notable lack of interest. They made empty protests and belated declarations in the United Nations, but they demonstrated a lack of understanding and imagination toward the colossal import of the issue involved.

It is a truism for students of international relations that by far the greatest international problem of our times rests in the global cleavage between the Communist bloc and the free world. Truism or not, the consequences seem not to be entirely obvious even to responsible statesmen. This conflict cannot be left indefinitely unsolved; the "Islamic" conception of Communism according to which the Communist creed will one day lose its bellicose and aggressive proselytism, as Islam once lived out its impetuosity, becomes irrelevant when one considers that Islamic aggressiveness lasted for many centuries.[22] It may be that our era of nuclear weapons will not permit us to wait as long. To a realistic observer it appears at the present that the East-West conflict can only be solved by one side gaining the upper hand over the other; this may come about peacefully or in war. There seems to be mutual desire, dictated by the

* This characterization of the Suez incident is adapted from General Omar Bradley's statement concerning the Korean conflict in the MacArthur hearings before the Senate Foreign Relations Committee. See the Committee's document, *Military Situation in the Far East* (Washington, 1951), Part 2, p. 73.

suicidal character of a nuclear encounter, to seek the solution by peaceful means; this is the interpretation of "peaceful coexistence," by which the Soviets hope to achieve world conquest through the adoption of "Socialism" by all peoples of the world. For Western statesmen peaceful victory over World Communism would mean that the populations of Communist countries, assumed to be hostile toward their regimes, might overthrow their governments.

In the East-Central European satellite area in October–November 1956, the fragility of Soviet domination and of Communist Party rule had become pronounced. In Poland a complete break was barely avoided. Then Hungary freed herself from the double bondage. Developments were still unpredictable. The whole area was seething with unrest, and the government of Bonn, uncertain of Western reactions, discreetly tried to calm down its East German brethren.[23] The crisis in which the Soviet Union found itself as a result mainly of the Hungarian Revolution has been thus described by Tito:

> It should be borne in mind that the Soviet Union, too, is now in a very difficult situation. Their eyes have now been opened and they realize that . . . [Hungarian] workers in factories and mines, that the whole nation is fighting. Soviet soldiers go unwillingly, with heavy hearts. Therein lies the tragedy.[24]

This tragic situation of the Soviet Union and World Communism might have been exploited for the benefit of the free world; the liberation of the satellite area — to which the United States was allegedly committed [25] — would have been a deadly blow inflicted on the Communist camp. It is believed, more for intangible than tangible reasons, that the present regime of the Soviet Union could hardly have survived the loss of its European satellites. No less a witness than Milovan Djilas wrote:

> Had the Hungarian Revolution been saved from Soviet intervention, it would have been difficult indeed for Moscow to obscure its internal conflicts by means of foreign conquests and the "world mission." The Soviet system would soon have been confined to its own national boundaries, and there, too, the citizens would be forced to reflect on their position and their destiny . . . Thus, new processes would begin in the Soviet Union, too.[26]

It is, of course, erroneous to pretend that in October–November 1956 only the fate of Hungary was at stake. The Hungarian uprising was only one outward sign of the general unrest that existed throughout the satellite area, and any Eastern or Western move regarding Hungary necessarily affected all the other parts of that area. The question was only superficially one of Hungary; in fact, it was a question of Soviet domination in East-Central Europe, and implicitly one of Soviet-Communist imperial power sustained or in demise.

If we compare the relative importance of the Hungarian issue in its wider significance — that is, the question of Soviet survival in its present imperial position — with that of Egyptian control over the Suez Canal, it seems obvious where the choice had to lie. Without any belittlement of the importance of the Suez problem, developments following both the Hungarian and the Suez affairs have given us clear answers. The present control exercised by Egypt over the canal, while undoubtedly affecting British and French prestige in the Arab world, has not been otherwise detrimental to the balance of power between East and West. The outcome of the Suez crisis strengthened Nasser and the Arab national movement, but it failed to strengthen Soviet power, nor did it significantly weaken the resistance potential of the West. It could not be pretended that a successful outcome of the Suez invasion for Britain and France would have resulted in any significant advantage to the West in the global Manichaean conflict, except that it might have thrown the Arabs more wholeheartedly into the Soviet camp. Thus the Suez incident, whatever its outcome, would not have been of paramount significance in the most vital conflict of our times.

The Suez action would have been avoided by Britain and France — if only for the sake of a concerted action in the Soviet crisis — had they pursued a policy of larger horizons and of sound imagination. If the Israelis had proceeded independently, their Sinai campaign alone would have weakened Egypt without necessarily dividing the Western allies, and would not have prevented concerted action against the Soviets. The untimeliness and shortsightedness of the Franco-British maneuver at a time when much larger issues were at stake must remain a model of ill-advised statesmanship.*

* Sir Anthony Eden, himself responsible for the ill-timed Suez action, has written concerning procrastination of the Hungarian question in the United Nations: "Five days passed without any further Council meeting upon Hungary, despite repeated attempts by ourselves and others to bring one about. The United States representative was reluctant, and voiced his suspicion that we were urging *the Hungarian situation to divert attention from Suez.* The United States Government appeared in no hurry to move. Their attitude provided a damaging contrast to the alacrity they were showing in arraigning the French and ourselves." *Full Circle* (Cambridge, Eng., 1960), p. 609 (italics added). Thus, the Western powers reproach

Neither did the United States recognize the priority which should have been accorded to the Hungarian Revolution and the ensuing Soviet plight in its East-Central European theater of domination. For six or seven days there was a recognized Hungarian government which was eagerly waiting for Western (and Yugoslav) diplomatic support, a government which, under the menace of Soviet armed might, had declared its country uncommitted and neutral. During those days no efficient action was initiated by the United States except the lukewarm appeal to the Security Council. From October 28 to November 3 even this action was set aside,[27] just when there existed in Budapest a government which would have welcomed United Nations observers or even a United Nations police force. In view of the developments in Hungary and preparations for a new Soviet military action, a "wait and see" policy prompted by the fear that interference would precipitate Soviet aggression[28] totally misjudged the situation and the character of Soviet aggressiveness. Neither the surgical operation undergone by Secretary John Foster Dulles, coming at the critical moment of November 3, nor the forthcoming presidential election could excuse the lack of attention to the Hungarian events.[29] Presumably the Hungarian issue took a distant second place in the priorities of the National Security Council in Washington as soon as the Suez conflict emerged.

It is not for the present analysis to spell out in concrete form what might have or should have been done. Suffice it to say that the possibilities in the diplomatic-military field were very wide. The response might have included the calling of an international conference; the recognition of Hungary's neutral status with a threat against an aggressor; actions of many kinds jointly with Yugoslavia; military and fleet movements. The risk of a war, in view of the Soviet plight and the unpopular issue (causing disgust and secession in Communist parties all over the world), was a relatively slight one. In any case, the faction within the Soviet Presidium that opposed the second military intervention would have been strengthened by any move of the West demonstrating that they *might* mean business, and this faction would possibly have defeated the interventionist group. There is no doubt that, up to the final fatal decision, the

each other for having, each in its own way and own field, diverted attention from the events of Central Europe and from the crisis which threatened the Soviet Union. An inquiry into the world's press on November 2, 1956, illustrates how world attention shifted away from Hungary to Suez; *One Day in the World's Press: Fourteen Great Newspapers on a Day of Crisis,* ed. Wilbur Schramm (Stanford, Calif., 1959).

Soviet Presidium had been hesitant. Any positive action of the West would have been apt to exploit this hesitancy and the political embarrassment which characterized Soviet diplomacy for some days.[30]

As it happened, the lack of concerted actions by the Western powers may go down into history as one of those tragic "lost and never recurring opportunities," such as the absence of a clear declaration of intentions by the British in 1914 (which might have prevented World War I), and the lack of action against Hitler's occupation of the Rhineland in 1935 (which might have prevented World War II). Future historians will perhaps regretfully register the absence of appropriate Western actions in 1956 that might have forestalled World War III, should there be any historiography after a nuclear holocaust.

25

The Second Soviet Intervention—Kádár versus Nagy

/\/

Had you for Greece been strong, as wise you were,
The Macedonian had not conquered her.

Inscription on statue of Demosthenes

Moscow could no longer preserve Hungarian Communism; it now
faced the choice of either leaving Hungary or occupying it. Thus,
its imperialism dropped its last "socialist" mask.

MILOVAN DJILAS

The task which lay before the Soviet Presidium when it had
to reach a decision on how to proceed in Hungary was dictated by
multifarious considerations, some international and some implicit
in the nature of Communism, and still others purely military. The
conspiratorial interpretation which Moscow, and Communists in
general, place upon international events seemed to have been confirmed by actual events: the Suez conflict may genuinely have appeared to them as a huge "capitalist" conspiracy intent on subjugat-
ing, with Israeli help, the Arab world, an uncommitted area open
to and suitable for the subversive Communist advance. The stand of
the United States against its allies in the Suez episode may have surprised the Moscow rulers. At the outset they could not, however,
be aware of the split in the West; and from the moment the British-
French ultimatum became known in Moscow, the Soviet High Command feverishly hastened preparations for any eventuality.* The

* Because the outbreak of the Suez crisis was looming on the horizon and Britain
had sent reinforcements to Cyprus and Malta, the Soviet Army Command had been

Soviet Presidium, with its distorted world image, was ready to meet "conspiracy" with a "conspiracy" of its own making. Nor did the Hungarian withdrawal from the Warsaw Treaty in any way affect the Russians' course. Only a threat from the West persuading them to use moderation could have prevented their decision and its implementation; but no such threat was forthcoming.

The Hungarian Premier, ever since assuming his second term of office, had been subjected to enormous pressure from two sides: the Russians and the Hungarian Stalinists wanted him to make use of strength (Soviet strength, naturally, since no Hungarian strength was available); the Hungarian people refused to cooperate with him unless he adopted their views and became instrumental in persuading the Russians to leave Hungary. Nagy had chosen the latter course, and thus had to become the victim, together with the Hungarian people, of the second Soviet military aggression, which its perpetrators tried to camouflage behind the technicality of a "new" government asking help from the Soviet Union under the Warsaw Treaty. Since Imre Nagy and his collaborators were unwilling to be used for such purposes, the Soviet intervention, as it proceeded with the extirpation of the Revolution and its government, laid the foundation stone for the new Communist rule, commonly called the Kádár regime.

THE OMINOUS DECISION

In the last days of October there appeared to be some disaccord between Soviet political and military leadership. The evacuation of Budapest, despite the agreement reached, was extended for three days and only completed on October 31; and meanwhile the military movements on October 30 and 31 along the eastern Hungarian borders offered a self-contradictory picture. Some Soviet-Russian forces were leaving the country; others were making huge circular movements; others were entering Hungary — all this at a time when Mikoyan had formally promised that Soviet forces which entered

---

preparing operational forces in the Kiev and Odessa military districts. These included mechanized and tank units, light and heavy artillery, paratroopers, units trained for desert warfare. Altogether five army corps (about thirty-five divisions) were concentrated in the huge corner between the Black Sea, Rumania, Carpatho-Ukraine, and Polish Galicia. Some of these units had entered Poland during the Polish crisis around October 19, but had subsequently been withdrawn. After the outbreak of the Hungarian Revolution, some of these forces had been moved into the Carpatho-Ukraine and into Transylvania; others had entered the Moldavian and Wallachian provinces of Rumania. See Béla Király, "Reconquest of Hungary," in *Facts about Hungary*, ed. Imre Kovács (New York, 1959), pp. 102–108, and an anonymous analysis in the *Wehrkunde* (Munich), December 1956.

Hungary subsequent to the revolt would be withdrawn.[1] It may, of course, be argued that this promise, like many later statements relative to troop movements, was mere deception; but we believe that *at this juncture* the Soviet military moves were just a part of the operational preparations to meet the potential dangers of the Suez conflict. Plans for an eventual second intervention in Hungary may also have been in the mind of the Soviet High Command, eager to re-establish its military prestige after its signal unsuccess in the streets of Budapest. The desire by the military to create a *fait accompli* by pouring troops into Hungary under the pretext of the Suez crisis may have significantly turned the balance within the Presidium in favor of the politico-military coup.[2]

The decision to remove the Hungarian government by military action and to reinstall a subservient full-fledged Communist regime was taken in the Kremlin shortly after Mikoyan and Suslov's return on Thursday, November 1. On that day, the massive invasion of Hungarian territory by Soviet tanks and armor began. To that evening can be traced the beginning of the political conspiracy which led to the formation of a new Hungarian government *on Soviet soil* two days later. Up to the evening of November 1, the Hungarian Stalinists, as well as Kádár and his friends, had been left in jeopardy by the Soviets; that night Kádár already knew what to do. The group of high-ranking Hungarian officers that had just returned to Hungary from Moscow had already been initiated to the plans for the Soviet coup.

On November 1 and before, the Presidium "after having thought about it a long time," "had to make a decision" whether "to help or stand aside."[3] It must be borne in mind that the Hungarian issue, though the most urgent, was not the only question which had to be considered by the Kremlin. Since the Suez conflict was now entering its most crucial phase, the latter must have had a bearing on the decision reached with regard to Hungary.[4] On November 1, the position of the United States seemed to emerge with outspoken clarity in opposition to Israeli and Franco-British actions. The members of the Soviet Presidium had been closely watching Western reactions to the Polish and particularly the Hungarian events. What they perceived may have been something entirely different from what Khrushchev so naturalistically described later: "The saliva of the imperialists was running in their mouths at the prospect of Hungary's leaving the Socialist camp . . . They thought that one by one they could sever the Socialist countries from their united base."[5]

Instead, the main Western powers were at loggerheads because of Suez, and no sign of military preparation seemed to threaten from the American side (in contrast to the military preparations of the Soviets). The much desired split in the West — if only on a limited issue — could be predicted. Besides the Suez distraction, the United States was also in the throes of a presidential election, a circumstance which certainly did not escape the attention of the Soviets. The moment must have appeared highly propitious for a ruthless action, especially within an area which Soviet policy had been accustomed to regard, since the end of World War II, as its private hunting preserve.

The effects of the armed suppression of the Hungarian Revolution on world public opinion in general must have been placed on the scales, too; but the Soviet leaders, though susceptible to the impact of public opinion, were always likely to disregard its unfavorable reactions when facing the prospect of tangible gains. Hungary would be saved for Communism once and for all, whereas an outraged world opinion would, in the course of time, be effaced. After all, as history has shown, the world has a short memory. And the United Nations machinery now had been thoroughly geared to deal with the Suez conflict: a full devotion to this task would exclude any other painstaking preoccupation. The Security Council had already postponed sine die its consideration of the merits of the Hungarian problem.

The Presidium seemed to have been more concerned with expected reactions by Yugoslavia and by Communist parties outside the Soviet orbit than by those of the "imperialists." [6] Propaganda was to be put in high gear to convince the comrades that Hungary and the Hungarian Communists were threatened by a White Terror, a new Horthy regime, fascists, and the Arrow Cross, and that thousands of Communists were being cruelly exterminated only for being Communists. In addition, Yugoslavia had to be told that Soviet troops would be withdrawn as soon as order was restored.[7] Relations with Tito might deteriorate but everything could be subsequently explained; besides, as Moscow must have known, alarm and disconcertedness ruled supreme in Belgrade.

Mikoyan and Suslov had briefed the members of the Presidium on their personal experiences in Budapest. They must have reported about the plight in which "faithful" Communists had found themselves in Hungary, about the hopelessness of restoring any measure of control by peaceful means, that is, by free elections. They also

informed the Presidium of the possibility of Hungary's leaving the
Warsaw Treaty system and becoming a neutral country. The masters
of the Kremlin might have gathered from these reports that the
central government in Hungary was still endeavoring to re-establish
its control over the country; that in Budapest, and more so in the
provinces, revolutionary organizations had superseded the state and
Party administration; that within days or weeks even the remnants
of the former Communist administration would be swept away and
the country would be reconsolidated on a pronounced anti-Communist and anti-Soviet basis. Imre Nagy had to be described by the
Soviet emissaries as a man full of "naïve" good will but incapable of
resisting the influence of his advisers, both Communist (who were
depicted as revisionists of the worst kind) and non-Communist. It
is not known whether either Mikoyan or Suslov advocated a coup,
but they must have advised that a coup, to be successful, had to be
speedy and ruthless.

Speed and Draconic measures were the counsel which the Presidium must have obtained from Party leaders in the satellite countries; alarm about a chain reaction promoted by the Hungarian
events was felt over the entire East-Central European vassal area of
the Soviets. Areas particularly affected were the former Hungarian
parts of Czechoslovakia and Rumania, and East Germany. In addition, Gomulka's rule in Poland seemed to be jeopardized by the
impact of the Hungarian Revolution and by Hungary's freedom
from the monopolistic Party rule. The Soviet Presidium must have
been aware that a non-Communist neutral Hungary would become
an irresistible attraction for its Communist neighbors; they knew,
as did the Yugoslav leaders, that emancipation from Soviet-Communist domination would not only unmask the shortcomings and
abuses of the dictatorship of the proletariat but would also provide
a glaring denial of the frivolous contention that a Communist regime is a "people's" government. There was already an obvious concatenation of events between Poland and Hungary; the Kremlin
now became apprehensive of the explosive situation which prevailed
in its entire satellite domain, and perhaps also of the instability of its
own existence in the face of a rampant crisis.

Not only the stability of the Communist camp but also the Soviet
view of power politics in the world must have weighed heavily in
persuading the Presidium to resort to massive military action. The
relinquishment of Hungary as a Soviet dependency would have upset
the basic considerations of Soviet policy as it had been conducted
since the end of World War II. To surrender "real estate" without

adequate compensation or without being forced to do so by the threat of a powerful adversary must have seemed the quintessence of folly to the masters of the Kremlin. From the West there was no offer or plan which could have "saved the face" of the Soviets and rendered the sacrifice less unattractive for them. No reciprocal "sacrifice" was to be expected from the NATO powers, no withdrawl of American forces from Italy or elsewhere, no "neutralization" of Greece or Turkey: evidently the capitalists wished to get something for nothing. An idealistic approach toward the Hungarian problem, the acknowledgment of the wishes of a people and of a government that merely wished to be independent and uncommitted, was alien to the sophisticated ideology of Soviet power politics. It was evidently not for them to suggest any compensation, for this would have been construed as a sign of weakness. The lack of any initiative from the West could only confirm the Soviet view that spheres of influence had been created in Europe which even the United States was ready to recognize implicitly, even while paying lip service to a policy of liberation.[8]

The Soviet Presidium was aware of the dangers inherent in any procrastination of a decision on Hungary. They had to act swiftly and deftly before the Western world, then mesmerized by the Suez incident, could come to its senses. A *fait accompli* had to be created before either the West or the United Nations would be ready to act. The greatest danger came from the existence of a government in Budapest that amenable to Western influences and would not be reluctant to seek assistance from the West in case of need. This possibility had to be avoided. Therefore no rupture could occur before the proper moment; no premature revelation of the forthcoming coup could be tolerated. On the other hand, not only did rapid military preparations for the armed coup have to be made immediately (the Army Command had seen to it that forces should be assembled to invade Hungary in as full strength as required), but a puppet government had to be set up that would take over at the moment when Imre Nagy's government was attacked. These were the decisions which the Soviet Presidium took on the morning of November 1.[9] The military actions were quickly intensified. Instructions were sent to Andropov, the Soviet ambassador in Hungary, and to other Soviet agencies in that country. And the Presidium members were designated who would be responsible for the implementation of the "political preparations." The conspiratorial action to reimpose Soviet-Communist rule in Hungary was set in motion.

HUNGARY'S WITHDRAWAL FROM THE WARSAW TREATY

Imre Nagy, who had just assumed the personal direction of foreign affairs, cabled to Marshal Voroshilov, Chairman of the Supreme Soviet, on November 1, referring to the Soviet declaration of October 30 and requesting that negotiations be held over the evacuation of Hungary by Soviet forces.[10] Nagy also summoned Andropov, the Soviet ambassador, to protest that Soviet troop movements were a violation of the Warsaw Treaty and the agreements reached during the discussion with Mikoyan and Suslov. The Soviet ambassador promised to obtain information from Moscow. At noon he telephoned to say that Soviet troops had only penetrated Hungarian territory to relieve other troops stationed there, and would be eventually withdrawn. The Prime Minister refused to accept this explanation, since, in the meantime, news had arrived that Soviet units had occupied Hungarian airfields.[11] Shortly thereafter more detailed reports reached the cabinet: an estimated number of 3,000 tanks had crossed the Hungarian border from Carpatho-Ukraine and Rumania. The aggressive intention to overthrow the Hungarian regime appeared obvious.[12] At 2 P.M., Imre Nagy telephoned Andropov to warn him that if the Soviet government continued to flout its own declaration of October 30, Hungary would be compelled, in protest against the violation of the Warsaw Treaty, to withdraw from the treaty. At 4 P.M., the Hungarian cabinet convened, and after a discussion unanimously accepted the Prime Minister's proposal for Hungary's withdrawal. The representatives of the political parties in the Council of Ministers, including the Communists, had previously obtained the consent of their organizations for this action.[13] At 5 P.M. the Soviet ambassador was received by the entire Council of Ministers (which included János Kádár) and was told by the Prime Minister that Hungary, in view of Soviet violations of the Warsaw Treaty, no longer considered herself bound by it and declared herself to be a neutral country. Nagy further told the ambassador that Hungary wished to inform other great powers of her neutral status and to protest the Soviet invasion of Hungary before the United Nations. Andropov acknowledged receipt of the declarations and promised to convey them to his government; he again assured the cabinet that Soviet troops would be recalled and asked the Prime Minister not to complain to the United Nations. Imre Nagy refused, but declared himself ready to withdraw the protest should Soviet troops in fact be recalled.[14] Later in the evening Andropov informed the Prime Minister that Hungarian airports had been taken over by the Soviet forces only to protect the evacuation of Soviet civilians from Hungary.[15]

The Hungarian public announcements of the withdrawal from the Warsaw Treaty refrained from mentioning that the action had been carried out in retaliation against Soviet treaty violations. On the other hand, the notes sent to the Secretary-General of the United Nations and to heads of missions of the great powers in Budapest briefly reviewed the history of Hungarian protests against the entry of Soviet forces. The Prime Minister requested the Secretary-General to place on the agenda of the forthcoming General Assembly "the question of Hungary's neutrality and the defense of this neutrality by the four Great Powers." [16]

The text of this November 1 note to the Secretary-General left the question open as to whether it requested the submission of the matter of Hungary's neutrality to the special emergency session of the General Assembly, meeting to discuss the Suez Affair, or to the General Assembly sitting in regular session. A procedural distinction might have enabled the emergency session to deal right away with the Hungarian request. But as it happened, the differentiation was immaterial; in the confusion created by the Suez incident, the Hungarian Prime Minister's note remained unnoticed somewhere on the desk of the Secretary-General until, upon renewed urgent appeals from Hungary, the Soviet aggression came up before the Security Council on November 3. A second note cabled on November 1 by the Hungarian government to the United Nations accrediting its new representative (after the recall of Péter Kos, alias Leo Konduktorov) remained equally unnoticed, a fact which later caused much unnecessary discussion and delay.[17]

The Hungarian repudiation of the Warsaw Treaty, with its accompanying declaration of neutrality, has been given different interpretations. Some construe it as one of the concomitant causes of the second Soviet intervention;[18] the repudiation was unrealistic, we are told, and intolerable to the Soviet Union,[19] and Imre Nagy ought to have shown greater understanding of Soviet susceptibilities than to commit himself a "violation of an international agreement." These commentators confuse cause and effect: the withdrawal from the Warsaw Treaty — as firsthand information clearly indicates[20] — was a result of Moscow's treaty infringements, its contemptuous conduct with regard to the Warsaw Treaty and other agreements. The repudiation of the Warsaw Treaty was made in response to the Soviet military invasion in preparation for the overthrow of the government. Any government may feel justified under international law to declare null and void a diplomatic instrument which the other party to it has openly broken. The questions to be discussed may thus be restricted to whether the formal repudiation of this treaty was, in fact, a contributing cause of the Soviet action, and secondly, whether it was an expedient and appropriate measure to resort to under the prevailing circumstances.

The Soviet die had already been cast when Hungary declared her neutrality. The movements of the army to occupy all strategically important points of the country outside Budapest, to seal off the Western border of Hungary, and to prepare for the deadly blow, were already under way when the withdrawal from the Warsaw Treaty was conveyed to the Soviet government. The Soviets could not have attributed any value to the formal adherence to this treaty by a state which ideologically and politically had already deserted the Communist camp. Had Hungary not repudiated this treaty and had the second Soviet aggression been withheld, how could a non-Communist country have cooperated with the Soviet Union according to the provisions of this diplomatic instrument? Would a non-Communist country have been permitted to participate in the Soviet bloc's palavers, whether military, political, or economic? What status could have been held by an independent Hungarian representative in the councils of the Warsaw Treaty? Certainly, the position of a non-Communist country would have been intolerable both from its own point of view and to the members of the Communist camp.* What mattered for the Soviet leaders was, in essence, whether Hungary was to remain a Communist country loyal to Soviet leadership, and not whether she preserved the mere formality of allegiance to a treaty.

We should also remember that the Soviet government did not even find it necessary to protest overtly against the repudiation of the Warsaw Treaty. Not a word of complaint was to be heard from Ambassador Andropov while the Nagy government exercised its functions. When it was swept away by the Soviet onslaught, the Warsaw Treaty was naturally upheld by the government which had been installed by Soviet intervention. Had the Soviet government really been prompted by the Hungarian move to resort to retaliation it would no doubt have said so and protested loudly. Thus, the *post*

---

* Although the Warsaw Treaty provided for the accession of other states "irrespective of their social and state systems" (on the condition that all members to the treaty agree with the accession), this writer believes that a symbiosis between a genuinely democratic country and the Soviet Communist bloc within the framework of a close association, as the Warsaw Treaty system is supposed to be, would be impossible.

hoc, ergo propter hoc argument may not be validly invoked with regard to the Hungarian repudiation of the Warsaw Treaty and the Soviet intervention three days later.

The abstention from the declaration of neutrality would thus not have saved the Nagy government from annihilation. Our second question for consideration is whether, from the point of view of that government as it stood on November 1, the renunciation of the Warsaw Treaty and its declaration of neutrality was, in any case, an expedient and appropriate measure. Our answer is in the affirmative because the Hungarian government had no other alternative; the action was a measure of despair, the last straw, and had its impact been properly grasped by the Western powers, the significance of this move would not have been lost.

The authors of the Hungarian declaration of neutrality wished to facilitate Western diplomatic intervention for saving Hungary's independence. At the same time, they intended to meet Soviet anxieties and give guarantees to Moscow that Hungary did not wish to join the Western alliance system. In their view — and they were certainly right — nothing could have saved Hungary but Western pressure, similar to that which had assured Austria's independence and neutrality.[21] If we consider the extremely difficult position in which Hungary's government found itself, faced by the menace of Soviet military intervention and by its own inability to put up a serious defense against it, the resort to this measure does not appear unreasonable. It was no gamble because Hungary had nothing to lose by it; the Soviet aggressive intent had become obvious. She could only gain by her declared neutral status, since it would have enabled the Western powers to enter by diplomacy the door that they now found ajar. When the Warsaw Treaty had been applicable to Hungary, a request for Western intervention or for United Nations protection would have been incompatible with the treaty stipulations. Now, the Warsaw Treaty having been set aside, it could no more be invoked as preventing this resort.

In Hungary the declaration of neutrality was greeted with enthusiasm; it had formed one of the demands insistently submitted to the government by many revolutionary organizations. Imre Nagy himself was easily persuaded to embark on this course when foreign policy motivations also counseled it. In his dissertation he had already advocated Hungary's neutral status and independence from the East-West global conflict. Though the withdrawal into neutrality had to be declared under inauspicious and critical circumstances, the Prime Minister must have been glad to be obliged to this historic move. His address to the nation, announcing Hungary's neutrality, is witness to the significance which he was ready to attribute to the decision:

The Hungarian national Government, imbued with profound responsibility toward the Hungarian people and history, and giving expression to the undivided will of the Hungarian millions, declares the neutrality of the Hungarian People's Republic. The Hungarian people, on the basis of independence and equality and in accordance with the spirit of the United Nations Charter, wishes to live in true friendship with its neighbors, the Soviet Union, and all the peoples of the world. The Hungarian people desires the consolidation and further development of the achievements of its national revolution *without joining any power blocs* [italics added]. The century-old dream of the Hungarian people is thus fulfilled.[22]

If the draftsmen of the declaration of neutrality did not achieve the objective they hoped for — the diplomatic support of the West and of the United Nations — it was not their fault. Unfortunately, the Hungarian declaration, though widely publicized by the press, elicited no response in the chancelleries of the West. Either Suez had attracted all the attention or else unpreparedness for meeting the surprises of the Hungarian situation prevented Western diplomacy from swiftly grasping and exploiting the opening furnished by this event.

The Soviet government seemed to ignore the Hungarian move. No reaction was forthcoming from Moscow until their politico-military conspiracy burst forth. The Soviet ambassador displayed his ingenuity for gaining time; at the Council of Ministers meeting on November 1, after having listened to the official declarations, he made a long, entirely pointless speech, thus delaying the Prime Minister for an hour from signing the diplomatic notes to the United Nations and other powers concerning Hungary's neutrality.[23] On November 2, Andropov invited the Hungarian government to appoint members of two delegations, a political and a military, to discuss the withdrawal of Soviet troops from Hungary and political problems that had arisen with regard to the Warsaw Treaty. This message was in reply to the Hungarian Prime Minister's cable to Voroshilov suggesting negotiations on these subjects. The corresponding Soviet military delegation was to be ready to start talks on the following day, whereas the Soviet political negotiators had yet to be designated. This Soviet communication created a temporary atmosphere of relief in Hungarian government circles; the real background of this cat-

and-mouse game was not fully recognized until later. The Hungarian government promptly appointed its two delegations. But irrespective of Soviet promises, the occupation of important Hungarian strategic points continued. The Soviet Army had commandeered Hungarian railroads in the East, and now not only tanks, trucks and armor poured in, but also large supplies of fuel and other goods. The Soviet forces acted in a manner resembling a full-fledged warlike operation. On this same Friday, November 2, Hungary again sent a note of protest to the Soviet Union and again informed the Secretary-General of the United Nations what was going on.[24]

Soviet Ambassador Andropov remained in frequent contact with the Prime Minister. Once he asked to see him privately. Andropov, we are told, suggested on that occasion that despite the withdrawal of Soviet forces, the Soviet Union might be allowed to maintain rocket launching sites on Hungarian soil, whereupon Imre Nagy unceremoniously dismissed his visitor. It is possible that the Soviet diplomat was cautiously sounding out the chances of cooperation with Imre Nagy under certain contingencies.[25]

POLITICAL PREPARATIONS: THE GOVERNMENT OF UZHGOROD

The Soviet Presidium could not have been satisfied by overthrowing the multiparty government without replacing it by a government and regime desirable in the eyes of Moscow. A military coup can bring fruitful results only when accompanied by a reshaping of the political structure of a country. The vacuum caused by the downfall of the Imre Nagy government was to be filled immediately, partly to prevent foreign interference, partly to support the semblance that the "counterrevolutionary" regime had been overthrown by Hungarian popular forces. Therefore, a "puppet government" had to be set up and kept in readiness "to take over" as soon as the military forces had attained their objectives.

The Soviet leaders were not novices in forming "puppet" or "shadow" cabinets. For one thing, many such "governments" had been set up during the Russian revolutionary period for the purpose of controlling secessionist or recalcitrant nationalities or regions through deception. But the most conspicuous of such cabinets had been installed at the outbreak of hostilities with Finland, on November 30, 1939, at Terijoki, on the Finnish side of the frontier near Leningrad. The Finnish People's Government, under the chairmanship of Otto Kuusinen, would have been moved to Helsinki had the Soviet forces been able to conquer Finland. In March 1940, the

Kuusinen government was allowed to disappear; it never became more than a government of Terijoki.[26] Otto Kuusinen later became a member of the Soviet Presidium in Moscow.

The selection of the leading member or members of a puppet government is always a delicate matter for the "parent" government. In Hungary there were still some prominent Communists who, fearful of losing their jobs and of being made answerable for past abuses, were only all too ready to throw in their lot with a Soviet conspiracy to restore the dictatorship of the proletariat under their leadership. The optimum solution for the Soviets would have been to win the collaboration of Imre Nagy, the Prime Minister himself; they undertook on several occasions, both prior to the *Putsch* and afterwards, to obtain his cooperation, but in vain. The second-best solution seemed to be Kádár; he was neither a notorious Stalinist nor a discredited muscovite, nor was he Jewish. He and his group, though inimical toward Rákosi and other Stalinists, had never, even during the revolutionary successes, given up their longing to work with and for Moscow. They had felt abandoned and frustrated by the Soviets, and for days had no other choice than to accept the multiparty regime, the legitimization of the revolutionary organizations, the withdrawal from the Warsaw Treaty, and Hungary's neutrality. Since the most dangerous weapon used against Communists of any description was their "alliance with the Soviet aggressors," Kádár and his group did their best to appear as true Hungarian patriots, and surpassed even Imre Nagy in their demands for Soviet withdrawals and the independence of the country. On November 1 at the 5 P.M. cabinet meeting announcing Hungary's withdrawal from the Warsaw Treaty, Kádár gave his consent to the measure both as First Secretary of the Party and also personally. He further stated that as a "Hungarian Communist" he would fight with his bare hands against the Soviet tanks, if that were necessary — while Ambassador Andropov nervously listened to this peroration.[27] At that time Kádár had not yet learned of the impending Soviet coup.

The Soviet Presidium had not given serious thought to the idea of bringing back either Rákosi or Gerö; they were too obviously discredited and compromised and had been blamed for the revolutionary outbreak in Hungary. Nevertheless, these men could be used as bugbears against Kádár and his friends to force them into obedience. Otherwise, in view of the scarcity of reliable Communist personnel, less notorious Stalinists might also be made use of, and, of course, a number of muscovites, too. Ferenc Münnich, an anti-Rákosi muscovite, had been selected as go-between to persuade János Kádár and some other future cabinet ministers of the government to place their services at the disposal of the impending politico-military conspiracy.

On the night of November 1, after the inaugural session of the new Communist Party and the announcement of its formation over the radio by First Secretary Kádár, who emphasized the readiness of his Party to collaborate with other democratic parties, Kádár was seen in the company of Münnich in front of the Soviet embassy; shortly thereafter he disappeared from Budapest.[28] He was taken by a Soviet aircraft from a Soviet-controlled airfield to the town of Uzhgorod, the capital of the Carpatho-Ukraine, a formerly Hungarian-Czechoslovak region. Other reliable comrades, to whom had been imparted the joyful news of the imminent events, soon joined them.*

The talks which accompanied the official formation of the Kádár government on November 3 were led by representatives of the Soviet Presidium. It can be reasonably assumed that Khrushchev was among those present at Uzhgorod to give the Presidium's blessing to Kádár.[29] Naturally, the performance was conspiratorial and the formation of the new government was only announced with the opening crash of gunfire in Budapest at about 5 A.M. on November 4. The Soviet leaders must have discussed with Kádár and his associates the plan of maneuver for taking over the reins of government, and also the government's future program.

Much conjecture has centered around the question: what persuaded Kádár to abandon Nagy's government and join the Soviet bandwagon? Kádár's participation in Rákosi's crimes before his own imprisonment, the blackmail possibilities stemming from his tape-recorded prison conversation with Rajk, and his jealousy of Imre Nagy, are invoked as reasons for his conversion.[30] The decision of Kádár and his friends to join the Soviet coup can be explained by their personal uncertainty regarding their future, and even more by the Soviet attitude displayed since Gerö's departure. Communists loyal to the Soviet leadership must have felt that Moscow had abandoned them as it had previously abandoned other Communist

* For over three years it was not known where the Kádár government was formed; the guesses varied from the Hungarian town of Szolnok to some place in Czechoslovakia, or Moscow. After Khrushchev's visit in Hungary on the occasion of the Hungarian Party Congress in December 1959, Kádár accompanied his guest to the Carpatho-Ukraine and in a speech made at Uzhgorod admitted that it was to this town that he had come "three years ago when the Hungarian people had been in great trouble." When his government asked for "brotherly help from the Soviet people, this support had been given and so the counter-revolution had been defeated." *Népszabadság*, Dec. 8, 1959.

Parties for ulterior motives. In vain had they offered their services to the Kremlin; the Kremlin seemed to have succumbed to its own slogans of "independence, equality, and democracy" for the satellites. The Soviet forces had given up fighting in the streets of Budapest, and the declaration of October 30 also seemed to indicate that no force would be used to re-establish the *status quo ante*. Mikoyan had personally discouraged Kádár and his group from placing their hopes on Moscow's renewed intervention. But as soon as Kádár was told that Moscow had reconsidered its stand and was now ready to impose its will by force, and when he was offered the leading role in a future Communist Hungary, this vain and impressionable person quickly grasped where his and the Party's interest lay.

The personnel selected by Moscow to staff the government to be imposed upon Hungary was not only purely Communist, but was restricted to Kádár's centrist group and to Stalinists of lesser notoriety. In the beginning the personnel available for posts was limited, since it seemed inadvisable to entrust the secret of the conspiracy to many. Münnich was the second important personage of the group. Among Kádár's confidants, only György Marosán was taken to Uzhgorod. Imre Horváth, another muscovite, had been Foreign Minister before Imre Nagy took over his portfolio while he was en route to the United Nations; instead of going to New York he journeyed to Uzhgorod via Vienna and Prague. Antal Apro, István Kossa and Imre Dögei had all occupied ministerial posts before the Revolution. Sándor Ronai, one of the few former Social Democrats who had been spared by Rákosi, now stood repudiated by his erstwhile Party comrades and was ready to join the forces backed by the Soviet Union.

The new Kádár regime needed a Prime Minister. The Russians would have preferred Münnich for that post, because Kádár's appointment to the premiership would go against the principle initiated after Stalin's death (and only transgressed by Khrushchev) that the leading Party post should be kept separate from that of the Prime Minister. But Münnich himself suggested that Kádár was more suited to add the premiership to his Party Secretary post because "he (Münnich) had been away for a long time and people were less familiar with his views and actions." [31] This convinced the representatives of the Soviet Presidium, and Kádár was chosen also as Premier. Perhaps they also had in mind that Kádár, as Prime Minister, might be replaced by Imre Nagy, should the latter become amenable to Soviet entreaties. The somewhat inappropriate name chosen for the new government was "Hungarian Revolutionary Worker-Peasant Government."

It was not unique for a satellite Prime Minister to be anointed by Soviet leaders: this had happened to Imre Nagy himself in June 1953. The remarkable characteristic of this inauguration consisted in the fact that this time a Communist countergovernment was to be installed against a government led by another Communist and supported by Communists. The cleavage within Hungarian Communist ranks thus had to be officially admitted. The announcements of November 4 asserted that the government of Imre Nagy "had come under the pressure of the reaction" [32] and that through its weakness and "through the increased influence of counter-revolutionary elements who edged their way into the movement," [33] the Socialist achievements and the worker-peasant power had become endangered. The revisionists and the Communists in name only of the rightist faction were not only shoved aside, but because of their refusal to cooperate and their maintenance of the traditions and aims of the Revolution, were ostracized and in many cases prosecuted and condemned. The Soviet Presidium was able to create a puppet government by openly splitting the leadership of the Hungarian Party and turning one part against the other in a life-and-death struggle. The government of Uzhgorod thus represented the consummation of the scission that had been noticeable for many years and had been influential in the outbreak of the uprising. The dividing line now became clearly one between Hungarian national sentiment and subservience, under the cover of Communist affiliation, to Soviet Russian aggressive imperialism.

THE OVERTHROW OF THE NAGY GOVERNMENT

In Budapest on Saturday, November 3, while the counter government was being secretly inaugurated at Uzhgorod, business between the Nagy government and the Soviet ambassador and Soviet authorities became intensified. Around noon, negotiations opened in the Parliament building between the two military delegations on the question of Soviet evacuation. The members of the Soviet delegation were the Generals Malinin, Cherbanin, and Stepanov. The Prime Minister himself ceremoniously opened the talks. Agreements were reached on such issues as the formalities of Soviet troop departures (greetings to be exchanged with Hungarian units, and so on) and the maintenance of Soviet military memorials (or their replacement when damaged).[34] Concerning the date of Soviet troop withdrawal, the negotiators remained divided: the Hungarians proposed December 15 whereas the Soviet officers insisted on January 15, 1957.

At that point the negotiations were adjourned, and set to continue at 10 P.M. at Tököl, the Soviet military headquarters on Csepel Island, south of Budapest. As we now know, the time and place of the continued negotiations was established to trap the military leaders of revolutionary Hungary. The negotiations themselves served to decoy the Hungarians into an unwarranted optimism, and also to thwart any vexatious United Nations resolutions, at least before the time set for the overt intervention. That same day the United Nations Security Council at 3 P.M. New York time (9 P.M. in Budapest) again considered the Hungarian Question after six days of recess. More than two full days had passed since the Hungarian Premier's appeal based on Hungary's invasion by Soviet forces. Four hours later, upon the Soviet representative's assurances that negotiations were under way between Hungarian and Soviet delegations concerning the withdrawal of Soviet troops from Hungary, the Question was again adjourned. Four hours after that, the all-out Soviet onslaught was to be launched.

By November 3 the Soviet forces had occupied all the points needed as bases of operations. They had surrounded Budapest, cut off the main roads leading toward the West, and put up stations near important industrial centers and Hungarian garrisons. In addition to the four divisions employed for the first armed intervention, another seven divisions have been identified as operating during the second phase of the military action.[35] An even greater number of reserves were kept in readiness.[36] The political setting of the coup had also been completed. General Serov, Chief of the Soviet State Security Authority (KGB), had been dispatched to Hungary to take charge of operations leading to the speedy suppression of resistance. His first action was the arrest of the Hungarian military delegation at the midnight session of the commission discussing the withdrawal of troops in Soviet military headquarters at Tököl. General Pál Maléter, the Hungarian Minister of Defense; General István Kovács, Chief of the General Staff; and Colonel Miklos Szücs were taken prisoner despite their immunity under international law as negotiators accredited by their government, an act that brought disgrace on the Soviet Army.[37]

The imminence of Soviet armed action was first realized by members of the Nagy government when communications between the Prime Ministry and the Hungarian military delegation were interrupted. Nagy ordered the delegation to return, but in vain.[38] When

Soviet forces entered Budapest and concentrated around a block known to be manned by Freedom Fighters, the Prime Minister still refused to give orders to shoot.[39] Only when a Soviet artillery barrage rendered the situation all too obvious did Imre Nagy approach the microphone at 5:30 A.M. to make an historic pronouncement:

This is Imre Nagy speaking, the President of the Council of Ministers of the Hungarian People's Republic. Today at daybreak Soviet troops attacked our capital with the obvious intention of overthrowing the legal Hungarian democratic government. Our troops are in combat. The Government is at its post. I notify the people of our country and the entire world of this fact.[40]

The Prime Minister only referred to facts and did not request help, although he has been accused — and condemned — for having called for "an overt and armed intervention of the Western imperialists against the Revolutionary Worker-Peasant Government and against the Soviet troops whose assistance had been requested by the said Government." [41]

What might have been the idea of Nagy when making his broadcast? It was the same belief in intangibles which had prompted him to resort to his declaration of neutrality. Since the stand of his government and the fate of the Revolution, he realized, would become hopeless as soon as the Soviet Union had made up its mind to crush Hungarian independence, he placed his hope in *historic imponderables:* in Western pressures and their unforeseeable effect on the Soviet mind; in Soviet restraint moved by reasons of farsighted perspicacity; in a new *volte-face* within the Soviet Presidium caused by an ideological or realistic assessment of the consequences. There was really nothing else for him to do, unless he was prepared to join hands with those who were ready to serve Moscow. It was said that the Prime Minister had to choose, at this moment, between his Hungarian national sentiment and Communism as prescribed by the Kremlin.[42] In reality, Imre Nagy had made his choice when, after his dismissal in 1955 and his expulsion from the Party, he had repudiated in his writings any Soviet claim to supremacy over other Communist parties and other nations. He had sought the implementation of this doctrine with patience and determination. He had shown utmost moderation toward Soviet claims and susceptibilities; it was the Revolution and the different groups of revolutionaries as well as rightist members of the Party who had led him to translate his concepts into action. Nevertheless, he was glad "to ride out the crest of the revolutionary tide," [43] as this direction mostly coincided with his ideas. He had been wavering on the multiparty issue, but much less so on the question of neutrality for Hungary. Concerning Soviet intervention he never wavered, since he had acquired the clear vision that Soviet interference was the main cause of all the evil in East-Central Europe.

Shortly before leaving the Parliament building for the last time he dictated a statement which later found its way into the United Nations official records. The statement was reproduced by a witness, and may not be a literal version of Nagy's words, but in essence it rings with evident authenticity, in the light of his known conduct at that juncture and later. We may take this as his genuine last testament:

This fight is the fight for freedom by the Hungarian people against the Russian intervention, and it is possible that I shall only be able to stay at my post for one or two hours. The whole world will see how the Russian armed forces, contrary to all treaties and conventions, are crushing the resistance of the Hungarian people. They will also see how they are kidnapping the Prime Minister of a country which is a Member of the United Nations, taking him from the capital, and therefore it cannot be doubted at all that this is the most brutal form of intervention. I should like in these last moments to ask the leaders of the revolution, if they can, to leave the country. I ask that all that I have said in my broadcast, and what we have agreed on with the revolutionary leaders during meetings in Parliament, should be put in a memorandum and the leaders should turn to all the peoples of the world for help and explain that today it is Hungary and tomorrow or the day after tomorrow, it will be the turn of other countries because the imperialism of Moscow does not know borders, and is only trying to play for time.[44]

The emotion evident in these words is understandable, in view of all that happened on that morning. The Prime Minister and members of his entourage — availing themselves of a standing invitation extended a few days earlier — took refuge in the Yugoslav embassy. Cardinal Mindszenty found shelter in the legation of the United States. Some members of the cabinet stayed in the Parliament building until the Soviet forces arrived and occupied the premises of the Prime Ministry.

The National Guard and a few military units, outnumbered and outflanked by Soviet forces, which this time appeared intent on ruthlessly crushing any armed resistance, fought for several days in Budapest and turned to guerrilla warfare thereafter, as described earlier. Workers' units put up heroic resistance in industrial suburbs and towns.[45] The armed resistance collapsed mostly because of lack of ammunition rather than complete defeat of the defenders. Close to two hundred thousand refugees — a great many of them Freedom Fighters — managed to escape to Austria, and after the closing of that border, to Yugoslavia. Armed resistance came to an end around November 14, though passive and political resistance continued. The Revolution that had originated in an armed revolt and drawn much of its strength from the readiness of its supporters to fight and die, could hardly survive the physical suppression of its resistance by overwhelming force.

CONCLUDING COMMENTS ON THE REVOLUTION

It would be presumptuous to try to explain the meaning of the Hungarian Revolution in a few words or to fit it into any of the known categories of revolutions. The world has witnessed national, democratic, and social revolutions, those directed against internal autocracies and those against foreign oppressors. The Hungarian Revolution bears characteristics of all these revolutionary patterns; and while being essentially a popular revolution it included, too, within its short history a revolution within the Communist Party, a fact which induced some commentators to describe it as some expression of "national Communism." [46] Were we to portray this Revolution through the mirror of its central personality, Prime Minister Nagy, the picture obtained would lend itself even less to sharp classification. The positions the Revolution wished to achieve and had actually attained varied in the course of its short term from October 23 to November 4. It has rightly been said that there were different "Imre Nagys," [47] but there were different phases of the Revolution too. A complicated political and social process, as the Hungarian Revolution proved to be, can only be analyzed when dissected into its various chronological stages and functional components; we have tried in earlier chapters to comply with this task, and here we wish to sum up the results of the analysis and evaluation.

The Yugoslav secession from the Soviet bloc was not a popular revolt; it was the revolt of the Yugoslav Communist Party against Soviet supremacy. The Polish October was an internal revolutionary action of the Polish Communist Party with the aim of emancipating it from an oppressive domination of the Soviet Communist Party. Both were expressions of "national Communism." In Hungary, a popular revolt, using revisionist and national Communist slogans, tried to provoke a change in Party leadership. After the attack by Soviet forces, the national character of the uprising became more obvious, and under its pressure and success, a revolution took place within the Party itself, catapulting into leadership the national Communist elements. From October 26 to October 30 the government of Hungary may, indeed, be considered a national Communist government. During the next few days it could not be considered Communist at all.

The national revolutionary movement brought into effective power broad popular strata of the population, which appeared no longer committed to Communism of any denomination. Many revisionist revolutionaries, having given up a painful dissimulation, also revealed themselves as democratic nationalists. The multiparty system adopted by the weight of the popular demand dethroned a disintegrated Communist Party from its monopoly of power. After October 30, Hungary ceased to be guided by a Communist government; it had become a multiparty democracy, with free elections and a parliamentary system in prospect. The reformed Communist Party, having accepted democratic multiparty rule, appears to have given up claims for the dictatorship of the proletariat: it had become a democratic Communist Party. Public opinion categorically rejected the one-party rule, and emphatically required political and personal liberties, but appeared to be willing to maintain existing Socialist institutions, especially the Socialist ownership of mining and big industry. National resentment against Soviet interference strongly burst forth in demands for a neutral and uncommitted status for Hungary.

The popular demands fitted exceedingly well into the conceptual framework of the Prime Minister. The only exception to this was the effective multiparty system. Nagy, in his writings, while admitting the possibility of other parties, seemed to insist on the leadership of a Communist Party. Even here, however, the leading role of the Party was not to be restricted to leading the proletariat like a "military General Staff." The Party had to establish "a close and lasting relationship . . . [with] the widest possible segment of the non-Party masses." [48]

As for the other popular demands, when he listened to the *vox populi* he must have had the impression he was listening to his own voice. He was always against an ossified interpretation of Marxism-Leninism, and considered the interpretation that had been applied within the Soviet Union to be inapplicable outside that country. He insisted on a national adaptation of "Socialism." He had even foreseen a merger of capitalistic and Socialist structures. An edition of his dissertation published in Paris in the Hungarian language contains the remarkable statement that "the conditions of

Socialism are ripening and to a certain extent already existing in capitalism; thus there are certain elements of Socialism already in capitalism just as various remnants of capitalism survive for a long time in Socialism." [49]

He absolutely disapproved of a dichotomous world picture. Hungary's neutrality between the two contending power groups had always been the cherished idea to which he gave eloquent expression in his writings. The following passage written in January 1956 throws light on his later willingness to repudiate the Warsaw Treaty: "The Hungarian people have become convinced by the terrible experiences of the two world wars that they cannot and must not become participants in the rivalries of free power groups."[50]

Imre Nagy always considered himself a Communist. He has often been described as a national Communist, but if we insist on styling him and his ideas as such we are compelled to emphasize that his brand of national Communism differed essentially from that of both Tito and Gomulka.[51] As a result of free elections in Hungary, Imre Nagy and the rejuvenated Communist Party would probably have been rejected by large masses of the people, but we can conjecture that many of his ideas would have survived.

Protagonists and ideas of the Hungarian Revolution have been slandered as fascist, reactionary, and counterrevolutionary by their antagonists of the Soviet and Kádár regimes. On the other hand, unbiased observers tend to discover in the Hungarian experience an attempt at a synthesis, in the Hegelian terms, of rival socio-economic world systems,[52] or, to quote Djilas, "a new phenomenon, perhaps no less meaningful than the French or Russian Revolutions." [53] The correct assessment of the Hungarian Revolution of 1956 will certainly remain a current topic of discussion — on both sides of the Iron Curtain. In the Soviet orbit, official Party propaganda undertakes and will undertake to belittle and denigrate its content and import, but the popular imagination, especially in Hungary herself, is bound to develop an idealized and idolatrized view of its aims and achievements. The criteria of "Socialist acceptability" developed by the postrevolutionary regime will one day boomerang against them by giving greater weight and circulation to its libertarian antithesis. The last phase of the Revolution — the open national effort to resist Soviet Russian aggression and defend the country's freedom — was inspired by nationalistic motivation. Therefore the legend of the Hungarian Revolution will survive in the minds of Hungarians and other satellite populations as a national struggle against an arrogant and oppressive foreign foe. It is unlikely that the Kádár regime or any other will ever be able to efface this image from the memory of present or future generations. History proves that the legend of past national glories and sufferings becomes even more vivid and compelling in later decades than immediately after the events themselves. The memories of the Hungarian fight for freedom of 1848–49, and the Napoleonic inspiration in France both acquired a greater political and social significance under generations that were not active participants in the historic happenings that inspired their souls and conditioned their deeds.

THE FIFTH PHASE

Aftermath of a Revolution
1 9 5 7 – 1 9 6 1

Solitudinem faciunt, pacem appellant
They make a wasteland, calling it peace.

TACITUS

26

Consolidation, Restoration, and Repression

/\.\/\

An intelligent victor will, whenever possible, present his demands
to the vanquished in installments.

HITLER

Soviet military might had swept away the Hungarian multiparty government and after ten days of fighting suppressed all open
armed resistance. With the elimination of the source and mainstay of
the short-lived Hungarian independence and freedom — the fighters
of the Revolution — and in the absence of a restored and consoli-
dated Hungarian Communist regime, Soviet military administration
had to step in temporarily to fill the vacuum thus created. But at
the same time remnants of the revolutionary organizations still
survived, albeit precariously, until the "new" Communist Party
and the Revolutionary Worker-Peasant Government were able to
gain a more solid footing in the country.

To forestall renewed repercussions the Kádár regime only gradually imposed its rule and that of the Communist Party over the
Hungarian masses. To this end it did not refrain from using decep-
tions of a manifold character that were also employed by its Soviet
protector. Following the consolidation of Party control and Security
Police surveillance, it had begun, by the summer of 1957, to resort
to harsher measures of repression. The internal resistance slowly
faded under the increasing pressure, and once again assumed the
role of a disguised and concealed opposition. The Kádár regime,
by the end of its first anniversary of tenure, had succeeded in re-
establishing its control and authority, but it was unable to dispense

with the Soviet forces stationed in the country, and these were its ultimate support.

SOVIET MILITARY ADMINISTRATION

The new Kádár regime claimed that the Nagy government had been overthrown by a "revolutionary counterattack of popular Hungarian forces with the assistance of Soviet troops." [1] The United Nations Special Committee, on the other hand, stated that "there is no evidence that during the fighting from 4 to 11 November there were any soldiers or groups of Hungarians, whether organized or unorganized, who fought against each other." [2] All fighting took place exclusively between Hungarians and Soviet armed forces; a limited number of Hungarian Security Police personnel had placed themselves at the disposal of the Soviet Command, but these rendered only noncombatant services.

When the fighting stopped there was generally no central or local Hungarian administration to transmit instructions and orders to the population or otherwise perform governmental duties. For four days after the original announcement of the new Revolutionary Worker-Peasant Government (when the Soviet forces struck on November 4) its representatives remained silent. They did not reach Budapest until November 7, at which time they were sworn in by István Dobi,[3] the ever-ready Chairman of the Presidential Council, who during the preceding ten days had also sworn in the various incarnations of the Imre Nagy government. But even after weeks of residence in Budapest, the Kádár government was still impotent and totally dependent on the Soviet armed forces that had enabled it to enter the capital. Maintenance of order and the provision for urgent administrative needs, where no longer in the hands of functioning revolutionary organs, fell to Soviet military commanders who, seemingly without much hesitation, were ready to assume the tasks. Their assumption of a civil role was tantamount to an admission of the lack of popular support for the new government.

Soviet military commanders issued orders for the maintenance of order, for regulating the hours of curfew, for arranging food supplies, for the resumption of work and the continued service of public utilities. Such orders were known to have been issued in the cities of Szombathely, Pécs, Miskolc, and Nyíregyháza.[4] On November 6, Major General of the Guards Grebennik, the military commander of Budapest, "with a view to re-establishing order and normal life in Budapest" issued instructions to the populace. He also prescribed that "everyone must unconditionally obey the patrols of the Soviet

Military Command and carry out their instructions and orders without question." [5]

Since most of the Soviet military orders remained unheeded, they were followed by reprisals and sanctions carried out by the Soviet Army and their security organs. In many cases the Soviet military authorities took over telephone exchanges and radio stations, issued permits to cars, delivered exit visas, and operated the railroads. They proceeded to arrest suspects, carried out summary executions, and surrounded barracks of the Hungarian Army, disarming the inmates and arresting the officers. The deportation to the Soviet Union of thousands of Hungarian citizens, many of them civilians who had not participated in the fight, was the subject of a resolution by the United Nations General Assembly on November 21.[6]

The Soviet Command ordered the dissolution of all "counterrevolutionary" national committees. Nevertheless, in many places revolutionary councils survived until the new government was able to substitute its own organs. The workers' councils were not disbanded by either the Soviet Command or the government, and they continued, after the second Soviet intervention, to control mines and factories, in fact the whole industrial life of the country. Since the resumption of work depended on the councils, the Soviet Command was compelled to have dealings with these revolutionary institutions. During the first two weeks following the elimination of the Nagy government, Soviet officers, often with the help of tanks or guards that were placed in factories, tried to persuade, intimidate, or force members of the workers' councils to induce the factory workers to resume work. These attempts were mostly unsuccessful; only a limited number of workmen returned.

The coordination between the Soviet Command and the Kádár cabinet seemed far from perfect during those weeks. Kádár and his colleagues principally tried persuasion where the Soviet Command resorted to threats; promises made by the former were mostly belied by the actions of the latter. Members of the workers' councils who were finally able to contact Kádár in the Parliament building, where he was surrounded by Soviet officers and advisers, clearly perceived that, like themselves, the Revolutionary Worker-Peasant Government was closely supervised by the Soviet Command.

Although the Soviet Command soon availed itself of the voluntary help of Hungarian Security Police personnel, the army's clumsiness and deficient knowledge of persons and affairs prevented it from effective work of consolidation, beyond the suppression of open, armed resistance. After the middle of November the Soviet Command conceded more and more authority to the Kádár government, and only intervened when it disagreed with government instructions or when Kádár needed physical assistance in the implementation of his plans. Such interventions were frequent, however, at first. It seems that Kádár was even encouraged at this time by the Soviet authorities to make empty promises for the sake of placating the regime's foes and for promoting the much required consolidation of the country. It also appears that Kádár and his government were obtaining advice from Soviet civilian sources rather than from the Military Command. In this period of reduced Soviet interference in Hungarian internal matters Kádár and his government were assisted by the Soviet Security forces in struggling with the workers' councils. After January 1957 direct Soviet military administration slowly disappeared. Many signs of an "enemy" occupation would, however, be felt for a considerable time to come.

THE REVOLUTIONARY WORKER-PEASANT GOVERNMENT

In the early morning hours of November 4, 1956, Ferenc Münnich had delivered a radio message, transmitted by some unknown station, announcing that he and three of his colleagues, members of the Nagy government, had broken off relations with that government on November 1 and initiated the formation of the Hungarian Revolutionary Worker-Peasant Government.[7] The speaker said that he and his friends were prompted to act thus because the government of Imre Nagy "had come under the pressure of reaction and become impotent."

Later in the morning János Kádár's appeal was heard on the radio announcing the program of the government.[8] He praised the achievements of the past twelve years but admitted that, at the same time, the clique of Rákosi and Gerö had committed "grave mistakes and gravely violated legality." The reactionaries had then "raised their hands" against the People's Democracy, misled many honest workers and "particularly the major part of the youth." And so, honest patriots had joined the movement aiming at the supposed strengthening of Hungary as a sovereign state. For this reason "it is wrong and criminal" to accuse them of having taken part in the revolt. But subsequent excesses had been committed by the counterrevolutionary forces utilizing the weakness of the Nagy government, and the time had now come to put an end to the counterrevolution. The points of Kádár's governmental program had largely been borrowed from the programs of Nagy's successive cabinets and from popular demands presented in the course of the Revolution. Thus we see assurances concerning Hungary's national independence, the democratic and Socialist system, the management of factories by the workers, the abolition of compulsory deliveries by the farmers, the cessation of pressures to join cooperatives, and democratic elections. No mention is made, however, of a multiparty system. The government is further said to have requested the Soviet Army "to help the nation in smashing the sinister forces of reaction and restoring order and calm in the country." Kádár promised that after the restoration of calm and order his government would open negotiations with the Soviet government and with other participants of the Warsaw Treaty about the withdrawal of Soviet forces from Hungary.

Originally the government headed by Kádár as Prime Minister included only seven other members: Ferenc Münnich was Minister of the Armed Forces and Public Security Forces; György Marosán, Minister of State; Imre Horváth, Minister of Foreign Affairs; István Kossa, Minister of Finance; Antal Apro, Minister of Industry; Imre Dögei, Minister of Agriculture; and Sándor Ronai, Minister of Commerce. After the cabinet had set up its headquarters in Budapest, Kádár experienced considerable difficulty in trying to persuade influential Communists to join his government.

Kádár also undertook to "broaden" his cabinet by including representatives of the three other "coalition" parties, the Smallholders, the Social Democrats, and the Petöfi (National Peasant) Party. He assured them he was ready to start negotiations with Imre Nagy should the latter consent to leave his place of asylum, the Yugoslav embassy in Budapest. Kádár conferred with Zoltán Tildy of the Smallholders, Professor István Bibo of the Petöfi Party, and an unidentified leader of the Social Democrats; the talks seemed to be progressing well when the plan for a coalition government was unexpectedly vetoed by Soviet officials, and also by the Soviet Command.[9] This happened in the second half of November, at approximately the same time as another event that damaged the Kádár regime — the abduction of Imre Nagy.

The Yugoslav government, as soon as it was able to approach the Premier of the new Hungarian government, made several propositions for solving the problem raised by the asylum of Imre Nagy and his associates in the Yugoslav embassy. Yugoslavia suggested that Nagy and his friends should either be allowed to return unmolested to their homes or else be allowed to proceed to Yugoslavia. Kádár, on the other hand, prompted by the Soviet Union, offered Nagy and his group asylum in one of the Socialist countries (preferably Rumania). Another alternative was that they should volunteer self-criticism and declare themselves for the Revolutionary Worker-Peasant Government. The latter suggestion, in particular, was made to both Imre Nagy and Losonczy; both the Soviets and Kádár attached special importance to a renunciation by these two leaders of their national Communism and reformism. Kádár's offers were rejected by the Nagy group. On November 21, Kádár gave the written guarantee, requested from him by Yugoslavia, of a "safe conduct" to their homes and immunity from arrest.[10]

The Yugoslav government appears to have been very eager to dispose quickly of the Imre Nagy issue — a source of acute embarrassment. It must have been aware, however, that without a Soviet commitment Kádár's guarantee would be of little value.* At any rate, when Nagy and his associates left the Yugoslav embassy on November 22, they were at once kidnapped by Soviet military personnel and taken to some unknown destination.

Tito's government protested to Kádár and expressed its surprise to the Soviet government for having prevented "the implementation of the above-mentioned agreement which was to have provided a friendly settlement of a disputed issue." The Kádár government insisted that Imre Nagy and his party had voluntarily left for Rumania.

The Nagy story demonstrates the impotency of the Kádár regime in November 1956 and the position of duplicity in which it was placed by Soviet orders. It also demonstrates the dangerousness of the former Prime Minister and his close advisers from the Soviet point of view. Whereas leaders of the other coalition parties were still allowed to move about freely and negotiate, heretic Communists, like Nagy and Losonczy, were outlawed by the Hungarian regime. They were said to be "guests" of Rumania, but it will appear that their status was of a very special kind.

Despite the revulsion created by Nagy's kidnapping, the three coalition parties were still ready to discuss with Kádár their possible inclusion in the government. And Kádár sorely needed their participation in order to regain a modicum of popular support; he must have known that the vast majority of the country regarded him as a traitor to the national cause and a Soviet stooge. A plan drafted by

* It has also been suggested that Yugoslav officials had a foreknowledge of what was going to happen to Nagy before he and his group left the embassy building; see Richard Lowenthal, "Tito's Affair with Khrushchev," *The New Leader*, Oct. 6, 1958, p. 15.

Professor Bibo, a Minister of State in the Nagy cabinet, had obtained a wide circulation after November 9, and had been endorsed on November 14 by the newly established Workers' Council of Greater Budapest. The Bibo proposal, entitled "A Plan to Solve the Hungarian Question on a Compromise Basis," relied on the assumption that the Soviet government, in view of the passive resistance which its troops had encountered and the difficulties of the Kádár regime, could be persuaded to release Hungary from the Warsaw Treaty under certain international guarantees.[11] The non-Communist parties, on December 8, drafted and submitted a ten-point program which was intended to be their condition of cooperation with the Kádár government; they would go no further than to recognize that the Communists must play "an important" though not "leading" role.[12] On the same day, however, the Hungarian Socialist Workers Party (as the Communist Party had called itself since November 1) resolved not to surrender any share of its authority to other parties.[13] The situation still remained fluid, and contacts between Kádár and non-Communist Party leaders were still maintained; the decision whether monopolistic Communist Party rule should be re-established evidently rested with the paramount power, the Soviet Union. And the Soviet Union, through its spokesman, Suslov, had given to understand on the anniversary of the Bolshevik Revolution that for all Socialist states the establishment of political rule by the vanguard of the working class, that is, the Party, remained the supreme principle.[14]

Kádár's attempts to re-establish Party unity and create multiparty assent to his regime coincided with the ideological battle fought between Polish adherents of "domesticism," on the one hand, and Soviet, Czechoslovak, and East German leaders condemning national Communism and the imitation of the "Yugoslav road," on the other.[15] The dispute, waged in the shadow of the Hungarian events, was not again to be allowed to penetrate into Hungarian intra-Party circles, where it had already proved explosive. The Soviet Union, being in the position to enforce its will by the presence of its armed forces, was intent not to permit any further deviation from the strict Moscow-inspired Party line or any insubordination against Soviet leadership of World Communism. Five Communist Party leaders (Soviet, Bulgarian, Czechoslovak, Rumanian, and Hungarian), held a meeting in the battered city of Budapest between January 1 and 4, 1957, the purpose of which was to impress upon the Hungarian Communist leaders surrounding Kádár the correct way to handle the affairs of the Hungarian Party and of their country. The dissenting member of the Soviet camp, Poland, was absent. The Soviet Party was represented by Khrushchev, apparently somewhat discredited by the revolutionary events in Hungary, and by his rival, Malenkov, who, it was being rumored, would soon succeed the former in the Party leadership. The meeting was also to emphasize the collective character of the pressure put upon Kádár and associates as distinguished from unilateral Soviet insistence.

The dilemma for Kádár was whether to try to appease Hungarian resentment already violently provoked by the brutality of Soviet intervention, or to resort to Stalinist measures of repression and terror. He had been told by his Soviet and other comrades to choose repression if persuasion should not be sufficient. Furthermore, he was dissuaded from any attempts at collaboration with other parties except with the clear understanding of the Communist Party's undisputed leadership. He was also told to refuse to recognize any split in the political representation of the working class, and to re-establish the monopoly of Communist Party rule in factories, mines, local administration, and all other activities.

On January 5, well briefed by the Budapest meeting, Kádár made a declaration on the "major tasks" facing his regime. This time it was no more the "weakness" of Imre Nagy but "his treachery" that had opened the road to the counterrevolution. Kádár now clearly stated that the aim of the government was to promote the dictatorship of the proletariat; political activity was to be the privilege of the Communist Party and of persons who, though non-Party, were ready to follow its lead and policy. Consequently, policy direction might emanate from the Party only. And the People's Patriotic Front, guided by the Party, "will unite all democratic forces." The Prime Minister and Party leader also asserted that henceforward directors of enterprises would be appointed by the government (and no longer elected by the workers' councils) and would be responsible to the government alone. He made no mention of negotiations for a withdrawal of the Soviet forces. Kádár offered, however, to admit to important posts members of other parties or non-Party persons who were prepared to accept his policies and support proletarian dictatorship.[16]

The most urgent problem of the government was the liquidation of the institutional residue of the Revolution. The hardening of the Kádár regime's attitude, in accordance with the directions received from the Communist leaders' meeting, had the effect of solving this problem. The Kádár group also attempted to destroy the *spiritual* residue of the Revolution by imposing a proper interpretation of revolutionary events. In both institutional and intellectual matters relating to the Revolution, Kádár displayed a gradualism which was reminiscent, to some extent, of what Rákosi had once called "salami tactics" (slice by slice). Until the beginning of January Kádár inspired hopes that a multiparty system might be re-established. With a straight face he uttered assurances such as the following statement to the representatives of the workers' councils on November 15, 1956: "We surrender the Party's monopoly: we want a multiparty system and clean and honest elections. We know that this will not be easy, because the workers' power can be destroyed not only by bullets but also by ballots. We must reckon with the fact that we might be thoroughly beaten at the elections, but we undertake the election fight because the Communist Party will have the strength to gain once more the confidence of the working masses." [17] He also kept alive the hope that other revolutionary achievements would be maintained: participants in the revolutionary events would not be prosecuted, compulsory instruction of the Russian language would not again be introduced, and so on. Later, however, he disavowed all these and other promises.

A natural assumption would be that Kádár was lying deliberately; but it appears likely that for some time he had hoped to be able to pursue a more liberal policy, and if so, he may have been honest in at least some of his pronouncements. The frivolity of his promises could be explained by the helpless and total dependency in which he found himself vis-à-vis the Soviets. He had never excelled as a man of principles. Kádár coupled a narrow, limited intellect with an astuteness for self-assertion. He was little equipped to fulfill the agonizing task of a satellite leader under the confused situation as it existed in postrevolutionary Hungary. His contacts with Soviet military and Party personnel were rendered even more awkward by his ignorance of the Russian language. He was nevertheless imbued with a longing for power. After his sufferings in prison he wished to minimize the hazards of satellite Communist leadership. To follow the guidance of the Soviet comrades must have appeared to him as the safest way both toward power and security — if only these comrades would always clearly express what they wanted him to do and never withdraw their protecting hand as they almost seemed to have done during the desperate days of the Revolution. When Kádár was clearly given to understand that Hungary and her Communist Party had to be aligned to the "faithful" People's Democracies and avoid falling into her prerevolutionary errors or the errors of Yugoslavia, when it became clear to him that he should not try to imitate even Gomulka, the path to follow remained no longer doubtful.

LIQUIDATION OF THE REMAINS OF "DUAL POWER"

The Kádár regime's gradualism and Pavlovian tactics in the liquidation of "dual power" — that is, power exercised simultaneously by revolutionary and "legal" institutions — were nowhere more apparent than in its dealings with the workers' councils. After the suppression of armed resistance these bodies continued to wield powers that made them serious rivals of a government supported by all the might of the Soviet Army. Even revolutionary councils and committees prolonged their existence for some time. A resolution of the Council of Ministers on November 12, 1956, even called for collaboration between revolutionary organs and competent local authorities, simultaneously inviting government and municipal employees to return to work. Revolutionary bodies were summoned to "purge from among their membership the counter-revolutionary elements hostile to the government and the social order." On December 8, the government reproached these bodies for "harming and impeding the activities of regular authorities" and decreed their immediate disbandment.[18]

To eliminate the workers' councils was not, however, such an easy task. After the installation of the Kádár government, the workers, fearful of a return of past exploitation and wishing to preserve the autonomy of their factories, rallied even more strongly to their freely elected councils. These independent organs even widened their scope of activity by creating broader territorial federations. On November 13 and 14 the workers' councils of the metropolitan area of Budapest set up the Greater Budapest Workers' Council, controlling practically all industries in the area, and empowered it to present the workers' demands to the government. During the ensuing conversations, Prime Minister Kádár made the reassuring promises, already quoted, concerning the multiparty system and free elections. The workers' representatives asked for a decree allowing them to organize a supreme national directorship of all workers' councils. Kádár, for his part, requested that they refrain from work stoppages. These parleys extended for some weeks while the deadlock continued. The government tried to re-establish Communist Party cells in the factories, to recruit a workers' militia (mostly among former AVH members), and to intimidate the councils by arresting and torturing some of their members. The Greater Budapest Workers' Council replied by declaring new strikes, whereupon the government declared that incitement to strike was a counterrevolutionary act, and that the Greater Budapest Workers' Council as well as all subordinate councils above the factory level must be dissolved.[19] The Council responded by staging a general strike on December 9 and 10. This was followed by the arrest of Sándor Rácz and Sándor Bali, the Chairman and Secretary of the Greater Budapest Workers' Council, which thus came to an end.

The individual workers' councils of Hungary by then had been deprived of their control over factory funds; now they could no longer support striking members and their families. The infiltration of plants by former Party functionaries, the powers exercised by the government-appointed managers, the re-establishment of Party cells and of the spy system undermined the position of the councils. They could no longer protect the workers or exercise political authority. In vain did they try to prevent the imposition of a Party organization upon factories and mines, the mass arrests, and the torture of council members. Economic necessity finally broke the spirit and will of the resistance. On January 5, when Kádár's attitude was stiffening, a governmental decree reduced that activity of the workers' councils; their function was now "to elaborate the wage and bonus system" together with the government authorities, and to see "that workers adhere strictly to government instructions." Thereupon many councils refused to function, thus rendering their plants leaderless.[20]

Kádár's struggle to regain the confidence of the industrial workers had proved an impossible task. The workers had not failed to realize that their economic position, standard of living, and freedom were closely coupled to questions of national independence. The Kádár regime was determined to reduce wages, which had been raised during the Revolution. The workers' innate national sentiment had thus been strengthened by their self-interest; the wage struggle had now been added to their nationalist objectives. Kádár had promised that he would negotiate with the Russians about their withdrawal as soon as "order was re-established," but soon it was realized that Kádár's "order" meant the earlier form of Party rule with its pressures and intimidations. Consequently, the councils endeavored to prevent the return to the old order of things. Kádár, on the other hand, tried to turn the workers' councils into instruments of the Party; in this, however, he failed.

In the summer of 1957 the government was faced with the problem of whether to abolish the workers' councils altogether. Although their political importance had vanished, their mere existence was felt to be an embarrassment. As long as they were freely elected by the workers, they were still "operated by elements which made them servants of counter-revolutionary interests." [21] Nevertheless, the government wished to maintain the semblance of worker participation in the factory management. After some months of hesitation, on November 17, 1957, the government officially declared the workers' councils dissolved, and substituted "shop councils" for them. Two thirds of the members of these new councils were to be trade-union officials elected by the trade-union committee of the plant (which was controlled by the Party), and only the remaining one third was to be elected by workers. The plant manager, chief engineer, accountant, and the Party secretary were *ex officio* members of each shop council. They were given the tasks of "strengthening the dictatorship of the proletariat" as well as protecting public property.[22] The last remnant of revolutionary institutions of October 1956 had thus disappeared.

Revolutionary organizations of intellectuals had been dissolved in December 1956 after making desperate attempts to have their voices heard. On November 24 of that year, less than three weeks after the Soviet Army intervened to crush the Revolution, representatives of the Revolutionary Council of Intellectuals issued an appeal, signed by 110 leaders of Hungarian intellectual life, identifying themselves with "the heroes who are pursuing the battle for the freedom of Hungary." [23] In December several writers and journalists were arrested. Writers and journalists, except a few adherents of the regime, refused to write. The government undertook, by creating the State Information Office, to reorganize its regimentation of the press and of all literary work. Originally, a certain liberalism was maintained which allowed journalists a relative freedom of expression. By December, however, the government drastically intervened in all publications, exercising severe censorship and prohibiting many writers from publishing at all.

The Writers' Association, though not a revolutionary creation, had for a long time been the center of spiritual resistance. After the downfall of the Revolution, it again carried on the opposition struggle. On December 28, 1956, the Writers' Association held a session *in camera* and passed a resolution against the Kádár regime and its Soviet military origin. The meeting, by 150 to 8 votes, branded the Soviet intervention "a historic mistake." This session was rightly called the last "free meeting" in Hungary.[24] On January 17, 1957, in the wake of general increase of government pressure, the Writers' Association was temporarily suspended. It was finally dissolved by decree on April 21 for having "assaulted the Socialist system."

Lectures in the universities of Hungary could not be resumed until February 1957; even then, in the various universities and colleges 20 to 40 per cent of the student bodies were missing. In one case, the Faculty of Forestry in Sopron, teachers and students alike had fled the country. Communist youth organizing also had to be started afresh: on February 26, in the place of DISZ, the Federation of Communist Youth (KISZ) was set up, and the revolutionary organization of students, the MEFESZ, was banned. The university youth, among the foremost promoters of the demonstrations leading to the Revolution, were now recognized by the regime as its potentially most violent enemy. Their number was reduced even further by the exclusion of openly hostile elements, and by forbidding admittance to students of bourgeois descent beginning in October 1957. Marosán, the Minister of State, had complained on January 29 that the universities were exploited by reactionary and counter-revolutionary elements; consequently, the teaching of Marxism-Leninism had to be intensified.[25]

By the latter half of 1957 the attitude of each individual toward the Revolution of 1956 had become the decisive criterion for obtaining any emoluments or position from the government or a public institution. The "meaning" of the Revolution had thus become an outstanding factor in intra-Party relations, and dictated the standing of persons in the eyes of the regime.

GRADUALISM AND SELECTION IN REPRESSION

Kádár, in his speech of November 4, 1956, had pledged on behalf of his government that it "would not tolerate the persecution of workers under any pretext, for having taken part in the most recent events." [26] These promises were reiterated personally by Kádár in the course of November, and special assurances were given to Imre Nagy and his associates regarding their past activities.[27] Meanwhile the Soviet military authorities, aided by their AVO lieutenants, were not only hunting down armed opponents but also exercising punitive measures — haphazardly and sporadically — against civilians. After the gradual withdrawal of the Soviet military regime the Kádár government, with the help of its hurriedly reorganized Security Police (called "R-groups," or "Security Force Regiments"), staffed mostly by former members of the ill-famed AVH, began to round up those who either still were overtly resisting or "conspiring" against the regime. Also arrested — generally on the basis of private denunciations — were persons who had committed some individual violent action during the Revolution. The rounding up of prisoners who had been released during the revolutionary days also commenced.[28]

"Simplified" criminal procedures to deal with murder, intentional manslaughter, arson, robbery, and looting had been decreed on November 12, 1956. Later, on December 11, the reticence against formally declaring martial law was given up, and the government decreed summary proceedings before a military court against perpetrators of the above "counterrevolutionary crimes," as well as persons in possession of firearms without license and conspirators in general, apprehended in the act. Death sentence had to be passed whenever the accused was found guilty. On January 15, 1957, an "accelerated criminal trial procedure" was introduced; this was to extend not only to the crimes previously listed but also to the damaging of public utilities or "other establishments declared indispensable by the government"; to "organizing against the People's Republic or against the people's democratic order"; and to "revolt" and "treason." Whereas the court-martial had to sentence to death the persons found guilty, judges under the accelerated procedure could hand down prison sentences of not less than five years, with the right to appeal; on the other hand the death penalty could be imposed not only against adults but against juvenile defendants.[29] Special benches of the ordinary courts had been given jurisdiction under the accelerated procedural rules. A decree issued on April 6, 1957, created in the Supreme Court of Hungary a special People's Court Bench to conduct summary trials, either as a court of first and last instance, and to act as appeal court to supervise sentences of lower courts. This special tribunal was empowered to re-try cases already tried by other courts. The Chief Public Prosecutor was empowered to select the court (either of a lower echelon or the special bench in the Supreme Court) he wished for the conduct of the trial.[30]

Equipped with such an array of summary procedural weapons, the government slowly extended the circle of those it wished to bring to trial, not only for current opposition to the regime, but for activities carried out in the Revolution. These procedures had retroactive application, and, starting about January 1957, participation by mouth or by deed in the revolutionary movement was considered unlawful; therefore practically the entire nation could have been brought to trial. Since this was neither possible nor expedient, it remained for the government and its agencies of prosecution to select the persons it wished to be condemned, either to death or to imprisonment. The initial restraint that had been observed by the Kádár regime in prosecuting participants in the "counterrevolution" had been entirely abandoned by the summer of 1957. The selection of those to be prosecuted seemed to depend on their attitude *subsequent* to the Revolution (unless they had committed some outstanding "crime" or had played a leading role in the events). Otherwise many Party members, now ostentatiously supporting the Kádár regime, could have been incriminated. János Kádár himself could have been indicted on charges for which Imre Nagy was later sentenced to death: he had voted for the introduction of the multiparty system, and had, in his capacity of Minister, endorsed the declaration of neutrality and praised the Revolution as a "popular uprising." Clearly, certain selections had to be made and were made, leaving a large part of the population in constant fear and making them dependent on the good will of the government.

The machinery for punishment of the "counterrevolutionaries" took some time to rumble into full operation. For one thing the prisons became overcrowded. Besides, there was a problem with the judiciary. With the Revolution and the disintegration of the Communist Party, the Courts of Justice (along with the army, police, and even Security Police) had temporarily ceased to be the willful tools of the regime. Ordinarily, the "independence" of Communist courts, although constitutionally decreed, is simply another façade, like the democracy of elections, for concealing the real state of affairs. Communist courts may be independent of the government but they are not independent of the Party. They are just as subject to Party instructions as are other administrative organs; the courts also have Party organizations and Party cells, as well as Party secretaries. However, as a consequence of the Revolution, the Party organizations in the Hungarian Courts of Justice had evaporated as in all other sections of the community. Thus the "independent" courts had become genuinely independent during the Revolution, and as long as the newly reorganized Communist Party was unable to extend its grip over the courts, again, many judges shrank back from the implementation of the repressive measures against the "counterrevolutionaries," whom they, no doubt, regarded as national heroes rather than criminals.

Soon the government found that the courts were not properly fulfilling the punitive tasks that fell upon them: persons were acquitted or sentences were too lenient. Minister Münnich at a conference of law court presidents in February 1957 openly complained that "some judges and courts have been very reluctant to resume work. They are evidently under the influence of the principles of the independence of judges . . . which was misinterpreted by many people." And the acting Minister of Justice, Ferenc Nezvál, explained that "the most important task of the court is to defend and strengthen the People's Democratic State order, to pass sentence in the spirit of the class struggle . . . against subversive counter-revolutionary elements." And the Chief Public Prosecutor, Géza Szénási, added: "Legality must fully correspond to the interest of the dictatorship of the proletariat." [31]

Oppressive measures against political opposition other than arrest and trial before courts were available to the Kádár regime. These were: internment (forced labor) and police surveillance often coupled with deportation to another part of Hungary. Internment camps had been dissolved at the beginning of Imre Nagy's first premiership. A presidential decree of December 13, 1956, reintroduced this instrument of repression, providing that: "Whoever endangers public order or public security by his activity or behavior . . . may be interned." [32] The method of ordering internment, its length, and the conditions in which the internee was to live were subsequently made more and more severe. Beginning March 19, 1957, internments could be ordered by the police, subject to later approval by a state attorney, their duration became indefinite, and interned persons could be put to work. Police surveillance, with or without enforced domicile (deportation), could be imposed on any person considered "dangerous to the state, to public security or to the Socialist order . . . or disquieting important state interests . . . or detrimental for economic reasons." [33] Surveillance could be ordered by the police. Persons under surveillance, whether living in their ordinary domicile or confined to another residence, had their movements restricted and were not allowed to use the telephone.

Among the opponents of the postrevolutionary regime who were targets of these copious instruments of repression the most vigorous were the members of the working class, an industrial proletariat that now appeared violently hostile. The chief weapon of the proletariat as recognized by Marx — the strike — had been successfully utilized during the Revolution to enforce democratization of the regime, and also after the uprising had been crushed by the Soviet forces. The decree-law of January 15, 1957, that introduced the "accelerated criminal procedure" also instituted the crime of "intentionally disturbing the functioning" of factories of public interest (plants regularly employing 100 people or more) "by inciting others or calling upon others to strike." [34] Thus, the industrial strike had become an offense punishable by death — which it had never expressly been even under Rákosi, though strikers then had been prosecuted under various headings of the criminal law.

The new regime's foremost endeavor was the reconstitution and reorganization of the Communist Party. Only with the help of a disciplined "vanguard" of workers aided by an efficient political police would they be able to dispense with the direct reliance on the Soviet Army, a condition which constantly reminded everybody of the primary source of the government's power and manifested all too overtly its satellite status.

27

The New "New Party" and Its Government

∧∨∧∨∧∨∧∨∧∨∧∨∧∨∧∨∧∨∧∨∧∨∧∨∧∨∧∨∧∨∧∨

He who fights for Communism must be able to fight and to renounce fighting, to say the truth and not to say the truth, to be helpful and unhelpful, to keep a promise and to break a promise, to go into danger and to avoid danger, to be known and to be unknown. He who fights for Communism has of all the virtues only one: that he fights for Communism.

BERTOLT BRECHT (East German Communist)

THE enormous problems and disadvantages with which the Kádár government had to cope during the first year of its tenure were partly compensated by the limited objectives it set at the beginning, and by its abundant use of both "gradualism" and of the *divide et impera* principle. The Pavlovian method as practiced by Kádár prescribed that all those forces or strata of the population which at the time of the suppression of the Revolution were not considered aggressive or otherwise dangerous should, at first, receive kid-glove treatment. Thus, in the beginning, farmers were favorites of the regime: the abolishment of compulsory deliveries, decreed during the Revolution, was maintained, and the Minister of Agriculture issued a decree on November 27, 1956, sanctioning the disbandment of kolkhozes.[1] The churches were spared: attending classes of religious instruction was favored.

From the experiences of prerevolutionary events the Kádár regime concluded that criticism and opposition from inside the Party could be far more dangerous than from outside the Party.

Accordingly, the new Party was to be based on elements which would not endanger its unity of purpose. However, the difficulties of restoring any Party machinery proved to be more formidable than expected, and therefore the pious endeavor to realize "ideological unity" had to be shelved for the sake of re-establishing Party rule at all.[2]

The paucity of leadership in the Party determined the composition of the government. The dangers implicit in any popular demonstration induced the government to postpone the elections that were due in the spring of 1957. Measures of consolidation achieved toward the end of that year made it possible to effect certain administrative changes, to hold elections in the fall of 1958, and even to convoke a Party Congress in 1959. As soon as the Party seemed organically reconstituted, more attention was devoted to the "ideological" attitude of members or of those the Party leadership wished to include among its ranks. Party "ideology" was throughout influenced by the experiences of the "counterrevolution" and also by the example of the Soviet Party. Kádár and his group aligned themselves so closely to Khrushchev's policies and leadership that the Kádár regime depended, for its stability, more heavily on the personal successes and prestige of Nikita Sergeyevich than any other Soviet satellite regime in East-Central Europe.

RESTORATION OF THE PARTY

The origin and name of the newest Party dates back to November 1, 1956, when the "disgraced" former Communist Party was considered dissolved, and the "Communists who fought against the despotism of Rákosi decided . . . to form a new Party."[3] But this Hungarian Socialist Workers Party of November 1, apart from its name, had little in common with its reincarnation on November 4. Only its voice was Jacob's — its hand was Esau's. Among the seven members of its original "preparatory committee" only Kádár himself survived. The other founding members (Imre Nagy, Donáth, Losonczy, Kopácsi, Lukács, and Szántó) were placed incommunicado after the second Soviet onslaught. The Party leadership, to efface the memories of its "doubtful origin," preferred to base its origin on the valiant act of the four "former members of the Imre Nagy government" who dissociated themselves from the Revolution and appealed for Soviet help. Kádár, together with Antal Apro, István Kossa, and Ferenc Münnich, formed the first directorate of the new "new Party." The four-member directorate co-opted more and more members to form a new Central Committee; and in

February 1957 the committee, consisting of 23 members, increased its number to 37 by further co-optation. An eleven-member Politburo continued to be the supreme source of authority.

In order to establish a proper organizational frame for the "new" Party a National Conference was called for June 27–29, 1957, in Budapest. This conference adopted the Party's new statute (by and large a replica of the "old" Party's statute of 1954) and annulled all the resolutions of the Hungarian Socialist Workers Party taken before November 4, 1956, because of their alleged opposition to Marxism-Leninism.

The foremost concern of the Party leadership was the reconstitution of the Party machinery and administration; for this purpose the membership had to be recruited anew. The Communist Party, which had claimed over 800,000 members before the Revolution, claimed only 100,000 in January 1957.[4] On May 5 the Party secretariat announced that the number of its members had increased to 300,000; at the same time it acknowledged that many former members were refusing to apply for readmittance.[5] During the month of April 118,-000 were said to have entered the Party; at that time the cadre system had been re-established making Party affiliation the prerequisite of a great number of jobs. The increase may also, however, represent a change of tactics by those who were hostile to the regime and now, giving way to increasing pressures, preferred to combat the Party from within. On September 11 it was announced that Party membership had further increased to 370,000 and "was stronger than the Hungarian Workers Party had ever been." [6] By subsequent increases the claimed membership reached 400,000 and stayed around that level. Kádár prided himself that the "new" Party was to become a "Party of the elite" and not that of numbers.[7] The greatest difficulties came in recruiting industrial workers and intellectuals. While the workers' councils were active they even managed to prevent the establishment of Party cells in the factories. Similar resistance against joining the Party came from the intellectuals.[8] In both cases nationalist and anti-Soviet motivations overshadowed opportunistic reasons or any ideological Communist conviction.

Before the Revolution half of the declared membership of 800,-000 comprised industrial workers, but the contribution of genuine workers to the membership is now relatively small. Of an alleged Party membership of 400,000, it is estimated that approximately 50,000 are functionaries of the Party; 130,000 are members of the new security agencies regrouping former members of the AVH, frontier guards, and militia men; and another 50,000 are government and municipal employees.[9] Thus more than half of the Party membership belongs to the class of the privileged, and less than half of the members are persons not directly and exclusively dependent on the Party or on the state for their material existence.

The leadership of the Party now is concentrated in the hands of Kádár and some of his personal friends. Notorious Stalinists have been debarred from holding Party or governmental key positions; but some weathercocks, having held leading positions both under Rákosi and also Nagy, have succeeded in preserving their status in the Party or government. But neither the Party nor the government could dispense with Rákosi supporters at the medium and lower levels; they are to be found in almost every post below the leadership and also among members of the Central Committee.

The key Party posts, at this writing, are held by Kádár, the First Secretary of the Party, and Gyula Kállai, a rising young member of the Politburo who seems headed for the highest governmental post, as we shall see later in our discussion of personnel changes in the government. Béla Biszku, Politburo Member and Minister of the Interior, appears to be third most powerful member of the Kádár team. György Marosán, former Minister of State, and later a Party Secretary, also belongs to this group though his star seems to have been waning since the Party Congress of December 1959.

Like Kádár, Kállai and Marosán had been imprisoned under Rákosi, and together with Biszku they appear to belong to the close personal entourage of Kádár. Other Politburo members after December 1959 (when the membership was increased to twelve) included Ferenc Münnich, the only muscovite member of the Politburo; Antal Apro, Károly Kiss, and Sándor Ronai, all of whom had served in high positions under Rákosi but had been able to befriend Kádár in good time. The remaining Politburo members were junior followers of Kádár, namely Jenö Fock (a Party Secretary), Lajos Fehér (the agricultural expert of the Party who had previously served under Imre Nagy), Miklos Somogyi, and Rezsö Nemes. The predominance of Kádár's personal friends or adherents on the Politburo clearly shows where the locus of power resides — always with the reservation, of course, that the ultimate power resides outside Hungary.

It has been intimated that the developments of June 1957 in the Soviet Union which permitted Khrushchev to "unmask the anti-Party plot" of Molotov, Kaganovich, and Malenkov, and to secure for himself the uncontested leadership of his country and of the entire Soviet bloc, greatly strengthened Kádár's position in the

Hungarian Party. A personal contact seems to have developed between Khrushchev and Kádár analogous to that which had existed between Stalin and Rákosi, but with the differences growing out of the characters of the persons involved. Khrushchev, who acted as godfather to the Kádár regime, may feel personally responsible for the success or failure of his protégé, whose country he more frequently honors with his visits than any other Soviet satrapy. (He visited Hungary in January 1957, April and June 1958, and December 1959.) The direct chain of communication between the Kremlin and the Hungarian Party's First Secretary is no less firm than it had been during the heyday of Stalinism. It may be even firmer, in view of Kádár's weakness of character compared with Rákosi's force and consummate political skill.

OPPOSITION WITHIN THE PARTY

The Party strives for "ideological unity," but the existence of rifts has been admitted. Factions, hardly concealed by the apparent conformism of the leading Party members, are prevalent within the Party. The danger of revisionism or rightism, on the one hand, and that of sectarianism or dogmatism, on the other, is continually stressed. The existence of these deviations was stated on September 11, 1957, by Károly Kiss, member of the Politburo. "At present," he said, "the chief danger in the political and ideological field is rightist opportunism and revisionism. But the dogmatic application of Marxism and Leninism and the sectarian policy arising from it constitute no less a danger." [10]

It has also been admitted that "misinterpretations" of nationalism have been causing much confusion in the people's minds since the Revolution; the "ideological remnants of the counter-revolution" have rendered the relation between the Party and the masses "extremely difficult." [11] Kádár himself stated that sectarianism "separated the Party from the masses." [12]

In the fall of 1957 the notion of rightist deviation was coupled with imprecations against Imre Nagy — presumably still somewhere in Rumania. These attacks became more virulent in December when the ideological monthly of the Soviet Communist Party, *Kommunist*, joined in and accused Nagy and "his accomplices" of having intended "to provoke a split in the Socialist camp by pitting one Communist Party against another," and of having tried, "by advancing the slogan of so-called 'national Communism,'" to undermine the unity of the Socialist countries.[13] The Hungarian Party press followed this up by proclaiming that "the Hungarian National Communists were misleading the masses and with their dangerous political ideas had infected the population. Against these *still effective revisionistic* tendencies, the ideological fight must be continued and strengthened" (italics added).[14]

Before Khrushchev's visit to Hungary in April 1958, newspapers and periodicals published many articles dealing with the unity of the Party. The danger of revisionism was again emphasized, though leftist deviations were not forgotten either. An article in the *Társadalmi Szemle* stated that "the most injurious thing is not to see clearly the difference between the errors and deviations of revisionism and dogmatism." The author further enlarged on these differences in saying:

Rákosi and his co-leaders did not always commit sectarian mistakes; their work was not always characterized by dogmatism . . . The 1956 counter-revolution in Hungary has shown in a very demonstrative manner, and in action, what revisionism is. The rightist Imre Nagy-Losonczy faction was fully revealed as a revisionist group which denied all basic principles of Marxism-Leninism . . . though it is true that leftist errors and leftist deviation created a favorable soil for revisionism.[15]

These and other statements revealed not only the political and ideological confusion which must have existed within the ranks of Party members, including the leadership, but also a rivalry for leadership between intra-Party groups. Statements made by Marosán and Apro appear to have supported a tougher line of policy while Kállai and Kiss took the same middle course favored by Kádár.

Khrushchev in Budapest praised the "correct policy of the Hungarian Socialist Workers Party and its Central Committee." He had even greater praise to bestow on Kádár, "who possessed the magnificent qualities of a fighter and a leader," and whose leadership "is a guarantee that the Party in the future will avoid the mistakes of the past." The Soviet leader also reminded his Hungarian audience of the ideological difficulties which had to be eliminated by the leadership of the "new" Party. These difficulties arose "on the one hand from the revisionist trends which gathered momentum within the Party, on the other, from the sectarian and dogmatic mistakes committed by the former leadership which had no longer been flexible enough and could no longer appraise the situation correctly enough; it was uncertain and hesitant in the implementation of the Party line."[16]

The joint statement signed by the Soviet and Hungarian Party leaders at the end of Khrushchev's trip in Hungary in April 1958 condemned "dogmatism and sectarianism within the working class and Communist movement." From Kádár's point of view, this statement served to persuade his "leftist" opposition that they should not count on Soviet support. The statement also underscored the "duty to continue the resolute struggle against revisionism" and warned "against the attempts of the enemy to make use of nationalism for fanning hostility and hatred among the peoples." This was in line with the attacks on Imre Nagy that had been going on for months. Indeed, on the same day, April 9, Khrushchev in a speech before the workers of Csepel violently denounced Imre Nagy and "his band of traitors" as representatives of "the worst sort of revisionism." [17]

It seems that the condemnation of rightist deviationism in 1957 and 1958 was carried to the extent of even making Kádár vulnerable to attacks. Had he not supported the Nagy government and its policy until November 1? There were many texts bearing the signature of Kádár, which might expose him, too, as a former representative of "the worst sort of revisionism." Because of his vulnerability Kádár often appears to be rather a buffer between the different factions of the Party than the convinced adherent of a middle-of-the-road policy. The difficulty of his position also lies in the fact that it has been well-nigh impossible to give a clear definition — articulated in everyday understandable terms — either of "revisionism" or of "dogmatism-sectarianism."

For the benefit of its readers, *Népszabadság*, the official Party daily, had undertaken to provide a current definition of *revisionism:* "A compromise with the capitalist system, the abandonment of the aim of overthrowing bourgeois power, of the proletarian dictatorship and Socialism." The paper further differentiated between the internal and external sources of revisionism. The internal sources are "the conservative inclinations of the petty bourgeoisie and the small peasantry, and the pressure they are able to exert." The external sources were "imperialist propaganda and threats," which exert an impact on "internal reactionary forces." [18]

The same daily, on another occasion, professed also to furnish the definition of *dogmatism*. It stated that although the fundamental tenets of Marxism were "irrefutable facts of absolute value," there exist some Marxist-Leninist tenets which are not of absolute value and which apply to "particular periods and conditions only." The newspaper quoted as "an example of dogmatism" the opinions of those who maintain that war is inevitable although the Twentieth

Congress of the Soviet Communist Party had declared "that it could be averted." [19]

THE DOGMATISTS (STALINISTS)

The average reader of the Hungarian Party daily may have been somewhat disappointed over this characterization of dogmatism. He had to conclude that the practical difference between Kádár's policy and that of his leftist opponents consisted in considering war either avoidable or unavoidable. Any attempts to treat other "condemned" aspects of the strongly reproved Stalinist-Rákosian regime might induce the readers to draw parallels between those days and their present predicament. This comparison might even expose some of the Stalinists who, despite their dogmatism, still occupied high positions under the Kádár regime. Nor would it be possible to admit that, when former Stalinist leaders were censured and excluded from key positions, the reasons were not ideological but personal. Those of Rákosi's and Gerö's innermost circle who had been directly or indirectly responsible for the imprisonment, torture, and humiliations inflicted on Kádár and his friends were now to pay for their luck of having escaped disaster during Stalin's reign of terror. A certain bias against muscovites who had remained immune under Rákosi's *Yezhovshchina* was also discernible in the treatment of former Stalinists by the Kádár regime.

All the members of the old notorious Stalinist "foursome" were still alive when the postrevolutionary era began. Rákosi and Gerö remained in the Soviet Union, where each had found hospitable asylum after his demotion. A third member, Mihály Farkas, and his son Vladimir, the torturers of Kádár and his co-prisoners, were both sentenced to sixteen years of imprisonment on April 25, 1957.* The fourth member of the "foursome," Jozsef Révai, the Party theoretician, had returned from the Soviet Union in January 1957. Soon after his arrival he founded the Táncsics Circle,[20] a sort of pro-Soviet Petöfi Circle, inappropriately named after the only political prisoner released by the Hungarian Revolution of 1848. It was to be a debating society on problems of Marxism-Leninism. Little is known about the activities of the Táncsics Circle, except that it became a meeting place of left-wing Communist elements. Révai also sponsored the publication of *Magyarország*, a weekly which reflected his and his faction's views. Révai, on March 7, 1957, pub-

---

* Both father and son were pardoned and released on March 30, 1960 (see next chapter).

lished an article which vehemently impeached Nagy but had only
mild words of criticism against Rákosi's policies. The ruling Kádár
clique must have felt uncomfortable because of the existence of a
Stalinist forum; on January 1, 1958, *Magyarország* ceased its publication, and in its last issue announced the dissolution of the Táncsics
Circle. There were hints at that time that the forthcoming visit of
Kádár to Yugoslavia had prompted the Hungarian leaders to act with
some severity against the Stalinists, as they were more accustomed to
do against the rightist opposition.

Révai died in the summer of 1959. In the meantime all of the
former Stalinist leaders had percolated back to Hungary, except
Rákosi and Gerö. The decision to permit the re-entry of most of the
leading Stalinists was taken by the Central Committee in late February 1958; all except Rákosi and Gerö were also offered the possibility of rejoining the Party.[21] A few members of the Central Committee also sponsored the return of Rákosi, but this move met with
"some hostile reaction." [22] It was given to understand, however, that
the return of both Rákosi and Gerö could be contemplated within
three or four years. An official spokesman of the government denied
on March 4, 1958, that the Hungarian Party would turn back to
what he described as the "old line," or that any of the returning
Stalinists would re-enter political life.[23] The principal figures
affected by the Central Committee's resolution were the former
Prime Minister Hegedüs; General Bata, former Minister of Defense;
Piros, former Minister of the Interior; and the former members of
the Party secretariat, Szalai, Végh, and István Kovács.[24] The ill-
famed judge of many rigged trials, Olti, and the chief prosecutor,
Alapi, also reappeared in Hungary after their sojourn in the Soviet
Union.

The pressures that made the return of these Stalinist elements
possible may have come partly from the Soviet Union, where their
presence might have been an embarrassment, and where the Khrushchev regime seemed chary of resorting to methods which had
enabled Stalin to get rid of superfluous foreign Communists. The
pressures no doubt came also from the Stalinists in Hungary, holding
the majority of medium-level Party positions in their hands and also
having sympathizers in the higher echelons. It would have been
only human for them to try to establish themselves more firmly
and even to obtain some of the key positions for their exiled associates. For the leadership, however, the return of Rákosi or Gerö
to an important position is a nightmare, not to be dispelled until and

unless Moscow becomes thoroughly convinced that the reins of Hungary may safely be entrusted to the present leadership.

Renewed attempts by Stalinists to regain lost ground were reported in September 1958 when Kádár and other centrists were accused of failing to develop Marxism-Leninism and not stamping out revisionist sympathies in cultural and political life.[25] The resolutions adopted by the Central Committee on March 6, 1959, after it listened to Kádár's report on the Twenty-first Soviet Party Congress, were widely interpreted as a partial abandonment of the middle course in favor of a return to a more orthodox type of Bolshevism.[26] The change has been linked with the influence of the Czechoslovak Communist Party. After his return from Moscow, Kádár visited Prague, and thereafter joined a bit more vigorously in the campaign which the Soviet bloc was by now waging against Yugoslavia. He stated on March 13, 1959, that "many people wrongfully pushed aside" had regained their positions, meaning Stalinists who had earlier been eliminated from some important Party posts.[27] The widespread view that dogmatism had again obtained the upper hand was based mostly on a new drive to further agricultural collectivization, and on the re-establishment of the "Socialist work competitions" in plants "along correct lines."[28] The suspicion cannot be excluded that the returned arch-Stalinists, despite their being kept at a distance from key positions, were able to impress Kádár with the necessity of returning to more efficient methods of building Socialism.

But rumors concerning Kádár's removal and replacement by a foremost Stalinist must be considered refuted by events. Kádár again earned the praise and approval of Khrushchev at the Hungarian Party Congress in December 1959. As late as 1961 none of the former leading Stalinists had regained any leading position in the Party. The fight against dogmatism and sectarianism remains a fight against the leaders of the Rákosi-Gerö era. On the other hand the return to harsh methods in collectivization, in the handling of Church affairs, and in the "production drive" have demonstrated that the Kádár regime does not abhor practices of the past when these are found necessary and are approved by Moscow. For Kádár the only thing that really matters and influences his policies is the attitude of the Kremlin, embodied in the smile or frown of Khrushchev.

It appeared that the following words of Khrushchev on December 2, 1959, would for some time guarantee Kádár's leadership in Hungary:

The successes . . . in expanding industry, in the development and Socialist reconstruction of agriculture, in raising the living standards of the working people, in welding the unity of the working class, the peasantry, the intellectuals, of the entire people, bear out the great viability of Marxism-Leninism, the correct guidance of your Party, its Central Committee headed by Comrade János Kádár, the true son of the Hungarian people.[29]

This praise was coupled with placing the major part of blame for the Revolution on the former leaders of the Hungarian Communist Party "who took it into their heads that they could do no wrong, that anything was permitted to them, and that they could disregard the objective conditions and the opinions of the working people." So long as Khrushchev is prepared to attribute the major share of responsibility for the "counterrevolution" to the mistakes of "armchair leaders" of the Rákosi kind, Kádár may feel secure in the saddle from the danger which might threaten him from his "leftist" opposition. This opposition will, however, continue to cause him headaches, partly because his position is now linked to Khrushchev's leadership and life expectancy, partly because the Stalinists, often operating as a close clique, will never fail to criticize his actions when they can be interpreted as concessions to the ubiquitous revisionists inside or outside the Party.

THE REVISIONISTS — DISGUISED AND UNDISGUISED

The revisionists and the rightists (or reformists), two allied factions that supported Imre Nagy's government down to its fall — though the revisionists with some reservations — saw their leaders exiled, imprisoned, or silenced in the months following the establishment of the Kádár regime. These two factions remained numerically strong, though not many of their leaders could be identified. The academic differentiation between the two groups is made difficult by the complete ostracism and criminal prosecution of all those who openly sided with the revolutionaries of October–November 1956. From the beginning of 1957, adherents of the rightists would restrict themselves to voicing only revisionist demands. The time for dissembling one's real sentiment and opinion had come back, and while revisionism was upbraided and its adherents risked exclusion from the Party or loss of their jobs, reformism or rightism became identified with counterrevolutionary attitudes and its supporters risked imprisonment, internment, or forcible changes of domicile.

The rightist leaders, among whom we may safely class Imre

Nagy after his last experiences with Soviet imperialism, were imprisoned. Géza Losonczy mysteriously died in prison. Imre Nagy was executed around June 17, 1958, as will appear in our next chapter. Ferenc Donáth was sentenced to twelve years. Miklos Gimes and Jozsef Szilágyi, also considered as belonging to this group, also suffered the death penalty. Sándor Kopácsi received a life sentence.

On the other hand, "notorious revisionists" like Professor György Lukács and Zoltán Szántó were released from their internment in Rumania, a status which they originally shared with Nagy and associates. Lukács was allowed to return to Budapest as early as April 1957. Neither of them was prosecuted, but Szántó was forced to appear as a "witness" in the secret trial of Imre Nagy.[30]

Writers and journalists who had been imprisoned because of their behavior during the Revolution and because they refused to admit guilt or cooperate with the Kádár regime were also classified as revisionists and supporters of the counterrevolution. In general, it was held that the "counterrevolutionary rising" was "launched by an alliance of revisionists, of traitors to the people, reactionary bourgeoisie and imperialists."[31] The revisionists had denied "the role of the workers' party," and there could be "no compromise on principles" with them.[32] Still, after the first waves of repression passed, the government instituted no criminal actions against those who were merely found to be revisionists but otherwise not engaged in counterrevolutionary activity.

During the first six months of Kádár's tenure of office, when the recruiting of the Party membership became an urgent business, the Party was glad to receive former members back into the Party without any brain-searching about their real feelings. We have previously described the difficulties in inducing workers and intellectuals to join the new Party. When eventually some of them joined, they did it with all the mental reservation pertinent to the circumstances. Among Party functionaries and the new Central Committee members, outward orthodoxy is a more stringent requirement than for the rank and file, but we ought not to be amazed if one day many of them revealed themselves as revisionists — if that appeared to be the opportune line of conduct. On the whole, the Central Committee, as in the past, has remained a servile body that is only too eager to follow or even anticipate the wishes of Moscow. But the great majority of the rank and file of the Party can now rightly be considered as revisionists in their hearts, if indeed they are Communists at all.[33]

The Party leadership appears now to take the reliability of

their members less for granted than did the leadership before the Revolution. Despite the reduced number of Party members and the constant scrutiny of their loyalty, doubts are often expressed by official quarters; the danger of "disguised" ideological attitudes has also been voiced in these circles. Thus *Népszabadság* of December 8, 1957, in an article entitled "Crisis and Reality," stated that revisionists "disguising themselves as Communists" had helped the "imperialist attack" during the Revolution, that revisionists were still to be found in all the sectors of society, and that it was necessary to unmask them. The prevalence of right-wing deviationists, even in the leading stratum of the Party, has been revealed by a number of purges which cannot be considered a routine expulsion of unreliables. The Deputy Minister of the Interior disclosed in April 1958 that the Central Committee "was obliged to expel" from the Party during the previous months "several thousand army and police officers," including nine generals, three former ministers, and ten former deputy ministers, for their "revisionist and nationalist tendencies." The same official added that "we have to reckon there are still at least 700,000 class enemies in the country ready any minute to attack the people's democratic regime." [34]

Many Party members are genuine revisionists, that is, Gomulka-like Communists who nevertheless condemn dictatorial aspects of the regime and its servility toward the Soviets. Other revisionists go further: they are nationalists of the Tito type; agreeing with Communism as such, they reject and despise the Kádár regime because it came to power through the support of the Soviet Army. Other revisionist Party members practice this sort of heresy only to harass and oppose the Party and the government with arguments and slogans taken from the "wellspring" of Marxism-Leninism, but are otherwise not Communists at all. This concealed and disguised opposition has become more widespread in the postrevolutionary period than before the October events, and broad sections of the population avail themselves of it. Nationalism, as a result of frustrations experienced by the Soviet invasion of the country, and deep-seated resentment judiciously hidden under the cover of apparent conformism are the sort of revisionism which many indulge in. Still others have retreated into political apathy. That a frustrated national sentiment lies at the bottom of all kinds of rightist deviations has been discovered by Party leaders, as suggested by the following passage in the Party ideological monthly (the italics are ours):

One has to reckon with the fact that a notable section of Hungarian society still remains hesitant and inclined to accept bourgeois ideological influence. In these circumstances the appearance of revisionist theories, *disguised as Marxism,* is especially dangerous. The most important obstacle to cultural and ideological development is *nationalism,* and the political and ideological struggle must accordingly concentrate on rightist views, revisionism, bourgeois and petty bourgeois tendencies.[35]

That the revisionists and pseudo-revisionists are numerous is proved by the popularity of personalities harboring what can only be considered revisionistic ideas. It is no wonder that the Party and government consider it important to extort recantations or self-criticism from those who lapsed into errors of rightist deviationism. The cases of Professor Lukács and Erik Molnár are typical in the popularity and approval accorded to their writings by Party members and others, and typical in the solicitude of the ruling circles to counteract their devastating influence.

After his return from captivity in Rumania, Professor Lukács was expected to make a declaration denouncing the Revolution and revoking his ideas expressed in the course of the events in October–November 1956. Since he refused to do so (and we may imagine that the Party had used all its machinery of pressure against the 74-year-old philosopher without resorting to violence) his case had to be discussed openly. At a meeting of the Hungarian Academy of Sciences on October 22, 1958, the Party philosopher Béla Fogarasi read a paper entitled "The Struggle of Marxism and Revisionism in Science" in which he asserted that Lukács' political mistakes could not be dissociated from his philosophical views. Fogarasi assailed his victim by stating that "according to Lukács, the principal conflict is not between Capitalism and Socialism, but between reaction and progress." He accused Lukács of having failed to understand the real nature of the Revolution, and said his book, *The Destruction of Reason,* was entirely an idealist work and "absolutely anti-Marxist and revisionist." [36] He also said Lukács advocated a "vague anti-Fascist democracy" only, and summed up his errors as follows: "We clearly saw the dualism in him, but we hoped that ultimately he would take up his position on the side of Marxism. Unfortunately, this has not been the case. Both on the fundamental questions and on the question concerning the *character of the counter-revolution* [italics ours] Lukács maintains his erroneous ideas." Fogarasi, in his assessment of revisionism, emphasized that the "social function" of present-day revisionism is "the ideological preparation of the counter-revolution." [37]

The airing of the Lukács controversy was necessitated by the popularity which the philosopher's seclusion and silence, imposed on him by circumstances, gained for him with students and intellectuals. His stubborn silence and refusal to discuss his "errors" condemned the regime more effectively than words could have done. Caught in a dilemma, the regime resorted to overtly denouncing the philosopher, and thereby further popularized his views.

Erik Molnár, several times Minister of Justice and also of Foreign Affairs, one-time ambassador in Moscow, was known to be a follower of Rákosi, whom he had served as defense counsel in Horthyist times. This "mild" Stalinist published a book in the summer of 1959 which evidently, owing to the reputation of its author, escaped the close scrutiny of the censor. His work, entitled *Some Economic Problems of Contemporary Capitalism*,[38] unexpectedly contained daring revisionist errors. It was made the subject of a debate in which leading Marxist economists attacked Molnár for such heretical theses as these:

Marxist laws of the growth and decline of capitalism can be nullified by conscious actions and the collaboration of various classes within the framework of a capitalist society.

Marxist principles about class struggle and the inevitable pauperization of the workers' class and about the constant increase of proletarian exploitation are no longer valid.

The Stalinist thesis of the general crisis in the capitalist system has lost its validity since World War II.

The intellectual upheaval caused by the writings of the 66-year-old "Marxist" scholar, suddenly revealing himself as an archrevisionist, can be assessed by the accusations that had been leveled against him: "Molnár's book presents a relatively favorable image of contemporary Capitalism," and "Marxists, under the impression of the book, had declared that . . . they cannot see any more the necessity of a Socialist revolution." [39] Molnár, defending himself in the debate over his book, refused to recant his principal theses, and retorted to his adversaries: "I do not agree with those . . . who seek to switch the struggle against revisionism from politics to science." He insisted that "dogmatism is the principal danger in our science [and] in economics." [40] The significance of this controversy and of its impact on the public may also be assessed in the light of an attack made by Politburo member Kállai against Molnár's heretical book — without, however, mentioning the name of its author — in the open session of the Hungarian Party Congress in December 1959.[41]

Revisionism, that is, ideological and veiled political opposition against the official course of the regime, had grown to be as popular and fashionable a trend among intellectuals as was any form of anti-Stalinism in the prerevolutionary epoch. No wonder that the Central Committee had to resort to drastic steps before the opening of the 1959 Party Congress. Eleven prominent members were expelled from the Party for propounding revisionist ideas, whereas twenty others who had practiced self-criticism for the same errors were only reprimanded. Those who were expelled, according to the Central Committee, had "systematically opposed the Party" and supported "revisionist traitors." And the committee added that many of the expelled had sided with the counterrevolutionaries during the 1956 uprising, a circumstance which had not been disclosed when they were admitted to the "new" Party.[42]

In November 1960, a year later, complaints were made by the deputy chief of the Party's cultural and scientific department that the large majority of the Hungarian intelligentsia was hostile to Marxist-Leninist ideology, and that nationalism as one of the most "destructive forms of bourgeois ideology" was still largely existent in Hungary.[43]

After the airing of the ideological dispute between the Chinese and Soviet Party leaders at the Moscow conference of November–December 1960 (where Kádár naturally sided with Khrushchev's views), the arguments were taken up in the Hungarian Party. Kádár, reporting to the National Assembly on his experiences in Moscow, revealed that the Hungarian Party had been assailed for being "too obdurate against revisionists and counter-revolutionaries," on the one hand, and also for being "itself revisionist" on the other.[44] Evidently Kádár wished thus to stress the correctness of his line.

All these revelations support the view that there exists a deep-rooted "ideological" rift within the Party membership, as far as its higher echelons, and centering around the meaning and theoretical assessment of the Revolution of 1956, the main ideas of "building Socialism," and the world situation. The existing cleavage rests on Hungarian nationalist as opposed to pro-Soviet tendencies. It would present far less difficulty for the regime and would assemble far fewer persons in the antiregime camp if revisionism were merely an ideological deviation from the official Party line. As a cloak for antiregime sentiment and activities, it remains far more dangerous.

GOVERNMENT, ELECTIONS, AND NATIONAL ASSEMBLY

The government of János Kádár as constituted in November 1956 has undergone two important changes, one in 1958 and the other in 1960. On January 27, 1958, Kádár handed over the premiership to Ferenc Münnich, up to then First Deputy Premier, and Gyula Kállai's post as Minister of Culture to Valéria Benke. Kádár stated: "Comrade Kállai and I should be relieved of our present duties in the government which are full-time occupations, so as to be able to work more effectively as Secretaries of the Party's Central Committee." Kádár took the occasion to explain that the original intention in Uzhgorod had been for Münnich to be Premier and that he (Kádár) had only temporarily taken over this post together with the leadership of the Party. Münnich subsequently added that "this change of personnel in the leadership of the government is in no way a political change." [45]

The second important change in the cabinet occurred on January 16, 1960, when Kádár announced the following re-shuffle: Kállai became First Deputy Premier relinquishing his Party secretaryship, while Marosán resigned as Minister of State and joined the Party secretariat and the Presidential Council. Perhaps as a result of far-reaching differences concerning the excessive speed of the agrarian collectivization drive or its organizational failures, Imre Dögei resigned as Minister of Agriculture (and was sent as ambassador to Peking), and Pál Losonczi,* so far head of a very successful model kolkhoz, succeeded him in the ministerial chair.[46]

These two cabinet reconstructions, though representing changes of emphasis among certain members of the political leadership, do not reflect modifications in the political line. The real guidance, apart from Soviet control, rests with the Party, the Politburo, and, on some questions of principle, with the Central Committee. The government remains an executive agency of the Party, more so now than during any phase of the prerevolutionary history. But the elevation of the fast-rising Kállai to the deputy premiership shelved Marosán's and Apro's claims on the second cabinet post, while the aging Münnich, the official Prime Minister, was reduced to a merely representative role. The bypassing of Apro, chief among the neo-Stalinists as a contender for the premiership, and Marosán's removal from his cabinet post can be interpreted as a strengthening

---

* Losonczi is no relation to Géza Losonczy, who had been kidnapped with Imre Nagy and had died in prison.

of Kádár's line of policy, denying to the Stalinists a future share of power.

The term of the National Assembly elected in May 1953 was supposed to expire in May 1957. But the government could not then, six months after the Revolution, risk an election campaign; the promises of free elections were too vivid in the memories of the people for them to accept meekly a single-party list. Consequently, the National Assembly, by an amendment to the Constitution, prolonged its own life. The postponement of the elections was officially supported by the argument that an election would impede reconstruction, and that all attention had to be devoted to this important task.[47] The elections were held on November 16, 1958; the single list of candidates was officially presented by the People's Patriotic Front. The government and the Party exerted every effort to insure a complete turnout to the polls. But a week before the balloting, complaints were heard that not only "class enemies" but also "wider circles of people" were showing apathy toward political life and refraining from demonstrating their loyalty by displaying enthusiasm for the elections.[48] The day before the vote Radio Moscow broadcast a Budapest report that leaflets were being distributed in all parts of the country, inciting voters to abstain from participating in the election and threatening those who went to the polls. This "provocation," according to the report, remained without effect.

The results of the national elections are thus summarized:

Voters 6,600,683
Votes cast .... 6,493,680 (98.4 per cent)
Valid votes 6,460,483
Valid votes for the single list ...... 6,430,822 (99.6 per cent)

In the local elections held simultaneously, out of 89,192 candidates for local council membership only 91 names were crossed out. When elections had been held under Rákosi's personal dictatorship, it had been claimed that 98.2 per cent of the electorate had voted for the official list. Thus Kádár had outdone Rákosi.[49]

The new National Assembly included 338 members. A breakdown of their numbers reveals that 139 were paid functionaries of the Party. Only 27 per cent of the deputies were industrial or manual workers. The Assembly included 53 members of the Party's Central Committee, which by this time had been enlarged to 73 members.

The most remarkable name in the new Assembly was that of Béla Kovács, former Secretary-General of the Smallholder Party and a Minister of State in the last Imre Nagy cabinet. Kovács underwent a series of pressures; he was harassed into inducing the peasantry to enter kolkhozes and approve the regime. A sick man, he reluctantly gave way, issuing cryptic warnings to the farmers, and died in 1959 without ever appearing in the National Assembly.[50]

Before the elections the regime did everything in its power to defend the "democratic character" of the single ticket, and to play down the conspicuous Communist character of the ballot. The People's Patriotic Front, the official sponsoring agency, was referred to as representing the nation as a whole, "embracing all Hungarian citizens who wish to work for the future of their country for the building of Socialism." Objections by the "class enemy" against the administration of such elections were answered by the Party press (italics ours):

> What will the enemy say? . . . He will say that in Hungary there is no democracy, the elections are not democratic and that in Hungary one "cannot elect, only vote" . . . During the elections, the enemy will certainly revive its slander again against our best friend, the Soviet Union. He will again begin with his *nationalistic chauvinistic incitement* and will bring up and state again that Hungary is *not an independent state.* But our national independence is secure from a political and economic point of view . . . The government is not under the influence of a single imperialist power. No interest foreign to the Hungarian people exists in the country.[51]

It was reported that, before and after the elections, debates were going on within the Party. A number of functionaries advocated frankness with the electorate, similar to that practiced by Gomulka during the Polish elections in January 1957. The voters should be told that "what they do is not a matter of choice but of geography." [52] Despite the attractiveness of the argument, the Party leadership refrained from references to "geographical circumstances," for that would have implicitly accused the Soviet Union. And since one would gather from the official announcements that the voters had been in an "enthusiastic mood," the elections were an outstanding success without any resort to "geopolitical" arguments.

POLITICAL ORGANIZATIONS GUIDED BY THE PARTY

With the reconstruction of the Party and the restoration of its power more or less assured, the Kádár regime wished to break from its isolation and regain the cooperation of at least some additional segments of the population. The People's Patriotic Front had been dormant since the Revolution. Its revival was suggested by the press in September 1957. Within the framework of such organizations Kádár and associates hoped to include leaders of former non-Communist parties in political life without, at the same time, resuscitating the multiparty system. The objectives of the People's Patriotic Front were summarized thus: "To rally the patriotic elements around the working class, the Party; to draw the non-Party masses into the conduct of national and local affairs; and to create cooperation with those internal forces which, although not agreeing in matters of detail with the Communists, identify themselves with them as far as consistent peace policy is concerned." [53] To make collaboration more attractive, the Party was now willing to allow individual membership in the front against payment of a small fee. But certain categories of persons (former landowners, large capitalists, leading officials of the former regime, military and police officers, war criminals, and "counterrevolutionary criminals") were not to be admitted. The view was expressed that henceforward "the Front should play an active part in Hungary's political life. The leaders of the Party and the government must cooperate more effectively with the People's Patriotic Front. They should, for example, discuss national problems with its National Council." [54]

This National Council met in October 1957 and decided that the front would be opened to people "who do not adhere to Communist ideology and even to individuals who may entertain religious beliefs." In order to avoid competing with other organizations, the front also decided not to issue membership cards nor generally collect fees. On January 27, 1958, Kádár's right-hand man, Gyula Kállai, became President of the People's Patriotic Front. In a speech before the National Assembly, Kállai stated that the front "was now led by the Hungarian Socialist Workers Party." [55] But by that time it was clear that the front had encountered difficulties, and the fear was expressed that some non-Party members might be attempting to use this organization against the Party. They were warned that "the Front must not become a forum for hostile views; counterrevolutionary objectives must not be allowed to predominate in the organization." [56] The People's Patriotic Front must not be changed into a kind of "petty bourgeois peasant movement." [57]

The front had played its role in the preparation of the elections, serving as the official sponsor of the single-list ticket and as the forum for campaign speeches. After the elections, the Party, not wishing to see its creature get out of hand, reduced the tempo of the front's activities. All in all the People's Patriotic Front remained what it had been in the prerevolutionary era: a tool of the Party and government for attracting non-Communists and inducing them to follow a course of limited cooperation with the regime. This is generally known, and nobody seems to be misled by it. If independent-thinking persons declare themselves ready to work within the framework offered by the front, they do it for opportunistic reasons and with all the mental reservations accompanying that attitude.

The new organization of the Communist youth, the KISZ, established early in 1957, had the purpose of weaning the youth away from the revolutionary legend. KISZ meetings condemned those young people "who supported the counter-revolution with arms." But those who had since admitted their errors, and "now genuinely support Socialist construction," were not to be rejected.[58] The problems that arose at the time of the resurrection of the Communist youth organization were later revealed by Kádár.[59] Even after the KISZ was founded, four other youth movements were operating, including movements of workers, peasants, and university students. Their simple unification would not have answered the question: "Which class would be leading the new, united organization?" Therefore the KISZ had to be bolstered and made into an organization of the "Socialist revolution, of Communism, of the working class." Unless the youth could be uniformly and centrally organized, the Party could not maintain control. Youth movements based upon occupational differences increased the danger of anti-system tendencies. But the universal youth organization was not to be restricted to one social stratum, for "to be a bourgeois or a child of the bourgeoisie were two different matters . . . a bourgeois child might join the KISZ but a bourgeois cannot join the Party." [60] The centralization took place in March 1957. In October it was admitted that only a minority of Hungarian youth belonged to the KISZ, a circumstance evidently due to difficulties of recruitment. The fact that the rather less talented or less industrious youths entered this organization may be inferred from a complaint that some enterprises in Budapest and in the provinces had given less advantageous duties and more menial work to KISZ members and functionaries — a tendency which "should be fought most energetically." [61]

The government did not spare its efforts to increase KISZ membership. A governmental decree issued on November 21, 1957, recognized KISZ "as the representative of the whole Hungarian youth." This organization was to ensure "a better education of the youth." The decree called for priority in admission to college for those who had done physical work in industry or agriculture before starting their studies, and invited state organs and other organizations to consult the KISZ in all questions concerning youth.[62] The first national conference of KISZ, on October 25, 1957, had stated that the broad masses of Hungarian youth in general and the young proletarians and peasants in particular were then "more faithful to the Party" than they had been earlier, but it deplored the reluctance of members to do propaganda work among the youthful masses. It recognized that the organization then had only 37,000 members in Budapest.[63]

Attempts were made in 1958 and 1959 to strengthen the "Communist character" of KISZ and to turn it into a "strong and militant" organization, but apparently with little success. The KISZ was criticized in the Party for the "cynicism" and "nihilism" of its members, terms that really meant anti-Communist or anti-Soviet attitudes.[64] The Hungarian leaders had recognized the antiregime attitude of the overwhelming masses of the youth that had led to the Revolution. They could do little more than try to strengthen, by administrative measures, this organization designed to convert the youth to orthodox Communist doctrines. The success of such indoctrination is no longer taken for granted and official caution prevails. The task has been rendered manifestly more difficult by memories of the Revolution and nationalistic reactions provoked by the Soviet intervention, events that particularly appeal to the imagination and enthusiasm of the young people.

Among other organizations guided by the Party, the National Women's Council has striven to bring women closer to the idea of Socialism. It is the successor of the Democratic Federation of Hungarian Women, and it wishes to gain increased membership by tackling problems of interest to women, such as better housing, more places in day nurseries, and more classrooms. The extent of its membership is not known and the relative scarcity of references in official statements to its activities may be due to its modest role and the limited attention paid to it by the public.

FALLACIES AND REALITIES OF THE KÁDÁR REGIME

Restored regimes are often characterized as having learned nothing and forgotten nothing. The same criticism may be lodged against the postrevolutionary Communist regime in Hungary. Still, such an accusation, while justified by the regime's behavior, may not correctly epitomize the inner working of the leaders' minds. The similarity of method between the Kádár restoration and the

Rákosi *ancien régime* may not so much reflect the new group's intentions as the intrinsic nature of the system under which it operates and the circumstances that brought it into being. In other words, though the restored government might wish to avoid errors of the past and learn from the lessons of its predecessor, it soon finds itself obliged to resort to "mistakes" of the past and to reiterate all that made the former system unpopular and detested by the people.

Because the restored Louis XVIII had not been forceful enough to prevent Napoleon's return and the Hundred Days, thereafter he and his successor felt obliged to insist on an autocracy based essentially on the divine right of the monarch — and this conception, in turn, again brought the downfall of the Bourbons. When Kádár undertook to come to terms with the workers' councils and non-Communist parties he was told by them to divest himself of the sole foundation of his regime, the Soviet Army. Even if it had been within his power to comply with that demand, a demand supported by the entire Hungarian nation, his compliance would have meant the annihilation of his regime. Consequently, he had no other choice than to resort to measures very similar to those for which Kádár himself had reproached the Rákosi dictatorship, mistakes that had ultimately led to the Revolution.

Any regime installed and maintained by foreign armed forces constantly faces an insoluble dilemma. Public opinion will demand the withdrawal of the foreign army as a condition of its cooperation with a government which, for its continued subsistence, is bound to rely on the foreign forces that had brought it into power. Emperor Maximilian collided with this dilemma in Mexico. He was summoned by popular demand to rid himself of the French Army that had established his regime; when, eventually, the French withdrew he lost his throne and his life. The Kádár regime has confronted a Hobson's choice. It can choose nothing but Soviet control and Soviet assistance. It cannot erase either from the memories of the Hungarian people or from the realities of its existence the tarnished title to which it owes its power. Tied inescapably to Soviet support, it cannot attain the popularity which is necessary for its internal consolidation, and it is obliged to behave and act contrary to popular demands and to resort to measures of oppression and violence against a hostile population.

Kádár's tarnished claim to power badly needed reinforcement. Like the tyrants of ancient Greece who tried to sanction their rule with mythological support, thus imitating the priest-kings of former regimes, or who introduced the doctrine of "popular will" to legitimize their status, the new Communist regime felt obliged to expound a theory whose fictitiousness could not have been doubted even by its own authors. The fiction may thus be formulated: abuses of Rákosian dictatorship had created discontent among the working class; "counterrevolutionary elements" profiting by this discontent had organized a revolt; but the "working people" — helped by the Soviet Army — had defeated the counterrevolution and secured the workers' government. It is on this watery theory that the Kádár regime is compelled to float its ship of state. This spurious basis, added to the equally fictitious dictatorship of the proletariat, is officially insisted on by the regime, which evidently hopes that after a number of years the much-repeated lie may be accepted as truth — mythology recognized as reality.

Rákosi had been able to establish and operate his tyrannical government on a semblance of constitutional legality with a minimum of direct Soviet interference, but the obviousness and brutality of Soviet armed intervention had urgently forced upon Kádár the necessity of making an official explanation of his source of power. Consequently, every possible manner of persuasion has been utilized for the acceptance of the "official thesis." An ostentatious parroting of the accepted version of the Revolution has become the requirement for Party admission or acceptance by the regime. This "test" is required of writers and journalists, and also of philosophers like Lukács. To fail this test establishes suspicion of counterrevolutionary mentality, or at least that of revisionism. There can be little doubt that Imre Nagy was also ordered to "accept and pronounce" the Party thesis of the Revolution.[65] His refusal meant that he was irredeemable.

The adoption of the counterrevolutionary thesis — together with the acknowledgment of Rákosian mistakes and abuses — logically determines the internal course of policies for the Kádár regime. This theoretical underpinning requires the government to resist pressures by the Stalinist opposition within the Party and endows it with the prestige to refuse Stalinist claims on leading Party posts. On the other hand, the official version of the revolutionary events enables the regime to suppress unrepentant revisionists and to use methods nothing short of those known as Stalinist in persecuting whomever it chooses to place in the counterrevolutionary category, including would-be counterrevolutionaries. While insistence on avoiding the errors of Rákosi certainly exercises a restraining influence on the regime, it does not preclude the use of Stalinist methods whenever *raison d'état* or Soviet instructions so demand. This was demonstrated, for instance, by the collectivization drive of 1958–1960. However, Party and government try to impress the public that Socialism is now being built "in a different way" from that practiced by Rákosi and Gerö, though the public can hardly be persuaded of a difference that is often not too obvious. The field where the regime has most abundantly profited by the experiences of the past is in the management of public economy. There is also some tolerance in art and literature. But the persecution of counter-revolutionaries and the handling of church affairs are likely to remind the people daily of the much deprecated Stalinist period.

If manifold signs seem to suggest the regime's intention to "learn from past mistakes," [66] the human material of Hungary with which it has to deal has in some measure also changed. The Revolution obliterated many of the misbeliefs, erroneous appraisals, and reticences of the past. It demonstrated that the anti-Communist and anti-Soviet national sentiment, especially on the part of the youth, was more prevalent than anyone suspected. Simultaneously, the fragility of the Party (previously described as "monolithic") and the paucity of reliable Communists became public knowledge. Consequently the Revolution had the effect of increasing the self-consciousness of the non-Party masses and significantly decreasing their servility toward those in power. Opportunism, still widely practiced, has become more openly admitted and is mostly explained by reasons of economic survival. On the whole, the Hungarian public has become more realistic both in its appraisal of Communist weaknesses and of the Soviet willingness to intervene on behalf of the regime. Submission to Kádár's government has become rather a conscious adaptation to the necessities of life than a fearful and fatal submission to the inevitable. The dependence of the regime on Soviet support has alerted many persons to the dangers of closer cooperation with rulers whom the public considers "traitors to the nation," and has restricted opportunism to the basic needs of carrying on one's profession. It has also convinced people that their predicament is bound up with the international *status quo*. The sense of frustration, however increased by Soviet guns, has now been hidden in the deeper recesses of the mind to wait for a time and opportunity when resentment may be able to burst forth, perhaps in a less violent but nevertheless in a more persistent manner than in 1956.

The Kádár regime has gained the knowledge that the people of Hungary, including the industrial proletariat, have turned against

Communism and are violently anti-Soviet. Though unable to change the popular trend, the regime has sought to mitigate resentment and gain some measure of popular support. It has refused to increase by pressure the number of Party members above a manageable size; it has abandoned the thesis of the superiority of Party members over ordinary citizens;[67] and it has officially endorsed the necessity of seeking popular confidence and the consensus of the governed for a wide field of questions. Propaganda saturation, accompanied by preposterous or childish slogans and symbols, has largely been abandoned or soft-pedaled. Worship of the Soviets has been brought down to a more realistic level. After the year of transition when the Soviet presence was openly demonstrated, the Soviet forces again became less visible, at least in most parts of the country. Despite these manifest attempts to win more popular support — without, however, giving up any of the paraphernalia of dictatorial rule — the Kádár regime has had to reckon with a solid though more subtle front of national opposition. This nation-wide opposition, while more outspoken in personal contacts between neighbors or colleagues than in the prerevolutionary era, is now even more deliberately sublimated in communications between superiors and subordinates, or between complete strangers. This sublimation is likely to deceive cursory visitors or lay observers.[68]

The Revolution, for the great majority of Hungarians, is not only the reflection of national sentiment and deep-seated resentment but also the dividing line between them and the scanty number of genuine supporters of the regime. The governmental thesis of the Revolution, which the regime cannot give up without ideologically endangering its existence, and the general knowledge of the spuriousness of this thesis have created an unbridgeable chasm between the regime and the Hungarian public. The impassioned image of the national cataclysm of 1956 harbored by the present generation contrasts diametrically with that which the official spokesmen wish to impose on the public mind. A regime that has to continue to rely on such a thesis cannot hope to obtain genuinely wider support or popularity. Condemnations, executions, and other persecutions of "counterrevolutionaries" (national heroes in the public eye) counteract the government's permissive measures, including bribes in the economic field. The execution of Imre Nagy will eventually prove a greater obstacle to Party unity and a more permanent blemish on the regime than Rajk's body was for the prerevolutionary system.

Furthermore, the abortive Revolution is no longer dismissed

by public opinion as a tragic negative. Though time has not yet raised this national event to a saga of "unsurpassed heroism" (as it is bound to emerge in the eyes of future Hungarian generations), or its martyrs to national symbols, the Hungarian public has already recognized the more positive aspects of that frustrated national effort. Any improvements over prerevolutionary or Stalinist conditions — carefully advertised by government or Party agencies — are not attributed by the public to the clemency or wisdom of the regime but are considered to be *achievements of the Revolution.* A diminishing Soviet economic exploitation, an undoubtedly higher standard of living, increased tactfulness toward national susceptibilities (though violently belied by some of Khrushchev's inept innuendoes) are all believed to be accomplishments of the uprising. Immediately after the suppression of the revolt it was felt that "all had been in vain," but in subsequent years this lethargic view has been transformed into one of positive appraisal. Thus the gap between the fictitious official standpoint and what the public believes concerning the nature and results of the revolutionary events, instead of being persistently closed, appears to be wider now than in 1957.

28

Means of Coercion and Control:
Soviet and Domestic

/\/

If you do not like my criticism, swallow it anyway; otherwise you
will have to swallow your own sour spittle later.
                                    KHRUSHCHEV in Hungary, April 18, 1958

KHRUSHCHEV'S thesis of internal de-Stalinization and equality
among Communist parties under Soviet leadership within a Communist commonwealth[1] was sorely tested in Russian relations with
the Hungarian People's Republic. De-Stalinization had opened the
way for a national revolution denying both Communism and Soviet
hegemony, and the suppression of the uprising had to be carried
out by the Soviet Army in a manner more Stalinist than a Stalin
could have used. The maintenance of the Communist regime
required special measures of coercion and control both by the
imposed national government and by the Soviet state and Party. But
neither the construction of a terrorist police system by the Hungarian government nor the maintenance of strict Soviet control and
supervision in Hungarian matters could take place without major
alterations in form and substance. The new ideological framework
governing relations between Socialist countries, the Yugoslav resistance and criticism, the Polish liberalization, offered powerful obstacles and inhibitions against unmitigated terrorism and military
control. More subtle methods had to replace Stalinst brutality and
the unpredictable exercise of *force majeure*.

The factors conditioning the 1956 bankruptcy have been studied both in Moscow and in Budapest.[2] Cocksure confidence in Hungarian armed forces is no longer assumed, though ways and means are being sought to increase their reliability. Without at least the promise of assistance by Soviet forces (whether inside the country or outside), the regime cannot feel secure. Increased vigilance in forestalling upheavals or unmasking nests of organized opposition without the use of indiscriminate methods of terrorism are explored and practiced. Four years after the reconquest of the country it was more difficult to distinguish clearly between Soviet and non-Soviet Hungarian coercive agencies than during the period immediately preceding the Revolution. The watchfulness dictated by past events and the proven unreliability of Hungarian control elements have caused the Soviet and Hungarian leaders to establish a more intricate system where agencies are skillfully penetrated by disguised or overt Soviet agents. Accordingly, Soviet citizens of Hungarian descent, now renaturalized, play an even more pervasive role than in prerevolutionary Hungary.

PATTERNS OF SOVIET CONTROL

After the initial months of Soviet military administration and unrestrained interference, the Soviet Union faced the problem of any government exercising military and political rule over a hostile territory — the maintenance of security control without outward show and without unnecessary meddling in those affairs that can safely be left to the exclusive authority of the domestic government. In the case of Hungary the concealment of the exercise of control assumed first-class political importance both from the internal and international points of view. The prestige of the Kádár government and of the Hungarian Communist Party had to be strengthened; the "independence" of Hungary had to be made more plausible in face of the accusations made openly abroad and silently acknowledged within the country. The delicacy of this task and its inherent contradictions explain the early equivocations that marked the transfer from overt Soviet control.[3] We can judge the true nature of this control starting in the fall of 1957 from an examination of various actions, appointments of persons, and other events.

The principal Soviet control and supervision continues to be exercised via the Party-to-Party channel. There is no reason to doubt that the Soviet Party bureau dealing with affairs of sister Parties regularly sends directives to the Hungarian Party and expects it to report to Moscow. This close contact is facilitated by personal communication between Party leaders, delivered in telephone conversations and personal visits. Whereas a Soviet Party representative is always available in the Hungarian Party headquarters, no Hungarian would be allowed to occupy a similar post in the Kremlin. We can assume that the peremptory language used in the Stalinist era and immediately afterward has now changed. Instructions are more in the form of invitations than commands. But the essence of the relation between the paramount authority and its subordinate has not changed. We must assume that if the language is more polite the spirit is no less domineering, and that Soviet messages are received in Hungary with as much humility as are Khrushchev's oral admonitions.

The nature of the relationship can be inferred from the tone used by Khrushchev during his first official visit after the Revolution in April 1958; it was undisguisedly that of an overlord visiting a vassal state. The Hungarian Party and its head were commended for their "correct policy"; Kádár's person was to be a "guarantee that the Party in the future will avoid the mistakes of the past." [4] In another speech, Khrushchev scoldingly warned the Hungarian Party leaders that they should not "stand around like idiots with their mouths open" when in possession of power, but should use it to beat the enemy.[5] Again he challenged the Hungarian Party leaders by saying: "You must help yourselves. You must be tougher, so tough that the enemy will always be aware that the Hungarian working class will not waver for a single instant." He added that "your class consciousness must be strengthened and you must be able to distinguish clearly between friends and foes." [6]

Khrushchev's overbearing attitude must have prompted some adverse comments, too. On his official visit to the Hungarian Party Congress in 1959, before commenting on Kádár's speech and the Hungarian Party report he expressed a hope that "his pronouncements would not be regarded as intervention in internal affairs" and that the questions raised would be settled by the Party Congress.[7] In subsequent speeches, however, he again forgot himself, and his comparisons between the tsarist military intervention in 1849 and the Soviet action of 1956 can hardly be interpreted as compatible with country-to-country equality.

Two contradictory tendencies are discernible in Soviet relations with Hungary, as with other satellite countries. There is a tendency to foster autonomy and independent decision-making in the satellite Communist parties. Simultaneously, independent actions by those Parties are watched with suspicion and are discouraged.[8] Especially, actions by satellite Parties that are considered "weak," such as the

Hungarian, are closely studied and strongly criticized. These weak Parties are also inclined to ask more frequently for "advice" and "guidance" than the stronger ones. A synchronization of doctrine and policy is expected by the Kremlin, a collaboration that could hardly be achieved without direction and control. The Hungarian Party is ready to accept and follow the Soviet lead: subordination of power is naturally followed by ideological and political dependence.[9]

Alongside the Party chain of command, other lines of control and supervision are maintained. The Soviet ambassador in Budapest fulfills a role that cannot be described as mainly diplomatic. Ambassador Andropov, who was on hand during the Revolution, afterward assumed the role of co-ruler of Hungary together with the Commander in Chief of the Soviet Army in Hungary. General Malinin, who had directed the military operations, was soon replaced by General Lashchenko, who, together with Andropov, directed the period of consolidation.[10] General Serov, head of the Soviet State Security Commission (KBG), spent several months in Hungary to organize and direct the repression. General Kazakov, subsequently Soviet Army chief in Hungary, is more conspicuous and openly active than his predecessor before the outbreak of the Revolution.

The importance of the Soviet ambassadorship to Hungary is emphasized by the fact that after Andropov's recall a superior officer occupied this "diplomatic" post. Colonel General Terenti Fomich Shtykov (who had been Soviet ambassador to North Korea at the outbreak of the Korean War) served as ambassador to Hungary until his replacement in July 1960 by an even more important Soviet political personality, Vladimir Ivanovich Ustinov, formerly First Secretary of the Moscow city Party organization.[11] The appointment to the Hungarian ambassadorial post of a Soviet Party functionary who had previously occupied a position from which Khrushchev had risen into his present paramount status is certainly not due to Hungary's relative importance within the Soviet bloc but rather to the delicacy of this diplomatic assignment.

Though muscovites seldom now occupy high-ranking Party posts, their number in administrative and diplomatic positions and in the Hungarian Army and Security Police has significantly increased. Soviet citizens of Hungarian parentage or "naturalized" Russians of the Kos-Konduktorov type exercise a clandestine but efficient control on behalf of their Soviet fatherland.* Apart from these

---

* On August 24, 1957, the Soviet and Hungarian governments concluded an agreement for the elimination of "double citizenship"; those who could claim citizenship of both countries were to choose one of them and abandon the other

unofficial Soviet "experts" who have penetrated many of the strategic positions, the Hungarian Army, the Security Police, and the ministries of Foreign Affairs and Foreign Trade are crowded with official Soviet advisers and experts. Soviet solicitude for the avoidance of any crisis in Hungary contradicts the principle of the expansion of domestic autonomy. Hungarian problems, as well as problems of the other satellite countries, are now receiving a more thorough consideration by the leaders of the Soviet Union than before the events of 1956. Khrushchev himself seems to be well briefed on Hungarian affairs, and this is the impression given by other Soviet leaders when they visit Hungary. Despite this care and attention devoted to the affairs of the "child of sorrow" among the People's Democracies, the masters of the Kremlin have not felt secure enough to dispense with their principal organ of control in Hungary, the Soviet armed forces.

THE SOVIET ARMY

The Soviet forces that suppressed the Revolution amounted to three army corps, which included eight tank and armored divisions, two infantry divisions, and additional artillery, air forces, and other ancillary units. These forces were successively reduced during the following three years. In March 1958 (before Khrushchev's visit), 17,000 men were ostentatiously withdrawn from Hungary as part of the Soviet attempt at partial disarmament. In 1959 the number of Soviet soldiers on Hungarian soil was estimated at some 45,000 to 50,000 men.[12] Their distribution in the country revealed, according to military experts, the real purpose of their presence. While officially it is claimed that the Soviet Army, under an agreement with the Hungarian government concluded in accordance with the terms of the Warsaw Treaty, is stationed in Hungary for protecting that country and the Communist bloc against potential aggressions of the imperialist West, its geographical allocation confirms its function as a force of occupation in hostile territory. The troops were concentrated around Budapest and some other industrial cities, or else stationed in encampments within easy approach to the capital, whereas the western and southern borders (with Austria and Yugoslavia) were not guarded by Soviet forces. The pressure exercised by the Soviet Army against internal uprisings in Hungary was enhanced by the presence of considerable Soviet troop concentrations in the Carpatho-Ukraine and on the Rumanian side of the Hungaro-Ru-

---

(*Népszabadság*, Aug. 25, 1957; *Magyar Közlöny*, Jan. 3, 1958). This agreement made possible the adoption of Hungarian citizenship by those Soviet citizens who had been residing in Hungary and had been descendants of some former Hungarian citizen.

manian frontier, at places from which Soviet troops poured into Hungary during the Revolution.[13]

Since the end of 1957 the Soviet forces have tried not to be noticeable, except near their garrisons. Officers, when in towns or when attached to Hungarian military or police headquarters, wear mufti. Both officers and men are again strictly isolated from the Hungarian public. The Soviet Military Command with its hundreds of officers is located in Budapest; but these quarters, together with the Soviet embassy, form a Soviet enclave in the city where officers, officials, and their families are accommodated and have their special shops and other facilities.

The slender legal basis for Soviet forces in Hungary was strengthened in the aftermath of the Revolution. Prior to the 1956 events, no agreement had been made public concerning stationing of Soviet troops in Hungary under the Warsaw Treaty or otherwise. With unashamed tardiness, on May 27, 1957, an agreement was signed between the Soviet and Hungarian governments in Budapest "on the legal status of Soviet forces temporarily stationed on the territory of the Hungarian People's Republic." [14] The agreement emphasized that the "temporary presence of Soviet forces . . . in no way affects the sovereignty of the Hungarian state" and that these forces "do not interfere in the internal affairs of the Hungarian People's Republic." The numerical strength of Soviet forces and the places of their stationing are to be determined by special agreements between Hungary and the Soviet Union. In criminal cases involving members of Soviet forces, if the victim happens to be a Hungarian citizen, Hungarian courts have jurisdiction. No case has been reported in which Hungarian courts have tried Soviet servicemen or officials. The agreement also includes stipulations for payment of damages caused to Hungarian property by actions of Soviet military units, but needless to say the provisions are not retroactive to October–November 1956. No provision is included that asserts which of the two states must pay for the maintenance of these Soviet units.

The stationing of Soviet troops in Hungary had been the principal complaint voiced throughout the nation during and after the Revolution. The crushing of the revolt by those troops and the resolutions of the United Nations General Assembly demanding their withdrawal focused world attention on their presence in Hungary. Prime Minister Kádár, in his radio address of November 8, 1956, and in his negotiations with workers' councils and other representative bodies, promised the withdrawal of foreign troops "as soon as peace and order are restored." On the other hand,

General Grebennik, the Soviet commander of Budapest, had replied to a similar demand made to him by representatives of the workers' councils: "Soviet troops will leave Hungary only when crayfish whistle and fishes sing." On November 19, 1956, the Soviet Foreign Minister, Shepilov, said in the United Nations General Assembly that "by agreement with the Hungarian government Soviet troops will be promptly withdrawn from Budapest, once normal conditions are restored in the Hungarian capital. At the same time, the Soviet government will begin negotiations with the government of the Hungarian People's Republic, as a party to the Warsaw Treaty, on the question of maintaining Soviet troops on Hungarian territory." Willingness to negotiate for the withdrawal had been declared by "both sides" — the Soviet government and the Hungarian government which it had installed by force. Soviet pronouncements and those of the Kádár regime referred to the Soviet declaration of October 30, 1956, which laid down the principle that Soviet forces could only be withdrawn from Hungary after an agreement to this effect among all the members of the Warsaw Treaty.[15]

The question of withdrawal from Hungary has not ceased to occupy foreign and Hungarian public opinion. It is coupled with another: would Soviet forces, once withdrawn from Hungarian territory, again intervene in case of another revolt against the regime? This is a question that also concerns satellite countries in which no Soviet forces are stationed, and also affects any international settlement which might induce the Soviet Union to withdraw its forces from East-Central Europe. Khrushchev during his visit to Hungary in April 1958 made contradictory statements on this issue. On April 5 he declared in Sztalinváros: "You must not again depend on the Russians coming to your assistance in the event of another counter-revolution. Therefore, you must become stronger and stronger." [16] On April 8 he said he had been misquoted by Western journalists, and he really meant to say that Hungarian Communists "should manage their efforts so that there should be no new counter-revolution and we Russians should not be obliged to come to your assistance." [17] Subsequent to these pronouncements, the principle of assistance by the Soviet Union and other Socialist countries in case of a "counterrevolution" in any Socialist country seems to have been adopted.

Another trial balloon was launched by Kádár himself when he declared on August 20, 1959, that "the time will come when Soviet troops will be withdrawn from Hungary." [18] A whispering campaign presaged an official announcement of this withdrawal at the Hun-

garian Party Congress scheduled for December of that year. It was
not Khrushchev, present at the Congress, but Kádár who disappointed wishful thinkers by declaring that "Soviet troops will only be
withdrawn when their presence is no more warranted by the international situation." [19] Two weeks before the Kennedy-Khrushchev
meeting in Vienna of June 1961, Kádár told a meeting of factory
workers that Hungary's friends cannot be expected "to defend our
frontiers and national independence to the end of time." These
words he said with reference to antiaircraft missiles recently supplied
to the Hungarian forces by the Soviet Union.

Hungarian public opinion, convinced that the Soviet Army could
always return if not obliged by international convention to abstain
from renewed interventions, desires their withdrawal for reasons of
national prestige and in order that the demands of the Revolution
may be fulfilled. The people, moreover, hope that the absence of
foreign troops would have a restraining effect on the government
and oblige it to give greater heed to the public interest. They hope
that with the departure of Soviet troops, external influence would
diminish, opening the way for an evolution more in conformity with
national sentiment.

THE HUNGARIAN ARMY

As we have seen, the untrustworthiness of the Hungarian Army
as an instrument of Soviet-Communist aims had become glaringly
manifest during the Revolution. How to reorganize this army so as
to make it reliable became a major problem for both the Kádár
regime and its Soviet supporters. During 1957 this task was to be
performed directly by Soviet military organs with limited cooperation by the Hungarian authorities. The Soviet forces, after November 4, 1956, had proceeded to disband those Hungarian units whose
members had assisted the revolutionaries. Most of the officers of the
Hungarian Army were placed under Soviet guard in a barracks camp
near the Soviet headquarters of Tököl. All the officers were compelled
to "take the test," that is to sign an Officers' Declaration agreeing
with the decision to ask for Soviet help and recognizing the legality of
the Kádár regime. Those who refused — and about 80 per cent of
them did so — were immediately dismissed, and many of them were
later imprisoned or interned. Members of the officer corps who had
signed the declaration were screened again and again by mixed Soviet-Hungarian commissions. High-ranking officers had to undergo
special interrogations. All officers who had behaved in a suspicious
manner during the Revolution were court-martialed. The Soviet

Army confiscated all heavy material belonging to the Hungarians, including the entire Hungarian bomber force.[20]

After March 1957 the slow and circumspect reorganization of the army began. This task was entrusted to General Géza Révész, who succeeded Münnich as Minister of the Armed Forces. Révész had been a muscovite, a Comintern agent, and a Soviet Army colonel before his return from Moscow in 1945. His new assignment cannot be interpreted except as a common Soviet-Hungarian appointment. While he was Defense Minister, purges against the officer corps continued. On May 18, 1960, General Révész, having evidently completed his task, was relieved as Minister of Defense and appointed Hungarian ambassador to Moscow.[21]

In 1959 the reconstructed Hungarian Army was estimated to number about 120,000 men, less than half of its prerevolutionary strength. It was composed of one artillery division, an armored division, a motorized mechanical division, and six or seven rifle and motorized rifle divisions. The Hungarian Air Force remained deprived of its bombers.[22]

What new methods could possibly be invented for rendering the Hungarian forces more reliable? Their smaller size and a more carefully selected and indoctrinated officer corps appear to be the only guarantees of higher loyalty. A larger percentage of officers on active service have received instruction in Soviet military colleges than was the case during the Revolution. Training in the Soviet Union appears, however, to be no safeguard against "chauvinism" or anti-Soviet sentiment; many of the officers, including high-ranking staff officers, who were purged during 1957–1959 had received their military instruction in Soviet training centers. The army, because of continuous purges that have drained the best elements out of its ranks, is badly lacking in experienced instructors, both commissioned and noncommissioned. The Ministry of Defense, during the summer of 1959, invited officers and noncommissioned officers of the former Horthyist army to join as instructors provided they had displayed a "politically loyal attitude" since 1945 and had not participated in the Revolution of 1956.[23]

The former methods of control and supervision have all been re-established in the army — the Communist Party cells in all units, the political officers, and the watchful eyes of the security officers. The Soviet military advisers have returned and are again attached to Hungarian units down to divisional (with certain units to the regimental) level. Supervision of the Hungarian Air Force is especially rigid: its flights are closely controlled and carried out in cooperation with Soviet Air Force units stationed in Hungary. Arms and supplies provided to the Hungarian forces by the Soviet Union are stringently rationed, and the accumulation of large stocks is prevented. All in all, the Hungarian Army seems more rigidly ruled by Soviet military organs than it ever was before the Revolution. Its capacity to fight a foreign enemy is questionable and its morale and degree of reliability are low. By now the Soviet Command must have become resigned to dismissing the Hungarian Army — and probably other satellite armies — from its war planning. We have to interpret within this context the words of General Ilku, Chief of the Political Section in the Hungarian Ministry of Defense, who stated at the end of November 1956: "For years to come, the Army will only act in a police capacity and will not be trained for battle maneuvers." [24] The defense budget for 1957 was consequently reduced to 1.9 billion forints as compared with 4.2 billion forints in the 1956 budget.[25]

POLICE, SECURITY POLICE, WORKERS' MILITIA, FRONTIER GUARDS

The Hungarian regular police had proved to be the weakest link in the chain protecting the Communist regime. Nevertheless, no large-scale purges of its officers and men were reported as in the case of the army. Evidently, all the blame for the passivity of the police was to be heaped on the shoulders of a few leading police officers, prominently on Sándor Kopácsi, the Chief of Police. The reorganization that was carried out concerned mostly questions germane to the incorporation of the Security Police into the regular police.

During the Revolution the dissolution of the Security Police (AVO) became a plank of the governmental platform, and afterward the move was endorsed by the Kádár regime. Though no formal document implementing the dissolution is known, a governmental decree of December 30, 1956, recognized its termination and alloted "investigations of crimes against internal and external security" to the jurisdiction of the regular police.[26] It appears, however, that the AVO did not really vanish. It only stopped being a separate section, and without leaving the Ministry of the Interior was placed *in toto* within the section that controlled the regular police. It acted, henceforward, as the "Political Investigation Division" of the Central Office of the Police.[27] We can also assume that most of its functionaries continued in their jobs, and that only a few of them were purged or dismissed. The enormous task of repression and investigation of "counterrevolutionaries" and other opponents of the regime had made the maintenance and stability of the government dependent on the operation of trained and seasoned Security Police personnel.

The Security Police in the prerevolutionary period was not restricted to investigation and interrogation officers; it also included an armed force, placed under the authority of the AVO, specially trained and indoctrinated to perform praetorian services for the Communist regime. This military arm was divided up and given various names at the beginning of the Kádár restoration. These units were known as "Security Force Regiments" (*Karhatalom*); the "R" groups, short for *Riado Csoport* (Alarm Group); "Home Guards" and "Factory Guards." Still others formed the core of an organization subsequently called the "Workers' Militia." The functioning of these units was supported by the Soviet Command, and their collaboration was close during the first year of the Kádár regime.[28] Eventually, these Security forces were brought back under the control of the Hungarian Ministry of the Interior, which handled them as part of the police. They are, nonetheless, militarily trained and organized armed forces that do not perform ordinary police duties but are kept in reserve for the defense of public buildings and in case of major disturbances.

The popular wrath so violently expressed against the Security Police during the Revolution was a lesson to this organization and to the government. At first, to be sure, when investigating real or presumed "counterrevolutionaries" and other opponents of the regime, the "new" Security Police showed itself as ruthless as during the Stalinist era. During Kádár's first year, it was often accused of brutality in its treatment of prisoners, and there is no doubt that the repression after the Revolution was carried out with the usual totalitarian methods of torture and "brain-washing" that must have led to a number of extorted confessions, the victimization of innocents, and illegalities on a large scale. After this initial year of terrorism the activities of the Security Police became more discreet and less provocative. Indiscriminate and arbitrary arrests were stopped, and those who kept themselves aloof from politics seemed no longer to have reason to fear arrest.[29] Though the concepts of rightism or counterrevolutionary mentality are somewhat vague, they do not appear to be given such a wide interpretation as in the Rákosian era or immediately after the collapse of the Revolution. Orders for arrest for political crimes are given out more sparingly and probably not by the head of the Security Police alone but with the consent of the Prosecutor General or persons in high Party echelons. Since the liquidation of most of the counterrevolutionary cases, complaints against Security Police terrorism have become more scarce. But lack of constitutional guarantees and the secrecy that covers the activities of this organization always leaves open the possibility of a recrudescence of mass arrests and unbridled brutality. The confidential cooperation between the Hungarian Security Police and similar Soviet organs was demonstrated by the handling of the Imre Nagy case, to be described presently.

During the Revolution the workers' councils had assigned "workers' guards" to protect factories. The Kádár regime distrusted this revolutionary agency of plant protection, and stated that "in certain establishments, criminals and counter-revolutionary elements slipped among the workers' guards." [30] On February 19, 1957, the workers' guards were declared dissolved and replaced by the Workers' Militia, led by former AVO personnel and directed by a commander in chief instead of by the individual plants.[31] The Workers' Militia soon developed into an instrument of intimidation and terrorism against industrial workers; its cohorts are only officially workers, and their main task consists in the regimentation of workers, the supervision of factories, and denunciations of those under suspicion. In 1959 their number was estimated at around 25,000.[32] They were equipped with tommy guns, which, however, were issued to them only for drill and parades.

In 1956 the Soviet invaders, deployed along the western frontiers of Hungary, undertook the temporary replacement of the untrustworthy and partly disbanded Hungarian Frontier Guard. The Soviet troops, unfit for such service, unacquainted with the terrain and environment, and assembled in large units from fear of the Freedom Fighters (especially at night), were highly ineffective as border guards. From November 1956 to February 1957 they allowed 175,-000 Hungarian refugees to enter Austria. In the meantime, the Frontier Guard was being screened and purged by the regime, and was finally restored in strength and returned to its watch on the border. By the summer of 1957 full control of the frontier was left to the Hungarian units by the Soviet Command. Mine fields and barbed wire installations which had been removed early in 1956 were hurriedly reinstalled in February and March 1957. Later they were reinforced by concrete pillars, and electric current was introduced into the barbed wire so as to render the border impregnable. Escapes thus became rare. Most of those who tried it in the years 1958–1961 were Frontier Guard personnel.

The Frontier Guard is subordinate to the Ministry of the Interior, and is a force "advised" by Soviet specialists. Its membership has been recruited from among enlisted soldiers, and these were encouraged to serve several terms. The officers, many of them subsequently dismissed because of disloyalty toward the regime, were selected from among the most reliable noncommissioned officers of the army or members of the Security Police.

The most heavily protected frontier is the Austrian. Next, it is the Yugoslav border that is given particular attention. After the Revolution of 1956, especially when the surveillance along the western frontier made escape hazardous, about 20,000 refugees crossed into Yugoslavia, a fact which compelled the reinforcement of Frontier Guard units along the southern border as well. Relatively few units are guarding the frontiers against fraternal Socialist countries, Czechoslovakia, the Soviet Union, and Rumania.

CONDEMNATIONS, INTERNMENTS, AND DEPORTATIONS

We have seen how the Kádár regime gradually equipped its judiciary with the legal means of dealing swiftly and discreetly with those charged with counterrevolutionary crimes and offenses against the security of the state. Summary procedure was officially abolished on November 3, 1957;[33] but a careful scrutiny by the International Commission of Jurists has established that this repeal primarily affected those summary proceedings that had been introduced shortly after the collapse of the Revolution in November–December 1956. It did not end proceedings of a summary nature practiced by the People's Chambers or by the Supreme Court acting as criminal court of first and last resort. As further pointed out by the International Commission of Jurists, there was still no requirement for a written indictment nor for an advance notification of the date of the trial. Only the public prosecutor could make arrangements for the presence of witnesses, and the accused could not be represented by a counsel of his own choice.[34] The secrecy surrounding political trials has been increased since the summer of 1958.

The political victims were recruited from all strata of the population. Their number is difficult to assess, and so is the number of people who have been executed.[35] The Hungarian press reported 105 executions up to the end of July 1957, while private estimates spoke of 2,000 and the number of imprisoned persons was estimated at 20,000.[36] The official spokesman of the Kádár government stated on April 26, 1958, that no statistics were available but that "the number of people condemned or awaiting trial on charges of counterrevolutionary crimes and activities" was "very much smaller" than that circulated in the West, where people "seem to have a liking for large figures." [37]

Prime Minister Münnich declared on February 18, 1958, that Hungarian judicial authorities "have completed the investigation of counter-revolutionary crimes and the calling to account of counter-revolutionaries." Since the beginning of 1959 emphasis is no longer laid on counterrevolutionary crimes but on the "defense of social property," on the fight against "juvenile delinquency" and alcoholism.[38] Despite official announcements, condemnations for revolutionary activities in 1956 have evidently not come to an end. During the summer of 1959 the case of the Workers' Council of Ujpest came up for trial; eleven were sentenced to death and eight of them executed.[39] Reports about condemnations and executions of juveniles, as soon as they had attained the statutory age of eighteen, were vehemently denied by the Hungarian government, but, in view of manifold contradictions, these statements were given little credence.[40]

At the Party Congress of December 1959, Béla Biszku, the Minister of the Interior, stated that 63,000 persons were in prison in Hungary, without disclosing the proportion of political and common prisoners.[41] This number does not include those interned or deported. Though two of the principal internment camps were unofficially reported to house 20,000 inmates each, the Prosecutor General admitted the existence of only one, containing 1,869 inmates, in December 1957. The obvious falsehood of the latter statement fosters incredulity toward official statistics of the regime.[42]

Sentences were passed against active participants in the Revolution. Those who fought with arms were usually convicted of murder, while those who were only found guilty of membership in a revolutionary group or organization were convicted of "associating to overthrow the People's Democracy." Incitement or exhortation to fight the Soviet Army was also classed as an action against the people's democratic system; concealment of arms or ammunition, incitement to rebellion, and illegal associations were construed as major offenses whenever "social factors" favored condemnations.[43]

Among the professional groups of the condemned, we find students and workers who fought as Freedom Fighters, members of workers' councils, soldiers and officers, priests, intellectuals, writers, journalists. The sentencing of leading members of the National Council for Transdanubia was reported in August 1957; its militant chairman, Attila Szigeti, had earlier attempted suicide in prison, according to reports, and has been presumed dead.[44] Major Pálinkás-Pallavicini, head of the unit which liberated Cardinal Mindszenty and paraded him to Budapest, was sentenced to death.[45] A group of "counterrevolutionary" Roman Catholic priests who had "raided" the State Church Office during the Revolution were sentenced to prison in January 1958, one of them, Father Turchányi, receiving a life sentence.[46] Professor István Bibo, a Minister of State in the last Imre Nagy cabinet, received a life sentence. György Ádám, Chairman of the Revolutionary Council of Intellectuals, drew eight years, and the writers Tibor Déry, Gyula Háy, Zoltán Zelk, and Tibor Tardos, between two and four years. Also condemned to prison were Professor Domokos Kosáry, historian, Dezsö Keresztury, Director of the Academy Library, and many others.[47] Though "counterrevolutionaries" and rightists were sentenced by the thousands, the only known instances of condemnation of Stalinists are the cases of former Defense Minister Mihály Farkas and his son Vladimir.[48]

Political prisoners who had temporarily been released before October 23, 1956, or had been liberated during the Revolution, if apprehended in Hungary, were taken back to prison, except those whose sentences were annulled. Szénási, the Prosecutor General, announced that 3,012 past convictions had been re-examined up to November 1957 and that only 399 deserved annulment.[49] It is not clear, however, whether these cases under review included ones that had been re-examined prior to the Revolution. At any rate, those favorably decided did not include cases of persons who had left Hungary after the collapse of the Revolution.

In March 1958 the government opened its campaign to "cleanse" the profession of practicing lawyers of "alien elements." [50] Already certain leaders of the Budapest Chamber of Advocates, as reconstituted during the Revolution, had been sentenced. A decree of March 30, 1958, abolished the National Committee of the Chambers of Advocates and also the autonomy of individual Chambers. Henceforward the profession of the law had to be exercised within "cooperatives" of attorneys. The purge of lawyers resulted in the disbarment of 720 of the 1,600 lawyers in Budapest.[51]

Early in 1960 the inmates of internment and forced-labor camps were estimated to number 35,000; those under police surveillance, 30,000; and those assigned to forced residence outside their domicile, 10,000.[52] The fate of those who had been deported to the Soviet Union shortly after the Revolution remains unknown.

After a partial amnesty issued in April 1959, a more substantial release of political prisoners was decreed on March 31, 1960. This amnesty extended unconditional pardon to those political prisoners sentenced before December 31, 1952, who had served half their sentence. It suspended the sentences of those who had been imprisoned for six years or less for antistate offenses before May 1, 1957. In addition, a few prisoners received individual pardons, including the writer Tibor Déry. As a gesture toward the leftist Party opposition, the two Farkases, father and son, were also released.[53] Gábor Péter, head of the Security Police under the Rákosi regime, who had been serving a life sentence since 1953, had already been released early in 1959.[54]

Though many prisoners sentenced as a consequence of revolutionary activities have thus been freed, the amnesty did not extend to crimes of "homicide" or "damaging of public property," for which many revolutionaries had been condemned, nor did this measure relieve the situation of those serving heavy prison sentences. The same decree ordered the dissolution of internment camps before June 30, 1960, but the three months' delay in implementing this measure raised the suspicion that some of the inmates of the internment camps may have received judicial condemnations to prevent their release. The same thing was done in 1953, when the internment camps had to be evacuated under the New Course.

One of the causes contributing to the acute resentment that led to the outbreak of the Revolution in 1956 had been the terrorism of the Rákosi regime, its mass imprisonments, executions, and tortures. One cannot escape the conclusion that the postrevolutionary terrorism may eventually have new repercussions in the life of a nation like Hungary. Kádár and many of his friends, having themselves been purge victims, ought to be in a position to know that the persecution of political adversaries, whether in judicial or nonjudicial form, can have reactions similar to those that occurred when such a widespread martyrdom whipped popular wrath to a revolutionary aggressiveness that overthrew the Communist regime. The new storm of judicial terror that swept over Hungary in the wake of the Revolution can perhaps be attributed to Soviet demands for revenge and repression rather than to the genuine desire of Kádár's ruling clique. If so, it demonstrates a lack of understanding of the national psyche, an ignorance or shortsightedness by the Soviets that once before had borne its "grapes of wrath." Outstanding among these acts of political myopia was the martyrization of Prime Minister Nagy and his associates.

THE EXECUTION OF IMRE NAGY

By entering the Yugoslav embassy on November 4, 1956, Prime Minister Imre Nagy became a pawn in the Khrushchev-Tito chess-play; in kidnapping him the Russians were intent on using him for their political purposes. Though Imre Nagy's person and his future statements still were matters of highest consequence in Hungarian politics, Kádár had no important part to play in Nagy's fate. His role was restricted to that of cat's paw of the Soviets.

To Khrushchev, in his policies toward Tito and toward strengthening the Soviet-Communist regime of Hungary, "self-criticism" by Nagy could have had great significance. Stalin would probably have extorted a confession from Imre Nagy and exhibited him in a theatrical trial on the Rajk and Kostov model. Khrushchev, after the denunciation of Stalin's crimes, could not resort to such methods. Yet a public renunciation of the revisionist and neutralist heresies would probably have provided Khrushchev with a satisfactory reply to Tito's renewed heresy. It would have given an uplift to the Kádár regime. It probably would have saved Nagy's life. It might even have opened the way for Nagy's return to politics, though it would have meant the end of his popularity and of his role as a national symbol. There is no doubt that during his internment in Rumania under the custody of the MVD, Nagy had been approached both by representatives of the Soviet Presidium and by emissaries of the Kádár regime. Zoltán Szántó and Zoltán Vass, who had fled with Nagy to the Yugoslav embassy and who originally shared his internment in Rumania, were reported to have acted as intermediaries between Kádár and Nagy.[55]

A change in the official attitude toward Nagy was perceptible in December 1957, more than a year after his kidnapping. The change coincided with the worsening of Soviet-Yugoslav relations after Tito's refusal to sign the Declaration of Communist Parties in November.[56] The Stalinist theoretician Révai had asked in March 1957 that Nagy be brought to trial,[57] and by December Münnich was saying about him that he "sank as low as to encourage the imperialist powers . . . to make an armed intervention in defense of the counter-revolution." [58] Intensified attacks appeared then in the press and in official speeches, and the fourth volume of the Hungarian White Book on the Revolution devoted a whole chapter to the role of Imre Nagy, concluding that in "violating his oath, Imre Nagy failed to defend the state order of the Hungarian People's Republic against the hostile attack: on the contrary, he headed this offensive." [59] At the same time it was affirmed that Nagy was still in Rumania.[60]

In January 1958, Western press agencies reported that Imre Nagy would probably be brought to trial during that year, basing their stories on a press conference by Prime Minister Münnich on January 17. In December and January the ideological organ of the Hungarian Communist Party devoted two articles to the revisionism of Nagy, saying that he had "envied the revisionist parties for their glory" (a reference no doubt to Yugoslavia) and had followed "the policy of betrayal of the dictatorship of the proletariat" because, "together with Djilas, he was attempting to establish an anti-Soviet federation which would have incorporated Hungary, Yugoslavia, and Austria." The periodical further accused Nagy of having wanted to change Hungary into a state-capitalistic structure following the pattern of India, as well as to establish a "nationalistic bourgeois regime" in Hungary.[61] At the same time, in Moscow, the ideological monthly of the Soviet Communist Party published an article with similar overtones.[62]

Preparations for the Nagy trial were abandoned when, in March 1958, Kádár paid a precipitous visit to Tito (see Chapter 30). The fate of Imre Nagy must have been one of the chief subjects of discussion. Evidently Tito received assurances that Nagy would not be tried "for the time being." [63] During Khrushchev's visit to Hungary in April, his objurgations against Nagy were left out of the official version of his speech.[64] The next reversal of policy and the decision to have Nagy executed took place after the last unsuccessful contact between the Soviet and the Yugoslav Parties after the Seventh Congress of the Yugoslav League of Communists on April 22–26. The deterioration of relations between Yugoslavia and the Soviet-Chinese Communist bloc, together with Imre Nagy's consistent refusal to refute his own ideology and actions, wrote Nagy's death warrant.

The antecedents and timing of Nagy's execution betray the real motives and objectives of this business. His head was to be thrown to Tito and to other potential Communist heretics and schismatics as a warning.[65] The Kremlin ignored or miscalculated Hungarian reactions, and contemporary and subsequent effects on Hungarian attitudes toward Communism and the Soviet Union, in the urge to throw down the gauntlet before a recalcitrant Tito and his sympathizers. The Kádár regime's role in the tragic outcome remained that of an accessory before and after the fact; no resolution of the Hungarian Central Committee or cabinet has even been cited that ordered the trial of Nagy and his associates. The secrecy that surrounded the "proceedings," the deficient reporting of the "trial," the absence of names (judges, prosecutor, and counsel for defense) and precise data (place and time of trial), the failure to cite the laws and procedures under which the accused were tried and condemned, and, finally, the omission of the usual *stylus curialis,* the Hungarian court language, bear witness that the trial of Nagy, if trial there was, rested on an ill-disguised cooperation between Soviet and Hungarian security organs, and that the initiative must have come from the Soviet agents under the orders of the Kremlin.

A communiqué, broadcast first in Moscow and then in Budapest, announced late on June 16, 1958, that the "Hungarian legal authorities concluded the proceedings in the case of the leading group of those persons who on October 23, 1956, started a counter-revolutionary armed uprising." The People's Court of the Supreme Court had declared the defendants guilty and passed the following sentences: Imre Nagy, General Pál Maléter, and two advisers of Nagy, Miklos Gimes and Jozsef Szilágyi, were sentenced to death. The former police chief, Sándor Kopácsi, was sentenced to life imprisonment. Sentences ranging from twelve to five years were handed out to Zoltán Tildy, former president of the Republic; Ferenc Donáth, the rightist leader; Ferenc Jánosi, clergyman son-in-law of Imre Nagy; and Miklos Vásárhelyi, the journalist.[66] The sentences were "nonappealable" and "the death sentences have been carried out." *

Statements by government and Party spokesmen in Budapest and in Moscow, including the official Hungarian publication that dealt with the trial and execution of Imre Nagy and his associates,[67] have not shed in substance any more light on the circumstances of the proceedings. Detailed analyses, both legal and political, of the judgment and the scanty though manufactured reports of the "trial" have demonstrated its factual and juridical fallacies as well as its evident contradictions and deficiencies.[68] Nagy was accused of having betrayed his oath of office; on the other hand, he was indicted for having obtained by conspiracy and revolt the post of Prime Minister. One of the grounds for the charge of "high treason" was that his cabinet had approved the multiparty system, and another was the withdrawal from the Warsaw Treaty; but none of these actions could legally be considered treason or conspiracy, and the question arises why other ministers, like Kádár, who had consented to these acts had not been brought to trial. Nor could the request

* In the amnesty of March 31, 1960, Tildy, Donáth, and Jánosi, received individual pardons and Vásárhelyi was released under the general provisions of the decree.

for help from the United Nations under the provisions of the Charter be considered as a crime under Hungarian law. The judgment does not mention the safe conduct promised to Nagy and associates by the Kádár regime; the asylum allegedly granted to him by the Rumanian government; his extradition (if any) by that government; the pledges for his safety given by Kádár to Yugoslavia and in public announcements; and the immunity as an envoy to which Maléter was entitled vis-à-vis the Russians. Such an obviously rigged political trial defies any serious legal scrutiny.

From the Hungarian point of view, the impact of the execution of Imre Nagy can be well compared, in its historical perspective, with the brutal slaughter of Prime Minister Batthyány and the thirteen generals of the 1848–49 Revolution, an equally ill-advised and shortsighted act of revenge that poisoned the relation between the Hungarian people and the Hapsburg dynasty for decades.* Nagy had been seeking to reconcile Communism with genuine Hungarian nationalism. In case of political disengagement in Central Europe, he could have been commonly trusted by East and West and also by the Hungarian people. Moscow's ukase not only destroyed those constructive potentials but also created an even wider gulf between Soviet influence and Hungarian national sentiment than that which already existed. Though Soviet military intervention, however brutal and unjust, might have sprung from the rationale of Soviet state interest, the execution of Nagy and his associates, twenty months after the suppression of the Revolution, could not even be defended on that ground.

After the creation of "heroic myth" of the Revolution, likely to become a greater motivating impulse to future generations than to the present one, the Soviet leaders had presented to the nation its gallery of martyrs. They finally succeeded in making their muscovite Communist Imre Nagy into a national hero whose role and example will be bound to electrify later leaders and the masses they command to the disadvantage of the much heralded "Soviet-Hungarian friendship." A future posthumous rehabilitation of Imre Nagy and Pál Maléter, a usual harbinger of changed Soviet policies, would certainly have effects no less tempestuous than the posthumous rehabilitation of Rajk. The martyrization of Rajk was exploited by

* Even after the "compromise" — the official reconciliation with Austria in 1867 — Hungarian governments had to rely on majorities in the Hungarian National Assembly that came, under a restricted ballot, mainly from parts of the country inhabited by national minorities, while the pure Magyar population voted predominantly for "independence" parties which opposed the dual system with Austria.

dedicated anti-Communists; Imre Nagy's personality will serve to solidify a broader and more genuine patriotic sentiment.

Nagy is already regarded as an embodiment of national virtues and aspirations, and will become even more so. His humanity and affability, even his mediocrity as a politician, will serve to enhance the contrast existing between him and most of the other Communist leaders. These others have been in most cases mendacious or muddled; they are products of disordered psychological conditions or otherwise may be useful subjects for teratological studies. Nagy's common sense and peasant-like ingenuousness recommend him to the man in the street and equate his tragedy, symbolically, with that of the average citizen. The execution of Nagy and his associates has rightly been called a "tragic event in which these men, symbols of the hope of a nation for freedom from foreign domination, were secretly sent to death in circumstances which call for full exposure, in violation of solemn undertakings that their persons would not be harmed." [69]

29

Synchronizing a Satellite

/\\.\\/\\.\\/\\.\\/\\.\\/\\.\\/\\.\\/\\.\\/\\.\\/\\.\\/\\.\\/\\.\\/\\.\\/\\.\\/\\.\\/\\.\\/\\.\\/\\.\\/\\.\\/\\V

We must make a sensible use of the great advantages of the socialist system and strengthen the world of socialist camp in every way. We must not fall behind or go too far ahead. We must, figuratively speaking, synchronize our watches.

KHRUSHCHEV in Hungary, December 1, 1959

AFTER consolidating its grip on the country, the Kádár regime felt obliged, partly under directives received from Moscow and encouragement from other People's Democracies, partly by its own initiative, to pursue and implement certain policies that would bring its country more into harmony with other more advanced "Socialist" systems. The building of Socialism, besides being an ideological necessity, also served the purpose of forcing certain potentially dangerous elements of the population to conformism or dependence upon the regime.

The Hungarian Party and government, simultaneously catering for popularity, found themselves faced with crucial alternatives on these issues of Communist alignment. Whether the measures to be taken concerned spiritual matters or the socio-economic system, it was always a choice between a policy of *quieta non movere* and further steps on the road toward "Socialism" with their concomitant hostility from those parts of the population that would be hurt. Recent history seemed to recommend stopping or slowing down the pursuit of Communist objectives, as in Gomulka's Poland. On the other hand, the dependence of Kádár on Soviet "advice," and the neophytic zeal of the Hungarian Party leaders to fall into line with the more docile and orderly People's Democracies, such as Czecho-slovakia or Rumania, favored decisions that would appear precocious for a Party which had been so recently in a state of collapse. Espe-cially, the precipitate and violent collectivization of agrarian hold-ings seems to have been a measure inexplicable according to ordinary political reasoning. Beyond doubt, Kádár desired popularity at home, but his desire could not match his solicitude to please his Soviet protectors and Communist colleagues.

In the realms of the mind and spirit, particularly in matters of education, the government was determined to lose no time in recon-verting to prerevolutionary practices. Revolutionary demands and postrevolutionary promises were quickly shoved aside. Since the attitude of the youth had become one of gravest concern, their education in Communist orthodoxy and away from antiregime tendencies had to be taken care of as soon as circumstances permitted. A renewed emphasis on the teaching of Marxism-Leninism and the reintroduction of Russian as the only obligatory foreign language at secondary schools[1] were the main devices by which the regime promoted the better indoctrination of youth. It was again the problem of the youth which prompted many of the steps the government took to curb church activities and spurred endeavors of the Party to rally the writers and other intellectuals.

THE CHURCHES

During the Revolution all the churches recovered their autono-mous status and swiftly discarded both the personnel and the restrictions imposed on them since 1948. The Calvinist and Lutheran Churches, which had been more intensively infiltrated by fellow traveler clergymen than the Catholic, removed the unpopular col-laborationist bishops, and elected in their stead persons enjoying popular support. In the Catholic Church most of the conspicuous peace priests were removed from their offices, and representatives of the Office of Church Affairs disappeared. Cardinal Mindszenty's return to his archbishopric as Primate of the Hungarian Catholics was an outward symbol of the resurrection of independent church authority.

The Kádár regime approached church affairs with a certain caution. Cardinal Mindszenty, it is true, was attacked from the begin-ning, and was officially forbidden to carry out ecclesiastical functions from the United States legation in Budapest, where he had taken refuge. A decree, retroactive from October 1, 1956, was issued on March 23, 1957, making the validity of ecclesiastical appointments dependent on the approval of the Presidium of the People's Republic. Two years later another decree provided that removal or transfer from one ecclesiastical post to the other also required government consent. A post remaining vacant for over three months might be filled by order of the state authority. An oath of allegiance was also required from holders of church offices.[2] But meanwhile, through gestures of tolerance, the government was trying to mitigate the implementation of state control: in June 1957 the ill-famed Office of Church Affairs was dissolved and the function once again returned to the jurisdiction of the Ministry of Education. In the fall of 1957 agreements were reached between the government and the churches for resumption of the state subsidies which had been paid before the Revolution.[3] The Priests' Peace Movement, a center of pro-Communist collaborationism, was dissolved and replaced by another organization, the *Opus Pacis,* sponsored by the Bench of Catholic Bishops.[4]

All denominations shared the victimization of many of their clergymen for "counterrevolutionary" activities. The Protestant churches, however, fared less well at the beginning of the Kádár regime than the Catholic: their bishops installed during the Revolution were all removed, and the former ones reinstated. A Protestant Peace Council was created with compulsory membership of the Protestant clergy.

Prime Minister Münnich stated on January 16, 1958, that relations between the state and the Roman Catholic Church were "excellent," and that Archbishop Grösz, acting head of the Church in absence of Cardinal Mindszenty, had contributed to that result. These excellent relations did not, however, stop the government from deciding that some bishops could not exercise their offices; for example, Bishop Badalik of Veszprém and Bishop Pétery of Vác are known to have been "suspended for excessively reactionary attitudes."[5] Kádár, speaking before the National Assembly, expressed the desire of the government to eliminate differences with the Catholic Church. He said that the problem for Catholic believers was that if they obeyed the Pope they came into conflict with their duties as citizens and if they acted as good citizens they might come into conflict with their obedience to the Pope. He advised Catholics to "think this over" and the Church to "adopt a positive attitude to this problem."[6] The press emphasized that the Party wished to "coexist and cooperate" with everybody on the basis of fighting for peace and the building of Socialism. The Party, however, had to draw the line somewhere; it "cannot practice the virtue of patience with Party officials" who are religious.[7]

Despite the official statements, the friction between the state and the Catholic Church continued. In March 1958 the Vatican, in order to counteract excessive collaborationist activities and the distortion of the true intentions of the Church, excommunicated Richard Horváth and Miklos Beresztoczy, two charter members of the Priests' Peace Movement.[8] By this time the Hungarian press was increasing its attacks on the Church, but when Münnich received the Bench of Roman Catholic Bishops in July, "the meeting was devoted to a friendly exchange of views on topical questions in state-church relations." [9] In September the government tried to exercise pressure by threatening to reduce the state subsidy by 25 per cent; but subsequently, "as a sign of the further strengthening of good relations" it agreed not to do so.[10] This threat and concession appeared to be an inducement for the churches to persuade their followers to vote for the regime in the elections of November 1958.*

The uneasy truce between church and state came abruptly to an end after those elections. The apostolic delegate who administered Cardinal Mindszenty's archdiocese was removed from his office. Five Catholic archbishops and bishops were submitted to a humiliating oath of allegiance in the Parliament building (the decree requiring this oath had not previously been enforced). Similar oaths were administered to the Protestant bishops. For weeks in April and May 1959 the Hungarian press reported that groups of priests of all denominations were swearing allegiance to Communist state functionaries. The press did not go into the methods of persuasion nor the priests' mental reservations. On June 2, 1959, the Office of Church Affairs was re-established. Security Police agents again took their places in ecclesiastical offices to supervise all activities. Theological seminaries were screened by the police, and many novices had to be expelled.

A violent press campaign against religion was set in motion. The teaching of religion in schools, first encouraged after the Revolution, was hindered and often rendered impossible in many ways. The regime's aims were twofold: first, to obstruct the teaching of religion and prevent religious influence on youth; second, to turn the exist-

* It was reported that at a mass held by Archbishop Grösz to celebrate the coronation of the new Pope, a peace priest mounted the chair and read a circular inviting the faithful to vote. The audience "immediately started coughing and sneezing, while children cried. Everybody seemed suddenly afflicted by a dreadful cold." *The Times* (London), Nov. 14, 1958.

ing churches into willful instruments of the Party. "The churches have to adapt themselves to the state order of People's Democracy and must respect the proletarian dictatorship as the order of the state." "The primary task of atheist education in the family is prevention . . ." [11] Provincial papers were particularly outspoken in saying that thus far "events of the counter-revolution had interrupted the systematic struggle against religion," since the conduct of such a campaign must "at all times be subordinated to the interests of political and economic policies." But now, "the time has come to fight." [12]

In seeking to subdue the churches, and especially the powerful Roman Catholic Church, the Hungarian Communist regime acted in harmony with Czechoslovakia and Rumania, but in contrast to the mutual toleration between church and state in Poland. Antichurch strategy differs as among the satellite countries. Where Eastern Orthodoxy is predominant, as in Rumania, allegiance to the Patriarch of Moscow (a tool of the Kremlin) is the appropriate way to achieve the desired results. Where a schismatic "national" Catholic Church can be created, as in Czechoslovakia and also in China, Communists seek to achieve the enslavement of religion through a victory by this church over the one recognizing the primacy of the Pope. In Hungary up to 1961 the Communists, though they had fostered the abject peace priests, had not been able to promote a secessionist "Catholic" Church. Most of the clergy are compelled to cooperate, in different degrees, with the restrictions of the regime. The cooperation is humiliating, but, paradoxically, the clergical opposition to Communism, because of its very elasticity, may be more difficult for the regime to conquer than a stubborn resistance.

For want of new appointments by the Vatican that can be approved by the Hungarian government, half of the Catholic bishoprics remained vacant, administered by vicars elected by the Chapters under government pressure.* Some apostolic administrators of dioceses have been banned by the government; on the other hand, the government-sponsored vicars have not received approval by the Vatican. At the parish level, priests in constant touch with their congregations cannot be rigidly controlled. Churches are centers of silent resistance. They are crowded with believers, and even non-

* After protracted negotiations between Archbishop Grösz and the Hungarian government, the Presidium of the Hungarian People's Republic approved four appointments of apostolic "administrators" made by Pope John XXIII for the administration of two vacant dioceses and two vacant archdioceses, including that of Cardinal Mindszenty. *Magyar Közlöny*, July 25, 1959.

believers who are in reality disguised political demonstrators against the regime. And the Primate of the Hungarian Catholic Church, though separated from his flocks, continues to exercise an electrifying effect on the people.[13]

THE WRITERS

After the unsuccessful talks between government and literary leaders, the collapse of all plans to resuscitate a "national" coalition regime, the dissolution of the Writers' Association and of the Union of Journalists, and the imprisonment of many prominent members, the majority of writers took refuge in a self-imposed silence. For the government, the problem was to prevent recurrence of a literary revolt which might again be the forerunner of political events. For the silent intellectuals, the problem was one of economic survival. In search of compromise, the literary weekly *Élet és Irodalom* (Life and Literature) called on Hungarian writers in August 1957 to submit their complaints and to state the conditions under which they would resume work in order to end the "chaos" endangering cultural life in Hungary. Gyula Kállai, then Minister of Culture, while threatening, on the one hand, to "free the culture life of Hungary from the counter-revolutionary elements," complained on the other that "unfortunately Communist intellectuals on whom the government could rely were not very numerous." [14] At the same time it was revealed that talks between the government and various groups of writers were in progress. Some agreement may have then been reached, because 263 writers were reported in September 1957 to have signed a protest against the Report of the United Nations Special Committee on Hungary.[15] The publication of two new literary periodicals was announced: *Kortárs* (Contemporary) and *Uj Hang* (New Voice), which was especially reserved for "young writers." On September 8, after a dormancy of ten months, the daily *Magyar Nemzet* also reappeared as the organ of the People's Patriotic Front.

Two prominent journalists, Jozsef Gáli and Gyula Obersovszky, were sentenced to death in July 1957; the intervention of the International Pen Club saved their lives and their sentences were changed to life imprisonment. The sentencing of Déry, Háy, Zelk, and Tardos came on November 13, 1957. The relations of the Hungarian writers with the regime continued unsettled; evidently the majority of them still refused to cooperate. Though the centrist elements around Kádár were willing to allow the writers a certain amount of freedom, the Stalinist wing of the Party and the handful of Stalinist writers opposed any concession.[16] In March 1958 it was admitted that the attitude of writers represented "a negative aspect of our life," because for many of them the psychological process of emerging from the blind alley of "internal emigration" and making the path back to the people had been "slower than for other intellectual strata." Significantly, the Kossuth Prize for literature was not awarded in 1958.[17]

Parallel with these developments, controversies arose among the literary papers. First these disputes centered around the person of the late novelist Dezsö Szabo. Whereas *Kortárs* in its issue of December 1957 wished to rehabilitate this writer who had a reputation of belonging to the extreme right, *Népszabadság* replied on February 2, 1958, by calling him a fascist and associating him with adherents of national Communism, and *Élet és Irodalom* declared on February 28 that "just as Szabo . . . was swept into an alliance with the Capitalists and wealthy landowners against the Soviet Union . . . so the Hungarian national Communists were swept into servile support of the same forces." These attacks were simultaneous with those against Professor György Lukács in the *Társadalmi Szemle.**

In June 1958, the month when Imre Nagy's execution was announced and the campaign against "revisionists" was going strong, an all-out attack was launched against writers and intellectuals in general. The Party daily first condemned teachers and students of the University of Budapest for having learned nothing from the past errors and having "tried to smuggle the mistaken methods of leadership back into the work of their Party organization of the University." Another periodical recognized that "we have been unsuccessful in attracting firmly to our side a part of the university professors and teachers, either ideologically or politically." It lectured the university teachers, saying that in addition to the bourgeois and revisionist views which they shared with the students, "a strong sham-humanism is alive among them, and illusions about the leading position of the intelligentsia." As for the students, the strongest of their hostile views was *bourgeois nationalism*. This was evident in two forms: anti-Sovietism and irredentism. At the University of Budapest great influence had been achieved by the "so-called third-road travelers and the so-called 'national Communist' ideology, the bourgeois democratic illusions and — especially at the Faculty of Social Sciences — the wrong anti-Marxist views of

---

* The Polish newspaper *Polytika* commented on January 11, 1958, on the attack against Lukács and compared it with the proceedings against Galileo.

some Populist writers." The Hungarian Populist writers were then selected as the main target for attacks.[18]

An article in the July 1958 issue of *Társadalmi Szemle* defined the attitude of the Party's Central Committee toward these Populist writers. In the Horthy era they had "earned historical merits for having kept the social problems of the peasantry in the forefront of public interest," but during the Revolution they had "shifted to the right hour by hour under the pressure of reactionary forces." The article flattered the Populists — "appreciation for their talent as writers has in no way diminished" — but invited them "to revise the ideology of their movement in the light of the recent trend of events and to repudiate their mistakes." Inasmuch as the Party and the state "cannot approve of their organization into a political body or literary clique," the Central Committee wishes "former Populist writers, as individuals and personalities of literary and political life, to play a more effective part in the work of building a People's Democracy." The article referred by name to some of these writers, to Péter Veres, last president of the Writers' Association before its dissolution, to the playwright László Németh, to the essayist Gyula Illyés, and to the novelist Áron Tamási, stating that they had become "allies of revisionism and counter-revolutionary elements."

None of these efforts seems to have borne satisfactory fruits. Though many of the originally "silent" writers were compelled for economic reasons to publish translations, reprints of their former works, or reviews, not many supported the regime as had been expected from them. Resignation is expressed by Bölöni, editor of *Élet és Irodalom,* in a radio interview: "A completely new generation of writers would bring about a new flowering of our present day literature . . . the philosophy of the older generation of writers could not be changed. Nor do we want to change them. It would be impossible . . . to transplant them into different worlds. All we ask of the old writers is not to be hostile to this new world." [19] Characteristic of the anodyne and ambiguous approach practiced by those who had been compelled to write again in order to eat is the first public statement made by the Populist writer Tamási after two years of silence: "We fully recognize the primacy of the working class, that is of the Party . . . but we demand equality for the peasants and the intellectuals. We fully recognize the importance of Socialism." [20]

Evidently more for the use of the "new generation" of writers than for the incorrigible "old" ones, the Communist Party early in

1959 issued a guide for the clarification of the "Party's literary political objectives." [21] This article, with strong Zhdanovite overtones, underlined the importance the Party attributed to literature, "this powerful weapon of cultural development." The Party was fighting for a literature that "identifies itself with the Leninist principle of Party-mindedness" and that wishes to portray "reality based on the ideology of the proletariat and on the Marxist-Leninist view." The article assumed the unenviable task of again defining "Socialist realism," upon whose very "existence" the revisionists had "tried to cast doubts." Socialist realism is "a creative method which conceives and understands life in motion, portrays its contradictions in motion and, therefore, shows the truth more deeply than any other art or literature" — but this portrayal must imply "the victory of the arising new over the dying old."

"Party guidance" and "successful organization of literary life" evidently were behind the reorganization of the Writers' Association which took place on September 25, 1959. In its revived version, the association acquired a board consisting only of Stalinist and collaborationist writers, most of them third-rate and little known. The absence of talent is suggested by a pronouncement of Gyula Kállai: "If some authors still withdraw into themselves, it will be primarily to their disadvantage, not to ours." [22] And at the Party Congress of December 1959, Kádár himself said that "the revolution on the cultural front is to some extent lagging behind the results achieved in the political and economic spheres . . . Literature and the arts are still far from having paid their debt to the people." [23]

Talks again took place during the first half of 1960 between the government and leading Populist writers. The Populists, because of the regime's criminal stigmatization of the revisionists, had by now become the most significant group of Hungarian writers,[24] enjoying not only great popularity but also personal contacts with prominent centrist members of the regime, especially with Gyula Kállai. Those who best fit that description seemed to be László Németh, Áron Tamási, Gyula Illyés, and Géza Féja. The regime no doubt continued to hope that the prominent Populists would become fellow travelers; but the price asked for such a "surrender" was still too high. The writers demanded, among other things, the liberation and reinstatement of Professor Bibo, and the leftist wing of the Party, led by Apro, Kiss, and Marosán, still opposed major concessions. In the absence of clear Soviet "advice" on such issues, even a limited agreement that would bring back into public life a number of influential writers was not forthcoming.[25]

In the meantime the regime and writers continued to observe a tacit bargain that permitted the recalcitrant but nationally respected writers to publish non-Communist writings, and even to make figurative or esoteric expression of anti-regime feelings.[26] But the endeavors of the regime to acquire the unequivocal spiritual endorsement of prominent Hungarian intellectuals had not succeeded. The meaning of the 1956 Revolution, the disapproval of Soviet intervention, the spuriousness of Kádár's title to power, are the main obstacles that prevent writers and intellectuals from collaborating wholeheartedly with the regime.

ECONOMIC ALIGNMENT WITH THE SOVIET BLOC

The Revolution and Soviet invasion placed the economy of Hungary in a chaotic condition. The loss to the national economy was estimated at from 18 to 20 billion forints, caused partly by material damage (to buildings, plants, and inventories), partly by reduced production and productivity.[27] The departure of nearly 200,-000 persons, many of them technicians and skilled workers, was itself an economic blow. The ensuing budget deficit was met by foreign credits and gifts, by radical curtailment of investments, and by inflating the currency.

The Soviet Union extended credits amounting to 1,138 million rubles, part of this sum in convertible currency, and three fourths of it in long-term loans. Other Communist states also gave assistance. Gifts in the form of goods received from the Soviet Union amounted to 40 million rubles, and from Communist China, $7.5 million. There was also Western aid, but its value remained unannounced.[28]

By August 1957 the general price level had increased by 20 to 30 per cent over that of October 1956. In order to combat inflation the government drastically reduced wages effective from August 31, 1957, thus undoing an increase that had been made at the beginning of the year. As a result of foreign aid and an excellent harvest, real incomes in 1957 were said to have surpassed the 1955 level.[29] On the other hand, a study issued early in 1958 by the Economic Commission for Europe largely refuted the optimistic statements from Hungarian sources concerning the state of the national economy. Production appeared to have stagnated, probably because expansion was sought in those sectors that could contribute to redressing the balance payments. Likewise, wage stabilization resulted in low labor productivity; there were shortages of many goods; and food prices on the free market had risen by 29 per cent compared to those of mid-1957.[30]

The imbalance in foreign trade which had threatened Hungary's economy since 1955 considerably worsened during the year after the Revolution. Imports in the first nine months of 1957 increased by 1.5 billion forints over the corresponding period of 1956, while exports fell by 1.1 billion forints. Owing to Soviet-bloc credits and the lack of Western currencies, the proportion of imports received from Soviet-bloc countries increased.[31] The intensification of trade relations with other Communist countries thus occurred as a necessity rather than as a planned policy. Hungary's acute need of essential raw materials for her production and for her export trade made her government a champion of the correct distribution of effort among "Socialist" countries. For the same reasons the over-ambitious policy of heavy industrial development was again soft-pedaled.

The final trade balance for 1957 showed a deficit of about two billion forints. Imports from the Soviet Union were twice as high as in the previous years; imports from Czechoslovakia and the German Democratic Republic increased by 40 per cent and from Poland by 30. Hungary's imports from Yugoslavia were in 1957 four times greater than in 1955 and 60 per cent greater than in 1956. On the other hand, Hungarian purchases made in capitalistic countries sank by 26 per cent as against 1955. Two thirds of Hungary's exports were directed to Communist countries, particularly to the Soviet Union. These exports remained, however, 30 per cent below those of 1955 and 12 per cent below those of 1956. Exports to capitalist countries decreased 17 and 10 per cent as compared with 1955 and 1956 respectively. It was announced that the foreign trade gap could no longer be filled by loans and that productivity must be increased to prevent an adverse trade balance.[32]

Frantic efforts early in 1958 were directed toward increased productivity, discipline in production, and the development of foreign markets.[33] It was pointed out that unless everybody cooperated in eliminating waste, extravagance, and laxity, the recent increase in living standards would have to be forfeited. In the budgets for 1958–59, no more provisions were made for foreign loans to balance income and expenditure.

The all-out effort for an improvement of the trade balance bore fruit in 1958, though it resulted in greater dependence on Communist markets other than Yugoslavia. Total exports increased by 21 per cent, while imports declined 12 per cent; the deficit of 1957 was replaced by an active trade balance of 587 million forints.[34] In 1938 Hungary's first supplier was Germany and the second Austria, which were also the first and second markets for her exports. By 1949 the Soviet Union already ranked first and the United Kingdom second as suppliers to Hungary, and the Soviet Union and Czechoslovakia first and second as purchasers of Hungarian exports. In 1958 the Soviet Union, Czechoslovakia, and East Germany took the three leading places, both as suppliers and purchasers.

According to Hungarian statistics the national income increased by approximately 5 per cent during 1958 (the smallest increase of all East-Central European Communist countries), but the per capita income of the agricultural population decreased by approximately 8 per cent. Real wages increased by less than 2 per cent as compared to an increase of 15 per cent for the previous year. The year 1958 saw a notable increase of investments. Plans for 1959 and subsequent years included such measures as the greater integration of the Hungarian economy with that of other Communist countries through the CEMA (Council of Economic Mutual Aid) and an increase in the volume of foreign trade.[35] The new Five-Year Plan started in 1960, at the same time as similar plans in other Socialist countries.

The plenary conference of CEMA in Moscow in January 1958 marked the beginning of a better and more comprehensive cooperation among the member states.[36] For Hungary, poor in raw materials but sufficiently industrialized to export industrial products, the vast markets of the Soviet Union and China appeared as promising outlets for her exports — provided she could import the necessary primary materials. Thus official Hungary had become a fervent admirer of the principles voiced in connection with CEMA, and ready to adjust her investment budget to develop industries fitting into the plans of this organization.

Since the economic incentive was one of the more successful devices of the Kádár regime for popularizing itself in the country, the idea of a "division of labor" among Communist countries was increasingly voiced. This division seemed to hold immense possibilities for the Hungarian economy; it seemed to open the way for ambitious projects that would revolutionize her production. Among such projects are the hydroelectric station to be built on the Danube in collaboration with Czechoslovakia, planned for 1975, that would meet 10 per cent of the power requirements in Hungary; new atomic power stations to be created within the framework of CEMA; and a pipeline leading to Hungary and Czechoslovakia from Soviet oil wells beyond the Volga.

The economic alignment to the Soviet-bloc countries is viewed with interest and consent by the realistic-minded elements of the population, not because the idea of closer relationship with the Soviet Union is cherished, but because a betterment of living conditions is hoped for. A cautious and suspicious public opinion will not automatically assume that all the plans in view are projected for the genuine interest of the Hungarian national economy. The public will doubt whether the increased trade and economic ties with the Soviet Union are equally beneficial to the Hungarian trade partner. The mystery beclouding economic agreements with Moscow, and especially the lack of published figures on commodities delivered or received will add to the lack of enthusiasm expressed by many in reviewing the achievements of CEMA.

Studies of trade terms between the Soviet Union and the People's Democracies of East-Central Europe in the years after 1956 have revealed that a discriminatory price system still operated. Soviet exports were overpriced; Soviet imports from the satellite areas were underpriced. For example, in 1957 the satellite countries had to pay 8 per cent more for Soviet imports than for similar commodities imported from the West, and received 18 per cent less for their exports to the Soviet Union than world market prices would indicate.[37] Other evidence has been presented that wheat shipments made by the Soviet Union to Hungary in 1957 had been overpriced $10.48 per ton (or 14.6 per cent) with respect to world market prices.[38] The political dependence of the smaller Communist countries was apparently still being used for economic exploitation by the Soviet Union, despite the warnings imparted by events in Hungary and other satellite countries.* Such exploitation cannot be altogether concealed, and will be used as an additional incentive for centrifugal nationalistic sentiment against economic integration.[39] On the other hand, we cannot presume that the Soviet Union would be ready to sacrifice its own economic, financial, or political interests to the shoring up of the satellite economy.

"The proof of the cake lies in its eating"; a synchronization of planning and the effective implementation of long-term objectives in the field of economic cooperation remains the test of CEMA. A warning by the Soviet government to its East European allies that it will be obliged to revise fundamentally its trading policy in 1965,

---

* Revolutionary demands in October 1956 asked for publication of secret trade agreements with the Soviets and clarifications on the exploitation of the uranium ore in Hungary. Details of trade agreements (and especially prices) are still shrouded in mystery as this is written. As to the uranium mines, *Társadalmi Szemle*, May 1960, disclosed that the "Soviet government had greatly and in many respects helped us to start on working" these mines. The Soviet Union — according to this article — declared itself ready "to purchase at a price above the world market price uranium ore not needed for the purposes of the Hungarian national economy."

because of increased commitments at home and in the underdeveloped areas of Asia and Africa,[40] casts doubt upon the prospects for a sustained economic cooperation within the CEMA framework. Whether the present Hungarian Communist government will be successful in achieving the rational integration of Hungary into the Communist economic orbit depends on the attitude of the Soviet leaders and on the content of this cooperation.

COLLECTIVIZATION OF AGRICULTURE

During the Revolution, more than half of the agricultural cooperatives (kolkhozes) were dissolved and about 63 per cent of the land under collectivization was returned to individual owners. For two years the peasantry was allowed to live in relative tranquility. The abolishment of compulsory deliveries and the ensuing "sellers' market" gave the farmers a measure of prosperity they had not enjoyed since the beginnings of the Communist regime. The idea of socializing agriculture was not abandoned in principle, but, as in Gomulka's Poland, no steps were taken toward the realization of this goal. A thesis on the agrarian policy of the regime was published in the Party's theoretical magazine, *Társadalmi Szemle,* in August 1957. The peasantry was to be grouped in five categories according to their reliability toward the government: (1) members of the kolkhozes, who were considered the nucleus around which "the Socialist transformation" of agriculture would take place; (2) agricultural laborers and semi-proletarians working mainly in the Socialist sector, who were considered to be loyal to the regime; (3) small peasants cultivating three to eight Hungarian acres* of land, who were said to be ready to enter kolkhozes; (4) middle peasants, who had recently gained much strength and whose capitalistic tendencies were to be checked and their holdings limited to about 25 Hungarian acres; (5) village exploiters or kulaks, defined as those owning larger plots than they could cultivate by the labor of members of their household, who could not be considered loyal and, without resort to violent methods, required attention so that their "political influence might be curbed." [41]

Despite the relative prosperity of the single-plot agrarian population, Hungarian agricultural production declined. With the depletion of livestock and the low level of average yields, especially of wheat, Hungary even fell behind other People's Democracies. In December 1958 it was admitted that Hungary, one of the historic

* The Hungarian acre, the cadastral "yoke," equals 0.57 hectares or 1.42 English acres.

breadbaskets of Europe, had not exported wheat since 1953 and in some years she was even compelled to import wheat. The deterioration in the agricultural picture applied equally, if not more stringently, to agricultural cooperatives. In spite of considerable support from the state, livestock-breeding was neglected, since farmers who had joined had sold their breeding animals.[42] At the end of 1958, Hungary was the least collectivized among the People's Democracies with the exception of Poland. There were 2,755 agricultural cooperatives cultivating an area of about 1.5 million Hungarian acres, representing 15.6 per cent of the total arable land. Their membership amounted to about 144,000 persons.

Now that the elections of November 1958 were out of the way, a sharp debate took place in December within the Party's Central Committee on the subject of collectivization. For the first time since the 1956 Revolution, it was officially reported that rightist and leftist deviationism had clashed within the Committee's precincts. After the debate, however, the Central Committee passed a unanimous resolution favoring an increased drive for collectivization. This resolution underlined the important role of agricultural cooperatives in the "Socialist transformation of agriculture" and condemned the "incorrect notions" according to which collectivization would unavoidably lead to a decline in production (the main argument used by the rightist opposition). On the other hand, the resolution pointed out that the aim of a correct agrarian policy is the "Socialist reorganization of agriculture together with a steady increase in agricultural yields." Government policy since the Revolution had proved to be correct, for it had strengthened the material position of the individual farmer as well as that of those belonging to kolkhozes. The political and economic situation, however, "allows a much faster rate of development of the cooperative movements," though allowance must be made to the fact that conditions for "a sudden great revolution" in agriculture "are not yet at hand in Hungary." [43]

The Central Committee's resolution proposed a series of measures to ensure accelerated progress in collectivization. Party organization should strengthen the peasants' confidence in collectivization. State farms and industrial enterprises should give constant support to cooperatives. The government would contribute by paying to the cooperative a "ground rent" according to the amount and type of land that new members had brought in.

The final decision to implement the Central Committee's recommendations was not made until after Kádár's return from the

Twenty-first Congress of the Soviet Communist Party at the end of January 1959. The Hungarian Politburo then decided to go much further and take what amounted to the "big leap forward" toward agricultural collectivization. Kádár stated that every effort had to be made to fill the existing gap in collectivization between Hungary and the other People's Democracies. "This must be our great lesson from the Twenty-first Congress in Moscow," [44] he announced, adding that conditions were now ripe for the move.

The government decree implementing the decision promised that the kolkhozes would be joined by "politically conscious specialists who possess high professional qualifications, have rich experience in the work of leading political and organizational work, and are loyal to Socialism." The weakest among the existing cooperatives, and all those to be formed in the future, were called to elect chairmen who would fulfill these requirements. Intensive farming was to be encouraged by governmental assistance with respect to fertilizers, seeds, machinery, and stock-breeding. To qualify for this help, the cooperatives had to comply fully with the provisions of their statutes, distributing half of their revenue among members on the basis of work units and assigning 10 per cent of their revenue to investment purposes.[45] Other government measures added new inducements such as the cancellation of certain debts to those who joined kolkhozes. Higher taxes were levied on those who did not.

The new campaign to herd farmers into agricultural collectives developed during February and March 1959. Early in April the government stated that more than 1,300 new kolkhozes had been formed, 354,000 farmers had joined, and 35 per cent of arable land was now cultivated by cooperatives. This, together with the acreage of state and municipal farms (the so-called "Socialist sector"), had reached 50 per cent of all arable soil.[46] The development had taken place mainly in Transdanubia, up to then largely immune to collectivization. Some of the methods by which peasants were forced to join could be gleaned from a Hungarian periodical. Articles state, for instance, that influential farmers were summoned to the village hall and detained until they had signed their application for kolkhoz membership. Simultaneously rumors were spread by Party agitators that farmers had been arrested because they refused to sign up. Industrial workers were sent home to their parents in villages on vacation *without pay* and were not permitted to return to work until they had persuaded their parents and relatives to join cooperatives. In some places the "transition to Socialism" was simply announced on a public loudspeaker and orders were issued to everybody to sign up for membership in cooperatives.[47] We may safely assume that these pressures, reported in a press under governmental censorship, were milder than some of those actually practiced but unreported.

An organizational lull accompanied the agricultural season from spring to fall, and then the collectivization drive was taken up again in December 1959. This time the onslaught on individual farmers was pursued in all parts of the country and was characterized by even greater coercion. Consequently, the results were even more "miraculous" than in the winter before. The developments in collectivization were reported week by week like sports results. On January 11 the Socialist sector of agriculture reached 57 per cent, on January 29, 66.2 per cent, and on February 12, 70 per cent. This campaign overreached itself to the extent that even Moscow considered it overzealous. The very day that Kádár returned from an agricultural conference of Communist states in Moscow, the Central Committee, quickly convoked, halted the collectivization drive until further notice.[48]

It appears from the Hungarian press[49] that the fast pace of the drive, coupled with skillful camouflage and willful sabotage on the part of the peasantry, had created disorganization and chaos that would endanger production. In many villages adherence to collectivization had been merely formal, and kolkhoz members continued to cultivate their formerly owned property, but in such a way as to satisfy only their needs. Migrations to towns, lack of discipline, and resort to premeditated slow-downs caused many newly-formed cooperatives to be unremunerative units, dependent on government sustenance. Widespread unrest that occasionally developed into local riots gave the Communist leadership warning that political strategy dictated a temporary consolidation of gains. Opposition within the Party, numerically increased and more outspoken as a result of the collectivization drive, also advocated caution. Imre Dögei, who was replaced as Minister of Agriculture on January 16 by Pál Losonczi, chairman of a successful agricultural collective,[50] presumably had been made scapegoat because of the use of terroristic methods on the villages.

Contrary to expectations the collectivization drive was taken up again in the winter of 1960–61. The regime seemed to be intent on following in the footsteps of East Germany and bringing into collective farms the remaining land still in private hands. The Central Committee decision to proceed with this drive until complete "victory" was achieved over the private agricultural sector was taken in October, but not made public until early December.[51] On February 19, 1961, the Hungarian Communist Party announced that 90 per cent of all arable land had by then been incorporated into the Socialist sector, and that private farming had thus come to its expected end in Hungary. Kolkhozes account for 69 per cent and state farms for 21 per cent of the cultivated land. The remaining ten per cent are tiny plots left to kolkhoz members.[52]

Though the methods employed in the "campaigned" collectivization of Hungarian agriculture have become widely known, the reasons and circumstances of the decision to proceed in this direction are less well established. For the purposes of this study, Kádár's attempt to succeed where Rákosi had so utterly failed may be assessed as a sign of his regime's dependence on the Soviet Union rather than of his desire either to follow in the footsteps of his Stalinist predecessor or to triumph over difficulties where the other had stumbled. Compulsion to agricultural communization must have appeared to Kádár as a means of subduing that important stratum of the Hungarian population that had managed to remain economically independent: the individual farmers cultivating their own plots. The opposition against the agricultural campaign had revealed more than any other issue the continuing rift in the Party. Furthermore, the coercion accompanying the implementation of the collectivization plan had also revealed the influence that "dogmatist" Party functionaries could often wield against the presumed desires of the Party leadership.

The circumstances of the opening of the campaign and of its sudden halt indicate that the plan had received Moscow's approval. Kádár's remarks about the necessity of falling in with the line pursued by other Socialist countries and Münnich's similar arguments[53] are evidence that the Hungarian Party experienced pressure both from Moscow and from the People's Democracies before it embarked upon the campaign. The political and ideological character of this decision appears self-evident. But the Hungary of Kádár could not afford to insist on her own road toward Socialism, as Gomulka had so far succeeded in doing with regard to the collectivization of Poland's agriculture. Moscow's method of controlling a satellite is not the same as it was in the Stalinist era. Whereas Stalin's ukase would have been directly issued and promptly implemented, Khrushchev's more diplomatic instructions are first discussed within the local Party leadership, and persuasion is used in the first instance rather than force. But the instructions are no less compulsory.

In Hungary, the collectivization question was first submitted to the Central Committee. Within that body was a strong opposition against "campaigned" collectivization. At the same time there was a small but vocal opposition against "soft" collectivization methods, which would fail, in their view, because of the "fascist" ideology of the Hungarian peasantry. Regardless of the differences of opinion the Central Committee, after having been briefed on Soviet wishes, decided to open the drive at a suitable moment and without resorting to "administrative measures." Equipped with this resolution, Kádár received his final "advice" during the Twenty-first Congress in Moscow, and thereupon the campaign was set into motion. Leftist Party functionaries saw to it that warnings counseling restraint from physical intimidation should be disregarded; hence the surprising success of the operation. Lajos Fehér, the Central Committee member in charge of agriculture (and former collaborator of Imre Nagy), who had worked out a more moderate collectivization program, himself pointed out in January 1960 the reasons for the campaign's marked success. He attributed it to: (1) the favorable East-West international situation (the impending negotiations at the Summit), meaning that Hungarian peasants could not hope for any political and moral support that might strengthen their resistance; (2) the realization, after the Revolution of 1956, that the Soviets had, in practice, been given a free hand in Eastern Europe; and (3) the conviction that any resistance was bound to be hopeless since the government was able to use such economic measures as could lead to their annihilation.[54]

The collectivization drive is Hungary's major political event since the liquidation of the Revolution of 1956. Whether it again will prove to be a Pyrrhic victory for the regime, as Rákosi's similar campaigns had been, history will show. Resistance was evidently reduced by the peasants' recollection that past attempts at total collectivization had collapsed in 1953 and in 1956; they hardly expected the collectivization to "stick" anyhow. In any case it would take more than one generation to accustom the Hungarian peasantry to methods of collective farming, and it is questionable whether the regime will be able to secure such a continuity. Until the fall of 1958 the Hungarian peasantry, though inimical toward the regime, had been a rather passive and not aggressively dangerous element of the population. The collectivization drive has made the peasants an utterly discontented element. It will require unrelenting vigilance by the regime to keep the lid clamped on their discontent.

30

International Implications of the Hungarian Situation

/\\.\\/

Today it is plain that the policy of the USSR toward the People's Democracies is a total failure. It has led to the disintegration and threatening dissolution of the Socialist camp. The resistance of the People's Democracies against the hegemony of the USSR is part and parcel of the revolt of popular masses against the Stalinist Party and government apparatus and its methods.

WOLFGANG HARICH's "Testament of a Party Rebel" [1]

THE anti-Soviet and anti-Communist uprising in Hungary has opened many new avenues in the field of international relations, both within the Communist orbit and outside. It exercised considerable influence on the relations between the Soviet Union and its satellites and also affected Hungary's ties with her Communist neighbors. Hungarian events weighed heavily upon Soviet-Yugoslav relations and were a contributory cause to the new rupture between the Soviet-led camp and Tito's domain. The Hungarian situation touched upon the cold war. Soviet relations with uncommitted countries were affected. The Hungarian fiasco had an erosive effect on the prestige of the United Nations, largely counteracting gains from the world organization's handling of the Suez conflict. The effects of the events in Hungary and the present Hungarian situation are still being felt in the theater of international politics despite studious Soviet endeavors to obliterate them.

The influence exercised by the Hungarian Revolution on national and international workers' organizations and workers' parties was and still is no less significant than its impact on relations among states. As a result of Soviet intervention in Hungarian affairs, leading Communists and intellectual sympathizers (like Jean-Paul Sartre) have broken openly with Soviet Communism in France, Britain, Italy, and elsewhere.[2] Socialists all over the world have been strengthened in their resistance to Communist infiltration. Anti-Soviet spiritual trends and political movements have gained inspiration from the Hungarian experience.

The principles and demands of the Hungarian revolutionaries, workers, and students have haunted Soviet and other Communist leaders ever since the revolt. Because the contradictions between claims for national self-determination and Soviet-supported Party dictatorship have manifested themselves in an incontrovertible manner, it has become very difficult to find formulas and explanations with which to refute them. The Soviet-Communist contention, based on orthodox Marxist-Leninist tenets, that popular revolutions can only further the triumph of "Socialism" seems to have been utterly contradicted by the course of Hungarian events: hence the fictitious and exorbitant allegations that a counterrevolution had been fomented by foreign imperialists and reactionaries. On the other hand, the restoration of Soviet-Communist rule in Hungary and fears of renewed schismatic tendencies in Communist Parties or attempts at nationalist self-expression in the satellite area have made necessary a policy of "mutual" assistance whenever achievements of "Socialism" seem again to be endangered. The suppression of the national Revolution in Hungary provoked the Communist leadership of other satellite countries to resort to measures of prevention and oppression, creating situations rightly characterized as "neo-Stalinism." [3] All in all, the Hungarian events have brought into the forefront latent problems of "Soviet colonialism," stronger doubts about the "proletarian" character of Communist regimes, and disbelief in the Marxist-Leninist doctrine.

HUNGARY AND THE SOVIET "MONROE DOCTRINE"

When questioned on the "lesson of Hungary," an expression widely used by the Communist press, Khrushchev explained that it meant the "fraternal Socialist solidarity always and in everything." All the Socialist countries "are linked together by their common interests" and "fraternally help one another and are always ready to come to one another's help." [4] The principle to "defend Socialism," that is, to intervene in favor of maintaining Communist rule, thus goes beyond the obligation to come to the assistance of the allied states "in the event of armed attack in Europe" as laid down by the Warsaw Treaty of 1955.[5] Though this treaty provided for Soviet fraternal help to a satellite country against *outside aggression,* it neglected to provide for Soviet fraternal help to preserve the *internal status quo.* This principle, recalling the Holy Alliance, had to be enunciated as a consequence of the Hungarian Revolution. It has been several times reiterated,[6] notwithstanding its contradiction of principles of nonintervention in internal affairs of other countries (one of the famous Five Principles of Peaceful Coexistence), and its contradiction of arguments asserting the inviolability of countries "having chosen their own forms of government." [7] This head-on clash of principles was especially shattering in Minsk on January 22, 1958, when Khrushchev in a single breath referred to the Soviet "fraternal help" that "routed in three days the counterrevolutionary bands in Hungary and restored revolutionary order," and exclaimed that "we want absolute nonintervention in the internal affairs of other states," and "we have strictly observed and shall continue to observe this inviolable rule." [8]

Consequently, intervention into the affairs of Socialist states to preserve or restore the "workers' power" is deemed to be nonintervention, whereas even a discussion of the conditions in the East-Central European area is interference in the domestic affairs of these countries. Soviet policy evidently aims at establishing a kind of Monroe Doctrine for the areas under its domination, both to exclude foreign influences and to maintain a *status quo* created by the military presence of the Soviet Army in this area since 1945. In contrast, the Soviet Union lately repudiated the time-honored American Monroe Doctrine in connection with events in Cuba.[9] Whereas this doctrine, established since 1823, was primarily aimed at preventing the restoration of Spanish colonial rule in the Americas, the Soviet "Monroe Doctrine" evidently is designed to preserve Soviet "colonial" rule in the East-Central European area.

The explanations of the Soviet government for its intervention in Hungary varied in accordance with the circumstances in which they were used. The official position first taken was that Hungary had applied for Soviet help under the terms of the Warsaw Treaty, having been attacked by "counterrevolutionary" elements and "imperialist agents," and that the Soviet government was obligated to render help. Subsequently, less stress was placed on legal arguments, and it was alleged that "by assisting the Hungarian people, the USSR had done its international duty to the working people of

Hungary and other Socialist countries, in keeping with the interest of world peace." [10] Or it was alleged that "the participation of Soviet Army units in crushing the Fascist rebels was a supreme act of proletarian solidarity." [11] Khrushchev gave still another explanation of the intervention: it was a "spontaneous" action of Soviet soldiers stationed in Hungary, suppressing the "bloodbath" instigated by the sinister forces of reaction.[12] Every version, regardless of how put, conveyed the same message to the world: the Soviet motive had been the preservation of a Soviet-Communist system in Hungary. And meanwhile the presumed *cause* of the revolt varied. The revolt had been set off by imperialist and reactionary counterrevolutionary attacks. Or it had been an uprising prompted by Rákosi's Stalinist dictatorship.

The genuine Hungarian reactions toward Soviet excuses for the armed intervention may be inferred from the frequency of the officially inspired statements, articles, and meetings, stressing Soviet-Hungarian friendship. The celebration of the fortieth anniversary of the Bolshevik Revolution in 1957 brought forth "theses" analyzing the "new conception" of Soviet-Hungarian relations.[13] Münnich, after becoming Prime Minister, called Soviet-Hungarian friendship "the alpha and omega of our national existence"; and Kádár excelled in giving a neo-Stalinist meaning to "progressiveness": "In our opinion, no man living in any country of the world can call himself progressive unless he is loyal to the USSR and the People's Democracies." In the same speech Kádár solemnly stated that the "temporary" stationing of Soviet troops in Hungary "was not determined by the internal situation of Hungary" but by the international situation.[14] Only a few days before Kádár's eulogy of Soviet-Hungarian friendship, the Party daily, denouncing "bourgeois nationalism" among the university youth, said that "in the eyes of students . . . every problem . . . is outweighed by one question: would the Soviet troops . . . be withdrawn from the country?" The article added that to these students "alliance with Mindszenty is *more Hungarian* than a militant joining of forces with the Soviet workers." [15]

Khrushchev's impromptu references to the intervention of Tsar Nicholas I in 1849 — during his visits to Hungary in April 1958 and December 1959 — must have had a devastating effect, even in Communist Party circles. This may be judged by the articles which undertook to minimize the impact of such utterances on the national consciousness. An obviously Party-inspired article, analyzing the meaning of "national independence," concluded that it "represents the endeavor to ward off external violence from the path of social development." This fundamental idea, the author continues, was applicable in 1848–49. But the situation was completely different in 1956, when social progress was in danger of being turned back with the help of "international reaction." According to the author, the 1956 Soviet intervention cannot be compared with that of 1849. Some people, he says, "maintain that both in 1849 and on November 4, 1956, the Russians marched into Hungary. Yet they forget the 'unimportant' factor that in 1849 the soldiers of the Tsar came to our country but in 1956 they were soldiers of the Soviet people who expelled the Tsar." [16] In his concluding remarks the author attacks "superficial analogies."

Also in history the essential causal connections can be analyzed and a difference can be made between scientific truth and superstitions originating from superficial analogies. Those who understand this will learn from history, but for those who do not, history is a not quite harmless storybook.

The reader may wonder whether these remarks were not directed against Khrushchev's injudicious reference to the 1849 intervention. But Khrushchev, in seeing an analogy between the 1956 intervention and that of 1849, was perhaps a better historian than he intended to be. Both Tsar Nicholas I and the Soviet Union of 1956 intervened in "reaction" against revolutionary changes. The Tsar, in the true spirit of the Holy Alliance, gave a helping hand to his brother emperor in restoring autocratic rule in Hungary. The Soviet Union reinstated the *ancien régime* of Communism in Hungary. The principle of immutability of an existing regime is now translated by the Soviet Union to include the empire that it had succeeded in building up after the end of World War II. From the point of view of the Hungarian revolutionaries, the true counter-revolutionaries in the picture were the Soviet invaders. Soviet Russian imperialism is characterized by a rigid insistence on the *status quo* in the Soviet-dominated area, but by subversion and revolution in Asia and Africa; a Monroe Doctrine for the satellite area, but intervention elsewhere.

The Hungarian Revolution increased the Soviet leaders' watchfulness over their East-Central European domain. It had happened — they undoubtedly knew — without Western assistance. Nevertheless, the Western powers had to be discouraged from "trying to put their pig snouts into the Socialist orchard." [17] This was a danger even more acute than the isolated revolt of an oppressed people. The West must "forget about the possibility of turning the People's

Democracies of East Europe to Capitalism once again. What is lost is lost." [18] On the other hand, the "cold war" must be brought into areas that thus far were effectively excluded from Soviet interference: Cuba and the Congo. Repetition of satellite revolutions could best be forestalled by daring attacks into the heartland of the enemy.

HUNGARY AND THE YUGOSLAV ROAD TO SOCIALISM

The anti-Communist developments in the latter stages of the Hungarian Revolution had raised the misgivings of Belgrade. The second Soviet armed intervention, installing a regime headed by Kádár but introducing, in practice, Soviet military rule, did not fail to leave bitterness in the mouths of the Yugoslav leaders. While many Yugoslavs openly sympathized with the Hungarian bid for freedom, the government adopted a line of reserved approval of the Soviet action in Hungary, mixed with severe criticism of this action.[19] The train of ideas was fully developed in Tito's speech of November 11, 1956, at Pula, which we quoted earlier. The first Soviet intervention was disapproved of, whereas the second armed intervention was considered *necessary* by Tito *"if it meant saving Socialism in Hungary."* On principle — so Tito said — he was against any interference, and from this point of view, the second intervention "was also bad." His official thesis reflected the idea that the handling of Hungarian affairs had been utterly mismanaged by the Soviets. Although the censure included the forceful intstallation of Kádár, the latter action might retrospectively be considered a favorable thing, "if it leads to the preservation of Socialism in Hungary . . . and to peace in the world . . . *provided that the Soviet troops withdraw* the moment the situation in that country is settled and quiet." (All the italics are ours.) The mishandling of Hungarian matters was attributed by Tito to "irresponsible Stalinist elements," both in the Soviet Union and in other Communist parties: "They sowed the wind and are reaping the storm." [20]

Tito's speech evoked sharp polemics in the Soviet-dominated press. Not only were the passages dealing with Hungarian events violently criticized but all differences between Yugoslavia and the Soviets were reviewed on this occasion.[21] The abduction of Imre Nagy by Soviet personnel, despite the safe conduct promised him by Kádár, led to the renewal of acrimonious dialogues. Tito, his eyes dimmed by his ambivalence toward the Soviet intervention, allowed himself to be duped by Kádár's assurances which, in the absence of any formal Soviet confirmation, would have struck any objective observer on the spot as illusory.

Yugoslavia received a diplomatic defeat and loss of prestige as a consequence of the Hungarian events. She wanted a "national" Communistic regime established in the territory of her northern neighbor, and instead saw a new puppet government created by Soviet bayonets, more subservient to Moscow than even Rákosi's despised regime. The man and the party group that Tito had wished to see at the helm of Hungary had become outlaws or Soviet prisoners. The "national road to Socialism" was barred, not only to Hungary, but, as a consequence of Hungarian developments, to all other People's Democracies save Poland. Even Poland was helpless or unwilling to promote any evolution that would have conformed to Tito's image of a Communist commonwealth. The defense of Socialism, as even Tito had to admit, had become more paramount than the "independence of Socialist countries and Communist Parties from the Soviet Union and from the Communist Party of the Soviet Union." [22] Of course, there were somewhat differing interpretations in Yugoslavia of the Soviet action in Hungary, too: the Yugoslav Vice-President, Edvard Kardelj, in a speech before the National Assembly, described the Soviet intervention as aimed at "saving the balance of power in Europe" rather than saving Socialism in Hungary.[23]

For several months, Soviet-Yugoslav relations were affected more by Hungarian events than anything else. Yugoslavia's hesitations were evident in her votes in the United Nations General Assembly. She sometimes voted against condemning Soviet intervention in Hungary and sometimes abstained from voting. On the whole, Yugoslavia did not formally object to United Nations endeavors to solve the Hungarian problem; she only voted against resolutions that included such items as the immediate withdrawal of Soviet troops and the holding of free elections under United Nations auspices. In short, she tried to save a Socialist Hungary that would not unconditionally be subject to Soviet power.

The flirtation which Tito had pursued with Nagy and other elements of the Hungarian Party likely to follow a course of national Communism was continued with some caution in regard to Kádár and his regime. Tito may have cherished hopes that Kádár, whom he had met on the occasion of Gerö's inauspicious journey to Yugoslavia in October 1956, would be able to pursue a national Communist line. His early appraisal of Kádár and his regime was summed up in his speech at Pula, when he said that, "viewing current developments in Hungary from the perspective of Socialism or counter-revolution, we must defend Kádár's present government, we must help it. We must help it because it is in a very difficult situation." [24]

Blaming much on the "errors of the Rákosi regime," Tito emphatically declared that "one cannot impose a leader on a people; that is impossible." Whether or not Tito was conscious that his words might apply to Kádár as well as Rákosi, he evidently cherished hopes that Khrushchev's disciple would follow the master's steps. The narrow policy followed by Tito in the Hungarian affair — rigid insistence on Communist dictatorship without Soviet control — was to continue, and hopes were now placed in the person of Khrushchev, who was engaged in a deadly struggle with his Stalinist and anti-Stalinist opponents in the Kremlin in the first six months of 1957.

In whatever direction Yugoslav-Soviet relations moved, Yugoslav-Hungarian relations followed, though not always immediately. After Khrushchev's triumphal emergence from his struggle for supreme Soviet leadership, and especially after the hopeful though inconclusive meeting of the Soviet and Yugoslav leaders in Rumania on August 1 and 2, 1957, the tie between Belgrade and Budapest miraculously fattened. Kardelj, earlier a severe critic of Kádár's regime, had friendly talks with the Hungarian leaders on his way to the Moscow Conference of Communist leaders in November 1957.[25] In Moscow bilateral talks were conducted between the Yugoslav and Hungarian delegations. Yugoslavia's Day of the Republic was enthusiastically celebrated in Budapest on November 29.[26] Meanwhile, however, the Moscow declaration of November 7 had failed to register the signatures of the Yugoslav delegates. Perhaps the Hungarian leadership had not been properly informed on the precariousness of Yugoslav-Soviet relations before and after the Moscow conference. On the other hand, we may assume that Hungary had been instructed by the Kremlin to maintain cordial relations with her southern neighbor, to serve as a "bridge" as long as there was hope that the deviating brother might still return to the fold.

In January 1958, Kádár was still able to refer to the "healthy development of good-neighborly relations" between Hungary and Yugoslavia, and his forthcoming visit to Yugoslavia was being predicted.[27] The future of Imre Nagy was evidently one of the subjects to be discussed. For Tito it was a matter of both prestige and policy to save the life and even the political future of Nagy, who, despite his "weaknesses" toward reactionaries, was still considered a leading representative of national Communism. For Kádár, Tito's friendship was a valuable asset for the strengthening of his domestic position, but he was by no means eager to have Nagy, a formidable rival, back in Hungary.

The "comradely meeting" between Hungarian and Yugoslav leaders was held sometime in late March 1958 at Karadjorjevo where "questions concerning the two Parties were discussed in a friendly atmosphere." *Borba* was, thereafter, able to pay its first tribute to the Hungarian regime after the uprising, and Tito was confident that "the friendly relations between Yugoslavia and Hungary will continue to strengthen in the interest of the preservation of peace in the world and Socialist development." [28] It is believed that Kádár gave Tito a genuine account of his Party's weaknesses and that they also discussed the ideological and economic coordination of the two regimes, the case of Imre Nagy, and the question of an atom-free zone in Southeast Europe similar to that proposed in the Rapacki Plan.[29] Kádár may have given assurances that Imre Nagy would not be tried. In any case he seems to have obtained an unconditional endorsement from Tito.

Already, however, the props of Hungarian-Yugoslav friendship were being kicked away and the structure was bound to fall. The Draft Program of the League of Yugoslav Communists had been published on March 13. This document, though addressed to the Yugoslav Seventh Party Congress to be held in Ljubljana from April 22 to 26, was couched in terms so general as to apply to other Communist parties. As it made the rounds of Europe it stirred up sharp and growing opposition from Moscow and its satellites. Nonetheless, the Yugoslav Party Congress adopted it.

"Yugoslavia's Way," as it came to be called, was cleansed of its original anti-Soviet references before adoption by the congress. But it contained the "heresies" of Titoist deviationism, methodically arranged and digested. It condemned "unequal relations" among Socialist countries. It refused to accept the Manichaean cleavage of the world.[30] The Yugoslav Program caused a violent reaction in the Communist orbit in that spring of 1958. Though Yugoslav "heresies" were widely known before, their ostentatious publication was a revolt against orthodoxy comparable by historic analogy to the publication of the Ninety-five Theses of October 31, 1517, that earned Martin Luther excommunication by Rome.

After an attack in the *Kommunist* of Moscow, the campaign was joined by the Hungarian Party journal, *Társadalmi Szemle*. The Yugoslav Program, according to this organ, "does not mention the constant machinations of the imperialist bloc, especially of the

U.S.A., against the Socialist countries." The imperialist governments "have included in their official 'program' the 'liberation of the Eastern European countries.' We must not underestimate this fact of the imperialist intrigues, especially after the counter-revolutionary attempt in Hungary. It can hardly be denied that a victory of the counter-revolution could have meant a very great danger also to Socialist Yugoslavia." The Hungarian periodical then took the plunge: "We feel that we must take a definite stand regarding views which in the recent past exerted strong influence in Hungary as well, and the practical effect of which proved bad." [31]

One of the signals for an open break between the Soviet block and Tito's Yugoslavia was the human sacrifice of Imre Nagy, announced in June. This led to a Yugoslav protest to Hungary and the exchange of recriminative notes. The Hungarian delegate to the Czechoslovak Party Congress declared on June 19 that the "defense of the purity of Marxism-Leninism against the revisionist views published in the Yugoslav Party Program is our internationalist duty." [32] The exchange of sharp diplomatic notes continued throughout the fall of 1958. Hungary alleged that the Yugoslavs had interfered in Hungarian internal affairs with regard to the case of Imre Nagy; that they had maintained conspiratorial contacts with Hungarian "counterrevolutionaries" for many months before the revolt broke out; and that they had allowed Imre Nagy to direct insurgents from the Yugoslav embassy. The Yugoslavs expressed their resentment over the accusations.

The ambiguity of Yugoslavia's position was again demonstrated by that country's voting against the inclusion of the Hungarian Question on the agenda of the United Nations while asserting simultaneously that Hungary had "not only violated certain of their explicit obligations towards us on a very sensitive question [i.e., Imre Nagy's execution] . . . but moreover began to accuse us publicly and without justification." [33]

During the second half of 1958, Czechoslovakia, considered to be the most reliable satellite, was apparently entrusted by Soviet leaders with the role of urging the Hungarian and Rumanian Communist parties to establish a common front against Tito. In December, at a reception in Prague, the Hungarian delegate, Marosán, made a direct attack on Yugoslavia that caused the Yugoslav ambassador to walk out. These attacks were repeated whenever Hungarian and Czechoslovak Party leaders met. Kádár's criticism of Yugoslavia when visiting Prague in February 1959 evoked sarcastic comments from Yugoslavia: "It emerges from Kádár's speech in Prague that

Hungary was a victim of Yugoslav revisionism and not of dogmatism and Stalinism . . . It is interesting, and to some extent symptomatic, that János Kádár broaches a subject . . . at the time when the same policy, the same concepts, and the same practices which brought Hungary to the brink of catastrope are again coming to the fore, both with regard to Yugoslavia and within the camp itself." [34]

At the Hungarian Party Congress in December 1959, First Secretary Kádár explained that "our relations with the Yugoslav League of Communists have deteriorated and there is no official contact at the moment between our Parties." He further stated that the Yugoslavs had "revised" Marxism, and he chose as an example of their diversion from the correct path the fact that in December 1956 he had been advised by them "not to make hopeless experiments" for the reorganization of the Party, but to "build our political system upon the so-called workers' councils." [35]

Kádár, perhaps against his better judgment, was forced to follow the circuitous path staked out by Khrushchev in his relations with Tito. For one small moment, meeting the Yugoslav dictator in March 1958, he might have thought himself the motor and not the wheel; soon thereafter, he was put in his proper place by Khrushchev. His servile acceptance of the renewed anti-Titoist campaign, coupled with its new "Rajk affair" — the judicial murder of Imre Nagy — vividly demonstrate Hungarian dependence on Moscow's policies. The attraction of Tito's Yugoslavia for Hungarians, as in the Stalinist times, is not so much Yugoslav revisionism but the coupling of this term with "independence," freedom from Soviet control. Thus, any anti-Yugoslav campaign pressed upon the Party and the country is likely to become once again an advertisement in favor of the "Yugoslav road to Socialism."

Yugoslav interest in Hungary, during the postrevolutionary period, continued to pursue egoistic Titoist aims: how to recruit proselytes from among Hungarian Communists for establishing a regime in Hungary that was Communist and yet not dominated by the Soviets. If Yugoslavia had registered a frank and unequivocal disapproval of Soviet aggression in Hungary, if she had used all diplomatic means to support national (whether Communist or non-Communist) resistance, if she had cooperated diplomatically with the West, her efforts might have borne fruit. But Tito's persistence in seeking a narrow Communist goal, in contrast to the wishes of many of his countrymen (including, of course, Milovan Djilas) instead of facilitating some realistic and humane solution of the Hungarian question, did not help Hungary or any other satellite.

It only resulted in a new political isolation for his country.[36] Short-sighted egoism in international politics may one day turn against its own promoter. Tito's conduct toward Hungary "revealed that Yugoslav national Communism was unable in its foreign policy to depart from its narrw ideological and bureaucratic class interests, and that, furthermore, it was ready to yield even those principles of equality and noninterference in internal affairs on which all its successes in the struggle with Moscow had been based." [37]

HUNGARY'S PLACE IN THE COMMUNIST COMMONWEALTH

The national Revolution in Hungary and the revolt of the Polish Communist Party against Soviet supremacy more effectively stirred up the inherent contradictions inside the Communist camp than even the Yugoslav search for a compromise formula with the Kremlin after the Soviet Twentieth Party Congress. Differences over the meaning of the Hungarian Revolution in the context of Marxist-Leninist thinking sowed dissent among Communist countries. The Party in Poland, along with many of the Western Communist parties, refused to give the meaning of "counterrevolution" to the uprising of October 23, 1956, and disapproved, though with some hesitations, the Soviet intervention of November 4. Stalwart Communist parties like the East German and the Czechoslovak condemned the Hungarian events outright as counterrevolution and hailed the Soviet intervention as an outstanding act of proletarian solidarity.[38] Poland's dissent over the handling of the Hungarian affair manifested itself in her refusal to send representatives to the Budapest meeting of Soviet and satellite Party leaders in January 1957.

During that same winter, Chinese Party leadership came to the rescue of Moscow. The Polish evolution and particularly the events in Hungary had not failed to create deep impressions in certain Party circles in China, and even raised hopes among opposition groups that analogous developments might take place in their own country.[39] After noteworthy hesitations, the Chinese Party, while giving support to Gomulka's regime, condemned the Hungarian revolt and approved Soviet armed intervention in Hungary.[40] Then came Chou En-lai's "good will" tour to European Communist capitals. He could not extract a recognition of Soviet supremacy from Poland, but he joined Kádár in a brotherly statement in which they acclaimed the Soviet Union as the "leader of the Socialist Camp" and denounced the counterrevolution organized by imperialist forces.[41] The Chinese personage impressed the Communist leaders of East Europe, and for some time thereafter China was regarded as a proper mediator of their differences with Moscow. Kádár returned the Chinese visit in October 1957, and his reception eclipsed that given to a Soviet delegation under Aristov.[42] In a speech at Peiping the Hungarian, while still emphasizing the leading role of the Soviet Union, stated that it was now impossible to solve any international issue without China. He also declared (perhaps with Imre Nagy in mind) that the bonds of understanding and mutual assistance in the international proletariat were more important than the Five Principles of Peaceful Coexistence formulated between China and India.[43]

Meanwhile the Hungarian Revolution had greatly struck the imagination of people living in neighboring Transylvania and Slovakia, and not just the Hungarian minorities in these regions. It was only natural that the governments of Rumania and Czechoslovakia attached a special importance to the stabilization of the Kádár regime. The Hungarian government, in turn, wished to entertain close relations with these two neighbors. The new Party-to-Party intimacy was attested on various occasions. In December 1957, the Hungarian Deputy Foreign Minister, István Sebes, reported to a committee of the National Assembly that Hungary's ties with Rumania and Czechoslovakia were "very strong," the general policies of all three governments being identical. In February 1958 a Hungarian Party delegation led by Kádár and Kállai visited Bucharest and the resulting joint statement exuded solidarity. The outstanding demonstration of friendship with Czechoslovakia was a visit by Hungarian Party representatives to Prague in December 1958. Kádár being absent because of illness, Marosán delivered Hungary's conviction of the unanimity of views. Czechoslovakia, he said, was to be a model for Hungary in both the political and economic spheres, since "proletarian internationalism and the equality and brotherhood of peoples had become a living reality" in that country. The joint statement of the two delegations emphasized "ideological purity" and denounced revisionism, including the Yugoslav brand.[44] Hungary and Czechoslovakia also joined in economic agreements, both general and specific. Kádár visited Czechoslovakia in February 1959 on his way back from the Soviet Twenty-first Party Congress, and an important Czechoslovak delegation visited Hungary in April 1958. Nevertheless, frictions were occasionally reported on the subject of the Hungarian minority in Slovakia.[45]

Expressions of warm friendship were also exchanged on numerous occasions between Hungarian Party leaders and those of Bulgaria and East Germany. Kádár visited Bulgaria in June 1958, and the next month attended the Fifth Congress of the Socialist Unity Party of Germany. These visits were sedulously returned, and personal contacts between the respective Party leaders developed almost to the extent practiced by Hungary with Czechoslovakia and Rumania. Exchanges of visits also took place between Hungary and all other countries of the Communist bloc, including Albania, the Mongolian People's Republic, North Korea, and North Vietnam.

Polish-Hungarian relations developed more sluggishly than the others. If Kádár's "orthodoxy" might have been in the beginning questionable in the eyes of Czechoslovak and German Communist leaders, the reason for Wladyslaw Gomulka's inhibitions toward the Hungarian Party leader stemmed from contrary motives. Public opinion in Poland severely condemned Soviet military intervention and the installation of a puppet government in Hungary. Gomulka was skillful enough to utilize the Hungarian collapse both for restraining Polish nationalism and obtaining concessions from Moscow; but he preferred, because of domestic pressures, to refrain from approving Hungarian developments or endorsing Kádár's regime.[46] Eighteen months passed before Gomulka fell in with the tactics required by the Kremlin. In May 1958 he said the Soviet intervention in Hungary had been "correct and indispensable" and an "international obligation on the part of the Soviet Union in the interest of the Hungarian people, of all Socialist states and of peace." [47]

This recognition of Kádár (never before spelled out in Poland) came on the occasion of a visit that Gomulka made to Hungary. A month later Gomulka faced simultaneously the question of Yugoslavia's Way (on which he had not yet publicly expressed himself) and the execution of Imre Nagy. On June 28, 1958, in a speech at Gdansk, he both disapproved the heretical Yugoslav Program and denounced Nagy as a revisionist whose punishment, though "severe," was deserved because he had given way to the counterrevolution and had been about to destroy Socialism in Hungary. Gomulka also ridiculed press reports stating that he had protested to Khrushchev against the execution of Nagy and his associates or otherwise criticized it in the Polish Party.[48]

With the friendship between the Polish and Hungarian Parties thus established, a Hungarian Party delegation attended the Third Congress of the Polish Communist Party in March 1959. An article in the Hungarian press by Gyula Kállai praised Gomulka, a "dynamic leader" of a Party that was able to struggle successfully both against revisionism and dogmatism. Kállai stated, nevertheless, that difficulties still existed in Poland for the successful development of the dictatorship of the proletariat, i.e., the Party did not assert itself sufficiently in certain fields. These difficulties — so the article continued — were very much the same as those existing in Hungary also: the weakness of Communist youth organizations, the weakness of the Party vis-à-vis the Church and the intelligentsia (especially in institutes of higher education), and, finally, the difficulties with the peasantry "whose revisionist theories had prevented the Socialist transformation of agriculture." The author concluded that "it is characteristic of revisionist demagogy that its main argument against the cooperative movement was the same in Poland as in our country." [49] Kádár himself visited Warsaw in April 1960, but without visible signs of enthusiastic welcome, even by Party members. Polish-Hungarian economic cooperation also lagged behind that of Hungary and other People's Democracies.

All these actions toward fitting Hungary snugly back into the Soviet bloc after the Revolution stemmed from the Kremlin's view of political necessities. The bankruptcy of Soviet-satellite relations, highlighted by the events in Hungary, had to be remedied so as to ensure a modus vivendi for the Soviet-led Communist camp. Supreme control by the Soviet Party was maintained in different degrees over the satellites, but it had to be maintained in one way or another. Czechoslovakia, the German Democratic Republic, and Bulgaria maintained Stalinist traditions of conscious and willing submissiveness. Rumania was held in bond by the threatening presence of Soviet forces. Poland and Hungary had been the mavericks of the Communist camp. Poland continued to cooperate, however, and she subsequently aligned herself, with certain reservations, to the orthodoxy required by Moscow. Hungary was compelled by naked force to abandon attempts at independence and was invested with a government in the Kremlin's likeness. Khrushchev's preferred mode of relations with the satellites can be described as *controlled cooperation,* and neither Poland nor Hungary now could be easily fitted into that frame. Poland seemed to behave with too much independence, Hungary with too much submissiveness.

Soviet policy aimed at the swift rehabilitation and acknowledgment of the Kádár regime — at making it look like a real state in its own right. Accusations of satellitism — especially true in the case of the Hungarian puppet regime — had to be refuted by giving Kádár's government the status and prestige which it badly lacked outside the Communist bloc. Therefore close relations between Hungary and other members of the Socialist commonwealth were encouraged by the Kremlin. On the whole, Stalin's penchant for bilateral dealings with the satellites and his displeasure at close inter-satellite friendship were purposely abandoned by Moscow, not only in the economic but also in the political and cultural fields. No obstacles were laid in the way of their mutual relations, provided nothing contravened the basic political and ideological assumptions of "proletarian internationalism" as interpreted by the Kremlin.

Thus, Moscow successfully introduced Kádár into the salons of Communist aristocracy, though with some difficulty in the case of Gomulka. By 1960 Hungary has apparently recovered the status of reliability, and her dark past, the attempt to secede from the family of Socialist states, was seemingly forgotten. In September of that year Kádár, together with other Communist leaders, joined Khrushchev's court of honor on the *Baltika* and sailed to the heartland of Western capitalism to play his assigned role in the General Assembly of the United Nations. Two months later, at the Moscow conference of eighty-one Communist parties, Kádár staunchly supported his patron, Khrushchev, against Chinese "dogmatism." [50] Despite Kádár's earlier fraternization with the Chinese, we must conclude that he is bound by gratitude and necessity to side with the Kremlin in any showdown.

HUNGARY AND THE NON-COMMUNIST WORLD

The impact of Hungarian events on nations of the Western alliance systems and on the uncommitted nations varied according to their geographical position, their political or their religious sentiments, their temperament, and the nature of their government. The reactions of governments and peoples pursuing anti-Communist policies ranged from official declarations condemning Soviet armed intervention to popular demonstrations. Particularly violent demonstrations took place in Paris, The Hague, and London, and also in Luxembourg, where the Soviet legation was stormed. The shattering effect on Communist parties in the West (large sections of their intellectual membership protested against Russian aggression) was only comparable to the impact of the Ribbentrop-Molotov Pact in August 1939.[51] Similar reactions were noticeable when the execution of Imre Nagy and his associates was announced in June 1958.

Official and popular response was naturally less pronounced in those uncommitted areas that are more exposed to Soviet political or economic pressures. The official view taken by the principal "non-aligned" state, India, revealed a picture of utter ignorance and misconstruction; failure to exert prompt diplomatic influence on Moscow where India's voice might have been seriously weighed could not be remedied by subsequent rectifications and reappraisals. Prime Minister Nehru had evidently relied on information supplied to him in letters from Bulganin and Tito; so it happened that India on November 10, 1956, was the only non-Communist country to vote *against* a resolution in the United Nations General Assembly calling for free elections in Hungary under United Nations supervision. Subsequently, an Indian envoy was dispatched to Budapest, and in the middle of December, Nehru was able to report that the Hungarian revolutionary movement was a "national" one, supported by the great majority of industrial workers and students.[52]

Significantly, Moscow seemed to be more concerned about the adverse impressions created in uncommitted Asian countries than in the West, where Communist parties were once again left to re-form their faltering ranks as best they could. With Soviet advice and support a Hungarian political mission, led by Deputy Foreign Minister Szarka, toured Asian nations during August 1957 in order to proclaim the official Hungarian interpretation of the uprising. The abstention from voting for the United Nations resolutions on Hungary by most of the Arab countries and some other "neutral" governments in Asia and Africa encouraged the Kádár regime to strengthen economic and cultural ties with them. Frequent visits of Hungarian and neutralist leaders occurred. In some of these Asian and African states the Kádár regime was able to make significant headway both politically and economically. When Ceylon withdrew into a position of neutrality after having sponsored condemnation of the Soviet intervention in Hungary, and when a number of uncommitted countries increased their industrial purchases from Hungary, these could only be viewed as cases in which the Kádár regime had broken out of the diplomatic blockade imposed on it after its installation by the Soviets.[53]

Less successful were the advances of the Hungarian government to the European neutralist countries. The governments and populations of both Austria and Switzerland, as far as was compatible with their neutral status, expressed their displeasure over the developments in Hungary. Relations with Austria have been strained throughout the postrevolutionary years. The Kádár government has expressed its discontent over the warm reception which Austria gave the tens of thousands of refugees, and it protested against Austria's refusal to repatriate juveniles who did not wish to return. On the other hand, Austria has objected to the reappearance of mine fields and barbed-wire fences on her eastern border, and also to violations of her frontier, first by Soviet then by Hungarian guards. Since Hungary largely depends on transit through Austria for direct travel to the West, restrictions on the issue of visas by Austria has also been keenly felt by the Kádár regime.[54] The Hungarian government has also complained about the "press campaign" conducted in Switzerland and elsewhere against the Hungarian People's Republic. But diplomatic notes have not been able to convince the Swiss government that it had a right to interfere with its own free press or that such an attitude was in conflict with Swiss neutrality.[55]

The reluctance of most Western powers to deal with the Kádár regime eroded by the end of 1957. On January 1, 1958, Western diplomats "broke their boycott" of the Hungarian government when they, including the representative of the United States, presented New Year's wishes to the Chairman of the Presidium of the People's Republic. The Hungarian Party press jubilantly reported "a complete fiasco of the boycott policy" and said that "attempts by United States diplomacy and the diplomatists of some other states to isolate our country had been in vain." [56]

The United States, however, refused to "normalize" diplomatic intercourse and maintained only a chargé d'affaires in Budapest. The Kádár regime's attempts at "normalization" of its relations with the United States government had not been successful. The Soviets have considered the refusal by the United States to grant full recognition to the postrevolutionary Hungarian government as the greatest stumbling block in the way of eliminating the bitterness caused by its armed intervention. Khrushchev, when in Budapest in April 1958, pressed the Hungarians to make certain insignificant concessions for the improvement of their relations with the United States.* An effort to improve relations in accordance with the "principle of coexistence" found expression in an exchange of notes between Budapest and Washington. The essence of the American reply was that the Soviet Union was in "flagrant violation of its international pledges and willful defiance of the decisions of the United Nations resolution," and that the Hungarian government had acquiesced in the Soviet domination. Budapest came back with a new note which

---

* János Kádár at the reception given for Khrushchev on April 4, 1958, disclosed that the Soviet leader had discussed Hungarian-United States relations with him. Kádár added, "You can expect soon an interesting initiative on our part." He said, "I have never been a businessman, but as a worker I have dealt with businessmen. They are very intelligent and they know that it is useful to have good relations." A few days later two Hungarian employees of the United States legation in Budapest, who had been held by the Hungarian government without a trial for a year, were released. *New York Times,* April 18, 1958.

the United States returned on the ground that its "offensive tone" was inconsistent with the stated desire of the Hungarian government to eliminate the obstacles to normal relations; the United States said it would not enter into discussions "under threats." [57]

The United States would like to have discussed the problem of the satellites directly with the Soviet Union, but could not get consent. Moscow had refused to allow the question to be placed on the agenda of the Summit meeting of 1955. Again in the spring of 1958, when another Summit was being contemplated, both the United States and the United Kingdom suggested that the agenda include the problem of East-Central Europe, but again the answer was no. Khrushchev wrote President Eisenhower in June 1958 that "there is absolutely no foundation for all the talk about the so-called 'tension' in Eastern Europe . . . we have found no signs of 'tension' in the area." About that time, the execution of Imre Nagy poisoned the international atmosphere and helped to delay United States consent to a Summit meeting for more than a year.[58] When finally the highest leaders of East and West gathered at Paris in the summer of 1960 they discussed neither Hungary nor anything else. International discussion of the Hungarian situation has thus been restricted to the forum of the United Nations — without, however, bringing tangible results such as the United Nations has achieved in some other parts of the globe.

HUNGARY AND THE UNITED NATIONS

The Security Council, disabled by the Soviet veto, took no action in the Hungarian affair. The General Assembly on November 4, 1956, called upon the Soviet Union "to desist forthwith from all armed attack on the people of Hungary and from any form of intervention, in particular armed intervention, in the internal affairs of Hungary." But already that same day, the Nagy government, which had requested help, had already been suppressed by the Soviet aggression. On November 10 the General Assembly called upon the government of the Soviet Union "to withdraw its forces from Hungary without further delay," and expressed the view that free elections should be held in Hungary under United Nations auspices. It requested the Secretary-General to investigate the situation caused by foreign intervention. On November 20 essentially the same resolution was adopted again. But neither the Soviet Union nor the Kádár government showed any readiness to comply with any of these resolutions. No representatives of the United Nations were admitted to Hungary — not even the Secretary-General.[59]

On January 10, 1957, the General Assembly again condemned the Soviet Union for violation of the Charter in "depriving Hungary of its liberty and independence," and set up a five-nation Special Committee on Hungary. This committee, not being permitted to enter Hungary, was compelled to collect evidence outside that country. On June 20, 1957, it submitted its unanimous report to the General Assembly.[60] The report concluded that "the events which took place in Hungary in October and November of 1956 constituted a spontaneous national uprising," and that "the present Hungarian regime had been imposed on the Hungarian people by the armed intervention of the Union of Soviet Socialist Republics." On September 14 the General Assembly endorsed the Report by a vote of 60 in favor, 10 against (Albania, Bulgaria, Byelorussia, Czechoslovakia, Hungary, Poland, Rumania, Ukraine, USSR, and Yugoslavia), and 10 abstentions (Afghanistan, Ceylon, Egypt, Finland, India, Indonesia, Nepal, Saudi Arabia, Syria, and Yemen).

In December 1957, Prince Wan of Thailand, who had been appointed Special Representative of the General Assembly on the Hungarian problem, reported no progress in his endeavors. On December 13, 1958, the General Assembly denounced the execution of Imre Nagy and his associates, reiterated its condemnation of the Soviet Union and of the Hungarian regime for their neglect to carry out the previous Assembly resolutions, and elected Sir Leslie Munro of New Zealand, former president of the General Assembly, to report on developments "relating to the implementation of the resolutions" on Hungary. This resolution of December 13 was carried by 54 votes in favor, 10 against, and 15 abstentions (Ethiopia, Ghana, Iraq, Lebanon, Libya, Morocco, and Sudan having joined the group of abstentionists, while Nepal now voted for the resolution). At the 1959 session of the General Assembly, Sir Leslie Munro reported no progress in his attempts to discuss the question with Soviet and Hungarian authorities. On December 9, 1959, the Assembly "deplored" the continued disregard of its previous resolutions by the Soviet Union and the regime of Hungary by 53 votes to 10, with 17 abstentions, and extended the mandate of its Special Representative.

To the General Assembly in the fall of 1960, Sir Leslie Munro submitted a new report that recalled the Hungarian events of the preceding year, especially the violations of human rights by the Hungarian authorities. He still could report no progress in his endeavors, and he summed up his findings in general terms such as: "No small state can feel secure in the enjoyment of its independence if the doctrine is maintained that a great power may by armed intervention overthrow the government of a small neighbor and replace it by another sponsored by itself." [61]

The credentials of the Kádár representatives in the United Nations were often challenged. Starting with the fall of 1957, the General Assembly neither recognized nor refused these credentials, a procedure which, nevertheless, allowed the Hungarian representatives to participate in the work of the Assembly.[62]

The General Assembly, at its 1960–61 session, placed the Hungarian question on its agenda by 54 votes in favor, 12 against, and 31 abstentions. The spurt in the number of abstentions was due to the admission of additional African states, newly independent. As the Assembly approached its next debate on the merits of the Hungarian affair, the relative decrease of affirmative votes made it seem possible that the Assembly would not much longer adopt resolutions taking a stand against Soviet interference in Hungary. Under the United Nations Charter, resolutions on important questions must be approved by a two-thirds majority of those present and voting. By the spring of 1961 the influx of new states had raised the membership to approximately one hundred nations. On April 22, 1961, the General Assembly concluded its fifteenth session without again discussing the merits of the Hungarian problem. This point of the agenda, together with the issues of Tibet, Korea, and others, was transferred to the Assembly session to open in the fall of 1961.

Notable in the history of the United Nations is the double standard followed by some of the Asian and African states in their attitudes toward the domination of one country by another. This double standard first became noticeable when the Suez crisis distracted attention from Soviet activities in Hungary. In the Suez conflict *all* the Asian and African states sternly rebuked Israel, Britain, and France for their actions, and urged application of sanctions against them. Actions were taken by the United Nations, even to the extent of sending a police force. Concerning the Soviet intervention in Hungary, resulting in the ouster of a legitimate government and in the military subjugation of an entire country, many of the same states were lukewarm in their reactions and have been lukewarm during the succeeding years. They tried to dilute the condemnatory resolutions, and then abstained from voting upon them. No sanctions, economic or otherwise, were formally proposed, though the years passed without Soviet or Hungarian compliance with any of the recommendations of the General Assembly.

The public reasons for the reluctance to oppose vigorously the aggression in Hungary have been: (1) that the resolution under consideration was not sufficiently "conciliatory"; (2) that any resolution would only aggravate the "situation" and stiffen the cold war; (3) that compliance with a resolution was not to be expected; (4) that voting for the resolution would be incompatible with the neutrality of the voting state or would be harmful to its interests. India, for instance, the leading practitioner of the double standard (despite Nehru's astute appraisal of Hungary, quoted at the beginning of this book), generally relied on motives 1 through 3. Others, like the United Arab Republic and other Arab states, preferred to mention their neutralist attitude. Afghanistan or Finland, bordering on the Soviet Union, did not wish to anger their powerful neighbor.*

The distinction drawn between national self-assertion by European nations and national self-assertion by Asian or African peoples plays into the hands of the Soviet Union. The government of that country deliberately supports such a dual policy, wishing on the one hand to exclude discussion of the Hungarian problem (and for that matter any "satellite" question) under the pretext that it is within the exclusive domestic jurisdiction of Hungary,[63] and on the other hand favoring consideration by the United Nations of questions involving the struggle against "aggression, imperialism, monopolies" and the "domination over peoples achieved by any means whatsoever," provided that the area in question is situated outside the Communist orbit. The entry of the United Nations forces into the Congo to replace Belgian troops received, at least originally, the Soviet blessing. With regard to Cuba the Soviet Union stated that the right to use and exploit natural resources was inherent in the sovereignty of that country. The Soviet government vehemently condemned "foreign" intervention against Castro. Such principles, if applied in the case of Hungary, would be in accord with the United Nations resolutions and would be helpful in solving the Hungarian problem.

One wonders whether Asian and African neutralist states that

---

* The relative indifference shown by former colonies with respect to Soviet colonialism is thus aptly described by Henry A. Kissinger: "The close identification of nationalism with the memory of colonial rule also accounts for the seeming blind spot of so many newly independent states with respect to Soviet colonialism. The leaders of the uncommitted nations may condemn such Soviet actions as the repression of the Hungarian revolt. They may dislike Soviet control of the satellite orbit. But they will not be prepared to consider it the same phenomenon which causes their own frustrations. Until they develop a stronger sense of personal identity and until their nations can develop purposes not drawn from the struggle for independence, they will require anti-colonialism, and it must have an anti-Western connotation. For beyond anti-colonialism lies psychological chaos." *Nuclear Weapons and Foreign Policy* (New York, 1957), pp. 259–260.

play, by reason of their numbers, such a decisive role in the activities of the United Nations will become aware of the inconsistency and peril inherent in the "double standard" principle. To adopt condemnatory resolutions only against those states which are likely to comply with them is tantamount to encouraging ruthless aggression that is contemptuous of world opinion. To remain "neutral," that is to say, passive, when principles of international solidarity and security and the "indivisibility of peace" are at stake may one day boomerang on the very government that remained aloof as long as its own immediate interests were not harmed. The restriction of the principle of national self-determination to areas outside the Sino-Soviet Communist orbit would mean that whenever a nation found itself engulfed in this orbit, its right to national independence would be forfeited. This ultimate result of the double standard could hardly be welcome to the uncommitted nations of Asia and Africa which diligently invite the world organization to rely in its resolutions on the "irresistible forces of Nationalism." [64]

Nationalism versus Communism

I am a man of peace! God is my witness how I love peace. But
I hope never to be such a coward as to confound oppression with
peace.

KOSSUTH (1851)

These things surely lie on the knees of the gods.

HOMER

31

Nationalism versus Communism

Λ.Λ.Λ.Λ.Λ.Λ.Λ.Λ.Λ.Λ.Λ.Λ.Λ.Λ.Λ.Λ.Λ.Λ.Λ.Λ.Λ.Λ.Λ.Λ.V/

OUR analysis of political developments in Hungary from the advent of Communist rule to the present days has revealed a great number of characteristics and symptoms, not generally obvious without specific research, pertinent to a Party dictatorship under Soviet guidance. It also has brought to light attitudes and resentments within the Party in Hungary, and the frustrations and ensuing aggressiveness of the population. Also we have examined the psychological experiences of the Revolution of 1956, the "vacuum" created by the disintegration of the Party during this Revolution, and the adjustments required by the elimination of the revolutionary structure. It remains here to recapitulate some of the principal conclusions reached in the past chapters and to test their wider applicability.

CONCLUSIONS — GENERAL AND SPECIFIC

We have found throughout this study that the most powerful motivation leading to a rift within the Communist Party of Hungary was a conscious or unconscious *national sentiment*. And this national sentiment was the main force that hopelessly divided a narrow Communist leadership from the rest of the population. National sentiment had been deeply frustrated first by the depravities of the Stalinist dictatorship, then by the disappointments of the New Course, later by Soviet military intervention in October and November 1956, and finally by the imposition, as a result of this intervention, of a new dictatorial regime. Hurt national feelings manifested themselves in the form of overt combativeness during the Revolution. Motivations of national resentment showed up in the deviationist interpretations of the Communist doctrine. These motivations formed the base of Imre Nagy's revisionist theories. They caused many dedicated Communists to be converted away from Communism. They furnished an impulse for revolutionary aggressiveness. They formed the molten core of collective hatred. Antagonism against the theory and practice of Communist principles was fostered by a resentment of adopting "foreign" ideas imposed by an alien power. In the fall of 1956 both Hungarian nationalism and Soviet Russian imperialist nationalism hurtled into the open and met in a head-on collision.

A secondary, but still outstanding, motivation for the intra-Party split and the nation-wide opposition against the regime was the aspiration for *freedom* and *democracy*. Frustrated national feeling and frustrated resentment against totalitarian despotism reciprocally enhanced each other's momentum, even to the extent that these motives often became undistinguishable to those who cherished them. Still other motivations that contributed to the accumulations of tension were resentment over economic hardships, offended religious sentiment, fear of physical violence, personal sufferings of many kinds, and a longing for the Western style of life (also a part of the aspirations for freedom). Deep-seated group resentments, we have seen, could find expression in disguised or concealed patterns of opposition. Even petty occasions, such as sports events, could open valves and release bursts of emotion that were far disproportionate to the immediate circumstances. We have also seen how important is the interaction between political developments in the "Socialist Fatherland" and those on the Hungarian puppet stage; the life and death of Stalin, the rise and rule of Khrushchev had their Hungarian repercussions.

Peoples, like individuals, are susceptible in diverse degrees to frustrations and resentments. Their reactions will differ according to ethnic, cultural, and other variables; factors influencing anti-Soviet and anti-Communist attitudes of the individual East-Central European nations have been mentioned earlier. The reactions will also differ according to the intensity of frustration, that is, in proportion to the pressures and pains inflicted on the nation in question. It is generally agreed that "frustration equals aggression" and that there is a "cultural threshold of frustration" for groups, as there is for individual personalities.[1] This threshold is determined by stimulating and restraining factors, historic, ethnic, cultural, and religious. In Hungary the threshold was passed when some additional impact closed the circuit that set off the explosion.

The question arises whether and how far conclusions derived from the Hungarian experience may be applied to other areas of the Soviet-Communist world. Certain reservations are necessary when embarking on such a slippery path. The standardization of Communism wherever it occurs — its uniformity of doctrine and of organizational and administrative methods — often induces scholars to extend indiscriminately the conclusions of their research to areas outside their proper field of scrutiny. Since the same dogmas and methods prevail in both the Soviet Union and its controlled area of East-Central Europe, there is a tendency nowadays to assign the East-Central European satellite area to students of Soviet affairs as their exclusive domain. Before World War II, who would have thought of applying the results of Russian studies to the Central European or Balkan countries? In their underlying historical, social, and political structures, East Germany, Poland, Czechoslovakia, Rumania, Hungary, Bulgaria, and Albania differ not only from Russia but also from one another to an extent that unhinges easy generalizations. Their apparent Communist uniformity does not make them alike under the skin. Such sweeping terms as "Polish-Hungarian events" may betray a lack of understanding of meaning of those events and the differences between them. We are thus rightly warned against drawing unwarranted general conclusions from the Hungarian experience.

At the same time, historical analogies, principles of national and mass psychology, and much empirical present-day knowledge indicate that reactions similar to those manifested by the events in Hungary may, under certain circumstances, be expected in other countries under Communist domination, particularly in other satellite countries of East-Central Europe.

We can safely assume the existence, in all satellite countries, of frustrations and resentments comparable to those in Hungary. And we can surmise that the chief motivation for such resentment is to be found in offended national sentiment, and, in varying degrees, in lack of freedom, violation of human rights, and other factors. It is impossible to disagree with the view[2] that disaffection in the East-Central European countries is a political factor which, as in the cases of Hungary and Poland, may, from one day to the next, place both Moscow and the West before agonizing dilemmas. As it is impossible to measure the intensity of resentment in the individual countries

and to foresee current political developments in one nation or in the
East-Central European area in general, prediction of reactions may
remain more or less a matter of guesswork. But the Hungarian experience can, nevertheless, point toward certain types of reactions
likely to occur in other satellite countries.

Since these countries are bound together by certain similarities
in their historic experience and by their desire for independence —
so hard to preserve between the colossi of the East and West — we
may thus face the question: why did Hungarians behave differently
from other peoples under Soviet-Communist rule? The extra resentment and aggressiveness in Hungary are due to the tradition of
Hungarian nationalism, the intensity of Stalinist terrorism and
despotism, the frustrated hopes of Imre Nagy's first premiership, the
obstinacy of Hungarian Communist leaders, the blunders and provocations of the Soviet leaders, and finally to foreign military aggression. Hungary's national character and history, Hungary's different
experience under Soviet-Communist rule abundantly explain why
Hungarians reacted in one way and other satellite peoples in another. The juxtaposition of the various aspects of the Hungarian experience with similar factors affecting the East German, Polish,
Czech and Slovak, Rumanian, Bulgarian, and Albanian ethos would
no doubt provide specific answers — country by country — to our
query. For instance, a satisfactory reply to the often reiterated question "why did the Czechs not revolt in 1956?" is that this people,
apart from other factors (pro-Slav affinities, frustration by the West
in 1938, unsuccessful local revolts in 1953), had been taught by history to embark on an all-out revolt only when its case was already
won, as happened both in 1918 and 1945. The Hungarians lacked
such lessons, and furthermore were forced into their uprising by
circumstances analogous to those in 1848–49, which rendered them
first unable, then unwilling, to stop halfway.

How far experiences of the Hungarian events may be helpful in
assessing the internal Soviet situation is questionable. Hungarian
frustration and reactions were typical of an East-Central European
nation attached by strong ties to Western culture, one which had
gone through a historical evolution entirely different from that of
the Russian people. The Hungarians' reactions to Communist rule
are predominantly national because they are living under foreign
control. The Russians are not living under foreign control. The
Russian people, too, having always lived under iron absolutisms of
one form or another, do not have quite the same attitudes toward
freedom and democracy. On the other hand, some of the attitudes

of the non-Russian nationalities in the Soviet Union — since they consider themselves foreign-dominated — may not be essentially different from those of the East-Central European satellite peoples.

IDEOLOGY — COMMUNIST AND NATIONAL

The interplay between the competing ideologies of Communism and nationalism has become one of the powerful influences of the world, affecting the evolution not only of Hungary but also of many other Communist and non-Communist states — and helping to determine the course of international relations. We have already examined the dual nature of Soviet expansionism, consisting of an intermixture of Russian nationalism and Communist internationalism. The significance of nationalism in relations between China and the Soviet Union need not be stressed here, though it can be said in passing that nationalism is likely to become stronger, not weaker, as a Sino-Soviet factor. In Yugoslavia, nationalist sentiment has been a towering force behind the Titoist deviation. As for the satellite area of East-Central Europe, there is general recognition that nationalism may pose the greatest challenge to Soviet domination, and the events in Poland and Hungary are often cited as illustrations.[3] The study of developments in Hungary substantiates the correctness of such an analysis.

In some lands and on some occasions, Communism and nationalism have clashed head-on. In other circumstances a diluted form of Communist doctrine with nationalistic tendencies has attempted to find a working compromise between Marxist tenets and requirements of a national ideology. Tito's national Communism first presented itself as a schismatic Communist movement, refusing to accept primacy of Moscow, but as in religious schisms it soon developed its own body of "heretical" doctrine. On the other hand, the ideas of Imre Nagy and some of his followers appear to be an amalgam of Marxist principles with postulates of national and humanistic thinking. This studious attempt to find an intermediate solution in Hungary reflects the fact that an unaltered form of orthodox Soviet Communism had been repudiated by the majority of the Hungarian people.

The global competing ideologies, Communism and nationalism, differ so basically that we might well consider it nothing more than a convenience to use the same term — "ideology" — for both of them, for the word perhaps cannot be quite proper to one if proper to the other. Marxist-Leninist Communism is an all-embracing quasi-religion, whereas nationalism is the approximation of a devotional outlook with emotional and utilitarian undertones. The two concepts differ not merely in substantive content — the beliefs and assertions that adherents must accept and act upon. More importantly, they differ in formal structure, and one of the ways in which they differ in formal structure is that Communism *has* a substantive content while nationalism has little or none. It is true that nationalism can be calculatedly given a deterministic set of dogma, as Hitler did. But the "old-fashioned" undogmatic nationalism that now is figuring importantly as an opponent of Communism is a much vaguer thing. And it is this very vagueness that brings difficulties to the presentation of nationalism as "ideology" in juxtaposition to the Marxist-Leninist creed.*

But if a point-by-point comparison of Communism and nationalism as "ideologies" — content and all — is infeasible, a systematic comparison of their formal structures becomes even more necessary. Failure to clarify the formal discrepancies often leads to the parallel examination of noncorresponding trends and notions.[4] Competing as they do in many places, Communism and nationalism, through the inherent characteristics of their basic structures, make different requirements of society and individuals, and these differences weigh heavily on the decision to choose between them.

The Marxist-Leninist Communist ideology bears the following basic structural characteristics, which affect its substantive principles and bind the entire creed together into a monolithic cohesiveness:

Communist ideology is *normative* and dogmatic; its principles are laid down in formal texts, fixed assumptions, socio-economic and political rules. Venerated scriptures composed by authoritative "prophets" contain these norms and dogmas which are authoritatively interpreted by approved agencies (Communist parties), and in case of doubt, by the supreme Party authority in Moscow.

This ideology is *determinist,* that is, its principles claim to determine and preordain inescapable historical, social, and economic developments. It is therefore chiliastic and possesses an eschatology of its own (attainment of "Communist society," withering away of the state, and so on).

The Communist creed is *fideistic;* it demands faith in the sources of its wisdom, reliance on the authorized organs of interpretation,

* Thus Zbigniew K. Brzezinski finds himself compelled to call nationalism "the most basic, even the most primitive, modern ideology" without providing a well-outlined definition (as does not seem possible), whereas he has been able to summarize the elements of "modern revolutionary ideology" in a series of numbered points. *The Soviet Bloc* (Cambridge, Mass., 1960), pp. 384–386.

and obedience to its superiors. There is no possibility of partial or modified endorsement of its tenets; you take it or leave it.

Communist ideology is *universalist* and therefore expansionist; its principles are said to be valid throughout our globe and are to be accepted by all peoples. Consequently, it is Messianic and driven forward by missionary zeal.

Traditional nationalism (like many other political, social, or economic philosophies) is generally characterized by the following structural features:

It is *undogmatic*, loose, and mostly liberalistic in interpretation; its principles are not laid down in any formal text and may be freely advanced and construed.

This "ideology" is *subjectivist;* it usually relies, as to past and future developments, on human free will and volition rather than on determinism.

Nationalism does not require uncritical acceptance of its principles; it may be *skeptical* toward ideas and programs submitted by superior leaders.

Nationalism is by nature *parochial*. It does not claim universal acceptance for its tenets; it wishes to gratify only a particular segment of humanity, without the absolute necessity of imposing its own principles on other nations.

This writer does not suggest that a national ideology could serve as a panacea against all international problems of our age. Far from this, nationalism, in its crudest forms, has frequently revealed itself as a source of international evils. Excessive and self-dominated national zeal is scarcely a goal toward which to strive. Our purpose, therefore, is not to elevate nationalism in the abstract, but to contrast the structural characteristics of nationalism with those of Communism, and thereby to provide further explanation of the adoption or rejection of one or the other in specific geographical areas. In any case, the significant role of nationalism as an antitoxin against Communism in the Soviet satellite area is beyond all dispute.

The structural discrepancies between Communist ideology and the principles of nationalism, the demands set on individuals and peoples by the one and the other, the spiritual bondage required by the one, and the relative freedom of interpretation and implementation left to the individual by the other, have often been more influential in gaining adherence than their intellectual content. Evidently Marxist-Leninist dogmas suit better one sort of people than another, just as the peoples of a certain region have been more susceptible to a given religion than others.* Though the germ of this creed originated in Western Europe, Lenin transformed it into a monolithic framework of revolutionary content. Consequently, Marxism as implemented by Lenin on Russian soil, may rightly be considered as of autochthonous Russian origin, just as the Sinic form of Buddhism, which originated in India, has taken on an indigenous Chinese character. The dogmatic-determinist and fideistic-Messianic Soviet version of Marxism, while possibly congenial to the Russian soul is certainly regarded as alien in the Westernized society of East-Central Europe.

The Hungarian experience has convincingly contradicted assumptions of a strong Communist doctrinal influence on the people of Hungary. The Soviets deluded themselves on this score. There is no doubt that Communist indoctrination has now penetrated deeply into the layers of Russian society — though how deeply is still questionable — but in Hungary the thin crust of Communist indoctrination promptly collapsed under the first impact of revolutionary action, revealing the profundity of popular sentiment hostile to the alien creed. The crust of Communist doctrinal adherence may vary among the satellite countries; but we can fairly assume that everywhere in this area it has remained only a crust. In the satellite area, Communist ideology has remained for the large majority of the population an esoteric and incomprehensible gibberish, and, for the more sophisticated, a ritualistic Mumbo Jumbo with overtones of ridiculousness. The bulk of the people watch the ideological squabbles of their leaders with amused interest just as Gulliver beheld the dispute on the opening of a boiled egg, or as a captive unbeliever anxiously follows the voodoo ritual trying to guess the real significance that may be decisive to his predicament.

In Hungary the hostility shown toward the institutionalized, rigid, and doctrinaire Communist ideology, and also toward its peculiar jargon, at the time of the Revolution led the Hungarian Communist leadership to abandon the Marxist-Leninist phraseology and replace it for a while with pragmatic, commonplace language. This quick change was one of the symptoms suggesting that Communist ideology in the satellite area has remained the exclusive domain of a tiny Party leadership, who employ it as a framework in which they can pronounce policies and communicate with other

* Arnold Toynbee points out that the "creative germ of Islam was not alien from, but native to, the Syriac Society" that favored its sweeping advance over regions inhabited by Semitic-Syriac populations, many of them, in opposition to Hellenic rule, devotees to Monophysitic and Nestorian heresies. *A Study of History* (abridgement), Volumes I–VI (New York, 1947), pp. 20–22.

Communist leaders. Ideology serves as a motivating and directing source for the leadership, as the basic blueprint for intra-bloc relations, and as a guide for foreign policy. But it is not the ideology of the people at large. And the basic ideological antagonism between the rulers and the governed in the satellite countries can be expected to persist in the years to come as a principal source of fragility and precariousness for both the Communist leadership in the parochial states and their superiors in the Kremlin.

Nationalism and contingent aspirations for freedom and democratic government are the principal obstacles to the final consolidation and perpetuation of Soviet-Communist rule in the East-Central European theater. This fact deserves particular emphasis when seen in the light of Soviet political tactics employed outside their bloc, and especially in the colonial or formerly colonial regions of Asia and Africa. Here, the foreign policy objectives of the Soviet Union are served by the nationalism of other peoples and by their demand for self-determination. Thus, aggressive and revolutionary nationalism is being fostered outside the bloc, and suppressed and castigated inside: *Vérité au-delà des Alpes, erreur ici.*

NATIONALISM IN THE SERVICE OF COMMUNISM

Asian nationalism and anticolonialism has been a vehicle for Communist expansion since the times of Lenin. After the unhappy experience with the Kuomintang, Stalin became more reserved in encouraging Asian national movements. It remained the task of Stalin's successors, and in particular, Khrushchev, to embark on a systematic policy of alliance with and support of nationalistic forces in Asia, Africa, and Latin America. The political and economic support given to nationalist regimes, a policy condemned by Chinese Communists, has developed into a strategy on three continents aiming at the conquest by peaceful means of the uncommitted section of the world community, thus preparing the ultimate "burial" of Western capitalism.

The former colonies, now independent, would react violently — and have done so in some cases — toward overbearing Communist parties, attempts at Communist seizure of power, or any other operation by the Communist side to deprive them, in whole or in part, of their newly-won "national identity." Therefore the usual Communist drive for political power was softened or halted. Instead, national emotions were roused against the common foe, the foreign "imperialists." Hostile policy toward the Western powers was encouraged. Foreign capitalistic exploitation was condemned.

Campaigns were waged against selected enemies, like "Yankee imperialism" in Latin America, Israeli "intruders" in Arab countries, and (for Indonesian consumption) Dutch "colonialism" in New Guinea. In November 1956 the Soviet Union, while pouring military forces into Hungary, offered "volunteers" for the defense of an Egypt invaded by "imperialists," and even threatened the use of ballistic missiles. In 1957, after having imposed a regime on Hungary by physical force, Moscow denounced the temporary stationing of United States forces in Lebanon at the request of the Lebanese government. In 1960 and 1961 the Soviet Union posed as champion of the independence of Cuba and kindled passions by charging the United States with armed intervention and economic exploitation. In the same year Moscow fervently supported complaints against Belgium before the United Nations and urged resolutions inviting that country to withdraw her troops from the Congo. But United Nations resolutions for a withdrawal of Soviet forces from Hungary remained unheeded.

After World War I the Wilsonian principle of national self-determination was applied (with notable exceptions) in Europe while it remained unimplemented in Asia and Africa. At present, the world may behold a reverse spectacle. Europe now is the sphere where self-determination is least regarded.

Asian and African statesmen whose view has been obfuscated by anti-Western anti-imperialism may be temporarily confused as to the real state of affairs existing in the countries of East-Central Europe since World War II. The governments of those countries, of course, claim to be independent. But the people of those countries do not take the claim seriously, and neither should the statesmen of Asia and Africa. As we have seen, Stalinist rigid uniformity was somewhat alleviated in the area in question. But even Poland, which has been given considerable autonomy in internal affairs, must align her foreign policy with the requirements of Soviet strategy and tactics — scarcely a badge of independent nationhood.[5] In the only case of overt revolution against Moscow's writ in the post-Stalinist period, secession was thwarted by military might. There is no reason to doubt that should Khrushchev's persuasion fail and new secessions occur, the Kremlin — in the absence of an outside deterrent — would again forcibly prevent withdrawal from the Socialist commonwealth. This determination to use military coercion would not be applicable to Communist states that had never been submitted to rigid obedience of Moscow's commands or had in the past successfully revolted against it, like China and Yugoslavia. Nevertheless, the experience of Hungary makes the conclusion inescapable that the "autonomy" enjoyed by the satellites of East-Central Europe is only a conceded "jurisdiction" that may be restricted or even revoked when it appears contrary to Moscow's basic principles.[6]

Inevitably there must come a time in the life of any new nation of Asia and Africa when its own nationalism is no longer supported by the Communists but instead begins to clash with Communism, and maybe with Soviet or Chinese nationalism as well. Viewed in this light, the conflict between nationalism and Communism in East-Central Europe takes on an additional meaning for the new nations. The awareness of Soviet colonialism in Europe might give them special reasons for not putting their nationalism into the service of today's biggest colonialist power.

NATIONALISM AGAINST COMMUNISM IN EAST-CENTRAL EUROPE

The East-Central European satellite area extends over seven countries (East Germany, Poland, Czechoslovakia, Hungary, Rumania, Bulgaria, and Albania) with a population nearing a hundred million, that is, not much less than half the population of the Soviet Union. The area's industrial production is over half, and its gross national product two fifths, of the Soviet Union's.[7] In cultural values, though a gauge of comparison is lacking, we can assume that these countries at least match the Soviet Union. The value of these lands — stretching from the Baltic Sea to the Mediterranean and the Black Sea — to whoever holds political, economic, or military possession is suggested by their diversity, by their closeness to industrial and strategic centers (e.g., the Ruhr, or the Turkish Straits), and by their own recognized strategic value in terms of conventional warfare.[8] The secession of Yugoslavia from the Soviet-led bloc, considered a transitory event by Stalin's successors, has driven a large and dangerous wedge into the otherwise compact satellite area and has separated Albania from the rest of the bloc. Another "foreign body" set within the satellite area is West Berlin, the "sore ulcer" of the German Democratic Republic. The East German satellite cannot be rendered safe and sound according to Moscow's standard unless the freedom of West Berlin is eliminated.

If we except the Hungarian case, East Germany has always been for the Soviets the weakest vessel of the satellite fleet. German nationalism drives the inhabitants both toward unification with the other Germany and toward liberation from the Soviet-Communist yoke. The loss of East Germany, besides upsetting the balance of power by creating a unified Germany, oriented toward the West, would have far-reaching consequences in the entire satellite area, particularly for Poland and Czechoslovakia. In raising the Berlin question, Khrushchev wished to achieve two ends by one stroke: first, to conquer new territory for Communism; second, to make East Germany more impregnable against the waves of German nationalism.

Polish nationalism is divided in its antagonism between East and West: Soviet Russian imperialism is its present-day problem; the German danger and potential loss of the western provinces may be the problem of tomorrow. Unless the present pressure becomes unbearable, a rational assessment might prefer the uncomfortable status of today to the greater uncertainties of tomorrow. But nationalism is often more emotional than rational, and the precarious balance created by Gomulka could easily be upset from either the inside or the outside. Thus Polish nationalism constitutes a danger to Soviet rule that should not be underrated by appearances.

In Czechoslovakia, oppression has never been so violent as, for example, in Hungary. Economic conditions have also been more tolerable. At this writing there are no Soviet forces in the country, and the pro-Slav affinity still counts. Thus many are inclined to talk of Czechoslovakia as the "faithful satellite." The possibility of a resurgence of aggressive German nationalism softens local nationalism, at least in the Czech provinces. Nevertheless, this country could not be considered thoroughly reliable from the Soviet-Communist point of view, and certainly not in time of crisis.

In Rumania, where the morale of the Party membership is probably the lowest in the entire area, the "proletarian dictatorship" is opposed by sabotage, sloppiness, waste of public property, and widespread corruption. During the Hungarian Revolution the Rumanian Army was disarmed by Soviet forces — certainly not a sign of reliability.

In Bulgaria, where Communism had deep roots before the arrival of Soviet troops in 1944, an essentially Stalinist and ruthless leadership, steeped in conspiratorial practices, is able, despite considerable rifts in the Party, to rule in complete disregard of a national opposition. Strangely enough, such an extremist leadership has been able to maintain a greater independence toward Moscow than the other satellites, except Poland. Bulgarian national sentiment is glimmering underneath the outer surface of Communist loyalties, and may one day break into a holocaust when kindled by propitious circumstances.

Albanian nationalism, a relatively late development, is being stimulated by the danger of Yugoslav expansion. To many Albanians, a distant Soviet rule — or even a more distant Chinese rule — is preferable to the gaping jaws of the Titoist giant next door. But as in the Polish and Czechoslovak cases, Albanian nationalism fer-

CHART III

CAUSATION OF RESENTMENT

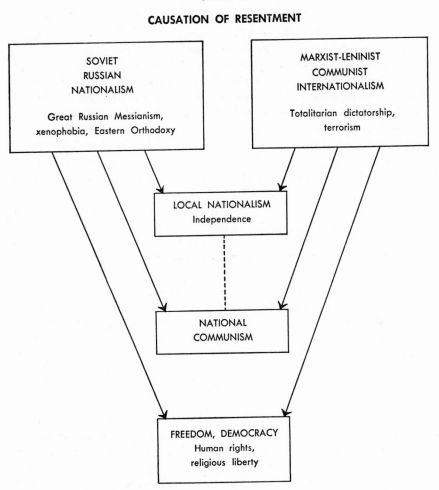

SOVIET RUSSIAN NATIONALISM

Great Russian Messianism, xenophobia, Eastern Orthodoxy

MARXIST-LENINIST COMMUNIST INTERNATIONALISM

Totalitarian dictatorship, terrorism

LOCAL NATIONALISM
Independence

NATIONAL COMMUNISM

FREEDOM, DEMOCRACY
Human rights,
religious liberty

vently desires the third alternative: complete immunity from both the present domination and the potential danger of the future.

Resentments in the satellite area are caused in somewhat the manner illustrated in Chart III. As shown by the arrows, both Soviet Russian *nationalism* and Marxist-Leninist Communist *internationalism* act upon *local nationalism*. They also act upon local aspirations for individual freedom. They act, too, upon the feelings of people who want Communism without foreign control, that is, national Communism; the resentment of these people is caused mainly by the impingement of Soviet Russian nationalism, but, to the extent that doctrinal differences occur, by Marxist-Leninist internationalism as well.

The intensity of the anti-Russian and anti-Communist resentments thus created in the satellite countries, and the strength of the resulting aggressiveness, are determined by a large bundle of conditions and circumstances, among which are: (1) the nature of national consciousness and national temperament; (2) historic precedents strengthening a desire for independence; (3) liberal sentiment and inclinations; (4) strength and traditions of local Communism; (5) pro-Slav and pro-Russian affinities or, contrariwise, anti-Slav and anti-Russian bias; (6) national phobias other than anti-Russian (e.g., anti-German); (7) religious sentiment and religious affiliations; (8) intensity and nature of local terrorism, oppression, or economic exploitation.

The Hungarian events of 1956 drew the Soviet Union's attention to the instability of its position in the satellite area. This problem was discussed with satellite Communist leaders, beginning with the hurried concourse in Budapest in January 1957. The common interest in preserving the Communist regimes in this area has been receiving priority over all other questions, including ideological ones. The Soviet Union has created comradely governments along its borders on the west, but these governments rule over hostile and nationalistic populations. Soviet imperialism has thus admitted an array of Trojan horses within its walls that might produce a result contrary to the foreign policy objectives of the Soviet Union. Had the Soviet Union shown greater foresight and self-restraint, as in the case of Finland after World War II, governments of the present satellite countries (apart from East Germany) might have become friendly but still independent ones. Of course Socialism might not have triumphed, but the Soviet Union would not have been, as it is now, committed to maintain by all possible means a status that is disliked by the populations of the countries concerned and is a potential threat not only to the existence of the Soviet regime but also to world peace in a nuclear age.

If Soviet and satellite leaders are alert to their perils, the same cannot be said of the West. The precariousness of Soviet-Communist rule in the satellite area offers explosive potentialities to the Western nations, too, because it is a danger to peace, as demonstrated by events in Hungary.* If we take the Hungarian warning seriously, and it appears there is sufficient reason to do so, then nationalism in the satellite states, its nature and intensity, in fact, the entire state of mind and psychology of the people behind the Iron Curtain cannot be irrelevant for the rest of the world.

The average man in the satellite orbit lives in what may be best described as a "prison atmosphere." His prison mentality focuses his attention on the main national issue: how and when to achieve freedom. Like a real prisoner, he is inclined to connect any outside event with his own predicament, and to interpret most events — human optimism being indestructible — in a light of hopefulness. Now and again he hears of international conferences, United Nations proceedings, or plans of meeting at the Summit. He is convinced that on any of these occasions his status will be discussed, and any report to the contrary he discards as Communist lies. The optimistic attitude may then be broken by streaks of despondency and frustration. Reactions springing from such a state of mind may be unpredictable. People in these circumstances, if national resentment drives them to utmost despair, can come genuinely to prefer even an all-destructive war to the continuation of their miseries. Thus we believe that the majority of the people in the satellite area are perhaps those rare inhabitants of the world who do not live in fear of a nuclear war. Immediate fears dispel more remote ones.

Another characteristic of satellite mentality is a basically and ostentatiously friendly attitude toward the West, especially the United States, Britain, and France. In some countries (Hungary, Rumania, and Bulgaria) there is friendliness, though perhaps to a lesser extent, toward Germany. Despite all the disappointments they have experienced in their frustrated hopes for liberation, and at a time when so much is heard about the "ugly American," the United States citizen is still the most popular foreign figure in East-Central Europe. Vice-President Nixon's enthusiastic reception in Poland

* Sharing this view, George F. Kennan has written: "Things cannot be expected to remain this way long. There must either be further violent efforts by people in that area to take things into their own hands and to achieve independence by their own means, or there must be the beginning of some process of real adjustment to the fact of Soviet domination. In the first of these contingencies, we in the West could easily be placed once more before the dilemma which faced us last year at the time of the Hungarian uprising; and anyone who has the faintest concern for the stability of the world situation must fervently pray that this will not happen." *Russia, the Atom and the West* (New York, 1957), pp. 34–35. Hugh Gaitskell, leader of the British Labour Party, when submitting his plan for a disengagement in Europe stated that he sees "grave dangers to peace in Central Europe in the event of new uprisings in East Germany or Hungary." *New York Times*, March 17, 1958.

would have been repeated had he gone to other satellite countries. If Khrushchev was chary of receiving the American President in the Soviet Union, the reason probably was that such a visit might have had untoward consequences for the Communist regimes of East-Central Europe. It was not without reason that the Kádár regime (and its Soviet overlords) refused the entry of the Secretary-General of the United Nations to Hungary in December 1956; this might have become a new occasion for a revolt.

We do not suggest that a revolution will occur in any of the satellite countries during the next few years. In Hungary the revolutionary fervor has certainly spent itself. But even if the Hungarian uprising is attributed to the "intervention of the accidental," [9] nothing assures us that another concatenation of events will not occur in one of the other countries in question. The Hungarian experience has proved the fallacy of the assumption that "real adjustment" to Soviet domination can be expected, and there is no reason to believe that the conclusion is valid for Hungary only.

History teaches us that *national* resistance is more tenacious than all other causes of dissent. National resentment may be stored up for many decades and centuries, as a Leyden jar stores electricity.[10] Some of this powerful current may drain away, but foreign domination provides a constant flood of new national resentment. The tension persists. Only the time and circumstances of its release are determined by outside events. Resentment continues until national aspirations are satisfied or until national identity is lost.

National revolts are more likely to occur at a time of relative relaxation than in the heyday of terror, as the Hungarian experience has shown. But they may also burst out at times of acute crisis when the attention or preoccupation of the leadership is diverted by other events. And generally it is not the underdog that makes the revolution but rather a relatively privileged section of the community. Therein lies the particular significance of an overt or disguised opposition among the Party membership — a privileged group indeed. It should again be remembered that in Hungary, students and workers, purported pets of the regime, were the spearhead of the revolutionary movement.

WHITHER EAST-CENTRAL EUROPE?

Western diplomacy toward the European satellite area may be implemented in three different territorial approaches: (1) in conjunction with the German unification question; (2) separated from the German question and thus excluding East Germany and Berlin but treating the rest of the area as one problem; and (3) fragmented, with individual attention given to each country concerned.

Sound diplomacy would simultaneously undertake all three of the approaches mentioned. There is little doubt that a combined solution for both the unification of Germany and the "de-colonization"[11] of the satellite area would be most desirable. George F. Kennan appears to argue that no permanent solution of the division is possible without solving the German question.[12] Evidently, the withdrawal of Soviet forces from Polish territory could only be expected when the Soviet occupation of East Germany had come to an end. The plan suggested by Hugh Gaitskell and favored by the British Labour Party foresaw a withdrawal of all foreign troops from both Germanies and from Poland, Czechoslovakia, and Hungary, and the neutralization and demilitarization of this entire area; the four countries were to be released from the North Atlantic Treaty Organization and from the Warsaw Treaty system respectively. But this was not an official plan and its endorsement by the great powers seems questionable. Its adoption would leave the status of Rumania, Bulgaria, and Albania unsolved.

Other suggestions have stressed the principle of self-determination for the satellite states rather than the unification of Germany. If East Germany were included in such a scheme it would no doubt achieve its unification with West Germany. If East Germany were not included, the de-Sovietization of Poland would seem questionable.

The effort to obtain de-colonization for individual nations is limited by geographical hindrances. Such a solution if viable at all, could only be achieved piecemeal, and first only for such states as are situated on the periphery of the Soviet empire, like Hungary, or Bulgaria, or Albania. The United Nations after the Hungarian Revolution proposed solutions for one satellite country: Hungary. Withdrawal of Soviet forces and free elections under United Nations supervision would certainly be agreeable for the West and the Hungarian people; but they are not even debatable as far as the Soviet Union is concerned.

The Soviet leaders can never be convinced by arguments alone; they may be influenced only by situations, by facts.[13] What would be considered by Moscow as a suitable "situation" or compensation for the loss of such valuable land as they control beyond their formal western borders? The proposals usually broached deal with some form of demilitarization or neutralization or both. For example, the plan suggested by the Polish Foreign Minister Rapacki aimed at the denuclearization of Germany, Poland, and Czechoslovakia. In its second version it also included a limited conventional demilitarization program. This plan would not solve any of the great political problems of Europe, not even the German question. Among the great powers only the Soviet Union endorsed the Rapacki Plan. We should remind ourselves that the peace treaties signed after World War II already contain military arrangements: they coupled the maintenance of Soviet troops in Hungarian and Rumanian territory with the occupation status of Austria, and those troops were supposed to be withdrawn when Austria achieved its independent statehood. Now, it is strange, but true, that the Soviet Union would expect some compensation if it carried out its obligations under the treaties.

The effect of a mere military withdrawal by the Soviet Union would vary according to the country concerned. In East Germany it would be tantamount to a total abandonment of the Communist system and its collapse. In Hungary it would significantly weaken the regime, but would not necessarily lead to its immediate downfall. The likelihood of a return of Soviet forces in case of revolt would thus acquire utmost importance. In Rumania, where no opportunity was given to national sentiment to ask for a withdrawal, the political impact of evacuation by Soviet forces would be slighter still, but would be important. There are no Soviet forces in Czechoslovakia and Bulgaria, nor officially in Albania. For Poland the consequences of a withdrawal of Soviet troops would strictly depend on two hypothetical questions: first, whether the German danger became imminent, and second, whether the Communist regime in Poland came into peril. If either of those questions could be answered in the affirmative, the return of Soviet troops could be expected.

Mere withdrawal of foreign troops might therefore be insufficient for a solution of the satellite problem, even if the Soviet Union would agree to pull back its troops in return for troop withdrawals from Western Europe, and even if the West would find such a plan acceptable. And those are conditions contrary to probability. On the one hand, the Soviet Union probably could not agree to any such program—could not knowingly expose its satellite governments to the danger of overthrow and risk precipitating a war by the potential return of its troops to rescue a regime. On the other hand, the Western powers probably could not consent to an arrangement that would remove American forces from the defense of Europe and would contain no provisions for the control of nuclear weapons. In the view of this writer an exclusively military solution of the problem of East-Central Europe is hardly feasible. Nor is a more general agreement on arms control or disarmament possible without solving at least some of the most burning political problems that divide East and West, thus creating an atmosphere of confidence that would favor settlement of the military questions.

What then would be the incentive that might induce the Soviet Union to give up its military and political hold over the satellite area? We believe that such an incentive could only be the emergence of a "greater evil," compared to which the Soviet retrenchment would be a "lesser evil." This greater evil is not easy to come by. The threat of nuclear war, which might have been successfully posed before the Soviet Union acquired nuclear capability, if the West had been morally prepared to employ such a threat, must now be excluded. Large-scale German rearmament might also have been the "greater evil" before Moscow became a nuclear power, but now such a course has become less meaningful. Since the Soviets might consider an all-out nuclear war to be the greatest evil of all, conceivably they might some day accept a global political and military covenant between East and West, including a reasonable solution of the satellite problem. At present, however, the likelihood of such a comprehensive arrangement seems even more distant than the conclusion of limited agreements on political and armament issues.

Though means of persuasion for the abandonment of the entire satellite area are elusive, the possibility of "compensating" the Soviet Union for forsaking an individual satellite country cannot be dismissed. In the first days of November 1956, a transaction for the relinquishment of Hungary in return for the neutralization of this country according to the Austrian model (as envisaged by the Imre Nagy cabinet), appeared to be within the limits of possibility, had this proposal been offered by the West.

The mental obstacles deterring the Soviet leaders from accepting a reasonable solution or price for the abandonment of their domination over peoples that are (as they must realize) hostile, may be summarized in two points:

1. Considerations of military strategy, economic exploitation, and political prestige tell them not to surrender real estate. Expansion, yes; retrenchment, no.

2. Ideological considerations tell them even more forcefully that the abandonment of souls they have claimed as converts would endanger the dynamism of their movement.

Concerning the first point, strategic positions of deployment have lost much of their value in an age of nuclear weapons. And the military worthlessness of the satellite armies for the defense of Communist regimes was strongly suggested by the Hungarian events. Economic exploitation has largely been abandoned anyhow, and the value of the satellite countries as equal trading partners may be greater than that of dependent economies. Soviet prestige in international affairs — especially vis-à-vis the uncommitted nations — might increase rather than decrease should the Soviet Union be willing in good grace to de-colonize East-Central Europe.

More important are the ideological reasons for refusing to give up the satellite area. A Messianic movement, like Communism, is bound by its very principles to expand. As Islam, in the times of its dynamism, fought fanatically against abandoning previously conquered soil to the "infidel," Communism is prepared to fight hard for the preservation of its *status quo,* as it did in North Korea and in Hungary. But even Islam could not stay forever in East-Central Europe.

The ideological rift between the Soviet Union and Communist China will have further repercussions in the satellite area. But the Communist parties of East-Central Europe (with the exception of Albania), are likely to cling to the Soviet position, and there will be no Chinese Titoism of any importance in their ranks. Therefore the Soviet hold over the area probably will not be weakened by a Chinese schism. If, however, the Sino-Soviet ideological rift were to widen into political antagonism on a Titoist scale (which is not now to be expected), a Soviet Union threatened on its long, vulnerable Asian front would indeed be compelled to loosen its grip on the satellite peoples.

The apparently "insoluble" character of the East-Central European question and a shift of emphasis to "soluble" problems[14] has profited only the Soviet Union. That country has thus been able to distract attention from its "weakness" and concentrate interest and discussion, in the United Nations and elsewhere, on questions which could be advantageously exploited in its own interest. The satellite problem is only "insoluble" because the Kremlin refuses to discuss it and not because it is per se incapable of being solved. The greatest disservice which the West could do to its own cause is to agree with the Soviet position of leaving untouched these matters that are deemed nonnegotiable. Not only political morality and the sanctity of treaties, but also elementary diplomatic strategy and constructive foreign policy, dictate a refusal to accept the permanence of the Soviet satellite situation. The cold war, like any other war, can never be won by defensive strategy or tactics. The restoration of independence in even a small part of the Soviet domain means much not only to the people involved but also in its effect on the Communist myth of irresistible advance. There is no more valid and worthy point that the West can raise than the question of satellitism in East-Central Europe — and no frailer and unworthier stand that the East can take. It is not without reason that the Soviet leaders tenaciously insist on stifling the discussion of this question; they would have no chance on the merits of their case.

Perhaps the best opportunity of reactivating the satellite problem is offered by the contest for the sympathies and support of the uncommitted nations of Asia and Africa. A clear Asian and African recognition of Soviet duplicity — its contradictory treatment of East-European and non-European problems — might have a sobering effect on Moscow's rigidity, both political and ideological. A necessary Soviet choice between the sympathy of these Asian and African nations and the maintenance of a "colonial empire" in the center of Europe might possibly influence its attitude concerning that problem. The belated acknowledgment of the truth in the Hungarian crisis by the Indian leader can no longer be helpful; but a conception of the satellite problem by the uncommitted nations and a readiness to exercise diplomatic pressure on the Soviet Union for the sake of its satisfactory solution might have an unpredictable value. This encircling diplomatic pressure might even grow into the "greater evil" beside which a dignified withdrawal from East-Central Europe might not seem so repugnant as before. The enlightenment of Asian and African leaders on their real kinship with the peoples of East-Central Europe should be a principal task of Western diplomacy.

The national sentiment of the peoples of East-Central Europe now under Soviet domination, their sustained confidence in their cause, and their longing for a "normalcy" that they cannot find even after fifteen years in their present situation, are solid guarantees of the fragility of the Communist regimes in these areas. A vigilant, strong West cannot and should not fail to observe the essential precariousness of these systems under the cover of apparent stability and firmness. The discontent of the captive peoples makes them natural allies of the uncommitted nations and Western Powers alike. The West, in its political and military planning, cannot ignore this state of instability. In international politics it is mostly the "unexpected that happens." That may stand as the final, pedestrian yet pertinent conclusion to be derived from the case of Hungary.

Bibliography

Aczél, Tamás, "The Honest Sinners," *The Review* (Brussels), June 1959, pp. 70–86.

Aczél, Tamás, and Tibor Méray, *The Revolt of the Mind.* New York, 1959.

Aptheker, Herbert, *The Truth about Hungary.* New York, 1957.

Aron, Raymond, "The Meaning of Hungary," *The New Leader,* March 24, 1958, pp. 5–19.

Bailey, George, "Remember Hungary: The War Goes On," *The Reporter,* November 24, 1960, pp. 36–39.

Bain, Leslie Balogh, *The Reluctant Satellites: An Eyewitness Report on East Europe and the Hungarian Revolution.* New York, 1960.

Balassa, Béla, *The Hungarian Experience in Economic Planning.* New Haven, 1959.

——— "Collectivization in Hungarian Agriculture," *Journal of Farm Economics,* February 1960, pp. 35–51.

Barghoorn, Frederick C., *Soviet Russian Nationalism.* New York, 1956.

Bass, Robert H., "Communist Fronts: Their History and Function," *Problems of Communism,* September-October 1960.

Berle, A. A., Jr. (ed.), see *Hungary under Soviet Rule.*

Bialer, Seweryn, "I Chose Truth," *News from behind the Iron Curtain,* October 1956, pp. 3–15.

——— "The Three Schools of Kremlin Policy," *The New Leader,* July 29, 1957, pp. 11–12.

Bibo, István, *Harmadik Ut* (Third Road). London, 1960.

Birke, Ernst, and Rudolf Neumann (eds.), *Die Sowjetisierung Ost-Mitteleuropas.* Frankfurt a.M., 1959.

Boffa, Giuseppe, *Inside the Khrushchev Era.* New York, 1959.

Borba. Daily of the Yugoslav Communist Party. Belgrade.

Borkenau, Franz, *European Communism.* New York, 1953.

Borsody, Stephen, *The Triumph of Tyranny. The Nazi and Soviet Conquest of Central Europe.* New York, 1960.

Brinton, Crane, *The Anatomy of Revolution.* New York, 1957.

Brzezinski, Zbigniew K., *The Permanent Purge.* Cambridge, Mass., 1956.

——— *The Soviet Bloc: Unity and Conflict.* Cambridge, Mass., 1960.

——— "The Organization of the Communist Camp," *World Politics,* January 1961, pp. 175–209.

Campbell, John C., "The European Territorial Settlement," *Foreign Affairs,* October 1947, pp. 196–218.

Cattell, David T., "Multilateral Co-operation and Integration in Eastern Europe," *The Western Political Quarterly,* March 1960.

Coulter, Harris L., "The Hungarian Peasantry: 1948–1956." *The American Slavic and East European Review,* December 1959, pp. 539–554.

CURPH, Columbia University Research Project on Hungary. Interviews with and manuscripts submitted by Hungarian refugees.

Dallin, Alexander (ed.), *Soviet Conduct of World Affairs.* New York, 1960.

Dallin, David J., *Soviet Foreign Policy after Stalin.* Philadelphia, 1961.

Delaney, Robert Finley (ed.), *This Is Communist Hungary.* Chicago, 1958.

Délmagyarország. Hungarian local paper published in the city of Szeged.

Deriabin, Peter, and Frank Gibney, *The Secret World.* New York, 1959.

Deutscher, Isaac, "Crisis in Moscow," *The Reporter,* November 15, 1959.

Djilas, Milovan, "The Storm in Eastern Europe," *The New Leader,* November 19, 1956.

—— *The New Class.* New York, 1957.

Dodd, Thomas J., "Hungary—The Missed Opportunity," *The Hungarian Quarterly* (New York), vol. 1, no. 1 (January 1961), pp. 14–20.

Ebenstein, William, "A Study of Totalitarianism," *World Politics,* January 1958, pp. 274–288.

Edwards, P., *The Natural History of Revolution.* Chicago, 1927.

Élet és Irodalom. Successor of the *Irodalmi Ujság* after the Revolution of 1956.

Ellenforradalmi Erök a Magyar Oktoberi Eseményekben (Counterrevolutionary Forces in the Hungarian October Events). 4 Vols. Budapest, 1957–1958.

Fábián, Béla, "Hungary's Jewry Faces Liquidation," *Commentary,* October 1951, pp. 330–335.

Fainsod, Merle, *How Russia Is Ruled.* Cambridge, Mass., 1953.

—— "What Happened to 'Collective Leadership'?" *Problems of Communism,* July–August 1959, pp. 4–11

Fejtö, François, *Histoire des Democraties Populaires.* Paris, 1952.

—— *La Tragédie Hongroise.* Paris, 1956.

—— *Behind the Rape of Hungary.* New York, 1957.

—— *Ungheria 1945–1947.* Torino, 1957.

Free Europe Committee, *Preliminary Results of Depth Interviews and Attitude Scales. Inquiry into Political and Social Attitudes in Hungary.* New York, 1957.

Fryer, Peter, *The Hungarian Tragedy.* London, 1956.

Gábor, R., *Organization and Strategy of the Hungarian Workers Party.* New York, 1952.

Ginsburgs, George, "Demise and Revival of a Communist Party: An Autopsy of the Hungarian Revolution," *The Western Political Quarterly,* September 1960, pp. 780–802.

Gomori, George, "Cultural and Literary Developments: Poland and Hungary," *The Annals of the American Academy of Political and Social Science,* May 1958, pp. 71–78.

Goodman, Elliot R., *The Soviet Design for a World State.* New York, 1960.

Griffith, William E., "The Revolt Reconsidered," *East Europe,* July 1960, pp. 12–20.

Gripp, Richard C., "Eastern Europe's Ten Years of National Communism: 1948–1958," *The Western Political Quarterly,* December 1960, pp. 934–939.

Gyorgy, Andrew, *Governments of Danubian Europe.* New York, 1949.

————— "The Ideology of Communism," mimeographed copy of lecture delivered in the Armed Forces Staff College, Norfolk, Va., January 1960.

Hallowell, J. H. (ed.), *Soviet Satellite Nations.* Gainesville, 1958.

Helmreich, Ernst C. (ed.), *Hungary.* New York, 1957.

Hovet, Thomas, Jr., *Bloc Politics in the United Nations.* Cambridge, Mass., 1960.

Hungarian White Books, see: *Ellenforradalmi Erök a Magyar Oktoberi Eseményekben;* and *Nagy Imre és Büntársai Ellenforradalmi Összeesküvése.*

Hungary under Soviet Rule: A Survey of Developments since the Report of the U.N. Special Committee, ed. A. A. Berle, Jr., et al. New York, 1957.

Hungary under Soviet Rule II: A Survey of Developments from September 1957 to August 1958, ed. A. A. Berle, Jr., et al. New York, 1958.

Hungary under Soviet Rule III: A Survey of Developments from the Revolution to August 1959, ed. A. A. Berle, Jr., et al. New York, 1959.

"Hungary's Four Years After," *East Europe,* November 1960, pp. 3–7.

Ignotus, Paul, "Hungarian Intellectuals under Fire," *Problems of Communism,* May–June 1959, pp. 16–21.

————— "Hungary's Craving for Normalcy," *Problems of Communism,* March–April 1960, pp. 24–30.

————— *Political Prisoner.* London, 1960.

International Commission of Jurists, *The Hungarian Situation and the Rule of Law.* The Hague, 1957.

Irodalmi Ujság (Literary Gazette). Hungarian Writers' Association periodical. Budapest.

Izvestiya. Daily of the Union of Workers' Deputies. Moscow.

Jaeger, H., "Der Tiefere Hintergrund des Falles Slansky," *Deutsche Rundschau,* December 1951.

Juhász, William, "Church and Society in Hungary," *Church and Society,* ed. Joseph N. Moody. New York, 1952.

Just, Béla, "*Un Procès Préfabriqué — l'Affaire Mindszenty.* Paris, 1949.

"Kádár's Congress in Hungary," *East Europe,* January 1960, pp. 15–21.

Kecskemeti, Paul, "Hungary's Communist Anti-Communists," *The New Leader,* February 10, 1958, pp. 24–25.

————— "Limits and Problems of Decompression: The Case of Hungary," *The Annals of the American Academy of Political and Social Science,* May 1958, pp. 97–106.

Kennan, George F., *Russia, the Atom and the West.* New York, 1957.

Kertesz, Stephen D., *Diplomacy in a Whirlpool.* Notre Dame, Ind., 1953.

————— (ed.), *The Fate of East Central Europe.* Notre Dame, Ind., 1956.

Király, Béla, "How Russian Trickery Throttled Revolt," *Life,* February 18, 1957.

————— "Hungary's Army under the Soviets," *East Europe,* March 1958, pp. 3–14.

————— "Hungary's Army: Its Part in the Revolt," *East Europe,* June 1958, pp. 11–15.

————— "Hungary's New Envoy in Moscow," *East Europe,* July 1960, pp. 26–28.

————— unpublished answers to a questionnaire on Hungarian and Soviet military affairs.

Király, Béla, and Árpád Kovács, "The Hungarian Revolution of 1956," *Thought Patterns,* no. 7 (publication of St. John's University, N.Y.), 1960.

Kommunist. Theoretical periodical of the Soviet Communist Party. Moscow.

Kortárs. Hungarian periodical. Budapest.

Kovács, Imre (ed.), *Facts about Hungary.* New York, 1959.

Kövágo, Jozsef, *You Are All Alone.* New York, 1959.

Lasky, Melvin J., *The Hungarian Revolution.* New York, 1957.

—————— "A Conversation with Kennan," *Encounter,* March 1960.

Lowenthal, Richard, "Why Was Slansky Hanged?" *20th Century,* January 1953.

—————— "Tito's Affair with Khrushchev," *The New Leader,* October 6, 1958, pp. 10–19.

Macartney, C. A., *October Fifteen — A History of Modern Hungary, 1920–1945.* Edinburgh, 1957.

Magyar Közlöny. Official gazette of the Hungarian government. Budapest.

Magyar Nemzet. Daily paper of the People's Patriotic Front of Hungary. Budapest.

Magyarország. "Stalinist" daily published in Budapest from 1957 to January 1958.

Medjunarodna Politika. Yugoslav periodical on foreign policy. Belgrade.

Meier, Victor, " 'Socialist Transformation' in the Countryside," *Problems of Communism,* September–October 1960.

Meissner, Boris, *The Communist Party of the Soviet Union.* New York, 1956.

—————— *Das Ende des Stalin-Mythos.* Frankfurt a.M., 1956.

—————— *Sowjetrussland zwischen Revolution und Restauration.* Cologne, 1956.

Mendershausen, Horst, "Terms of Trade between the Soviet Union and the Smaller Communist Countries," *The Review of Economics and Statistics,* May 1958, pp. 106–118.

Méray, Tibor, "The Crisis of the New Class," *The Review* (Brussels), June 1959, pp. 87–101.

—————— *Thirteen Days That Shook the Kremlin.* New York, 1959.

Mészáros, István, *La Rivoltà degli Intellettuali in Ungheria.* Torino, 1958.

Michener, James Albert, *The Bridge at Andau.* New York, 1957.

Mikes, George, *The Hungarian Revolution.* London, 1957.

Molden-Pogany, Josef, *Ungarns Freiheitskampf.* Vienna, 1957.

Molnár, Miklos, and Lászlo Nagy, *Imre Nagy, Réformateur ou Révolutionnaire?* Geneva, 1959.

Morgenthau, Hans, "The Revolution in U.S. Foreign Policy," *Commentary,* February 1957.

Morris, Bernard, "Soviet Policy toward National Communism: The Limits of Diversity," *The American Political Science Review,* March 1959, pp. 128–137.

Mourin, Maxime," "La Hongrie après l'insurrection," *Revue de Défense Nationale,* June 1959.

Nagy, Balázs, "Imre Nagy and the Hungarian Revolution," *The Review* (Brussels), April 1960, pp. 16–54.

Nagy, Ferenc, *The Struggle behind the Iron Curtain.* New York, 1948.

Nagy Imre és Büntársai Ellenforradalmi Összeesküvése (The Counterrevolutionary Conspiracy of Imre Nagy and His Accomplices). Budapest, 1958.

Nagy, Imre, *On Communism: In Defense of the New Course.* New York, 1957. Same book in Hungarian: *A Magyar Nép Védelmében.* Paris, 1957. French edition: *Imre Nagy: Un Communisme Qui n'Oublie pas l'Homme.* Paris, 1957. Introduction by François Fejtö.

Nehru, Jawaharlal, "The Tragic Paradox of Our Age," *New York Times Magazine*, September 7, 1958, pp. 13, 110–111.

Népakarat. Daily of the Central Council of Hungarian Trade Unions (after November 1956). Budapest.

Népszabadság. Daily of the Hungarian Communist Party after November 1, 1956. Budapest.

Népszava. Daily of the Central Council of Hungarian Trade Unions (until the Revolution of 1956). Budapest.

Népujság. Hungarian local paper published in the town of Salgotarján.

Norman, Daniel, "The Fate of Béla Kun," *The New Statesman*, September 1, 1956.

Nowa Kultura. Polish literary journal. Warsaw.

Orme, Alexandra, *Comes the Comrade!* New York, 1950.

Paloczi-Horvath, George, *The Undefeated*. London, 1959.

——— *Khrushchev: The Making of a Dictator*. Boston, 1960.

Papendorp, Theodore J., "Hungary in the Light of the Economic Integration of the Soviet Bloc." (Mimeographed, Cambridge, Mass.)

Polityka. Polish weekly of the Communist Party. Warsaw.

Potoczky, Kálmán, unpublished manuscript in Hungarian on events in Hungary, 1953–1956. New York.

Pravda. Daily paper of the Soviet Communist Party. Moscow.

Radio Broadcasts, *A Magyar Forradalom és Szabadságharc* (The Hungarian Revolution and Fight for Freedom), Hungarian radio broadcasts from October 23 to November 9, 1956, Free Europe Press. New York. 1957.

Rendületlenül. Organ of the Hungarian Freedom Fighters Federation, Inc., of New York.

Révay, István, *Hungarians in Czechoslovakia*. New York, 1959.

The Review. Quarterly, published by the Imre Nagy Institute. Brussels.

The Revolt in Hungary, a documentary chronology of events based on Hungarian radio broadcasts, ed. Free Europe Committee. New York, 1957.

"La Révolte de la Hongrie," a collection from works of Hungarian writers and poets (1949–1956), *Les Temps Modernes*, November–December 1956, January 1957.

Rude Pravo. Daily of the Czechoslovak Communist Party. Prague.

Ruff, Lajos, *The Brainwashing Machine*. London, 1959.

Savarius, Vincent, "The Silent Writers of Hungary," *Soviet Survey*, July–September 1958.

Scarlett, Dora. *Window onto Hungary*. Bradford, England, 1959.

Schapiro, Leonard, "Has Russia Changed?" *Foreign Affairs*, April 1960, pp. 391–401.

Schenk, F. and Lowenthal, R., "Politics and Planning in the Soviet Empire," *The New Leader*, February 5, 12, and 19, 1959.

Schorr, Daniel, "Cardinal in a Cage," *The Reporter*, November 24, 1960, pp. 39–40.

Seton-Watson, Hugh, *The East European Revolution*. New York, 1951.

——— *Neither War nor Peace*. New York, 1960.

Sinor, Denis, *History of Hungary*. London, 1959.

Spulber, N., *The Economics of Communist Eastern Europe*. Cambridge, Mass., 1957.

Sulyok, Dezsö, *Zwei Nächte ohne Tag.* Zurich, 1948.

Szabad Nép. Daily paper of the Hungarian Communist Party until the end of October 1956. Budapest.

Társadalmi Szemle. Theoretical periodical of the Hungarian Communist Party. Budapest.

Toma, Peter A., "Revival of a Communist Party in Hungary," *The Western Political Quarterly,* March 1961 (part 1), pp. 87–103.

Toynbee, Arnold J., *A Study of History,* abridged edition. Vols. I-VI, New York, 1954, vols. VII-XI, New York, 1957.

Trybuna Ludu. Daily of the Polish Communist Party. Warsaw.

Uj Szo. Hungarian paper in Bratislava, Czechoslovakia.

United Nations, *Report of the Special Committee on the Problem of Hungary.* United Nations, General Assembly, Eleventh Session, Supplement No. 18 (A/3592). New York, 1957.

Váli, Ferenc A., "The Hungarian Revolution and International Law," *The Fletcher Review,* Summer 1959, pp. 9–25.

——— "The Nagy 'Trial,' " *Rendületlenül,* May–June 1959, pp. 5–6.

Valoság. Hungarian monthly paper. Budapest.

Varga, Lászlo, *Violations of Human Rights in Hungary* (mimeographed). New York, 1960.

La Vérité sur l'Affaire Nagy. Paris, 1958. Preface by Albert Camus. English translations: *The Truth about Imre Nagy.* London, 1959. *The Truth about the Nagy Affair.* New York, 1959.

Watnick, Morris, "Georg Lukacs: An Intellectual Biography," *Soviet Survey,* January–March 1958, pp. 60–66; April–June 1958, pp. 51–57; and July–September 1958, pp. 61–68.

Wolfe, Bertram, *Stalin's Ghost.* New York, 1957.

Wszelaki, Jan, *Communist Economic Strategy: The Role of East Central Europe.* Washington, 1959.

——— "Economic Developments in East-Central Europe, 1954–1959," *Orbis,* Winter 1961, pp. 422–451.

Zinner, Paul E. (ed.), *National Communism and Popular Revolt in Eastern Europe.* New York, 1957.

——— "Hungary's Imre Nagy: Revolutionist at the End," *Columbia University Forum,* Fall 1958, pp. 6–10.

——— "Revolution in Hungary: Reflections on the Vicissitudes of a Totalitarian System," *The Journal of Politics,* February 1959, pp. 3–36.

Notes

/\/

1. Summons to the Kremlin

1. *Szabad Nép*, May 11, 1953.

2. *Ibid.*

3. The exact date of the meeting is not certainly known. It can be assumed, however, that the journey to Moscow took place shortly after the East German uprising on June 17, 1953. Miklos Molnár and Lászlo Nagy, *Imre Nagy, Réformateur ou Révolutionnaire?* (Geneva, 1959), put the journey in the week following the Berlin revolt (p. 59); Tamás Aczél and Tibor Méray, *The Revolt of the Mind* (New York, 1959), suggest June 24 as the exact date of the Moscow interview (p. 158).

4. Columbia University Research Project on Hungary (to be referred to as CURPH), report by György Heltai, *Hungary, 1953–1956*, p. 3. According to Heltai, Rákosi tried to have Imre Nagy's invitation canceled, but to no avail.

5. Imre Nagy, *On Communism: In Defense of the New Course* (New York, 1957), p. 250. This book is an English translation of various memoranda which Nagy had circulated in Hungary during 1955 and 1956.

6. Aczél and Méray, *Revolt*, p. 175.

7. The exact date of Beria's arrest is set at June 26. See Zbigniew K. Brzezinski, *The Permanent Purge* (Cambridge, Mass., 1956), p. 161. His arrest was officially announced on July 10, and his execution was announced on December 23. Khrushchev was able to establish himself as First Secretary of the Party in September 1953. After Malenkov relinquished this post, Khrushchev was handling Party affairs as senior Secretary but remained rather in the background until his official nomination to the first Party post. See Merle Fainsod, "What Happened to 'Collective Leadership'?" in *Problems of Communism*, July–August 1959, pp. 2–3.

8. The most complete picture of this scene can be extracted from various parts of Nagy's memoranda, cited in note 5 above. Other items of these dialogues are reported on the basis of statements given by leading Hungarian refugees who, in view of their status in the Party, were able to obtain first-hand information on the subject.

9. Imre Nagy, p. 66.

10. Tibor Méray, *Thirteen Days that Shook the Kremlin* (New York, 1959), p. 6; Aczél and Méray, *Revolt*, p. 159.

11. Imre Nagy, p. 250.

12. CURPH, Heltai report, p. 9.

13. CURPH, interview no. 500. According to this testimony, the Soviet Presidium members called Rákosi, Gerö, and Farkas every possible name.

14. In the Doctors' Plot of Jan-

uary 1953, the last purge initiated under Stalin, a number of eminent Moscow doctors were arrested and accused of a conspiracy to kill off prominent Soviet leaders. After Stalin's death the accused were released and rehabilitated. Ignatiev, Minister of State Security, and his deputy, Riumin, were made responsible for these illegalities. *Survey of International Affairs, 1953* (London, 1956), pp. 10–11.

15. For the decision of the Central Committee removing Beria from office and approving his arrest, see Boris Meissner, *The Communist Party of the Soviet Union* (New York, 1956), p. 44.

16. After the removal of Imre Nagy from the premiership in April 1955, Rákosi blamed himself (in Nagy's view, erroneously) for having recommended him as Prime Minister. "In his speech at the April meeting of the Central Committee, Mátyás Rákosi allegedly said that he felt heavy responsibility for the fact that I had become Premier on July 4, 1953, thereby suggesting that he at least 'recommended' me for Premier. For the sake of truth, it must be stated that it was not Mátyás Rákosi, but the Soviet comrades — Comrades Malenkov, Molotov, and Khrushchev — who recommended what Comrade Rákosi and all members of the Hungarian delegation accepted with approbation. Thus Rákosi is innocent in this question; there is no basis for his remorse, because he bears no responsibility at all for my nomination as Premier." Imre Nagy, p. 252.

17. For instance, Imre Nagy, p. 153.

2. The Historical Setting: Expansionism and Satellitism

1. "Marxian revolutionary internationalism [turned] into a pseudo-internationalism filtered through the sieve of Soviet national interest." Bernard Morris, "Soviet Policy toward National Communism: The Limits of Diversity," *The American Political Science Review*, March 1959, p. 130. See also Andrew Gyorgy, "The Ideology of Communism," mimeographed copy of lectures delivered in the Armed Forces Staff College, Norfolk, Va., January 1960, pp. 30–31.

2. "The "internationalist" and "socialist" Soviet Union is a much more nationalist state, with far more ethnocentric attitudes, than was Imperial Russia." Frederick C. Barghoorn, *Soviet Russian Nationalism* (New York, 1956), p. 177.

3. *Ibid.*, pp. 9, 22.

4. See Franz Borkenau, *European Communism* (New York, 1953), pp. 50–68.

5. "The International Situation and the Defense of the USSR," *Works*, vol. 10, August–December 1927 (Moscow, 1954), p. 53.

6. Zhdanov's and Dimitrov's sudden passing away as a consequence of illness might be presumed to be the result of the defeat of the "internationalists." The internationalist Tito was forced by the strength of circumstances to become a Yugoslav parochial nationalist. After the reconciliation of 1955, he renewed his ambition to achieve a leading stature in the international Communist movement, but his attempts failed when again Khrushchev insisted on preserving the leadership of Communist parties for that of the Soviet Union. Borkenau, pp. 518–548; Richard Lowenthal, "Tito's Affair with Khrushchev," *The New Leader*, Oct. 6, 1958, pp. 10–19.

7. Barghoorn, pp. 84–86. Such a state of affairs naturally favors Great Russian national and cultural expansions.

8. Information given by "M.I." in *Rendületlenül*, December 1959.

9. Text in *East Europe*, February 1958, pp. 55–56.

10. Tass translation, *New York Times*, Dec. 7, 1960.

11. See R. W. Seton-Watson, *The Rise of Nationality in the Balkans* (London, 1917), pp. 117–118; E. C. Corti, *Alexander von Battenberg* (London, 1959), pp. 77–109.

12. For a comprehensive picture of the Communist takeovers see Hugh Seton-Watson, *The East European Revolution* (New York, 1951), *passim;* Andrew Gyorgy, *Governments of Danubian Europe* (New York, 1949).

13. František Palacky (1798–1876), Czech historian, wrote that the arrival of the Magyars into present-day Hungary had been the greatest disaster to the unity of the Slav world. *Geschichte von Böhmen* (Prague, 1864), I, 195–196. For Hungarian history in general see Denis Sinor, *History of Hungary* (London, 1959); Dominic G. Kosary, *A History of Hungary* (New York, 1941); C. M. Knatchbull-Hugessen, *The Political Evolution of the Hungarian Nation* (London, 1908).

14. *New York Times*, Dec. 3, 1959.

3. The Communists Take Over

1. A characteristic example of such inconsistencies has been described by Stephen D. Kertesz, *Diplomacy in a Whirlpool* (Notre Dame, Ind., 1953), p. 172. The Hungarian Foreign Minister, János Gyöngyösi, in a note dated November 12, 1945, addressed to the three armistice powers (Britain, USA., and USSR), urged the revival and strengthening of international control over the Danube, with continued participation of nonriparian states; in August 1948 the same Foreign Minister solidly supported the Soviet view to exclude nonriparian participation in the Danube Commission.

2. It might be held that the conspicuous Great Russian nationalism and a deficiency in class-consciousness of the Soviet troops had been a result of the patriotic education with which they were more abundantly endowed after the German attack on the Soviet Union; see Frederick C. Barghoorn, *Soviet Russian Nationalism* (New York, 1956), pp. 13, 264–265.

3. Election results and subsequent events are analyzed in *Hungary*, ed. Ernst C. Helmreich (New York, 1957), pp. 116–118; and *Facts About Hungary*, ed. Imre Kovács (New York, 1959), pp. 59–64.

4. For the strategy employed by the Communist Party for the takeover of power see Hugh Seton-Watson, *The East European Revolution* (New York, 1951); Ferenc Nagy, *The Struggle Behind the Iron Curtain* (New York, 1948); Dezsö Sulyok, *Zwei Nächte Ohne Tag* (Zurich, 1948).

5. The Communist Party suddenly reversed its anti-irredentist attitude in March 1946, and advocated an extension of Hungary's frontier to the detriment of Rumania. When a Hungarian delegation met Stalin and Molotov in Moscow, certain ambiguous statements made by the Soviet leaders gave the impression that Hungary's territorial claim against Rumania would be supported by the Soviet Union. See Ferenc Nagy, pp. 209–210.

6. At the Paris peace conference (July–October 1946), Molotov opposed even a minor change in the Transylvanian border in favor of Hungary which had been proposed by the United States; Helmreich, p. 26; John C. Campbell, "The European Territorial Settlement," *Foreign Affairs*, 1947, pp. 211–213.

7. The Hungarian Foreign Ministry tried to have deportation of Germans restricted to those who had been

members of Nazi organizations. For Communist pressures see Ferenc Nagy, pp. 198–199. The Hungarian government decree of December 22, 1945, ordering a partial deportation of Germans from Hungary could not be entirely implemented because the Americans refused to accept any more deportees into their zone in Germany.

8. The Soviet government exerted great pressure on Hungary to agree to an "exchange" of populations. But since the number of Slovaks in Hungary was less than one seventh of that of Hungarians in Czechoslovakia, no equal exchange was possible. See Hugh Seton-Watson, p. 344; Helmreich, pp. 26–28; Kertesz, pp. 122–125.

9. Article 5 of the Paris peace treaty signed on February 10, 1947, made the "exchange" of 200,000 Hungarians dependent on an agreement between Hungary and Czechoslovakia. By 1949, however, both countries had full-fledged Communist governments and the matter was then dropped.

10. Under the Armistice Agreement of January 20, 1945, Hungary was obliged to pay to the Soviet Union $200 million in commodities over a period of six years, and $100 million to Yugoslavia and Czechoslovakia. The Soviet Union evaluated the goods in such a way as to double or triple the stated amounts. See Andrew Gyorgy, *Governments of Danubian Europe* (New York, 1949), p. 134.

11. The notion of "German assets" was interpreted by Soviet authorities in a most arbitrary and diffuse sense; thus they were interested in acquiring only the "assets," that is, the net property *without* its liabilities.

12. The Communist Minister Ernö Gerö signed in August 1945 a Soviet-Hungarian Economic Cooperation Agreement which, among other things, provided for the establishment of Soviet-Hungarian Joint Corporations. So additional Hungarian industrial and commercial firms became subject to Soviet control and economic exploitation.

13. Western chancelleries flooded the Hungarian government with their protests and requests for compensation, asking for such clarification that might enable them to proceed with the matter in Moscow. Because of Communist intervention, Soviet soldiers or the Soviet Army could never be indicated in diplomatic notes as perpetrators of the acts complained of (personal recollection of this writer).

14. See Miklos Molnár and László Nagy, *Imre Nagy, Réformateur ou Révolutionnaire?* (Geneva, 1959), p. 20.

15. *Népszabadság*, May, 9, 1957, quoted Imre Nagy's self-criticism after his arrival to Moscow in 1930; see also Molnár and Lászlo Nagy, pp. 18–19.

16. Molnár and Lászlo Nagy, p. 23.

17. Ferenc Nagy, pp. 190, 305.

18. The journalist Miklos Gimes, executed together with Imre Nagy in June 1958, was a member of this Swiss Group.

4. Party and State

1. *New York Times*, Jan. 23, 1949.

2. It is thus not without reason to speak of the "conspiratorial" character of the People's Democracies. Bernard Morris, "Soviet Policy Toward National Communism: The Limits of Diversity," *American Political Science Review*, March 1959, pp. 128–137.

3. August 20, Saint Stephen's Day (St. Stephen, first King of Hungary, 1001–1038) is the Hungarian national holiday. In order to provide an ad-

missible reason for celebrating the ancient sacred holiday, Rákosi arranged that the new Communist constitution be promulgated that day; thereupon it was declared "Constitution Day" and maintained as a state holiday.

4. For various peculiar provisions of the new Constitution, see *Hungary*, ed. Ernst C. Helmreich (New York, 1957), pp. 84–86.

5. Helmreich, pp. 125–126.

6. Hugh Seton-Watson in his foreword to Imre Nagy's *On Communism: In Defense of the New Course* (New York, 1957), pp. xi–xii, draws attention to the fact that out of 92 persons who had been members of the Central Committee between 1949 and 1954, only 46 were still members in 1954.

7. Merle Fainsod, *How Russia Is Ruled* (Cambridge, 1953), pp. 166–179.

8. The story of Szakasits' arrest and torture is recalled by George Paloczi-Horvath, *The Undefeated* (London, 1959), pp. 238–239. That author shared a prison cell with Szakasits.

9. Stalin, especially after World War II, exercised his authority via his private secretariat, especially Lt. General Poskrebyshev and Malenkov. Orders to the Security Police organs, to the military and other governmental offices were frequently issued through this secretariat, by-passing the "constitutional" Party channels. Boris Meissner, *Sowjetrussland zwischen Revolution und Restauration* (Cologne, 1956), p. 76. George Paloczi-Horvath, *Khrushchev: The Making of a Dictator* (Boston, 1960), pp. 120–121.

10. Rákosi was even ready to defend his procedure on a rather unorthodox basis. Imre Nagy, pp. 251–252, reports: "It is well known among Party leaders that when Mátyás Rákosi became Premier he alluded to Stalin in voicing the view with the Political Committee that it was necessary to *increase the role of the state* vis-à-vis the Party; that it was necessary to place the government more into the foreground, in the interest of wider and more direct connections with the masses: this, according to him, was required by the new situation. He indicated that placing the state and the government more into the foreground and increasing respect for them was an important task of the Party when the Council of Ministers came into the fore. I believe there is no need for commentary on this." (Italics are added.)

11. The controversy between François Fejtö (*Behind the Rape of Hungary*, New York, 1957) and Paul Kecskemeti ("Hungary's Communist Anti-Communists," *The New Leader*, Feb. 10, 1958, pp. 24–26) relates to the question of whether Communism in Hungary always had two faces, a "terrorist" and a "humano-social" faction within the Party, as Fejtö asserts, or whether such a view is only an "unhistorical" backward projection of the contrast, as submitted by Kecskemeti.

12. See the following CURPH (Columbia University Research Project on Hungary) interviews: no. 500 ("When the Social Democrats fell, I had no doubt at all that people like Szakasits and Marosán could be English spies. But when our close friends began to be arrested, then we started to have doubts."); nos. 459, 507, 519, 563, 616. See also Dora Scarlett, *Window onto Hungary* (Bradford, England, 1958), the report of a British Communist who worked in Hungary until the Revolution of 1956.

13. See especially George Paloczi-Horvath, *The Undefeated* (London, 1959), pp. 186–192. This is a pathetic confession of a former "obsessed" Communist who had to admit that even the much maligned Horthy re-

gime was preferable to Communism. His meetings with workers in prison who had also been Party members ("This rottenest of all the conceivable rotten systems is made possible by the great Communist lie") brought about his abandonment not only of Communism but also of Marxism of any kind.

14. "Fermentation" expression used in CURPH, interview no. 616. This writer had met, in August 1950, "I.G.," then a high official in the Ministry of Foreign Affairs and prominent Party member. He expressed fear of being pushed into the background because he was not of proletarian origin (his father was a district attorney). He bitterly complained that neither Rákosi nor Gerö was of such an origin. He further said that he and some of his friends had lately protested in the Party against such discrimination. A few weeks later I.G. was taken away from his Ministry, and the author met him again in prison in the fall of 1953 when I.G. was serving a life sentence. However, in September 1954, he was released and rehabilitated. In 1950, "R.H.," a high official in the foreign trade section of the Ministry of Commerce, complained to the author that he had a row in the Party where he was reproached for having his child baptized. He said that when the child was baptized, in 1948, the Party expressly invited him to do so in order to demonstrate religious tolerance. He showed thorough disappointment, especially when he was demoted into a less important post. In June 1951, "S.C.," head of a section in the People's Economic Council, in private company admitted his disgust about the way that deportations were being carried out. While maintaining that some deportations might be justified, he strongly inveighed against the method by which they were being implemented. He added that "many

in the Party" thought so too. Such instances could be multiplied.

15. CURPH, interview no. 500.

16. Imre Nagy, p. 8.

17. "Rákosi and the Party leaders, Gerö, Révai, and Farkas, seriously impaired the effectiveness of the Communist principle of criticism and self-criticism within the Party and government. They generally considered criticism from below as the voice of the enemy and acted accordingly. They did not criticize one another but shielded each other from criticism. They took even the mildest form of criticism as a personal insult. According to them, mistakes could be made only at the lower echelons. They themselves were infallible and could do no wrong." Imre Nagy, p. 279.

18. Helmreich (note 4, above), pp. 206–207.

19. For a good survey see Ilona Paul, "The Education Weapon," in This Is Communist Hungary, ed. Robert Finley Delaney (Chicago, 1958), pp. 141–164.

20. Rákosi expressly wanted the Szabad Nép to look like the Pravda. CURPH, interview no. 563.

21. For a good summary see Paul Landy, "Mass Media: 'Ignorance is Strength,' " in Delaney (see note 19, above), pp. 87–94; also see CURPH interview no. 152.

22. Landy, pp. 95–108; CURPH, interview no. 504.

23. Landy, p. 101; CURPH, interview no. 504.

24. For good summaries of developments in literature and art (though the authors widely differ in outlook and background) see: Ferenc Kormendi in Helmreich, pp. 170–181; István Mészáros, La Rivolta degli Intellettuali in Ungheria (Torino, 1958), passim; George Gömöri, "Cultural and Literary Developments: Poland and Hungary," The Annals, May 1958, pp. 71–78; Tamás Aczél and Tibor Méray, The

Revolt of the Mind (New York, 1959), pp. 3–143; CURPH, interviews nos. 152, 500, 508, 567, 616.

25. CURPH, interview no. 500; see also Helmreich, p. 178.

26. See, in particular, CURPH, interviews nos. 500 and 616; also a CURPH report by Miklos Molnár, "History of the *Irodalmi Ujság.*"

27. A very apt analysis is made by Aczél and Méray, pp. 57–80; an excellent analysis of Lukács' ideology is made by Morris Watnick, "Georg Lukács: An Intellectual Biography," *Soviet Survey*, nos. 23, 24, 25 (January–September 1958).

28. George Gömöri (note 24, above), pp. 72–74; Aczél and Méray, pp. 94–118.

29. A characteristic description and comment is in CURPH, interview no. 616.

30. Aczél and Méray, pp. 351, 353; CURPH, interviews nos. 616 and 500.

31. CURPH, interview no. 616.

32. *Ibid.*

33. CURPH, interview no. 152.

34. Characteristically, a frustrated Security Police (AHV) major thus saw (and hoped for) a solution of the crisis which he presumably thought would save his skin: "At the end we shall ask for admission, as a member state, into the Soviet Union, and this decision will automatically solve all our outstanding problems and difficulties." *Ibid.*

35. CURPH, interview no. 615.

36. A good description of the prevailing amorality is found in Mészáros (note 24, above), pp. 166–168. Perhaps one of the most immoral aspects of Party propaganda consisted of the slogan for making youth camps more attractive: "To give birth to children is the duty of married women, but a glory for unwed girls!"

37. These were the words of Jozsef Révai to intellectuals who complained to him. CURPH, interview no. 500.

38. George Paloczi-Horvath, *The Undefeated* (London, 1959), pp. 186–192; CURPH, interview no. 152.

39. See explanations by the Italian Communist journalist Giuseppe Boffa, *Inside the Khrushchev Era* (New York, 1959), p. 84.

40. Aczél and Méray, pp. 151–156; CURPH, interview no. 616.

41. Imre Nagy, p. 144.

5. Security Police: Purges and Terror

1. See Zbigniew K. Brzezinski, *The Permanent Purge* (Cambridge, Mass., 1956), pp. 28, 175.

2. Aladár Weisshaus and György Demény, non-muscovite Communist leaders who refused to cooperate with the Soviet-sponsored Rákosist Communist Party, disappeared in 1945 and 1946. Demény was still in prison in 1956 (personal recollection of the present writer). Both were personal enemies of Rákosi, which also accounts for the treatment reserved for them. See CURPH (Columbia University Research Project on Hungary), interview no. 152.

3. *Hungary*, ed. Ernst C. Helmreich (New York, 1957), pp. 136–141.

4. CURPH, interview no. 526. The interviewee, a historian-archivist, visited the AVH record offices when they were abandoned during the Revolution in 1956. He reports that their records, though still permeated with Communist phraseology, seemed more realistic than Communist Party or political papers but at the same time revealed the cynicism of the machines of terror. Despite their factualness, many of the reports he saw were distorted, full of stupid and muddled thinking. The interviewee concluded that the AVH was far from being the omniscient apparatus it claimed to be.

The present writer's personal experiences also confirm such a conclusion; the results achieved by the AVH and its successors are due only to the ruthless and brutal powers of which they can freely avail themselves, powers which are not at the disposal of any police bound by the rule of law.

5. George Paloczi-Horvath, *The Undefeated* (London, 1959), p. 194.

6. Nográdi, also a muscovite who prior to his return to Hungary worked for many years in the NKVD's service, had a mistress who was the wife of a former Horthyist officer. He reported his "liaison" to the Party. In 1952 the woman was arrested as an American spy, and it was then that Rákosi struck out to liquidate Nográdi. CURPH, interview no. 500. See also General Béla Király, "Hungary's Army under the Soviets," *East Europe*, March 1958, p. 12.

7. Miklos Molnár and Lászlo Nagy, *Imre Nagy: Réformateur ou Révolutionnaire?* (Geneva, 1959), p. 28.

8. Paloczi-Horvath, pp. 160–163.

9. István Stolte told his story personally to this writer in a prison cell in September–October 1956. See also Paloczi-Horvath, p. 194.

10. Concerning the tape recording, see CURPH, interview no. 152; Paloczi-Horvath, pp. 259–262. The use of tape recorders to secure subservience and to supervise Security Police personnel has apparently been used in other cases within the Soviet orbit. At Colonel Rozanski's trial in 1957 in Warsaw (the former Deputy Chief of the Polish Security Police was accused of torturing prisoners) a tape recorder produced by the prosecutor refuted the denial of the accused (information provided by Professor Zbigniew K. Brzezinski to this writer).

11. See, in particular, Merle Fainsod, *How Russia Is Ruled* (Cambridge, Mass., 1953), pp. 365–389; and Brzezin-ski, *The Permanent Purge*, pp. 65–97.

12. *Facts About Hungary*, ed. Imre Kovács (New York, 1959), p. 188.

13. This is a considerably smaller proportion of the population than is estimated to have been imprisoned or deported in the Soviet Union during 1937–1939 or after World War II, where even percentages running from 7 to 14 were mentioned (see Fainsod, p. 385); but Hungary had no Siberia to which prisoners could be deported. On the other hand, the proportion of intellectuals and high-skilled workers among prisoners must have been considerably greater in Hungary than in the Soviet Union.

14. For Merle Fainsod's interpretation of the *Yezhovshchina*, see his pp. 373–374.

15. For instance, when György Faludi, a writer of renown who returned to Hungary (having served in the American Army) after World War II, and who admitted under torture of having "spied for Edgar Allan Poe and Walt Whitman," was brought before the presence of Gábor Péter, the AVH Chief, he was told by the latter: "Aren't you an idiot to have come back, to return home, to this filth!" CURPH, interview no. 506; Paloczi-Horvath, p. 224.

16. To cite one example we refer to the case of Endre Havas, a Communist writer who, when tortured for some months, never ceased "to praise socialism" and to repeat that "Rákosi cannot be aware" of what is done to him. His torturers, having received instructions from Rákosi himself, and believing that Havas was making fun of them, increased the torture. Eventually he succumbed to his pains and died in the prison hospital. István Mészáros, *La Rivoltà degli Intellettuali in Ungheria* (Torino, 1958), p. 175; Paloczi-Horvath, p. 224; François Fejtö, *Behind the Rape of Hungary* (New York, 1957), p. 121.

17. For personal impressions of the AVH prisons, among many reminiscences the following seem most trustworthy and instructive: Paloczi-Horvath; Jozsef Kővágó, *You Are All Alone* (New York, 1959); Lajos Ruff, *The Brainwashing Machine* (London, 1959); Paul Ignotus, *Political Prisoner* (London, 1960); "The Muted Horror in Hungary" (anonymous), *East Europe*, August 1958, pp. 11–26.

18. See Béla Just, *Un Procès Préfabriqué: L'Affaire Mindszenty* (Paris, 1949); William Juhasz, "Church and Society in Hungary," in *Church and Society*, ed. Joseph N. Moody (New York, 1952).

19. The story is related by Jozsef Magyar in Robert Finley Delaney, *This Is Communist Hungary* (Chicago, 1958), pp. 49–54.

20. See Franz Borkenau, *European Communism* (New York, 1953), pp. 226–229.

21. *Survey of International Affairs, 1947–1948* (London, 1952), pp. 194–195.

22. Milovan Djilas wrote in the *Borba* (June 14, 1949), that Rajk, Gomulka, General Xoxe, and General Markos were being disgraced because they resisted subjugation of their countries to the Soviet Union.

23. *Survey of International Affairs, 1949–1950* (London, 1953), p. 206.

24. A partial explanation emerged at the Eighth Plenum of the Polish Central Committee in October 1956. Zbigniew K. Brzezinski, *The Soviet Bloc: Unity and Conflict* (Cambridge, Mass., 1960), p. 96.

25. Rákosi on September 30, 1949, in a speech before top-level Party functionaries in Budapest, exclaimed: "The lessons of the Rajk trial were not learned by us only, but by the worker movement of the whole world. During the trial it became clear that the American imperialists and their Yugoslav colleagues made similar plans in all the People's Democracies. Rajk, Pálffy, Brankov exposed these plans in great detail. They exposed the special role played by the Catholic reaction and the Vatican which prepared the downfall of democracy not only in Hungary but also in Czechoslovakia and Poland. Brankov reported that he was scolded by Ranković, because the work of the traitors did not make as much progress in Hungary, as it did in Czechoslovakia." *Szabad Nép*, Oct. 1, 1949; see also Béla Fábián, "Hungary's Jewry Faces Liquidation," *Commentary*, October 1951, pp. 330–335.

26. Franz Borkenau, p. 543; Richard Lowenthal, "Why Was Slansky Hanged?" *20th Century*, January 1953, pp. 18–23; H. Jaeger, "Der Tiefere Hintergrund des Falles Slansky," *Deutsche Rundschau*, December 1951, pp. 1079–1080.

27. CURPH, Heltai report, pp. 2–3. The emergence of anti-Péter investigations within the AVH was already noticed by prisoners in the spring of 1952; see Jozsef Kővágó, pp. 74–77. These investigations coincide with those led by Malenkov, Bulganin, and Khrushchev against Beria as early as 1951–52; see Peter Deriabin and Frank Gibney, *The Secret World* (New York, 1959), p. 167.

6. The Army of a Satellite

1. This and some of the further information in this chapter was obtained by this writer directly from General Béla Király in 1959. Still other facts were known to the writer through personal conversations in Hungary during 1951–1953.

2. The proportion of Soviet advisers to the Hungarian element in the Zrinyi Academy (Command and

General Staff College) is known. In 1951 there were one Soviet General and thirteen Soviet staff officers (mostly colonels, lieutenant colonels), as against about 400 officer students and personnel of administration. Information from General Király.

3. Draftees of three age groups were always in active service. Each is estimated at 70–75 thousand men, making a total of 210,000. Adding officers and noncommissioned officers, as well as Security Police troops and Frontier Guard units (who generally served over three years), one obtains the figures mentioned in the text. See *Hungary*, ed. Ernst C. Helmreich (New York, 1957), p. 149.

4. Béla Király, "Hungary's Army: Its Part in the Revolt," *East Europe*, June 1958, p. 5.

5. Percentage figures may be misleading, since in a Communist state the whole economy, all industrial, commercial, and other state-owned enterprises, are included in the budget. As for government expenditure alone, the defense expenditure of the budget amounted to 37.8 per cent of the total in 1953. Helmreich, ed., p. 224.

6. The most important aides of the advisers were their interpreters; they were generally Carpatho-Russians who also spoke some Hungarian (the region has a mixed population, partly of Hungarian stock). Many of them were of very low intellect, and their primitive interpretation was a constant source of misunderstanding and therefore a menace for the Hungarian commanders.

7. Merle Fainsod, *How Russia Is Ruled* (Cambridge, Mass., 1953), p. 407.

8. Information directly from General Király.

9. *Ibid.*

10. "I do not want to go into details. But whether the important questions of the equipment, personnel, or supplies of the army, war industry, or the modernization of national defense were concerned, I most emphatically supported the proposals of the Ministry of National Defense within the framework permitted by our political and economic possibilities. As a result of a more thorough knowledge of the actual situation, I went further and represented a more correct viewpoint in this field than did Mátyás Rákosi, who, as he used to say, had already burned his fingers once by fulfilling excessive demands. I have said enough on this subject. Details would touch on questions that I do not deem it proper to raise in public even before the Party." Imre Nagy, *On Communism: In Defense of the New Course* (New York, 1957), pp. 245–246.

7. Economics in Stalinist Hungary

1. The expression was used by Ernö Gerö. *Hungary*, ed. Ernst C. Helmreich (New York, 1957), p. 301.

2. Helmreich, ed., p. 294.

3. For an exhaustive survey see Béla Balassa, *The Hungarian Economic Planning* (New Haven, 1959), *passim*.

4. Balassa, p. 32. Imre Nagy speaks of "the irresponsible pre-1953 policy . . . having swallowed up nearly 120 billion forints." Imre Nagy, *On Communism: In Defense of the New Course* (New York, 1957), p. 67.

5. "Under socialist conditions . . . it is inadmissible that a numerically growing population should be forced to satisfy its needs at an unchanged or even declining level, as happened in this country between 1949 and 1953." Imre Nagy, p. 100.

6. Imre Nagy, pp. 131, 155.

7. Hugh Seton-Watson in his foreword to Imre Nagy, pp. xviii–xix. See also CURPH (Columbia University Research Project on Hungary), interview no. 500, where the interviewee refers to the "cursed" Stalinist dogma, "we cannot stand on one foot only," which means that the monopolistic rule of Party and government had to be extended to industrial and farmer population alike.

8. Helmreich, ed., p. 226; Balassa (p. 34) puts the reduction of the standard of living from 1949 till 1952 to 18 per cent. See also CURPH, Heltai report, p. 5.

9. CURPH, interview no. 616.

10. Helmreich, ed., pp. 295–299; Balassa, *passim*.

11. Helmreich, ed., p. 295.

12. Imre Nagy, pp. 186–188.

13. *Szabad Nép,* Oct. 20, 1954, an article he wrote while he was Prime Minister.

14. Imre Nagy, p. 187.

15. Tamás Aczél and Tibor Méray, in *The Revolt of the Mind* (New York, 1959), p. 10, give an apt description: "According to the Muscovites, the Soviet methods were always right, and the cause of their inapplicability was always to be found in the social and human backwardness of the native country. The Soviet methods were not only correct . . . but they were also the only expedient — in fact, the only enlightening — one. Nobody who desired or even suggested alternative methods (after analyzing the conditions and the circumstances) had to do so with malice aforethought, because the comparison was not between method and method, but between Soviet method and non-Soviet method."

16. Helmreich, ed., p. 302.

17. Helmreich, ed., pp. 286–287; the newspaper *Szabad Ifjuság* reported on Dec. 3, 1954, that Hungarian railroads had transported three million tons of stone marked as coal in 1953.

18. Helmreich, ed., p. 288.

19. CURPH, interviews nos. 152 and 466; Helmreich, ed., p. 329. Budapest, since 1896, already had a one-line subway of limited capacity on the Pest side.

20. Helmreich, ed., p. 239.

21. Imre Nagy, p. 206.

22. For an excellent summary see Béla Balassa, "The Hungarian Economy in the Communist Era," in *This Is Communist Hungary,* ed. Robert Finley Delaney (Chicago, 1958), pp. 228–233.

23. Balassa in *This Is Communist Hungary,* p. 231.

24. For instance, in 1950, cheese, entirely, and butter, to a considerable extent, disappeared from the market. Workers of the Magyaróvár cheese factory complained that even they and their families were unable to obtain cheese, which was all shipped to East Germany. This writer was also told that exported cheese was wrapped in paper bearing Cyrillic inscription to give the Germans the impression they were being helped by the Soviet Union.

25. For example, Hungarian-made fountain pens were sold in Cairo for one-tenth the price at which they were obtainable in Hungary. The construction of an electrical power plant at El Tabin, Egypt, was entrusted to Hungary because this country was the lowest bidder. The contract price was 1.6 million Egyptian pounds (about 6.4 million dollars), and eventually it was found that Hungary had to spend ten times this amount in her home currency to have the plant established. Balassa in *This Is Communist Hungary,* pp. 235–236. See also Imre Nagy, pp. 105–106, 184–185, 188–189.

26. Jan Wszelaki, *Communist Economic Strategy: The Role of East Central Europe* (Washington, 1959), pp. 60–61. For example, Hungarian bauxite was bought by the Soviet Un-

ion until 1954 at prices fluctuating from $4.90 to $7.50 per ton, while Czechoslovakia and East Germany paid from $10.80 to $12.70 per ton for the same bauxite. On the other hand, Hungary paid prices for Soviet synthetic rubber 11 to 13 per cent above the world price level and for Soviet lead, 34 to 70 per cent above the world price level. For Soviet cotton Hungary had to pay from $926 to $986 per ton, while the average price of cotton imported from Great Britain fluctuated from $798 to $822 per ton.

27. Balassa in *This Is Communist Hungary,* pp. 235–236. A well-known example is the purchase by the Soviet Union of Polish coal, and its resale to Czechoslovakia and Hungary with the middleman's large profit (Wszelaki, pp. 59–61).

28. A good summary of these events in J. Theodore Papendorp, "Hungary in the Light of the Economic Integration of the Soviet Bloc" (mimeographed, Cambridge, Mass.), p. 7.

29. Said Imre Nagy, p. 189: "It must be pointed out that, although the economic cooperation and mutual assistance between the socialist countries brought significant results, the activity of the CEMA from the point of view of industrial production and development was exceptionally limited during the period of the Five-Year Plan . . . Parallel manufacturing and the exaggerated trend toward autarky within the socialist camp, not only reduced our opportunities to export within the camp, but also deprived us of chances of importing basic and raw materials."

8. The Gladiators Square Off

1. Boris Meissner, *The Communist Party of the Soviet Union* (New York, 1956), pp. 42–43.

2. Imre Nagy, *On Communism: In Defense of the New Course* (New York, 1957), p. 66. His accusation that Rákosi concealed the resolutions from the public is on p. 73.

3. "The pre-June Party leadership, which the June, 1953, resolution of the Central Committee branded as 'clique leadership,' had serious consequences in the internal life of the Communist Party too. This legacy, which had to be liquidated and replaced by Leninist principles in Party life, was very onerous and became the biggest problem of the new Party leadership." Imre Nagy, p. 278.

4. *Szabad Nép,* July 5, 1953. Extracts from this speech are in *Documents on International Affairs, 1953* (London, 1956), pp. 177–181.

5. For the psychological reactions to Imre Nagy's speech see Tamás Aczél and Tibor Méray, *The Revolt*

of the Mind (New York, 1959), pp. 184–187.

6. See N. S. Khrushchev's report on the agricultural situation in the USSR made to the Central Committee of the Party on September 3, 1953, *Documents,* pp. 33–38.

7. *Szabad Nép,* July 12, 1953. These extracts are from *Documents,* pp. 182–188.

8. Paul Kecskemeti, "Limits and Problems of Decompression: The Case of Hungary," *The Annals,* May 1958, p. 100.

9. Beria appeared intent to establish personal contacts with anti-Stalinist satellite leaders. His contacts with East German leaders (Wilhelm Zaisser, Minister of State Security, and Rudolf Herrnstadt, editor of the Party daily) were revealed after his downfall. See Ulbricht's speech before the Central Committee of the Socialist Unity Party, *Neues Deutschland,* July 30, 1953.

10. See Beria's speech to the Su-

preme Soviet proposing Malenkov's appointment as Chairman of the Coun-

cil of Ministers on March 15, 1953, *Documents,* pp. 10–11.

9. Rivalry of Party and State

1. Imre Nagy, *On Communism: In Defense of the New Course* (New York, 1957), pp. 249–250 (italics added).

2. Merle Fainsod, *How Russia Is Ruled* (Cambridge, Mass., 1953), pp. 138–151.

3. Boris Meissner, *Das Ende des Stalin-Mythos* (Frankfurt a.M., 1956), p. 59.

4. Fainsod, pp. 273–285; Boris Meissner, *Sowjetrussland zwischen Revolution und Restauration* (Köln, 1956), pp. 66, 76.

5. On Khrushchev's speech of February 24–25 see Boris Meissner, *Das Ende,* pp. 196–197.

6. Imre Nagy, p. 251.

7. "These views led me to a correct Marxist determination of the relationship of Party and state. In neither my theoretical nor my practical work did I expound activities deviating from Marxist-Leninist teachings. At the Third Party Congress, for the first time in the life of our Party, I dealt exhaustively and in detail with Marxist state theory and with its practical application to the conditions unique in Hungary during the period of transition. I explained the relationship of Party and state, the role of the Party, and its functions in our popular democratic system. I dealt in detail and exhaustively with the operation and chain of command of the state apparatus. In my report, our entire state machinery and administration were placed for the first time on the solid ideological basis of Marxism-Leninism. Together with other arguments, this bears heavily upon the statement that the charge that I tried to set the state organs against the Party is groundless." *Ibid.,* p. 253.

8. *Ibid.,* p. 252.

9. *Ibid.,* p. 251.

10. *Ibid.,* p. 271.

11. "The result of these warnings and of more forceful action here and at home was that double-dealing became the chief method of the opposition." *Ibid.*

12. Tamás Aczél and Tibor Méray, *The Revolt of the Mind* (New York, 1959), pp. 208–231.

13. When Rákosi in his speech in the Politburo mentioned the "tremendous achievements of the Party in the last eight years," Nagy interrupted him: "There were plenty of mistakes in these eight years." "But there were also achievements," retorted Rákosi. Whereupon Nagy closed the dialogue with: "Let's not argue . . . I know what I know." *Ibid.,* p. 229.

14. Zbigniew K. Brzezinski, *The Soviet Bloc: Unity and Conflict* (Cambridge, Mass., 1960), p. 210.

15. Imre Nagy, p. 280.

16. *Ibid.,* p. 281.

17. *Ibid.*

18. *Ibid.*

19. *Ibid.,* pp. 281–282.

20. *Ibid.,* p. 143. Paul Kecskemeti ("Limits and Problems of Decompression: The Case of Hungary," *The Annals,* May 1958, p. 101) claims that Khrushchev's last remarks referred to the impending Hungarian Party Congress where three of Rákosi's adherents were to be dropped from the Politburo. This writer is inclined to attribute a wider significance to Khrushchev's words: he wished to stress the nonimplementation of the June program.

21. Imre Nagy recalls Rákosi's first open attempt to overthrow him in the following words: "The discussion of

the Kovács letter and the resolution of the Political Committee, both of which occurred during my absence, were the first crude attempt by Mátyás Rákosi to place the blame for the troubles arising from opposition to correcting old faults on the New Course and on me personally. The Central Committee's resolution concerning the Kovács letter, which the Soviet comrades said was 'lacking in Bolshevik frankness and deviated in the direction of compromise of principle' and which the Political Committee was obliged to change, willy-nilly, after it had been published, showed the true motives of Rákosi; even before the Third Party Congress, he tried to achieve what he did achieve in the spring of 1955. In short, assisted by baseless contentions, he used my absence enforced by illness to make the Political Committee accept a resolution condemning the policy of the New Course and putting the blame on me. Not only did Rákosi have this matter discussed at the Political Committee in my absence, but he wanted

to go to Moscow without me. The Soviet comrades felt this would be wrong and refused to give him permission. Thus Rákosi's attempts in May, 1954, were a fiasco. He was obliged to admit both in Moscow and before the Political Committee that he had made the Political Committee accept a resolution containing unfounded and misleading statements concerning collective leadership, unity of principle, and Party democracy, and that he had informed the Soviet comrades in this vein. The disclosure of this matter revealed the unethical political campaign directed against me, which had already started at that time." Imre Nagy, p. 282.

22. Boris Meissner, *Sowjetrussland,* pp. 99–100, where the author, *inter alia,* refers to impressions gained by the British statesmen Attlee and Bevan that Malenkov was still powerful at that time.

23. F. Schenk and R. Lowenthal, "Politics and Planning in the Soviet Empire," *The New Leader,* Feb. 5, 12, and 19, 1959.

10. The Third Party Congress and the People's Patriotic Front

1. *Szabad Nép,* May 25, 1954.

2. Nagy's initiative remained sterile; only a draft act on local councils was subsequently submitted for public discussion (a novel feature!) in August 1954, which, however, was no longer inspired by principles of decentralization (*Szabad Nép,* Aug. 19, 1954). For an analysis, see *Free Europe Press,* Research Report 13, Sept. 9, 1954, pp. 14–16.

3. *Free Europe Press,* Research Report, Hungarian Party Congress, May 24–30, 1954 (RR 1, July 1, 1954), pp. 35–41.

4. CURPH (Columbia University Research Project on Hungary), interview no. 451, reproaches Imre Nagy

of having believed that by drafting good memoranda he would be able to change the Party policy. Miklos Molnár and Lászlo Nagy, in their *Imre Nagy, Réformateur ou Révolutionnaire?* (Geneva, 1959) describe Imre Nagy's "naïveté" for not having tried to rally around his program others than Party leaders and functionaries (p. 85).

5. CURPH, Heltai report, p. 8.

6. Tamás Aczél and Tibor Méray, *The Revolt of the Mind* (New York, 1959), pp. 213–215.

7. Merle Fainsod, *How Russia Is Ruled* (Cambridge, Mass., 1953), pp. 134–135.

8. CURPH, interview no. 567.

9. Molnár and László Nagy, pp. 86–87.

10. Tibor Méray, *Thirteen Days That Shook the Kremlin* (New York, 1959), p. 22.

11. Robert H. Bass, "Communist Fronts: Their History and Function," *Problems of Communism*, September–October 1960, pp. 8–16.

12. Imre Nagy, *On Communism* (New York, 1957), pp. 207–208. A verbatim quotation of the "letter" sent to the Soviet Presidium is provided there — a rare document indeed.

13. *Szabad Nép*, March 9, 1955.

14. *Documents on International Affairs, 1947–1948* (London, 1952), p. 392.

15. *Free Europe Press*, Research Report 13, p. 8.

16. *Ibid.*

17. *Ibid.*, p. 9.

18. Kálmán Potoczky (unpublished manuscript in Hungarian) expressed the view that in Imre Nagy's conception the People's Patriotic Front was to serve as a transitory organization paving the way for a shift from the Communist Party's dictatorship toward a multiparty system (p. 95). CURPH, interview no. 567, also maintains that Nagy, at the time of the Congress, held out the possibility of introducing a multiparty system. This he may have done in private conversation only. Moscow would never have consented to a voluntary abandonment of the Communist Party's monopoly of power, and Imre Nagy had been entirely dependent on the Kremlin for the approval of his program.

11. Economic Problems of the New Course

1. "Who doesn't recall that up to June, 1953, it was Mátyás Rákosi, 'Mighty Ernö' [Ernö Gerö], and other 'left-wing' extremists who consistently disparaged achievements; who were never satisfied with them; who strained production and collection alike to such an extent that the matter of socialist building in our country all but arrived at a dead end. However, a complete change of attitude occurred in June, 1953, as the disclosure, ventilation, and criticism of past mistakes got under way. Thereafter, all their endeavors were aimed at concealing their mistakes and ending criticism as soon as possible. It was not without reason that Khrushchev said in June, 1953, that 'Mátyás Rákosi practiced self-criticism so that he would not be criticized any further.' After June, 1953, the persons who began to 'appreciate' Party achievements were the very ones who previously were the least satisfied with them. . . . Their aim was to hush up past mistakes and to divert public attention from themselves." Imre Nagy, *On Communism* (New York, 1957), pp. 262–263.

2. *Ibid.*, p. 141.

3. *Ibid.*, pp. 153–154.

4. *Ibid.*, p. 153.

5. *Ibid.*

6. *Hungary*, ed. Ernst C. Helmreich (New York, 1957), p. 242.

7. Rákosi's speech of October 31, 1953. *Társadalmi Szemle*, October–November 1953, pp. 893–912; *Documents on International Affairs, 1953* (London, 1956), pp. 206–209.

8. Quoted from Imre Nagy, p. 176. This resolution of the Central Committee does not appear to have been reported elsewhere.

9. *Szabad Nép*, Jan. 24, 1954; Imre Nagy, p. 183.

10. Imre Nagy, p. 181.

11. Some production figures and proof of a deficit spreading in industry are furnished by István Kovács, Party

Secretary for Budapest, in his speech of October 16, 1954. *Free Europe Press,* Research Report 19, October 22, 1954, pp. 4–5.

12. Helmreich, ed., p. 295.

13. Imre Nagy, p. 177.

14. Imre Nagy described as follows the period prior to the Central Committee's session in October 1954: "Thus, despite the resolution of the Third Party Congress, opposition could not and did not cease. It did not even diminish; on the contrary, it continued to grow and became dangerous. To arouse panic and to justify and make their proposals for undermining the June policy acceptable, opposition elements at the head of organs directing the Party, the government, and the economy began predicting inflation and unemployment — in a very misleading manner, as events proved. These proposals called for a general reduction of industrial output; a large-scale cut-back in social provisions for the workers; a great reduction in the standard of living of persons living on wages and salaries; and an increase in the burdens of the peasants. The anarchistic and inhuman manner in which rationalization was carried out contributed to all this and embittered a large section of the intelligentsia in the government. All these measures were so timed that their implementation would have occurred at the time when the local councils were holding elections and PPF committees were being set up. In this way the 'left-wing' opposition would have succeeded in turning all sectors of the population against the Party, the People's Democracy, and mainly the government. This was what they were getting ready to do; but the wide-scale political activity arising from the resolutions and from the October stand of the Central Committee succeeded in preventing this to a great extent." *Ibid.,* pp. 272–273.

15. Imre Nagy, p. 120.

16. Tamás Aczél and Tibor Méray, *The Revolt of the Mind* (New York, 1959), p. 271.

17. The Politburo refused to allow the publication of Nagy's speech and of the Central Committee's resolution. Nagy included parts of his speech in his *Szabad Nép* article of October 20, 1954, that was published without a Politburo approval.

18. *Szabad Nép,* Oct. 10, 1954.

19. *Ibid.*

20. Kálmán Potoczky, unpublished manuscript in Hungarian, p. 96.

21. For the role of the *Szabad Nép* rebels in repudiating the Politburo report, see Aczél and Méray, pp. 270–288; CURPH (Columbia University Research Project on Hungary), interviews nos. 500, 563, 564, and 567.

22. Imre Nagy, p. 191.

23. *Ibid.,* pp. 192–193.

24. *Ibid.,* pp. 189–190.

25. "The already difficult position of our foreign trade was further aggravated by an accumulation of unpaid debts in virtually all of the capitalist countries. Payments falling due on expensive short-term foreign credits constantly used up our foreign exchange income, making it impossible to use the exchange to purchase essential import products. Despite the fact that in the given international situation it would have been possible for us to convert our capitalist debts and concentrate them in just a few places, thereby reducing our payment balance, and despite the fact that on several occasions I specifically instructed the leaders of the Ministry of Foreign Trade to do this, our debts were not liquidated. This was primarily because the Political Committee, at the recommendation of Mátyás Rákosi, took the attitude that such a solution would be dangerous and should be resorted to only later and then with extreme caution. In

the meantime, other People's Democracies successfully solved similar problems in this way, and lightened their financial obligations in this way." *Ibid.*, pp. 191–192.

26. *Ibid.*, p. 193.

12. Political Prisoners — Liability and Peril

1. Inaugural speech before the National Assembly, July 4, 1953. *Szabad Nép,* July 5.

2. Imre Nagy had studied the files of many political trials. He is said to have discovered among the files of the Rajk case the fact that he himself, at one time, had been selected as a victim. Miklos Molnár and Lászlo Nagy, *Imre Nagy, Réformateur ou Révolutionnaire?* (Geneva, 1959), p. 28.

3. "The irrationality of totalitarian purges has been assessed as a means of exercising increased terror upon the population; irrationality is considered to discourage more effective resistance because the identity of persons aimed at by the purges can never be guessed and uncertainty thus created accumulated the desired effect." Zbigniew K. Brzezinski, *The Permanent Purge* (Cambridge, Mass., 1956), p. 111.

4. The Russian-born wife of a journalist did not show surprise (as her husband did) when AVH officers rang the bell at night and came to take away people, who then simply disappeared. CURPH, interview no. 616.

5. George Paloczi-Horvath, *The Undefeated* (London, 1959), pp. 242–246; Jozsef Kövágo, *You Are All Alone* (New York, 1959), p. 102.

6. Imre Nagy, *On Communism* (New York, 1957), p. 296.

7. *Ibid.*

8. *Ibid.*, pp. 295–296.

9. *Ibid.*, p. 296.

10. *Ibid.*

11. We may infer this from the fact that those detainees alone were released in August–October 1954, and also from Khrushchev's remark that Rákosi had ordered the arrest of the prisoners in question.

12. Imre Nagy, p. 296.

13. Tamás Aczél and Tibor Méray, *The Revolt of the Mind* (New York, 1959), pp. 245–255; Paloczi-Horvath, pp. 246–248; CURPH, Heltai report, pp. 12–15. Contrariwise, Dora Scarlett, *Window onto Hungary* (Bradford, England, 1959), p. 207, rightly points out that only former Party members had been then released although she mentions the release of a "few thousand prisoners."

14. Imre Nagy, p. 296.

15. *Ibid.*, pp. 296–297.

16. *Ibid.*, p. 297.

17. *Ibid.*

13. About-face in Moscow: Nagy's Fall

1. Imre Nagy, *On Communism* (New York, 1957), pp. 274–275.

2. Tamás Aczél and Tibor Méray, *The Revolt of the Mind* (New York, 1959), p. 282.

3. "After the October resolution of the Central Committee there was confusion in the ranks of the 'left-wing' opposition and an increase in double-dealing." Imre Nagy, p. 274.

4. *Irodalmi Ujság,* Oct. 23, 1954; Tibor Méray, *Thirteen Days That Shook the Kremlin* (New York, 1959), p. 24.

5. See Iván Boldizsár's editorial, "Forum, and not Show-Window,"

Magyar Nemzet, Oct. 3, 1954; for an analysis, see *Free Europe Press,* Research Report 19, p. 4.

6. Imre Nagy, pp. 274–275.

7. François Fejtö, *Imre Nagy: Un Communisme qui n'Oublie pas l'Homme* (Paris, 1957), pp. 26–27; Méray, *Thirteen Days,* pp. 24–25.

8. See the Eight Power Declaration of December 2, 1954, issued at the end of the Moscow Conference of the Soviet bloc, in *Documents on International Affairs, 1954* (London, 1957), pp. 64–70.

9. CURPH (Columbia University Research Project on Hungary), interview no. 500.

10. Imre Nagy, pp. 210–211.

11. Aczél and Méray, *Revolt,* pp. 292–295.

12. CURPH, interview no. 500; Aczél and Méray, *Revolt,* pp. 315–319.

13. Merle Fainsod, "What Happened to 'Collective Leadership'?" *Problems of Communism,* July–August, 1959, p. 4.

14. Zbigniew K. Brzezinski, *The Soviet Bloc: Unity and Conflict* (Cambridge, Mass., 1960), pp. 156, 165.

15. See for instance the article in *Pravda,* Feb. 3, 1955, quoting Khrushchev; Brzezinski, p. 156.

16. Méray, *Thirteen Days,* pp. 25; François Fejtö, *Un Communisme Qui n'Oublie pas l'Homme* (Paris, 1957), p. 24.

17. Fejtö's point is that Mao Tsetung was favoring the increase of heavy industrial output in the Soviet Union so that this country might be able to extend aid to China.

18. Fainsod, *loc. cit.*

19. CURPH, Heltai report, suggests February. Méray (*op. cit.,* p. 22) places the visit in January. The interview must have taken place before Khrushchev's speech of January 25 before the Central Committee.

20. Seweryn Bialer, "I Chose Truth," *News from behind the Iron Curtain,* October 1956, p. 8.

21. The most detailed narrative of the meeting is presented by Méray, *Thirteen Days,* pp. 25–28. Many of the items of accusation mentioned there can be found in Imre Nagy's writings (*On Communism*) though the source and place of the accusations are not indicated. Méray's account is also confirmed by other documents (Central Committee resolutions, etc.).

22. *Szabad Nép,* Oct. 20, 1954; Méray, p. 26.

23. Méray, *Thirteen Days,* p. 26.

24. Imre Nagy, *op. cit.,* pp. 234–235, defends himself against this accusation. The Nagy speech in question was delivered at the inauguration Congress of the People's Patriotic Front on October 24, 1954.

25. Méray, *Thirteen Days,* pp. 26–27.

26. Méray, *Thirteen Days,* p. 27.

27. Brzezinski, *The Soviet Bloc,* pp. 158–159.

28. "The very fact that the New Course did take into consideration the peculiar domestic facts existing in each case is a reflection of the change that had taken place in relations in the Soviet world since Stalin's death." Brzezinski, *The Soviet Bloc,* p. 164.

29. *Pravda,* Feb. 9, 1955.

30. Méray, *Thirteen Days,* p. 28.

31. CURPH, Heltai report, p. 16.

32. A medical bulletin in the Feb. 20, 1955, issue of *Szabad Nép* said Nagy had been suffering from coronary thrombosis since early February. His state of health much improved subsequently and he was presumably active again in the beginning of April.

33. Méray, *Thirteen Days,* p. 29; CURPH, Heltai report, pp. 17–18.

34. Méray, *Thirteen Days,* p. 29.

35. *Szabad Nép,* March 9, 1955.

36. CURPH, Heltai report, provides a different version; there it is maintained that Nagy was willing to

come to an agreement with Rákosi. According to this account, in order "to safeguard the unity of the Party," Nagy had been ready to resign, and keep his university chair only. (p. 17)

37. CURPH, Heltai report, p. 18.

38. Méray, *Thirteen Days*, p. 30.

39. Méray, *Thirteen Days*, p. 30.

40. The Central Committee's resolution of April 14, 1955, as printed in the *Szabad Nép*, April 18, 1955, said in part: "Comrade Imre Nagy, as a member of the Political Committee and as the Chairman of the Council of Ministers, represented political opinions which were sharply opposed to the over-all politics of our Party and inimical to the interests of the working class, the working peasants, and the people's democracy. Comrade Nagy tried to throttle the motor of socialist building, socialist industrialization, and especially the development of heavy industry, and in the provinces the movement of the agricultural cooperatives, which is the decisive method of socialist rebuilding of the villages. He tried to obscure and force into the background the Party leadership, and he attempted to pit the government agencies against one another, and the Patriotic People's Front against the Party. Comrade Imre Nagy by all this prevented the building of a solid basis for increasing the welfare of the people.

"These anti-Marxist, anti-Leninist, anti-Party views of Comrade Imre Nagy form a composite system, an attitude which spread to the various fields of political, economic, and cultural life. The activities of Comrade Imre Nagy have caused serious damage to our Party, our People's Democracy, and our whole socialist structure.

"Comrade Nagy in the interest of realizing his rightist, opportunist policies, resorted to un-Party-like, anti-Party and even factional methods, which are completely incompatible with the unity, the discipline of the Marxist-Leninist Party."

Nagy discusses this resolution at pp. xliii–xliv of *On Communism*.

41. In a secret document which was circulated in July 1955 by the Soviet leadership to Communist leaders abroad, and which Seweryn Bialer was able to consult, some reasons for Malenkov's removal were thus spelled out: "The policy of Malenkov, aside from the harm which it threatened in Soviet domestic matters, concealed serious dangers for the countries of the People's Democracies and for the relations of the Soviet Union with these countries, an example of which is the situation in Hungary." Seweryn Bialer, "The Three Schools of Kremlin Policy," *The New Leader*, July 29, 1957, p. 10.

42. CURPH, Heltai report, p. 18.

14. Rákosi Sole Master — but with Strings Attached

1. *Szabad Nép*, April 19, 1955.

2. According to Imre Nagy, *On Communism* (New York, 1957), p. 250, Molotov had said that when the Soviet Presidium discussed with Rákosi who should succeed him as Prime Minister in May 1953, Rákosi had "wanted a Premier who would have no voice in the making of decisions."

3. *Szabad Nép*, April 18, 1955. Nagy was greatly displeased at having

been censured and removed from office in such bad company as Mihály Farkas: "The April resolution of the Central Committee also implemented measures, much less severe than mine, against Mihály Farkas because he allegedly supported 'my' policies for a long time. This qualification of Farkas' act does not stand up; it is not sincere — it is deceptive. A much more severe punishment is in order for Mihály

Farkas, not on the basis of a motive prescribed in a resolution, but rather by the revelation of his criminal actions in matters of rehabilitation and of state defense. If anybody is burdened with responsibility because he supported the implementation of the June policies, it is not Mihály Farkas, of all people." Imre Nagy, p. 295.

4. A vivid description of the public mood and the spontaneous strike of farmers after Imre Nagy's fall is presented by Dora Scarlett, *Window onto Hungary* (Bradford, England, 1958), pp. 218–219. She describes how peasants attempted to become self-sufficient in expectation of a renewed collectivization drive.

5. Imre Nagy, p. 39, quotes Rákosi's speech of May 1955 at the Party Academy when the latter had said: "Imre Nagy overestimated the easing of the tension in the international situation."

6. CURPH (Columbia University Research Project on Hungary), Heltai report, p. 19.

7. See Rákosi's speech in Csepel on August 8, 1955. *Szabad Nép,* Aug. 9, 1955.

8. George Paloczi-Horvath, in *The Undefeated* (London, 1959), p. 255, estimated that 950,000 out of one million Communist Party members (1952), in addition to the rest of the population of Hungary, were anti-Communist. In the view of the present writer, by 1955 the proportion of anti-Communists was certainly no lower.

9. CURPH, interview no. 616.

10. *Pravda,* May 4, 1957.

11. See Tito's speech of July 28, 1955. *Documents on International Affairs, 1955* (London, 1958), p. 275.

12. Seweryn Bialer, "I Chose Truth," *News from behind the Iron Curtain,* October 1956, pp. 10–11. For a full description of the session see David J. Dallin, *Soviet Foreign Policy*

after Stalin (Philadelphia, 1961), pp. 227–233.

13. Dallin, pp. 227–233.

14. Merle Fainsod, "What Happened to 'Collective Leadership'?" in *Problems of Communism,* July–August 1959, p. 5.

15. *Documents on International Affairs, 1955* (London, 1958), p. 268.

16. See Tito's speech delivered in Pula on November 11, 1956. Paul E. Zinner (ed.), *National Communism and Popular Revolt in Eastern Europe* (New York, 1957), p. 520.

17. *Szabad Nép,* June 4, 1955, commenting on the Belgrade visit of Soviet statesmen, said that "normalization of the relationship between the Hungarian and Yugoslav states has been initiated." Rákosi said in his Csepel speech of August 8, 1955, "We shall do everything to improve the relations between our homeland and Yugoslavia and to turn it into a friendship." (*Szabad Nép,* Aug. 9, 1955) In this speech Rákosi accused the imprisoned Gábor Péter of responsibility for the rupture with Yugoslavia, as Khrushchev had charged Beria and Abakumov in Belgrade.

18. *Documents,* p. 271.

19. *Szabad Nép,* Sept. 26, 1955.

20. CURPH, Heltai report, pp. 23–24. János Kádár was the only one among the rehabilitated Party members to whom Rákosi spoke.

21. Paloczi-Horvath, p. 259; Dora Scarlett, pp. 221–222.

22. The Soviet Union cancelled $90 million of Yugoslavia's debt to meet her claims. *Annual Register of World Events, 1955* (London, 1956), p. 259.

23. Article 22 of the Treaty of Peace with Hungary of Feburary 10, 1947. For text of treaty see *The American Journal of International Law,* Supplement 1948, pp. 225–251. For analysis of Article 22 see Ferenc A. Váli, "The Hungarian Revolution and Inter-

national Law," *The Fletcher Review,* Summer 1959, pp. 11–12.

24. Seweryn Bialer, "The Three Schools of Kremlin Policy," *The New Leader,* July 29, 1957, p. 10.

25. The text of the Warsaw Treaty is reprinted in *The American Journal of International Law,* Supplement 1955, pp. 194–199.

26. Information obtained directly from General Béla Király.

27. *Szabad Nép,* July 17, 1955.

28. *Szabad Nép,* Oct. 14, 1955.

29. On Kotewala speech see extract in *Documents on International Affairs, 1955* (London, 1958), p. 412; for the pronouncements of the conference, see *Annual Register of World Events, 1955* (London, 1956), pp. 165–166.

30. *Documents,* pp. 472–475.

15. Imre Nagy: "Withdrawal" and "Return"

1. Imre Nagy's introduction to his memoranda, published in *On Communism* (New York, 1957), pp. xxxv-xxxvi.

2. Expression attributed to Imre Nagy by Tibor Méray, *Thirteen Days That Shook the Kremlin* (New York, 1959), p. 41.

3. Like Nagy's dissertation, Djilas' book was published in New York in 1957.

4. Imre Nagy, p. xxix.

5. Publisher's note in Imre Nagy, p. v.

6. For a discussion see Miklos Molnár and Lászlo Nagy, *Imre Nagy, Réformateur ou Révolutionnaire?* (Geneva, 1959), p. 148.

7. *Ibid.*

8. CURPH (Columbia University Research Project on Hungary), interviews nos. 118, 451, 500, 615, and 660; Molnár and Lászlo Nagy, pp. 52–53; *The Review* (published in Brussels by the Imre Nagy Institute for Political Research), no. 1 (1959), pp. 4–8 ("In Memoriam Imre Nagy"), and no. 3 (1960), pp. 89–98 ("Imre Nagy and Those Who Do Not Know Him"); Paul Zinner, "Hungary's Imre Nagy: Revolutionist at the End," *Columbia*

University Forum, Fall 1958, pp. 6–10.

9. Imre Nagy, p. 13.

10. *Ibid.,* p. 14.

11. *Ibid.,* p. 15.

12. *Ibid.,* pp. 16–17.

13. *Ibid.,* p. 43. This chapter is chapter 4 of Imre Nagy, *On Communism.*

14. *Ibid.*

15. *Ibid.,* p. 44.

16. *Ibid.,* pp. 47–50.

17. *Ibid.,* p. 51.

18. *Ibid.,* p. 53.

19. *Ibid.,* p. 55.

20. *Ibid.,* p. 56.

21. *Ibid.,* p. 57.

22. *Ibid.,* pp. 57–58.

23. *Ibid.,* p. 61.

24. *Annual Register of World Events, 1954* (London, 1955), p. 106.

25. Imre Nagy, p. 20. This chapter is chapter 3 of Imre Nagy, *On Communism* (New York, 1957).

26. *Ibid.,* pp. 22–23.

27. *Ibid.,* p. 27.

28. *Ibid.,* p. 28.

29. *Ibid.,* pp. 25–27.

30. *Ibid.,* pp. 23–24.

31. *Ibid.,* p. 40.

32. *Ibid.,* p. 244.

33. *Ibid.,* p. 38.

16. The Eager Flock of an Unsuspecting Shepherd

1. For an excellent analysis of Imre Nagy's popularity with various segments of the populations see Miklos Molnár and Lászlo Nagy, *Imre Nagy,*

Réformateur ou Révolutionnaire? (Geneva, 1959), pp. 133–136.

2. In the 1958 "trial" of Imre Nagy and associates, the question whether he had circulated his ideas in a wider circle was discussed, and he admitted to giving copies of his writings to a limited number of people only, according to the Hungarian White Book entitled *Nagy Imre és Büntársai Ellenforradalmi Összeesküvése* (The Counterrevolutionary Conspiracy of Imre Nagy and His Accomplices, Budapest, 1958), p. 20.

3. Tibor Méray, *Thirteen Days That Shook the Kremlin* (New York, 1959), pp. 45–49; CURPH (Columbia University Research Project on Hungary), Heltai report, pp. 30–31.

4. The story concerning these publications, with all the names concerned, is told by Tamás Aczél and Tibor Méray, *The Revolt of the Mind* (New York, 1959), pp. 332–334; and CURPH, Miklos Molnár, history of the *Irodalmi Ujság*.

5. CURPH, Molnár, *op. cit.,* CURPH, interview no. 500; Aczél and Méray, *Revolt,* pp. 339–344.

6. "Our writing was not centrally planned or coordinated . . . However, we did have a coordinated campaign demanding rehabilitation." CURPH, interview no. 500.

7. "The actions of Gimes and most of the rebellious Communists were not motivated by admiration for Khrushchev. They were, instead, motivated by shrewd intention to take advantage of the Moscow and Belgrade developments in order to get rid of Rákosi and his gang." Aczél and Méray, *Revolt,* pp. 335–336; CURPH, interview no. 567.

8. For the text of the Writers' Memorandum and names of signatories see Aczél and Méray, *Revolt,* pp. 343–350.

9. Characteristic was the attitude of Tamás Aczél, who, after having become Secretary of the Writers' Association, resolved "secretly to embark on a policy of rightist deviation." See CURPH, interview no. 500.

10. Sándor Haraszti had written the draft text of the memorandum, which was then turned into its final form by Aczél, with Vásárhelyi and Losonczy cooperating; its text had never been discussed with Imre Nagy. CURPH, interview no. 500.

11. Tibor Méray, *Thirteen Days,* p. 40.

12. *Ibid.,* p. 41.

13. *Szabad Nép,* Dec. 11, 1955.

14. Kálmán Potoczky, unpublished manuscript, p. 105.

15. "The system was agonizing for years, but determination to overthrow it, at any cost, came spontaneously, perhaps in the evening of October 23." CURPH, interview no. 616.

16. An interesting conversation on the merits of Communism is recorded in CURPH, interview no. 500: "During the summer of 1956 we dared to tell Imre Nagy that we thought Communism was a total failure. There was a tremendous debate, in which he (Nagy) called us revisionists and bourgeois objectivists . . . Imre Nagy said that Rákosi, and the Russians falsified Marxism, but that *real* Marxism was all right, and was a redeeming force. I [the interviewee] said: 'It had 35 years to prove itself a redeeming force, and look at it now . . .' Nagy said: 'Yes, but that is because of Stalinism.' I retorted: 'You are a subjectivist; the rottenness does not stem from the people or leaders, but from the system.' Nagy was angry at first, but eventually he agreed that there were structural mistakes, too. Those around him (Losonczy, Gimes, Vásárhelyi and Löcsei) broke with Communism sooner than he did."

17. For instance: Imre Mezö (Budapest Party Secretary, killed during the Revolution), Kálmán Pongrácz

(Chairman of the Budapest Council), Jozsef Mekis (Politburo member in 1955–1956), Jozsef Köböl (Central Committee member). Tibor Méray, in "The Crisis of the New Class," *The Review*, June 1959, p. 98, says that Mezö and Köböl even protested in writing against Imre Nagy's expulsion from the Party.

18. *Népszabadság*, June 18, 1958; Hungarian White Book (note 2, above), p. 10.

19. "The memory of the power which had once belonged to the *populus Romanus* lingered in the past . . . In the 6th century the factions ('demes') of the circus, Blues and Greens, appear as political parties, distract the city by their quarrels, and break out in serious riot. On one occasion they shook the throne ('Nike' revolt, 532 A.D.)." John Bagnell Bury, "Later Roman Empire," *Encyclopaedia Britannica*, Vol. 19 (1957), p. 440.

20. Leonard Schapiro, "Has Russia Changed?" *Foreign Affairs*, April 1960, p. 393.

21. "The interior fight against Communism does not choose, in the beginning, political issues as main targets, and as its weapon it used the trait inherent in Marxism and Leninism, namely the possibility to combat the system from within. The opposition, using Leninism against Stalinism, could attack 'legally.' This attack was carried out by Communist as well as non-Communist writers." CURPH, interview no. 616.

22. CURPH, interview no. 500.

23. Tibor Méray, *Thirteen Days*, p. 27.

24. Aczél and Méray, *Revolt*, pp. 242–243.

25. This writer met five or six members of the Békéssámson group in prison who told him their story.

26. See discussion in Walter Kolarz, "The Nationalities under Khrushchev," *Soviet Survey*, April–June, 1958, pp. 57–65: "The pro-Stalin demonstrations in Tiflis in March, 1956 . . . [had] a national Georgian character and for this reason were severely repressed." (p. 63) A description of the riots is in *New York Times*, April 22, 1956.

17. Effect Beyond Intent — Impact of the Twentieth Party Congress

1. Boris Meissner, *Das Ende des Stalin Mythos* (Frankfurt a.M., 1956), pp. 12–14.

2. According to one interpretation, Khrushchev, and also Mikoyan, recognized four forms of Socialist construction: (1) the Soviet; (2) the People's Democracies; (3) the Chinese, and (4) the Yugoslav. Soviet superiority to any of these forms was "soft-pedaled" in speeches made at the Twentieth Congress. Bernard Morris, "Soviet Policy Toward National Communism: The Limits of Diversity," *American Political Science Review*, March 1959, pp. 128–129. The same author considered the vagueness of these pronouncements to be the source of subsequent misunderstandings.

3. CURPH (Columbia University Research Project on Hungary), interview no. 500.

4. For the text of Khrushchev's secret speech, see Bertram Wolfe, *Stalin's Ghost* (New York, 1957).

5. According to Merle Fainsod's interpretation, Khrushchev's intention had been to demonstrate before the Party that they had nothing to fear from him, whereas those who had been implicated in Stalin's excesses were to be kept from positions of power. "What Happened to 'Collective Leadership'?" in *Problems of Communism*, July–August 1959.

6. The nations mentioned in Khrushchev's speech as having been deported by Stalin, were the Karachai,

the Kalmyks, the Chechen-Ingush, and the Balkars.

7. Among Communist commentators, only a few (Moravski in Poland, Togliatti in Italy) were ready to draw inferences from Khrushchev's speech on Stalin's crimes and errors with regard to the People's Democracies. Meissner, p. 37.

8. Articles and characteristic comments by Soviet and foreign Communist publicists and Party leaders on the results of the Twentieth Congress are to be found in Meissner, pp. 29–37.

9. Giuseppe Boffa, the Italian Communist journalist, refuses to recognize that the system was to be blamed for the "errors" committed during the "cult" period. He pretends that it was the *system* that saved the Communist regime: "The Socialist regime had made possible the impetuous progress of the USSR and this progress, which became incompatible with the despotic aspects of Stalin's regime, created forces which stopped that despotism." See Boffa's *Inside the Khrushchev Era* (New York, 1959), p. 84. It may well be asked why the system did not render Stalin's despotism impossible a priori and prevent his crimes committed during more than twenty years.

10. Togliatti's speech before the parliamentary group of Italian Communists; Meissner, p. 29.

11. *New York Times*, Dec. 2, 1959.

12. George Paloczi-Horvath, *The Undefeated* (London, 1959), p. 257.

13. Miklos Molnár and László Nagy, *Imre Nagy, Réformateur ou Révolutionnaire?* (Geneva, 1959), p. 123; Tamás Aczél and Tibor Méray, *The Revolt of the Mind* (New York, 1959), pp. 390–391; CURPH, Heltai report, p. 27; István Mészáros, *La Rivoltà degli Intellettuali in Ungheria* (Torino, 1958), pp. 179–180.

14. *Szabad Nép*, Feb. 18, 1956.

15. *Szabad Nép*, Feb. 21, 1956; Aczél and Méray, p. 400.

16. *Szabad Nép*, March 14 and 15, 1956.

17. *Szabad Nép*, March 29, 1956.

18. Prison guards made notes of these pronouncements, and other quotations were added by prisoners (unpublished manuscript by Kálmán Potoczky, p. 239; and personal recollections of the present writer).

19. *Szabad Nép*, April 17, 1956.

20. See Ernö Gerö's speech before the Central Committee; *Szabad Nép*, July 19, 1956.

21. Jan Wszelaki, *Communist Economic Strategy: The Role of East Central Europe* (Washington, 1959), p. 74.

22. Aczél and Méray, *Revolt*, p. 400; Potoczky manuscript, pp. 133–134.

18. Rákosi's Fall

1. For the expansionism of the Yugoslav ideology after the Twentieth Congress, see the thorough analysis by Zbigniew K. Brzezinski, *The Soviet Bloc* (Cambridge, Mass., 1960), pp. 195–203. For a study on Yugoslav ambitions in the international field see Richard Lowenthal, "Tito's Affair with Khrushchev," *The New Leader*, Oct. 6, 1958, pp. 11–12; David J. Dallin, *Soviet Foreign Policy after Stalin* (Philadelphia, 1961), p. 352.

2. For an analysis, see Brzezinski, pp. 198–200.

3. See Tito's speech at Pula on November 11, 1956, reprinted in

Paul E. Zinner (ed.), *National Communism and Popular Revolt in Eastern Europe* (New York, 1957), p. 520.

4. Tito's Pula speech, Zinner, pp. 523–524.

5. See Miklos Molnár and Làszlo Nagy, *Imre Nagy, Réformateur ou Révolutionnaire?* (Geneva, 1959), p. 128.

6. Zinner, p. 13.

7. For Tito's interpretation, and the direct quotations in this paragraph, see Pula speech in Zinner, p. 520. Tito said: "those same elements which provoked such resistance on the part of Yugoslavia in 1948 also live in these Eastern countries, in Poland, Hungary, and in others . . . During the time that we were preparing the declaration in Moscow on our party relations, mainly on the relations between the Yugoslav League of Communists and the Communist Party of the Soviet Union, this was a little difficult to settle. Here we could not completely agree, but, nevertheless, the declaration was issued which, in our opinion, *is intended for a wider circle than Yugoslavia and the Soviet Union*" (italics added).

8. *Ibid.*

9. CURPH (Columbia University Research Project on Hungary), interview no. 500.

10. It is recorded that in country districts, peasants came by cart and gave 100 forints for a copy of the *Irodalmi Ujság* (the ordinary price being one forint) to take it to their village, where it was subsequently handed from one family to another. United Nations, *Report of the Special Committee on the Problem of Hungary* (New York, 1957), p. 67.

11. Molnár and Lászlo Nagy, p. 127.

12. Imre Sarkadi, a Stalinist writer, addressed a letter to the *Szabad Nép* (April 1, 1956) deprecating the in-

cident. The issue of April 15 also referred to this scene.

13. A number of "shameful attacks" were recorded in an article bearing the title "For the Development of Party Democracy" (*Szabad Nép*, April 15, 1956); the author of the article undertook to demonstrate how internal Party democracy had been promoted since the Twentieth Congress and expressed concern about the "regrettable incidents" stemming from the excessive use of a democratic exchange of views — an excellent example of the concealed method for disclosing existing fissures in the Party. For a detailed description of these and other open attacks, see Tamás Aczél and Tibor Méray, *The Revolt of the Mind* (New York, 1959), pp. 392–396; CURPH, Heltai report, p. 29; CURPH, interview no. 616.

14. "Preparing this dissertation was not in vain, because when I reread it after the Twentieth Congress it strengthened my earlier conviction of the correctness of my stand on basic questions of principle." Imre Nagy, *On Communism* (New York, 1957), p. xxx.

15. According to a witness, "Imre Nagy was never free of a sense of obligation towards the Russians and he held deep loyalty to the Party. He was thus easily controlled by both, at least until October 24th." CURPH, interview no. 514.

16. An intimate insight into conversations with Nagy is revealed by this testimony: "We tried to push the old boy, we tried to tell him that refusal to organize a group outside the Party was all wrong, but without success. He had illusions." CURPH, interview no. 500. See also Molnár and Lászlo Nagy, pp. 143–145; Paul E. Zinner, "Imre Nagy, Revolutionist at the End," *Columbia University Forum*, Fall 1958, p. 10.

17. On Gerö proposition and Kádár tape incident see George Paloczi-Horvath, *The Undefeated* (London, 1959), pp. 259–262; CURPH, Heltai report, pp. 23–24, 31–32.

18. On the birthday celebration see Molnár and Lászlo Nagy, p. 129; Tibor Méray, *Thirteen Days That Shook the Kremlin* (New York, 1959), pp. 48–49; CURPH, Heltai report, p. 30; CURPH, interview no. 500.

19. For debates in the Petöfi Circle, see the comprehensive narrative in the unpublished manuscript by Kálmán Potoczky, pp. 35–54; Aczél and Méray, *Revolt*, pp. 399–412.

20. Aczél and Méray, *Revolt*, pp. 57–80; István Mészáros. *La Rivoltà degli Intellettuali in Ungheria* (Torino, 1958), *passim*.

21. The Lukács address is summarized in the *Szabad Nép*, June 17, 1956; see also Potoczky manuscript, pp. 41–42.

22. Potoczky manuscript, pp. 43–44; Aczél and Méray, *Revolt*, pp. 401–402. On Julia Rajk's imprisonment see Paloczi-Horvath, pp. 258–259.

23. *Szabad Nép*, July 3, 1956.

24. *Szabad Nép*, May 10, 1956.

25. *Szabad Nép*, May 19, 1956.

26. The story of Rákosi's ouster has been reported in slightly contradictory versions. This writer mostly relied on the narrative offered by Aczél and Méray, *Revolt*, pp. 412–419, which had been told to the authors by Kálmán Pongrácz, a Central Committee member. See also George Paloczi-Horvath's epilogue in Imre Nagy, *On Communism*, pp. 298–299; François Fejtö, *Behind the Rape of Hungary* (New York, 1957), pp. 128–129; Potoczky manuscript, pp. 66–68; CURPH, Heltai report, pp. 31–32.

27. Rákosi's valedictory speech, the Central Committee's resolution, and Gerö's inaugural address, all of which took place July 18, are printed in the *Szabad Nép*, July 19, 1956.

28. *Szabad Nép*, July 22, 1956.

29. Aczél and Méray, *Revolt*, p. 419.

30. "When increasingly strong dissatisfaction began to rise to the surface in the ranks of Hungarian Communists themselves, and when they demanded that Rákosi should go, the Soviet leaders realized that it was impossible to continue in this way and agreed that he should be removed." Tito's speech in Pula of November 11, 1956, quoted in Zinner (note 3, above), p. 524. See also Lowenthal (note 1, above), p. 12, where a similar view is held concerning the immediate cause of Rákosi's ouster.

31. Tito's Pula speech; Zinner, p. 524.

32. *Ibid.*

33. Quoted in Zinner, p. 18.

34. *Ibid.*, p. 27.

19. Rajk's Body and Imre Nagy's Return

1. *Társadalmi Szemle*, August 1956, p. 2.

2. *Ibid.*, p. 8.

3. *Szabad Nép*, Aug. 12, 1956.

4. *Szabad Nép*, Sept. 2, 1956.

5. *Szabad Nép*, Sept. 16, 1956.

6. *Társadalmi Szemle*, September 1956, pp. 8–9.

7. *Szabad Nép*, Sept. 10, 1956.

8. *Szabad Nép*, Sept. 16, 1956.

9. Unpublished manuscript by Kálmán Potoczky; George Paloczi-Horvath, *The Undefeated* (London, 1959), p. 259.

10. Tamás Aczél and Tibor Méray, *The Revolt of the Mind* (New York, 1959), pp. 235–236; François Fejtö, *Behind the Rape of Hungary* (New York, 1957), pp. 153–154.

11. CURPH (Columbia University Research Project on Hungary), interview no. 616.

12. Potoczky manuscript.

13. *Szabad Nép*, Oct. 7, 1956, reported that talks had taken place between the Hungarian group and the two Soviet leaders.

14. *Szabad Nép*, Oct. 7; descriptions of Rajk's funeral in Aczél and Méray, *Revolt*, pp. 437–440, and in Potoczky manuscript.

15. Béla Király, "Hungary's Army: Its Part in the Revolt," *East Europe*, June 1958, pp. 3–5; *Szabad Nép*, Oct. 14, 1956.

16. *Szabad Nép*, Oct. 11 and 13, 1956.

17. Potoczky manuscript.

18. Aczél and Méray, *Revolt*, p. 421.

19. *Nagy Imre és Büntársai Ellenforradalmi Összeesküvése* (Counterrevolutionary Conspiracy of Imre Nagy and His Accomplies), Hungarian White Book (Budapest, 1958), pp. 124–126.

20. Tibor Méray, *Thirteen Days That Shook the Kremlin* (New York, 1959), pp. 54–55; Miklos Molnár and Lászlo Nagy, *Imre Nagy, Réformateur ou Révolutionnaire?* (Geneva, 1959), p. 158; Potoczky manuscript, p. 82.

21. Potoczky manuscript, p. 79.

22. Paul E. Zinner, "Hungary's Imre Nagy, Revolutionary at the End," *Columbia University Forum*, Fall 1958, p. 9.

23. Méray, *Thirteen Days*, pp. 56–57.

24. Méray, *Thirteen Days*, pp. 57–59; Molnár and Lászlo Nagy, p. 161; Potoczky manuscript, pp. 82–85.

25. *Szabad Nép*, Oct. 14, 1956.

26. Molnár and Lászlo Nagy, pp. 161–162.

27. "The institutions which [Lenin] created were from the start fake institutions, in the sense that they were Party-controlled, and not the free elected bodies which they purported to be — soviets, trade-union councils, law courts and the like. This made it possible for the Party to preserve the semblance of popular democratic activity, and indeed in the course of time to destroy all memories of the real nature of free institutions, without in any way endangering executive control over all aspects of life." Leonard Schapiro, "Has Russia Changed?" *Foreign Affairs*, April 1960, p. 393.

28. For an excellent description of this literary "renaissance" see Aczél and Méray, *Revolt*, pp. 425–436.

29. Paloczi-Horvath, p. 275.

30. *Ibid.*; see also Aczél and Méray, *Revolt*, pp. 429–431.

31. *Szabad Nép*, Oct. 14, 1956.

32. Potoczky manuscript, pp. 95–98.

33. CURPH, interview no. 152.

34. CURPH, interview no. 526. The thesis that Gerö planned a provocation is also based on personal information obtained by the present writer, and is supported by Gerö's attitude on October 23 (see Chapter 20).

35. CURPH, Heltai report, p. 22; *Magyar Hirlap*, Jan. 9, 1960.

36. CURPH, interview no. 526; Páger's return was reported by *Szabad Nép*, Sept. 2, 1956. There were demonstrations against him when he appeared on the stage.

37. CURPH, interview no. 500.

38. For an analysis of the sentiment preliminary to the outbreak of a revolution see Crane Brinton, *The Anatomy of Revolution* (New York, 1957), pp. 28–69.

20. Yugoslavia Complies — Poland Rises — Hungary Revolts

1. Tito's speech at Pula on November 11, 1956, reprinted in Paul E. Zinner (ed.), *National Communism and Popular Revolt in Eastern Europe* (New York, 1957), p. 524.

2. Richard Lowenthal, "Tito's Af-

fair with Khrushchev," *The New Leader*, Oct. 6, 1958, p. 12.

3. Tito as reprinted in Zinner, p. 524.

4. *Ibid.*, p. 525.

5. *Szabad Nép*, Aug. 8, 1956.

6. *Szabad Nép*, Oct. 15, 1956.

7. Tito in his Pula speech approved of Kádár and his friends as representing that "which is most honest in Hungary." There Tito also pointed out that "they were persecuted under Rákosi, they were in prison." Zinner, p. 527.

8. For an excellent analysis see Zbigniew K. Brzezinski, *The Soviet Bloc* (Cambridge Mass., 1960), pp. 242-253.

9. *Ibid.*, p. 251.

10. See United Nations, *Report of the Special Committee on the Problem of Hungary* (New York, 1957), p. 69.

11. *Radio Broadcasts*, pp. 9–10. Full citation: *A Magyar Forradalom és Szabadságharc* (The Hungarian Revolution and Fight for Freedom), Hungarian radio broadcasts from October 23 to November 9, 1956, Free Europe Press (New York, 1957).

12. Tito's speech of November 11 at Pula, as reprinted in Zinner (note 1, above), p. 525.

13. For Gerö's speech see Zinner, pp. 402–407. For "fascist rabble" reports, see *U. N. Report*, p. 81. For possible explanation of Tito's "mob" statement see our note 20, below.

14. *U. N. Report*, p. 6.

15. The charge of the existence of a well-planned revolutionary movement organized with outside help was first made in an article in *Pravda*, Oct. 28, 1956, under the title "Collapse of the Anti-People Adventure in Hungary." This explanation found repetition in the Hungarian White Books, published after the Revolution, but was not found acceptable by Tito. (See Pula speech in Zinner.)

16. See *U. N. Report*, p. 82; Dora Scarlett, *Window onto Hungary* (Bradford, England, 1958), p. 262; François Fejtö, *Behind the Rape of Hungary* (New York, 1957), p. 186.

17. See the convincing analysis by Crane Brinton, *The Anatomy of Revolution* (New York, 1957), pp. 80–90.

18. William Ebenstein in his "A Study of Totalitarianism," in *World Politics*, January 1958, p. 284, wrote that the "double-edged nature of modern means of control is evidenced by the fact that in every uprising against modern totalitarianism, as happened, for example, in Hungary in 1956, the government radio station, the newspapers, and the prisons are among the first objectives of the rebels. Just as the possession of these three key media of control is of crucial importance to a totalitarian government, it is of equal importance to the rebels. Once in possession of these three elements of control, the rebels against a totalitarian system find it much easier to finish their job than would have been true in earlier ages." It is to be observed that the attacks by the insurgents against the radio building and the offices of the Party newspaper were made for specific reasons as explained in the text, while the main political prison of Budapest was not liberated before the early morning hours of October 30, at a date when the Revolution already had won its temporary victory. The Ebenstein's remarks, though certainly accurate, have less validity for the case of the Hungarian uprising, where revolutionary activity was entirely spontaneous, prompted by casual motivations, and also greatly hampered by Soviet military activity.

19. "In so far as any one moment can be selected as the turning point which changed a peaceful demonstration into a violent uprising, it would be this moment when the AVH, already intensely unpopular and universally feared by their compatriots,

attacked defenceless people." *U. N. Report*, p. 6; see also pp. 81–82.

20. See Miklos Molnár and Lászlo Nagy, *Imre Nagy, Réformateur ou Révolutionnaire?* (Geneva, 1959), p. 179; unpublished manuscript by Kálmán Potoczky, p. 270. The delegation of writers was led by Gyula Háy; in their presence Gerö used the word "mob" in his description of the demonstrators. Possibly his words pronounced at this occasion gave rise to the belief (which must have reached Tito via the writers and their Yugoslav contacts) that he availed himself of such expressions as "mob" in his speech.

21. *U. N. Report*, p. 82; Fejtö, p. 186; Béla Király, "Hungary's Army: Its Part in the Revolt," *East Europe*, June 1958, pp. 8–10; Tibor Méray, *Thirteen Days That Shook the Kremlin* (New York, 1959), pp. 86–87; Potoczky manuscript, pp. 275–277.

22. Király, "Hungary's Army," *East Europe*, June 1958, p. 8.

23. Méray, *Thirteen Days*, p. 89.

24. Marosán made the boast on July 25, 1957, in a Party meeting at Csepel. *Népszabadság*, July 26, 1957. See also *U. N. Report*, p. 52.

25. *U. N. Report*, p. 39; Méray, *Thirteen Days*, p. 107.

26. *U. N. Report*, p. 39.

27. *Ibid.*, pp. 39–40.

28. *Ibid.* See also Béla Király, "Reconquest of Hungary," in *Facts about Hungary*, ed. Imre Kovács (New York, 1959), p. 103.

29. See Ferenc A. Váli, "The Hungarian Revolution and International Law," *The Fletcher Review*, Summer 1959, p. 13.

30. Herbert Aptheker, *The Truth about Hungary* (New York, 1957); George Mikes, *The Hungarian Revolution* (London, 1957); Melvin J. Lasky, *The Hungarian Revolution* (New York, 1957); François Fejtö, *La Tragédie Hongroise* (Paris, 1956); Peter Fryer, *The Hungarian Tragedy* (London, 1956); James A. Michener, *The Bridge at Andau* (New York, 1957); Josef Molden-Pogany, *Ungarns Freiheitskampf* (Vienna, 1957), and others.

31. Friendly cooperation between commanders of Soviet units and revolutionary bodies has been recorded from the towns of Györ, Veszprém, Debrecen, and Jászberény. *U. N. Report*, p. 25.

32. According to Méray, *Thirteen Days*, pp. 125–128, by October 28 there remained only one center of resistance (the Kilián barracks) and that could have been crushed by the Soviet (and Hungarian) Army, had Imre Nagy not prevented this action. It is to be remarked that the Prime Minister had authority to prevent only the Hungarian military units, not the Soviet forces, from participating in an attack; the Hungarian units would hardly have fought against their countrymen on October 27 or 28, as they refused to do so on October 23. In fact, Soviet forces, carrying out an attack against the Kilián barracks on October 27, had been repulsed (Király, "Hungary's Army," *East Europe*, June 1958, p. 10), and after this event fighting slowly died out.

33. Information obtained directly from General Béla Király.

21. Party and Government during the Revolution

1. *Radio Broadcasts*, p. 16. Full citation: *A Magyar Forradalom és Szabadságharc* (The Hungarian Revolution and Fight for Freedom), Hungarian radio broadcasts from October 23 to November 9, 1956, Free Europe Press (New York, 1957).

2. François Fejtö, *Behind the Rape of Hungary* (New York, 1957), pp. 187–190; the narrative is based on

the testimony of a French correspondent of *Le Monde*. See also Tibor Méray, *Thirteen Days That Shook the Kremlin* (New York, 1959), pp. 89–94; Miklos Molnár and Lászlo Nagy, *Imre Nagy, Réformateur ou Révolutionnaire?* (Geneva, 1959), pp. 185–197.

3. *Radio Broadcasts*, pp. 19–20.

4. *Ibid.*; see also United Nations, *Report of the Special Committee on the Problem of Hungary* (New York, 1957), p. 35.

5. Nagy's status between October 24 and 26 has been interpreted differently. The *U. N. Report* (pp. 38–49) takes the view that he was a prisoner of Gerö. Molnár and Lászlo Nagy (pp. 190–191) explain Nagy's attitude by his timidity in the wake of events and misinformation from his entourage. Méray, *Thirteen Days* (pp. 92–106), claims that Nagy offered himself in the role of conciliator while yet not fully aware of what was going on in the streets of Budapest. Fejtö (p. 191) seems to favor the "prisoner" solution.

6. Imre Nagy, *On Communism* (New York, 1957), p. 144.

7. Radio address on October 24 at 12:10 P.M.; *Radio Broadcasts*, p. 21.

8. *Nagy Imre és Büntársai Ellenforradalmi Összeesküvése* (The Counterrevolutionary Conspiracy of Imre Nagy and His Accomplices), Hungarian White Book (Budapest, 1958), pp. 73–74.

9. See George Ginsburgs, "Demise and Revival of a Communist Party: An Autopsy of the Hungarian Revolution," *The Western Political Quarterly*, September 1960, p. 785. This study, however, ignores the role of Moscow in the removal of Gerö and, more generally, the impact of Soviet attitudes on the Stalinist and Kádár-led factions of the Party leadership.

10. *Radio Broadcasts*, pp. 54–55.

11. *Ibid.*

12. See Paul Kecskemeti's article,

"Hungary's Anti-Communist Communists," *The New Leader*, Feb. 10, 1958.

13. CURPH (Columbia University Research Project on Hungary), interview no. 500.

14. CURPH, interview no. 616.

15. The most conspicuous of these attacks was the siege and capture of the Budapest District Party building on October 30, when Imre Mezö, the Party Secretary for Budapest (a Nagy sympathizer), was one of those killed in the action. See Méray, *Thirteen Days*, pp. 153–155.

16. Paul E. Zinner (ed.), *National Communism and Popular Revolt in Eastern Europe* (New York, 1957), pp. 419–420.

17. *Radio Broadcasts*, p. 64. Hence the cautious expression used in the Central Committee declaration: "deems correct the election of workers' councils." In fact these councils were being elected without the "intermediary of the trade union organs," as further recommended in the resolution of the Central Committee.

18. *Radio Broadcasts*, p. 82.

19. See Jozsef Kövágo's pertinent testimony, *You Are All Alone* (New York, 1959), pp. 172, 186, 202, 207–216. See also *Radio Broadcasts*, p. 84, a statement by Béla Kovács to a correspondent of Pécs Radio denying his willingness to participate in any but a national government.

20. Zinner, pp. 429–432; *Radio Broadcasts*, pp. 101–103.

21. *Radio Broadcasts*, p. 98.

22. *Ibid.*, p. 102.

23. Zinner, p. 432.

24. *Szabad Nép*, Oct. 29, 1956; Zinner, pp. 449–451. The article in question was written by Miklos Molnár and it took issue with the *Pravda* article of the preceding day: "Collapse of the Anti-People Adventure in Hungary."

25. Unpublished manuscript by

Kálmán Potoczky, pp. 362–365, 369–370.

26. *Népszabadság*, Dec. 29, 1957, revealed that between September 30 and December 20 the total number of collective farms declined from 3,930 to about 2,000; the area under collectivization and cultivation (about 2,593,000 cadastral yokes) was reduced to a little over one million. See *Hungary, A Survey*, Part 1, The Kossuth Foundation (New York, 1959), pp. 3, 14; see also CURPH, interview no. 152.

27. See radio announcement by Antal Gyenes, the Minister of Crop Collections, *Radio Broadcasts*, p. 224. The Minister thereupon dissolved his ministry, distributing the "cadre" sheets to the employees; CURPH, interview no. 152.

28. Broadcasts by Radio Miskolc on October 26, 1956; *Radio Broadcasts*, pp. 72–73.

29. *Radio Broadcasts*, pp. 88–90; Méray, *Thirteen Days*, p. 138.

30. *Radio Broadcasts*, pp. 61–62; Molnár and László Nagy, p. 202.

31. *Radio Broadcasts*, p. 351; *U. N. Report*, pp. 86–87.

32. *Radio Broadcasts*, pp. 161–162.

33. *Ibid.*, p. 246; *U. N. Report*, p. 86.

34. Potoczky manuscript, pp. 427–429.

35. Kádár's October 30 speech is reprinted in Zinner, pp. 455–456.

36. *Radio Broadcasts*, p. 145.

37. *Ibid.*, p. 170.

38. Zinner, pp. 453–454; *Radio Broadcasts*, pp. 172–173.

39. *Radio Broadcasts*, pp. 173–174.

40. The members of the Smallholder Party's Executive Committee were: Jozsef Kövágo (former Mayor of Budapest), János Csorba, Sándor Kiss (Secretary-General of the Peasant Union), Imre Németh, Tivadar Pártay, István B. Rátz, István B. Szabo, Jozsef Adorján, and István Szemes; see Kövágo, *You Are All Alone*, pp. 193–194; and *U. N. Report*, p. 97.

41. *Radio Broadcasts*, p. 244; *Népszava*, Nov. 1, 1956; *U. N. Report*, p. 98.

42. *Radio Broadcasts*, pp. 269–270; *U. N. Report*, pp. 98–99.

43. The dominating role of "Christian-Democratic" parties in the satellite countries, were Communist rule to disappear, has been predicted as likely by *Ideology and Foreign Affairs*, a study prepared by the Center for International Affairs, Harvard University, at the request of the Committee on Foreign Relations of the United States Senate (Washington, 1960), p. 29.

44. *Radio Broadcasts*, p. 287.

45. *Ibid.*, p. 163.

46. *U. N. Report*, p. 99.

47. Kövágo (see note 19, above), pp. 207–215, describes his conversation with Béla Kovács upon the latter's arrival in Budapest.

48. *Radio Broadcasts*, pp. 338–339.

49. For statements on the general lines of policy of the new political parties, see *U. N. Report*, pp. 97–99.

50. *Ibid.*

51. Zinner, pp. 455–456.

52. See CURPH, interview no. 616. According to Molnár and Lászlo Nagy, p. 199, Miklos Gimes was the first who tried to persuade Imre Nagy of the advisability of reintroducing the multiparty system; the Prime Minister sternly opposed this measure ("never in my life!") but later gave way.

53. *Radio Broadcasts*, pp. 179, 189.

54. *U. N. Report*, p. 44; Méray, *Thirteen Days*, pp. 163–165; Kövágo, pp. 197–202.

55. *Radio Broadcasts*, pp. 277–278; Zinner, pp. 464–467.

56. Méray, *Thirteen Days*, p. 165.

57. The Council of Ministers adopted unanimously the declaration

of withdrawal from the Warsaw
Treaty and of Hungary's neutrality;
Kádár had also been present, and

there was no dissent. *U. N. Report*, p.
55.

22. Hungarian Armed Forces during the Revolution

1. For historical precedents on inadequate or belated resort to force,
see Crane Brinton, *The Anatomy of
Revolution* (New York, 1957), pp. 90–
95; L. P. Edwards, *The Natural History of Revolution* (Chicago, 1927),
passim; G. S. Pettee, *The Process of
Revolution* (New York, 1938), *passim*.

2. Paul E. Zinner, "Revolution in
Hungary: Reflections on the Vicissitudes of a Totalitarian System," *The
Journal of Politics*, February 1959, p.
29.

3. For Kopácsi's role see: CURPH
(Columbia University Research Project
on Hungary), interview no. 500; unpublished manuscript by Kálmán
Potoczky, pp. 353–354; *La Vérité sur
l'Affaire Nagy*, edited by friends and
former collaborators, preface by Albert
Camus (Paris, 1958), pp. 81–84; United
Nations, *Report of the Special Committee on the Problem of Hungary*
(New York, 1957), p. 38.

4. CURPH, interview no. 500.

5. *Radio Broadcasts*, p. 137. Full
citation: *A Magyar Forradalom és
Szabadságharc* (The Hungarian Revolution and Fight for Freedom), Hungarian radio broadcasts from October
23 to November 9, 1956, Free Europe
Press (New York, 1957).

6. Paul E. Zinner (ed.), *National
Communism and Popular Revolt in
Eastern Europe* (New York, 1957), p.
452.

7. *Radio Broadcasts*, pp. 186–187.

8. Potoczky manuscript, pp. 284–
285.

9. *U. N. Report*, p. 135.

10. See Judgment in the Imre
Nagy "trial," *Nagy Imre és Bűntársai
Ellenforradalmi Összeesküvése* (The
Counterrevolutionary Conspiracy of

Imre Nagy and His Accomplices),
Hungarian White Book (Budapest,
1958), p. 14.

11. *Ibid*.

12. Nehru's estimates in *Annual
Register of World Events, 1956* (London, 1957), p. 102.

13. See Béla Király, "Hungary's
Army: Its Part in the Revolt," *East
Europe*, June 1958, pp. 11–12.

14. *Ibid.*, p. 10.

15. The announcements mentioned
in this paragraph are in *Radio Broadcasts*, pp. 48, 51, 80, 93, 98. The
October 28 announcement calling
soldiers back to their units (*Radio
Broadcasts*, p. 93) rather refutes François Fejtö's thesis in *Behind the Rape
of Hungary* (New York, 1957), p. 199,
according to which Hungarian units
had been disarmed and disbanded by
their commanding officers in order to
prevent their participation in the
fighting against the Russians.

16. Király, in *East Europe*, June
1958, p. 11; and personal information
by General Király to this writer.

17. For Maléter's story see Fejtö,
pp. 201–203; also Potoczky manuscript,
pp. 322–325.

18. Fejtö, pp. 199–200; Király, in
East Europe, June 1958, p. 12. The
corps commander at Kecskemét was
General Lajos Gyurko, a graduate of
the Voroshilov Academy in Moscow;
on November 1 he fled to Soviet headquarters and only returned to his
staff after November 4.

19. See Fejtö, pp. 227–229; *Radio
Broadcasts*, pp. 209–210.

20. *Radio Broadcasts*, p. 186.

21. *Ibid.*, p. 152.

22. *Ibid.*, p. 178.

23. Király's story has been nar-

rated by himself in "How Russian Trickery Throttled Revolt," *Life*, Feb. 18, 1957, pp. 119–129; see also Fejtö, pp. 203–205; and *Radio Broadcasts*, pp. 212, 216.

24. *Radio Broadcasts*, pp. 340–341.

25. *Ibid.*, p. 178; Király, in *East Europe*, June 1958, p. 14.

26. Much confusion was created during Janza's ministry by the unwarranted separation of Budapest's "outer" and "inner" defenses, the former taken away from General Király's command and entrusted to Colonel András Márton, the commander of the Zrinyi Academy. See Király, in *East Europe*, June 1958, p. 14.

27. At the crucial hour of November 4 the commander of the Budapest garrison was betrayed by his own chief of staff; see Király, "Russian Trickery," *Life*, p. 129.

28. Information received directly from General Király; also see Király, in *East Europe*, June 1958, p. 14.

23. Revolutionaries and Revolutionary Institutions

1. See Merle Fainsod, *How Russia Is Ruled* (Cambridge, Mass., 1953), pp. 61–62; and Crane Brinton (who prefers the expression "dual sovereignty"), *The Anatomy of Revolution* (New York, 1957), pp. 139–144.

2. Paul E. Zinner (ed.), *National Communism and Popular Revolt in Eastern Europe* (New York, 1957), p. 420; *Radio Broadcasts*, pp. 93–95. Full citation: *A Magyar Forradalom és Szabadságharc* (The Hungarian Revolution and Fight for Freedom), Hungarian radio broadcasts from October 23 to November 9, 1956, Free Europe Press (New York, 1957).

3. Zinner, p. 454; *Radio Broadcasts*, p. 172.

4. United Nations, *Report of the Special Committee on the Problem of Hungary* (New York, 1957), p. 80, estimates the number of demonstrators on October 23 to have been at least 200,000 and perhaps 300,000.

5. Unpublished manuscript by Kálmán Potoczky, pp. 359–360.

6. Information provided to this writer by General Béla Király.

7. *U. N. Report*, p. 85.

8. In Debrecen, 20 per cent of the membership of the revolutionary council was reserved to university students, another 20 per cent to representatives of armed forces, and the remaining 60 per cent to workers' representatives.

9. *U. N. Report*, p. 85.

10. *Ibid.*

11. *Radio Broadcasts*, p. 246.

12. Jozsef Kövágo, *You Are All Alone* (New York, 1959), pp. 228–229.

13. See the Committee's appeal to the "World Peace Council" in Paris. *Radio Broadcasts*, p. 313.

14. *U. N. Report*, p. 88.

15. For instance, in the village of Kocsod the local organization of the People's Patriotic Front transformed itself on October 24 into a "revolutionary committee." See *Népszabadság*, Jan. 24, 1957; François Fejtö, *Behind the Rape of Hungary* (New York, 1957), p. 215.

16. *Radio Broadcasts*, p. 351.

17. In some Hungarian missions abroad the chief felt compelled to seek refuge elsewhere when the members of the mission revolted; thus, the Hungarian minister in Copenhagen fled to Moscow, the Hungarian minister to Austria moved to Prague, and the Hungarian ambassador in New Delhi asked for asylum from the government of India; *La Vérité sur l'Affaire Nagy* (Paris, 1958), p. 125.

18. *Radio Broadcasts*, p. 183.

19. *U. N. Report*, pp. 52, 56, 86.

20. *Radio Broadcasts,* p. 256.

21. Personal information to this writer by Dr. György Heltai.

22. See CURPH (Columbia University Research Project on Hungary), interview no. 602; this information about the planned turnover is also based on the personal knowledge of this writer.

23. This expression was first used, so far as this writer knows, by François Fejtö, *op. cit.,* p. 197.

24. See for instance, the ten points of the Petöfi Circle. *Szabad Nép,* Oct. 23, 1956; *U. N. Report,* p. 75.

25. Zinner, p. 422.

26. *U. N. Report,* pp. 91–92.

27. *Radio Broadcasts,* pp. 281, 297.

28. *U. N. Report,* p. 92.

29. *Ibid.,* p. 93.

30. Brinton, pp. 128–152.

31. Professor György Lukács, in an interview with a Polish journalist on October 31, made the following statement (italics ours): "The new Party will not be able to expect rapid success — Communism in Hungary has been totally disgraced. Collected around the Party will probably be small groups of progressive intellectuals, writers and a few young people. The working class will prefer to follow the Social Democrats. *In free elections the Communists will obtain five per cent of the vote, ten per cent at the most.* It is possible that they won't be in the government, that they will go into opposition. But the Party will continue to exist; it will save the idea; it will be an intellectual center, and after some years or some decades from now, who knows . . ." *Nowa Kultura,* Dec. 2, 1956, as quoted in Melvin J. Lasky, *The Hungarian Revolution* (London, 1957), p. 159.

32. For a summary of these demands see *Facts about Hungary,* ed.

Imre Kovács (New York, 1959), pp. 87–100.

33. See CURPH; also *Inquiry into Political and Social Attitudes in Hungary,* Free Europe Press (New York, 1957); and Marquette University Hungarian Research Program.

34. *Radio Broadcasts,* pp. 155–156; *U. N. Report,* p. 77.

35. *Radio Broadcasts,* p. 262.

36. Professor Lajos Jánosi, Hungarian atomic scientist of world renown, admitted in an interview on November 1 that he knew very little about the uranium extracted by the Soviet Union in Hungary (*Radio Broadcasts,* p. 273). See also an article written by Béla Balassa, in *This Is Communist Hungary,* ed. Robert Finley Delaney (Chicago, 1958), pp. 236–238.

37. *Facts about Hungary,* pp. 93–94.

38. See in this regard the criticism by Fejtö, pp. 207–209.

39. *Ibid.,* pp. 227–232.

40. Raymond Aron, "The Meaning of Hungary," *The New Leader,* March 24, 1958, p. 12; and Paul Ignotus, *Political Prisoner* (London, 1959), p. 187.

41. For Cardinal Mindszenty's radio speech see *The Revolt in Hungary* (New York, 1957), English translations of internal broadcasts by Hungarian radio stations from October 23 to November 4, 1956, pp. 79–80.

42. Zinner, p. 465.

43. *U. N. Report,* p. 20.

44. *Népszabadság,* Jan. 6, 1957.

45. Raymond Aron, p. 13.

46. *Radio Broadcasts,* p. 335. The issue in question was that of November 3.

47. See note 31, above.

48. *Radio Broadcasts,* p. 348.

24. Foreign Factors: The Soviet Union, Yugoslavia, and Suez

1. The *Pravda* editorial of October 28, bearing the title "Collapse of the Anti-People Adventure in Hungary," after blaming the "subversive activity conducted by the imperialist powers" for the outbreak of the "counterrevolution," recognized the "past serious mistakes" made in the field of economic management and the "violations of democratic principles and Socialist legality." The article took the optimistic view that the "anti-people venture had collapsed as a result of the measures taken by the leadership of the Hungarian Workers Party and the Hungarian Government." It further stated that the people's democratic system, while "severely tested," had "once more reaffirmed its enormous vitality." It cited the radio announcement from Budapest according to which a "new national government" had been formed "on a broad democratic basis." The article pursuant to this report indicated that the "enemy onslaught against the people's democratic system in Hungary had evoked a wave of anger and indignation"; it ended with overtones of hopefulness: the Hungarian working people "are determined to defend their people's regime and to continue on the path of building Socialism."

2. Khrushchev's speech before the Hungarian Communist Party Congress on December 2, 1959 (*New York Times*, Dec. 3, 1959). The simultaneous dispatch to Budapest of both Mikoyan and Suslov on October 24 and again on October 30 seemed to indicate the representation of the two schools of thought in the Kremlin.

3. On October 30, 8:05 P.M., the Hungarian frontier station of Záhony reported that "Soviet units are pouring out of Hungary"; similar reports came from Miskolc, where Soviet units

turned back and moved toward the Soviet frontier, and also from Nyiregyháza, which was passed by Soviet forces marching eastwards. See *Radio Broadcasts*, pp. 189, 196–197. Full citation: *A Magyar Forradalom és Szabadságharc* (The Hungarian Revolution and Fight for Freedom), Hungarian radio broadcasts from October 23 to November 9, 1956, Free Europe Press (New York, 1957). On October 31, 1:17 P.M., Radio Miskolc reported again the inward trend of Soviet forces; *ibid.*, p. 234.

4. *Pravda*, Oct. 31, 1956; Paul E. Zinner (ed.), *National Communism and Popular Revolt in Eastern Europe* (New York, 1957), pp. 485–489.

5. François Fejtö, *Behind the Rape of Hungary* (New York, 1957), p. 237, reports that Mikoyan and Suslov refused to agree to Hungary's withdrawal from the Warsaw Treaty whereas such a plan had only been tentatively suggested to the Soviet representatives on October 31 (personal information from György Heltai to this writer). About Tildy's conversation with Mikoyan see the convincing testimony of Jozsef Kövágo, *You Are All Alone* (New York, 1959), pp. 198–202. See also Tibor Méray, *Thirteen Days That Shook the Kremlin* (New York, 1959), pp. 164–166; Miklos Molnár and Lászlo Nagy, *Imre Nagy, Réformateur ou Révolutionnaire?* (Geneva, 1959), pp. 202–204.

6. The departure of Gerö, Hegedüs, Piros, and other discredited Stalinists was reported late on October 31. *Radio Broadcasts*, p. 242. It must have been under the impact of Soviet refusal to help that Ferenc Münnich had exclaimed: "The only thing left is to die with honor" (statement made to Wiktor Woroszylski, a Polish journalist; see Fejtö, *Behind the Rape of Hungary*, p. 241).

7. Concerning the negotiations in the Party headquarters on October 31 see United Nations, *Report of the Special Committee on the Problem of Hungary* (New York, 1957), p. 44. Münnich participated in these discussions; evidently his knowledge of the Russian language was also needed. He became a Party Presidium member on October 28, but was dropped from the leadership of the new Party on November 1.

8. See Merle Fainsod, "What Happened to 'Collective Leadership'?" in *Problems of Communism,* July–August 1959, p. 6.

9. Khrushchev, in his speech before the workers of the Ganz-Mavag plant in Budapest on December 2, 1959, made it abundantly clear that he and some other (unnamed) Presidium members sided with the plan "to help Hungary's working people against the counter-revolutionary forces." While "some Soviet comrades expressed anxiety that any aid would be misconstrued," Khrushchev asserted "that in time they would see we were right." *New York Times,* Dec. 3, 1959. Also see Giuseppe Boffa, *Inside the Khrushchev Era* (New York, 1959), p. 105.

10. From October 31 on, the Czechoslovak, Bulgarian, Rumanian, and East German satellite press vehemently assailed the Hungarian developments; the Hungarian papers in Slovakia and Transylvania particularly delighted in calling the Hungarian revolutionaries "fascists" (see the article of the Bratislava *Uj Szo* of October 31). On the other hand, Polish and Yugoslav press reports remained sympathetic until November 4. As to the presumed appeals of Communist leaders in the People's Democracies in favor of intervention, see Méray, *Thirteen Days,* pp. 199–200.

11. There had been student demonstrations in the universities of Bratis-lava in Czechoslovakia, and in those of Bucharest and Cluj in Rumania; similar reports have been made concerning demonstrations in the Leningrad and Kiev universities in the USSR. Méray, *Thirteen Days,* pp. 199–200; *U. N. Report,* p. 125; *The Annual Register of World Events, 1956* (London, 1957), pp. 248, 260–261; *New York Times,* Oct. 30 and Nov. 3, 1956.

12. In a statement issued on November 1, 1956, the government of the People's Republic of China commented on the Soviet declaration of October 30. The Chinese greeted with satisfaction the Soviet announcement, registered the Soviet admission of mishandling of some satellite problems, and approved Polish and Hungarian demands for "democracy," independence, and equality. They further noted with satisfaction that in Poland attempts to undermine the people's democratic system had failed, but refrained from any ulterior comment with regard to events in Hungary. Zinner, pp. 492–495.

13. See Tito's speech at Pula on November 11, 1956, as reprinted in Zinner, p. 525.

14. The letter was published in the *Politika* of Oct. 29, 1956; see also Zinner, pp. 446–448.

15. See Richard Lowenthal, "Tito's Affair with Khrushchev," *The New Leader,* Oct. 6, 1958, p. 14. The present writer is also indebted for valuable information on Yugoslav-Hungarian relations during the Revolution to Dr. György Heltai, the Deputy Foreign Minister under Imre Nagy.

16. Milovan Djilas' appraisal of the Hungarian Revolution is to be found in his article "The Storm in Eastern Europe," *The New Leader,* Nov. 19, 1956, for which three years were added to his existing sentence.

17. Yugoslav considerations of marching into Hungary are revealed by Richard Lowenthal, *loc. cit.*

18. The official Yugoslav comment appeared in the form of an editorial in *Borba*, Nov. 1, 1956; Zinner, pp. 495–496.

19. See Hungarian note to Yugoslavia of July 21, 1958. *Népszabadság*, July 23, 1958.

20. Richard Lowenthal, *loc. cit.*, asserts that Yugoslavia had been consulted by the Soviets in regard to the second armed intervention. He relies on reports received from a Yugoslav source; on the Hungarian reply to a Yugoslav note of July 21, 1958, protesting Imre Nagy's execution — a reply which contained a passage that "the responsible Yugoslav officials learned, on the basis of confidential information, that at daybreak on November 4" the Soviet attack was to be launched; and on such items as the Yugoslav Central Committee's circular of November 5, the Yugoslav U. N. delegate's behavior toward Anna Kéthly in New York, and the "misleading confidential information" sent by Tito to Nehru. The consultation of Tito was supposed to have been made personally by Khrushchev and Mikoyan on a visit to the Yugoslav leader in the first days of November. Lowenthal expresses no certainty that such a visit took place, but only reports information he received to that effect.

21. "You can rest assured that *we have never advised them* [the Soviets] *to go ahead and use the army*. We never gave such advice and could not do so even in the present crisis . . . Therefore, we should combat those rumors in our country" (italics added). From Tito's speech at Pula on November 11, 1956; Zinner, p. 530.

22. For an expression of the "Islamic" conception — though not applied specifically to Hungary, see Reinhold Niebuhr, *The Structure of Nations and Empires* (New York, 1959), p. 117.

23. *The Annual Register of World Events, 1956* (London, 1957), p. 222.

24. From Tito's speech at Pula on November 11, 1956; Zinner, p. 529.

25. See the lucid presentation of the question by James Burnham, *Containment or Liberation?* (New York, 1952), *passim*.

26. Milovan Djilas, "The Storm in Eastern Europe," *The New Leader*, Nov. 19, 1956.

27. For a history of the treatment of the Hungarian problem by the United Nations, see "Timetable of a Failure," in *Facts about Hungary*, ed. Imre Kovács (New York, 1958), pp. 115–150.

28. An expression of this policy of caution was given by President Eisenhower's address of October 31, 1956, assuring Americans that Poland and Hungary are not to be considered as "potential military allies" by the United States. *Documents on International Affairs, 1956* (London, 1959), p. 266.

29. On November 4, after the news of the second Soviet intervention had reached him, President Eisenhower sent a letter to Soviet Premier Bulganin urging him "in the name of humanity and in the cause of peace" to have Soviet forces withdrawn from Hungary; *Documents on International Affairs, 1956*, p. 491. We may assume that this message was received with an astonished disdain by the Kremlin, as dictators relying on their strength are used to assess appeals to humanitarianism. The *New York Times* reported on Nov. 5, 1956: "Some officials had suggested several days ago that the United States could have exerted some deterrent influence on the Soviet Union . . . But these ideas did not gain Administration favor, and there was no evidence that they were discussed at President Eisenhower's conferences during the day."

30. Henry A. Kissinger (*The Necessity for Choice*, New York, 1961,

p. 48) aptly contrasts the unwillingness of the United States to threaten the Soviet Union with nuclear bombing in the Hungarian crisis with Soviet threats to send missiles against Britain during the Suez conflict. He also emphasizes that, at that date, the Soviet Union was certainly inferior in that kind of warfare. See also Thomas J. Dodd, "Hungary — The Missed Opportunity," *The Hungarian Quarterly,* vol. I, no. 1 (January, 1961), pp. 14–20.

25. The Second Soviet Intervention — Kádár versus Nagy

1. See statement by General Pál Maléter on November 1, 1956; Melvin J. Lasky, *The Hungarian Revolution* (London, 1957), p. 176.

2. The information on the differing viewpoints between the Soviet High Command and the Presidium before the endorsement of the coup plan by the latter, has been given to this writer by Dr. György Heltai.

3. From Khrushchev's speech of April 4, 1958, in Hungary. *Népszabadság,* April 5, 1958.

4. The view that the Suez issue significantly influenced the Soviet decision to administer a military coup in Hungary is shared by most students of the Hungarian Revolution: Miklos Molnár and Lászlo Nagy, *Imre Nagy, Réformateur ou Révolutionnaire?* (Geneva, 1959), p. 208; Milovan Djilas, "The Storm in Eastern Europe," *The New Leader,* Nov. 19, 1956; Zbigniew K. Brzezinski, *The Soviet Bloc* (Cambridge, Mass., 1960), p. 228; Tibor Méray, *Thirteen Days That Shook the Kremlin* (New York, 1959), pp. 200–201. However, Raymond Aron, "The Meaning of Hungary," *The New Leader,* March 24, 1958, p. 18, maintains that the Suez expedition had no influence, and that if it had not taken place the Soviet Union would still have suppressed the Hungarian Revolution.

5. From Khrushchev's speech of December 2, 1959, at Budapest (*New York Times,* Dec. 3, 1959).

6. Suslov, speaking on November 6, 1956, at the anniversary of the Bolshevik Revolution, showed anxiety to allay suspicions by Communist parties.

7. Tito's speech at Pula on November 11, 1956; Paul E. Zinner (ed.), *National Communism and Popular Revolt in Eastern Europe* (New York, 1957), p. 529.

8. Hans Morgenthau has written: "The events of the fall of 1956 have opened up a gap between our verbal commitment to a policy of liberation and the actual policy we pursued when the opportunity, not to *initiate* liberation, but to support it after it had already been achieved, arose in Hungary. These events made obvious what some of us had suspected all along, that the United States was actually pursuing a policy of containment conceived in terms not of liberation, but of an implicit and thus far unacknowledged agreement to recognize the existence of spheres of influence. The American abstention in the face of the German uprising of 1953 and of the Polish and Hungarian revolts of 1956, coupled with the renunciation of force on the latter occasion, had made it perfectly clear that liberation, for the United States, is a matter of desire and hope, 'a consummation devoutly to be wished,' but not an objective of policy to be pursued by deliberate action. The United States, far from seeking out or creating opportunities for opening the door to liberation, has proven to be unwilling even to enter the door when a satellite nation kicks it wide open." "The

Revolution in U. S. Foreign Policy," *Commentary,* February 1957.

9. The Soviet decision to resort to a second armed intervention must have been taken after October 30 (the date of the Moscow declaration) and before noon, November 1 (when the massive influx of Soviet armor into Hungary began). We have also to assume that the Soviet Presidium had waited until its emissaries, Mikoyan and Suslov, returned from Budapest (during the night from October 31 to November 1). Accordingly, the morning hours of November 1 (Moscow time) appear as the presumptive date of the fateful decision.

10. Zinner, p. 462.

11. United Nations, *Report of the Special Committee on the Problem of Hungary* (New York, 1957), pp. 9, 54–56. This report tells the story of Hungary's withdrawal from the Warsaw Treaty.

12. See Molnár and László Nagy, p. 209; Balázs Nagy, "Imre Nagy and the Hungarian Revolution," *The Review* (Brussels), April 1960, p. 49; and information provided personally to the present writer by Dr. György Heltai.

13. *U. N. Report,* p. 55; Molnár and László Nagy, p. 210. According to Tibor Méray, *Thirteen Days,* p. 192, when the question of Hungary's withdrawal from the Warsaw Treaty and the declaration of neutrality were discussed by the leadership of the Communist Party, only György Lukács and Zoltán Szántó accepted the resolution with reservations. János Kádár and the others unreservedly rallied to the proposition submitted by Imre Nagy.

14. The scene is described in detail in unpublished manuscript by Kálmán Potoczky, pp. 493–492; see also *U. N. Report,* p. 55; Tibor Méray, *Thirteen Days,* pp. 193–194.

15. *Radio Broadcasts,* p. 282. Full citation: *A Magyar Forradalom és Szabadságharc* (The Hungarian Revolution and Fight for Freedom), Hungarian radio broadcasts from October 23 to November 9, 1956, Free Europe Press (New York, 1957).

16. *Népszabadság,* Nov. 2, 1956; Zinner, pp. 462–463.

17. See "Timetable of a Failure," *Facts about Hungary,* ed. Imre Kovács (New York, 1959), pp. 120–124.

18. For example, Tibor Méray, *Thirteen Days,* p. 198.

19. George F. Kennan, as reported in Melvin J. Lasky, "A Conversation with Kennan," *Encounter,* March 1960.

20. Molnár and Lászlo Nagy, p. 209; *U. N. Report,* p. 55; Jozsef Kővágo, *You Are All Alone* (New York, 1959), pp. 204–205; information by Dr. György Heltai to this writer.

21. See *U. N. Report,* pp. 55–56; *La Vérité sur l'Affaire Nagy* (Paris, 1958), pp. 118–120; Balázs Nagy (note 12, above), pp. 51–53; and information given to this writer by Dr. György Heltai.

22. *U. N. Report,* p. 55; Zinner, pp. 463–464.

23. Potoczky manuscript, p. 492.

24. For Hungary's three diplomatic notes to the Soviet Union on November 2 (concerning the two delegations and the violations of Hungarian sovereignty), and the note to the Secretary-General, see *Radio Broadcasts,* pp. 307–308; *U. N. Report,* p. 58.

25. CURPH (Columbia University Research Project on Hungary), interview no. 451; Potoczky manuscript, p. 491. Both of these sources report on the launching site suggestion made by Yuri V. Andropov; the "sounding out" of Imre Nagy on his willingness to cooperate is an assumption of this writer, supported by similar attempts made after the installation of the Kádár government.

26. *Survey of International Affairs, 1939–1946* (London, 1958), p. 74.

27. *La Vérité sur l'Affaire Nagy,* p. 120; *U. N. Report,* p. 44; Potoczky manuscript, p. 492.

28. Kádár's disappearance has been reported, albeit sometimes with slight variations, by all students of the Hungarian Revolution. See, in particular, François Fejtö, *Behind the Rape of Hungary* (New York, 1957), p. 241; Tibor Méray, *Thirteen Days,* pp. 208–209; *U. N. Report,* pp. 10, 44–45; Potoczky manuscript, pp. 507–513. There is no sufficient evidence for the allegation, occasionally made, that Kádár was seen in Budapest on November 2. He himself admitted that on November 2 he had already begun negotiations with the "Soviet comrades" with a view of defeating the "counterrevolution" and that on November 3 "everything was already decided." See *A Magyar Szocialista Munkáspárt Országos Értekezlétenek Jegyzökönyve* (Budapest, 1957), the minutes of the Hungarian Party's national conference of June 27–29, 1957. The negotiations mentioned by Kádár could hardly have been conducted in Budapest.

29. It has been stated that Khrushchev's siding with those members of the Presidium who advocated the second armed intervention turned the scales in favor of this move (see Isaac Deutscher, "Crisis in Moscow," *The Reporter,* Nov. 15, 1956; Tibor Méray, *Thirteen Days,* pp. 202–203). Khrushchev had been reproached by Presidium members for being responsible for the crisis in Hungary; it seems only reasonable to assume that he wished to belie the accusations leveled against him, and therefore, seconding the coup, assumed responsibility for the implementation of its political part. After the Revolution, Khrushchev showed particular solicitude toward Kádár's performance, and visited Budapest many times. Kádár's December 1959 visit, accompanying Khru-

shchev, to Uzhgorod, where memories of the formation of his government were recalled, had the air of a "family reunion" where Nikita Sergeyevich had played the role of godfather.

30. Kádár's reasons for quitting the Nagy cabinet are analyzed by Tibor Méray, *Thirteen Days,* pp. 206–209; this question is also discussed by the *U. N. Report,* pp. 44–45.

31. Kádár's speech of January 28, 1958. Kádár further said that "it was touch and go" on November 2, 1956, for Münnich to become Premier in Uzhgorod; he was "one of the first of us initiators . . . [who] saw the need for a new government and the need to end treason." *Népszabadság,* Jan. 29, 1958.

32. From the radio appeal by Münnich on November 4, 1956; Zinner, pp. 473–474.

33. From the program of government announced by Kádár on November 4, 1956; *New York Times,* Nov. 5, 1956; Zinner, pp. 474–478.

34. *U. N. Report,* pp. 45, 56.

35. See Béla Király, "Reconquest of Hungary," *Facts about Hungary,* ed. Imre Kovács (New York, 1959), pp. 105–106.

36. Khrushchev told United States Ambassador Charles E. Bohlen: "We think we have enough troops there, but, if need be, we will send in more and more, and more." Daniel Schorr, "Bohlen Returns to the Russian Challenge," *New York Times Magazine,* Oct. 18, 1959, p. 88.

37. The scene of the arrest of the Hungarian military delegation in the Soviet Army headquarters is fully described in the *U. N. Report,* p. 45. Concerning Pál Maléter, executed together with Imre Nagy, a Special Report of the United Nations Special Committee on the Problem of Hungary, dated July 14, 1958, stated: "The Special Committee, as noted earlier, found that General Maléter was ar-

rested on November 3, 1956 in the Soviet Headquarters at Tököl on Csepel Island, where, as Minister of Defence in the Nagy Government, he was leading the Hungarian military delegation, which was negotiating with the Soviet Command, *in which capacity he was entitled to special protection accorded under international law*. It should be noted that at the meeting of the Security Council on November 3, 1956, the representative of Hungary declared, and the representative of the USSR confirmed, that these negotiations were taking place." (Italics are added.)

38. The search for the military mission which "no longer replied" is dramatically depicted by General Béla Király, the man who was in charge of maintaining contact with Maléter, in "How Russian Trickery Throttled Revolt," *Life,* Feb. 18, 1957, p. 126.

39. *Ibid.,* pp. 126, 127; *U. N. Report,* p. 26. The Prime Minister's refusal to allow the Hungarian Air Force to bomb marching Soviet formations during November 1–3 had paralyzed all action until the occupation of the airfields, after which the launching of any attack became impossible.

40. This is the translation given by the *U. N. Report,* p. 45. The appeal was made not only in Hungarian but in many languages. See also Zinner, p. 472.

41. *Nagy Imre és Bűntársai Ellenforradalmi Összeesküvése* (The Counterrevolutionary Conspiracy of Imre Nagy and His Accomplices), Hungarian White Book (Budapest, 1958), p. 15.

42. "Imre Nagy got into a situation where a conflict between the Hungarian and the Communist in him became inevitable. The way he fought this internal fight is from a human viewpoint much to be admired." CURPH, interview no. 616.

43. This writer has borrowed the metaphor from Paul E. Zinner, "Hungary's Imre Nagy: Revolutionist at the End," *Columbia University Forum,* Fall 1958, p. 10.

44. *U. N. Report,* pp. 45–46; Potoczky manuscript, p. 572.

45. For a history of the fighting on November 4 and after, see Béla Király, "Reconquest of Hungary," in *Facts about Hungary,* ed. Imre Kovács (New York, 1959), pp. 109–111; same author, "Hungary's Army: Its Part in the Revolt," *East Europe,* June 1958, p. 15; Fejtö, pp. 253–255; Potoczky manuscript, pp. 574–606.

46. For instance, Zbigniew K. Brzezinski suggests that the experience of the Hungarian Revolution provided an abortive "Test Case of National Communism." *The Soviet Bloc,* pp. 207–235.

47. CURPH, interview no. 511.

48. Imre Nagy, *On Communism* (New York, 1957), pp. 255–256.

49. *A Magyar Nép Védelmében* (Paris, 1957), p. 17. The excerpt does not appear in the New York edition, just cited.

50. Imre Nagy, p. 33.

51. See in particular, the analysis of Nagy's concept in Balázs Nagy (note 12, above), pp. 22–33.

52. Raymond Aron (note 4, above), p. 16; CURPH, interview no. 616.

53. "Between the two events (the Polish and Hungarian revolts), although they happened almost simultaneously, there lies a whole epoch. The changes in Poland mean a triumph of national Communism, which in a different form we have already seen in Yugoslavia. The Hungarian uprising is something more, a new phenomenon, perhaps no less meaningful than the French or Russian Revolutions." Milovan Djilas, "The Storm in Eastern Europe," *The New Leader,* Nov. 19, 1956.

26. Consolidation, Restoration, and Repression

1. *Nagy Imre és Büntársai Ellenforradalmi Összeesküvése* (The Counterrevolutionary Conspiracy of Imre Nagy and His Accomplices), Hungarian White Book (Budapest, 1958), p. 119.

2. United Nations, *Report of the Special Committee on the Problem of Hungary* (New York, 1957), p. 101.

3. *Népszabadság*, Nov. 8, 1957.

4. *U. N. Report*, pp. 101–102.

5. The text of the order is reprinted in the *U. N. Report*, p. 102, along with an order issued by Major Kornusin, the military commander of Pécs.

6. Resolution of the General Assembly adopted by roll call of 55 to 10, with 14 abstentions (A/RES/407). Subsequently, the Special Committee commissioned by the General Assembly stated that it "has reached the conclusion that, since 4 November 1956, deportations of Hungarian citizens to the USSR have taken place in considerable numbers, which cannot be accurately assessed, but which run into thousands. The Committee has no proof that more than a part of the deportees has been returned to Hungary." *U. N. Report*, p. 127.

7. Melvin J. Lasky, *The Hungarian Revolution* (London, 1957), p. 237; Paul E. Zinner (ed.), *National Communism and Popular Revolt in Eastern Europe* (New York, 1957), pp. 473–474.

8. Zinner, pp. 474–478; *U. N. Report*, pp. 108–109.

9. *U. N. Report*, pp. 105–106, 115; this change coincided with Marshal Konev's visit to Budapest.

10. The negotiations for the termination of Imre Nagy's asylum in the Yugoslav embassy are fully covered by the *U. N. Report*, pp. 106–107. Much of the information was evidently received by the Committee from Yugo-

slav governmental sources, although this was not mentioned in the Report.

11. For the Bibo Plan see *Facts about Hungary*, ed. Imre Kovács (New York, 1958 edition), pp. 100–106. In addition to the plan, dated November 9, 1956, Bibo wrote a lengthy memorandum on the situation of Hungary in January 1957. Hungarian texts of both documents in *Harmadik Ut* (Third Road), published in London, 1960, pp. 357–379.

12. *U. N. Report*, p. 116.

13. *Ibid.*

14. Suslov's speech of November 6, 1956, is printed in *Izvestiya*, Nov. 7, 1956; see also Zbigniew K. Brzezinski, *The Soviet Bloc* (Cambridge, Mass., 1960), p. 273.

15. See Brzezinski, *The Soviet Bloc*, pp. 274–277.

16. *Népszabadság*, Jan. 6, 1957.

17. *U. N. Report*, p. 109.

18. *Magyar Közlöny*, Dec. 8, 1956.

19. *U. N. Report*, pp. 109–112; François Fejtö, *Behind the Rape of Hungary* (New York, 1957), pp. 281–291; *Facts about Hungary*, ed. Imre Kovács (New York, 1959), pp. 189–197.

20. *Népszabadság*, Jan. 12, 1957, denounced these refusals as provocative acts.

21. *Népszabadság*, June 28, 1957.

22. *Népszabadság*, Nov. 17, 1957.

23. *U. N. Report*, p. 118.

24. Fejtö, p. 294.

25. *U. N. Report*, p. 119.

26. Zinner, p. 477.

27. Note to Yugoslavia of November 22, 1956.

28. *U. N. Report*, pp. 104, 130.

29. See *Highlights of Current Legislation and Activities in Mid-Europe*, Library of Congress, January 1958, p. 22.

30. See "Judicial System of the Kádár Regime," *Facts about Hungary* (1959), pp. 232–240.

31. These two addresses of February 15, 1957, are quoted from in *U. N. Report,* p. 131.

32. Decree No. 31 of 1956; *Highlights* (note 29, above), p. 25.

33. Police surveillance was technically based on a World War II emergency decree (No. 8130/1939), but implemented and amended by the new provision (Decree No. 1 of 1957). Originally it was the Minister of the Interior who had been given such powers in 1939; now any police chief of a county or of the city of Budapest was authorized to apply these measures.

34. *U. N. Report,* pp. 112, 131. For full material and analysis of repressive meatures in Hungary up to March 1957 see *The Hungarian Situation and the Rule of Law* (The Hague, 1957), edited by the International Commission of Jurists.

27. The New "New Party" and Its Government

1. The Minister of Agriculture's Directive of November 27, 1956, and a joint Directive of the same minister and the Minister of Finance regulated the dissolution of collective farms. On December 13, the government appealed to the farmers to return illegally seized assets from disbanded collectives, and a decree of January 13, 1957, required the local councils to confiscate such properties *without recourse to punitive measures.* Other administrative measures, however, undertook to consolidate existing collectives, or even to have dissolutions of kolkhozes reviewed by their former members. See *Highlights of Current Legislation and Activities in Mid-Europe,* Library of Congress, February 1958, pp. 63–66.

2. François Fejtö, *Behind the Rape of Hungary* (New York, 1957), p. 303.

3. From Kádár's speech as quoted in Paul E. Zinner (ed.), *National Communism and Popular Revolt in Eastern Europe* (New York, 1957), pp. 465–466.

4. *Népszabadság,* Jan. 3, 1957.

5. *Népszabadság,* May 5, 1957.

6. Interview given by Politburo member Károly Kiss; *Népszabadság,* Sept. 12, 1957.

7. See Kádár's speech in Szeged on October 12, 1957; *Népszabadság,* Oct. 13, 1957.

8. See Fejtö, pp. 299–301.

9. Estimates conveyed to this writer by a confidential source of information.

10. *Népszabadság,* Sept. 12, 1957.

11. From Marosán's lecture at the Political Academy of the Hungarian Socialist Workers Party on November 18, 1957, on "Certain Questions Concerning Relations between the Party and the Masses." (*Hungarian Information Service,* November 19, 1957.)

12. *Népszabadság,* July 15, 1958.

13. "The Fraternal Communist Parties' Struggle against Present-Day Opportunism," by D. Shevlyagyn, *Kommunist,* December 1957, pp. 27–44.

14. Dezsö Nemes, "The Development of Hungarian Revisionism as Organic Part of the Ideological Preparation of the Counter-Revolution," *Társadalmi Szemle,* January 1958.

15. Article by Géza Kassai, *Társadalmi Szemle,* January, 1958.

16. *Népszabadság,* April 6, 1958.

17. Joint statement and speech are in *Népszabadság,* April 10, 1958, but the denunciation of Nagy was omitted from that report and is found in reports of Western correspondents who heard the speech.

18. *Népszabadság,* Jan. 14, 1958.

19. *Népszabadság,* Jan. 19, 1958.

20. United Nations, *Report of the Special Committee on the Problem of*

Hungary (New York, 1957), p. 118.

21. *The Times* (London), March 3, 1958.

22. *New York Times,* Feb. 22, 1958.

23. *Magyar Nemzet,* March 5, 1958.

24. Their return was announced in a speech by Kádár on October 15, 1958. Concerning the present occupations of leading Stalinists, see *New York Times,* Oct. 24, 1960.

25. *New York Times,* Sept. 19, 1958.

26. E.g., *Neue Zürcher Zeitung,* April 25, 1959.

27. *Népszabadság,* March 14, 1959.

28. From the resolution of March 6 of the Hungarian Central Committee; *Népszabadság,* March 8, 1959.

29. *Népszabadság,* Dec. 2, 1959; *New York Times,* Dec. 2, 1959.

30. *Nagy Imre és Büntársai Ellenforradalmi Összeesküvése* (The Counterrevolutionary Conspiracy of Imre Nagy and His Accomplices), Hungarian White Book (Budapest, 1958), p. 116.

31. Kádár, in an interview at Berlin while attending the Congress of the Socialist Unity Party of Germany in July 1958; *Leipziger Volkszeitung,* July 16, 1958.

32. *Népszabadság,* July 16, 1958.

33. *Népszabadság* (Jan. 5, 1958), anxious to refute the "slanderous allegation" that workers no longer wish to exercise power, stated (italics added) that "the political consolidation and strengthening of power may, however, create the *false illusion that we have won over the entire working class* . . . there are still waverers among the workers . . . Nevertheless administrative measures are no substitute for the ideological struggle . . . Internal contradictions can even exist in the working class . . . these, however are not antagonistic in character."

34. Deputy Minister Lászlo Földes in *Társadalmi Szemle,* April 1958.

35. "The Guiding Principles of the Socialist Workers Party's Cultural Policy" in *Társadalmi Szemle,* September 1958 (summarized in advance in *Népszabadság,* Aug. 20, 1958). See also "Nationalism — Ideological Weapon of the Counter-Revolution" in *Népszabadság,* Feb. 21, 1958.

36. This book had been published in (East) Berlin in 1955 under the title *Die Zerstörung der Vernunft: der Weg des Irrationalismus von Schelling zu Hitler* (The Destruction of Reason: The Road of Irrationalism from Schelling to Hitler).

37. Fogarasi's speech was published in the *Népszabadság,* Oct. 23, 1958. See also *New York Times,* Oct. 26, 1958.

38. *A Modern Kapitalizmus Néhány Problémája* (Budapest, 1959). For analyses of the book see "Modern Capitalism — Through Marxist Eyes," *The Review* (Brussels), July 1960; and *Hungary: A Survey,* Part 2 (mimeographed publication of the Kossuth Foundation, New York), pp. 30–48.

39. From a hostile review by László Háy in *Társadalmi Szemle,* October 1959.

40. *Társadalmi Szemle* (December 1959) published a summary of the debate, which was held on November 14, 1959.

41. *New York Times,* Jan. 10, 1960. See also "Kádár's Congress in Hungary," *East Europe,* January 1960.

42. *Népszabadság,* Nov. 21, 1959.

43. Sándor Szerényi in *Társadalmi Szemle,* November 1960.

44. *Népszabadság,* Dec. 10, 1960; *New York Times,* Dec. 10, 1960. See also *The Economist,* Dec. 24, 1960, p. 1305.

45. *Népszabadság,* Jan. 28 and 29, 1958.

46. *Népszabadság,* Jan. 17, 1960.

47. *U. N. Report,* p. 117.

48. *Hétföi Hirek,* Nov. 10, 1958.

49. *The Times* (London), Nov. 20, 1958.

50. Béla Kovács' article was published in *Magyar Nemzet,* Feb. 20, 1959.

51. *Társadalmi Szemle,* October 1958.

52. *The Economist,* Jan. 10, 1959, pp. 138–140.

53. *Népszabadság,* Sept. 5, 1957.

54. *Ibid.*

55. *Népszabadság,* Jan. 28, 1958.

56. *Magyar Nemzet,* Jan. 11, 1958.

57. *Társadalmi Szemle,* March 1958.

58. *Magyar Nemzet,* Oct. 15, 1957.

59. Kádár's speech at the first national conference of the KISZ on October 25, 1957; *Népszabadság,* Oct. 27, 1957.

60. *Ibid.*

61. *Népszabadság,* Oct. 26, 1957.

62. *Magyar Közlöny,* Nov. 21, 1957.

63. *Népszabadság,* Nov. 2, 1957.

64. For an analysis, see Maxime Mourin, "La Hongrie après l'Insurrection." *Revue de Défense Nationale,* June 1959, p. 1051.

65. See the report by the International Confederation of Free Trade Unions (*Spotlight,* October 1957) according to which Imre Nagy "is under intensive Soviet pressure. The Soviet authorities are trying to obtain from him a statement which would for all practical reasons explain and approve the Soviet armed intervention of 4 November 1956 in Hungary. According to this information, Imre Nagy should declare János Kádár's government, imposed by Soviet forces, as legal. That is the reason why the trial against Imre Nagy and his closest colleagues is being postponed."

66. See, for example, an article in *The Times* (London), April 29, 1960.

67. *Népszabadság,* July 17, 1958. This article further warned that "elements who join the Party indiscriminately must not be allowed to change its vanguard character." Therefore no "recruiting campaign" was to be launched and "appointments must not be made conditional on Party membership."

68. This circumstance may explain the glaring inconsistencies in reporting on Hungarian public opinion to which gullible visitors from the West are an easy prey. See the remarkably well-informed discussion by George Bailey, "Remember Hungary: The War Goes On," *The Reporter,* Nov. 24, 1960, pp. 36–39.

28. Means of Coercion and Control: Soviet and Domestic

1. See the exhaustive analysis by Zbigniew K. Brzezinski, *The Soviet Bloc* (Cambridge, Mass., 1960), pp. 165–181, 308–332, 376–382.

2. Soviet investigation into the causes and motives of the Revolution started immediately after the suppression of the uprising. See United Nations, *Report of the Special Committee on the Problem of Hungary* (New York, 1957), pp. 125–126, presenting evidence by Hungarian deportees who had been interrogated by MVD officers.

3. In 1957, Soviet officers were assigned to attend and also to address Party meetings, local councils, and school classes; this was later abandoned. See *The Times* (London), April 29, 1960.

4. *Népszabadság,* April 4, 1958.

5. *Népszabadság,* April 5, 1958.

6. *Népszabadság,* April 7, 1958.

7. *Népszabadság,* Dec. 2, 1959; *New York Times,* Dec. 2, 1959.

8. The tendency toward relaxation of satellite rule is described in an article by the *New York Times,* Dec. 26, 1959, where this decentralization is compared to that carried out by Moscow within the Sixteen Soviet member republics.

9. The recent developments and the present patterns of inter-Communist relations are brilliantly condensed in Brzezinski, *The Soviet Bloc*, pp. 395–400.

10. See François Fejtö, *Behind the Rape of Hungary* (New York, 1957), p. 301.

11. *New York Times*, July 7, 1960.

12. See *Hungary under Soviet Rule III: A Survey of Developments from the Revolution to August 1959*, ed. A. A. Berle, Jr., *et al.*, and published by the American Friends of the Captive Nations (New York, 1959), p. 7. *The Times* (London), on April 29, 1960, estimated the total of Soviet forces at some 37,000.

13. *Hungary under Soviet Rule III*, pp. 8–11; *Hungarian Freedom Fighter*, September 1959.

14. The agreement is published in the *U. N. Report*, pp. 60–62; the original Hungarian text was published in *Népakarat*, May 29, 1957.

15. For Grebennik statement (an adaptation of a Russian proverb), and Soviet pronouncements in remainder of paragraph, see *U. N. Report*, pp. 57–58.

16. *New York Times*, April 6, 1958. The Hungarian press did not report that passage of the speech.

17. *Népszabadság*, April 9, 1959.

18. *Népszabadság*, Aug. 21, 1959.

19. *Népszabadság*, Dec. 2, 1959.

20. *U. N. Report*, p. 104; *Hungary under Soviet Rule: A Survey of Developments since the Report of the U. N. Special Committee*, ed. A. A. Berle, Jr., *et al.* (New York, 1957), pp. 15–16; also *Hungary under Soviet Rule III* (see note 12, above), pp. 12–13.

21. The appointment of Révész as ambassador may also be due to a Soviet desire to be kept currently informed on Hungarian matters by a man in their confidence. See Béla

Király, "Hungary's New Envoy," *East Europe*, July 1960.

22. *Hungary under Soviet Rule III* (note 12, above), pp. 12–13.

23. *Szabad Magyar Tudosito*, July–August 1959, p. 21.

24. *Hungary under Soviet Rule* (note 20, above), p. 15.

25. On January 18, 1958, Prime Minister Münnich stated that the Hungarian military expenditure was very small because Hungary is a small country. About 2 to 3 per cent of the annual budget was spent for military purposes (Budapest Radio).

26. Decree No. 35 of 1956; its Section 1 announced: "As a consequence of the dissolution of the Office of State Security of the Ministry of the Interior . . ." (*Highlights of Current Legislation and Activities in Mid-Europe*, Library of Congress, January 1958, p. 26.

27. This appears from an article in *Népakarat*, May 31, 1957.

28. *U. N. Report*, p. 104.

29. *The Times* (London), April 29, 1960.

30. Decree No. 29 of 1956, ordering a complete inventory of arms and ammunition in the possession of the workers' guards. *Népszabadság*, Dec. 12, 1956.

31. Decree No. 13 of 1957. In its preamble the task of the Workers' Militia is thus defined: "to strengthen the defense of the people's democratic order, to assure tranquility among the toiling people and undisturbed production, as well as to create more effective protection against attempts of counter-revolutionary elements to restore [the capitalistic regime]." *Highlights*, January 1958, p. 27.

32. *Hungary under Soviet Rule III* (note 12, above), p. 14.

33. Decree No. 62/1957 issued by the Presidium of the People's Republic.

34. *The Hungarian Situation and the Rule of Law*, Supplementary Report by the International Commission of Jurists (The Hague, February 1958).

35. See the well-informed article "Repression under the Kádár Regime," *The Times* (London), Oct. 22, 1960.

36. *Hungary under Soviet Rule* (note 20, above), p. 17.

37. *Népszabadság*, April 27, 1958.

38. *Magyar Nemzet*, Feb. 22, 1958.

39. *Manchester Guardian*, July 16, July 31, and Aug. 15, 1959.

40. *Neue Zürcher Zeitung*, Oct. 10, 1959. János Kádár on November 30, 1959, and the Hungarian representative to the United Nations on December 8, 1959, denied the charges of the execution of 31 juveniles. The Minister of the Interior announced to the Party Congress on December 3, 1959, that "there were never and are not at present juveniles imprisoned. There are no juveniles among the formerly sentenced and those under investigation either." (*Népszabadság*, Dec. 4, 1959.) On the other hand, Hungarian court decisions (*Legfelsöbb Biroság Határozatai*) mention cases of juveniles who had participated in the "counterrevolution" and therefore had been given prison sentences. The case of the Workers' Council of Ujpest was first denied, then admitted by the official spokesman. Kádár, in a speech made September 7, 1959, in Salgotarján, unreported by the Budapest press but reported in the local paper *Népujság* of September 8, vehemently attacked the insurgents of 1956, and threatened further punitive actions against them. This speech must be considered together with unofficial reports concerning a hundred juveniles waiting trial in a Budapest jail, and the alleged execution of one youth of 18 in Budapest. Furthermore, the decree of "partial amnesty" of April 12, 1959, provided that "disregarding the duration of the imposed penalties, *juveniles under the age of 18* [italics added], pregnant women, etc. . . . who committed the criminal offense before May 1, 1957, receive full amnesty," but those persons were excluded from the amnesty if they were "the initiators and leaders of counterrevolutionary organizations, those sentenced for war crimes against the people . . . those sentenced for violent crimes against human life." (*Magyar Közlöny*, April 3, 1959).

41. *Népszabadság*, Dec. 4, 1959.

42. Estimate of 20,000 each is in *Spotlight* (publication of the International Confederation of Free Trade Unions), December 1957, the two internment camps being in Kistarcsa and in Tököl respectively; the estimate of *The Times* (London), Oct. 23, 1957, corresponds. Prosecutor General's statement is in *Népszabadság*, Dec. 22, 1957. He spoke of the internment camp of Kistarcsa which was made originally to house about 4,000 internees; it was reported by former inmates that the camp was overcrowded to the extent that prisoners were obliged to sleep in six-hour shifts.

43. For an authoritative appraisal of condemnations see the publication of the Hungarian Freedom Fighters Federation, Inc., *Criminal Justice in Hungary After the Revolution* (New York, 1959).

44. On sentencing see *Facts about Hungary*, ed. Imre Kovács (New York, 1959), p. 300. On Szigeti see *The Times* (London), May 27 and 30, 1957. The secret sentencing of Rácz and Bali, leaders of the Workers' Council of Greater Budapest, was reported in *Rude Pravo* (Prague), April 12, 1959; and the execution of Jozsef Kovács, Chairman of the Workers' Council of Szeged, was belatedly reported in *Délmagyarország* (Szeged), March 5, 1958.

45. *Népszabadság*, Dec. 10, 1957.

46. *Népszabadság*, Jan. 11, 1958.

47. *Neue Zürcher Zeitung*, July 10, 1958; *New York Times*, Aug. 21, 1958.

48. *Népszabadság*, April 25, 1957.

49. The Prosecutor General stated that "one of the slogans of counter-revolutionary demagogy was to mention violations of law" on the part of prerevolutionary prosecutors and courts, "but on investigation it was found that in the overwhelming majority of cases the procedure had been well-founded and lawful." *East Europe*, February 1958, p. 46.

50. *Népszabadság*, March 23, 1958.

51. *Hungary under Soviet Rule III* (note 12, above), p. 20; *Die Presse* (Vienna), April 22, 1958.

52. László Varga, *Violations of Human Rights in Hungary* (mimeographed, New York, 1960), p. 17.

53. *Népszabadság*, March 31, 1960.

54. Associated Press Report from Budapest, February 13, 1959.

55. *New York Times*, Sept. 18, 1957.

56. For the preliminaries and problems concerning the November 1957 Declaration see Brzezinski, *The Soviet Bloc*, pp. 308–315.

57. *Magyarország*, March 7, 1957.

58. *Népszabadság*, Dec. 16, 1957.

59. *Ellenforradalmi Erök a Magyar Oktoberi Eseményekben* (Counter-revolutionary Forces in the October Events in Hungary), published by the Information Bureau of the Council of Ministers, vol. IV [1957], p. 92.

60. As reported in *Die Presse* (Vienna), Jan. 7, 1958.

61. *Társadalmi Szemle*, December 1957 and January 1958; the first article was entitled "The Ideas of Imre Nagy and the Ideological Preparation of the Treason," the second "The Development of Hungarian Revisionism

as an Organic Part of the Ideological Preparation of the Counter-Revolution." The quotations are from the January issue.

62. *Kommunist*, December 1957; the article by D. Shevlyagyn attacked Imre Nagy and his "accomplices," who intended "to provoke a split in the Socialist camp by pitting one Communist Party against another." It said that "by advancing the slogan of so-called 'national Communism' the unity of the Socialist countries would have been undermined."

63. *New York Times*, March 30, 1958.

64. Khrushchev's speech of April 9, 1958, before the workers of Csepel, overheard by Western correspondents. *Népszabadság* of April 10 did not include references to Imre Nagy in its versions of the speech.

65. For an analysis of the Nagy execution as an anti-Titoist move, see David J. Dallin, *Soviet Foreign Policy after Stalin* (Philadelphia, 1961), pp. 485–486.

66. *Népszabadság*, June 17, 1958.

67. *Nagy Imre és Büntársai Ellenforradalmi Összeesküvése* (The Counterrevolutionary Conspiracy of Imre Nagy and His Accomplices), Hungarian White Book (Budapest, 1958).

68. *La Vérité sur l'Affaire Nagy* (Paris, 1958); English edition: *The Truth about the Nagy Affair* (London, 1959); *Facts about Hungary*, pp. 199–212; Special Report of the United Nations Special Committee, July 14, 1958; Ferenc A. Váli, "The Imre Nagy 'Trial,'" *Rendületlenül* (New York), May–June, 1959.

69. From the communiqué issued by the United Nations Special Committee on the Problem of Hungary of June 21, 1958.

29. Synchronizing a Satellite

1. *Népszabadság*, Jan. 27, 1958.

2. For decrees of March 1957 and March 1959 see *Hungary under Soviet Rule: A Survey of Developments since*

the Report of the U. N. Special Committee, ed. A. A. Berle, Jr., et al. (New York, 1957), p. 24, and Hungary under Soviet Rule III: A Survey of Developments from the Revolution to August 1959, ed. A. A. Berle, Jr., et al. (New York, 1959), p. 29.

3. Népszabadság reported on April 19, 1958, the amount of government subsidy to four religious groups (Roman Catholics, Calvinists, Lutherans, and Jews), and the fact that the churches themselves were expected to raise the same amount.

4. Hungary under Soviet Rule III, pp. 26–27.

5. L'Osservatore Romano, Jan. 11, 1958.

6. Népszabadság, Jan. 29, 1958.

7. Népszabadság, Feb. 11, 1958.

8. New York Times, March 11, 1958.

9. Népszabadság, July 24, 1958.

10. Népszabadság, Sept. 25, 1958.

11. Népszabadság, April 9, 1959.

12. Csongrádmegyei Hirlap, May 8, 1959.

13. For Cardinal Mindszenty's life in the U. S. legation see Daniel Schorr, "Cardinal in a Cage," The Reporter, Nov. 24, 1960, pp. 39–40.

14. Népszabadság, Aug. 6, 1957.

15. Népszabadság, Sept. 16, 1957.

16. See discussion in Neue Zürcher Zeitung, Jan. 10, 1958.

17. Magyar Nemzet, March 23, 1958; Népszabadság, March 15, 1958.

18. Népszabadság, June 18, 1958; Belpolitikai Szemle, June 1958. For a comprehensive analysis, see Paul Ignotus, "Hungarian Intellectuals under Fire," Problems of Communism, May–June 1959, pp. 16–21.

19. Broadcast by Radio Budapest, October 1, 1958.

20. Magyar Nemzet, Nov. 23, 1958.

21. Társadalmi Szemle, February 1959.

22. Élet és Irodalom, Oct. 2, 1959.

23. Népszabadság, Dec. 1, 1959.

24. See Paul Ignotus, "Hungary's Craving for Normalcy," Problems of Communism, March–April 1960, pp. 24–30.

25. News from Hungary (published in New York by Free Europe Committee), July 22, 1960.

26. This more tolerant attitude appears from the contents of the September 1960 issue of Kortárs, as interpreted in The Hungarian Quarterly (New York), Vol. 1, No. 1 (January 1961), pp. 58–62. See also William E. Griffith, "The Revolt Reconsidered," East Europe, July 1960, p. 20.

27. From the report of the Hungarian Central Statistical Office issued on February 1, 1958; Népszabadság, Feb. 2, 1958.

28. In addition to material aid, Communist China gave Hungary a loan of $25 million in free foreign exchange and the same amount of goods credit. The German Democratic Republic, Rumania, Czechoslovakia, Bulgaria, and also Yugoslavia extended credits. Medjunarodna Politika, August 1957.

29. Magyar Nemzet, March 19, 1958.

30. U. N. Economic Bulletin for Europe (Geneva), vol. X, no. 2 (1958).

31. Statement by the Minister of Foreign Trade, Népszabadság, Oct. 18, 1957.

32. Népszabadság, Feb. 25, 1958.

33. Népszabadság, March 20, 1958.

34. Economic Bulletin of the Hungarian National Bank, January–June 1958 and July–December 1958.

35. Statement of Árpád Kiss, Chairman of the Planning Office; Népszabadság, Dec. 9, 1958. See also announcements to the National Assembly in Népszabadság, Feb. 19, 1959.

36. See Zbigniew K. Brzezinski, The Soviet Bloc (Cambridge, Mass., 1960), pp. 282–290.

37. Horst Mendershausen, "Terms of Trade between the Soviet Union

and the Smaller Communist Countries," *The Review of Economics and Statistics*, May 1958, pp. 106–118. For figures of overpricing in 1958 and 1959, see Jan Wszelaki, "Economic Developments in East-Central Europe, 1954–1959," *Orbis*, Winter 1961, p. 440.

38. See the letter by Aleksander Kutt to the *New York Times*, April 23, 1960.

39. See David T. Cattell, "Multilateral Cooperation and Integration in Eastern Europe," *Western Political Quarterly*, March 1960, pp. 64–69.

40. *New York Times*, April 4, 1960.

41. The *Társadalmi Szemle* article emphasized that security and intensive production should be the guiding principles in respect to agriculture: "Above all we shall have to break with the concept of many years, according to which agriculture, in spite of its high degree of participation in national income, is expected to benefit in a very low proportion to state investments."

42. *Népszabadság*, Dec. 13 and 16, 1958.

43. *Társadalmi Szemle*, January 1959.

44. See article by Kádár in *Népszabadság*, Jan. 29, 1959.

45. Decree is printed in *Magyar Közlöny*, Feb. 1, 1959.

46. *Népszabadság*, April 4, 1959.

47. See the articles relative to collectivization in *Élet és Irodalom*, March 6, 1959 ("A Report on the Village 'Miracle'"); March 13 ("Why Did They Join?").

48. New York Times, Feb. 15, 1960. See also Victor Meier, "'Socialist Transformation' in the Countryside," *Problems of Communism*, September–October 1960, p. 52.

49. For a vivid description of a village after collectivization see *Élet és Irodalom*, Jan. 15, 1960.

50. *Népszabadság*, Jan. 17, 1960; New York Times, Jan. 17, 1960.

51. *The Economist*, Dec. 24, 1960.

52. *New York Times*, Feb. 21, 1961. See also the analysis in *The Times* (London), March 1, 1961.

53. "If the work of political enlightenment will improve, our agriculture may take a great step forward on the road to Socialism during 1959. It not only may, *it will have to,* because our friendly neighbors, Czechoslovakia and Rumania, are greatly ahead of us." From Prime Minister Münnich's statement on Christmas Eve, *Népszabadság*, Dec. 25, 1958.

54. The causes facilitating collectivization cited by Lajos Fehér may be found in his article in *Népszabadság*, Jan. 17, 1960.

30. International Implications of the Hungarian Situation

1. See *Bitter Harvest — The Intellectual Revolt behind the Iron Curtain*, ed. Edmund Stillman (New York, 1959), pp. 293–294. Harich was imprisoned in East Germany for deviationism.

2. For an analysis of the decline of Soviet prestige in consequence of Hungarian events see David J. Dallin, *Soviet Foreign Policy after Stalin* (Philadelphia, 1961), p. 446.

3. See Zbigniew K. Brzezinski, *The Soviet Bloc* (Cambridge, Mass., 1960), the section entitled "Neo-Stalinism in One Country," pp. 370–375.

4. *New York Times*, Oct. 10, 1957.

5. Article 4 of the Warsaw Treaty of May 14, 1955, provides: "In the event of armed attack in Europe on one or more of the Parties to the Treaty by any states or group of states, each of the Parties to the Treaty . . .

shall immediately, either individually or in agreement with other Parties to the Treaty, come to the assistance of the state or states attacked with all such means as it deems necessary, including armed forces." It would appear, paradoxically, that if Hungary was still a signatory of the Treaty (as Moscow claimed) when the Soviet Union attacked Hungary on November 4, 1956, other signatories to the Warsaw Treaty (Albania, Czechoslovakia, Bulgaria, the German Democratic Republic, Poland, and Rumania) were obligated under Article 4 to "come to the assistance" of Hungary.

6. The principle of maintaining the Communist *status quo* with the "fraternal assistance" of the Soviets was again announced by Khrushchev during his two official visits in Hungary, in April 1958 and in December 1959.

7. The refusal of the Soviet government to discuss under any circumstances the status of the East-Central European Communist-dominated countries has always been based on the argument that these countries had already chosen the form of government they desired; thus the principle of self-determination (agreed upon at Yalta) had already been applied to them.

8. *Pravda*, Jan. 26, 1958.

9. *Pravda*, July 17, 1960.

10. United Nations, *Report of the Special Committee on the Problem of Hungary* (New York, 1957), pp. 14–16, 50–52.

11. Joint Soviet-Hungarian Declaration of March 28, 1957, in Moscow; *Népszabadság*, March 29, 1957.

12. This explanation was suggested by Khrushchev on March 16, 1959, when receiving the delegation of the West German Social Democrat Party (personal information by Dr. Fritz Erler to this writer).

13. *Népszabadság*, Sept. 22, 1957.

14. *Népszabadság*, Jan. 29, 1958.

Before Khrushchev's visit to Hungary in April 1958, an official brochure, "Why Are Soviet Troops Stationed in Hungary?" was widely circulated; the text is in *Népszabadság*, April 13, 1958.

15. "Overcoming the Vestiges of Nationalism at Our Universities," *Népszabadság*, Jan. 21, 1958 (italics ours). See also "The Friendship of Fraternal Peoples," *Népszabadság*, April 13, 1958, in which criticism is aimed at a "small group which uses the slogan of a 'correct relationship' with the ulterior motive of undermining and attacking Soviet-Hungarian friendship."

16. "Spirit of 1848" by Lajos Mesterházy in *Magyar Nemzet*, April 23, 1958.

17. Khrushchev on April 5, 1958, in Budapest; *Népszabadság*, April 6, 1958.

18. From Khrushchev's press conference March 19, 1959; *New York Times*, March 20, 1959.

19. See article in *Borba*, Nov. 5, 1956.

20. Paul E. Zinner (ed.), *National Communism and Popular Revolt in Eastern Europe* (New York, 1957), pp. 529, 531.

21. See, in particular, the *Pravda* article of November 23, 1956; Zinner, pp. 541–563.

22. Quoted from above article in *Pravda*; Zinner, p. 557. See also Brzezinski, *The Soviet Bloc*, p. 235.

23. See *Annual Register of World Events, 1956* (London, 1957), p. 265.

24. From the speech of November 11, 1956; Zinner, pp. 534–535.

25. *The Times* (London), Nov. 5, 1957.

26. *Népszabadság*, Nov. 29, 1957.

27. *Népszabadság*, Jan. 19 and 29, 1958. Münnich stated that a meeting between Hungarian and Yugoslav leaders had been agreed on in Moscow.

28. *Népszabadság*, March 29 and April 5, 1958.

29. *Die Presse* (Vienna), March 30 and April 1, 1958; *New York Times*, March 29, 1958.

30. For the text of the program see *Yugoslavia's Way*, translated by Stoyan Pribechevich (New York, 1958). For a useful analysis see Brzezinski, *The Soviet Bloc*, pp. 318–322.

31. "Necessary Remarks on the Draft Program of the League of Yugoslav Communists," *Társadalmi Szemle*, May 1958.

32. *Népszabadság*, June 20, 1958.

33. *New York Times*, Sept. 23, 1958.

34. Commentary by Radio Zagreb, February 24, 1959.

35. *Népszabadság*, Dec. 1, 1959.

36. See Richard Lowenthal, "Tito's Affair with Khrushchev," *The New Leader*, Oct. 6, 1958.

37. Milovan Djilas, "The Storm in Eastern Europe," *The New Leader*, Nov. 19, 1956.

38. For an analysis of the controversies that followed the Polish and Hungarian events, see Brzezinski, *The Soviet Bloc*, pp. 269–277.

39. Wu Han, Chairman of the Democratic League (one of the Chinese "parties" that recognizes the leadership of the Communist Party), denounced three of his leading fellow party-members who held ministerial rank for having declared after the Hungarian uprising that the Chinese Communist Party must abandon its leadership, giving their own party equal status. *The Annual Register of World Events, 1957* (London, 1958), p. 341.

40. "More on the Historical Experience of the Dictatorship of the Proletariat," *People's Daily*, Dec. 29, 1956.

41. *Népszabadság*, Jan. 17, 1957.

42. *The Times* (London), Oct. 1, 1957.

43. *Neue Zürcher Zeitung*, Oct. 12, 1957.

44. *Népszabadság*, Dec. 14, 1957; March 2, 1958; Dec. 16, 1958.

45. For a comprehensive survey of the position of Hungarian minorities in Czechoslovakia, Rumania, and Yugoslavia, see the article by István Révay, "Hungarian Minorities under Communist Rule," in *Facts about Hungary*, ed. Imre Kovács (New York, 1959), pp. 250–258; and István Révay, *Hungarians in Czechoslovakia* (New York, 1959).

46. See Brzezinski's analysis of the Polish attitude toward the Kádár regime in *The Soviet Bloc*, pp. 260–265.

47. *Népszabadság*, May 11, 1958.

48. *Trybuna Ludu*, June 29, 1958.

49. "On the Third PZPR Congress," *Népszabadság*, March 29, 1959.

50. Hungary endorsed the Soviet view of "peaceful coexistence" in a statement issued before the conference. *New York Times*, Oct. 31, 1960.

51. See analysis in *Manchester Guardian*, Nov. 12, 1956.

52. *Annual Register of World Events, 1956*, p. 102.

53. In December 1958, Perera, ambassador of Ceylon to the United Arab Republic (and formerly alternate representative on the Special Committee of the United Nations on the problem of Hungary), gave a lecture in Budapest, where he stated that "the Hungarian question has not existed and does not exist now, and it was not at all necessary for it to be debated in the United Nations." *Népszabadság*, Dec. 24, 1958. A government delegation of Guinea visited Hungary in February 1959. Agreements on economic and cultural cooperation were concluded and political questions discussed. *Népszabadság*, Feb. 21, 1959.

54. *Magyar Nemzet* (July 6, 1958) commented on the situation in an article entitled "Good Neighborhood or Cold War."

55. A Hungarian government spokesman stated on March 4, 1958,

that for the past eighteen months Switzerland had "tolerated" on its territory "activities hostile to Hungary" and "subversive organizations hostile to the Hungarian government" and such an attitude was "manifestly contrary to the principle of Swiss neutrality." From the Swiss side it has always been stressed that neutrality meant the neutrality of the state and not that of one's conviction.

56. *Népszabadság*, Jan. 11, 1958.

57. For U. S. note of November 21, 1958, in reply to Hungarian note of September 20 of the same year, see Department of State press release 710, dated November 21 and reprinted in *Department of State Bulletin*, Dec. 8, 1958, p. 911. For department statement of January 31, 1959, on the returning of the next Hungarian note, see *Department of State Bulletin*, Feb. 16, 1959, p. 222.

58. For U. S. aide-memoire of March 6, 1958, see *Department of State Bulletin*, March 24, 1958, p. 459. For Soviet note of March 24, see *New York Times*, March 25, 1958. On May 28, 1958, the British ambassador in Moscow presented to Foreign Minister Gromyko an outline of ten items to be considered by a Summit meeting; Item 10 is entitled "Ways of Easing Tensions in Eastern Europe"; Supplement to *New Times* (Moscow), June 1958, No. 26. The same periodical quotes Khrushchev's letter to President Eisenhower of June 11, 1958. For Eisenhower's statement of June 18, 1958, declaring that the Nagy execu-

tion had dealt a serious blow to hopes for a fruitful Summit meeting, see *New York Times* of June 19. Popular pressure for the holding of such a meeting considerably relaxed after Nagy's execution.

59. See Ferenc A. Váli, "The Hungarian Revolution and International Law," *The Fletcher Review*, Summer 1959, pp. 15–18.

60. This United Nations *Report of the Special Committee on the Problem of Hungary* (New York, 1957), cited often in previous chapters, is a studious, well-documented work containing 784 paragraphs and 148 pages. The five members of the Special Committee were Alsing Andersen of Denmark, Chairman; K.C.O. Shann of Australia, Rapporteur; R.S.S. Gunewardene of Ceylon; Mongi Slim of Tunisia; and Professor Enrique Rodriguez Fabregat of Uruguay.

61. *New York Times*, Dec. 3, 1960.

62. Váli, "Hungarian Revolution and International Law," pp. 18–22.

63. Paragraph 7 of Article 2 of the Charter provides: "Nothing contained in the present Charter shall authorize the United Nations to intervene in matters which are essentially within the domestic jurisdiction of any state or shall require the Members to submit such matters to settlement under the present Charter."

64. From the speech of the representative of Indonesia (Wirjopranoto) in the Congo dispute before the Security Council on September 16, 1960. *New York Times*, Sept. 17, 1960.

31. Nationalism versus Communism

1. This writer relied on a penetrating analysis by Francis D. Wormuth, "Macropolitics: Aggression in Group Theory," *Audit*, Feb. 22, 1960.

2. Milovan Djilas, "The Storm in Eastern Europe," *The New Leader*, Nov. 19, 1956.

3. See, in particular, *Ideology and Foreign Affairs*, a study prepared at the request of the U. S. Senate Committee on Foreign Relations by the Harvard Center for International Affairs (Washington, 1960), pp. 16–20.

4. For instance, the study just

cited discusses the impact of Communist ideology and that of ideologies of Nationalism, Neutralism, and Internationalism in various parts of the world. The differences of structure between the Communist creed and the other undogmatic political philosophies are not identified; and the authors do not undertake to differentiate between a Party or government ideology and an "ideology" of the people.

5. For the "limits of Polish autonomy" see Zbigniew K. Brzezinski, *The Soviet Bloc* (Cambridge, Mass., 1960), pp. 359–364.

6. That the Soviet bloc's unity ultimately rests on Soviet military preponderance is well illustrated by Hugh Trevor-Roper, "Marxism and the Study of History," *Problems of Communism*, September–October 1956, p. 42.

7. See *Comparisons of the United States and Soviet Economies*, Joint Economic Committee, Congress of the United States (Washington, 1960), pp. 12–13.

8. The strategic significance, especially of Bohemia, for the domination of Europe had always been emphasized by Bismarck. The importance of East Europe, even for command over the world (but before the nuclear age) has been expounded by one writer in this eccentric form: "When our statesmen are in conversation with the defeated enemy, some airy cherub should whisper to them from time to time this saying: 'Who rules East Europe commands the Heartland: who rules the Heartland commands the World-Island: who rules the World-Island commands the world.'" Sir Halford MacKinder, *Democratic Ideals and Realities* (New York, 1919), p. 186.

9. Paul £. Zinner, "Revolution in Hungary: Reflections on the Vicissitudes of a Totalitarian System," *Journal of Politics*, February 1959, p. 36.

10. Francis D. Wormuth in *Audit*, p. 5.

11. Expression used by Paul Auer in his letter to *Le Monde*, Dec. 20, 1959.

12. George F. Kennan, *Russia, the Atom and the West* (New York, 1957), pp. 32–49.

13. *Ibid.*, pp. 23–24.

14. See Henry A. Kissinger, *Nuclear Weapons and Foreign Policy* (New York, 1957), p. 340.

Index

The display type used in this book is Corvinus. This type face was designed by Imre Reiner for Bauer type foundry; its name derives from Matthias Corvinus, King of Hungary (1458–1490).